W9-ABB-995

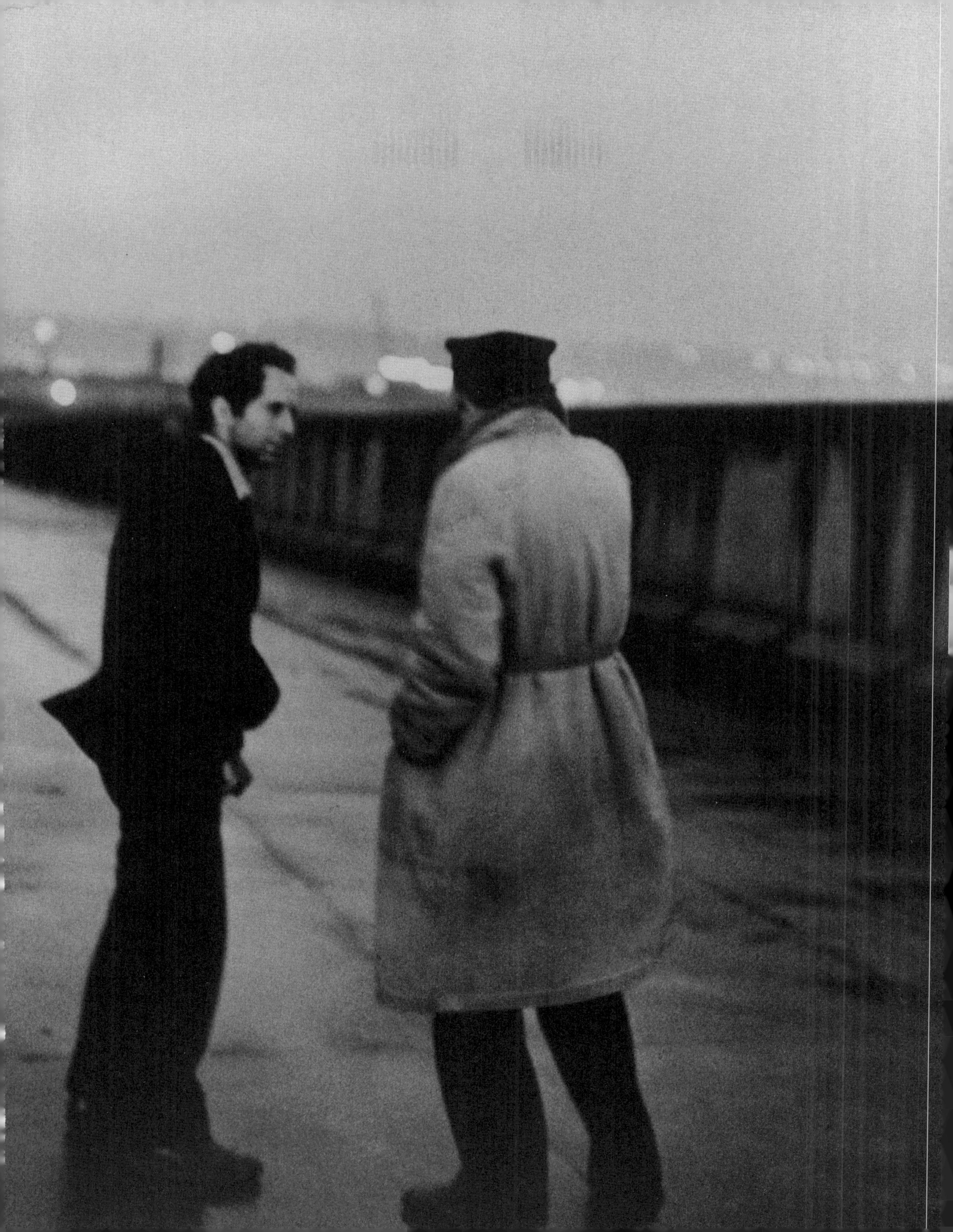

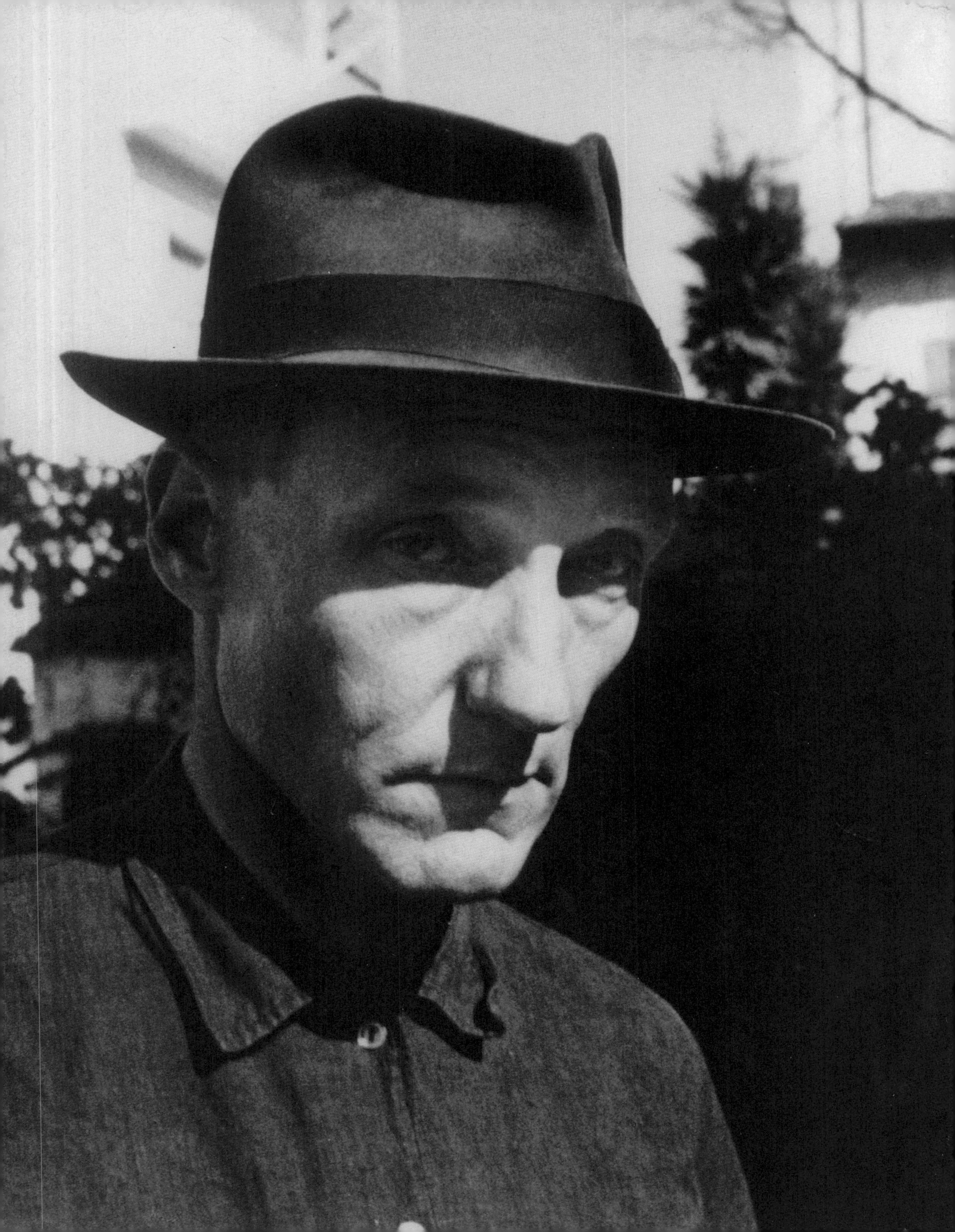

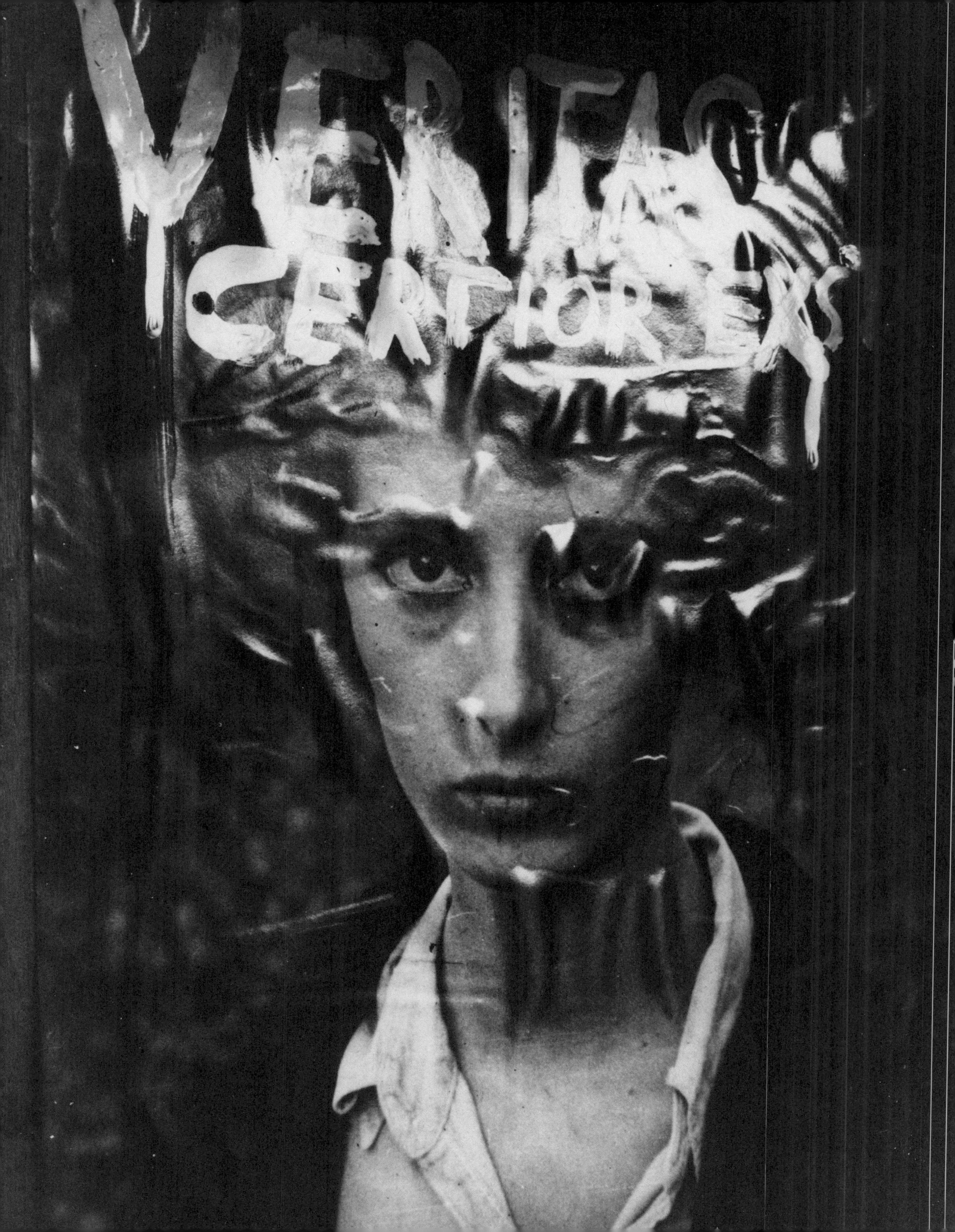

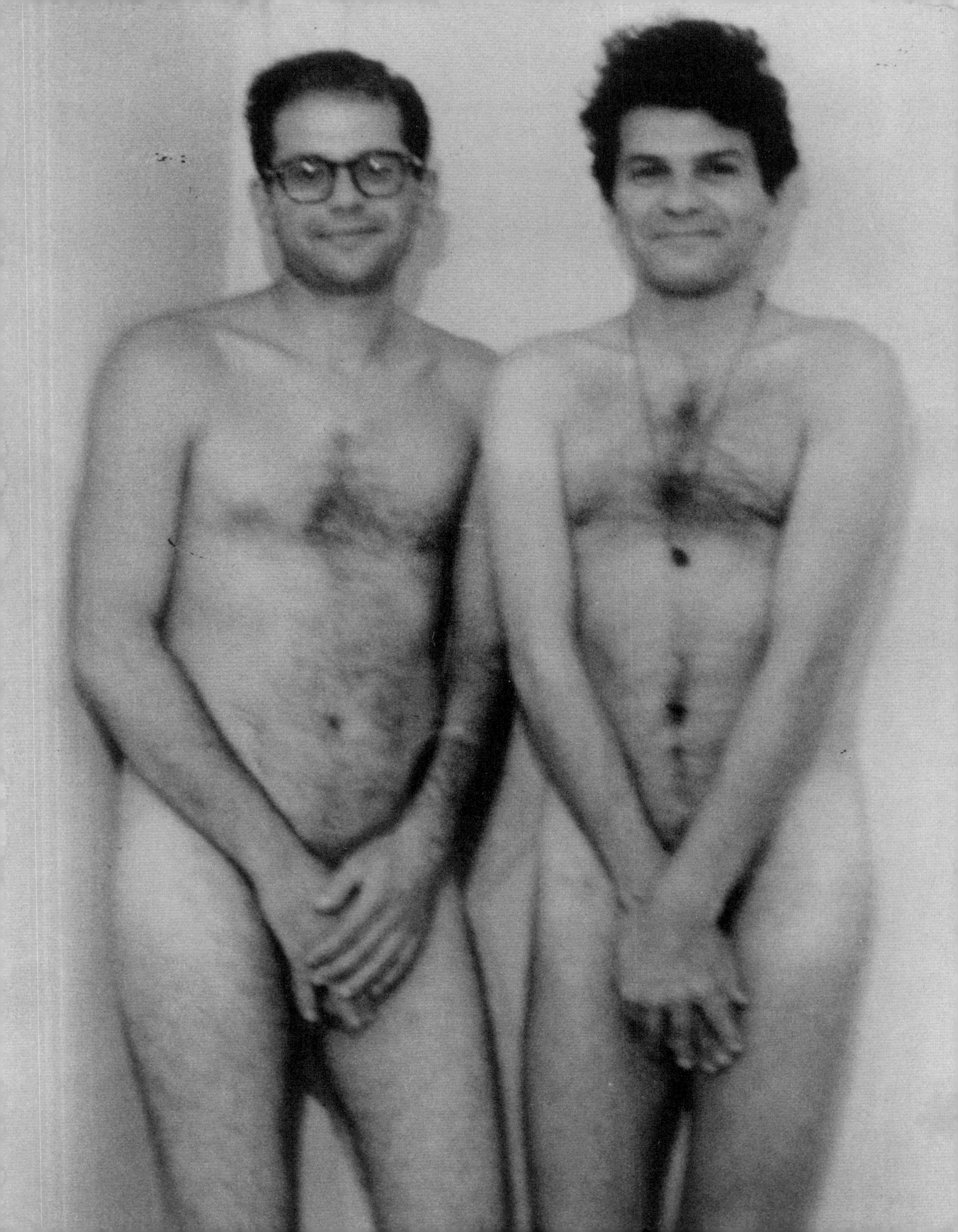

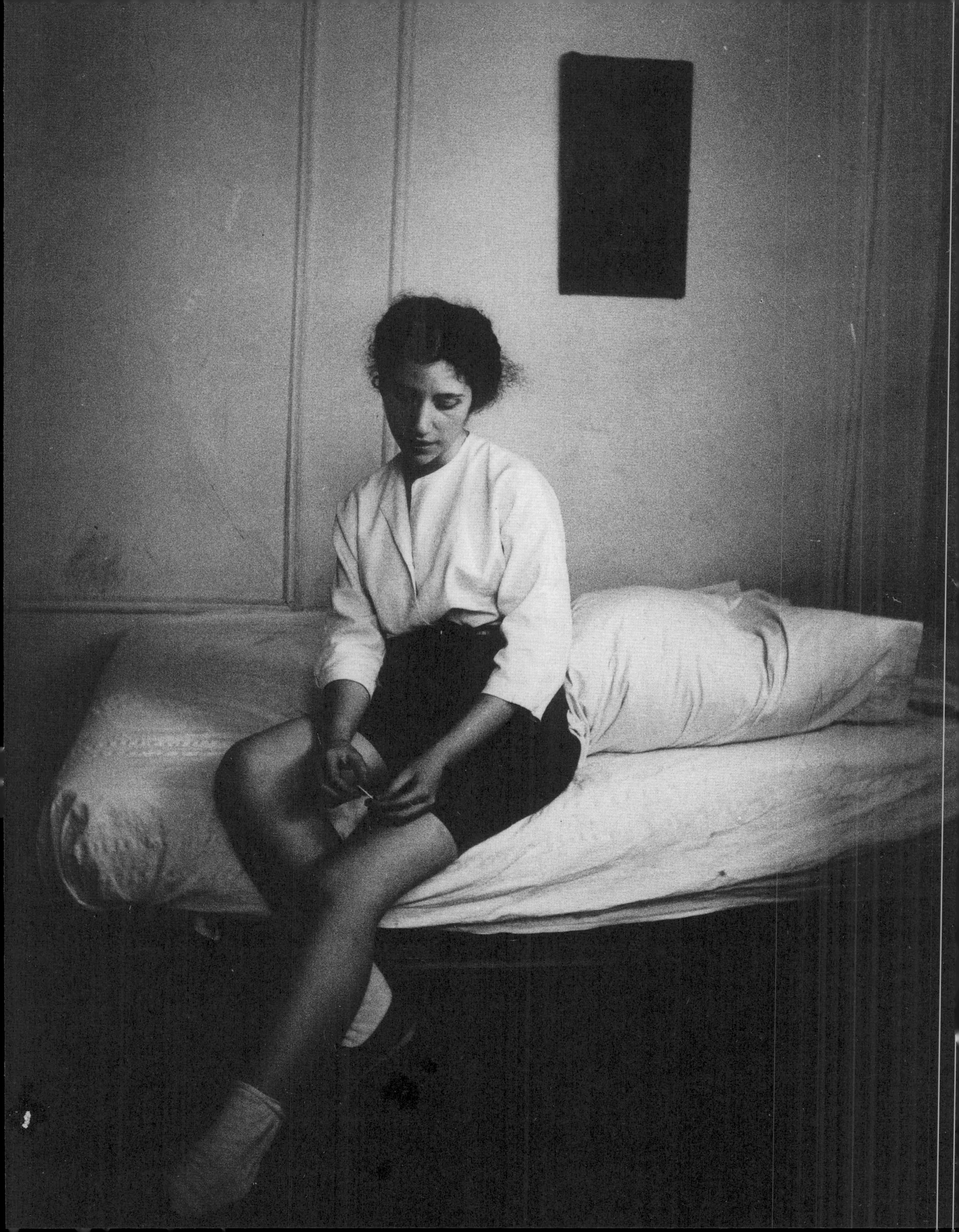

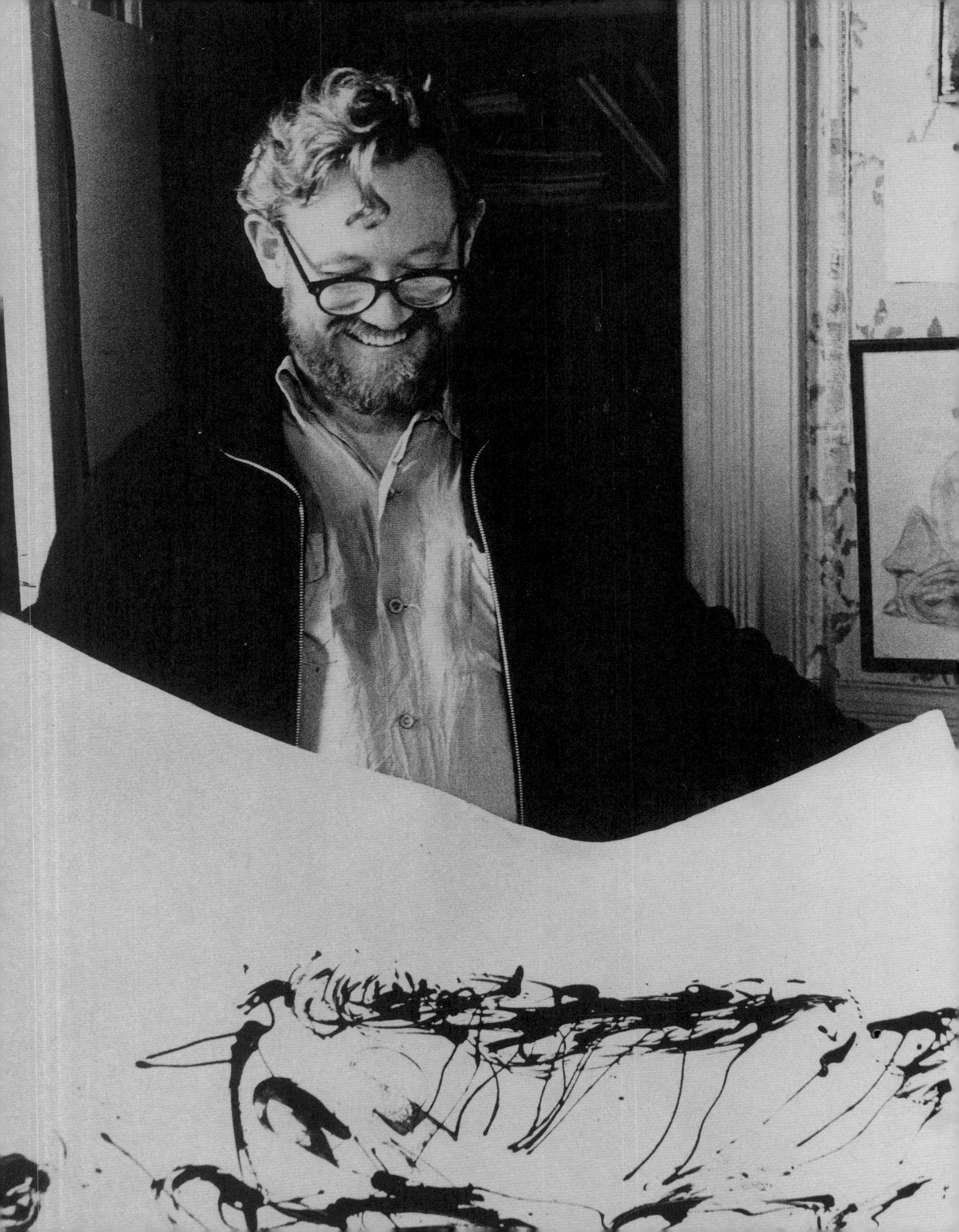

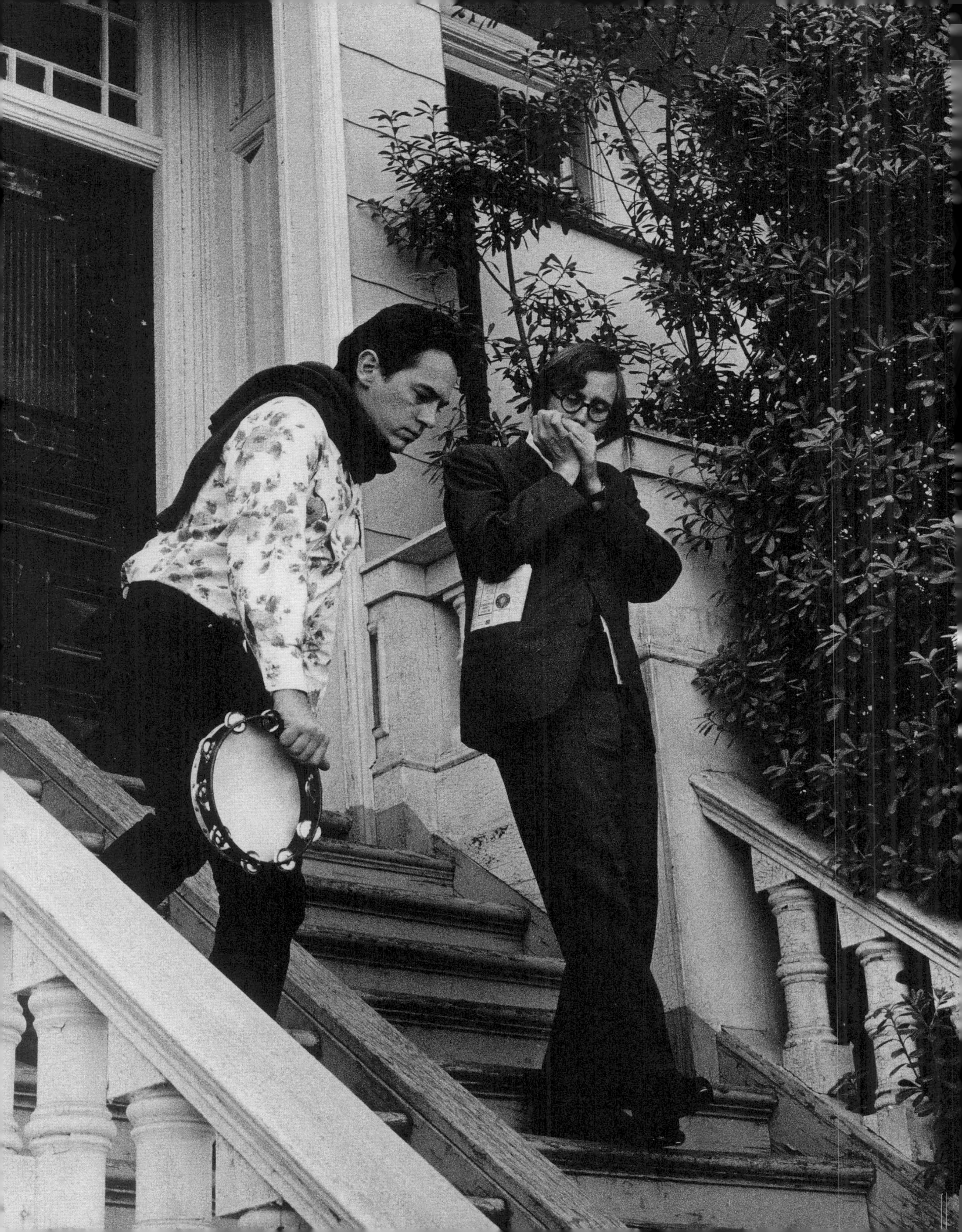

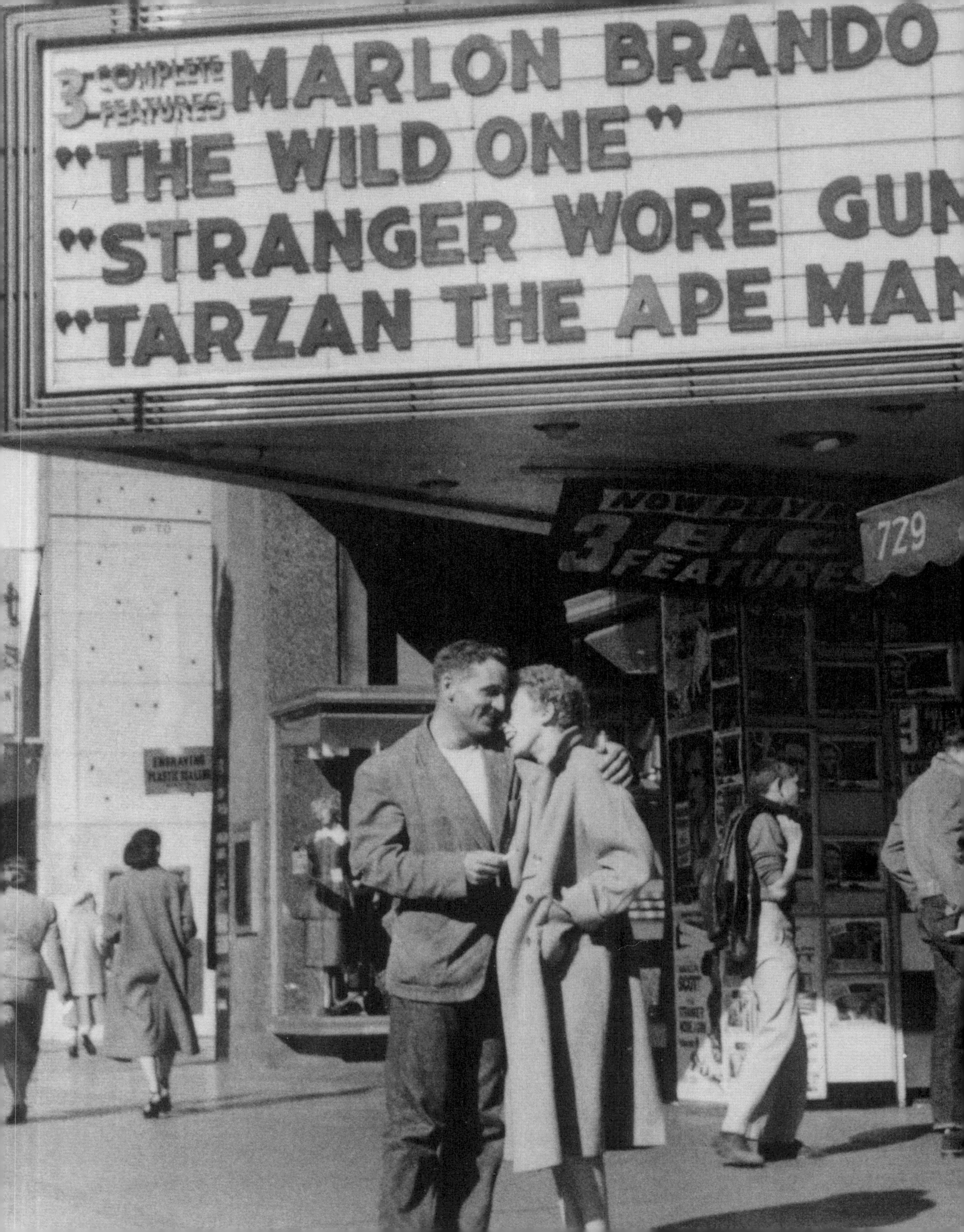

3 COMPLETE FEATURES
MARLON BRANDO
"THE WILD ONE"
"STRANGER WORE GUN
"TARZAN THE APE MAN
3 BIG FEATURES
729

Beat Culture AND THE New America: 1950–1965

LISA PHILLIPS

with contributions by
MAURICE BERGER
RAY CARNEY
MARIA DAMON
ALLEN GINSBERG
JOHN G. HANHARDT
GLENN O'BRIEN
MONA LISA SALOY
EDWARD SANDERS
REBECCA SOLNIT
STEVEN WATSON

WHITNEY MUSEUM OF AMERICAN ART, NEW YORK

in association with

Flammarion
Paris - New York

This book was published on the occasion of the exhibition
"BEAT CULTURE AND THE NEW AMERICA: 1950-1965"
at the Whitney Museum of American Art.

Exhibition Itinerary
Whitney Museum of American Art, New York
November 9, 1995–February 4, 1996

Walker Art Center, Minneapolis
June 2–September 15, 1996

M.H. de Young Memorial Museum,
The Fine Arts Museums of San Francisco
October 5–December 29, 1996

"Beat Culture and the New America: 1950-1965" is sponsored by the AT&T Foundation.
The exhibition is also made possible by a generous contribution from
Thomas H. Lee and Ann Tenenbaum.
Additional underwriting is provided by The Yamagata Foundation.
The National Endowment for the Arts and the National Committee of the Whitney Museum have made grants in support of the exhibition. Performance series is funded by MTV Networks.

Research for the exhibition and publication was supported by income from an endowment established by Henry and Elaine Kaufman, The Lauder Foundation, Mrs. William A. Marsteller, The Andrew W. Mellon Foundation, Mrs. Donald A. Petrie, Primerica Foundation, Samuel and May Rudin Foundation, Inc., The Simon Foundation, and Nancy Brown Wellin.

Cover images: Left: John Cohen, *Robert Frank and Larry Rivers, New York, 1959, during production of "Pull My Daisy"* (detail);
Right: Dennis Hopper, *Double Standard*, 1961 (detail);
Back cover image: Left: Larry Keenan, *Neal Cassady shaving at Allen Ginsberg's San Francisco apartment*, 1965 (detail)

Images for pages 1-8:
1: *Robert Frank and Larry Rivers, NYC, 1959, during production of "Pull My Daisy."* (detail). Photo © John Cohen
2: *Burroughs in Tangiers Under Hot Shadow*, 1961 (detail). Photo by Allen Ginsberg
3: *Veritas Crown of Flames*, 1957. Photo by Charles Brittin
4: *Corso and Ginsberg, Shy*, 1961 (detail). Photo by Allen Ginsberg
5: *Diane DiPrima*, c.1953-60. Photo by James O. Mitchell
6: *Philip Whalen with his drip portrait by Michael McClure at his San Francisco apartment*, 1965. Photo by Larry Keenan
7: *Michael McClure and Bruce Conner leaving Dave Hazelwood's apartment*, 1965. Photo by Larry Keenan
8: *Neal Cassady and Natalie Jackson under cinema marquee, San Francisco*, 1955 (detail). Photo by Allen Ginsberg

Library of Congress Cataloging-in-Publication Data
Phillips, Lisa.
Beat Culture and the New America, 1950-65 / Lisa Phillips, with contributions by Maurice Berger... [et al.].
p. cm.
Includes bibliographical references.
ISBN 0-87427-098-7 (alk. paper)
1. Arts and society—United States—History—20th century.
2. Subculture—United States—Influence. I. Title.
NX180.S6P53 1995
700'.1'03097309045—dc20 95-24764
CIP

ISBN 0-87427-098-7 softcover edition
ISBN 2-08013-613-5 hardcover edition (Flammarion)

Flammarion
26 rue Racine
75006 Paris
Numéro d'édition: 1059
Dépôt légal: November 1995

CONTENTS

DIRECTOR'S FOREWORD

Words like "beat" are generally the inventions of journalists and marketeers. Though not necessarily bad things, such popular descriptions of a generation often are at cross purposes with attempts to understand the richness and complexity of cultural history. Either hyperbolic or just banal, they bear little resemblance to the complex moments they purport to describe. The thirty-year romance with the term "hippie" and the current media preoccupation with "Generation X" are excellent examples of this phenomenon.

Though some contemporaneous critics understood well the depth and seriousness of Beat culture, the shallow narrow-mindedness of many postwar journalists led to a reactionary response to the art, literature, film, and nonconformist lifestyle of those who became known as the Beats. As a result, a strangely comforting characterization of beatniks emerged in the popular media: they were loony beret-wearing weirdos, conspiratorial communists, amoral homosexuals, filthy drug-addicted hipsters, or merely pathetic wannabe artists. These labels proved as useful to politicians looking for convenient scapegoats as to those seeking to build and manipulate the burgeoning youth market. Perhaps this was because the inherent radicality of bebop, abstract painting, and modern free verse made the Beats easy targets of class-based ridicule and derision. But more likely, it was because their attitudes opened up a closed-down culture.

In fact, the fifties and sixties found many Americans alienated from what was perceived as an increasingly hypocritical society. Psychically adrift, their energy flowed from an intuitive understanding of what this country could be, and what role they might play in the search pro-

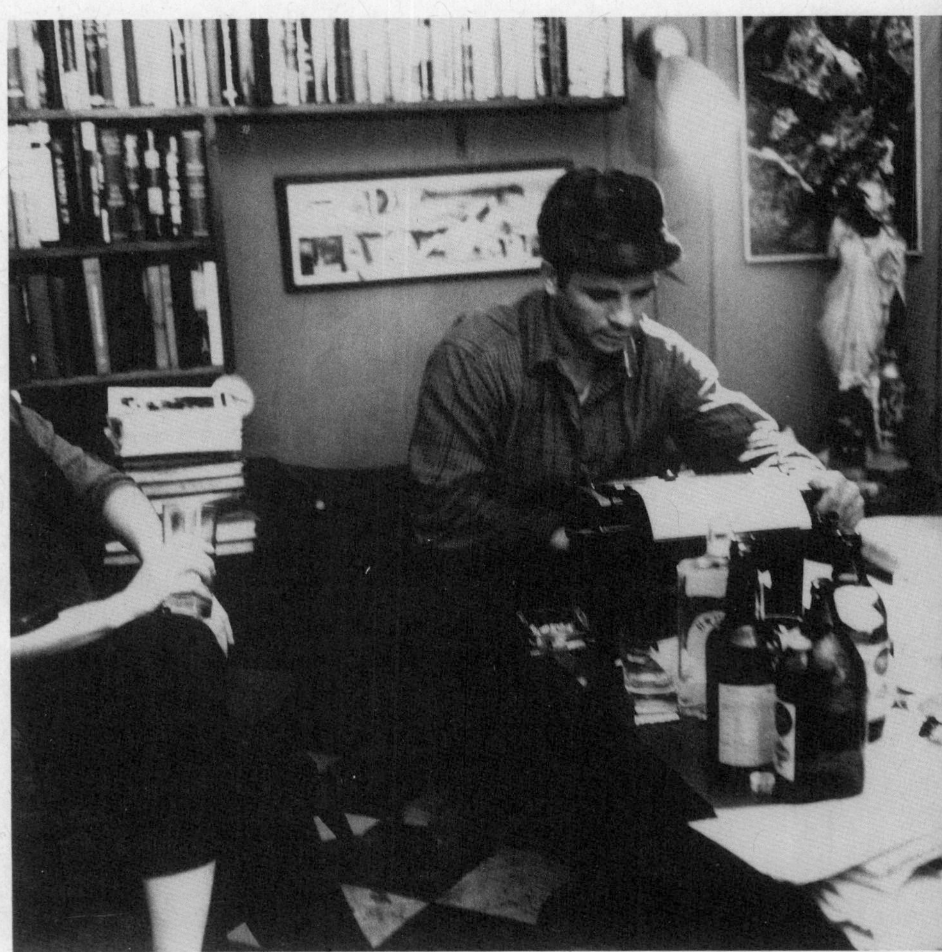

cess. Especially for those anguished by the virulent racism that continued to plague postwar America, the Beat engagement with black culture seemed a critical source for spiritual renewal. From another perspective, many artists struggling with their emerging sexual identities found the Beat world a nurturing place, where desire could be freely expressed and pleasure openly extolled. In more ways than can be simply listed, Beat culture offered an open road to a generation that feared itself lost in a no-exit world.

"Beat Culture and the New America: 1950-1965" is an attempt to put the cultural legacy of the Beat generation into the context of the social and artistic ferment of the 1950s and early 1960s. The exhibition of painting, sculpture, photography, film, and a fascinating range of documents and Beat ephemera is not concerned merely with defining what Beat was and was not, what it spawned or what it ignored. Whitney curator Lisa Phillips, who conceived and organized this exhibition, and the nine contributing writers to this catalogue have set out to define not only the historical roots of Beat culture, but also the relationship between its fuzzy edges and its molten center. Just as important, we believe that this exhibition will clarify the bridge between the current range and tone of American art, music, and literature and the residual forces which initially emerged during this complex moment in postwar American history and remain very much with us today.

We are extremely grateful to all the authors for their insightful contributions. In particular, I would like to personally acknowledge the great American poet Allen Ginsberg, whose intelligence and spirit are emblematic of Beat culture's special power; Ginsberg graces this book with a prologue, and he has provided thoughtful guidance to much of this project. The exhibition has provided the occasion for the production of a remarkable CD-ROM. In making this come about on time and on budget, John Carlin and Alice Rubin of the Red Hot Organization have shown tenacity and creativity in equal measure.

After its presentation at the Whitney, this exhibition will be seen at the Walker Art Center in Minneapolis and the M.H. de Young Memorial Museum, The Fine Arts Museums of San Francisco. We thank M.H. de Young director Harry S. Parker, III, and associate director and chief curator Steven A. Nash, as well as Walker Art Center director Kathy Halbreich and associate director and chief curator Richard Flood. Their collegial support and valued advice are deeply appreciated. We are, of course, obliged to the many lenders both private and public who have so graciously agreed to share their work with the three communities who will be viewing the exhibition. On behalf of the Trustees of the Whitney Museum and our colleagues in Minnesota and California, I extend thanks to each lender.

A number of enlightened individuals and organizations have provided the funding necessary to produce and tour this exhibition. We are again grateful to all our friends at the AT&T Foundation, and in particular to Suzanne Sato, for their continuing support of important exhibitions of American art. Similarly, I am relieved that I can still cite the National Endowment for the Arts as a public champion of important exhibitions such as this one. The exhibition was also supported by a generous grant from The Yamagata Foundation, and we thank Hiromichi Yamagata and Fred Hoffman for their belief in the significance of this project. Likewise, we are indebted to MTV Networks, which has helped underwrite the production of the educational materials for the exhibition.

I would like to acknowledge and extend our sincere appreciation to Whitney Museum Trustee Thomas H. Lee and to Ann Tenenbaum, who have made a major contribution toward the exhibition. And once again, in fulfillment of its important mission, the Whitney Museum's National Committee has helped underwrite the exhibition's US tour.

Our final acknowledgment is to the artists, writers, musicians, and assorted characters who are included in the exhibition. These men and women embody the soul of Beat culture.

David A. Ross
Alice Pratt Brown Director

Jack Kerouac typing, 1959. Photo © Fred W. McDarrah

ACKNOWLEDGMENTS

This project was an enormous undertaking that could never have been accomplished without the help and good will of so many people, including the sponsors, the staff at the Whitney Museum, the lenders, the artists, and countless other contributors. I am particularly appreciative of David A. Ross' support and encouragement of this project from the start.

I was extremely fortunate to have an extraordinary exhibition coordinator, Judy Hecker, who assisted with almost every aspect of the project, from the initial phases of research to the final realization. Jenelle Porter, my assistant, attended to the many details of the loans and catalogue and provided invaluable support, along with Ms. Hecker, in the development of the exhibition.

A very ambitious film and video program has been organized by Ray Carney, professor of American Studies at Boston Univeristy, together with Whitney curator John G. Hanhardt. It is a critical component of the exhibition which has profited from their considerable expertise. Matthew Yokobosky and Maria Christina Villaseñor in the Department of Film and Video were essential in coordinating the many films represented in the program.

The multimedia nature of this project entailed the contribution of several other skilled collaborators and I am grateful to all of them: the time line in the exhibition was prepared in collaboration with Steven Watson; the performances and educational programs were developed by Constance Wolf; an interactive CD-ROM and orientation film were produced by John Carlin and Alice Rubin of the Red Hot Organization in association with Voyager and the Whitney Museum; and the installation was designed by Christian Hubert.

Allen Ginsberg has been generous from the beginning, sharing insights, information, and suggestions and contributing as a writer, visual artist, and performer. I would also like to thank Bob Rosenthal, in Ginsberg's office, for all his assistance, as well as Althea Crawford and Peter Hale, who gave this project more than a fair share of their time.

I am indebted to Walter Hopps, who encouraged me early on to pursue this concept for an exhibition and for the knowledge of the period he shared with me. A number of others have been enthusiastic and supportive, especially Bruce Conner, George Herms, and Michael McClure; each has made valuable suggestions and imparted information along the way. Other poets, artists, critics, and curators who generously gave of their time and expertise include David Amram, Jacquelynn Baas, Bill Berkson, Tosh and Shirley Berman, Charles Brittin, Lawrence Ferlinghetti, Raymond Foye, Robert Frank, Hal Glicksman, Thelma Golden, Wally Hedrick, Jean-Nöel Herlin, Fred Hoffman, Dennis Hopper, Jess, Ted Joans, Hettie Jones, Larry Jordan, Allan Kaprow, Robert LaVigne, Ed Leffingwell, Alfred Leslie, Leah Levy, Judith Malina, Fred W. McDarrah, Arthur Monroe, Lawrence Rinder, Larry Rivers, Rebecca Solnit, Sandra Starr, David Sterritt, Dean Stockwell, Steven Watson, and William Wilson.

The generosity of the artists and lenders who are credited in this catalogue made the exhibition a reality, as did a number of other people who were especially helpful in securing loans: Paule Anglim and Ed Gilbert; Rita Bottoms of the University of California at Santa Cruz Library; Lisa Dennison of the Solomon R. Guggenheim Museum; Claudia Funcke of Columbia University's Rare Book and Manuscript Library; Peter Goulds; Michael Govan of the Dia Center for the Arts; Lisa Brower and Maryl Hosking of The New York Public Library; Margaret Kimball of Stanford University Library; Nicole Klagsbrun; Joan LiPuma; Lisa Lyons of the Lannan Foundation; Peter MacGill; Jonas Mekas; Arthur Monroe of The Oakland Museum; Nancy Reddin Kienholz; Rani Singh; John Sampas and the Estate of Jack Kerouac; Stephanie

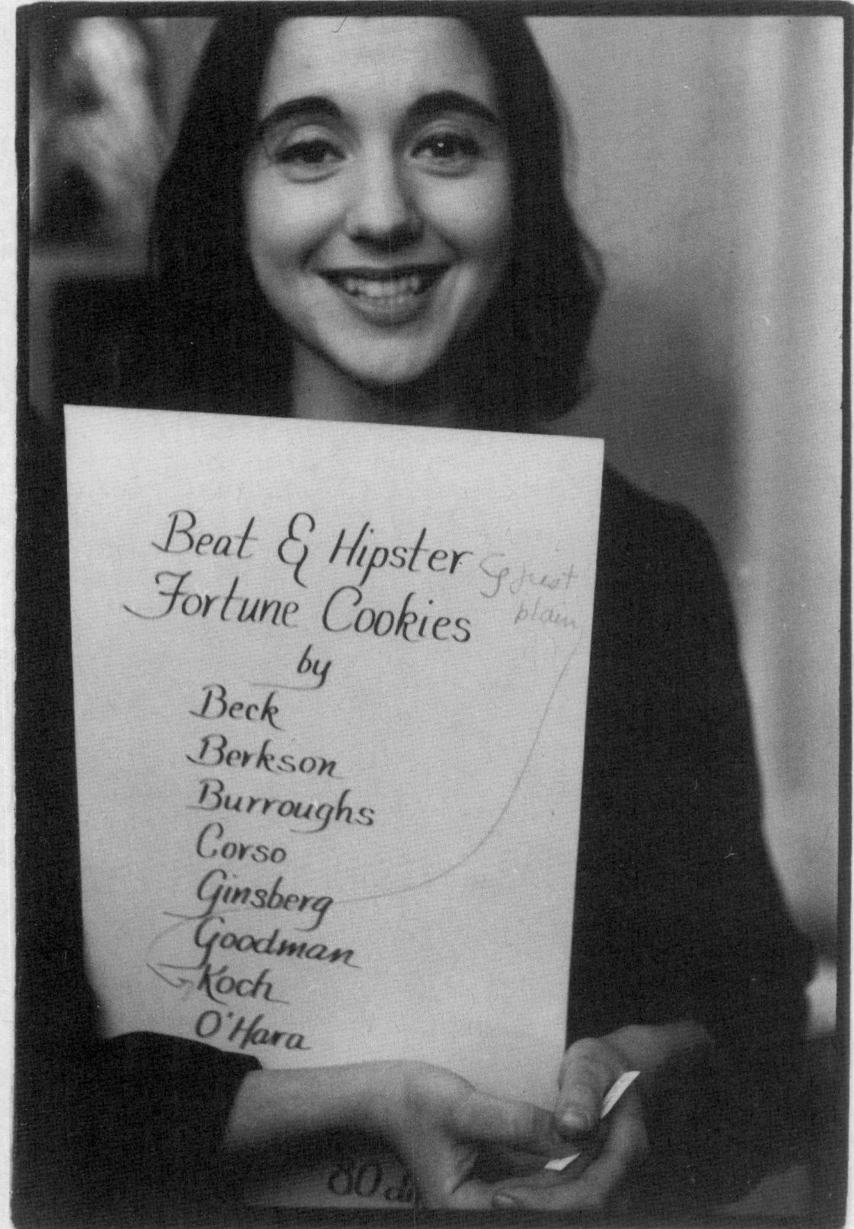

Beat & Hipster Fortune Cookies for sale at the Living Theater, c.1959.
Photo © Fred W. McDarrah

Barron and Robert A. Sobieszek of the Los Angeles County Museum of Art; Laela Weisbaum of the Archives of American Art; and David White.

One particular work in the exhibition deserves special mention: Jay DeFeo's *The Rose*. The restoration and removal of this work from the San Francisco Art Institute was a historic event, made possible through the encouragement and tireless efforts of Leah Levy and Ursula Cipa of the Estate of Jay DeFeo, and the support of the San Francisco Art Institute, Ella King Torrey, president, and Patti Quill, director of communications. A team of conservators, Anthony Rockwell, Anne Rosenthal, and Niccolo Caldararo, worked in concert with Nancy McGary, manager of the Permanent Collection of the Whitney Museum, on this most challenging restoration.

The publication of this catalogue entails a debt to a good many people: in particular to the authors for their excellent contributions—Maurice Berger, Ray Carney, Maria Damon, Allen Ginsberg, John G. Hanhardt, Glenn O'Brien, Mona Lisa Saloy, Ed Sanders, Rebecca Solnit, and Steven Watson. I would also like to extend my thanks to the designer, Lorraine Wild, to the publications department of the Whitney Museum, and to a number of interns who worked on aspects of the book over several summers: Julie Dobrow, Coleen McKenna, Jenny Meyer, Roxanne Richards, and Allyn S. Rippin. Justine Harari, Yeardley Leonard, and Ann Schneider contributed much appreciated research as well.

"Beat Culture and the New America" will be enjoyed by audiences around the country, and I would like to thank our partners in the project: the Walker Art Center, Minneapolis, Kathy Halbreich, director, and Richard Flood, chief curator; and the M.H. de Young Memorial Museum, The Fine Arts Museums of San Francisco, Harry S. Parker, III, director, and Steven A. Nash, associate director and chief curator.

Lisa Phillips

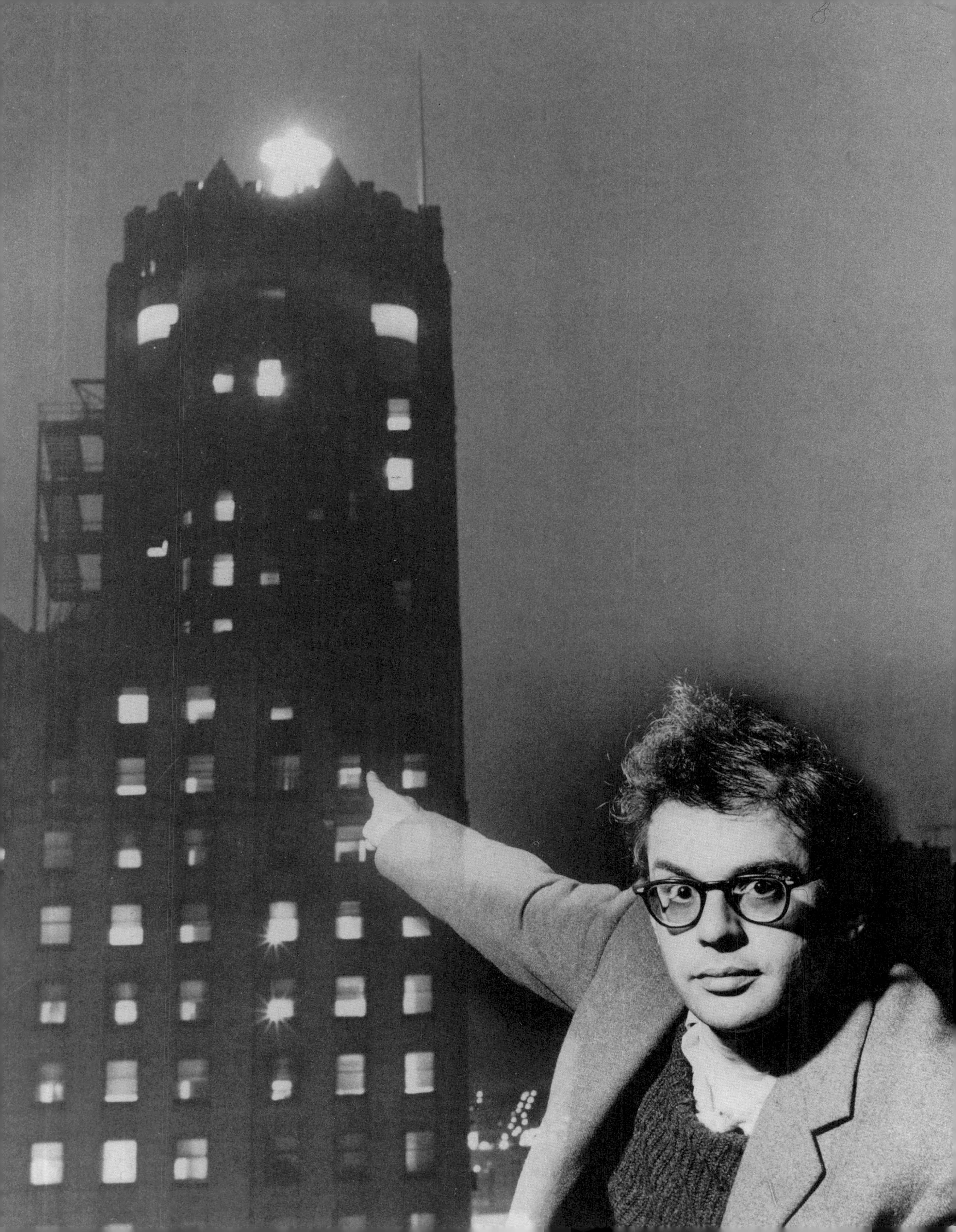

ALLEN GINSBERG

PROLOGUE

The phrase "Beat Generation" arose out of a specific conversation between Jack Kerouac and John Clellon Holmes in 1948. They were discussing the nature of generations, recollecting the glamour of the Lost Generation, and Kerouac said, "Ah, this is nothing but a beat generation." They talked about whether it was a "found generation" (as Kerouac sometimes referred to it), an "angelic generation," or some other epithet. But Kerouac waved away the question and said beat generation—not meaning to name the generation, but to unname it.

John Clellon Holmes' celebrated article in late 1952 in *The New York Times Magazine* carried

Allen Ginsberg and "Moloch," 1957. Photo by Harry Redl

the headline title "This Is the Beat Generation." That caught the public eye. Then Kerouac anonymously published a fragment of *On the Road* called "Jazz of the Beat Generation," and that reinforced the curiously poetic phrase. So that's the early history of the term.

Herbert Huncke, author of *The Evening Sun Turned Crimson*, and friend of Kerouac, Burroughs, and others of that literary circle from the forties, introduced them to what was then known as "hip language." In that context, the word "beat" is a carnival, "subterranean" (subcultural) term—a term much used then in Times Square: "Man, I'm beat," meaning without money and without a place to stay. It could also refer to those "who walked all night with shoes full of blood on the snowbank docks waiting for a door in the East River to open to a room full of steam heat and opium" ("Howl"). Or the word would be used as in conversation: "Would you like to go to the Bronx Zoo?" "Nah, man, I'm too 'beat,' I was up all night." So, the original street usage meant exhausted, at the bottom of the world, looking up or out, sleepless, wide-eyed, perceptive, rejected by society, on your own, streetwise. Or, as it once implied, "beat" meant finished, completed, in the dark night of the soul or in the cloud of unknowing. It could mean "open," as in the Whitmanesque sense of "openness," equivalent to humility. So "beat" was interpreted in various circles to mean emptied out, exhausted, and at the same time wide-open and receptive to vision.

A third meaning of "beat," as in beatific, was publicly articulated in 1959 by Kerouac, to counteract the abuse of the term in the media (where it was being interpreted as meaning "beaten completely," a "loser," without the aspect of humble intelligence, or of "beat" as "the beat of drums" and "the beat goes on"—all varying mistakes of interpretation or etymology). Kerouac (in various interviews and lectures) was trying to indicate the correct sense of the word by pointing out its connection to words like beatitude and beatific—the necessary beatness or darkness that precedes opening up to light, egolessness, giving room for religious illumination.

A fourth meaning that accumulated around the word is found in the phrase "Beat Generation literary movement." This phrase referred to a group of friends who had worked together on poetry, prose and cultural conscience from the mid-forties until the term became popular nationally in the late fifties. The group consisted of Kerouac, Neal Cassady (Kerouac's prototype hero of *On the Road*), William Burroughs, Herbert Huncke, John Clellon Holmes (author of *Go*, *The Horn*, and other books), and myself. We met Carl Solomon and Philip Lamantia in 1948, encountered Gregory Corso in 1950, and first saw Lawrence Ferlinghetti and Peter Orlovsky in 1954.

By the mid-fifties, this smaller circle—through natural affinity of modes of thought, literary style, or planetary perspective—was augmented in friendship and literary endeavor by a number of writers in San Francisco, including Michael McClure, Gary Snyder, Philip Whalen, and by 1958 some other powerful but lesser-known poets, such as Bob Kaufman, Jack Micheline and Ray Bremser, and the better-known black poet LeRoi Jones. All of us accepted the term beat at one time or another, humorously or seriously, but sympathetically, and were included in a survey of Beat manners, morals, and literature by *Life* magazine in a lead article in 1959 by Paul O'Neil, and by the journalist Alfred Aronowitz in a twelve-part series entitled "The Beat Generation" in the *New York Post*.

By the mid-fifties a sense of some mutual trust and interest was developed with Frank O'Hara and Kenneth Koch as well as with Robert Creeley and other alumni of Black Mountain College in North Carolina. Of that literary circle, Kerouac, Whalen, Snyder, poets Lew Welch, Diane DiPrima, Joanne Kyger, & Orlovsky, as well as myself and others were interested in meditation and Buddhism. (A discussion of the relationship between Buddhism and the Beat generation can be found in a scholarly survey of the evolution on Buddhism in America, *How the Swans Came to the Lake*, by Rick Fields).

The fifth meaning of the phrase Beat generation refers to the broader influence of literary and artistic activities of poets, filmmakers, painters, writers, and novelists who were working in concert in anthologies, publishing houses, independent filmmaking, and other media. These groups refreshed the long-lived bohemian cultural tradition in America. Among major interactive figures were: in film and still photography, Robert Frank and Alfred Leslie; in music, David Amram; in painting, Larry Rivers; in poetry and publishing, Cid Corman, Jonathan Williams, Don Allen, Barney Rosset, Lawrence Ferlinghetti. This energy fell out into the youth movement of the day, which was growing, and was absorbed by the mass and middle-class culture of the late fifties and early sixties.

Some essential effects of Beat Generation artistic movement can be characterized in the following terms:

Spiritual liberation, sexual "revolution" or "liberation," i.e., gay liberation, somewhat catalyzing women's liberation, black liberation, Gray Panther activism.

Liberation of the word from censorship.

Demystification and/or decriminalization of some laws against marijuana and other drugs.

The evolution of rhythm and blues into rock and roll as a high art form, as evidenced by the Beatles, Bob Dylan, and other popular musicians influenced in the late fifties and sixties by Beat generation poets' and writers' works.

The spread of ecological consciousness, emphasized early on by Gary Snyder and Michael McClure, the notion of a "Fresh Planet."

Opposition to the military-industrial machine civilization, as emphasized in writings of Burroughs, Huncke, Ginsberg, and Kerouac.

Attention to what Kerouac called (after Spengler) a "second religiousness" developing within an advanced civilization.

Return to an appreciation of idiosyncrasy as against state regimentation.

Respect for land and indigenous peoples and creatures, as proclaimed by Kerouac in his slogan from *On the Road*: "The Earth is an Indian thing."

The essence of the phrase "beat generation" may be found in *On the Road* with the celebrated phrase: "Everything belongs to me because I am poor."

This essay is a revised version of "A Definition of the Beat Generation," as published in *Friction*, 1 (Winter 1982), pp. 50-52.

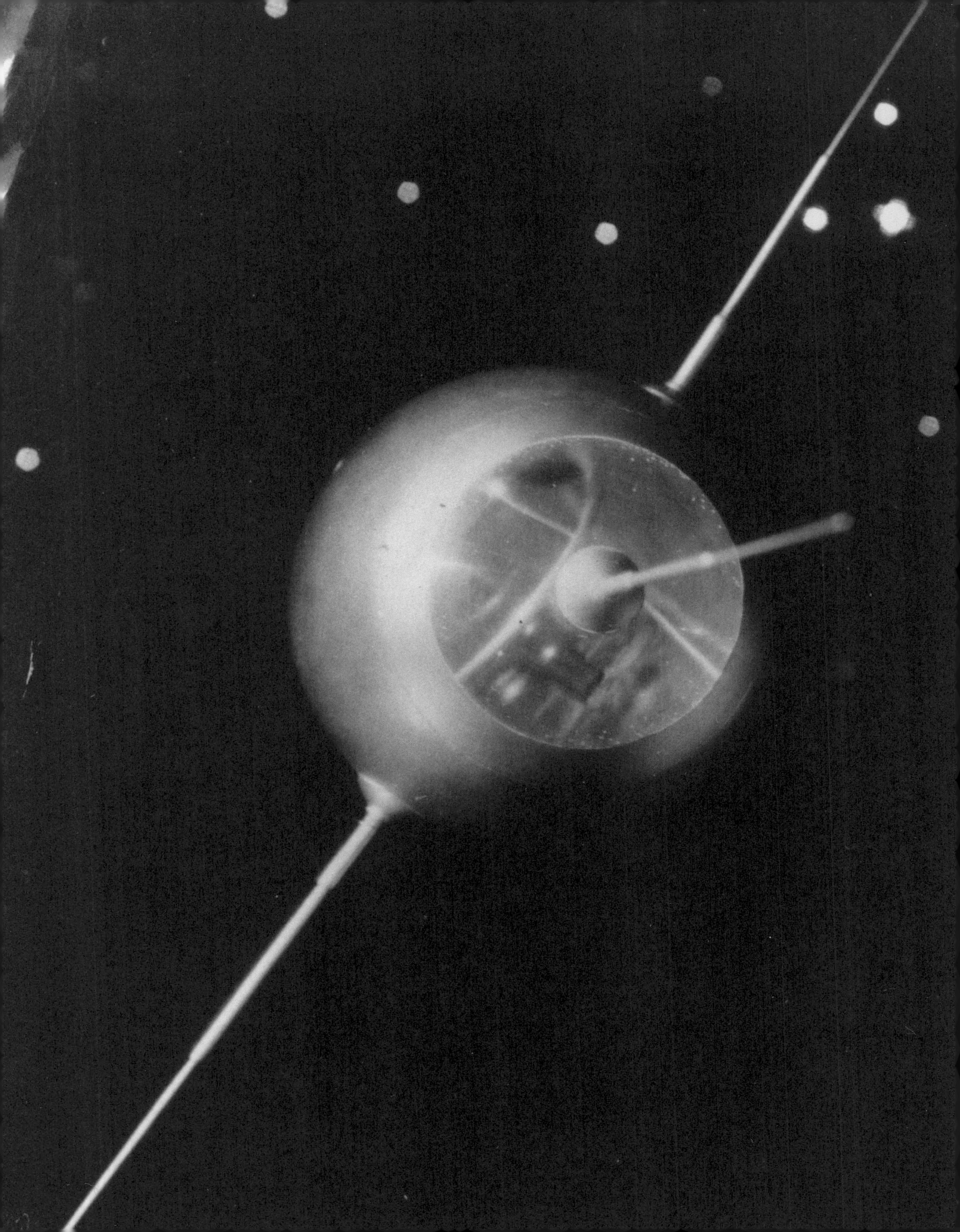

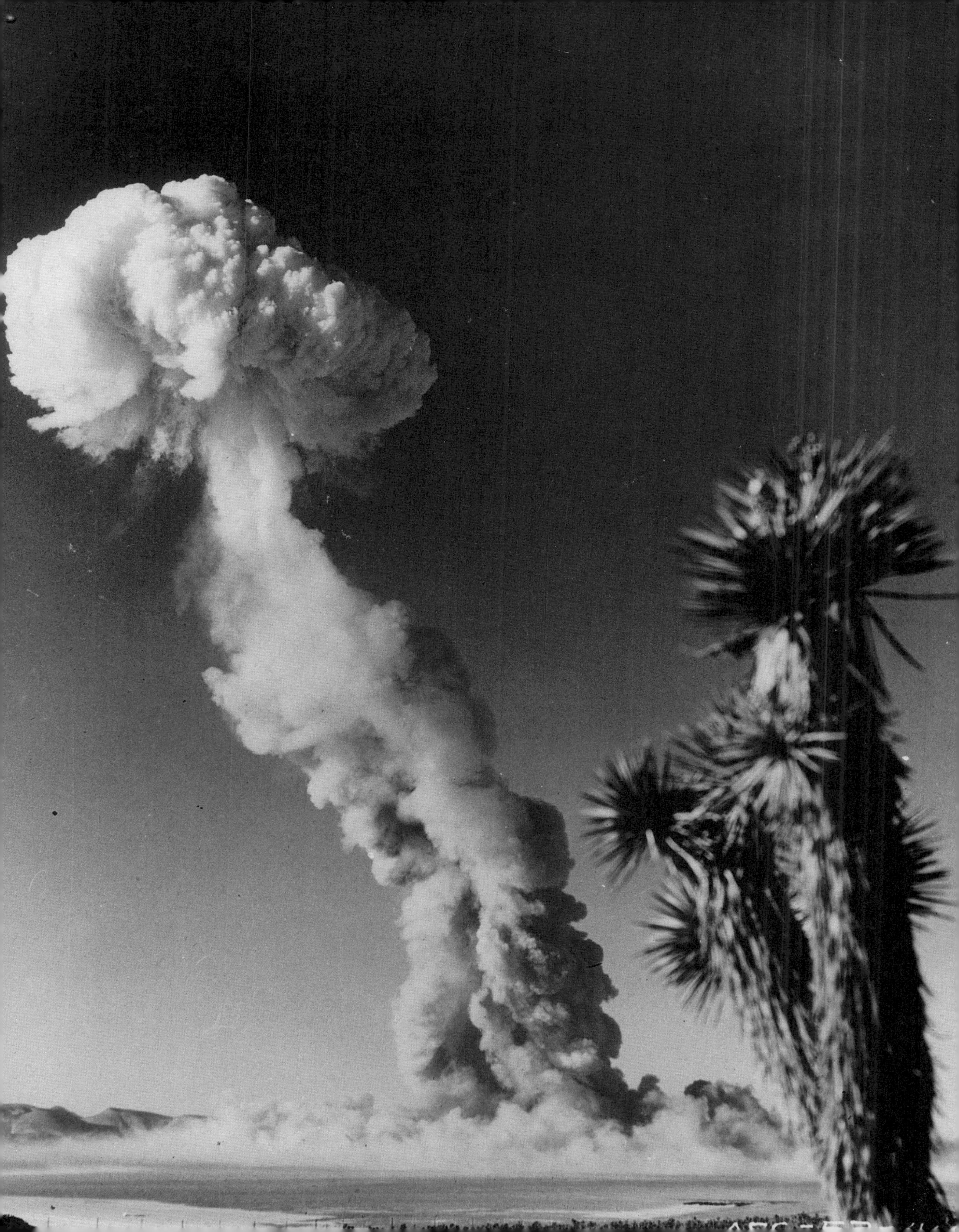

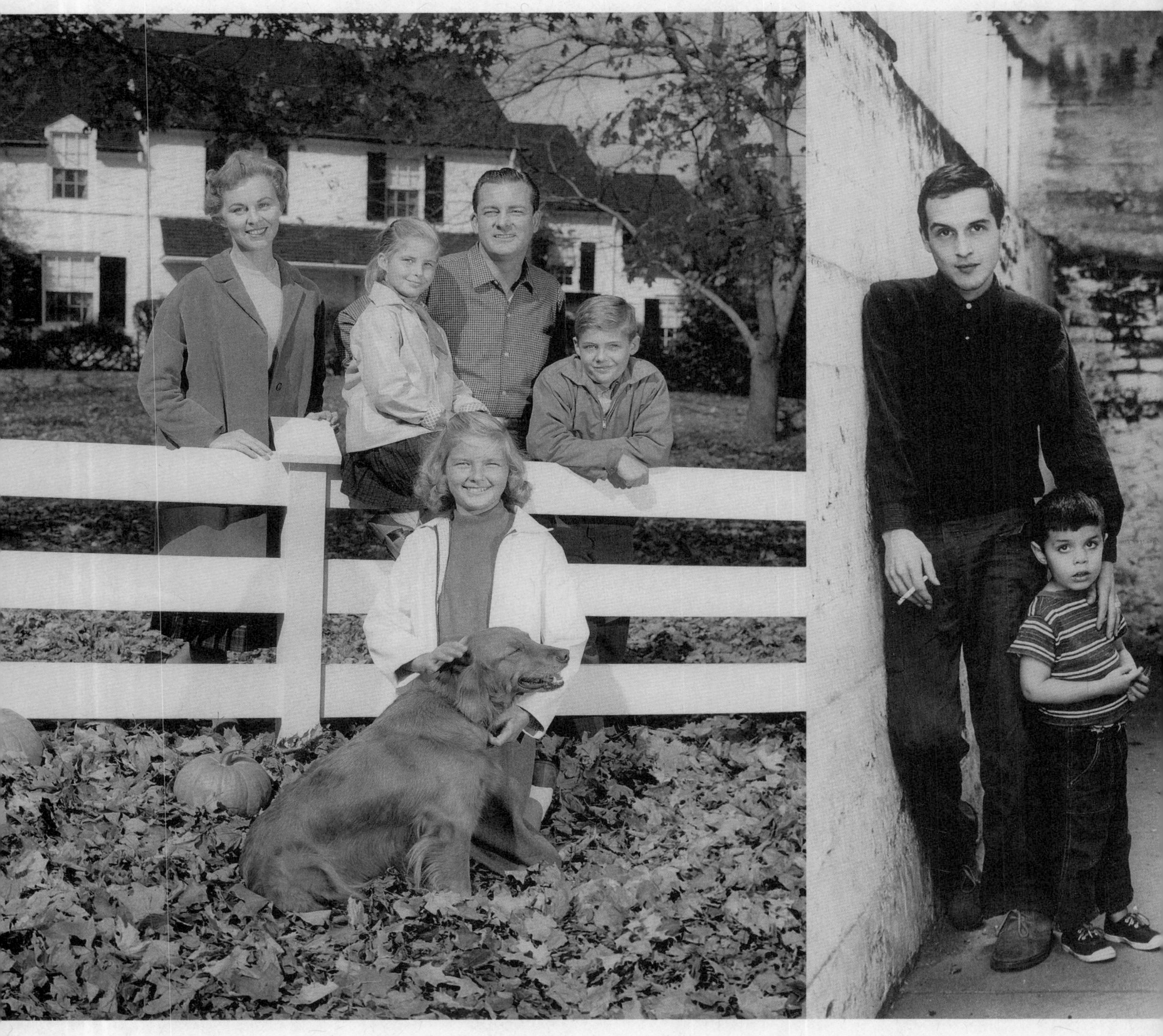

Previous page, left: **Model of Sputnik**, 1957; right: **Nevada atomic bomb explosion**, 1951

Above, left: **American family**, 1950s; right: **David Meltzer and family, San Francisco**, 1957. Photo by Harry Redl

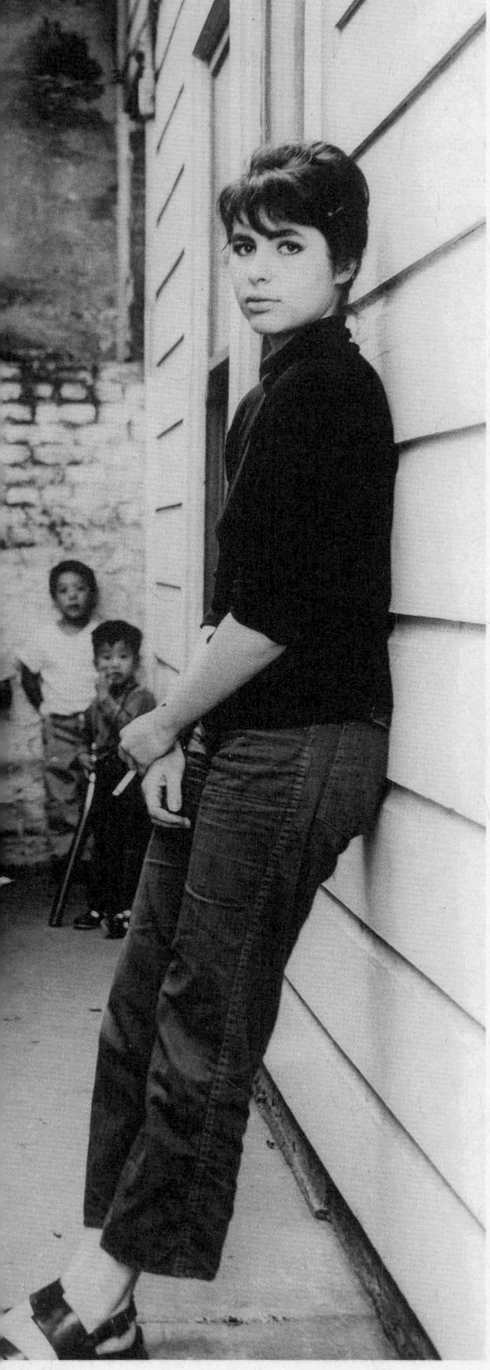

LISA PHILLIPS

Beat Culture: AMERICA REVISIONED

"We gotta go and never stop going till we get there."
"Where we going, man?"
"I don't know but we gotta go."
Jack Kerouac[1]

During the cold war, in the aftermath of World War II, a new generation emerged in America, known as the Beat generation. Disillusioned with the progress of science and Western technocracy, the Beats embarked on a quest for a new set of values out of which a new faith, a new tribal ethic was born. Although once rejected by mainstream society as outlaws, rebels, and morally dangerous, today the Beats are recognized as icons of America's counterculture and as one of the most influential cultural movements of the century. Their literary works, which aroused great controversy and academic disdain when first published in the fifties, are now part of the canon of American literature taught in universities around the country. Their archives are selling for vast sums of money to libraries and museums, and first editions of their books are highly sought after. Perhaps most important, the Beats continue to inspire younger generations of artists with their directness, courage, and intensity of vision.[2]

Despite such enduring achievement, the image many of us have of the movement often derives from the distorted media stereotypes that proliferated in the fifties and early sixties rather than from the works the Beats produced. There is the benign image of the cool hipster, dressed in black, playing bongo drums, and chanting poetry to a jazz backup; or the more sinister image of a rebellious, sociopathic, drug-using dropout. Both images conveyed an irreverence for authority and prevailing social norms.

What started as a small underground in the early fifties had, by the end of the decade, become big news. Thousands of words were written about the movement. Parodies, indictments, caricatures, and clichés were created for mass consumption in glossy magazines such as *Life* and *Look* and for TV and Hollywood movies. Most of the articles, like *Life* magazine's "The Only Rebellion Around," were double-edged. On the one hand, they stoned the Beats with epithets—"a few fruit flys...some of the hairiest, scrawniest and most discontented specimens of all time... who refuse to sample the seeping juices of American plenty and American social advance...."[3] On the other, the press gave the Beats credit for being the only rebellion around. They were alternately blamed for the rise of juvenile delinquency, narcotics addiction, sexual promiscuity, alcohol consumption among the young[4]—and heralded as a trigger for change, for giving voice to a new generation.

By 1960, as the country moved away from the constrained temperament of the postwar period, the beatnik had become a new cultural effigy. People rushed to cash in on the Beat boom, creating rent-a-beatnik parties, beatnik bus tours, and beatnik kits. The Beats themselves, who were vanguard and antimaterialist, could not fend off their own co-option, packaging, and containment as a *style*. In order to disassociate themselves from commercial exploitation, many of them took to the road again and explored foreign lands, others retreated into private worlds of work and, occasionally, self-destructive delusion. The original community began to disperse. Within one decade, an avant-garde movement had been absorbed by the mainstream, perhaps for the first time in history.

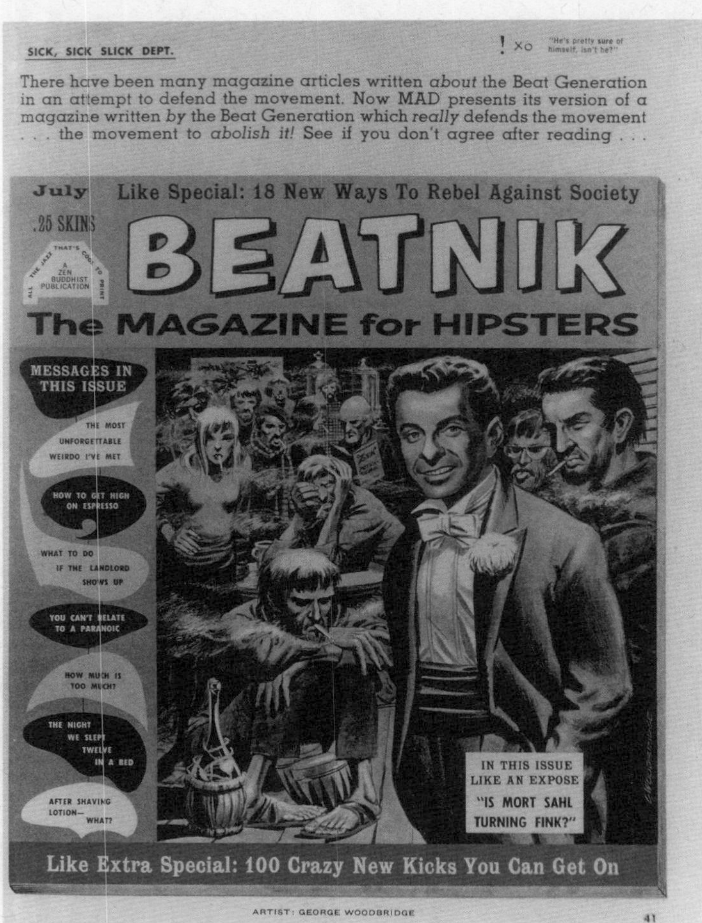

SICK, SICK SLICK DEPT.

"He's pretty sure of himself, isn't he?"

There have been many magazine articles written *about* the Beat Generation in an attempt to defend the movement. Now MAD presents its version of a magazine written *by* the Beat Generation which *really* defends the movement . . . the movement to *abolish it!* See if you don't agree after reading . . .

ARTIST: GEORGE WOODBRIDGE

41

George Woodbridge, illustration from **MAD**, September 1960

Hal Chase, Jack Kerouac, Allen Ginsberg, and William S. Burroughs, Morningside Heights, Budapest Degenerates, 1945. Photo by Allen Ginsberg

Jack Kerouac may have "opened a million coffee bars and sold a million pairs of Levis to both sexes,"[5] but Beat was in fact a state of mind. One has to cut through the haze of media myth and distortion to see the roots of the movement, its genesis, and its true accomplishments.

Half a century ago, in 1944, Jack Kerouac, Allen Ginsberg, and William Burroughs met in New York at Columbia University. They were introduced to the phrase "beat" in the mid-1940s by Herbert Huncke, a Times Square junkie and hipster friend of Burroughs. Kerouac began using it by the end of the decade (and was originally going to call *On the Road* "The Beat Generation"), and it first appeared in print in John Clellon Holmes' 1952 article for *The New York Times Magazine*, "This Is the Beat Generation."

Long before *On the Road*, *Naked Lunch*, and *Howl* were published, Kerouac, Burroughs, and Ginsberg envisioned themselves as a new school of literature, "the nucleus of a totally new historically important American creation."[6] They shared a vision of America and were attracted to each other by a mutual opposition to status quo conformity. They wrote about each other, solicited each other's criticism, and promoted each other's books. Despite their differences (according to Burroughs, you couldn't find three more different writers), their careers converged at a crucial moment that resulted in a shared outlook and sensibility.[7]

This accidental gathering in the forties lay the groundwork for the Beat movement, which soon swelled to include other avant-garde poets and writers, as well as filmmakers and visual artists on both coasts. As Ginsberg said, "Nobody knows whether we were catalysts or invented something, or just the froth riding on a wave of its own. We were all three, I suppose."[8] By the time the term Beat reached print in 1952, it was galvanizing a generation and provoking dispute. The real meaning of "beat"—upbeat, downbeat, deadbeat—was continually debated, as were the people who fit the term and who transcended it.[9]

This exhibition looks at the Beat movement in all its complexity—through the many cross-

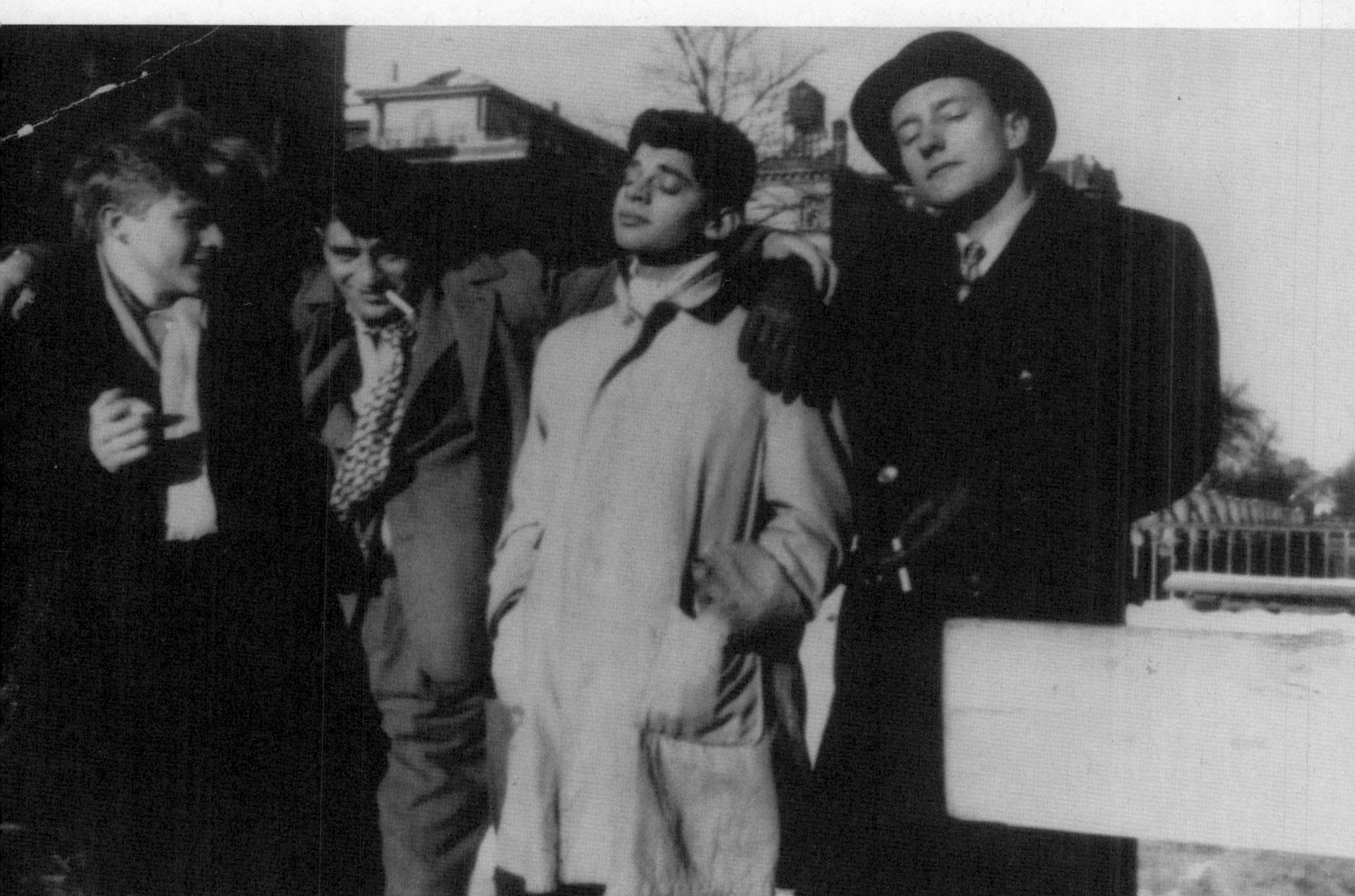

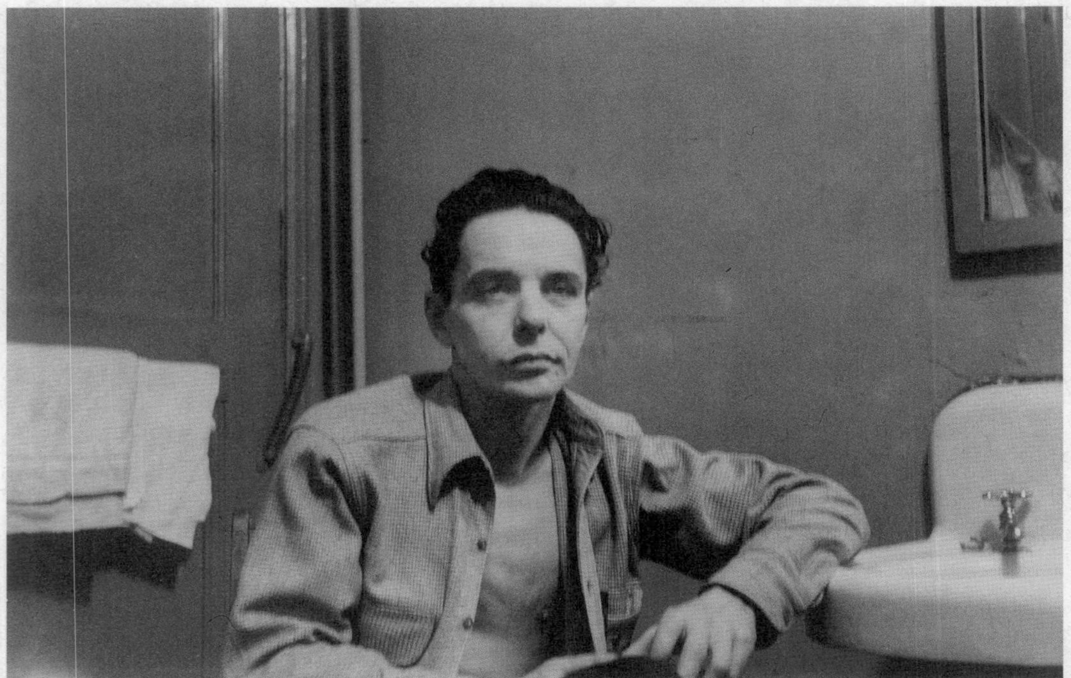

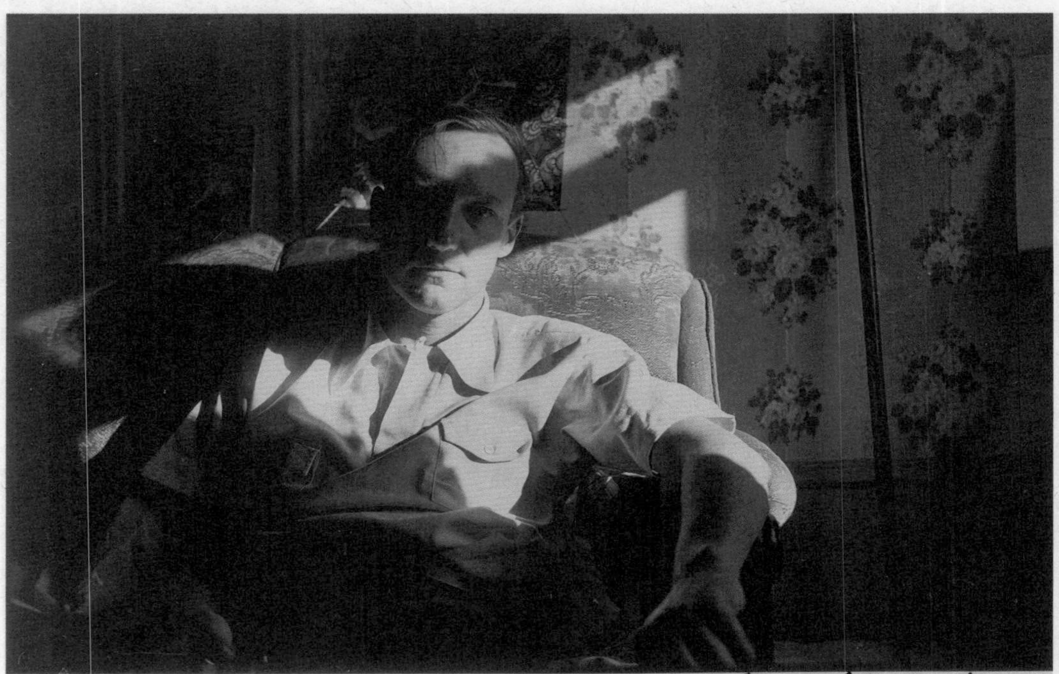

Rare Glimpse of Storyteller Herbert Huncke, 1953. Photo by Allen Ginsberg

Sad in Love, 1953. Photo by Allen Ginsberg

Jack Kerouac, Heroic Portrait, 1953. (detail) Photo by Allen Ginsberg

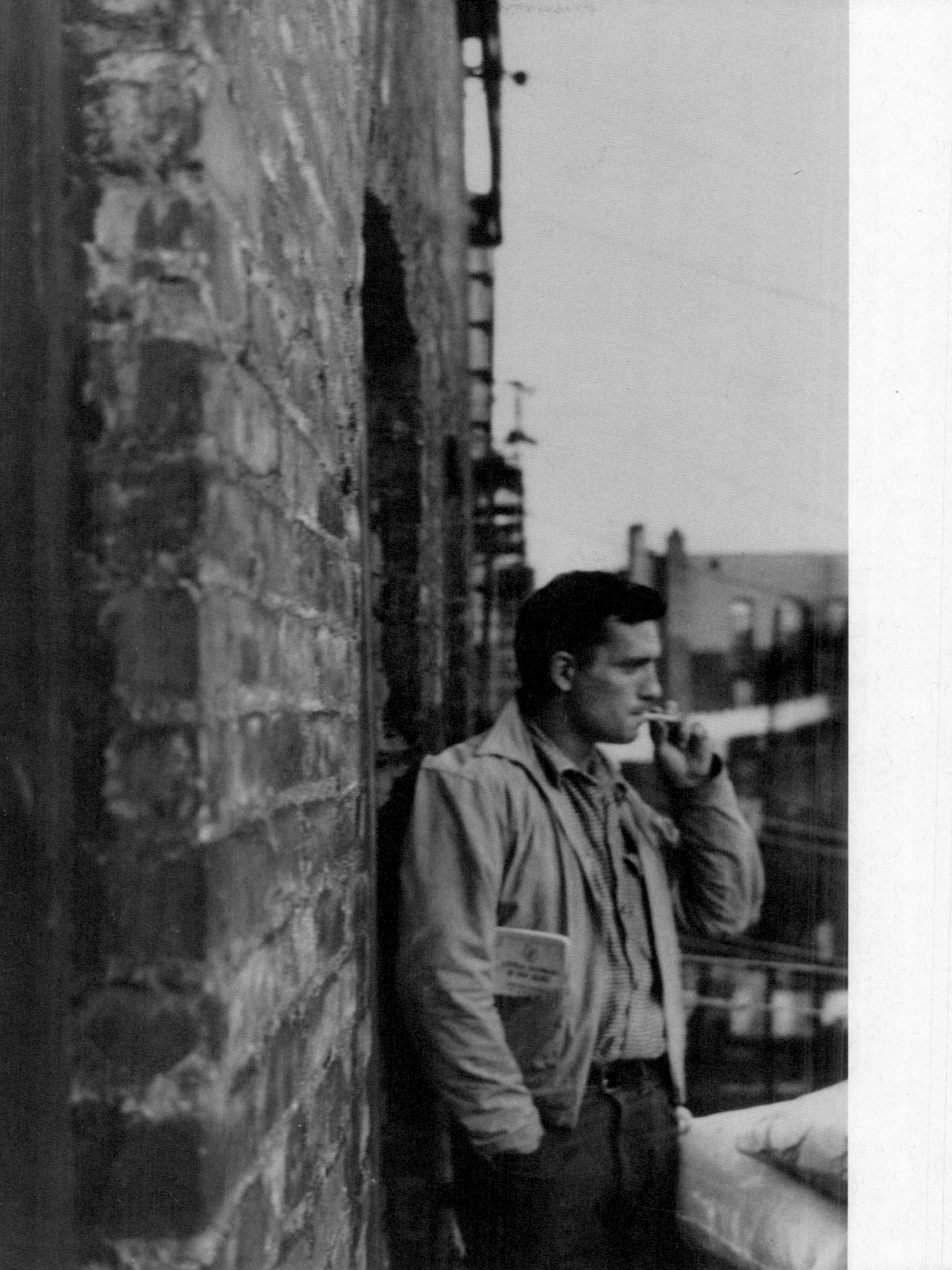

currents, rich exchanges, and collaborations among poets, visual artists, musicians, and filmmakers at work on both coasts during this period of intense creative ferment. By defining Beat as a broad cultural movement, it becomes evident that the Beat spirit and sensibility extended well beyond the now legendary literary accomplishments, permeating many forms of artistic expression, touching and transforming American artistic life.

Many of the Beats' fellow travelers resisted the label—for instance, painters, sculptors, and filmmakers never called themselves Beat artists—but they shared a strong affinity and spirit with the Beat poets as well as a close-knit bohemian community in New York's Greenwich Village, San Francisco's North Beach, and in the canyons of Los Angeles. They supported each other, collaborated with each other, encouraged freedom of expression across artistic lines, and provided an atmosphere of acceptance where advanced art could be made and could flourish. They expanded the notion of what art could be—valuing process over object and joining the commonplace with the ecstatic. Together they formed a potent underground that offered another view of American reality as an alternative to the conformity and consensus of official culture.

The Beats saw an enormous gap between America's promise and reality. Their response was to re-envision America according to their own rules and interests, celebrating life at the margins, the "great unknown and undiscovered peoples"[10] in America: the underprivileged, dispossessed, outcast, and outlaw subcultures of the African-American, the jazz musician, the junkie. They knew that you could love your country and still be a rebel.

The Beat rebellion gave form to an invisible turning point in American culture at mid-century. Born in the Depression, the Beats spent their adolescence in wars, both hot and cold, and matured in the shadow of nuclear holocaust. Amid the smug optimism of the Eisenhower years there was plenty of anxiety and discontent. Comfortable affluence and confidence in American values were compromised by fears about the spread of Communism and the threat of nuclear annihilation. The Beats detested the arms race, McCarthyism, and the seemingly forced migration to the suburbs. They stood opposed to the predominant climate of corporate values, consumerism, and conformity, finding the weight of convention punishing and exhausting. They were "beat," "beaten" down, worn out by it.

John Clellon Holmes recognized the effects of the social and cultural cataclysms upon the lives of his generation:

> The historical climate which formed its attitudes was violent, and it did as much violence to ideas as it did to the men who believed in them....Conventional notions of private and public morality have been steadily atrophied in the last ten or fifteen years by the exposure of treason in government, corruption in labor and business and scandal among the mighty of Broadway and Hollywood....Orthodox religious conceptions of good and evil seem increasingly inadequate to explain a world of science-fiction turned fact, past-enemies turned bosom-friends, and honorable-diplomacy turned brink-of-war. Older generations may be distressed or cynical or apathetic about this world....But the Beat Generation is specifically the product of this world, and it is the only world its members have ever known.[11]

Segregated water fountains in North Carolina, 1950

One has to look at the metaphysical mood of the generation to understand the Beat phenomenon. The Reverend Howard Moody, who presided over St. Mark's Church in New York—a center for avant-garde poetry, theater, art, and dance in the late fifties and sixties—made the following observation in his sermon "The Beatitude of the Beat Generation":

> **Should we be surprised that in the age of "the lonely crowd," "the organization man," and "the hidden persuaders" we would get a generation, or at least a segment, that is sickened on the inside and rebellious on the outside at having seen human existence being squeezed into organized molds of conformity? I wonder if it is as incongruous as we like to think—this generation we have spawned, whose primary interests seem to be fast cars, long trips, jive, junk, jazz and all other related kicks.[12]**

Sociologically, the Beats were the first large, self-conscious, and widely publicized group of middle-class dropouts and have sometimes been called American existentialists. They indeed shared a sense of acute alienation, of the absurd, and a belief in the importance of individual action with their European counterparts. They pursued their desire for risk and total experience through drugs, sex, and speed. However, the Beats also inherited a long tradition of dissent in America that runs from Emerson and Thoreau and Whitman to the pioneer-outlaw—a tradition of the individual forging an independent way against the majority. In fact, the Beat spirit can be traced back to the old pioneer and cowboy notion of the excitable, intense, and independent personality exemplified by frontier America.[13] By the 1950s, this spirit of self-invention and anti-assimilation was ready for renewal.

The Beats were not programmatically political, but were utopian in their belief that artist-citizens would be the leaders of a new society. Theirs was "a revolution of the soul,"[14] a revolution of the spirit—a utopia based on the intense embrace of experience, often evading logic, bypassing reason, and staying in the presence of sensation. Their heroes were mad prophets, seers, visionaries, and they felt a spiritual kinship with William Blake, with the Symbolists Rimbaud and Lautréamont, and with the Surrealists Cocteau and Artaud.

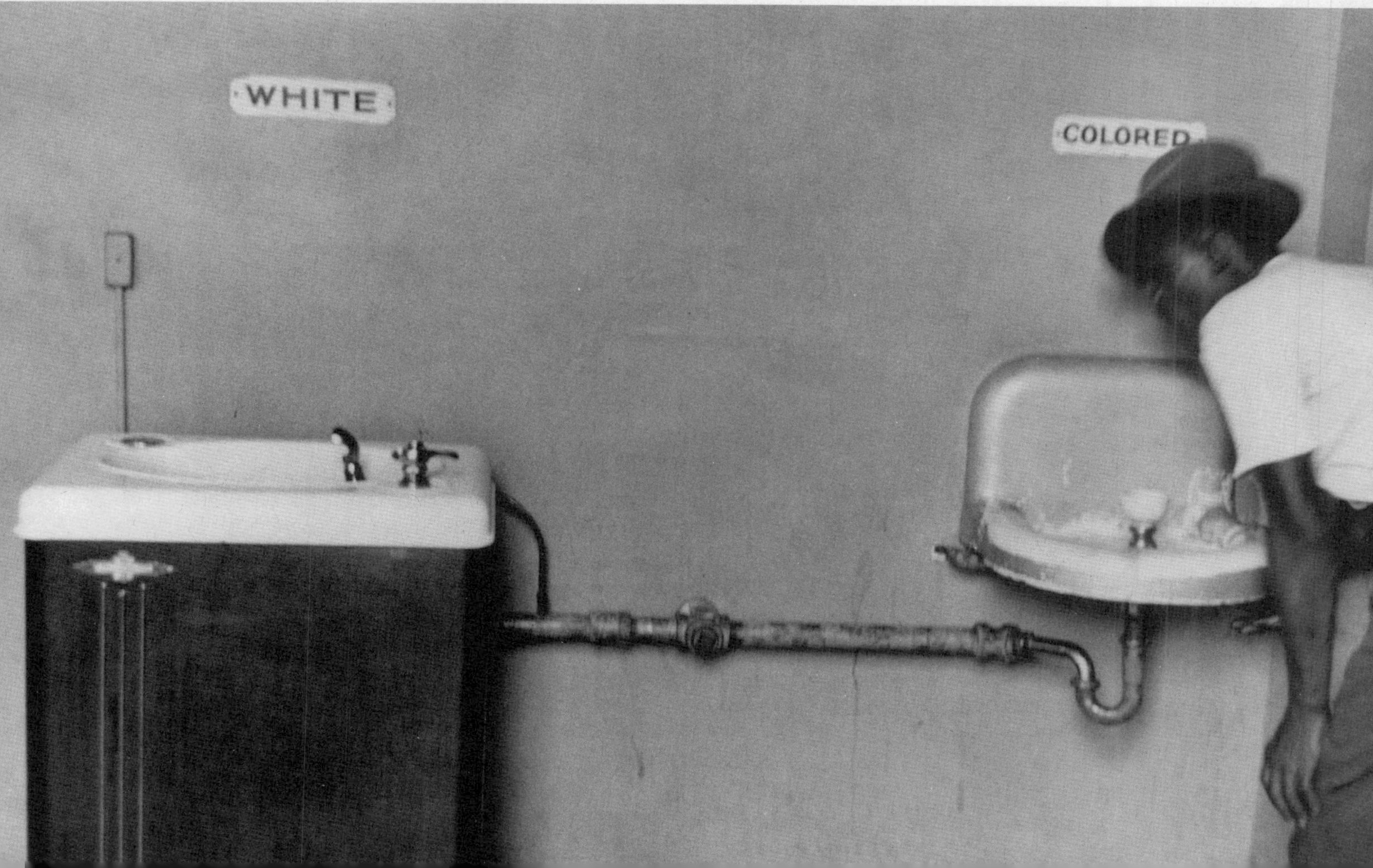

Madness was often privileged over reason. Who determined what was sane and what was not? ("I saw the best minds of my generation destroyed by madness, starving hysterical naked/ dragging themselves through the negro streets at dawn looking for an angry fix" ("Howl"). Or: "...the only people for me are the mad ones, the ones who are mad to live, mad to talk, mad to be saved, desirous of everything at the same time, the ones who never yawn or say a common-place thing, but burn, burn, burn, like fabulous yellow roman candles exploding like spiders across the stars..." (*On the Road*).[15] To the Beats, establishment culture and the military seemed criminal, and sinister—and their values could not be trusted. According to artist Bruce Conner, there was a common tendency among the Beats to "reverse assumptions about cause and effect, to reverse polarities."[16]

When Allen Ginsberg was asked to provide a "history of the Beats in overview" for a conference at New York University last year, he had one overriding observation: "...almost any of the seminal figures had had some kind of visionary experience....some sort of vision which they thought of as either supernatural or Buddhist or a variety of religious experience. William Burroughs from childhood has recorded any number of tricks of consciousness that were a break in the ordinary modality of consciousness for him. Good old men on the lawn in St. Louie, or little Martians, or other apprehensions later on as a result of junk withdrawal or junk or as a result of Yage experiments in South America...."[17]

Much of Beat art and attitudes were informed by visionary experiences—psychic visions or visions attained through meditation or drugs. Gary Snyder had a satori experience in 1948 of everything sentient and alive; Ginsberg had a vision of Blake in the same year; Kerouac in Rocky Mount fell backward with a golden light in his eye, realizing that the universe is golden ash. Gregory Corso had an experience of "skinless light" on Crete in 1960; Michael McClure's biological, ecstatic visions can be found in his early "Peyote Poem" as well as in his book *Dark Brown*. Herbert Huncke had a childhood experience of gigantic universal stillness; Philip Whalen achieved a number of small satoris as a by-product of meditation and Zen.[18] While taking peyote in 1956-57, Bruce Conner reconnected with a mystical experience he had had at eleven wherein he found himself transforming through decades, perhaps centuries.[19] "The Beat Generation is a vision," said Holmes, "not an idea."[20]

This was a generation searching for some kind of ecstasy, some marvelous vision of God—and drugs, jazz, and relentless mobility were all ways to get there. The Beat generation, as Kerouac said "is basically a religious generation....Beat means beatitude, not beat up. You *feel* this. You feel it in a beat, in jazz—real cool jazz or a good, gutty rock number."[21] Much of the Beats' frenetic activity is an overactivated form of search. They had an obsessive desire to believe but an inability to do so in conventional terms. This was the "hot" side of the Beats, who were always pictured as the essence of "cool." They experimented with all kinds of religions and mystical cults—Zen, the occult, yage, peyote, LSD, Catholicism, the Cabala—to attain an ecstatic radicalism, which they then transmitted through their art. This mystical strain was especially strong on the West Coast and can be seen in the works of Bruce Conner, Michael McClure, Wallace Berman, Jordan Belson, Jay DeFeo, Kenneth Anger, and Harry Smith, to name a few.

Burroughs Lying Down in Bedroom, 1953. Photo by Allen Ginsberg

Bill and Jack in Mortal Combat, 1953. Photo by Allen Ginsberg

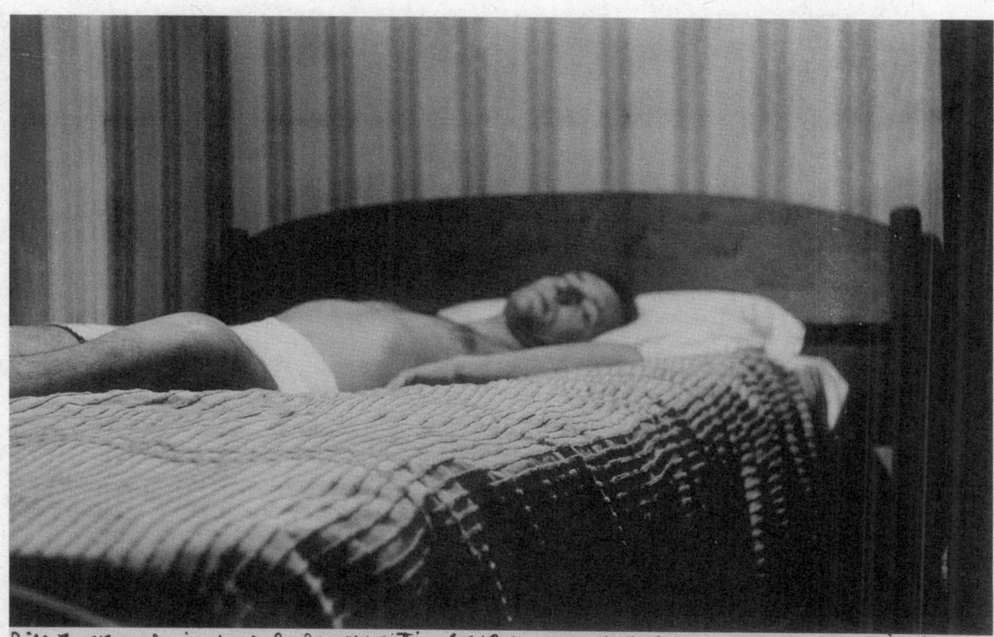

Bill Burroughs in back bedroom waiting for company, Apt. 16, 206 E. 7th St. "He is staying with me, I come home from work 4:45 and we talk until one AM or later, I hardly get enuf sleep, can't think about work seriously, am all hung up in a great psychic marriage with him for the month—" (letter to Neal Cassady, September 4, 1953.) New York, Fall '53.
Allen Ginsberg

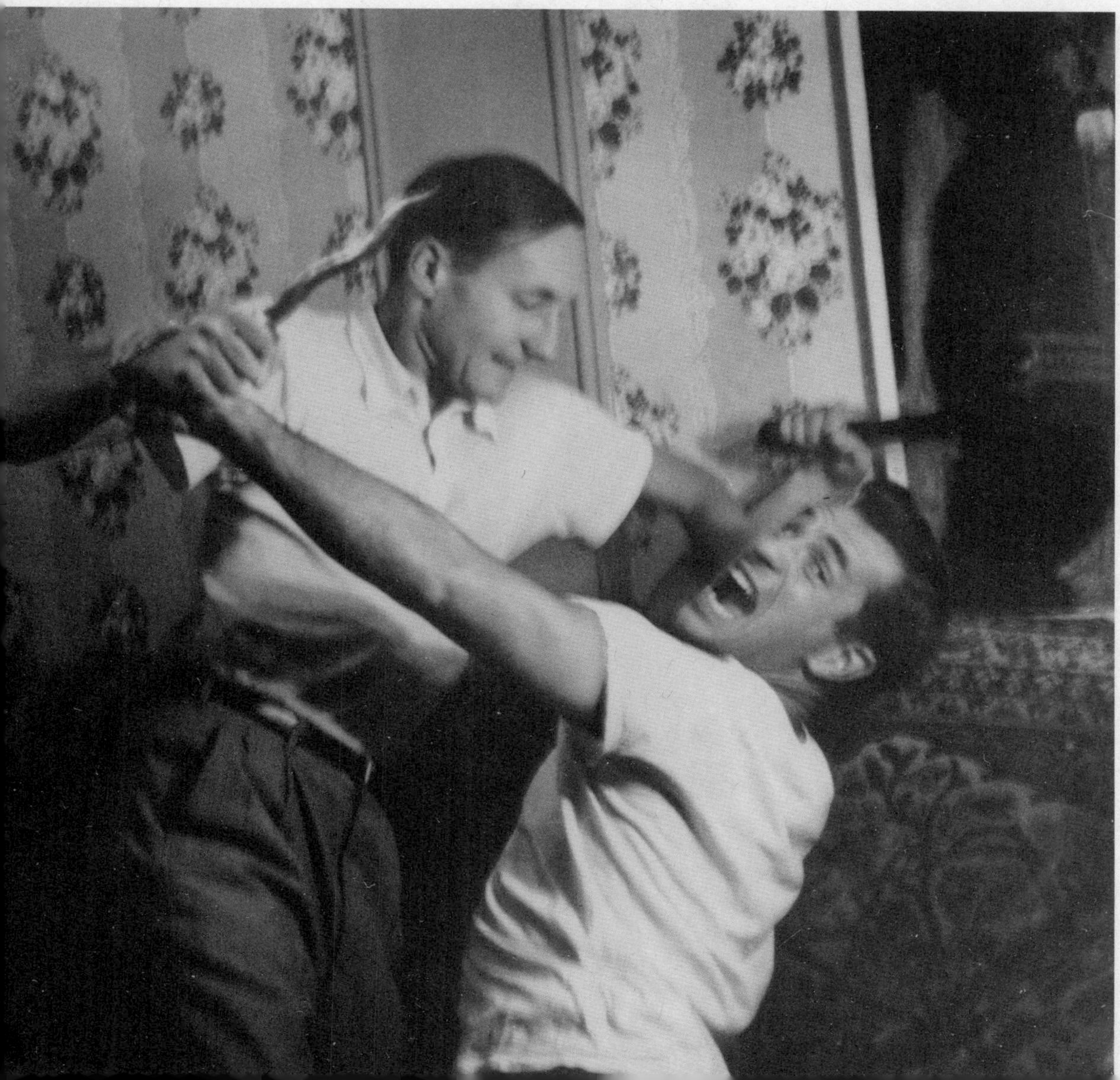

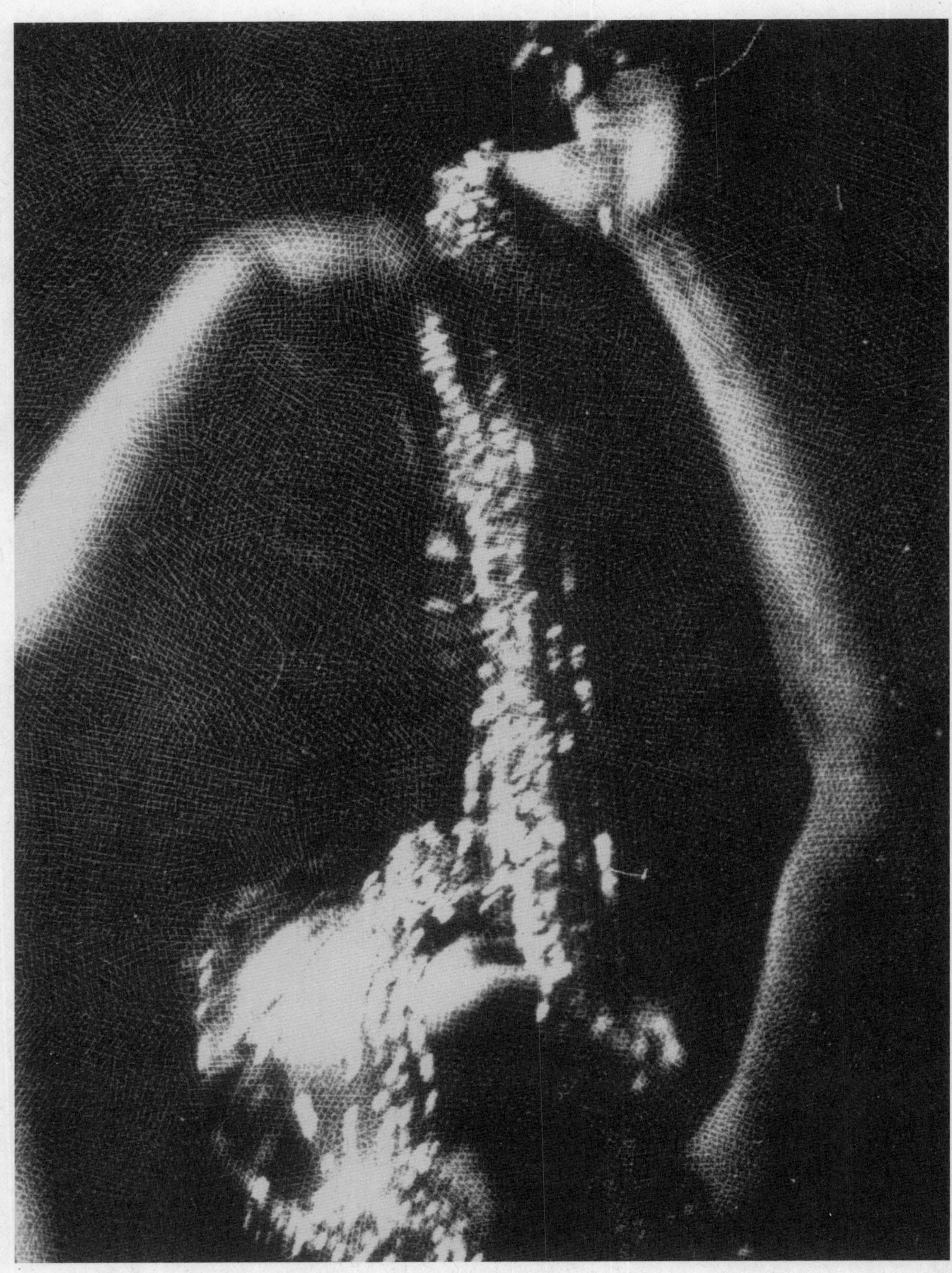

Wallace Berman and Jay DeFeo
Untitled (Jay DeFeo), 1958
Gelatin silver print,
5 1/2 x 4 3/16 (14 x 10.6)
Lannan Foundation, Los Angeles

The search for alternative consciousness, the mystical side of the Beats, goes hand in hand with their gritty realism and rebellion. These two sides—the ecstatic and the horrific, the beatific and the beaten, define the poles of Beat experience. The extremes of mystical wonder and squalid realism, the lofty and seedy, could be combined and expressed in the arts, but "were not translatable in politics."[22]

The Beat interest in these extremes and intensity of experience, in the mystical and the commonplace, in reversing expectations, converged with several other ground-breaking developments in the arts at mid-century. The Beats played a greater role than is generally acknowledged in the shifting cultural paradigm of this watershed period, overlapping and intersecting with such developments as avant-garde dance and theater, Neo-Dada art, Abstract Expressionism, American independent film, California Assemblage, Fluxus, and Happenings.

Most of these groups had shared goals and ambitions. Boundaries among media were traversed freely and often disrupted. Immediacy, spontaneity, and improvisation were stressed. The purity of the modernist canon was rejected, and the marginal, impure, and debased were redeemed as worthy subjects for art. (Kerouac: "I love it because it's ugly.") Art and life were inseparable, which brought a new kind of realism to art, and a new kind of freedom and self-expression to living.

One of the most revolutionary achievements of the Beat era was a change of venue for art: out of the academies, museums, and concert halls and into the streets, coffeehouses, and nightclubs. Artists, filmmakers, jazz musicians, and poet-performers mixed in places like the Black Cat Café, the Cellar, and the Coexistence Bagel Shop in San Francisco, the Gashouse in Los Angeles, and the San Remo, the Cedar Tavern, Café Bizarre, and the Five Spot in New York. A fluid café scene created a setting for aesthetic exchange among artists in all media. Another part of the circuit of informal meeting places was the artist co-op gallery—a phenomenon of the fifties that flourished in San Francisco, New York, and Los Angeles. The 6 Gallery in San Francisco was the site of the now legendary first reading of Ginsberg's "Howl" in 1955 (sometimes cited as the beginning of the Beat movement), while the Brata Gallery in New York sponsored the first jazz poetry readings in New York in 1958, organized by David Amram and Jack Kerouac. The Judson Memorial Church showcased cutting-edge poetry, art, and dance performances.[23] In addition, a number of small magazines and broadsides, such as *Semina*, *Yūgen*, and *The Floating Bear*, promoted a common forum for artists and writers, as did bookstores on both coasts: among them, the 8th Street Bookshop run by Ted Wilentz (Robert Smithson worked there in the late fifties) and Orientalia on 10th Street in New York; and City Lights Bookstore in San Francisco. *The Floating Bear*, run by Diane DiPrima and LeRoi Jones, published the work of poets, playwrights, dancers, musicians, and painters. *Semina*, published by Wallace Berman, was actually an assemblage of sorts, containing loose sheets of art and poetry on various papers boxed together.

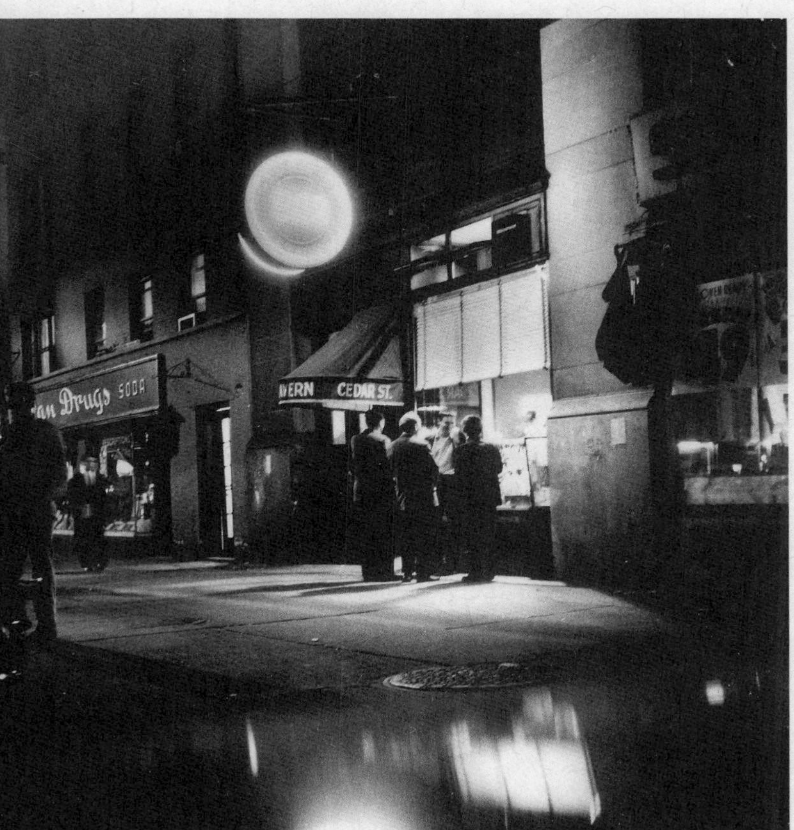

Cedar Tavern, 1959. Photo © Fred W. McDarrah

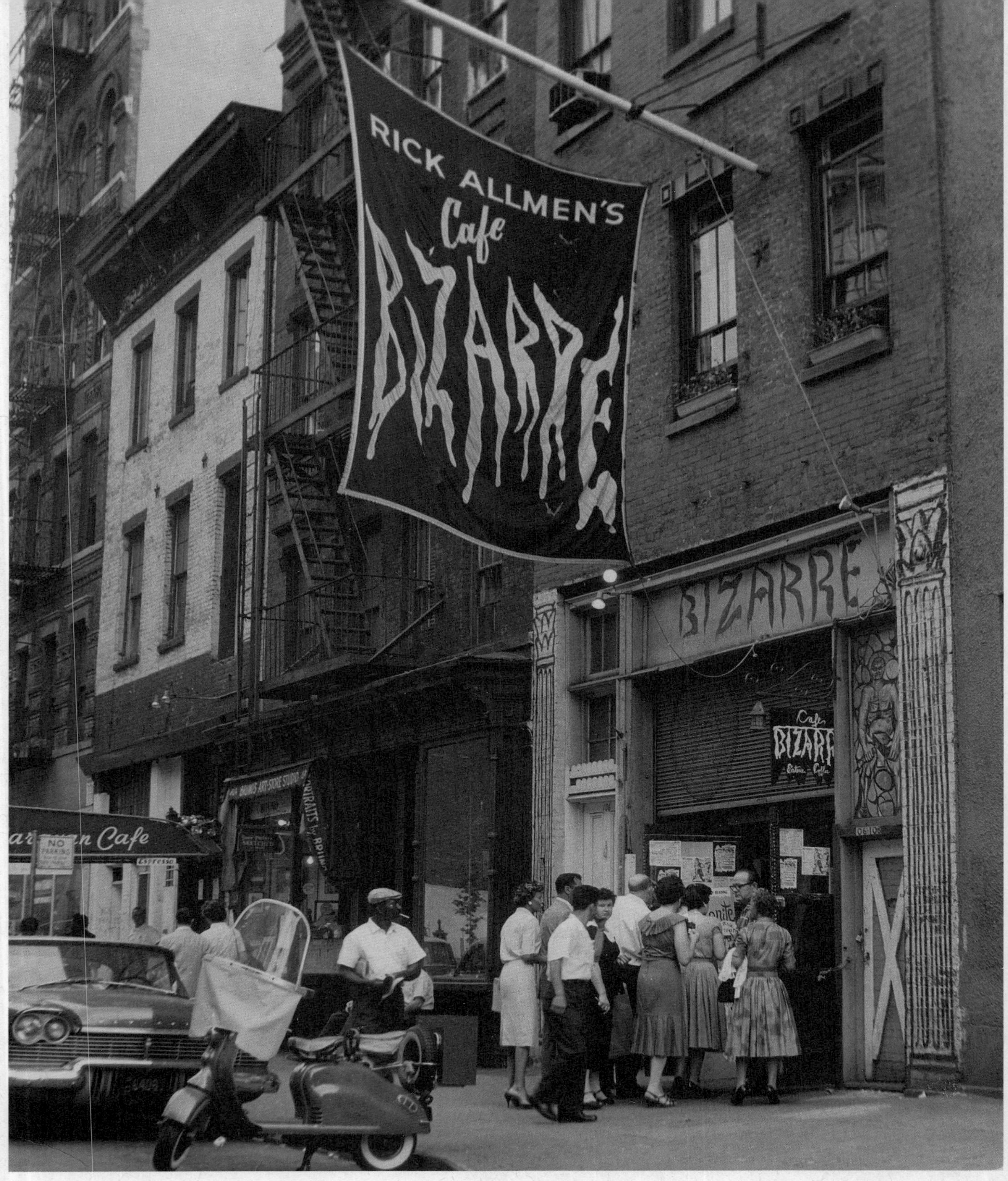

Café Bizarre, 1959. Photo © Fred W. McDarrah

Jack Kerouac leaving the Artist's Club after New Year's Eve party, 1958. Photo © Fred W. McDarrah

This synergy and boundary-crossing of the Beats produced works ranging from eloquent poetry and prose to jazz-poetry performances, to photographs, assemblages, drawings and paintings, book-jacket designs, experimental films, ephemeral installations, posters, and broadsides. Lines were never strictly drawn: visual artists made films, poets made paintings. Bruce Conner created collages, assemblages, drawings, films, installations; Berman made sculpture, photo-collages, poetry, mail art; Herms worked in a variety of formats that included poetry; Kerouac painted; Ginsberg took photographs; Burroughs made drawings and "cut-ups." Ferlinghetti, Ted Joans, and Michael McClure studied and made visual art. Claes Oldenburg and Jess composed poetry. There were numerous crossovers and collaborations from jazz poetry readings at the Five Spot or Living Theater to independent films like *Pull My Daisy*. Poets wrote about the artists (McClure on Pollock, Creeley on Chamberlain) and artists illustrated books by poets (Berman for McClure, Jess for Duncan, LaVigne for Ginsberg, Rivers for O'Hara) and artists designed sets for the poets' plays (Herms for McClure, Jess for Duncan).

Jack Kerouac
On the Road, 1951
Original manuscript, teletype paper scroll
Collection of The Sampas Family;
John Sampas, legal representative

I first met met Neal not long after my father died... I had just gotten over a
serious illness that I won't bother to talk about except that it really had som
thing to do with my father's death and my awful feeling that everything was
dead. With the coming of Neal there really began for me that part of my life
that you could call my life on the road. Prior to that I'd always dreamed of
west, seeing the country, always vaguely planning and never specifically tak
off and so on. Neal is the perfect guy for the road because he actually wa
on the road, when his parents were passing through Salt Lake City in 1926,
jaloppy, on their way to Los Angeles. First reports of Neal came to me th
Hal Chase, who'd shown me a few letters from him written in a Colorado reform
school. I was trmendously interested in these letters because they so naively
and sweetly asked for Hal to teach him all about Nietzsche and all the wonder
intellectual things of that Hal was so justly famous for. At one point Allen
I talked about these letters and wondered if we would ever meet the strange N
Cassady. This is all far back, when Neal wasnot the way he is tod
a young jailkid shrouded in mystery. Then news came that Neal wa
school and was coming to New York for the first time; also there
had just married a 16 year old girl called Louanne. One day I wa
the Columbia campus and Hal and Ed White told me Neal had just arrive
living in a guy called Bob Malkin's coldwater pad in East Harlem, the
Harlem. Neal had arrived the night before, the first time in NY, with beau
tiful little sharp chick Louanne; they got off the Greyhound bus at 50 St. and
cut around the corner looking for a place to eat and went right in Hector's, and
since then Hector's cafeteria has always been a big symbol of NY for Neal. They

In taking art off the pedestal and into the real life of cafés and the street, the Beats created a new kind of realism. Not only was the content raw and gritty, but so were the form and delivery. Process was stressed; improvisation and spontaneity were paramount. At the center of Beat culture was the performative, from an emphasis on spoken word poetry and the power of delivery to gesture and body expression in readings and art making. Both the lives and art of the Beats were part of one continuous carnivalesque performance of music, conversation, drinking, reading, working, smoking, sex, traveling, and making art that spilled over from their homes into bars, art galleries, and the street.[24]

Many of the poets greatly admired the Abstract Expressionists such as Jackson Pollock for their action painting. Pollock substituted process and performance for narrative pictorial space, acting out body rhythms and primal motions on canvas. For many Beats, such painting, along with jazz improvisation, was an important model for a new writing style. Kerouac, who also made paintings, referred to his writing as "sketching" and valued immediacy, rarely going back to edit or modify ("first thought, best thought"). His typing of *On the Road* in one sitting on a 100-foot roll of teletype paper was a performance piece, and the scroll is a relic of this performance. Ginsberg has described Kerouac's writing as "spontaneous bop prosody," connecting his direct intuitive expression of experience and syncopated breath patterns to jazz performance.[25]

Robert Creeley, the Black Mountain poet who was also part of the Beat circle in San Francisco, wrote about many visual artists, among them Franz Kline and John Chamberlain. He commented later that "possibly the attraction the artist had for people like myself—think of O'Hara, Ashbery, Koch, Duncan, McClure, Ginsberg; or Kerouac's wistful claim that he could probably paint better than Kline—was that lovely uncluttered directness of perception and act we found in so many of them....It may also have been the *energy* these people generated, which so attracted us..."[26] He also said, "...I hadn't realized as yet that a number of American painters had made the shift I was myself so anxious to accomplish, that they had, in fact, already begun to move away from the insistently *pictorial*...to a manifest directly of the *energy* inherent in the materials...."[27]

Michael McClure—another pivotal bridge figure between artists and writers—claimed that Pollock was integral to his own life and thought. It was the heroic engagement as well as the dynamic open rhythms of the Pollock surface that attracted the Beat consciousness of the

Jackson Pollock
Number 27, 1950
Oil on canvas,
49 x 106 (124.5 x 269.2)
Whitney Museum of American Art, New York; Purchase 53.12

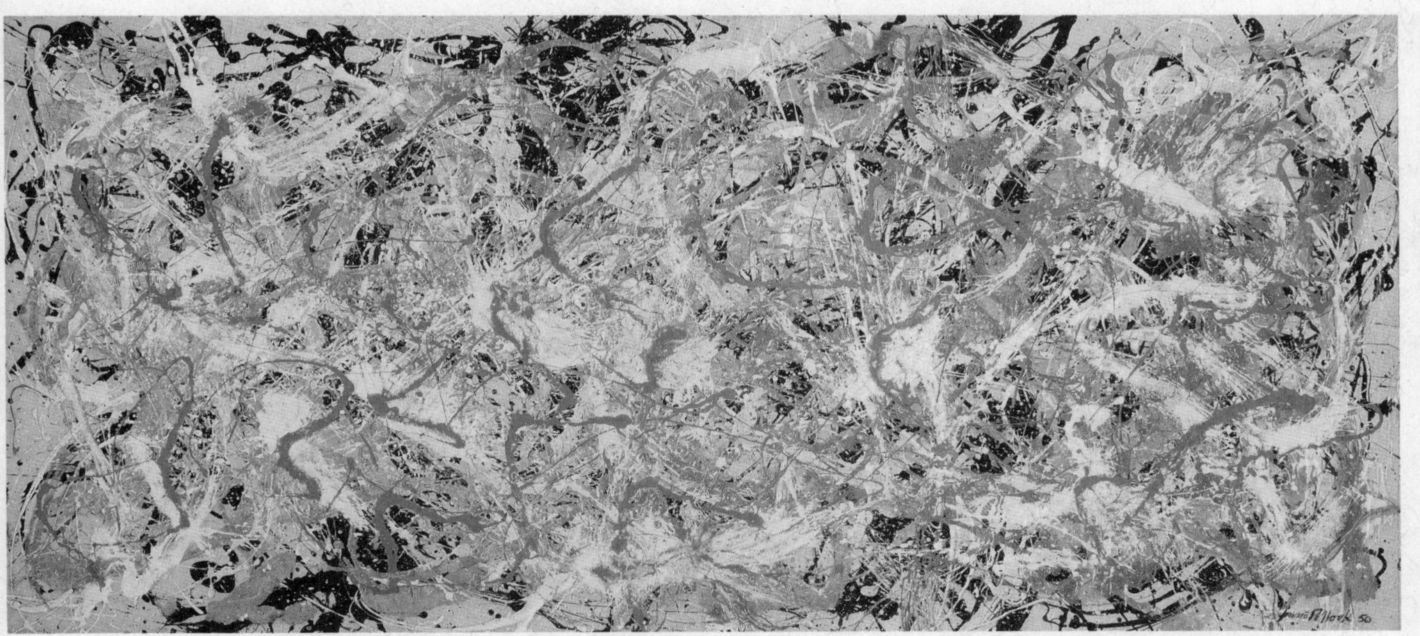

fifties.[28] But Kerouac drew a barrage of moral criticism because of the undeniably raw content of his writing. Pollock's work, on the other hand, was abstract and ambiguous. According to literary critic Seymour Krim, "in Kerouac's case people hardly noticed the method because the life he seemed to glorify—promiscuity, pot-smoking, the hot pursuit of speed, kicks, excitement—was so much more tangible than art."[29]

This tangibility—the street-level realism of much Beat writing from Kerouac to Ginsberg to Corso—was a harbinger of new emerging forms in the visual arts, namely junk sculpture, assemblage, and Happenings.[30] Younger artists strove to make art come to life, to make it an actual living thing. They took themes and materials from the street—junk, debris, scavenged refuse—and turned it into art. From Robert Rauschenberg's combines, to Bruce Conner's assemblages using photographs, beads, lace, and nylon stockings, to John Chamberlain's junk sculptures of smashed car parts, a raw, confrontational, and often dark aesthetic evolved. As Allan Kaprow stated in his 1958 manifesto "The Legacy of Jackson Pollock": "Pollock left artists at a point where they must become preoccupied with and even dazzled by the space and objects of our everyday life, either our bodies, clothes, rooms, or...the vastness of Forty-Second Street."[31]

This sense of everyday life was a hallmark of Beat poetry. All kinds of subject matter, from African-American slang to Walt Whitman to Hollywood movies to the garbage dump, were dynamically fused in a candid, confrontational realism. Traditional hierarchies of value were overturned—the commonplace was redeemed and the lofty brought down to earth, as in this passage from "Howl": "The world is holy! The soul is holy! The skin is holy! The nose is holy! The tongue and cock and hand and asshole holy!"[32]

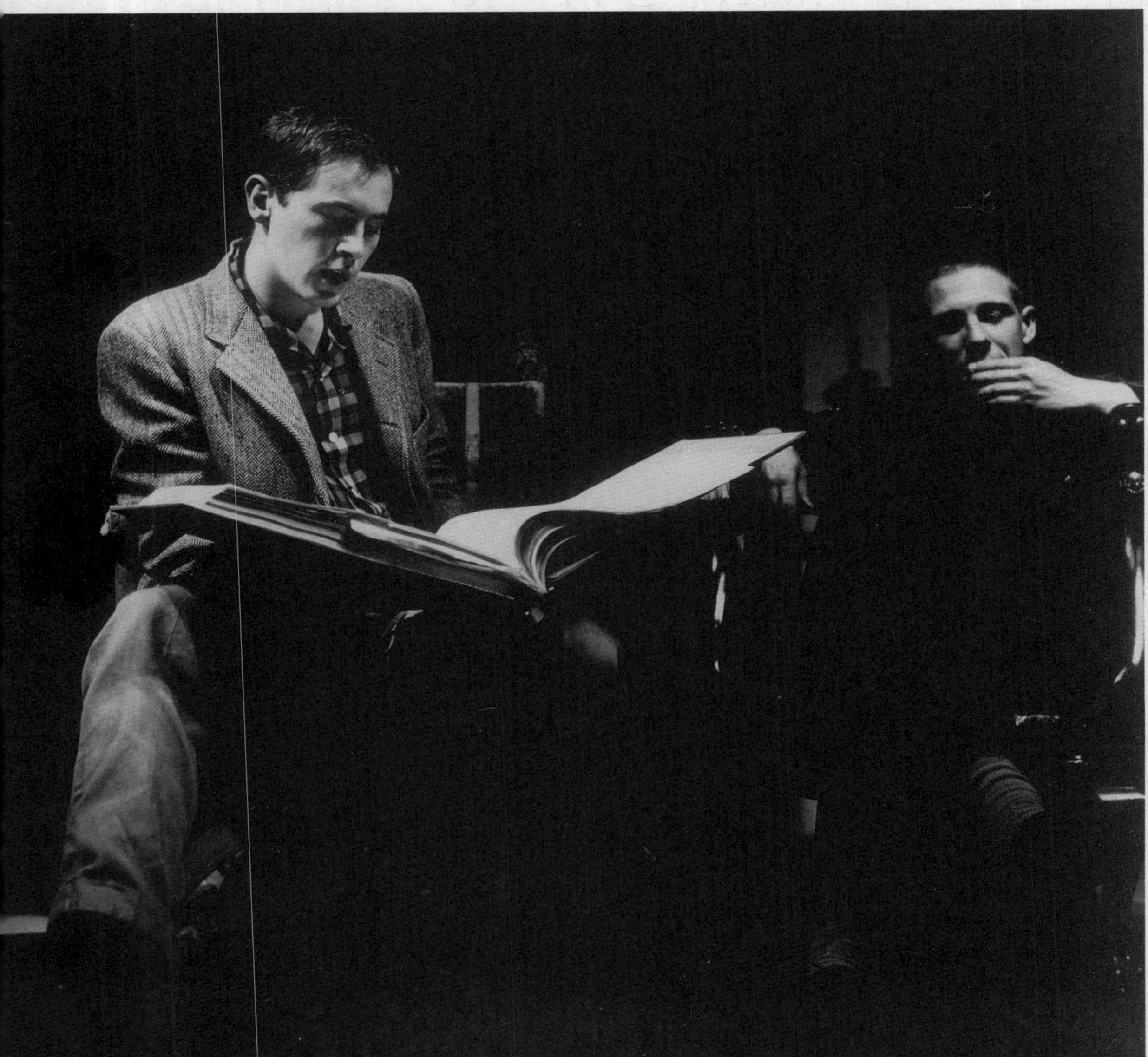

Michael McClure and Gary Snyder at a reading, Berkeley, California, 1958. Photo by Harry Redl

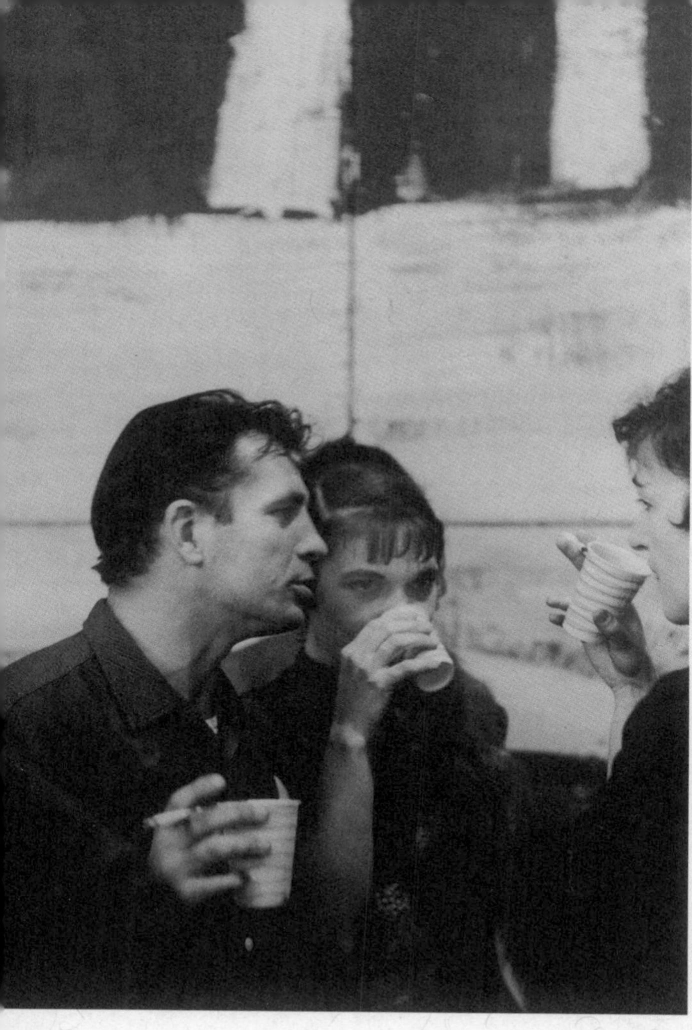

Jack Kerouac,
Dody Müller, and Cessa Carr at cast party in Alfred Leslie's loft for "Pull My Daisy," NYC, 1959.
Painting in background by Alfred Leslie.
Photo © John Cohen

Franz Kline
Dahlia, 1959
Oil on canvas, 82 x 67 (208.3 x 170.2)
Whitney Museum of American Art, New York; Purchase, with funds from an anonymous group of friends of the Whitney Museum of American Art 66.90

By the end of the decade, artists such as Kaprow, Oldenburg, and Dine had made living extensions of assemblage in their Happenings—elaborate installations that combined a junk aesthetic with performance and environmental scale to produce a completely new and radical intermedia art form. These artists substituted found objects—splattered rags, pieces of cardboard—for paint and canvas to make three-dimensional material textures. Their environments, such as Kaprow's *Apple Shrine*, Oldenburg's *Street*, and Dine's *Car Crash*, were monochromatic and conveyed a strong sense of decay and brutality. This work also opened up numerous avenues for later artistic exploration of mixed-media art forms, installation, body art, and performance art.

In the sixties, yet another generation took charge. Following the cataclysms of Vietnam and the Kennedy and King assassinations, many were mobilized, unlike the Beats, into political action. But the Beat credo of the individual, of self-discovery and realization as a metaphor for implicit truth continued to gain strength. It can be found everywhere in the culture that began to emerge in the sixties, from hippies forming their own communes to feminists exploring personal choices. The explosion of youth and counterculture in the sixties was built on the foundation of subversive nonconformity that the Beats had established in the fifties.

Today, the Beats are experiencing their biggest revival ever, and while they have always lent themselves to popularization, their current widespread recognition has far exceeded their original expectations and desires. There are CD sets, symposia, and documentary films in the works, a big resurgence of spoken word poetry, and art that is clearly indebted to the Beat aesthetic. City Lights Books reports record demands for Beat literature. There is both nostalgia for the origins of youth culture and for a genuine bohemian community, but also a reawakening of the spirit, a yearning for the utopian freedom found in the Beats' commitment to emotional intensity, exuberance for life, and their determination to avoid spiritual death.

The paradox of this recognition is that the Beats have now been historicized and categorized in a way they assiduously worked to avoid. How can one recount their history, "exhibit" it, and still preserve their anarchic sense of rebellion against institutions, their subversive spontaneity, their raucous spirit and electric performance? How can we enshrine a movement whose possibility and power came about precisely because it wasn't enshrined? The Beats deserve to be recognized by history and be represented in our cultural institutions, but as artists who made a virtue of breaking the rules, who challenged our expectations of what "official" history means—and who sought to unname, to undefine.

Notes

1 Jack Kerouac, *On the Road* (New York: The Viking Press, 1957), p.196.

2 For the continuing influence of Beat culture, see Glenn O'Brien's essay, "The Beat Goes On," pp. 169-87 below.

3 Paul O'Neil, "The Only Rebellion Around," *Life*, November 30, 1959, p. 115.

4 Norman Podhoretz, "The Know-Nothing Bohemians," *Partisan Review*, 25 (Spring 1958), pp. 305-18.

5 William Burroughs remembering Jack Kerouac in *The Adding Machine: Collected Essays* (London: John Calder Publishers, 1985), p.180.

6 Allen Ginsberg, letter to Jack Kerouac, 1951.

7 Edward Halsey Foster, *Understanding the Beats* (Columbia: University of South Carolina Press, 1992), p. 4.

8 Ginsberg, quoted in Glen Burns, *Great Poets Howl: A Study of Allen Ginsberg's Poetry, 1943-1955* (Frankfurt and New York: P. Lang, c.1983), p.404.

9 See Allen Ginsberg's "Prologue," pp. 17-19 above.

10 Jack Kerouac to Allen Ginsberg, letter, February 26, 1950, Stanford University, Ginsberg Archive.

11 John Clellon Holmes, "The Philosophy of the Beat Generation," *Esquire*, 49 (February 1958), p. 36.

12 Howard R. Moody, "Reflections on the Beat Generation," *Religion in Life*, 28 (Summer 1959), p. 427.

13 See Foster, *Understanding the Beats*, pp. 7-8.

14 John Clellon Holmes, *Go* (New York: Thunder's Mouth Press, l952), p. 36.

15 Allen Ginsberg, *Howl and Other Poems* (San Francisco: City Lights Books, 1956), p. 9; Kerouac, *On the Road*, p. 9.

16 Conversation with Bruce Conner, December l993.

17 Allen Ginsberg at "The Beat Generation: Legacy and Celebration" conference at New York University, May 19, 1994.

18 Ibid.

19 Conversation with Bruce Conner, December 1993.

20 John Clellon Holmes, *Passionate Opinions: The Cultural Essays* (Fayetteville: The University of Arkansas Press, 1988), p.50.

21 Quoted in Holmes, "The Philosophy of the Beat Generation," p. 35.

22 Conversation with Judith Malina, July 11, 1995. It was the Beat's belief that the personal is political, and their avoidance of a programmatic political stance that prompted many associated with the movement, like Malina, to move into more activist territory in the 1960s.

23 For the Judson Memorial Church and the avant-garde, see Robert E. Haywood, "Heretical Alliance: Claes Oldenburg and the Judson Memorial Church in the 1960s," *Art History*, 18 (June 1995), pp. 185-212.

24 Sally Banes sees the Beat generation as a major influence on the development of performance art in *Greenwich Village, 1963* (Durham, North Carolina: Duke University Press, 1993), p. 25.

25 Allen Ginsberg, "Improvised Poetics," interview, November 26, 1968, published in Donald Allen, ed., *Composed on the Tongue* (Bolinas, California: Grey Fox Press, 1980), p. 43.

26 Robert Creeley, "On the Road: Notes on Artists and Poets, 1950-1965," in *The Collected Essays of Robert Creeley* (Berkeley and Los Angeles: University of California Press, 1989), p. 371.

27 Ibid., p. 369.

28 Neil Chassman, "Poets of the Cities: Leveling of Meaning," in *Poets of the Cities: New York and San Francisco 1950-1965*, exh. cat. (Dallas: Museum of Fine Arts, 1974), pp. 16-17.

29 Seymour Krim, "King of the Beats," *The Commonweal*, 69 (January 2, 1959), p. 358.

30 See Jonathan Feinberg, *Art Since 1949: Strategies of Being* (New York: Harry N. Abrams, 1995), esp. chap. 7, "The Beat Generation: The Fifties in America."

31 Allan Kaprow, "The Legacy of Jackson Pollock," *Art News*, 57 (October 1958), pp. 24-26, 55-57; quoted in Haywood, "Heretical Alliance," p. 195.

32 Ginsberg, *Howl and Other Poems*, p. 27.

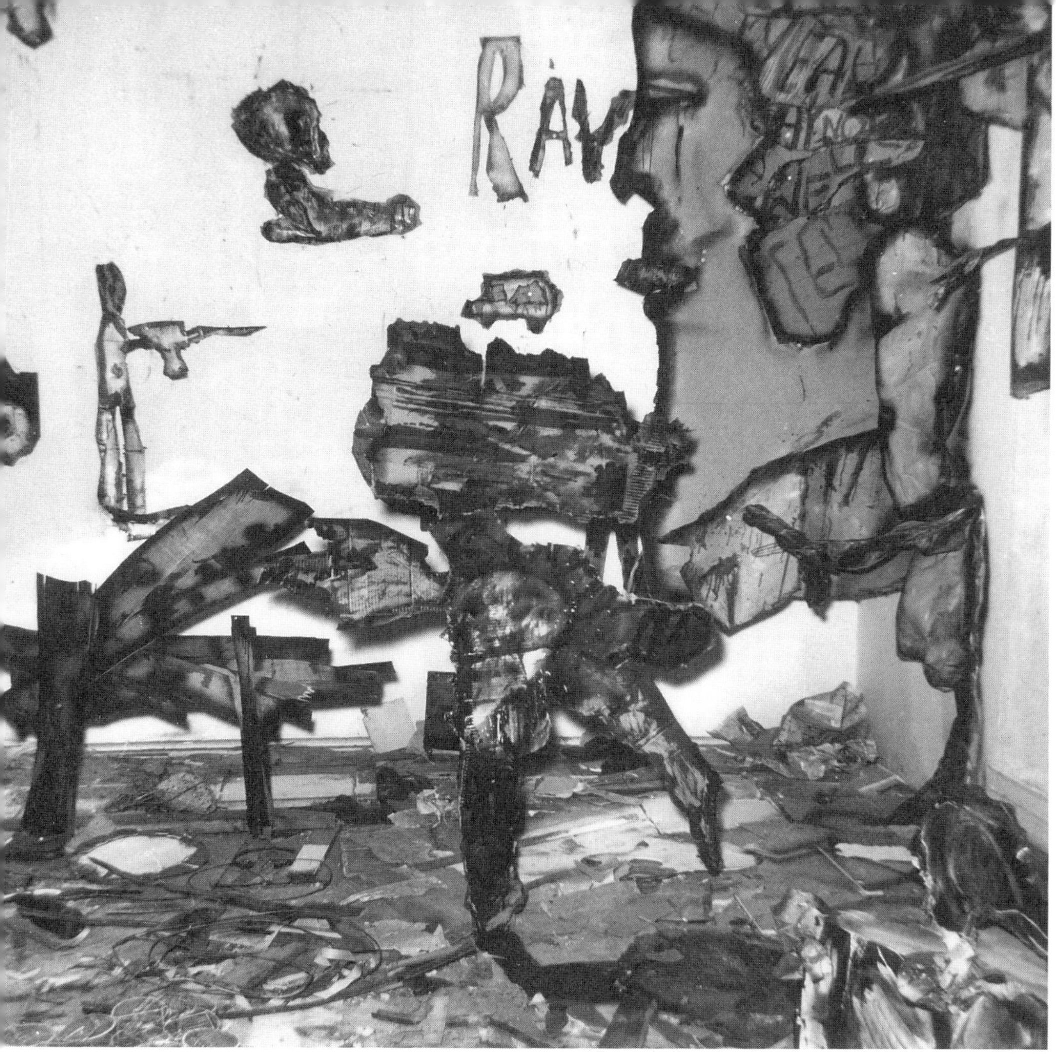

Above: **Claes Oldenburg's "The Street" installed in the Judson Gallery, Judson Memorial Church, New York, February-March**, 1960

Below: **Jim Dine and Judy Tersch in Dine's happening, "Car Crash," at the Reuben Gallery, New York**, 1960. Photo by Robert R. McElroy

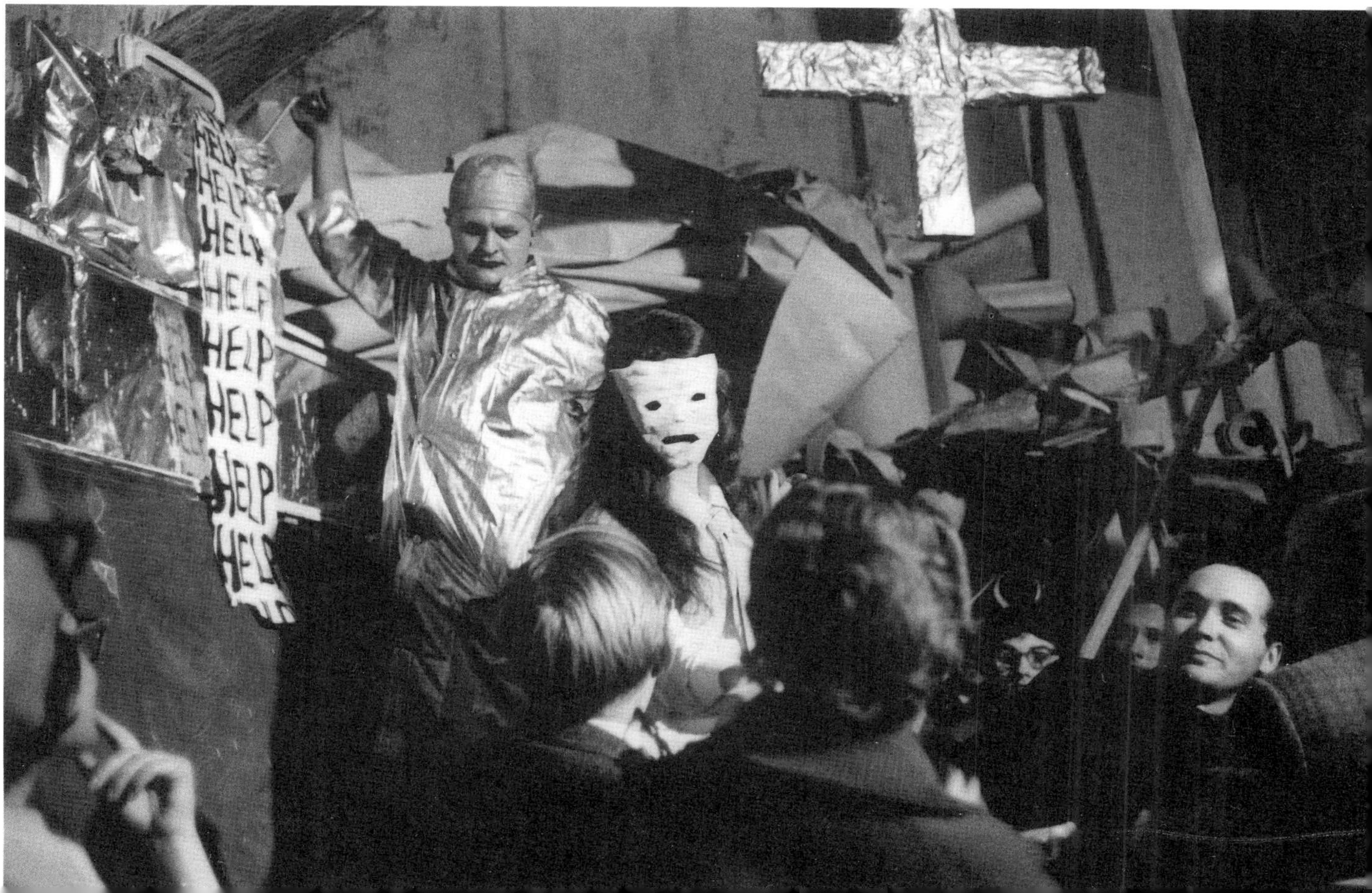

Robert Rauschenberg
Yoicks, 1953
Oil, fabric, and paper on canvas,
96 x 72 (243.8 x 182.9)
Whitney Museum of American Art,
New York; Gift of the artist 71.210

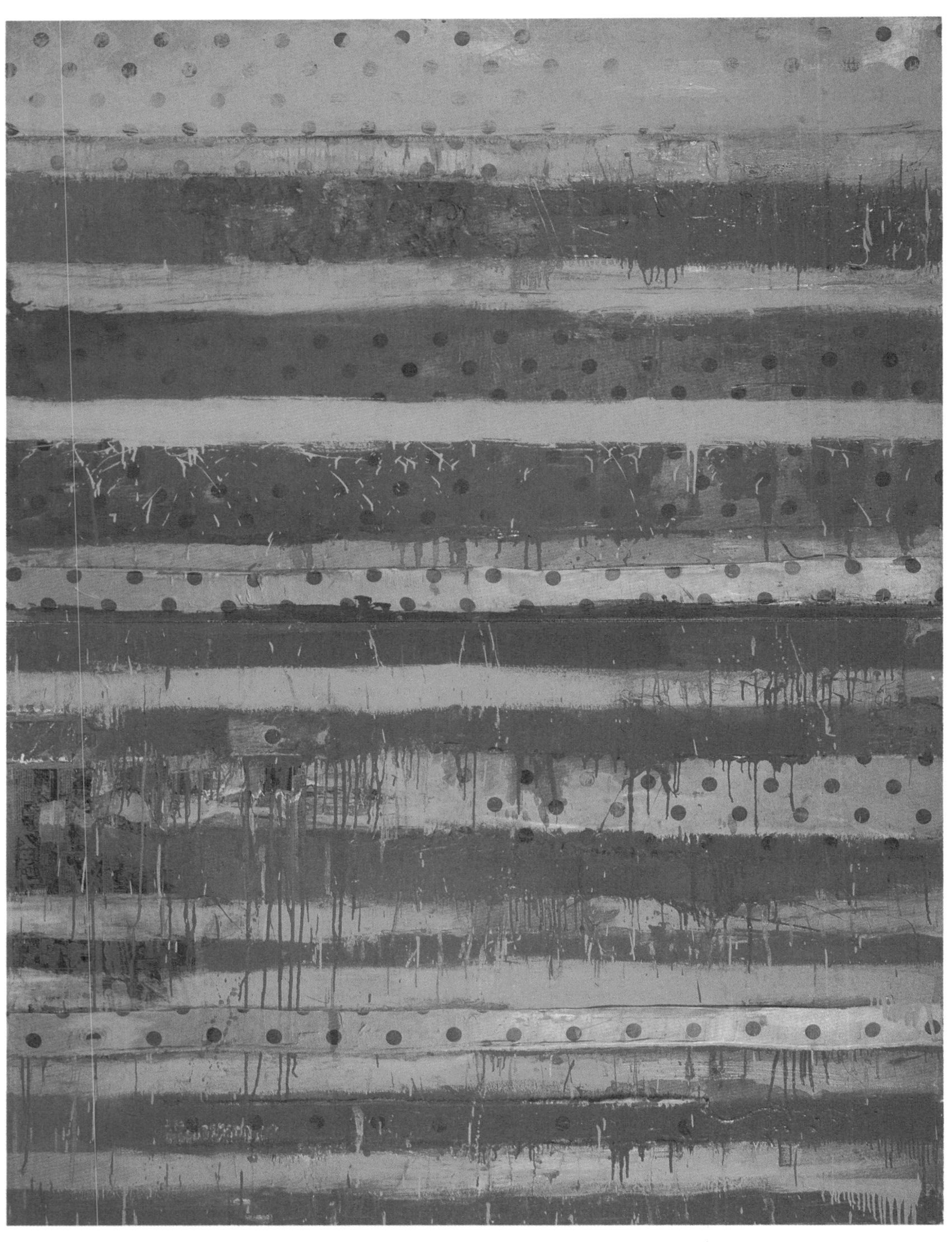

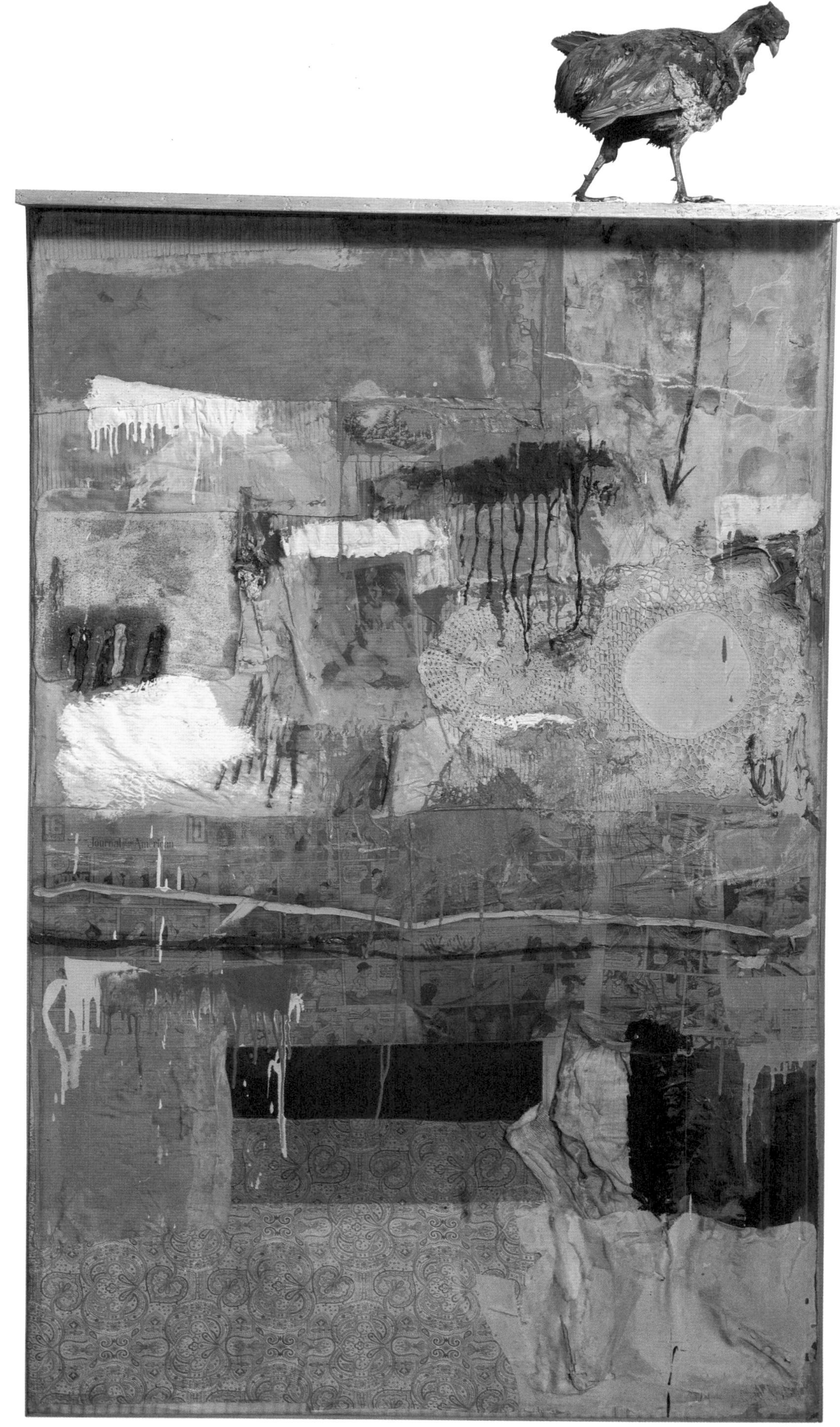

Robert Rauschenberg
Satellite, 1955
Oil, fabric, paper, and wood
on canvas with stuffed pheasant,
79 3/8 x 43 1/4 x 5 5/8 (201.6 x
109.9 x 14.29)
Whitney Museum of American Art,
New York; Gift of Claire B. Zeisler
and purchase with funds from the
Mrs. Percy Uris Purchase Fund
91.85

Michael McClure

A New Book/A Book of Torture, 1961

Ripolin enamel on paper, 42 x 27 1/2 (106.7 x 69.9)

Collection of the artist

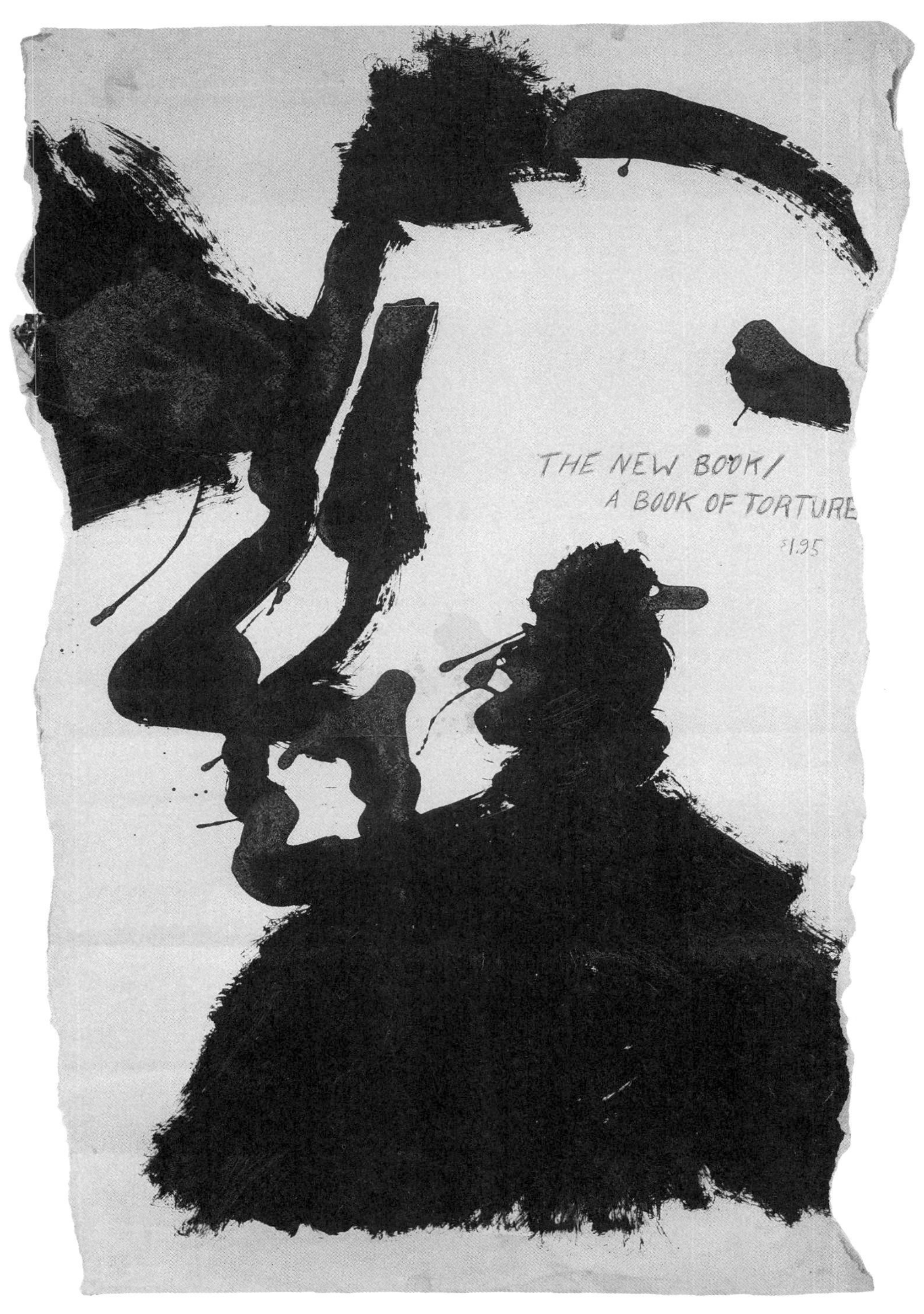

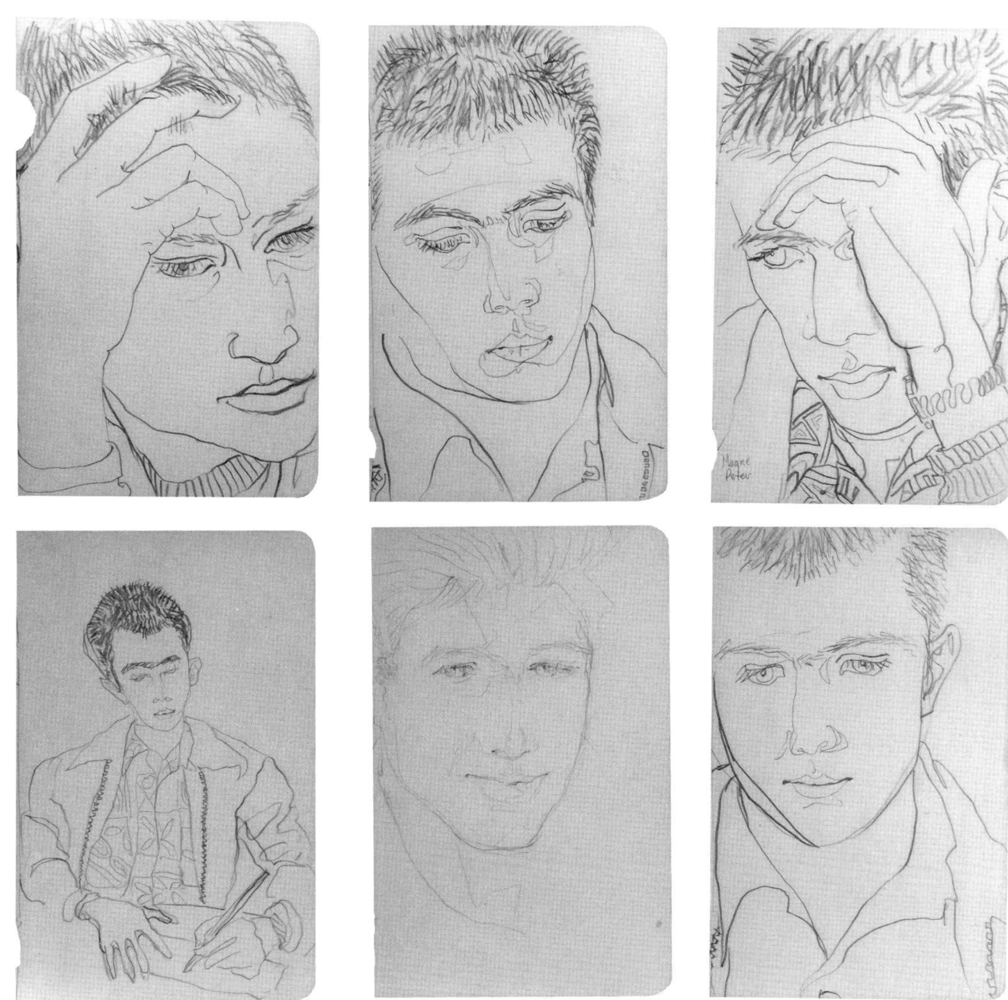

Robert LaVigne
Peter Orlovsky: Six Sketches, 1954
Graphite on paper, 8 x 5 (20.3 x 12.7) each
Rare Book and Manuscript Library, Columbia University, New York;
Robert LaVigne Collection

Larry Rivers and Kenneth Koch
New York 1950-1960, 1961
Oil and charcoal on canvas, 69 x 84 (175.3 x 213.4)
Private collection

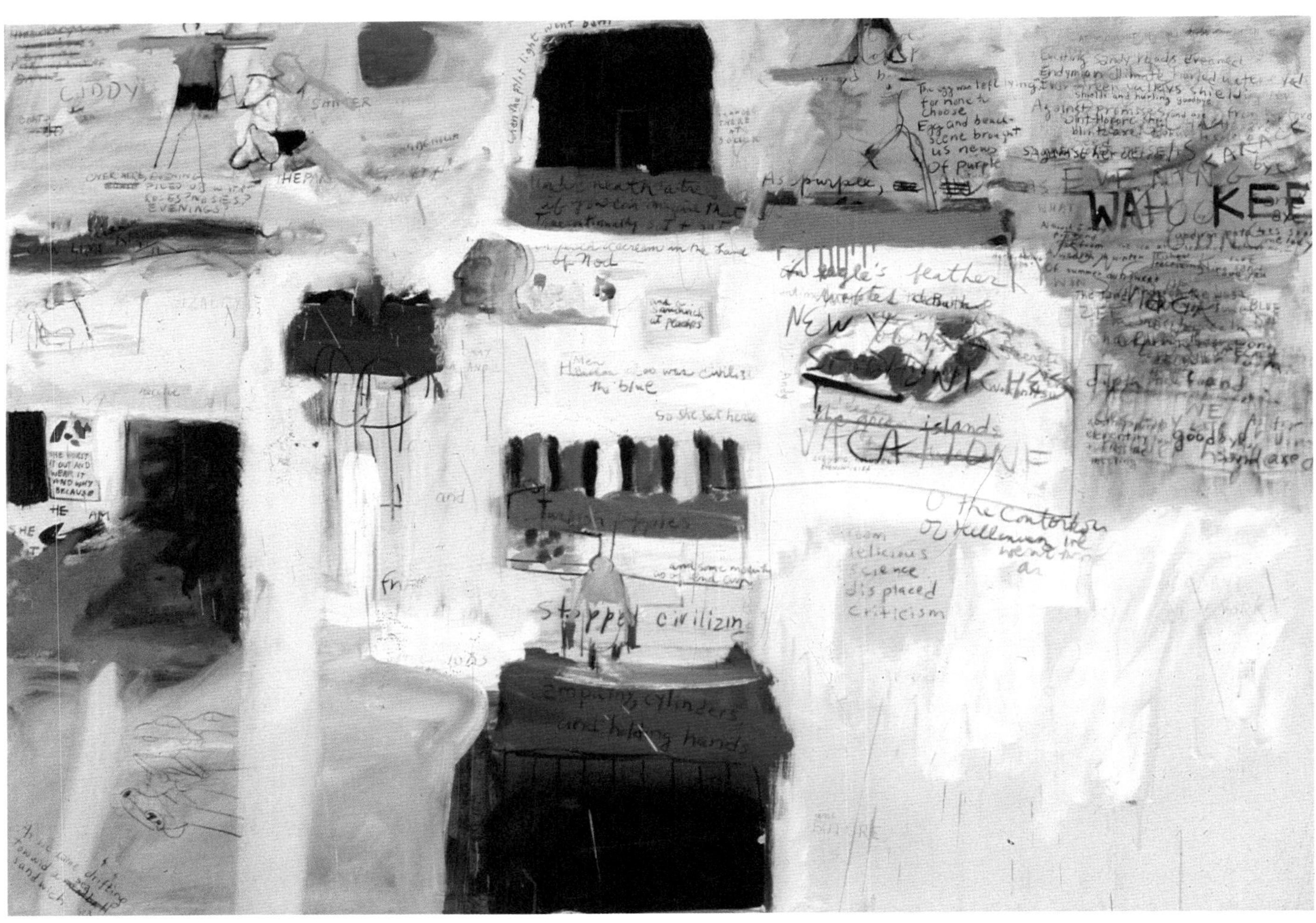

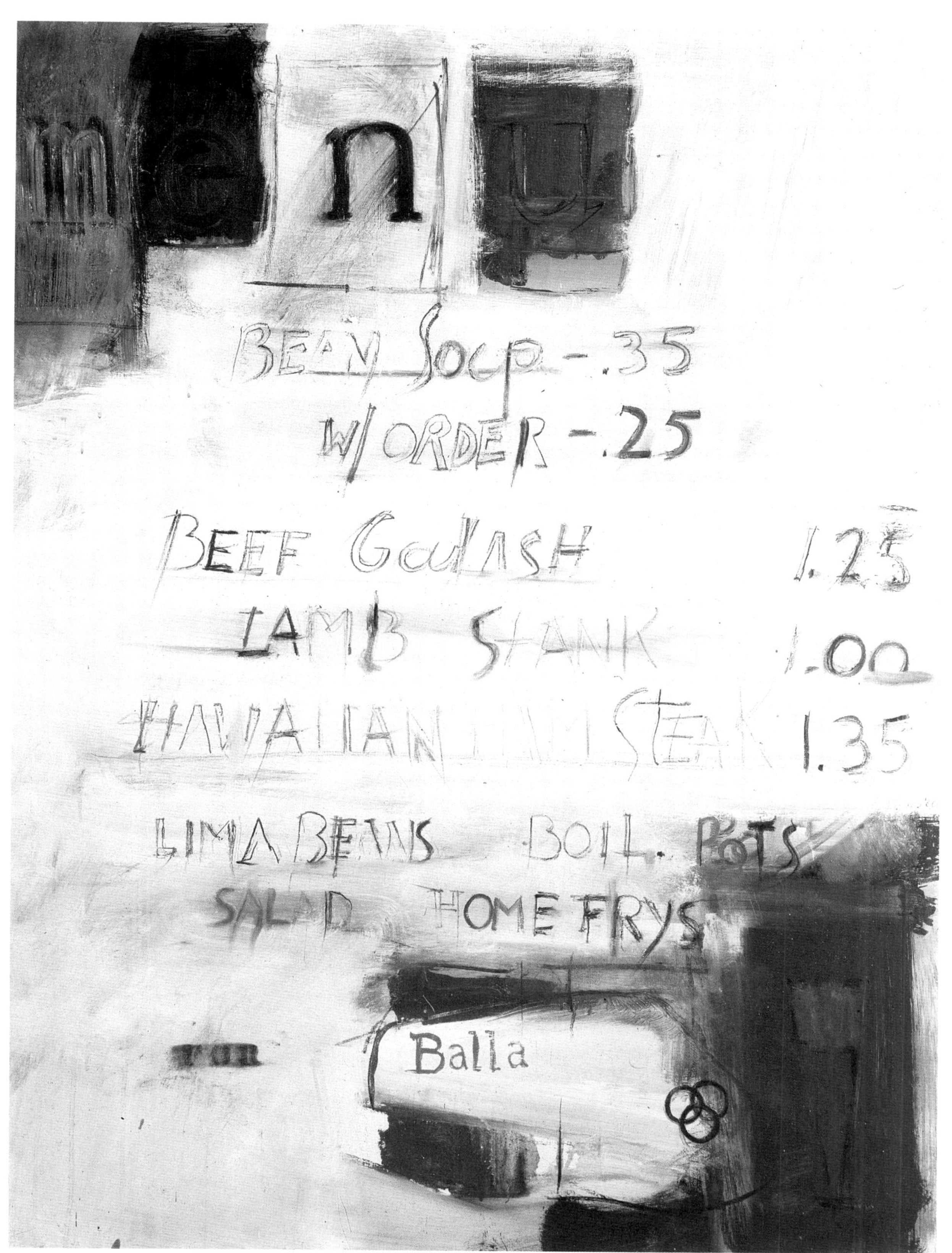

Larry Rivers
Cedar Bar Menu I, 1960
Oil on canvas, 47 1/2 x 35 (120.7 x 88.9)
Collection of the artist

Gregory Corso
Portrait of Robert LaVigne, 1956
Ink on paper, 10 1/2 x 8 (26.7 x 20.3)
Rare Book and Manuscript Library,
Columbia University, New York;
Robert LaVigne Collection

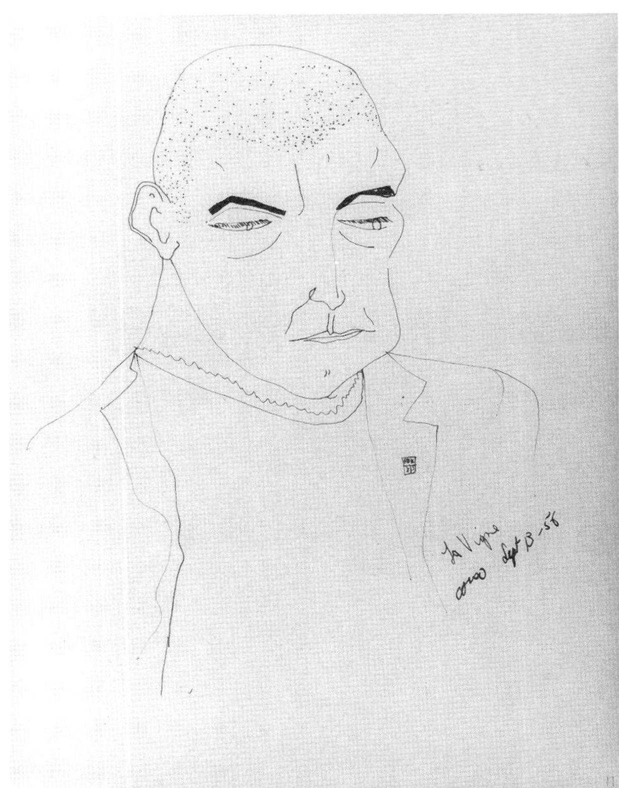

Gregory Corso
Self-Portrait, n.d.
Ink on paper, 11 x 8 1/2 (27.9 x 21.6)
Rare Book and Manuscript Library, Columbia
University, New York; Gregory Corso Collection

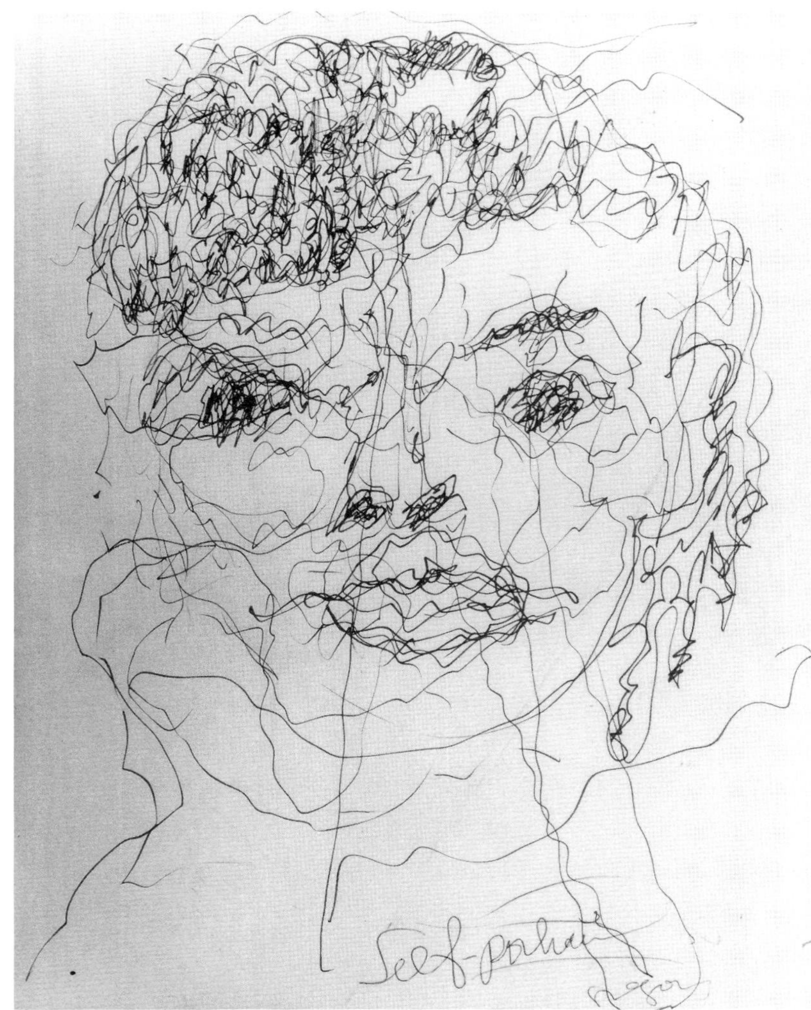

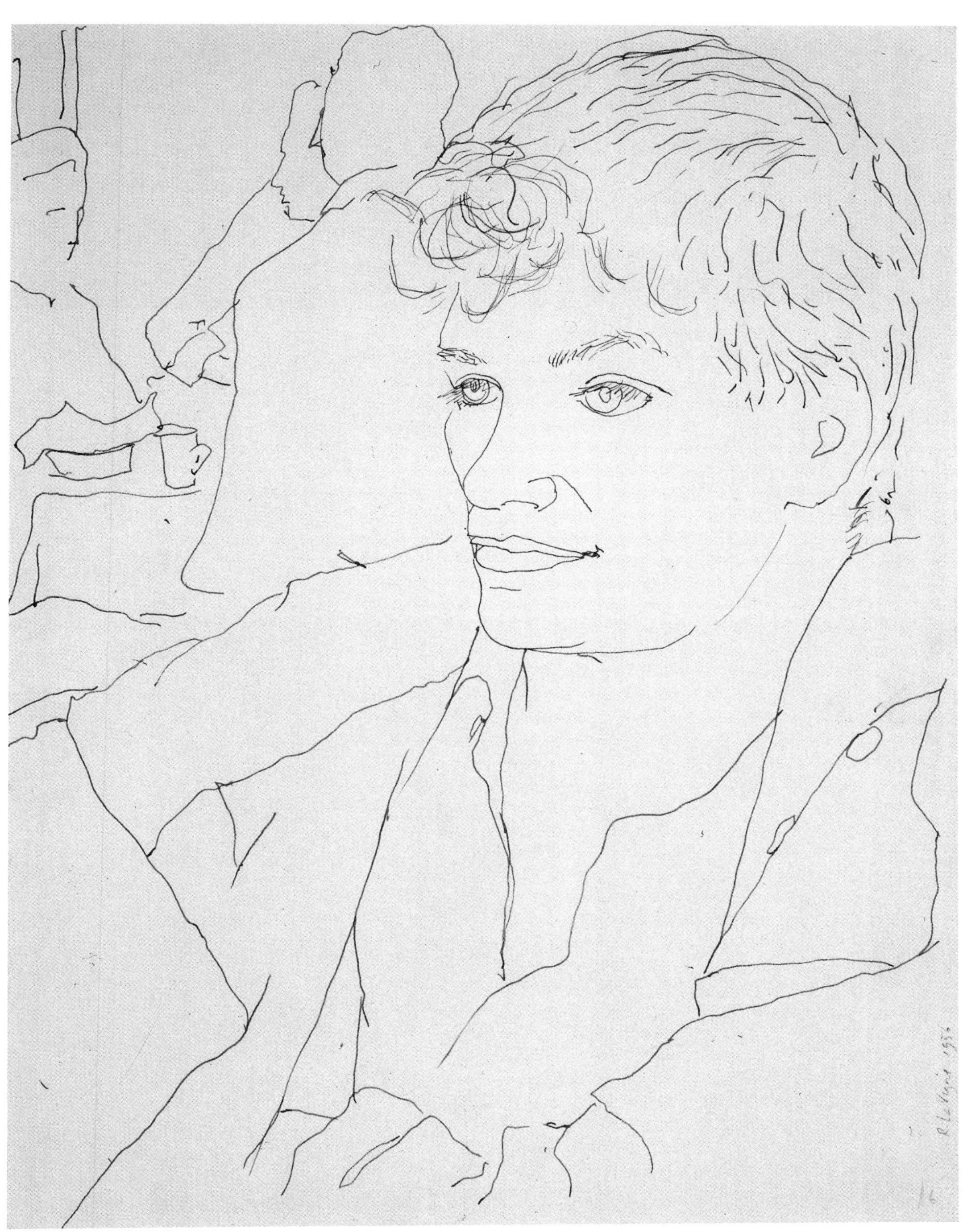

Robert LaVigne

Portrait of Gregory Corso, 1956

Ink on paper, 10 1/2 x 8 (26.7 x 20.3)

Rare Book and Manuscript Library, Columbia University, New York; Robert LaVigne Collection

Jack Kerouac
Buddha, 1956-60
Oil on canvas, 17 x 13 1/2 (43.2 x 34.3)
Collection of The Sampas Family; John Sampas, legal representative

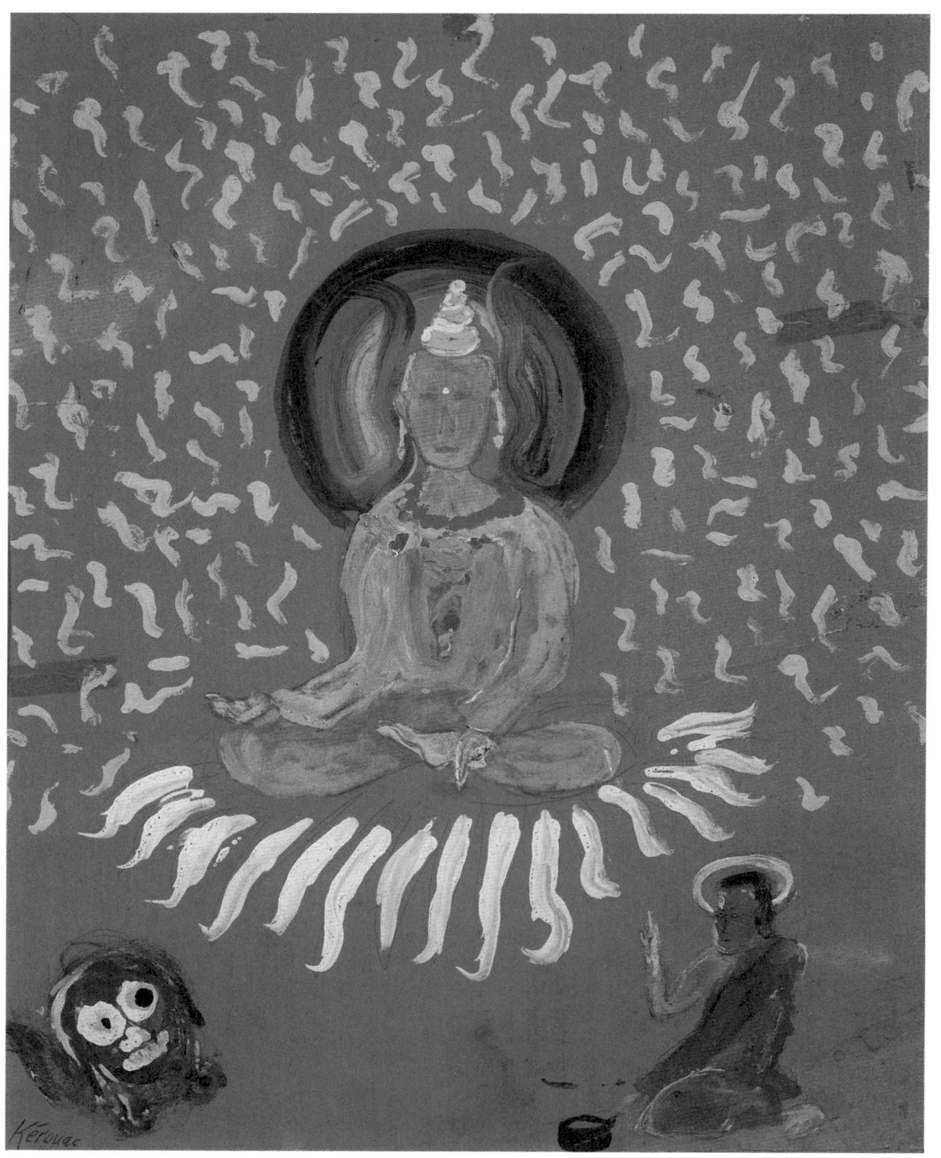

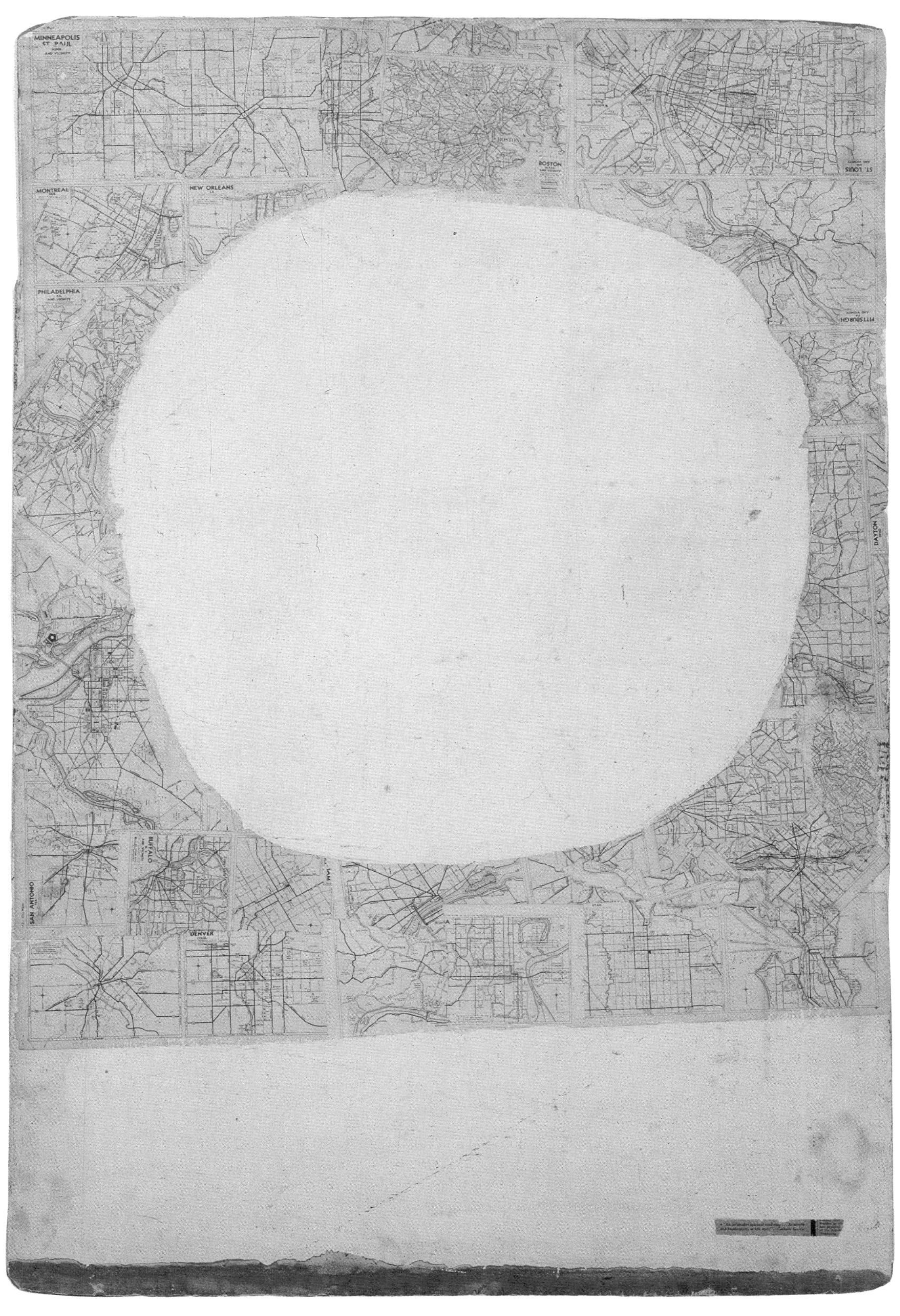

Robert Rauschenberg
Mother of God, c. 1950
Oil, enamel, printed paper, newspaper, and
metallic paints on masonite,
48 x 32 1/8 (121.9 x 81.6)
Collection of the artist

Jack Kerouac
Book of Dreams, c. 1952-54
Bound typescript with crayon on paper, 11 x 8 1/2 (27.9 x 21.6)
The New York Public Library; Astor, Lenox, and Tilden Foundations,
Henry W. and Albert A. Berg Collection of English and American Literature

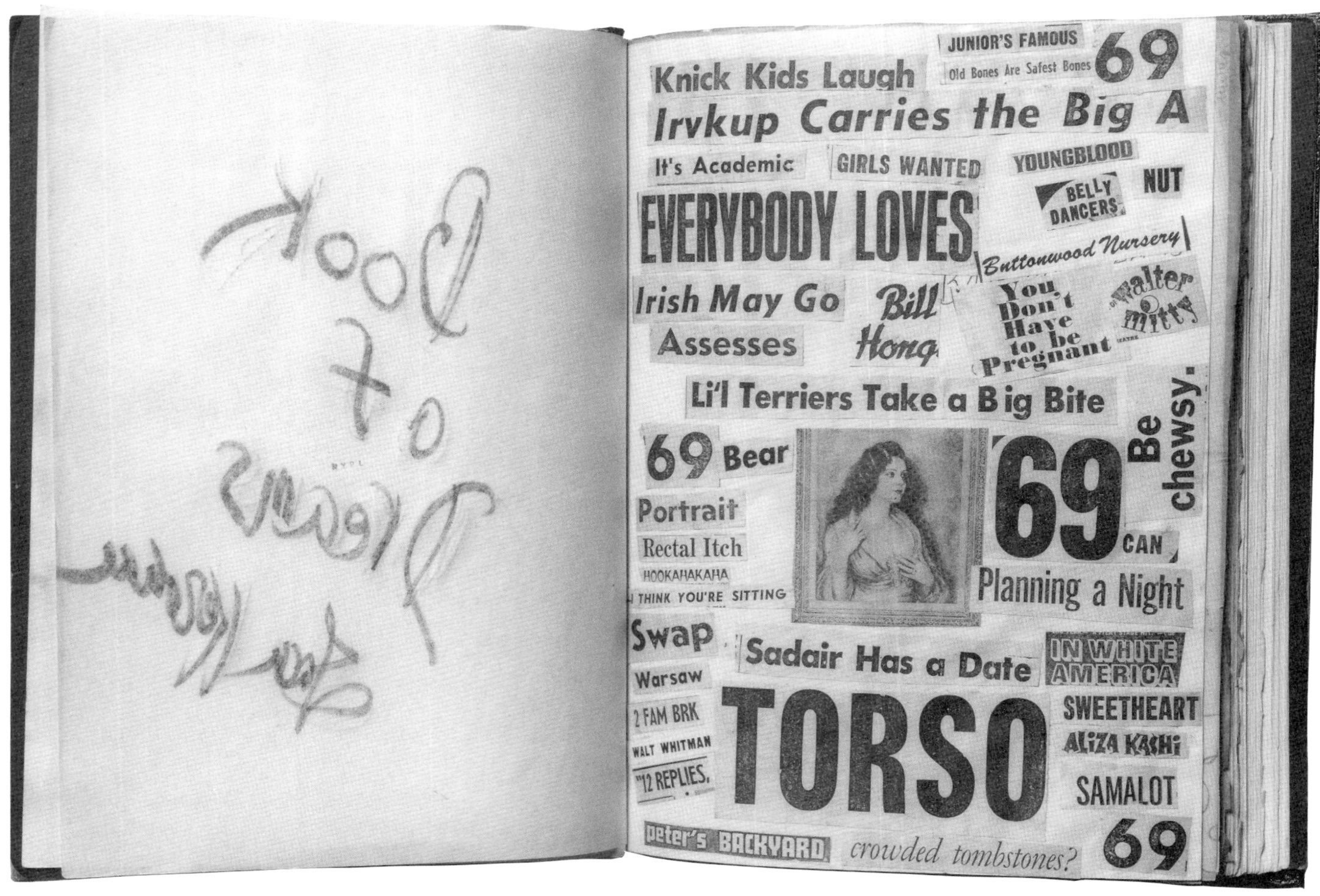

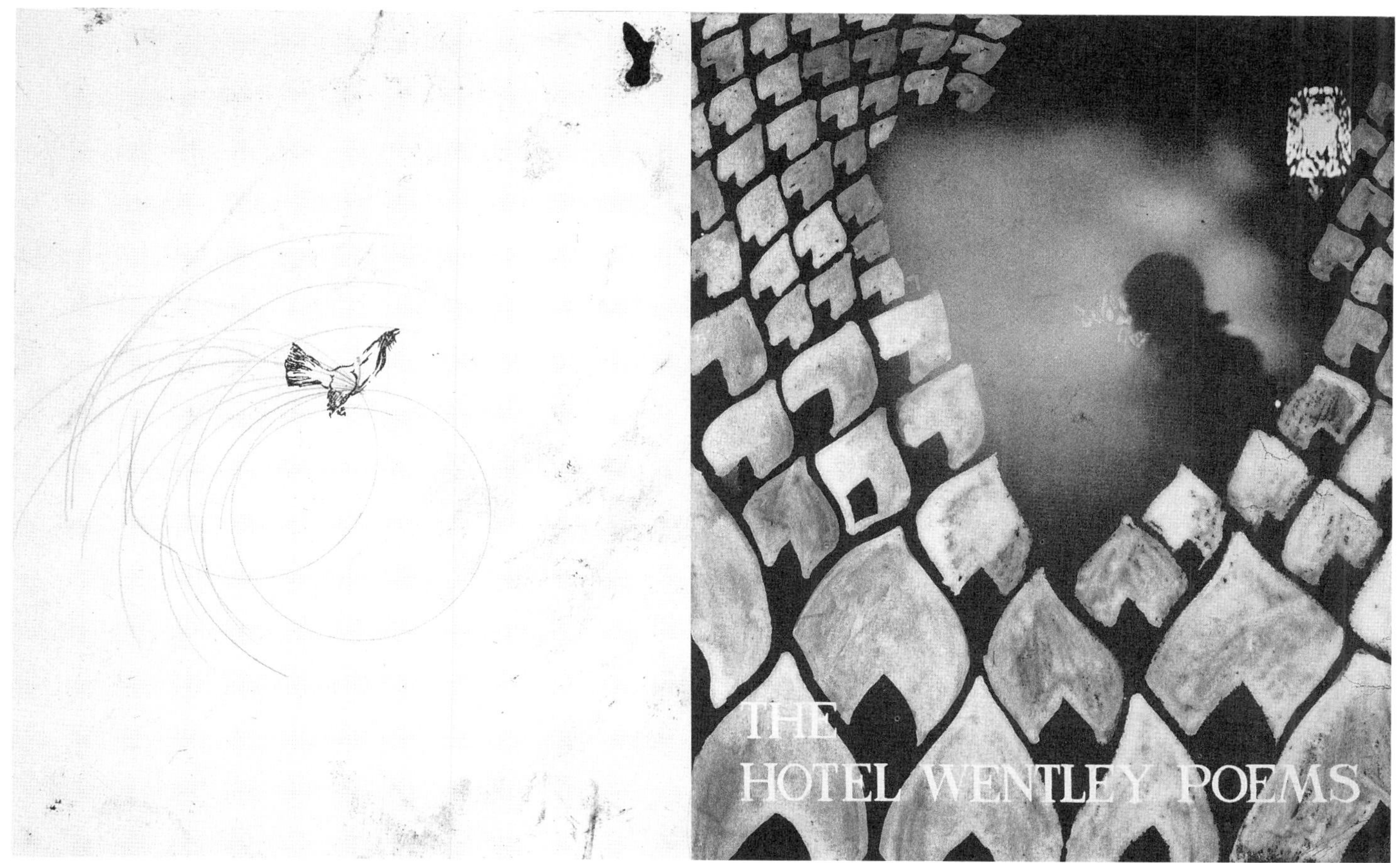

Robert LaVigne

Cover design for John Wieners' "The Hotel Wentley Poems," 1957

Ink, wash, and halftone on paper, 8 x 12 1/2 (20.3 x 31.8)

Rare Book and Manuscript Library, Columbia University, New York; Robert LaVigne Collection

Jim Dine
Bedspring, 1960
Mixed media on wire bedspring, 52 1/4 x 72 x 11 (132.7 x 183 x 28)
Solomon R. Guggenheim Museum, New York;
Purchased with funds contributed by the
Louis and Bessie Adler Foundation, Inc.,
Seymour M. Klein, President

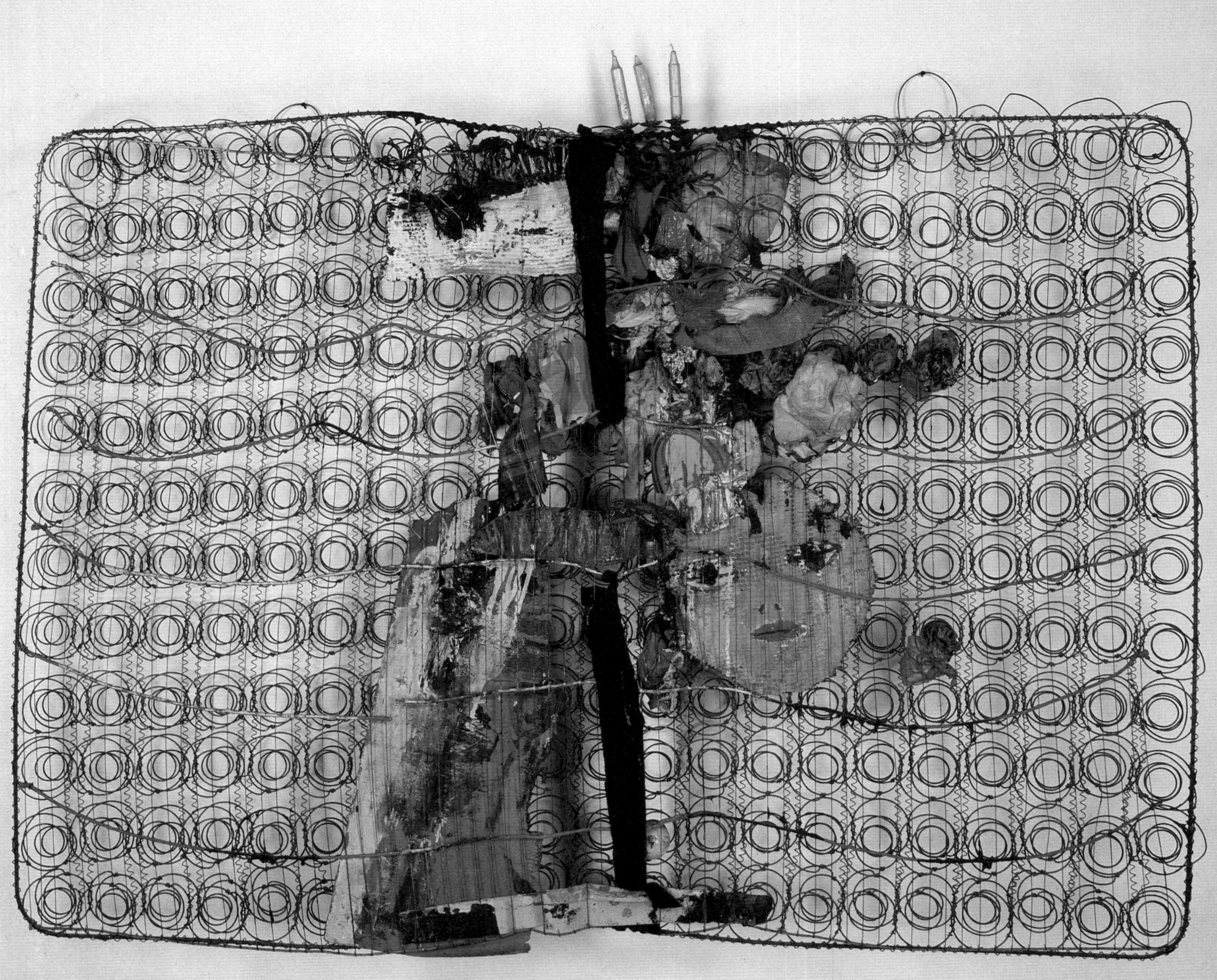

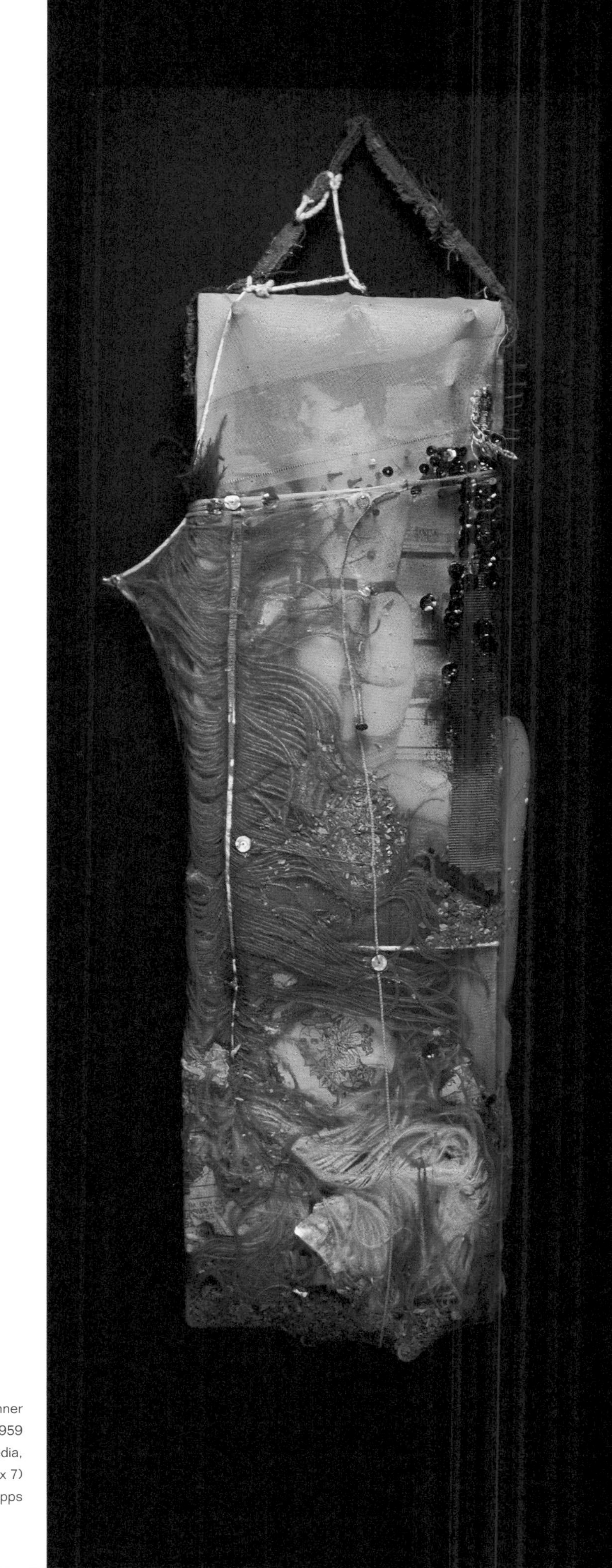

Bruce Conner
BLACK DAHLIA, 1959
Mixed media,
26 3/4 x 10 3/4 x 2 3/4 (67.9 x 27.3 x 7)
Collection of Walter Hopps

William S. Burroughs and Brion Gysin
Untitled (Tornado Dead: 223), from **The Third Mind**, c. 1965-70
Offset lithography, newsprint, ink, letterpress, and graphite on paper,
8 3/4 x 6 3/4 (22.2 x 17.1)
Los Angeles County Museum of Art; Purchased with funds provided by The Hiro Yamagata Foundation

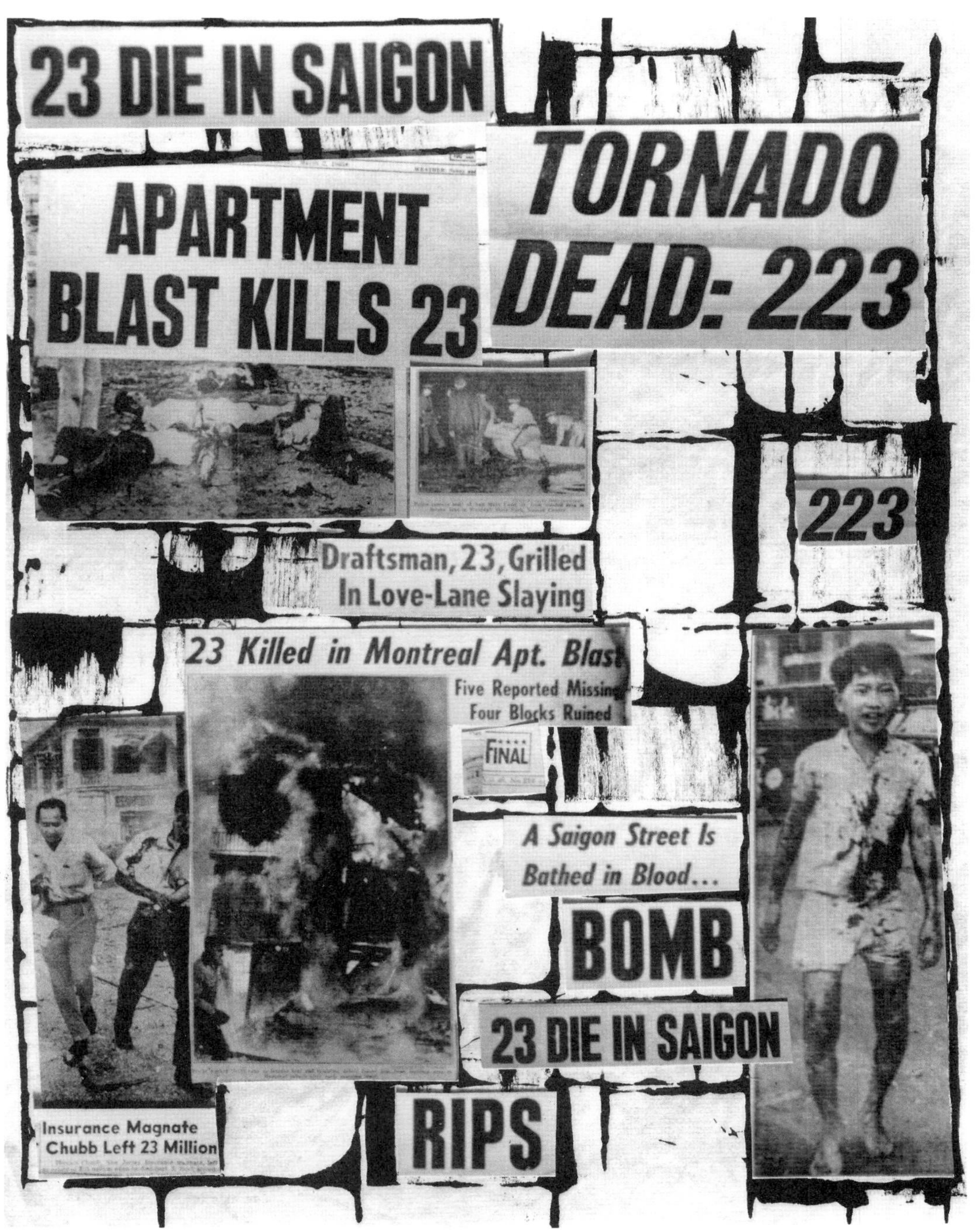

Carolee Schneemann

Quarry Transposed—Portrait of N., 1960

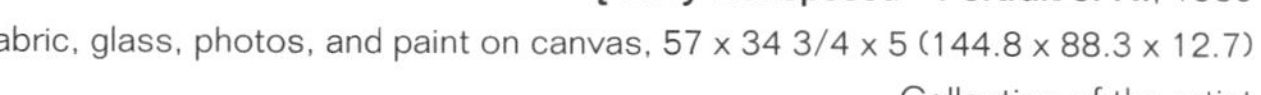

Fabric, glass, photos, and paint on canvas, 57 x 34 3/4 x 5 (144.8 x 88.3 x 12.7)

Collection of the artist

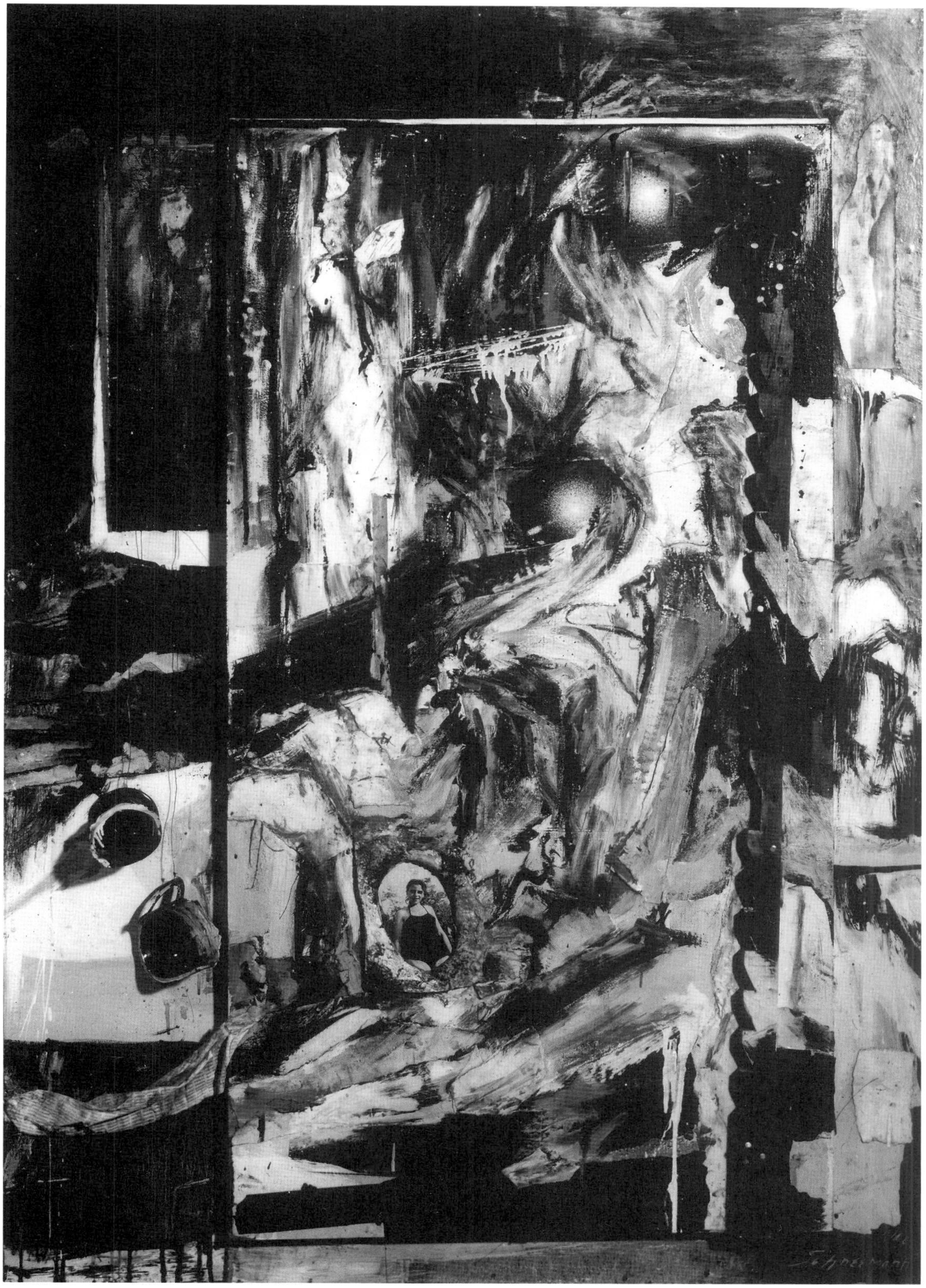

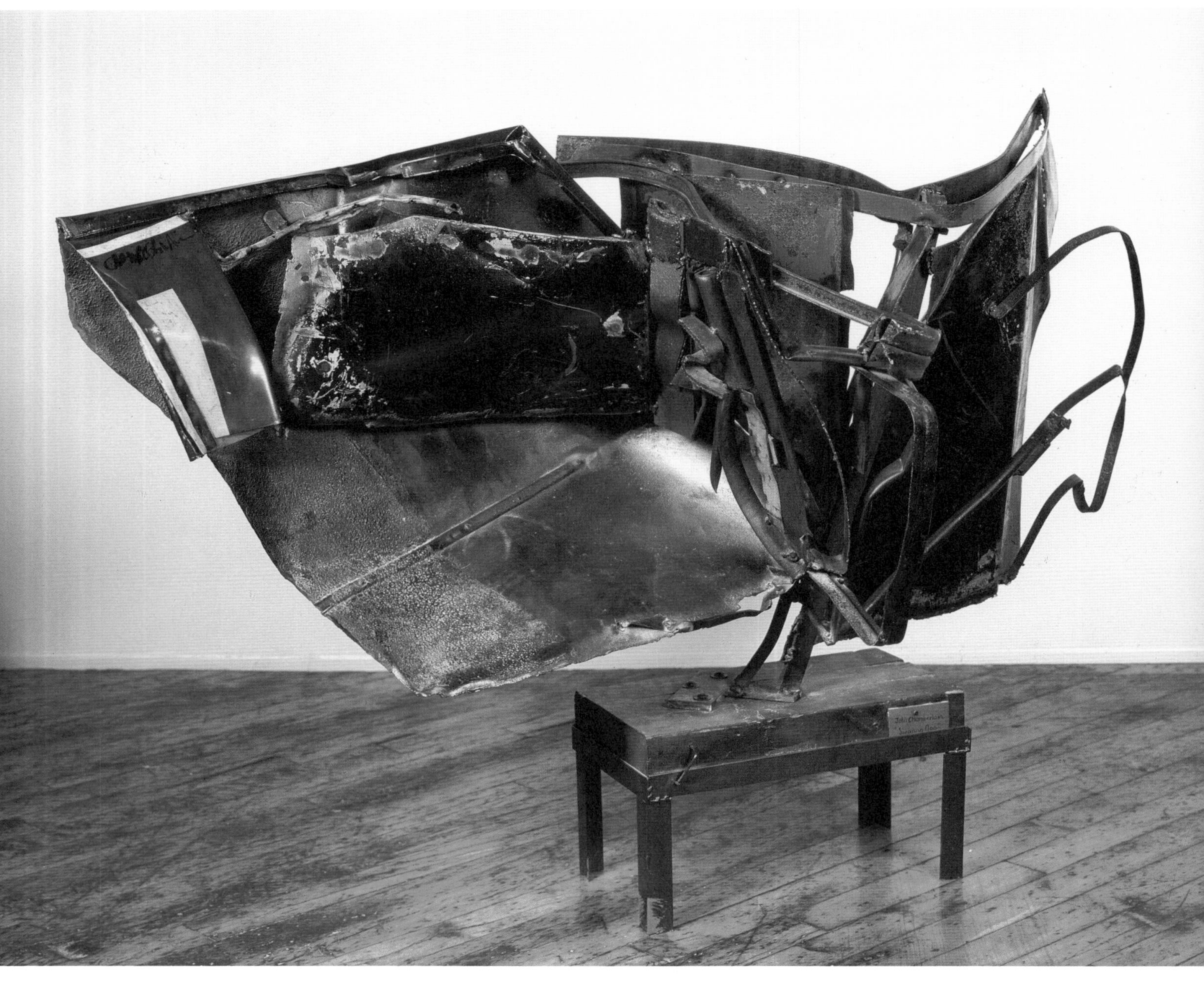

John Chamberlain
Swannanoa/Swannanoa II, 1959
Painted and chromium-plated steel, 45 1/2 x 66 x 25 1/2 (115.6 x 167.6 x 64.8)
Dia Center for the Arts, New York

Ray Johnson
Elvis Presley #2, 1956-57
Tempera and ink wash on magazine page,
11 x 8 1/2 (27.9 x 21.6)
Collection of William S. Wilson

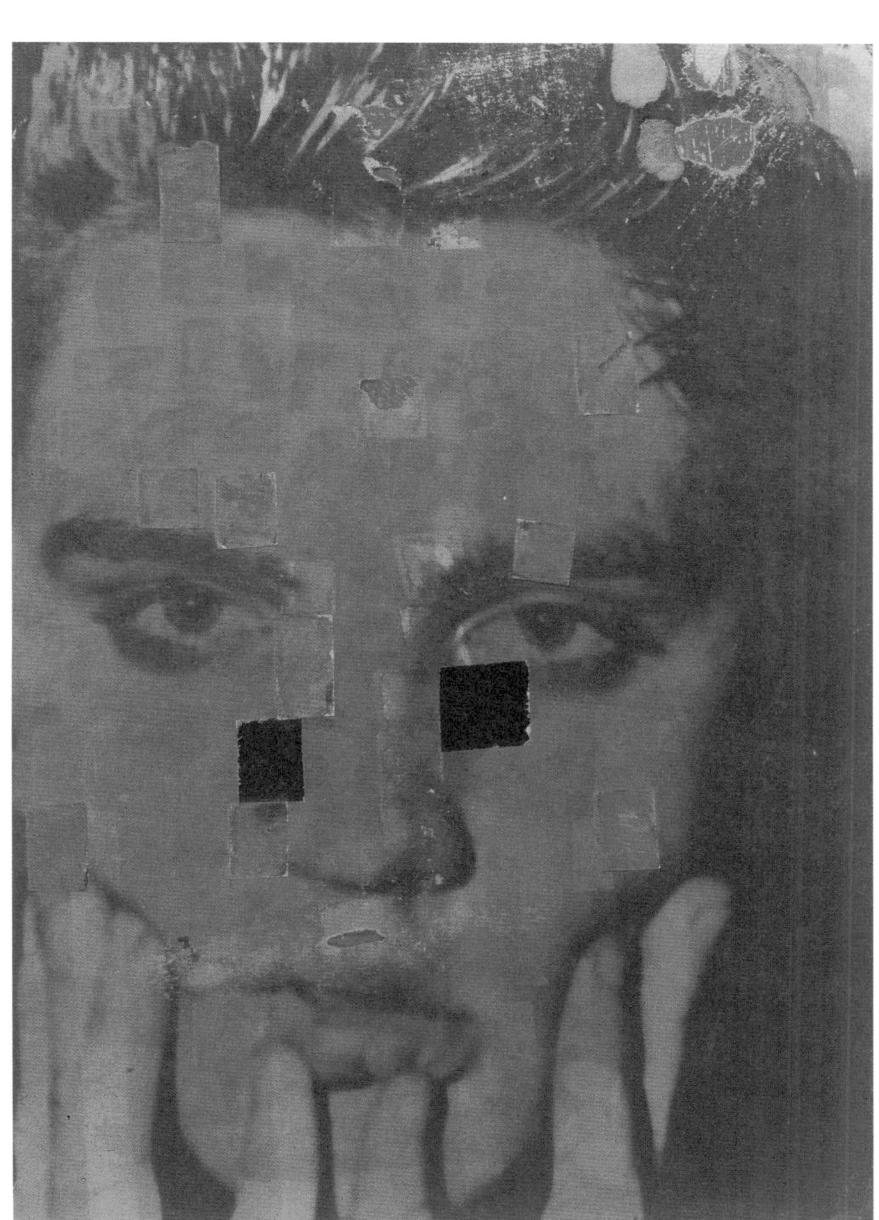

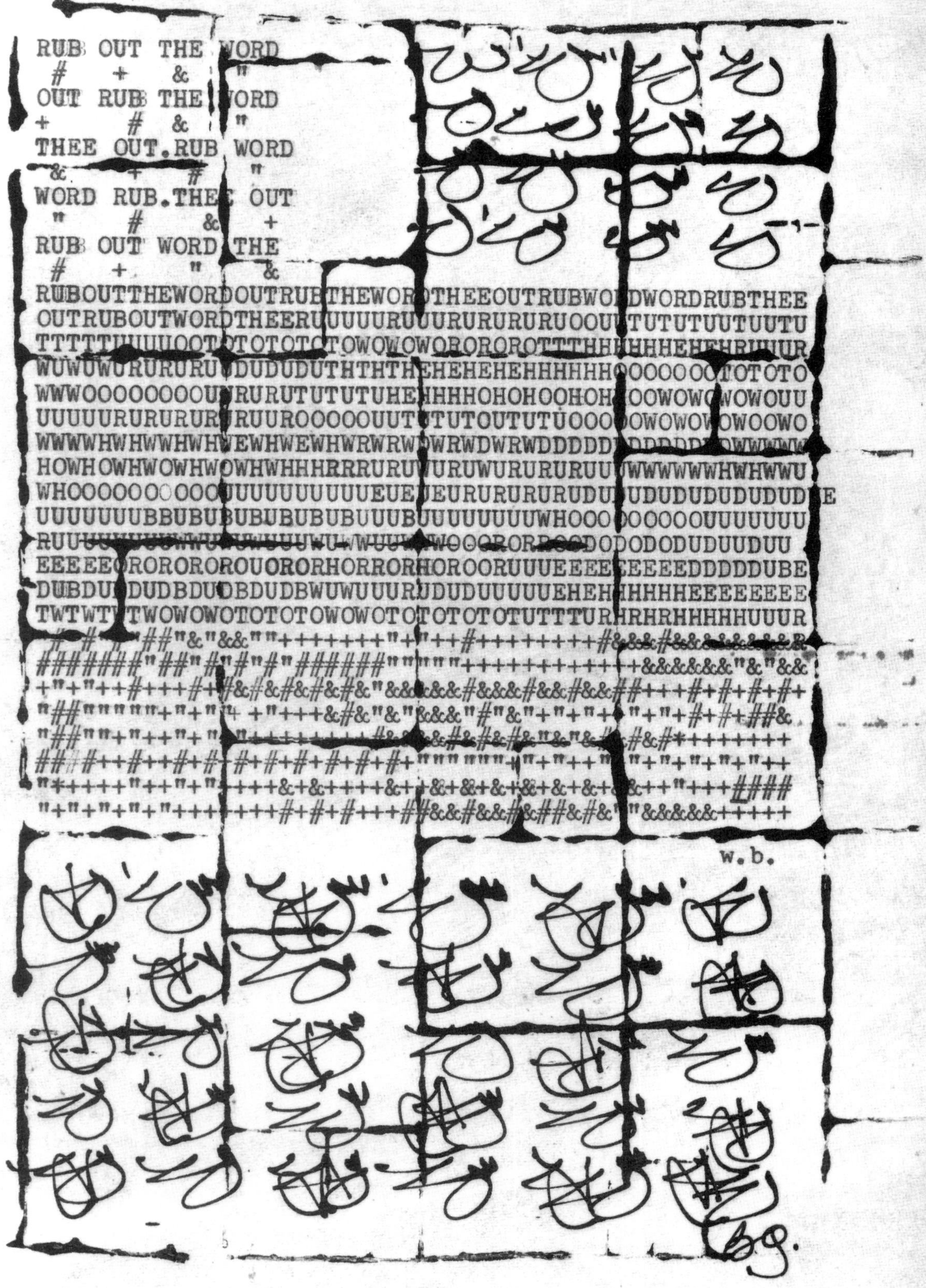
RUB OUT THE WORD
+ & "
OUT RUB THE WORD
+ # & "
THEE OUT.RUB WORD
& + # "
WORD RUB.THEE OUT
" # & +
RUB OUT WORD THE
+ " &
w.b.

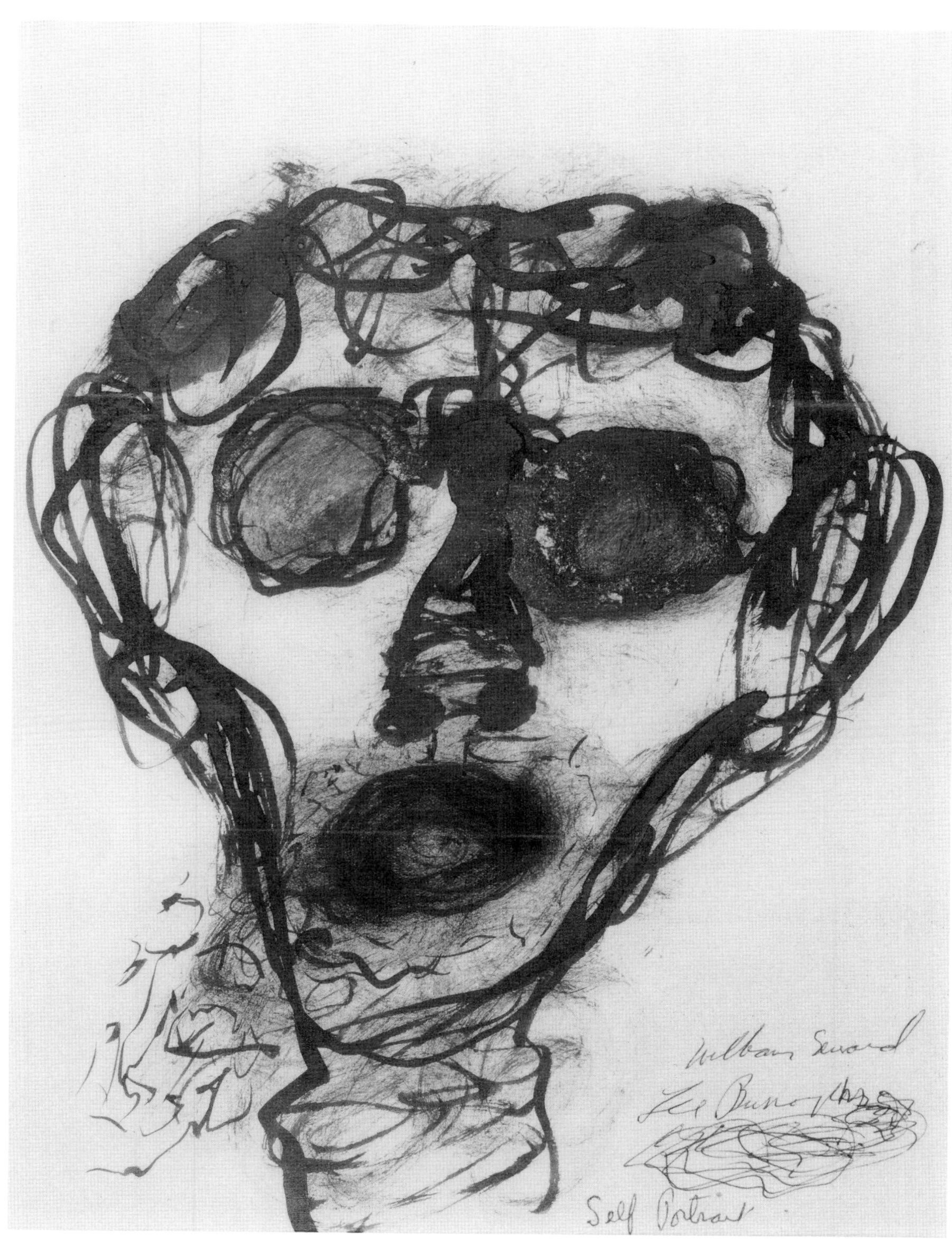

William S. Burroughs
Self-Portrait, c. 1959
Ink on paper, 11 x 8 1/2 (27.9 x 21.6)
Rare Book and Manuscript Library, Columbia University, New York; Allen Ginsberg Collection

William S. Burroughs and Brion Gysin
Untitled ("Rub Out the Word"), from **The Third Mind**, 1965-70
Typescript and ink on paper, 10 1/16 x 6 13/16 (25.6 x 17.3)
Los Angeles County Museum of Art; Purchased with funds provided by The Hiro Yamagata Foundation

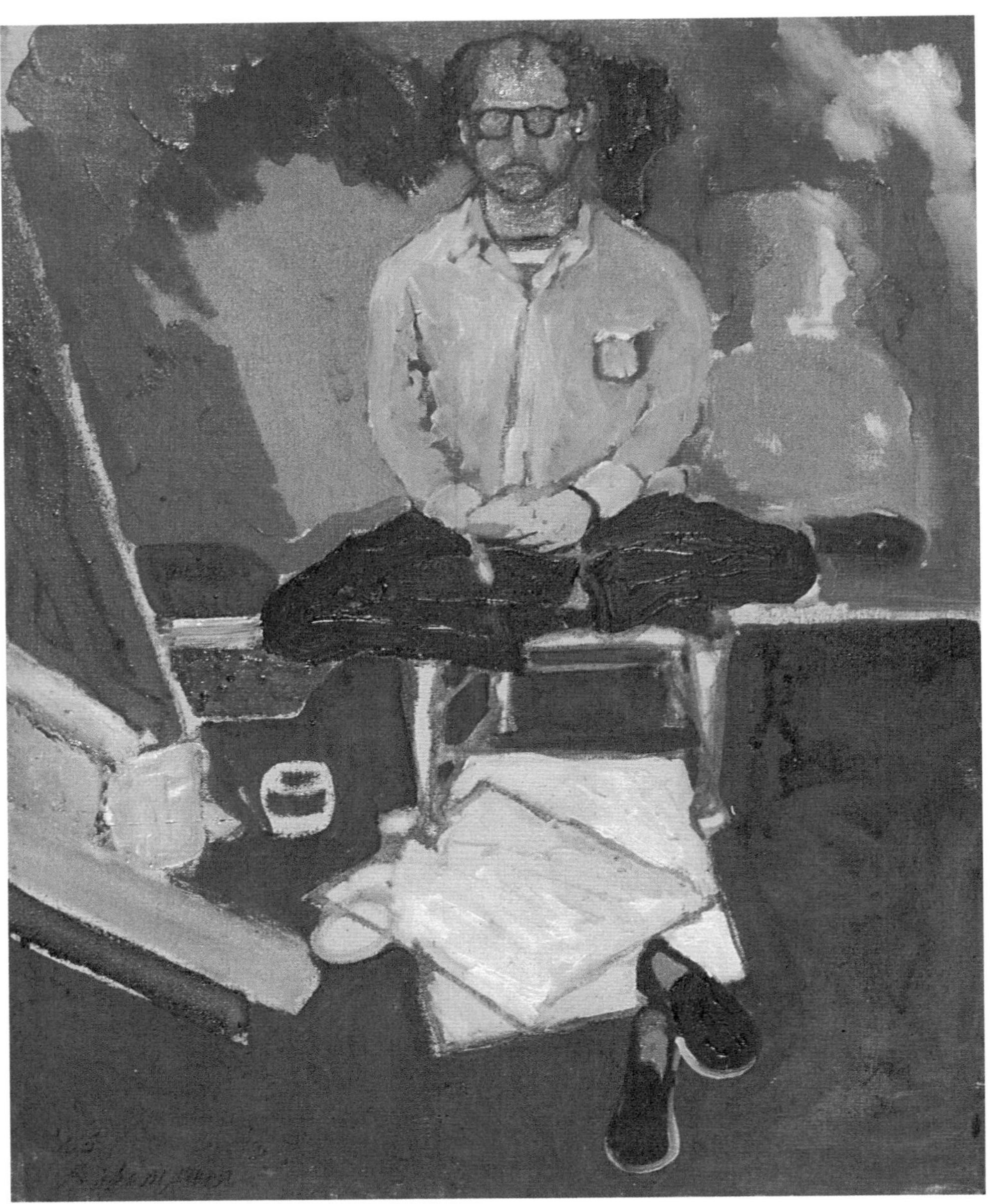

Bob Thompson
Portrait of Allen, 1965
Oil on canvas, 20 x 16 (50.8 x 40.6)
Collection of George Nelson Preston

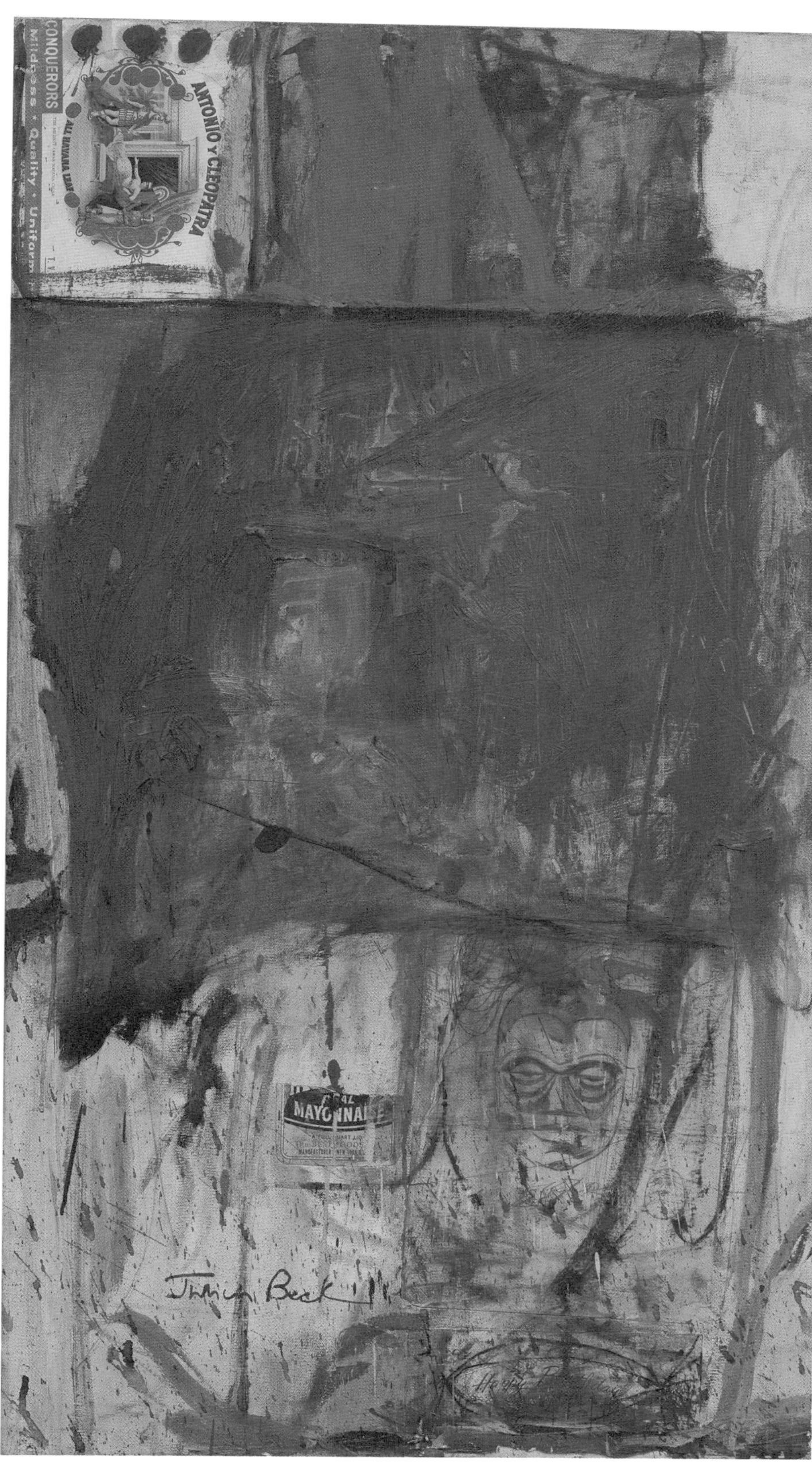

Julian Beck
Romeo and Juliet, 1957
Collage on canvas, 40 x 22 (101.6 x 55.9)
Collection of Sietske and Herman Turndorf;
courtesy Janos Gat Gallery, New York

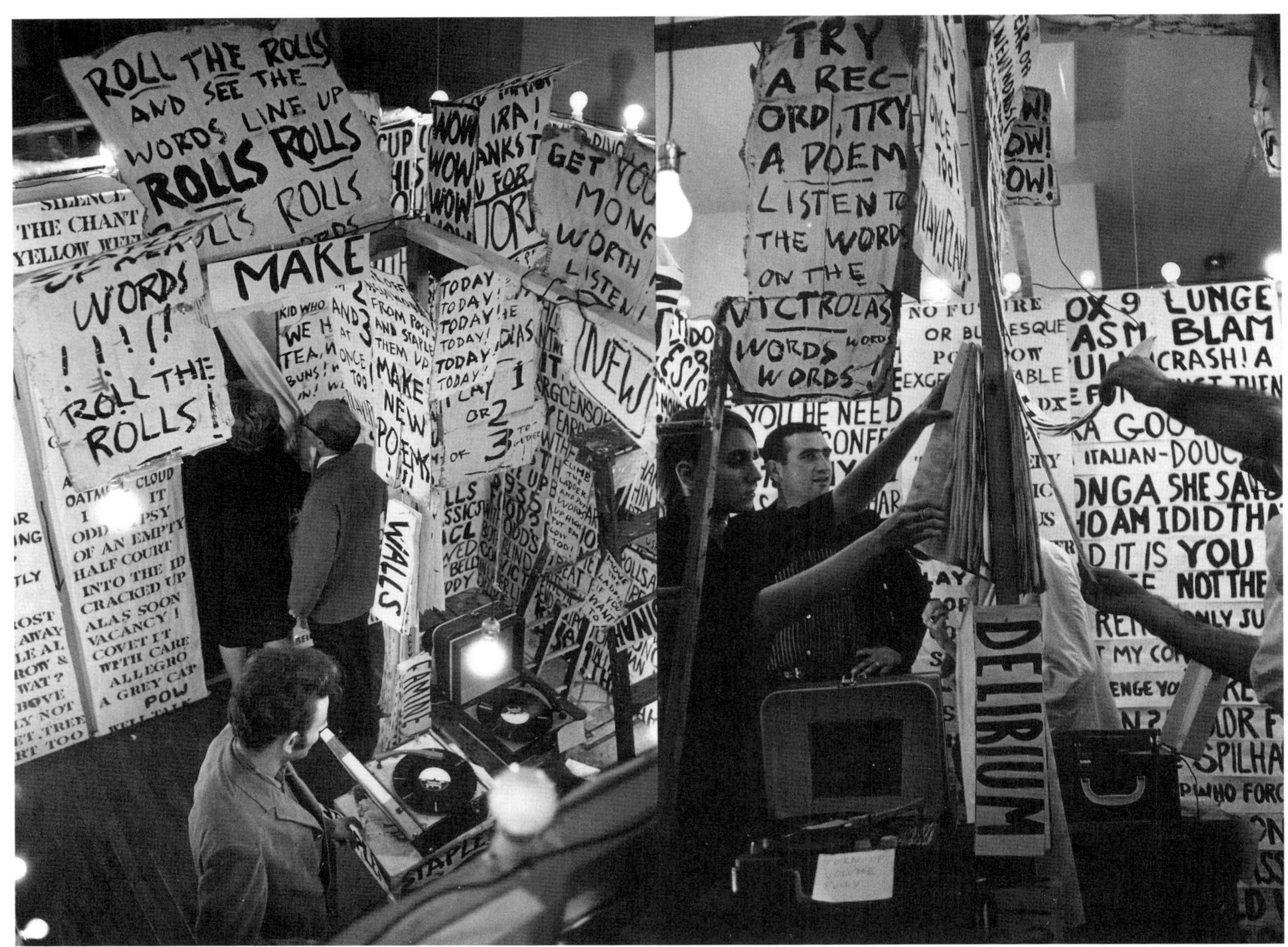

Allan Kaprow
Words, 1962; as installed at the
Smolin Gallery, New York
Photo by Robert R. McElroy

Allan Kaprow
An Apple Shrine, 1960;
as installed at the Judson Gallery,
Judson Memorial Church, New York
Photo by Robert R. McElroy

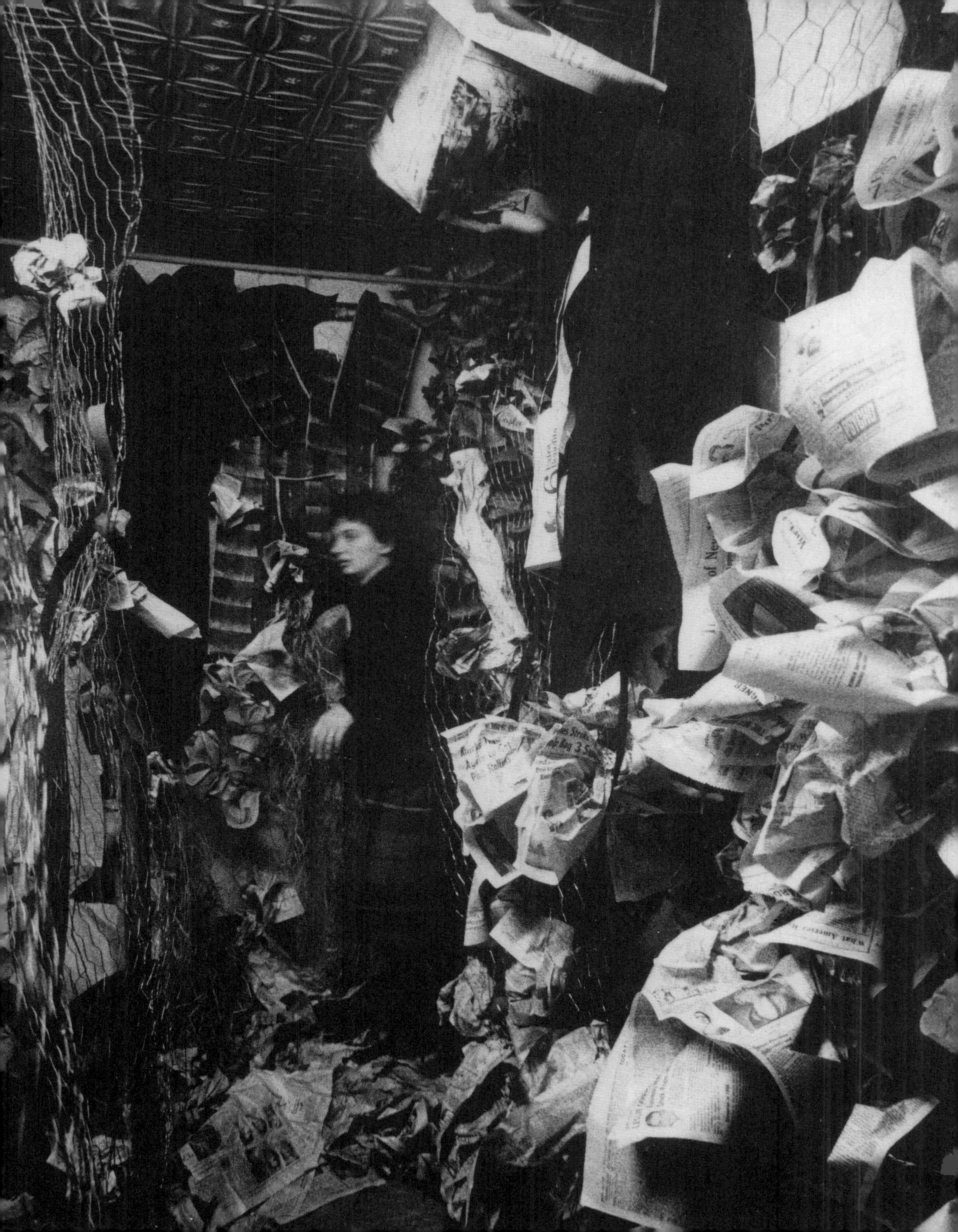

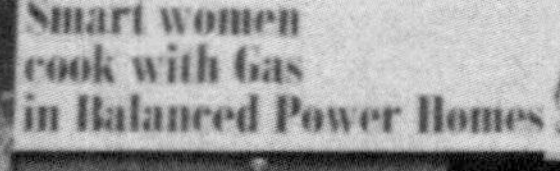
Smart women
cook with Gas
in Balanced Power Homes

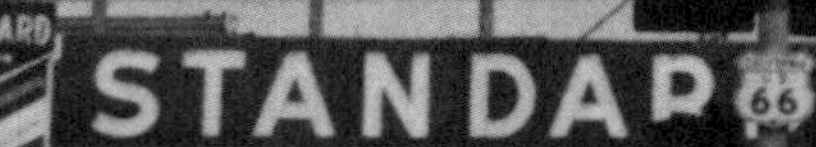
66

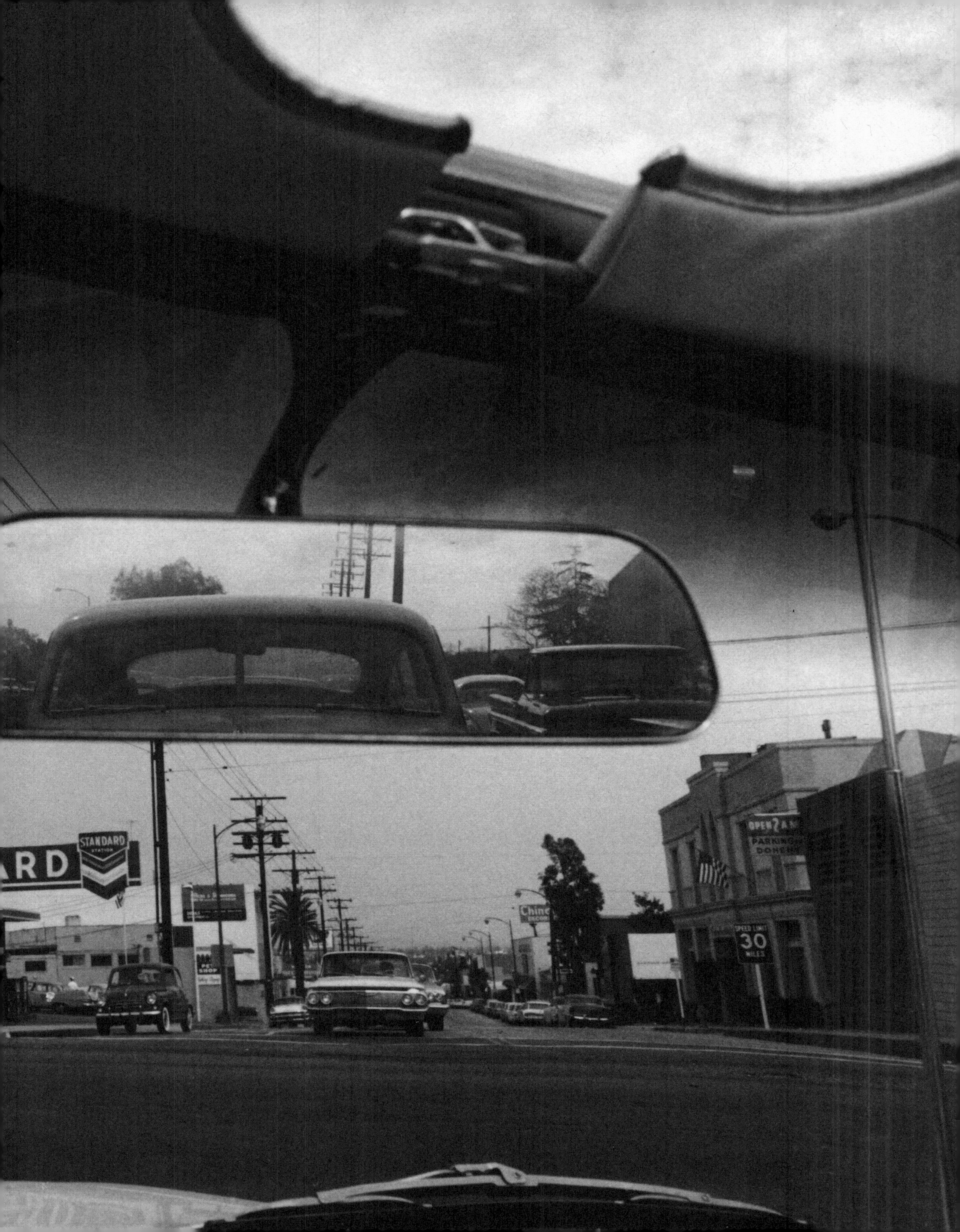
ARD
STANDARD
PARKING
DOHENY
SPEED LIMIT
30
MILES

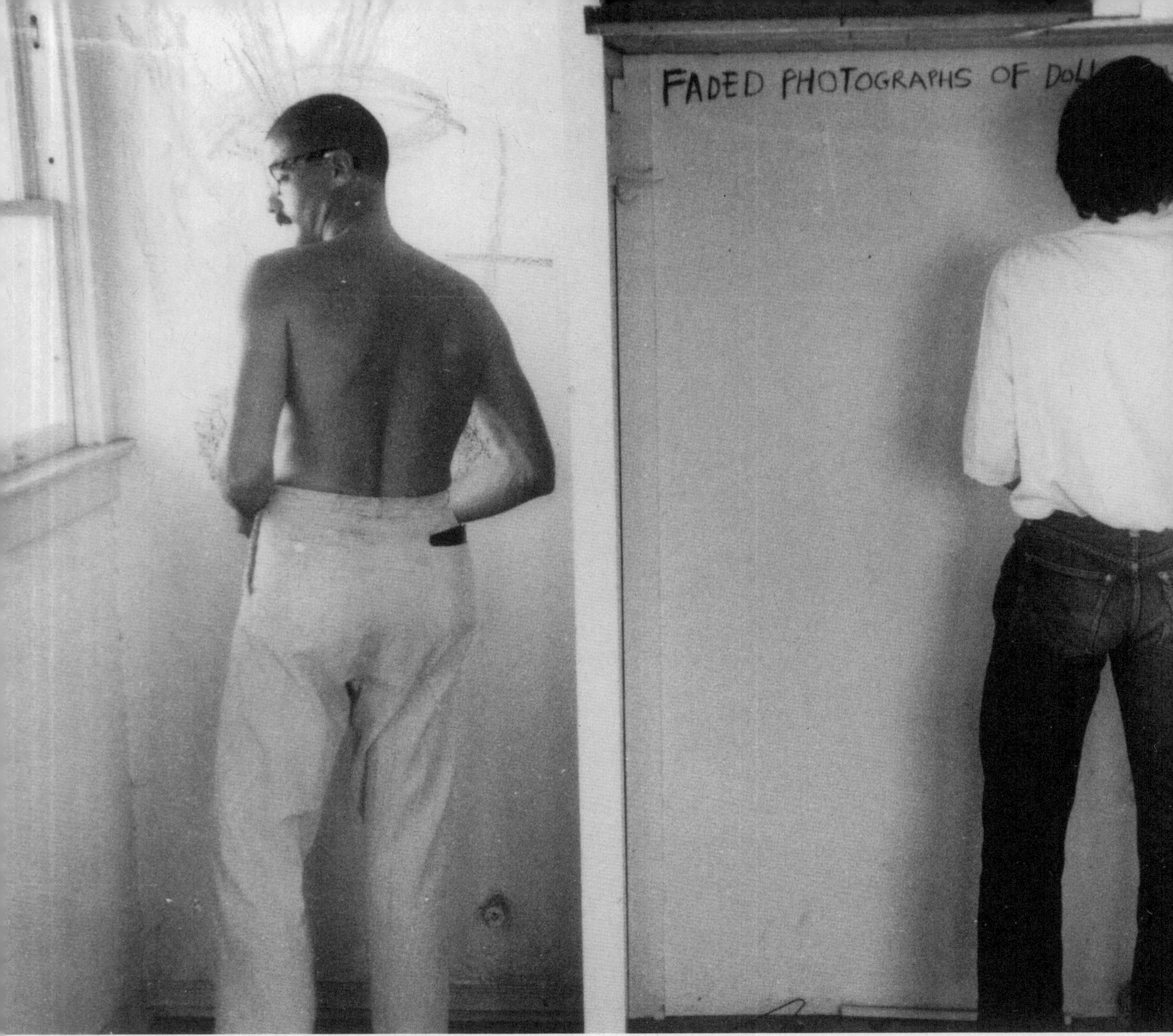

Previous page: **Double Standard**, 1961. Photo by Dennis Hopper

Above: **Robert Alexander and Wallace Berman writing on the walls in Venice, California**, 1956. Photo by Charles Brittin

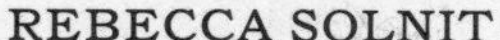

REBECCA SOLNIT

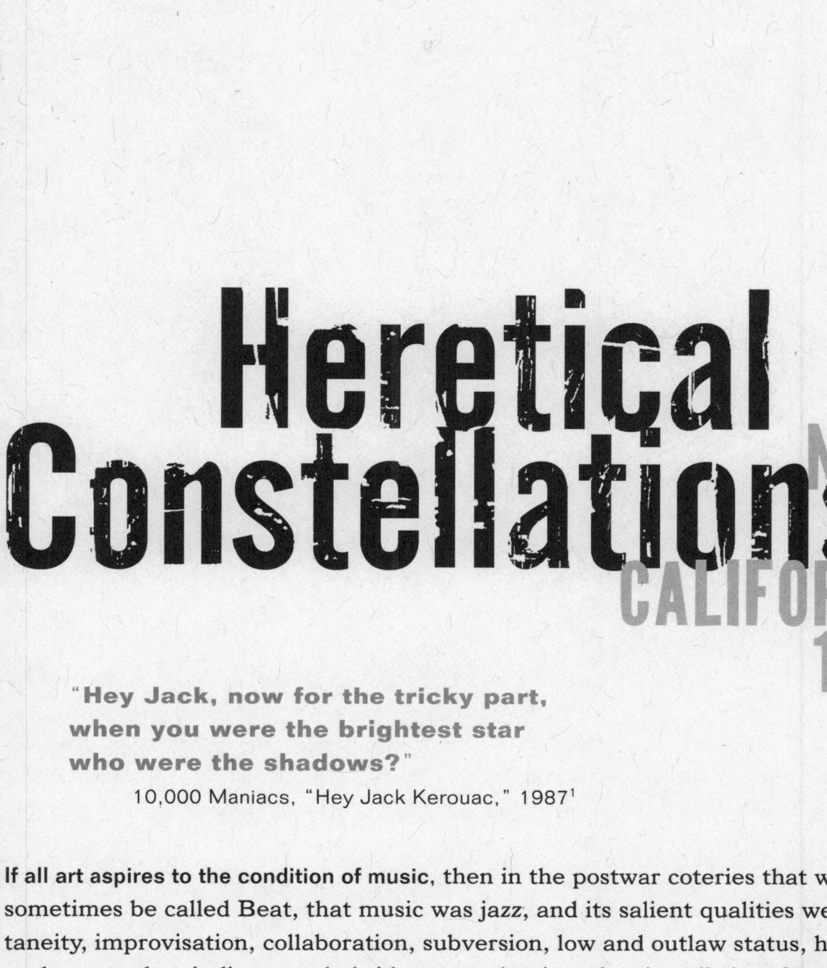

Heretical Constellations: Notes on California, 1946–61

> **"Hey Jack, now for the tricky part, when you were the brightest star who were the shadows?"**
>
> 10,000 Maniacs, "Hey Jack Kerouac," 1987[1]

If all art aspires to the condition of music, then in the postwar coteries that would sometimes be called Beat, that music was jazz, and its salient qualities were spontaneity, improvisation, collaboration, subversion, low and outlaw status, hipness/coolness, and an indigenous, hybrid, vernacular Americanism distinct from the Europhilia that had overwhelmed their predecessors. If a single point could be claimed as the beginning of California's subversive artistic avant-garde sometimes aligned and included with the Beats, that point might be the famous breakdown of the saxophonist Charlie Parker in a Los Angeles recording studio on July 29, 1946, a session at which the young artists Wallace Berman and Robert Alexander were present.[2] This was the first year of the peace that brought a sense of an utterly, irreparably changed world, the world after the revelations of the Nazi Holocaust and Hiroshima. In 1946, Levittowns were mushrooming, television sets had gone into mass production, America was booming while Europe was sifting through its ruins, the spectacular nuclear-test explosions on Bikini Island inaugurated the cold war, Los Angeles' horrific Black Dahlia murder took place, and Charlie Parker found the burdens of race, addiction, and genius insupportable. It was a time that demanded reassessment and invention just to survive.

Although many artists of the postwar period claimed jazz as an influence, Berman and Alexander had gone further, into a rapport with the musicians and an understanding of their world, acquiring familiarity with the drugs, slang, and style that would come to define their own

Wallace Berman's Larkspur Gallery, Larkspur, California, 1960. Photo by Charles Brittin

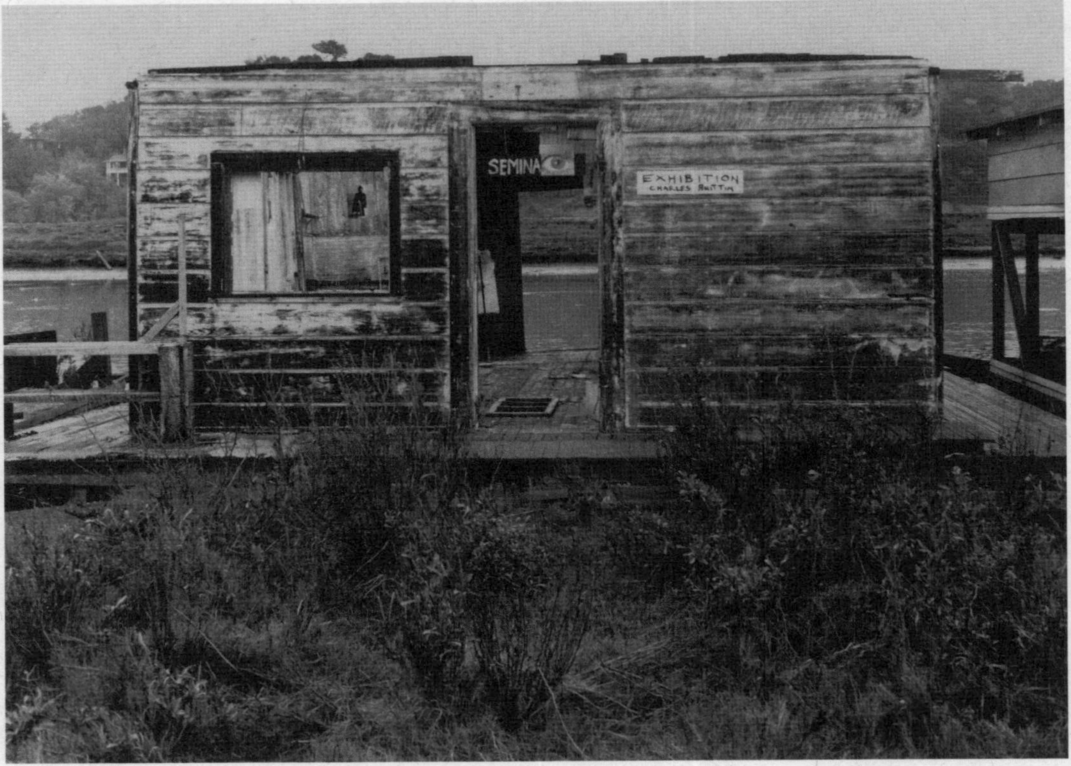

lives. Both first-generation American Jews, Berman and Alexander kept throughout their lives a sense of unassimilated marginal status, and of the dangers as well as the possibilities of art making. They dedicated themselves less to the making of objects than to the making of a culture in which it was possible to make the brilliant, risky, groundbreaking, sometimes soaring, sometimes outrageous art that would emerge from the subculture they brought into being in Los Angeles and contributed to in San Francisco. Their achievement cannot be measured only by the artifacts they left behind (though Berman's are remarkable) but by the richness and impact of the subculture or avant-garde they fostered and all the doors it opened to what would be called the counterculture and then to the culture at large.

Perhaps because outside support was so abysmally lacking in that time and place, the subculture is likewise distinguished by its friendships, correspondences, collaborations, gestures of support, and artist-run galleries, presses and publications, by artists who served as one another's audience and who worked to create a cultural infrastructure, a community. It was a culture that brought together artists and poets and filmmakers, particularly in San Francisco. It was a period of mixing it up, of bringing ideas and epiphanies from one medium to another, a period when not only jazz (and later, rhythm and blues and rock and roll), but esoteric and occult traditions, contemporary politics, popular culture, mass media, drugs, sex, and non-European traditions as well as Dada and Surrealism influenced and appeared in the work. From it emerged the great experimental films of Stan Brakhage, Bruce Conner, Larry Jordan, Kenneth Anger, the paintings of Jay DeFeo, Wally Hedrick, Jess, Artie Richer, Joan Brown, the collages and assemblages of Conner, Jess, Berman, George Herms, Edward Kienholz, and an array of great poetry—by Jack Spicer, David Meltzer, Robert Duncan, Michael McClure—which was tied to the other poets' circles that included Allen Ginsberg, Gary Snyder, Bob Kaufman, and many more.

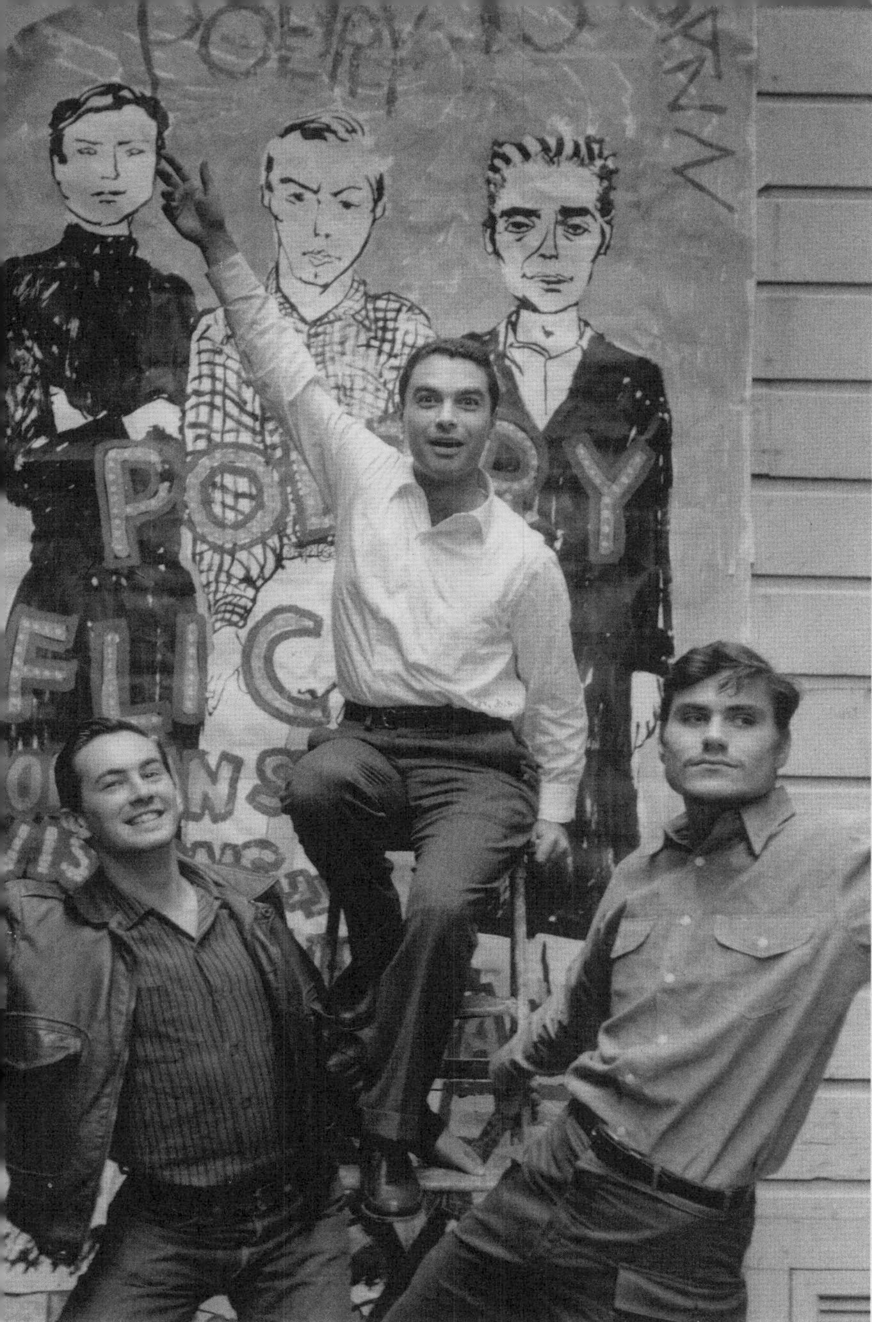

Any number of constellations can be picked out from the alignments and affinities among those gathered around Los Angeles and San Francisco, constellations based on proximities, projects, styles, media. Toward the end of the 1950s, one of this era's greatest artists, Bruce Conner, founded the Rat Bastard Protective Association. Its name derived from the slang term "rat bastard" that poet Michael McClure had picked up at the gym, from the Scavengers Protective Society (the San Francisco garbage collectors) and from the Pre-Raphaelite Brotherhood (PRB, like the Rat Bastard's RBP). A parody of societies, self-conscious movements, and historians' anxieties to pigeonhole art making, its members paid dues, had meetings, and were entitled to use the RBP seal of approval on their work. Among them were artists such as Joan Brown and Carlos Villa, a few poets, and the Auerhahn Press publisher Dave Hazelwood.

A flowering of anomalies and apostasies, these West Coast artists tend to be exceptional in the most literal terms—thus one can say that there was a distinction between the no-nonsense abstract painters of the period and the mystical-poetic assemblage artists—except that the assemblagist Kienholz firmly allied himself with the painters, while the greatest painter of the era, Jay DeFeo, was something of a mystic in her work, hung out with the assemblagists, and made a few immensely influential collages and assemblages. This fecund period is impossible to describe in terms of the neat linear genealogies of a genre or medium, since cross-pollinations were so central, since those working in each medium drew on friends and theories from other media, and since some of the most stellar figures worked in several media.

Berman counted some of LA's great jazz musicians among his friends, and his first extant works of art are academic-surrealist drawings of jazz figures within the iconography of their world, one of which became a bebop album cover. A homage to Parker would show up fifteen years later in one of the issues of *Semina*, the experimental publication Berman produced, and throughout his life, literature and music would inform his visual work far more than visual art traditions. And Berman's visual work, which included photography, film, printmaking, mail art, collage/print hybrids made on an early photocopier, assemblage, site-specific text pieces, and installation, represents the interdisciplinary approach that typifies the period. George Herms evolved into an assemblage artist by making objects to bear his poetry, while Michael McClure came to San Francisco in 1954 to study with Clyfford Still and Mark Rothko; finding them gone, he went on to use the ideas of gesture and Action Painting in the development of his distinctive poetic voice.

Poetry is Jazz (Michael McClure, Philip Lamantia, and Larry Jordan), 1957. Photo by Larry Jordan

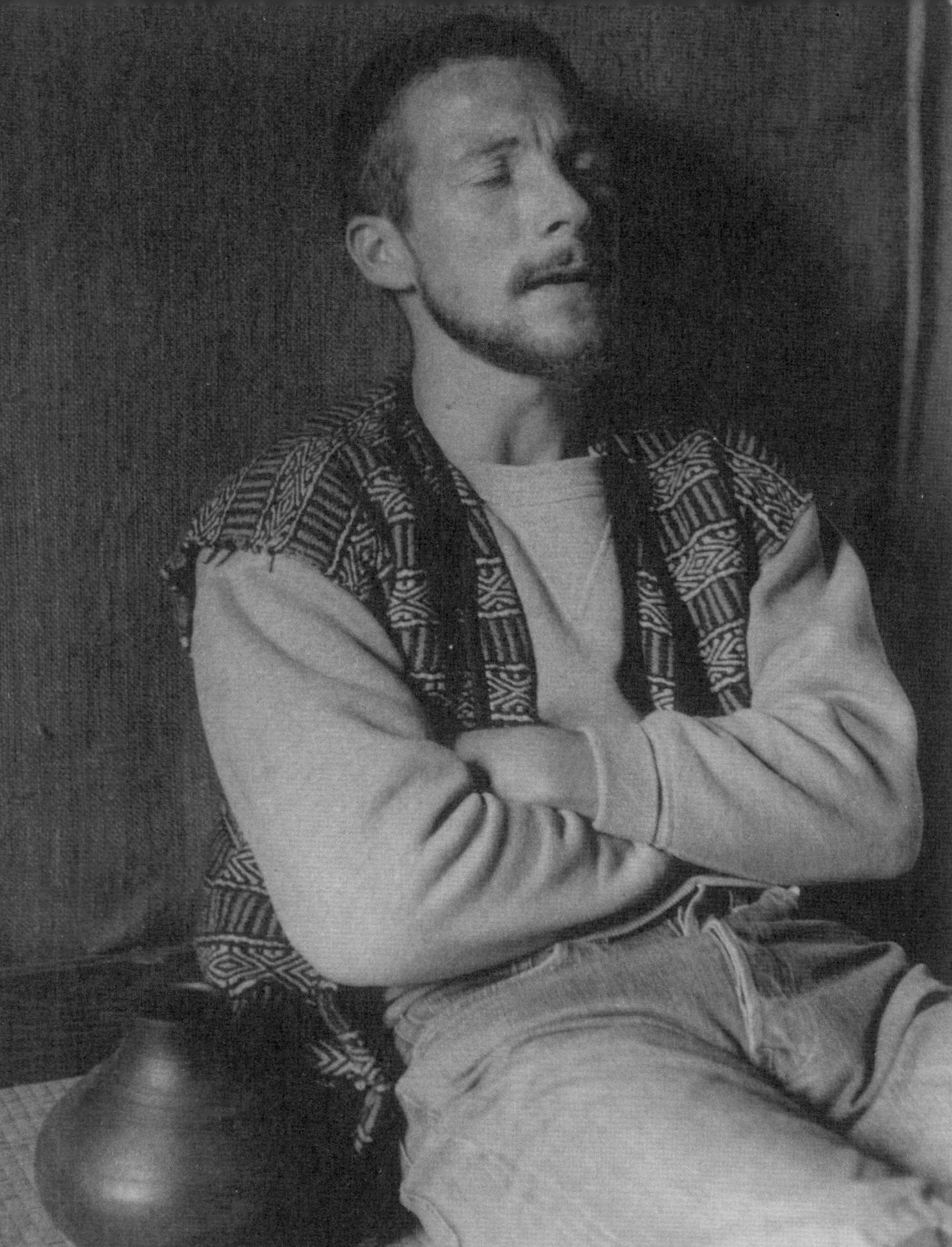

Gary Snyder, San Francisco, 1957.
Photo by Harry Redl

Another characteristic of the period is the lack of critics, curators, and other outsiders to sift through the abundance and set standards and draw lines. As a result, the names that crop up in these histories range from the internationally renowned to the largely forgotten—at King Ubu Gallery, for example, David Park, Elmer Bischoff, and Jess exhibited with little-known artists like Harry Jacobus and Lynn Brockaway Brown; at the time, there was little distinction between those who would become famous and those who would be nearly forgotten. Success was nowhere on the horizon, and its absence freed the artists to be as experimental, as outrageous, as personal as they liked, an exhilarating if not always an enviable condition. Between the looming cold war and the lack of an audience, there was little evident future for their work, which was made, like music, for the moment and for their fellow artists. They were remarkable for their commitment to work for its own sake, and their history is littered not only with acts of sabotage, but with abandoned and destroyed pieces, ephemeral gestures, and unstable materials. They established an idea of success that has everything to do with the caliber of one's acts and nothing to do with recognition, though some of them eventually became successes on both counts.

The central moment in West Coast Beat culture or in Beat culture generally, the moment Jack Kerouac mythologized in *The Dharma Bums* and everyone runs up against in addressing the era, is as much a triumph as the collapse of Parker nine years earlier had been a tragedy: Allen Ginsberg's first reading of "Howl" at the 6 Gallery on Fillmore Street in San Francisco in October 1955. The poem, and his public reading of it, was a watershed, but the homogeneous image of a movement founded and a momentum begun falls apart under closer examination. In this sense, the event illuminates the complexity of the scene. Five poets appeared with Ginsberg that evening. Philip Lamantia, who had close ties to André Breton and the Surrealists in New York, read the work of John Hoffman, who'd died of a heroin overdose a little while before, and so the reading was a memorial and a continuation as well as a beginning. Michael McClure and Gary Snyder read poetry whose open, surging lines may well be Beat but whose subjects—Coyote, a woman married to a bear, a whale massacre—forecast the environmental consciousness and indigenous traditions that would much later become key elements of West Coast culture. Philip Whalen, who was already immersed in Zen, also read. The anarchist Kenneth Rexroth, whose salons had kept radical culture alive in San Francisco since the 1930s, was the master of ceremonies and senior poet.[3]

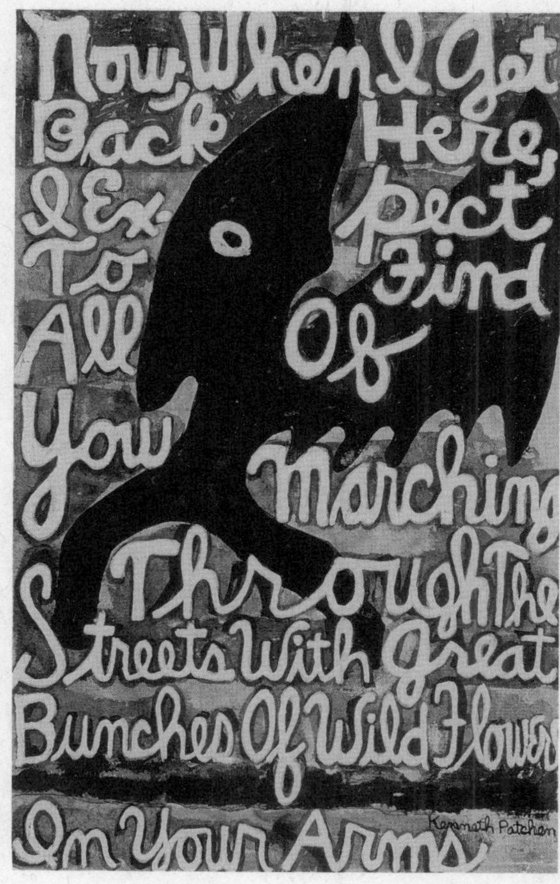

Kenneth Patchen
Now, when I get back here...,
c. 1960
Mixed media, 24 x 21 (61 x 53.3)
University Library, University of California, Santa Cruz; Special Collections, The Kenneth Patchen Archive.

So the event pointed to things that preceded and followed the insurrectionary moment that would be called Beat. The Beats who were to become so famous were largely strangers to the crowd who supported the 6; they lacked a community that maintained cultural spaces, resources, and connections that would make such readings possible. If Ginsberg had broken new ground, the 6 had made it possible. The reading was modeled after one Robert Duncan had given at the 6 Gallery earlier that year, with his lover Jess and friends Larry Jordan and McClure among the participants. And it was McClure who had invited Ginsberg into the community, and Ginsberg who brought Kerouac, a complete unknown in these circles. Another writer present, Jack Goodwin, described in a letter how "This Carrowac person sat on the floor...slugging a gallon of Burgundy and repeating lines after Ginsberg, and singing snatches of scat in between the lines; he kept a kind of chanted, revival-meeting rhythm going."[4] The 6 Gallery had taken over a space that Duncan, Jess, and Harry Jacobus had run for a year as the King Ubu Gallery, named after the riotous antihero of Jarry's 1896 play; the six who gave the place its new name were poet Jack Spicer and five of his students from the California School of Fine Arts (now the San Francisco Art Institute): John Allen Ryan, Deborah Remington, David Simpson, Hayward King, and Wally Hedrick, a mixed group in regard to color, gender, media, and sexual orientation.

These things happened in two closely linked and wildly different cities, San Francisco and Los Angeles. At the time, they seemed to have little more in common than a coast, and in the 1950s it was possible to deride LA as "Omaha with a beach."[5] The dominant culture of this sunny, sprawling city, whose main industries were real estate, aerospace, and defense as well as entertainment, was that of Midwesterners determined to stay Midwestern. There were many other cultures, however, which sometimes acquired enough voice to impinge on Omaha: the Spanish-speakers who had been the original Angelenos; the huge African-American community that had migrated during the war in search of defense industry jobs; the immigrant Jewish community in which the Hebrew letters so common in Berman's work were part of the everyday environment of kosher stores and Yiddish newspapers. There was, of course, Hollywood with its stars and hopefuls, as well as the *noir* tradition in film and fiction, which cast southern California in a different shadow, and the thriving black jazz scene in south-central LA from which such luminaries as Charles Mingus and Ornette Coleman emerged. European refugees such as Thomas Mann, Aldous Huxley, Bertolt Brecht, and Arnold Schönberg were Angelenos during the 1940s, and the rootless optimism of the place seemed to make it a prime spawning ground for utopian movements and religious cults, from Aimee Semple McPherson to L. Ron Hubbard to the Crowleyan magicians centered around the California Institute of Technology. What is probably still the greatest California assemblage was finished in south-central LA in 1954, Simon Rodia's *Watts Towers*, an uninhabitable palace of spindly mosaic-covered spires built by an immigrant tile setter. There was plenty of material for young artists in LA to work with, but it was so new, so unassimilated, that there was no precedent for making it into art.

Robert Irwin, who was one of the young painters brought to light by Ferus, the gallery Walter Hopps and Kienholz, with some help from Bob Alexander, founded in 1957, once remarked, "See, what I've always liked about this town, still do, is that it's one of the least restrictive towns in the world. You can pretty much live any way you want to here. And part of that is because the place has no tradition and no history in that sense. It doesn't have any image of itself, which is exactly its loss and its gain."[6] Kienholz himself remarked, "Christ, I was in Los Angeles without a sense of history of art. Like John Reed stole a book one time in Los Angeles and brought it into Ferus Gallery....I'd never heard of Schwitters. And that was in '57."[7] As Mike Davis puts it: "for the Los Angeles 'hipster' generation that came of age in the late 1940s and 1950s, there was little alternative but to form temporary 'communes' within the cultural underground that burgeoned for almost a decade. One of the

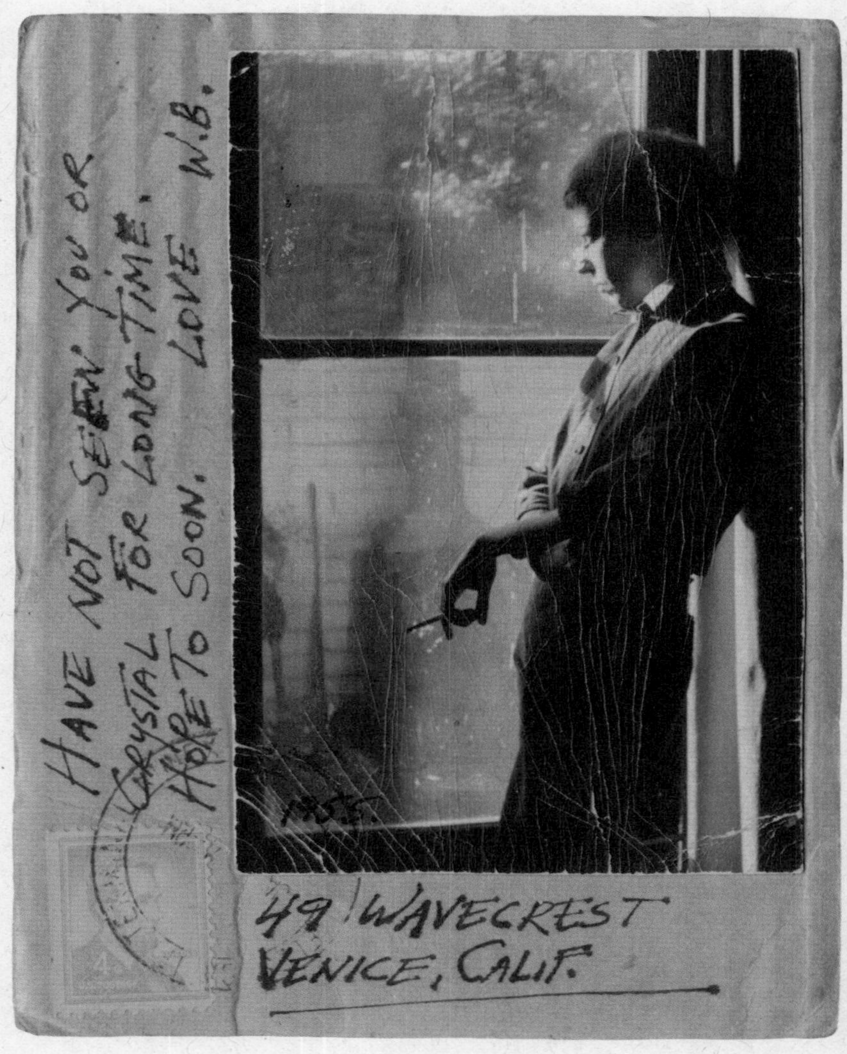

Wallace Berman postcard sent to Cameron, 1962. Estate of the artist

qualities shared by these diverse groups was their concern for critically reworking and re-presenting subcultural experience...."[8]

The two communes, to use Davis' term, in the visual arts were centered around Ferus and around Berman, with many ties between them. The poet and Cabalist scholar David Meltzer lived behind Ferus for a time, was close to Berman and his family, and knew both circles well. He saw them as radically different, calling the Ferus group "lumberjacks" because of the rugged shirts and rugged personas they affected:

> They were much more the professional artists....in the thirties and forties and fifties art was essentially male territory. These male prototypes of the bohemian, almost Hemingwayesque, Falstaffian, exploiters of women patrons. They're almost like Gully Jimson. Male display and male competition. They would be the contingency in the lumberjack shirts, and then you'd have the Berman contingency, the ethereal, exotic creatures out of a *Yellow Book*. One of the operative words that seemed to distinguish Artie [Richer] and [Robert] Alexander and Wally [Berman] was the notion of the personal. There was a great giving of work to each other in the group. There was much more cross-pollination than in the lumberjack camps—they rubbed shoulders, but they were into cars, talking paint—clean some brushes, get back to work. Even Wally's notion of work was baffling to a career artist who gets up no matter how hung over he is and clocks in his time....[9]

George Herms' "Secret Exhibition," a 1957 installation of assemblages on the foundations of some blocks of housing awaiting development, a show only Berman and John Reed ever saw before he moved and abandoned the work, is pretty far from the sense of purpose of the Ferus gang.

Still, Ferus was a leap forward for Los Angeles. Alexander had been a moving force in instigating the gallery, but it was a young art history student, Walter Hopps, and a painter, Ed Kienholz, who became the founding partners of this gallery on La Cienega Boulevard. They were complementary opposites, the refined and elusive connoisseur and the brash, imposing, hands-on artist, and together they did great things. Ferus began in the spring of 1957 with a group show, "Objects on the New Landscape Demanding of the Eye," which brought together the painters Hopps had admired in San Francisco—Jay DeFeo, Roy DeForest, Richard Diebenkorn, Frank Lobdell, Clyfford Still—with the lesser-known LA painters who would become Ferus' stable. (The painters with social ties to Ferus included John Altoon, Craig Kauffman, Allen Lynch, Ed Moses, Robert Irwin, and Billy Al Bengston.) A series of solo exhibitions followed, of paintings by Sonia Gechtoff, Hilda Levy, and then Wallace Berman's disastrous public debut. Kienholz was still bashing around in paint at the time, and his breakthrough into assemblage took place at the end of the decade, after which he became one of the most outspoken political artists in the US for many decades. Hopps too was still finding his métier with

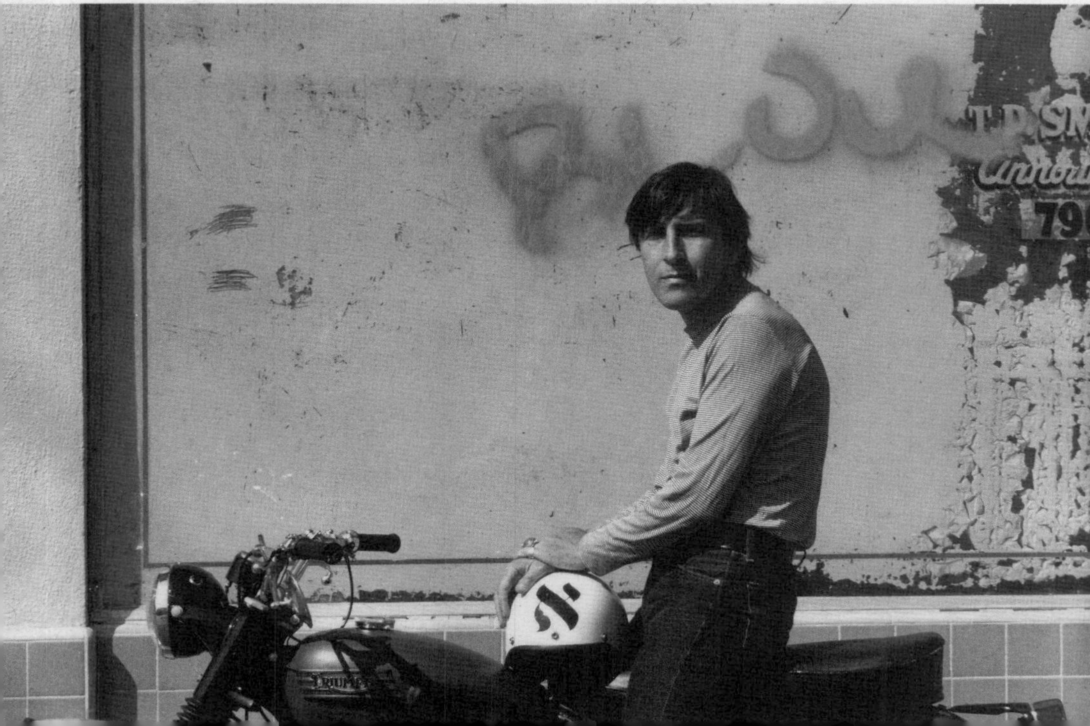

Wallace Berman, 1964.
Photo by Dennis Hopper

Ferus, and he later went far as a curator and museum director, beginning at the Pasadena Art Museum, where he mounted the first major retrospectives of Joseph Cornell and Marcel Duchamp. Hopps worked wonders in developing an audience of collectors for Los Angeles art, laying the foundation for a support network that eludes San Francisco still and eventually made LA into the second American city for contemporary art.

The Ferus gang seemed a hangover from an earlier time, a Cedar Tavern vision of what art could be; the Berman circle seemed to prefigure the sixties with its emphasis on art as part of a total environment, a life, with all the mixing of media and making of alternatives that involved. These people were often visionary, drawing from drugs and occult traditions, circulating their art as gifts that tied the community together. Berman was a catalyst here for many younger people, from David Meltzer to the assemblage artist George Herms to the actors Russ Tamblyn and Dean Stockwell, providing an example of someone living for and within art, providing places to gather, connections, esoteric information, and encouragement. His presence was said to be remarkable, and he had a talent for moving in many circles, from jazz musicians to the magician Cameron to Hollywood stars to these young artists.

Berman's publication *Semina*, begun in 1955, replicated this practice of gathering and disseminating. An unbound collection of unmatched pages of poetry, prose, photographs, and drawings, *Semina* was the first publisher for many young poets. It printed excerpts of *Naked Lunch* early on as well as brief pieces by great poets of the past. *Semina* embodied Berman's idea of a multimedia community. The name itself is drawn from the Latin root for such words as seminal and semen; it was in fact a seed packet, gathering and dispersing a new culture. When Dennis Hopper, another member of Berman's circle in the fifties, put him in *Easy Rider*, Berman played a commune member sowing seeds, a nice tribute to his real-life role. The poet Philip Lamantia recalls, "One of the things about Wallace Berman was that he seemed to have access, mysterious access....Something he was very emphatic about—when he talked about poetry, he seemed to be particularly impressed by the surrealist movement. 'They're the only group,' he said, 'that has remained together for'—by that time, late fifties, 'forty years.'"[10]

Another distinction between the Ferus and Berman circles was geographic. Nearly everyone around the Bermans, and the Bermans themselves, moved to San Francisco at some point in the latter fifties—Alexander, Meltzer, Herms, the artists Idell T. and Elias Romero, Artie Richer, John Reed—and some stayed. Berman's June 1957 Ferus show had resulted in a conviction and fine for obscenity. The complaint is said to have been for an exquisite drawing by Cameron of a supernatural copulating couple, which had been reproduced as a small page of *Semina* and placed among the objects on the floor of Berman's sculpture/installation piece *Temple*. The actual charges are said to have been based on another drawing, depicting interlocking male and female genitals dangling in a square frame from one arm of *Cross*; the police couldn't or didn't find the drawing. The bust and conviction unnerved and embittered Berman and he returned to the low-visibility position of influence he occupied for the rest of his life, seldom showing and otherwise limiting public access. The Berman family left for San Francisco soon afterward.

San Francisco appears in nearly everyone's accounts as a sanctuary during the 1950s, a place where the conservatism and conformity of the McCarthy era weren't so stifling, a tolerant, cosmopolitan city whose tone had been set by the festive adventurers of the Gold Rush. If Los Angeles was the American city of the future, San Francisco was in many ways like a European city of the past with its Italian cafés, its small, pedestrian scale, its charming Victorian architecture. For many artists, the swirling fog, innumerable vistas, and places like the decrepit amusement park Playland at the Beach gave it a particular magic. The city had strong unions, radical and anarchist traditions, but the bohemianism fostered there before the war isn't particularly impressive. The Bohemian Club itself, founded by journalists and writers in 1872, which had been in the early part of the century an actual bohemian haven of sorts, mutated into the right-wing-men-only politicians' summer camp now frequented by the likes of Henry Kissinger and

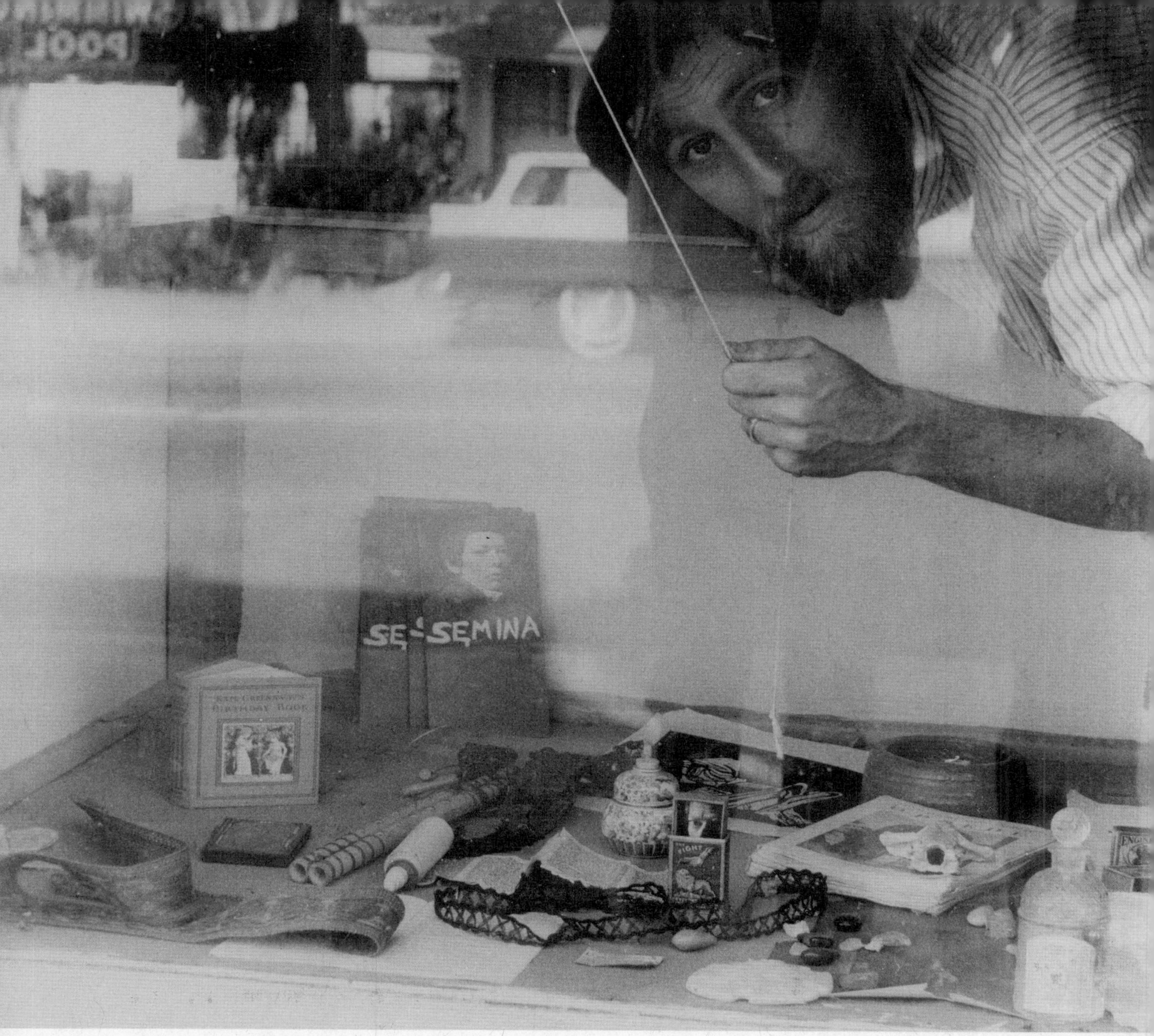

George Schultz. Though there were minor flurries of painting and mural making, the f.64 group of photographers was the only major art movement to come out of the region before the war. During the war, San Francisco had become a major center for poets, and there were several circles of them in the city and across the bay in Berkeley.

While Los Angeles had little more than private coteries, San Francisco had an art school whose postwar period opened up rich, diverse, and unlikely possibilities to its students. The golden age at the California School of Fine Arts began with the hiring of Douglas MacAgy as director; MacAgy had been assistant director at the San Francisco Museum of Art, the country's second modern art museum. He ushered in his radical era by covering up the school's Diego Rivera mural with sheets, and such acts of repudiation preceded much of the invention that

Stone Brothers Printing with Wallace Berman in window, 1957 (detail). Photo by Charles Brittin

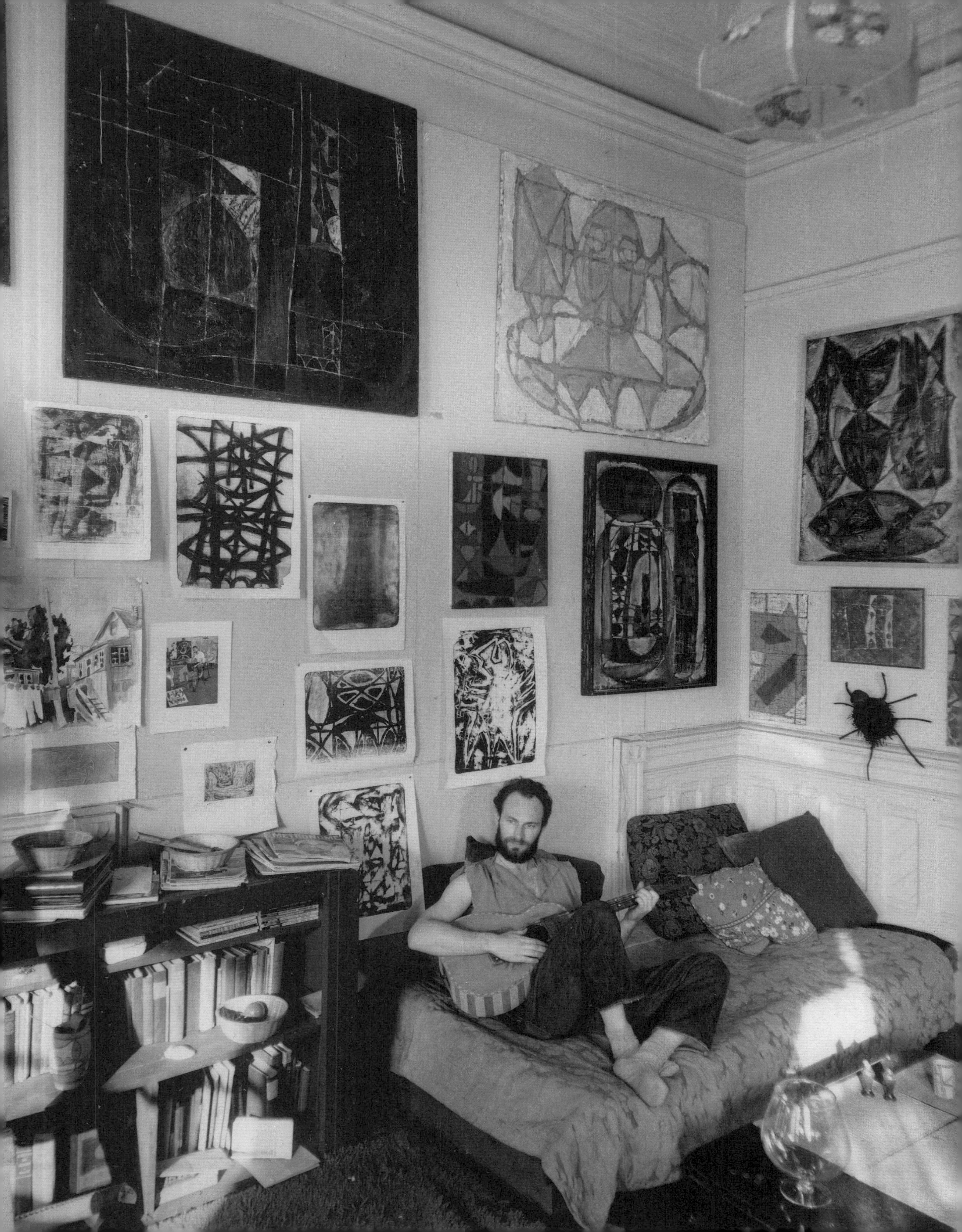

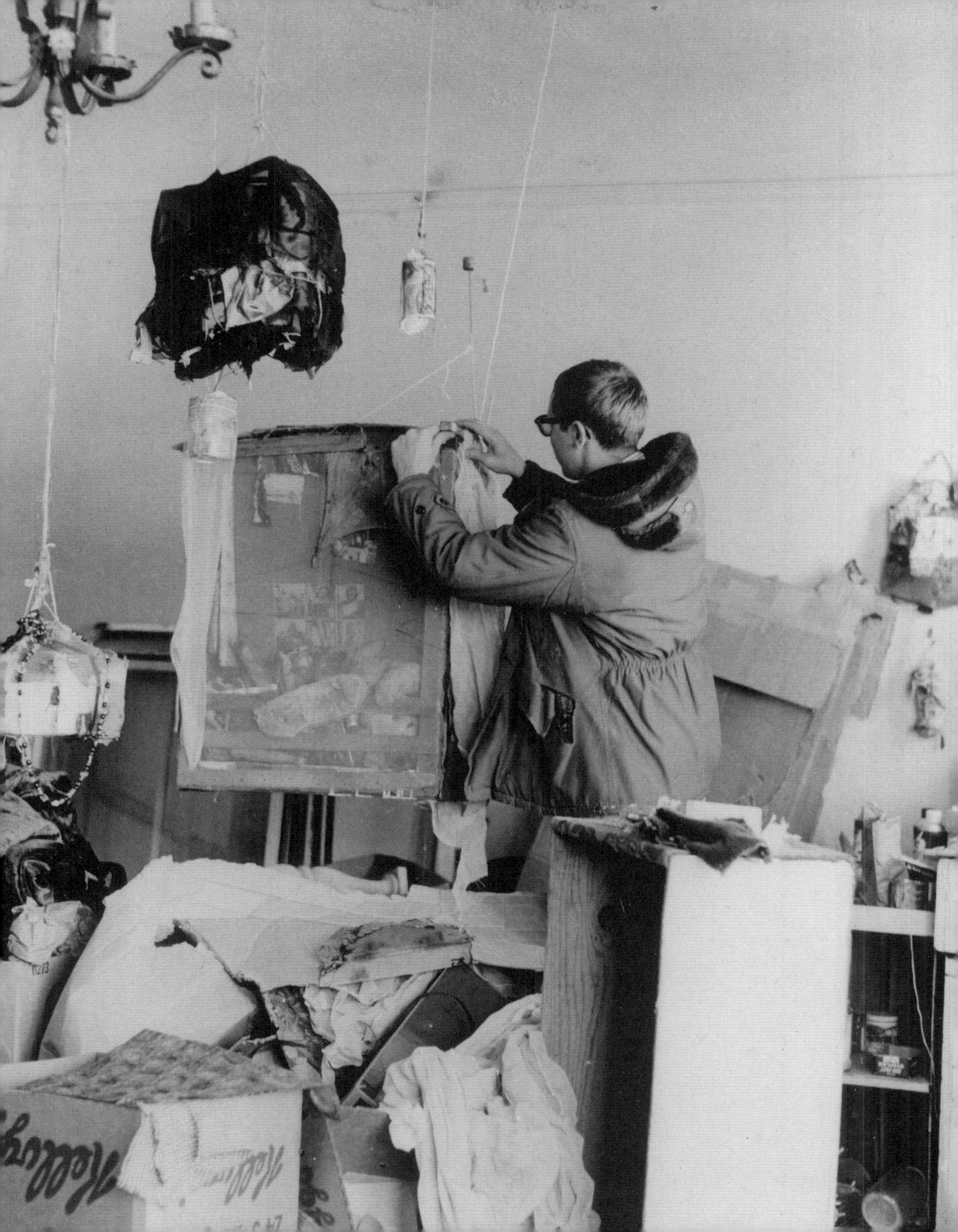

Opening exhibition at King Ubu Gallery; mural by Jess, sculpture by Miriam Hoffman, 1952. Photo by Nata Piaskowski

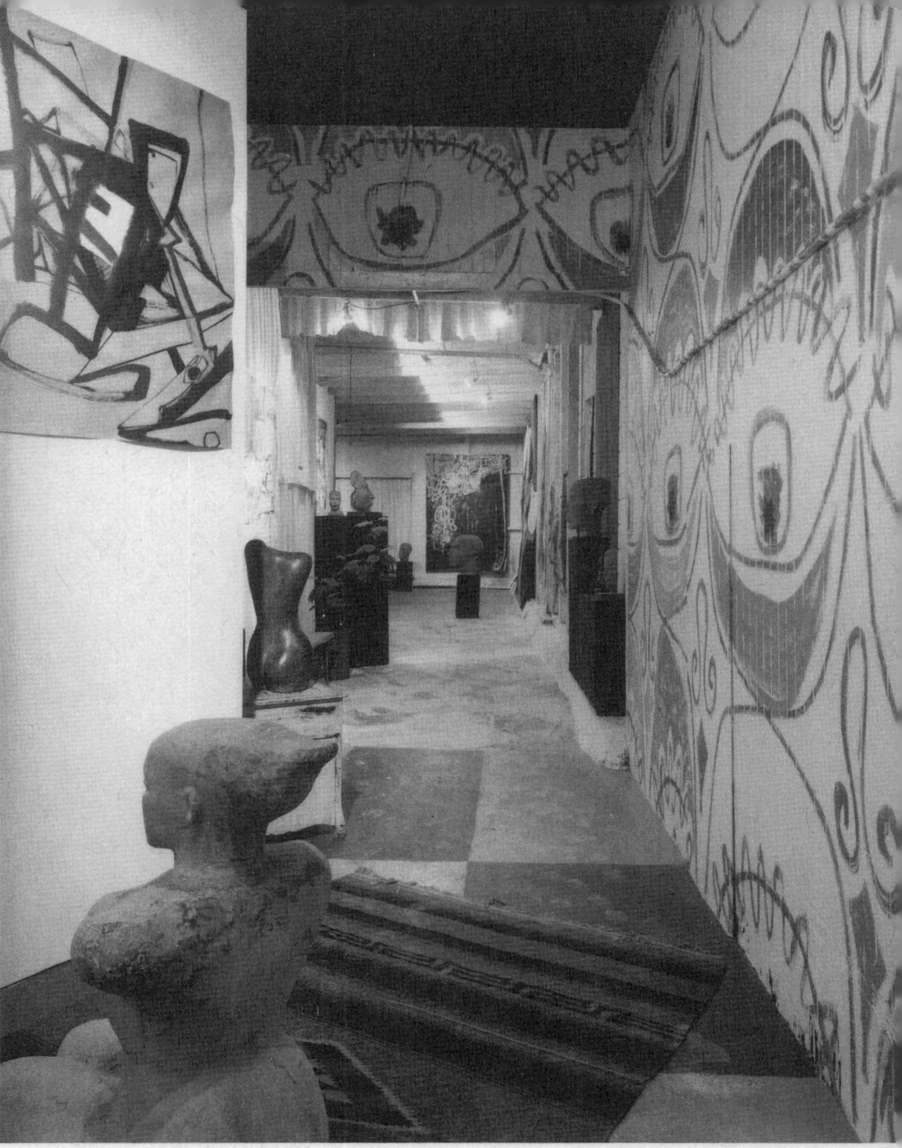

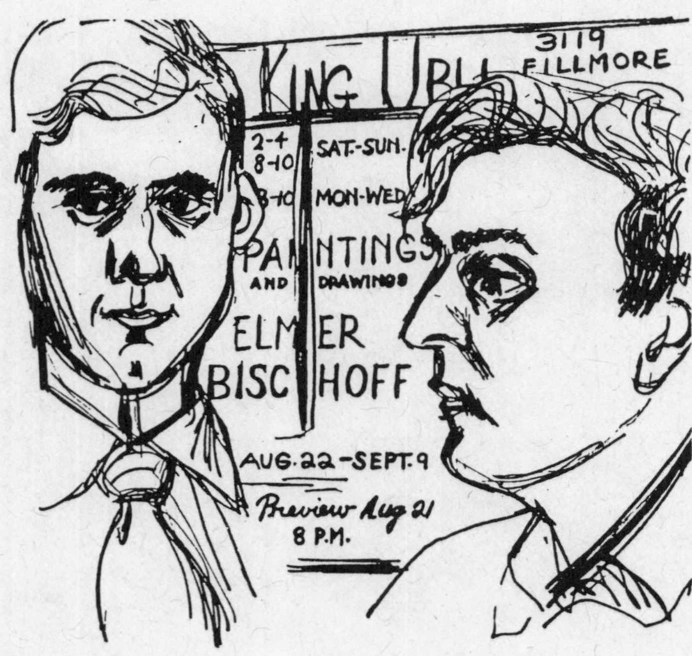

Elmer Bischoff, **Announcement for King Ubu Gallery exhibition with portraits of Robert Duncan and Jess**, 1953.

Previous page, left: **Wally Hedrick in his studio at the "Ghost House," San Francisco**, 1952. Photo by Nata Piaskowski; right: **Bruce Conner in his studio**, 1959. Photo by Jerry Burchard followed. His new faculty included Clyfford Still, Elmer Bischoff, Ansel Adams, and David Park (as well as Ad Reinhardt and Mark Rothko for summer sessions). Park broke with the abstraction that dominated the decade after the war by taking all his abstract paintings to the dump in 1949, and beginning to paint in the style that would be called Bay Area Figurative. He returned to representation that fall with a painting of the Studio 13 Jass Band, in which he played piano, MacAgy played drums, and Bischoff trumpet. (The band formed a bridge across stylistic coteries and was also the longest-lasting artists' institution to emerge from the era: Wally Hedrick would become the band's banjo player and plays in it still, as does the ceramic sculptor Richard Shaw and as did Dave Getz, who would later play in Big Brother and the Holding Company.) Park's second figuration was titled *Kids on Bikes*, a title that firmly rejects the stratospheric vaguenesses of Ab-Ex for the vernacular present. Though Park's heresy was widely regarded as reactionary, it meant that there was no orthodoxy at the school. When artists like Jess came, the whole range between Park and Still was theirs to explore.

Jess' repudiation was of an entire successful career in another field—as a chemist involved in refining the raw materials for nuclear bombs. He quit to go to art school in 1949, and having thrown out security and complicity so wholeheartedly (along with his last name), he was free to become an astoundingly radical artist, of the gentlest, quietest kind. Learning from both Still and Park, Jess made abstract paintings in which he allowed romantic images to emerge, sometimes obliquely, sometimes clearly. By 1950, he was involved with the erudite poet Robert Duncan, who had burned a few bridges of his own, notably by publishing the essay "The Homosexual in Society" in the magazine *Politics* in 1944, an essay that may be the first voluntary public acknowledgment in modern times of a gay man's gayness. Duncan and Jess set up house together in 1951, and until Duncan's death in 1987 they had an immensely rich collaborative life, contributing to each other's work and, for a year beginning in late 1952, running the King Ubu Gallery with a close friend, the painter Harry Jacobus (an abstractionist with a palette reminiscent of Bonnard's).

Jess began working in collage in 1951. "Collage was a way for me to construct imaginary scenarios in a more realistic rather than a nonobjective way. I really could not paint well enough at the time to create images as fantastic—in all senses of the word—as were available in *Life* magazine."[11] His collages drawn from *Life*, the *Dick Tracy* comic strip and Modess sanitary products ads, as well as from more hermetic sources, insist on finding the lyrical, the sublime, the ridiculous everywhere and together. With work in both painting and collage that was sometimes romantic, sometimes humorous, occasionally erotic, and taken from the most obscure and most obvious sources, Jess had gone beyond not only the forms but the terms of art making at the time, with work that didn't even want to be heroic or important or contemporary.

A wholly different kind of maverick was Wally Hedrick, a Korean War veteran from Pasadena who arrived at the California School of Fine Arts in 1952. At some point in the fifties, the figurative and abstractionist painters used to mock the rivalry between their camps with a game of softball, and Hedrick, who so clearly didn't belong to either camp, was the painter they entrusted with the role of umpire. He once described his subjects as sex, religion, and politics—a variation on the classical trio of figure, landscape, and still life—and he brought a boisterous irreverence to all of them. He painted strong iconic images, from an American flag with the word "peace" on it (which apparently preceded Jasper Johns' foray into flag painting) to a television that stood as tall and mystical as an Easter Island obelisk to early anti-Vietnam war pieces, such as the brilliant, explosive phallic *Anger* of 1959; he also made welded metal assemblages during the 1950s. Hedrick's own act of destruction began as early opposition to the war in the late 1950s, when he began to paint the flag images black. When they were all obliterated, he continued making black paintings through the end of the war.

Hedrick's wife, Jay DeFeo, went through a similar engagement with the cycles of obliteration and creation with her monumental painting *The Rose*. DeFeo was in fact primarily an abstract painter, but her concern with tight abstracted forms and huge accretions of paint didn't align her with anyone else painting in the fifties, and many of her friendships were elsewhere, among the assemblagists and mystics. Although she didn't take her forays into other media seriously herself, they made a huge impression on other artists. Manuel Neri's move to plaster sculpture was instigated by some site-specific studio pieces DeFeo made in that medium; Wallace Berman was tremendously intrigued by her photocollages; and Bruce Conner even credits her way of wrapping Christmas presents and dangling them from the ceiling as an influence on his assemblages, which often dangled or had pendulous attachments. But DeFeo was a painter, and one whose dedication and intensity inspired awe in those around her. Even Kienholz declared, "She just had a flow, a creative flow, coming from her that was fantastic to observe."[12] She herself said a year before her death in 1989, "I really felt that I had the respect of all my male friends who were artists. It wasn't an issue maybe because there wasn't any competition for wall space, even any competition for jobs at the time....Joan Brown, who was actually more mature than I—we kind of grew up together—I think Joan would answer the question the same way I do."[13] Brown is another artist history records as largely a painter, but during the 1950s she made marvelously funky assemblages, as did her future husband Manuel Neri (both were Rat Bastard Protective Association members and part of the most experimental edge of the small art community).

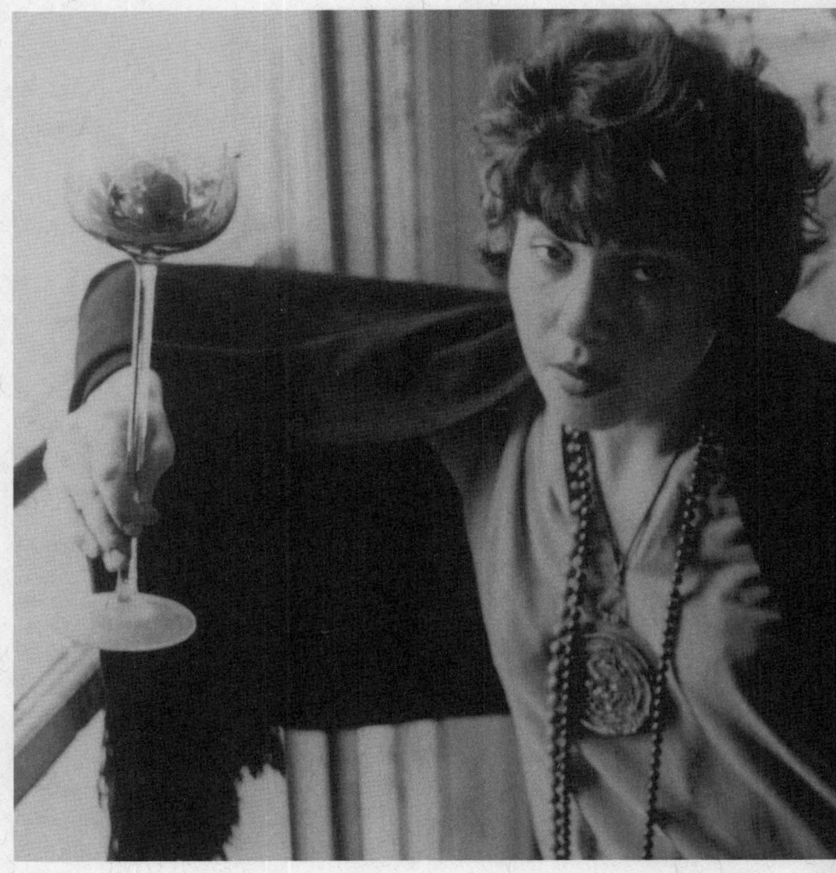

Jay DeFeo with shattered glass filled with rose petals, 1959 (detail). Photo by Jerry Burchard

In 1959, DeFeo began to work on a piece installed in the center of the bay window of the house she shared with Hedrick on Fillmore Street, a mandalalike radiating form called variously *The White Rose*, *The Death Rose*, and finally just *The Rose*. Building up and scraping away the surface of the piece, letting it evolve through "a whole cycle of art history" from primitive to Baroque to Neoclassical, taking it from a painted surface to a bas-relief of paint, she worked on it as a ritual, a performance, and an act of dedication for seven years. It came to an end when she and Hedrick were evicted from the building where Joan Brown, the McClures, and so many others had lived. The removal of the painting by cranes and moving men—it had grown to a weight of 2,300 pounds—was documented by Bruce Conner in a lyrical film later subtitled, "Jay DeFeo's painting removed by Angelic Hosts." Then the massive piece began to crumble, and it disappeared into conservation storage for twenty-five years, leaving nothing behind but a legend and, for DeFeo, lead poisoning from the white paint. Its departure marked the end of an era.

Bruce Conner had swept in at the height of that era, in the annus mirabilis of 1957, fleeing the draft (no one in Kansas was ever 4F, he said later) and rejecting New York, already a prolific, brilliant artist with an enormous sense of purpose. A friend of McClure's from their high school days in Wichita, he had been corresponding with the filmmaker Larry Jordan and arrived ready to start an experimental film society with him. (Stan Brakhage had introduced Conner to Jordan, who worked as Joseph Cornell's filmmaking assistant and used stop animation to make moving collage films himself.) An immensely talented painter, collagist, and draftsman beginning

Jay DeFeo
The Rose, 1958-65
Oil and mixed media on canvas,
129 x 92 x 8 (327.7 x 233.7 x 20.3)
Estate of the artist

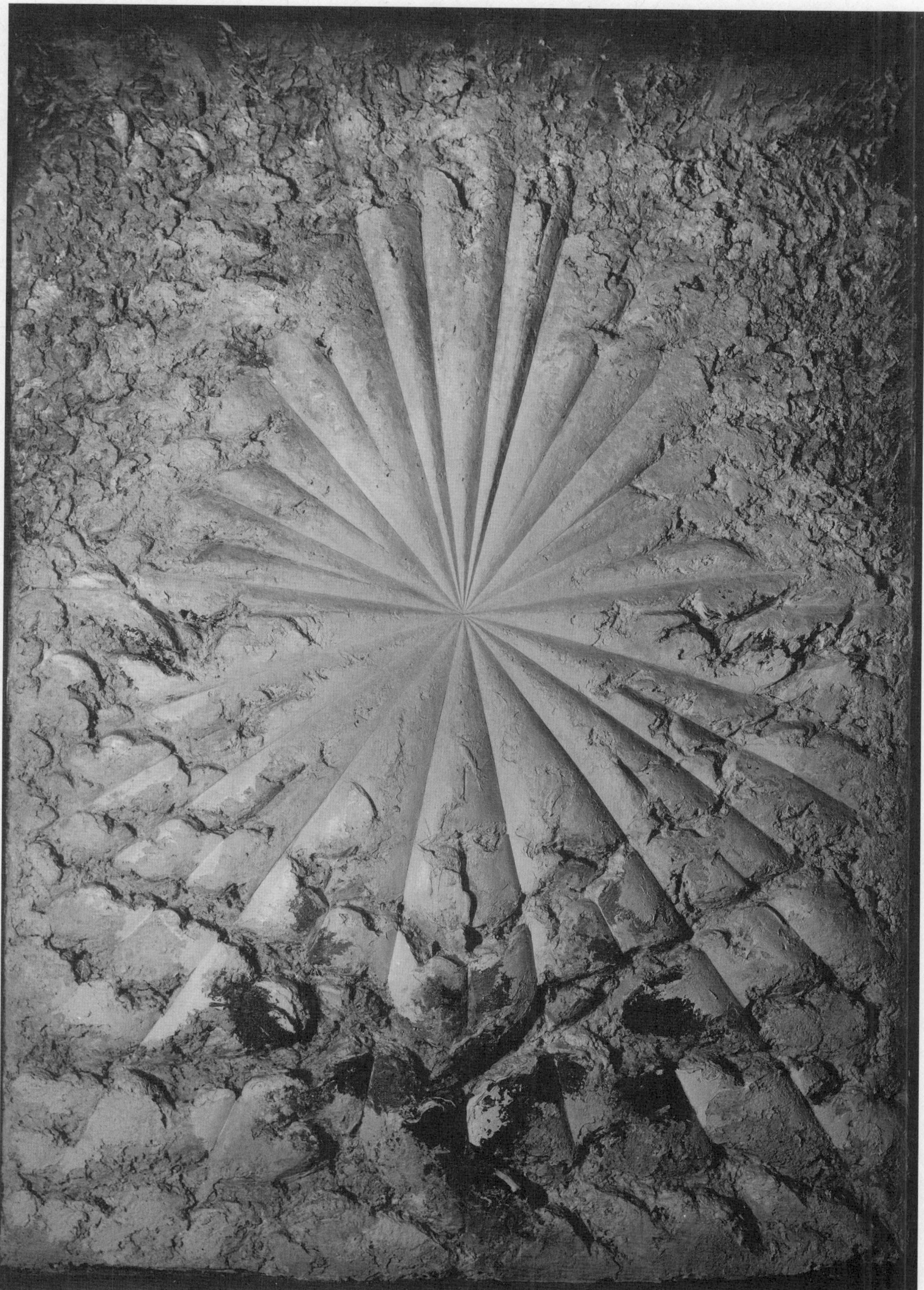

to explore assemblage, Conner completed his own first movie in 1958. A collage of available footage titled *A Movie*, it deconstructs the genres, elements, clichés, and cues of the editing and sequencing of moviemaking so brilliantly that it is still used as a sort of training film for would-be auteurs in art school. Other films explore sex, political life, the media, and the medium of film. Among the earlier works is *Marilyn Times Five*, which deconstructs a girlie film of a Monroe look-alike through repetitions that begin to suggest the pathos, the labor, and the loneliness involved; among the later are films using songs by the punk band Devo (*Mongoloid*, 1977) and by David Byrne and Brian Eno (*America Is Waiting*, 1981).

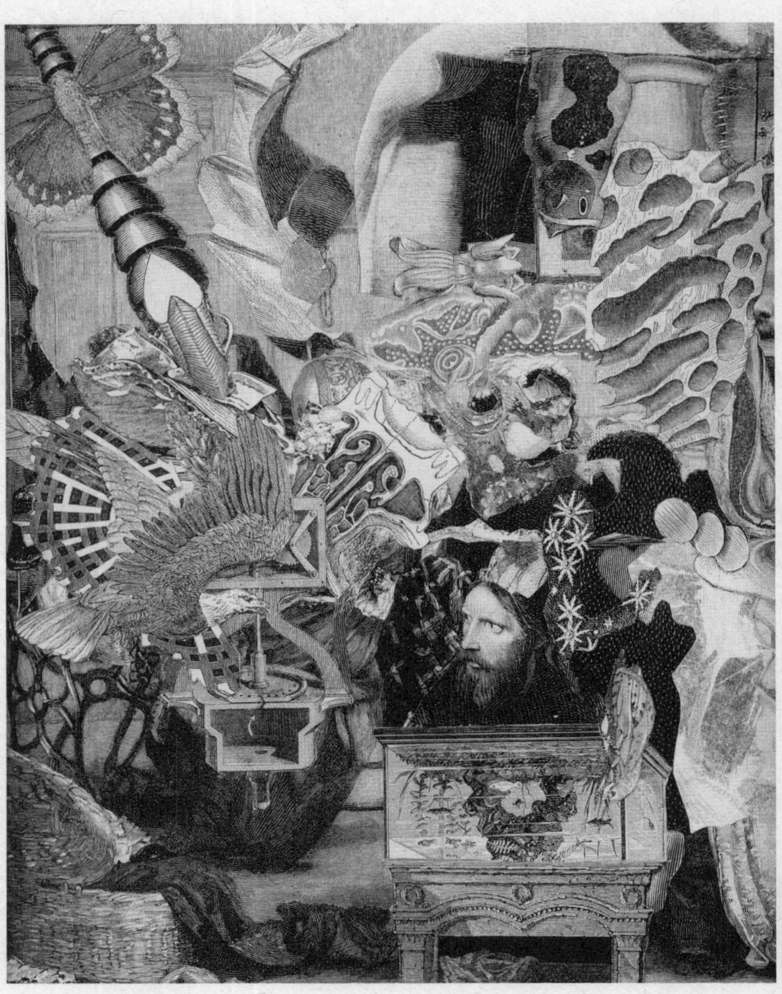

Bruce Conner
FROM THE DENNIS HOPPER ONE MAN SHOW, c. 1961,
One of seven collages from wood engravings
Collection of Dennis Hopper

A similar genius infused Conner's assemblages, in which scraps of lace, nylon stockings, girlie photographs, and jewelry, accreted into spooky compositions sometimes morbidly erotic, sometimes anguished, sometimes both. George Herms' assemblages seemed like redemptions of the rusty, rural debris he worked with, bringing order out of chaos; something darker was at work in Conner's pieces, which used textiles and other soft materials that often seem to move from order—perhaps social order—to the turbulence of dream, nightmare, violence, and vision. When asked in 1974 about this array of work, Conner said, "Well I think one of the themes of the work is an assumption that the creature is good. That the society which we have is alienating to the animal. It expresses power and violence and death and that's its main structure. And the signs of that are in the symbols that we see all around us in the art, in the clothes, in the roles that people play in the society. That people have to deal with this crucifixion of the spirit all the time; and that how well they shine through that is the triumph of those individuals."[14]

Assemblage has, since William Seitz's 1961 *The Art of Assemblage* show at The Museum of Modern Art (which included Herms, Jess, Kienholz, and Conner), been classified as a medium: a kind of sculpture made of mixed and found and recycled materials. But Conner's work in particular makes it clear that assemblage was nothing more—or less—than a working method that could be used to approach any medium at all. Only such a methodological rather than a material definition makes it possible to approach the breadth of what was going on in California in the 1950s. The poet Robert Creeley wrote in retrospect, "Coming of age in the forties, in the chaos of the Second World War, one felt the kinds of coherence that might have been fact of other time and place were no longer possible. There seemed no logic, so to speak, that could bring together all the violent disparities of that experience. The arts especially were shaken and the *picture of the world* that might previously have served them had to be reformed."[15] This reformation was achieved through assemblage.

Abstract Expressionism and the psychoanalytic and archetypal themes that had led to it seem to have been turning their back on this time and place in order to hold on to a logic, a logic that couldn't assimilate the new scope for cruelty, folly, and apocalyptic erasures, the holocaust

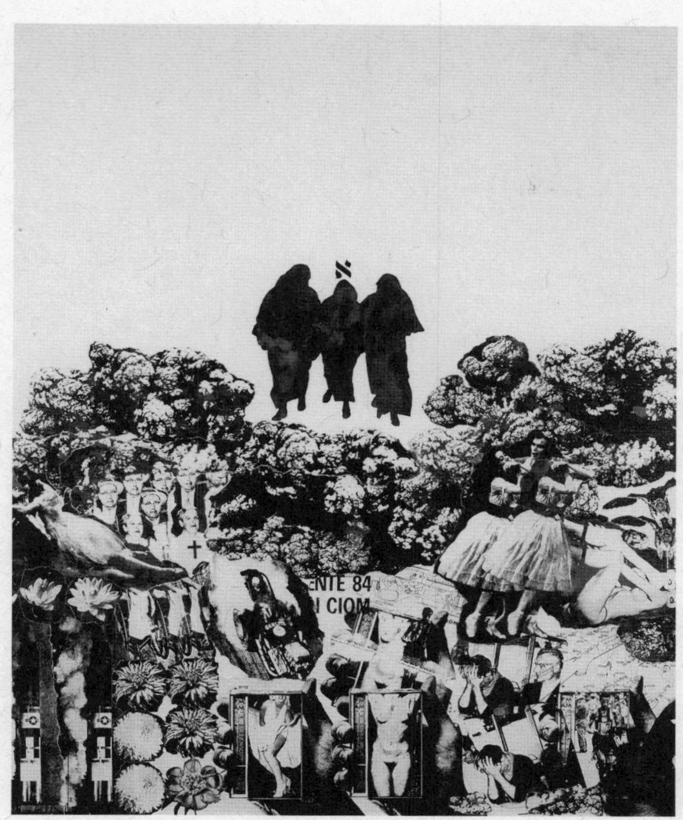

Wallace Berman
Scope, 1965
Verifax collage on canvas,
38 x 32 (96.5 x 81.3)
Collection of Dennis Hopper

and the bomb, the proliferation of popular culture, of products, of information and images both banal and obscure. In the official histories, it's Pop Art that's usually represented as the antithesis of Ab-Ex in the Hegelian dialectic of styles, but Pop too was usually cool, distanced, formal, whatever its subject matter. It's the art in between and elsewhere which seems to have performed a synthesis that was forgotten, to have found a way to make art that had room, as Jess' collages did, for the mysteries of the tarot and the delights of Dick Tracy, as did Conner's assemblages such as the *Temptation of Saint Barney Google*, as Berman did repeatedly in his Verifax collages of the 1960s and 1970s, in which the motif of a hand holding a transistor radio is repeated over and over, its face each time bearing another revelation: guns, starlets, mandalas, snakes, Buddhas, crosses, ears, roses. The California work was insistently both high and low, refusing the segregation that divided popular from high culture, spirituality from the street, and this perhaps is its principal resemblance to the poetry of the Beats, of Ginsberg and Kerouac.

Assemblage was a technique that could bring together the disparate ingredients of these artists' experience without imposing a false coherence, that could let the materials speak both of their original intent and the artist's—and the tension in between. It was a methodology that acknowledged the urban environment so central to the era, an environment of man-made materials endlessly decaying, becoming obsolete or outmoded, being replaced and accreting, a distinctly American environment. To work with materials which had already been made by others, already had meaning, was to acknowledge the status of the imagination in a world of used and artificed objects and images, if not quite of Baudrillardian simulacra. Its practitioners understood that to make from scratch, to start from nothing, is only to contribute, while to recontextualize what has been made is to critique. Theirs was an art of critical reading, reinterpretation. A piece such as Kienholz's massive assemblage environment *Barney's Beanery*, in which all the faces are stopped clocks, reinterprets with the deftness of drawing both objects and the human condition. Paintings such as those Wally Hedrick made with an overhead projector and old advertisements as well as Jess' *Translations*—luscious paintings of images translated paint-by-number style from such sources as old copies of *Scientific American* and old snapshots—rework images, giving them a new magic and context and framing creation as being about context and intent as much as facture. The contemporary blurring of the boundaries between making and interpreting seems to begin here, if anywhere.

Few of the artists in California achieved much recognition before the 1970s. Yet their influence was profound, broadening the definition of what art could be, carving out a place for West Coast artistic activity, providing examples of working artists (often as teachers) who were making California something more than New York's outback. In their wake came other groups: the tail end of the fifties scene, with artists such as Carlos Villa, Manuel Neri, and Al Wong in San Francisco, and Ed Ruscha, Llyn Foulkes, Vija Celmins, Betye Saar, and eventually Judy Chicago in Los Angeles; funky sixties artists up north like Robert Arneson, William Wiley, Robert Hudson, and Richard Shaw who carried on a tradition of personal symbolism, eclectic form, humor, and social commentary—and then their student, Bruce Nauman; sleek sixties artists down south like John McLaughin, Larry Bell, Joe Goode, and many of the Ferus artists in a later phase; Bay Area Conceptualism with Zen-influenced artists like David Ireland, Terry Fox, and Tom Marioni; southern California Conceptualism with Chris Burden and John Baldessari; light and space artists such as James Turrell (and arguably Earth Art: Michael Heizer, Dennis Oppenheim, and Robert Morris all have Bay Area roots); and onward, to artists and styles too many and diverse to list and classify.

The artists who came of age in the 1950s seem to have prefigured and in some ways generated not only a stable artistic tradition on the West Coast, but the counterculture which would change all of American society. Berman is acknowledged by his work in *Easy Rider* (a film Dennis Hopper says was influenced by Conner's cinematic techniques) as well as by his appearance on the cover of The Beatles' *Sgt. Pepper's Lonely Hearts Club Band* album, the album that was such a watershed in defining what rock could be. Conner worked on light shows with the North American Ibis Alchemical Light Company in the 1960s, making his most ephemeral and widely seen works and helping to define what would be considered psychedelic. Michael McClure became a mentor to Jim Morrison of The Doors and a friend of Bob Dylan's. It's hard to trace the permeation of drugs and esoteric religious traditions through the culture, but psychedelics, the tarot, the Cabala, and Zen make some of their earliest surfacings in American culture in these circles. Too, their willing outsider status, their radical resistance to the political mainstream, their experiments with collective institutions and communal living seem to forecast the broad breakdown of the narrow strictures of the society. When the colossal Human Be-in took place in 1967, Gary Snyder and Allen Ginsberg—two of the poets who had read at the famous 6 Gallery event twelve years earlier—held the stage; the small community they had found on Fillmore Street had become a mass movement in Golden Gate Park.

But for most of the artists, the indiscriminate revelry of the 1960s was more interesting than inviting. By the early sixties, Jess had already withdrawn from the turbulence of public culture into a more selective social life, and most of the artists had retreated from the urban epicenters. The kind of community they had created as a way of survival was no longer so necessary in a more tolerant, diverse society, and the experiments they had initiated collectively continued independently. The creation of the National Endowment for the Arts in 1965 and the subsequent growth of nonprofit arts organizations would assume, for better and worse, much of the responsibility for maintaining an artistic infrastructure, leaving artists to the creation of art rather than of culture. And the art is remarkable on its own grounds.

I have been contemplating this art for more than a decade, and every year another artist or movement or way of describing the world emerges that recontextualizes it, brings it in from the cold of anomalies to the thrones of ancestors. When Christian Boltanski burst on the American scene, his work bore an enormous family resemblance to Berman's, particularly to Berman's Verifax collages and assemblages of obliterated faces, accompanied by Hebrew letters and inscribed stones. DeFeo's engagement with *The Rose* spoke less of painting than of ritual, performance, installation, and the kind of extended involvements of Conceptual artists such as Linda Montano and Carolee Schneemann. Kienholz and Conner had, in very different ways in the very early 1960s, addressed the commodification/degradation/assault of women and of sexuality that would become a central subject of feminism; Kienholz, with the vast and scathing tableau *Roxy's*, a recreation of a brothel in which the women are made of furniture and animal bones, Conner with delicately terrifying pieces like *Black Dahlia* (with that work and the film *Crossroads*, about the 1946 Bikini nuclear tests, Conner addressed two of the milestones of the first year of the cold war). Appropriation, of course, recalled Jess' and Hedrick's forays into the medium, and the humor and critique of many of this group became hallmarks of postmodernism. Jess also seems like a godfather to the current queer art scene, with his refusal to be authoritative, major, modern, bold. And the insistence of these artists on being political, on making art that was engaged with the issues of the time, has finally become mainstream. Forty years later, the world seems ready for them.

Wallace Berman died in 1976, Jay DeFeo in 1989, Joan Brown in 1991, Edward Kienholz in 1994. The rest of them are still making art.

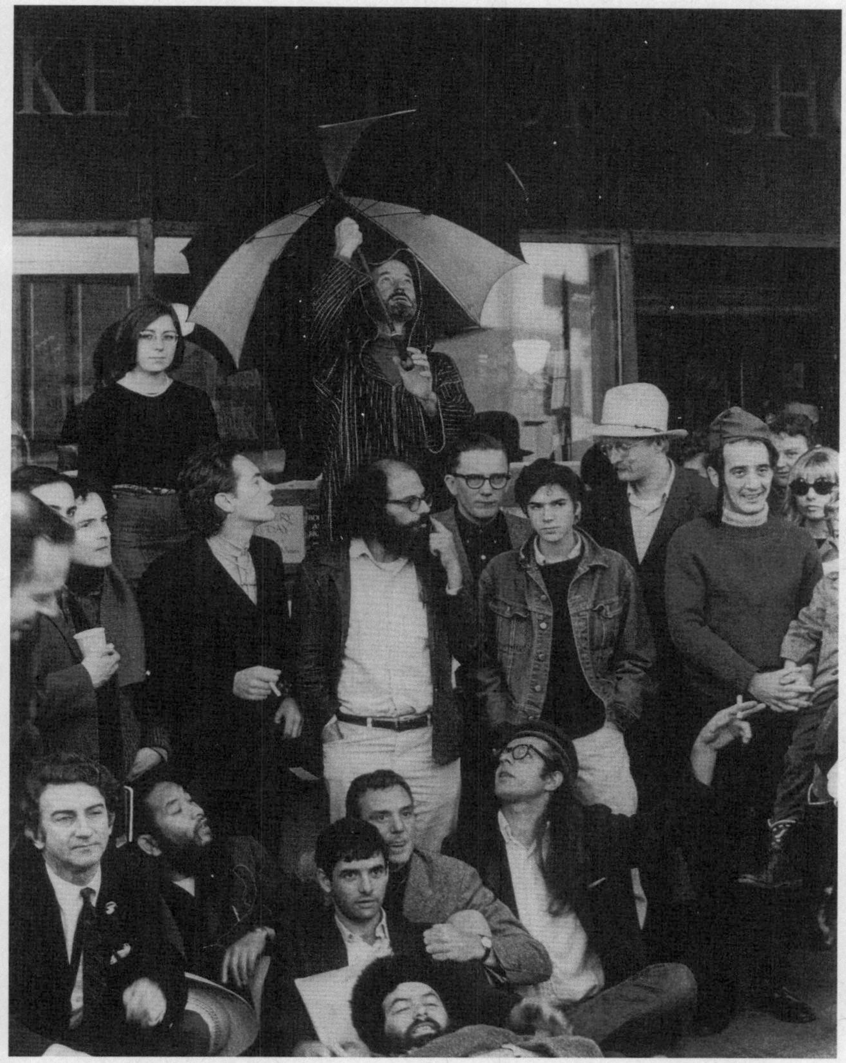

City Lights Bookstore last gathering of poets and artists, North Beach, San Francisco, 1965. Photo by Larry Keenan

Notes

1 10,000 Maniacs, "Hey Jack Kerouac," written by Robert Buck and Natalie Merchant, from the album *In My Tribe*, ©1987 Elektra/Asylum Records.

2 See Sandra Starr, *Lost and Found in California: Four Decades of Assemblage Art*, exh. cat. (Santa Monica, California: James Corcoran Gallery, 1988), p. 58. David Meltzer also spoke to me of this event, and the book *Jazz West Coast: The Los Angeles Jazz Scene of the 1950s* by Robert Gordon (London and New York: Quartet Books, 1986) covers it in more depth, from Parker's perspective.

3 See Michael McClure, *Scratching the Beat Surface* (San Francisco: North Point Press, 1982), pp. 11-17.

4 Jack Goodwin in a letter to 6 Gallery member John Allen Ryan, who was in Mexico at the time. The letter was included in a booklet assembled for the author by Goodwin in 1988.

5 See Henry T. Hopkins, "The Emerging Los Angeles Art Scene," in *Billy Al Bengston: Paintings of Three Decades*, exh. cat. (Oakland: The Oakland Museum; Houston: Contemporary Arts Museum, 1988).

6 Quoted in Laurence Weschler, *Seeing Is Forgetting the Name of the Thing One Sees* (Berkeley: University of California Press, 1982), pp. 50-51.

7 Kienholz, oral history interview with Laurence Weschler, library, University of California, Los Angeles, typescript, p. 17.

8 Mike Davis, *City of Quartz: Excavating the Future in Los Angeles* (New York: Vintage Books, 1992), p. 64.

9 David Meltzer, taped conversation with the author, May 1988.

10 Philip Lamantia, interview with the author, July 12, 1988.

11 Quoted in Michael Auping, *Jess: A Grand Collage, 1951-1993*, exh. cat. (Buffalo: Albright-Knox Art Gallery, 1993), p. 25.

12 Kienholz, oral history interview, p. 103.

13 Jay DeFeo, taped conversation with the author, 1988.

14 Bruce Conner, oral history interview with Paul Karlstrom, August 12, 1974, Archives of American Art, typescript, p. 23.

15 Robert Creeley, "On The Road: Notes on Artists and Poets 1950-1965," in *Poets of the Cities: New York and San Francisco 1950-1965*, exh. cat. (Dallas: Dallas Museum of Fine Arts, 1974), p. 56.

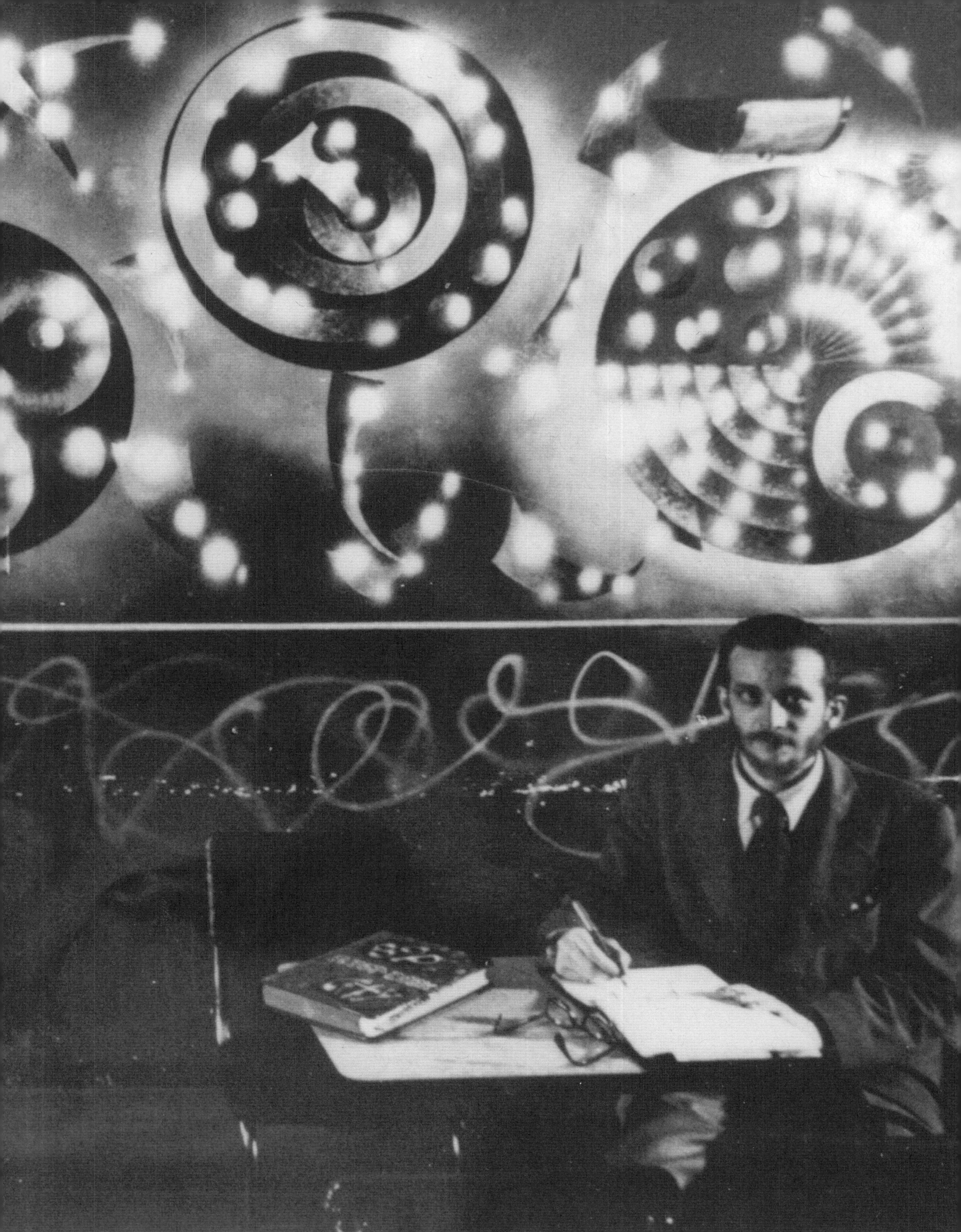

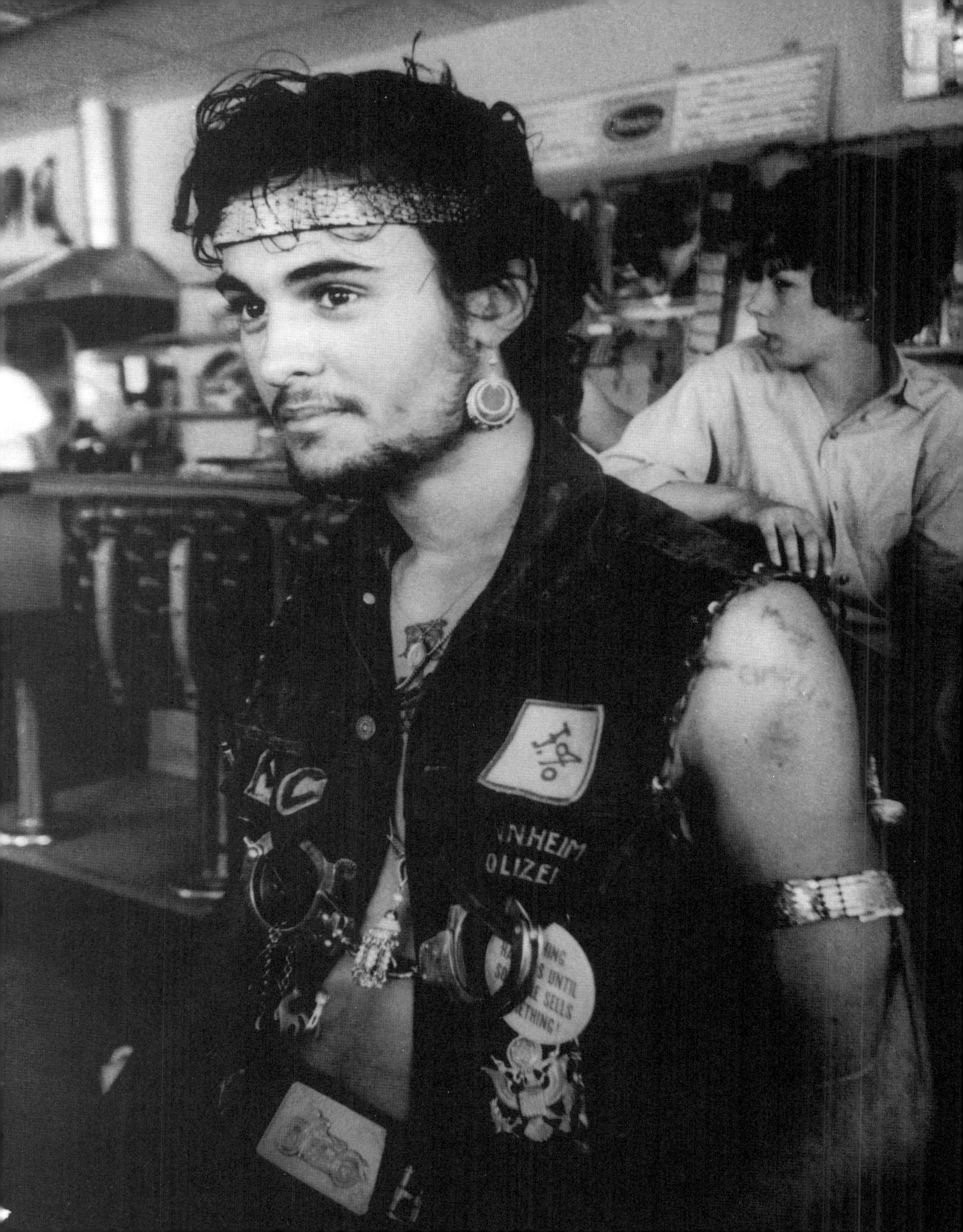

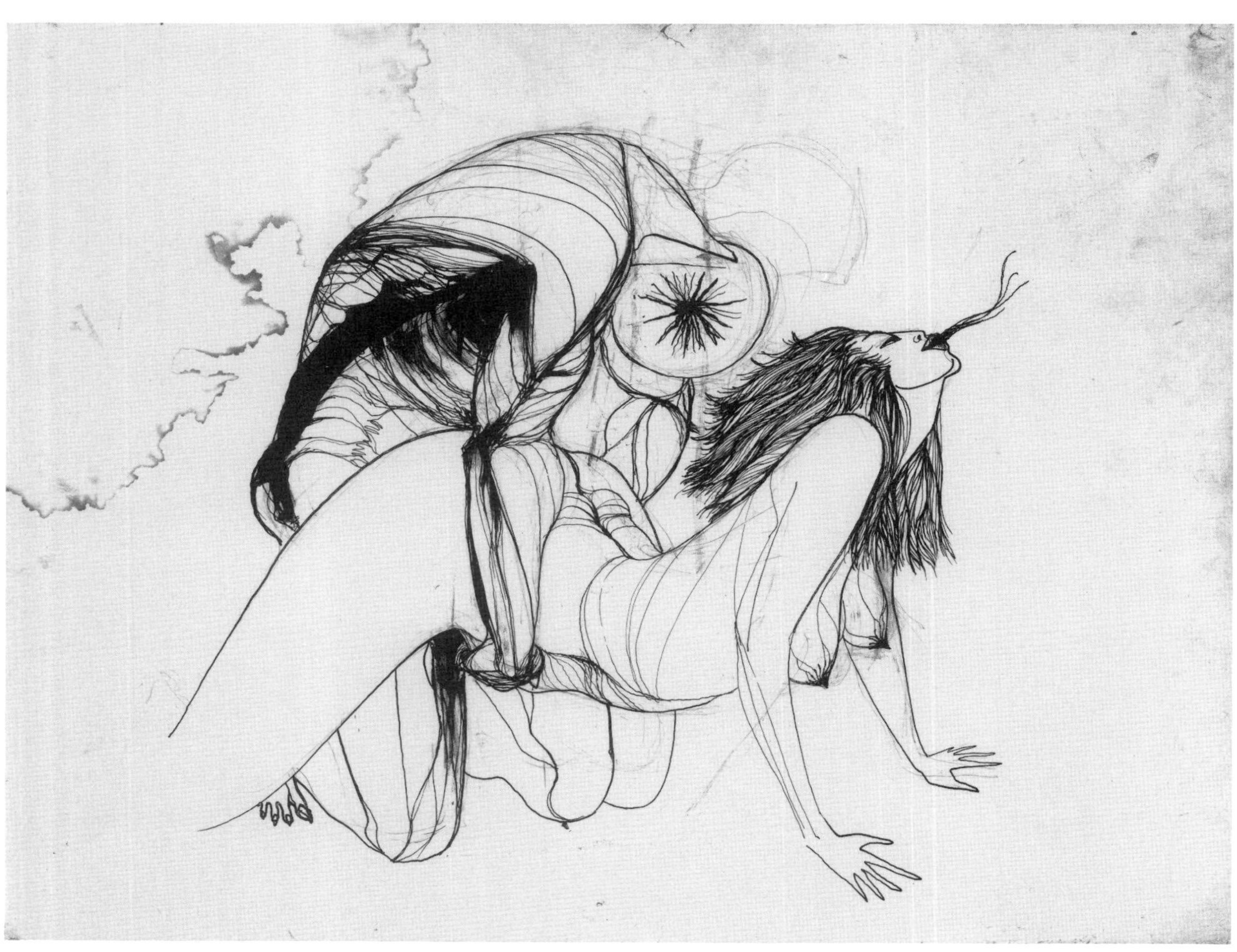

Cameron
Untitled, c. 1957
Ink on paper, 18 1/2 x 24 (47 x 61)
Estate of the artist

Wallace Berman
Semina, 1955-64
Printed papers, nine issues total, 5 1/2 x 3 1/8 to 11 x 9
(14 x 7.9 to 27.9 x 22.9)
Collection of Hal Glicksman

Previous page, left: **Harry Smith with his mural at Jimbo's Bop City**, c. 1952 (detail). Photo by Hy Hirsch
Right: **Biker**, 1961 (detail). Photo by Dennis Hopper

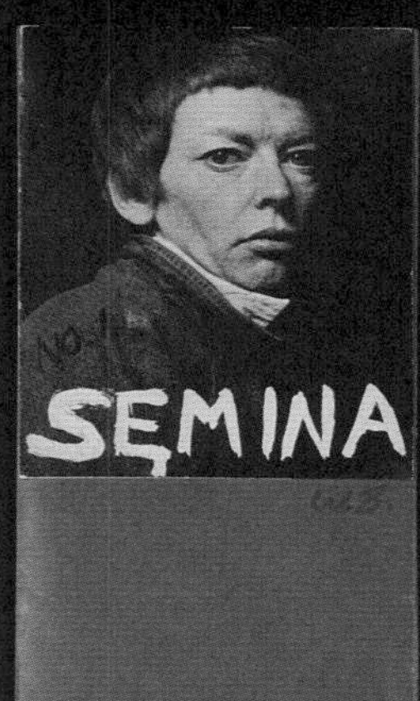
SEMINA

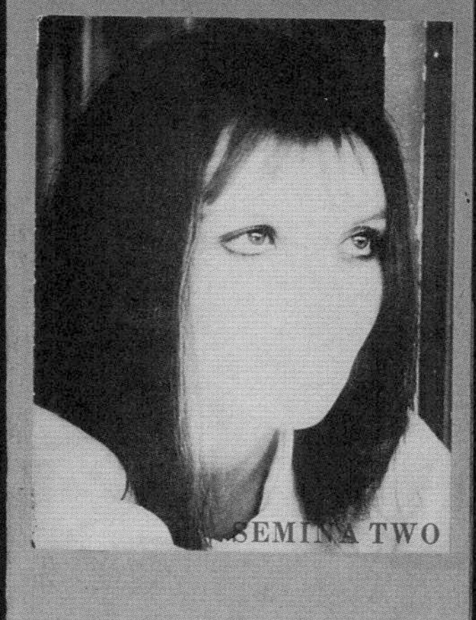
SEMINA TWO

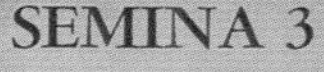
SEMINA 3

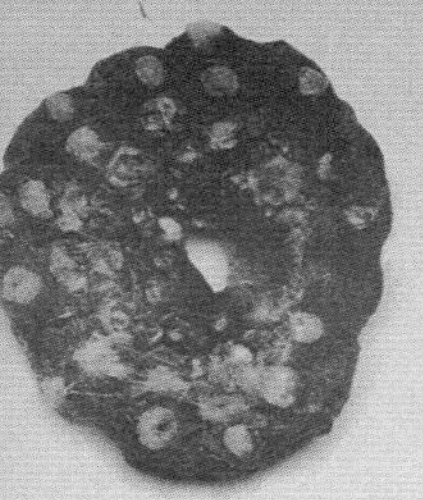
PEYOTE POEM

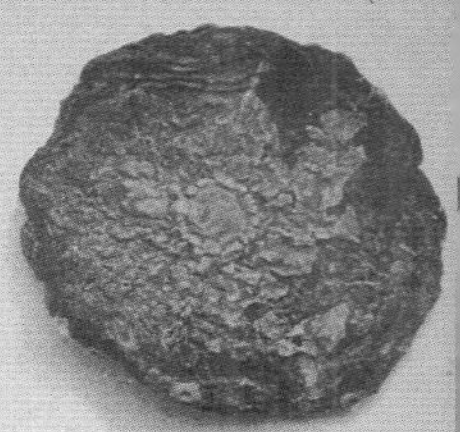

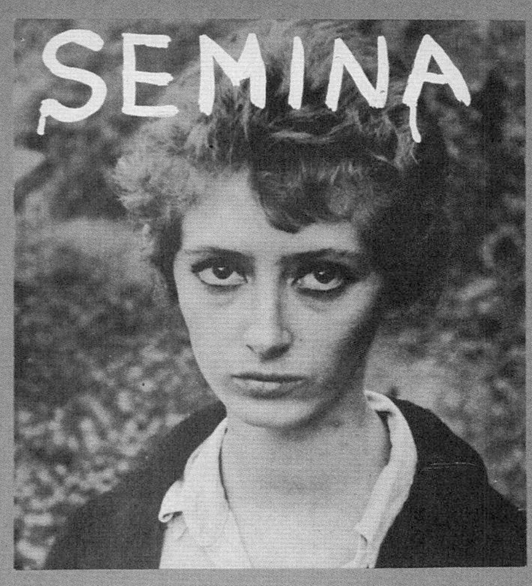
SEMINA

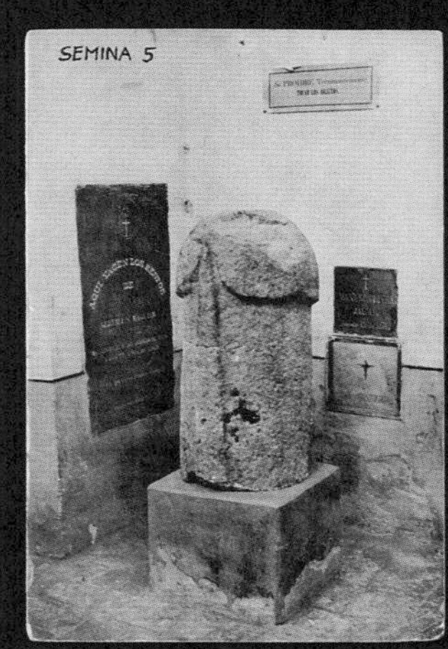
SEMINA 5

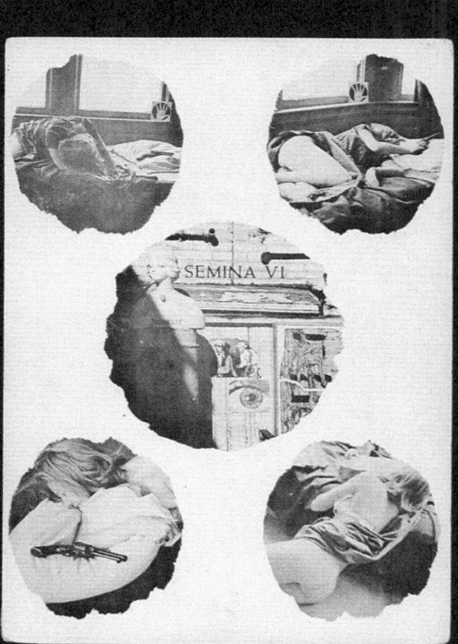
SEMINA VI

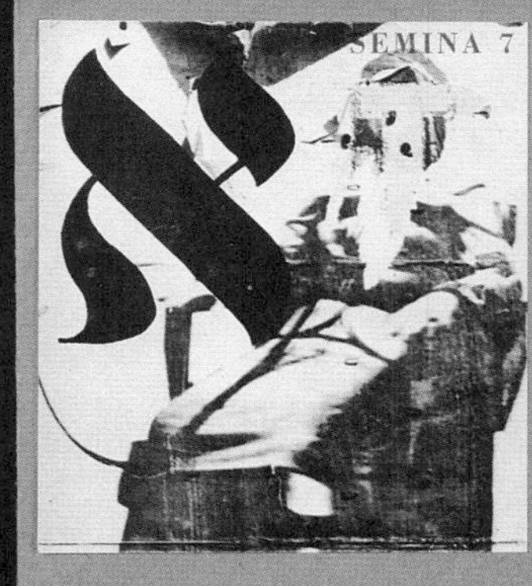
SEMINA 7

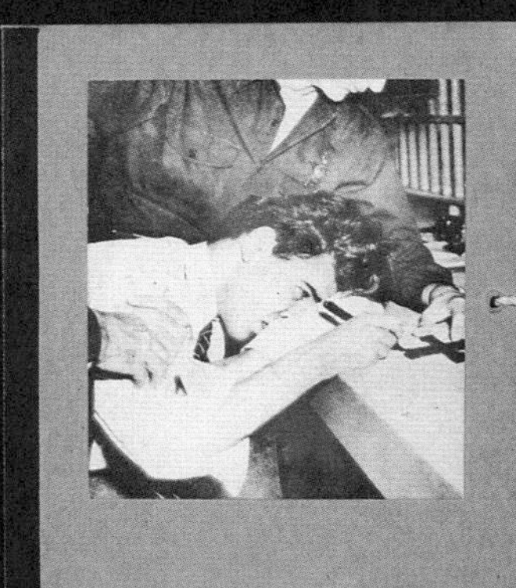

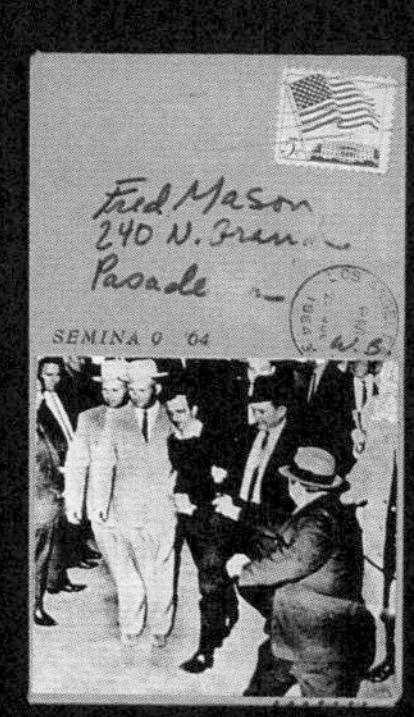
Fred Mason
SEMINA 9 '64

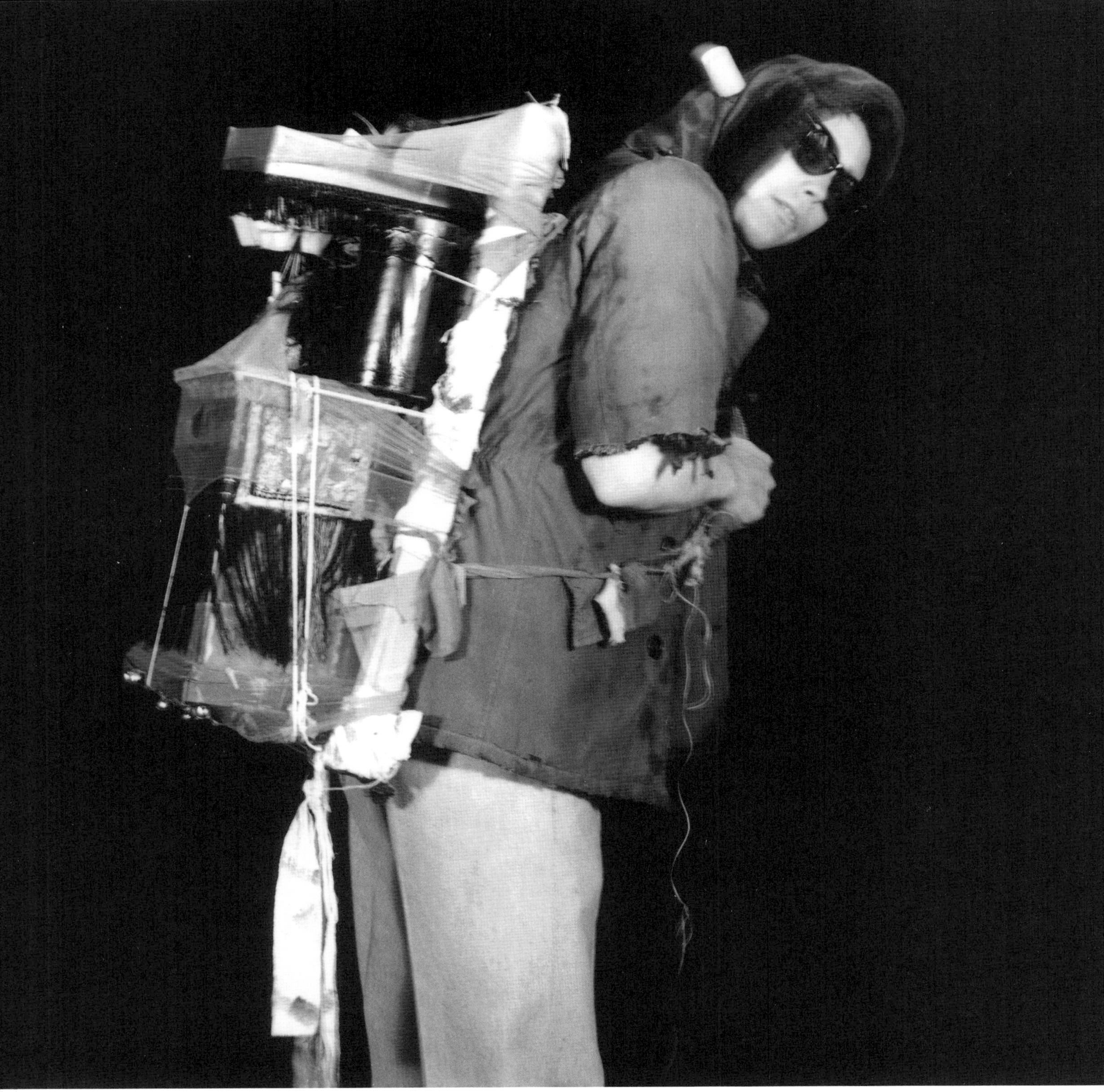

Bruce Conner
RAT BACK PACK, 1959
Mixed media
No longer extant

Bruce Conner
RATBASTARD, 1958
Nylon, wood, coat hanger, cloth, nails, canvas, newspapers, and photocopy, 9 5/8 x 8 x 2 (24.4 x 20.3 x 5.1)
Lannan Foundation, Los Angeles

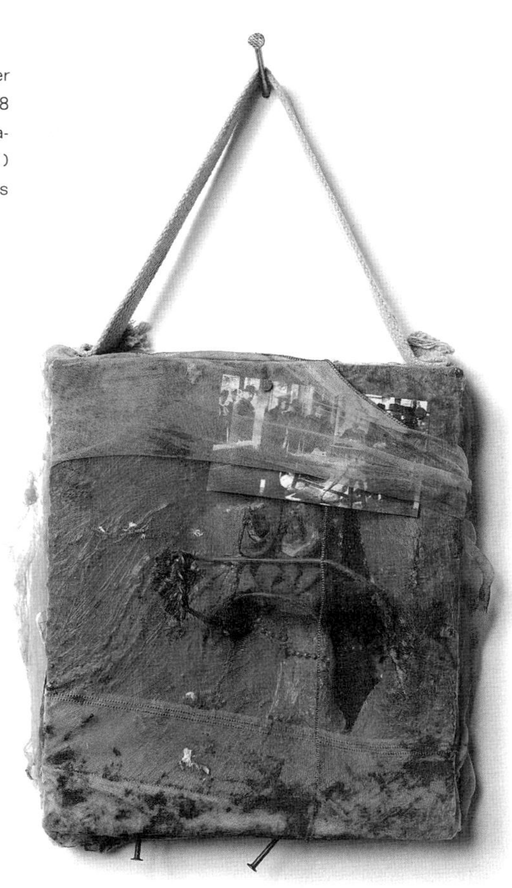

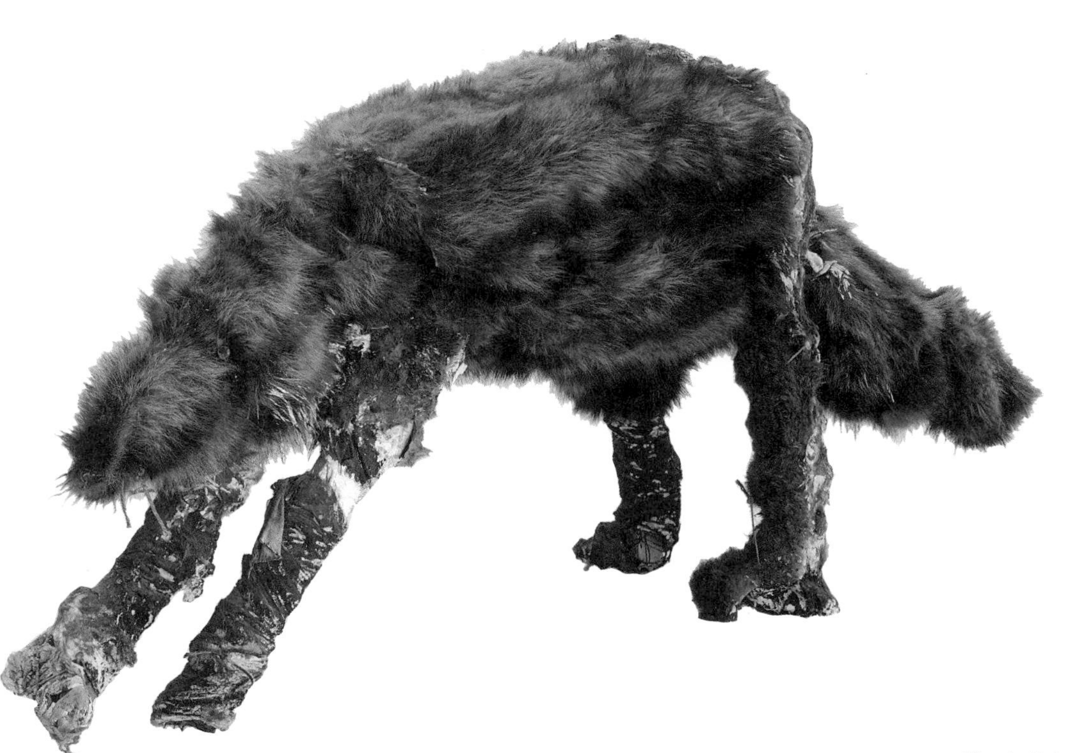

Joan Brown
Fur Rat, 1962
Wood, chicken wire, plaster, and raccoon fur, 20 1/2 x 54 (52.1 x 137.2)
University Art Museum, University of California, Berkeley; Gift of the artist

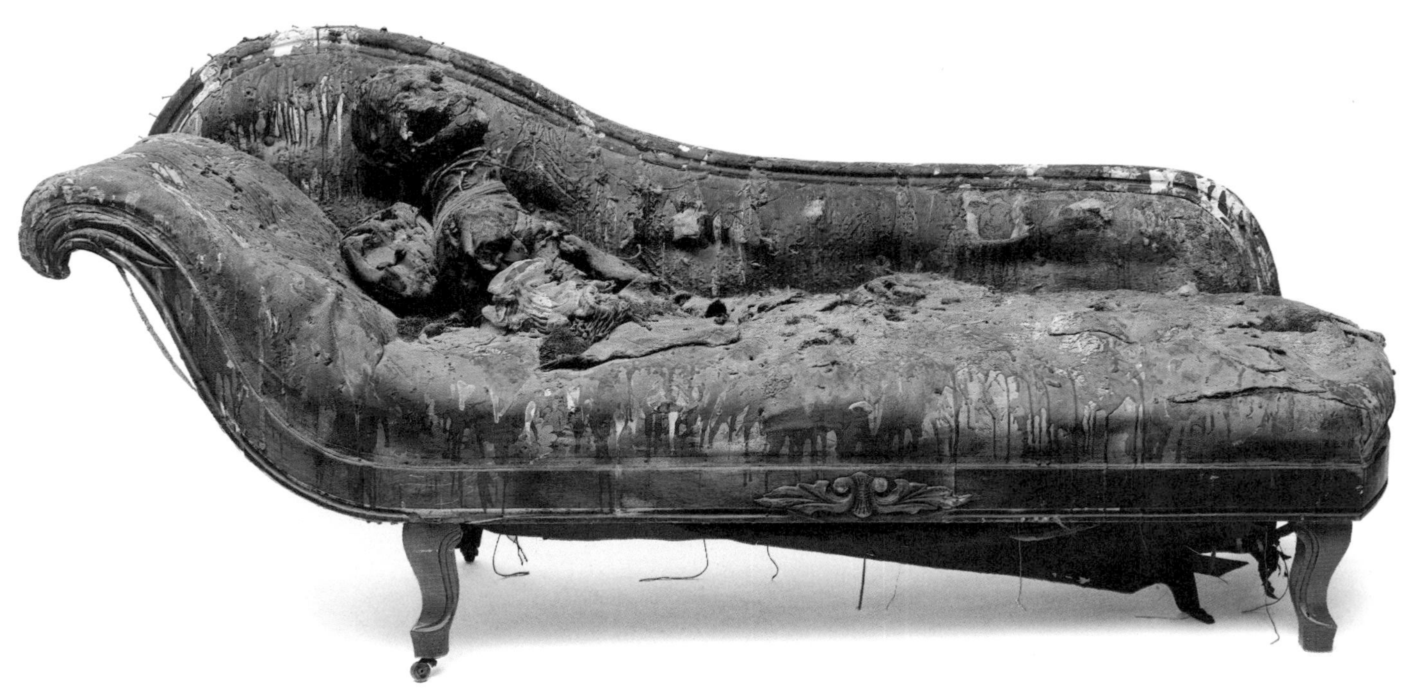

Bruce Conner
COUCH, 1963
Cloth-covered couch with wood frame, figure, cloth, and paint, 32 x 70 3/4 x 27 (81.3 x 179.7 x 68.6)
Norton Simon Museum, Pasadena, California; Museum Purchase with funds donated
by Mr. David H. Steinmetz, III and an Anonymous Foundation, 1969

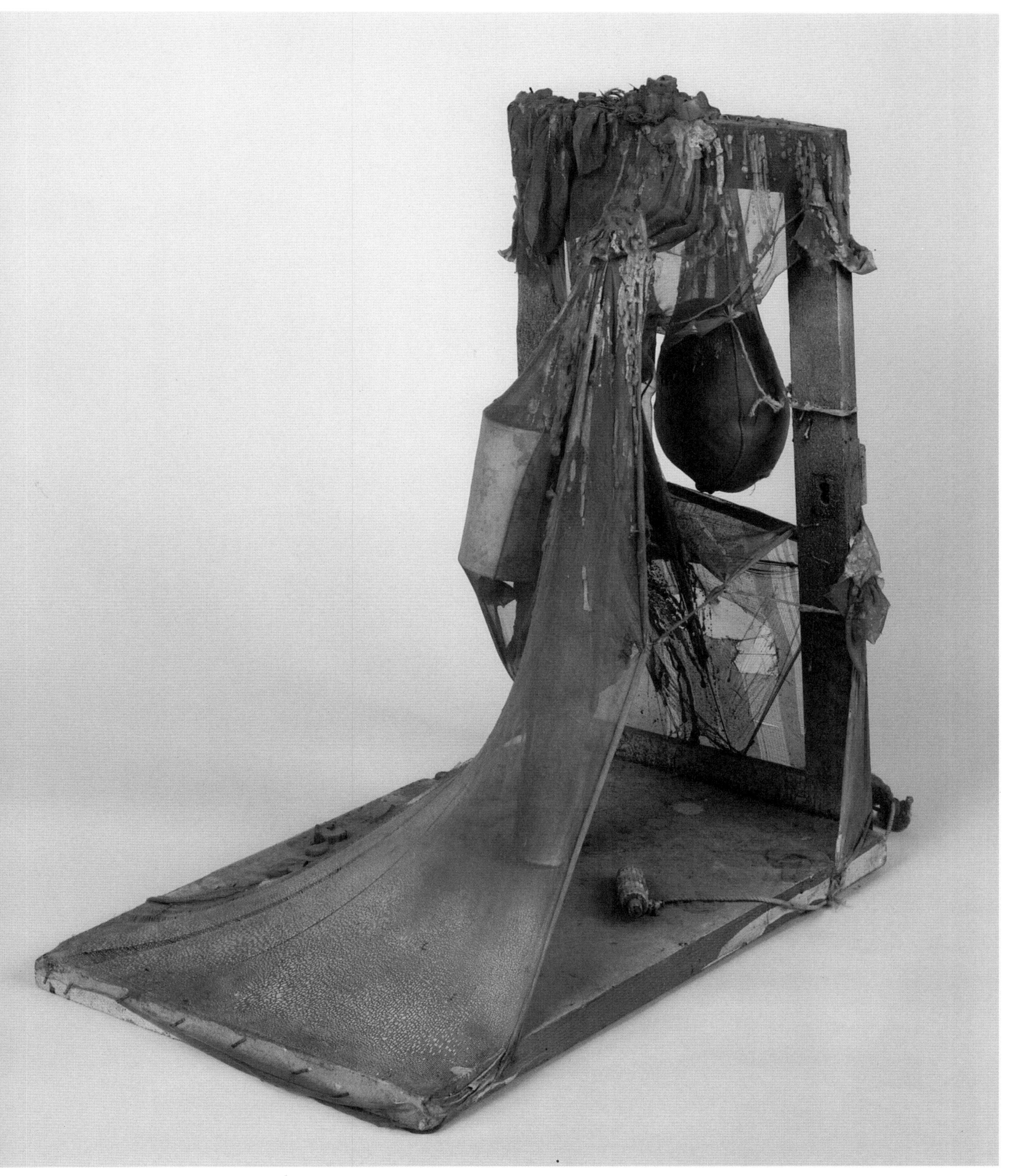

Bruce Conner
PORTRAIT OF ALLEN GINSBERG, c. 1960-61
Wood, nylon, tin can, candle, wax, spray paint, and assorted detritus,
20 x 19 x 11 1/2 (50.8 x 48.3 x 29.2)
Collection of Robert Shapazian

Stuart Perkoff
Untitled, 1959
Collage, 11 x 7 7/8 (27.9 x 20)
Collection of Hal Glicksman

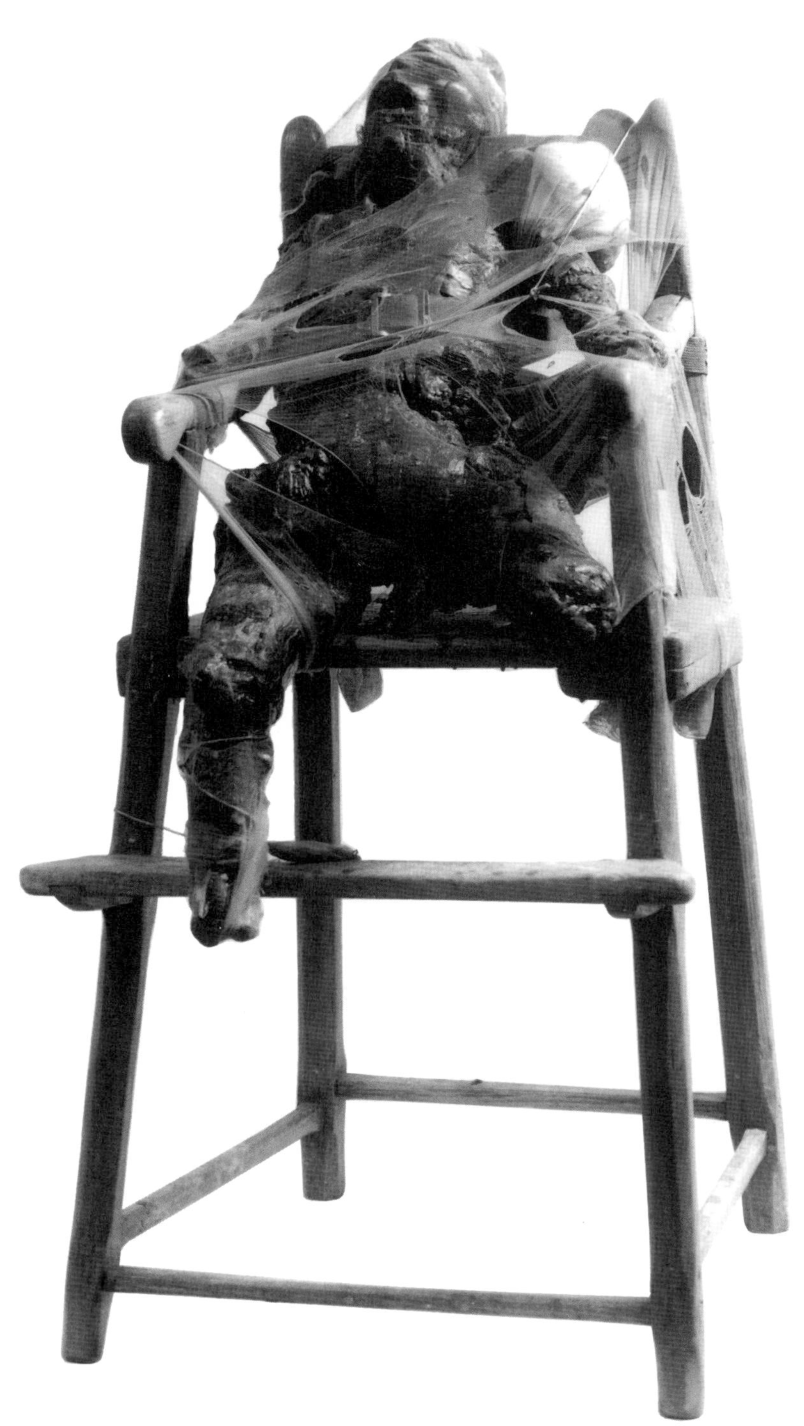

Bruce Conner
CHILD, 1959
Wax, nylon, cloth, metal, twine, and high chair,
34 5/8 x 17 x 16 1/2 (88 x 43.2 x 41.9)
The Museum of Modern Art, New York
Gift of Philip Johnson, 1970

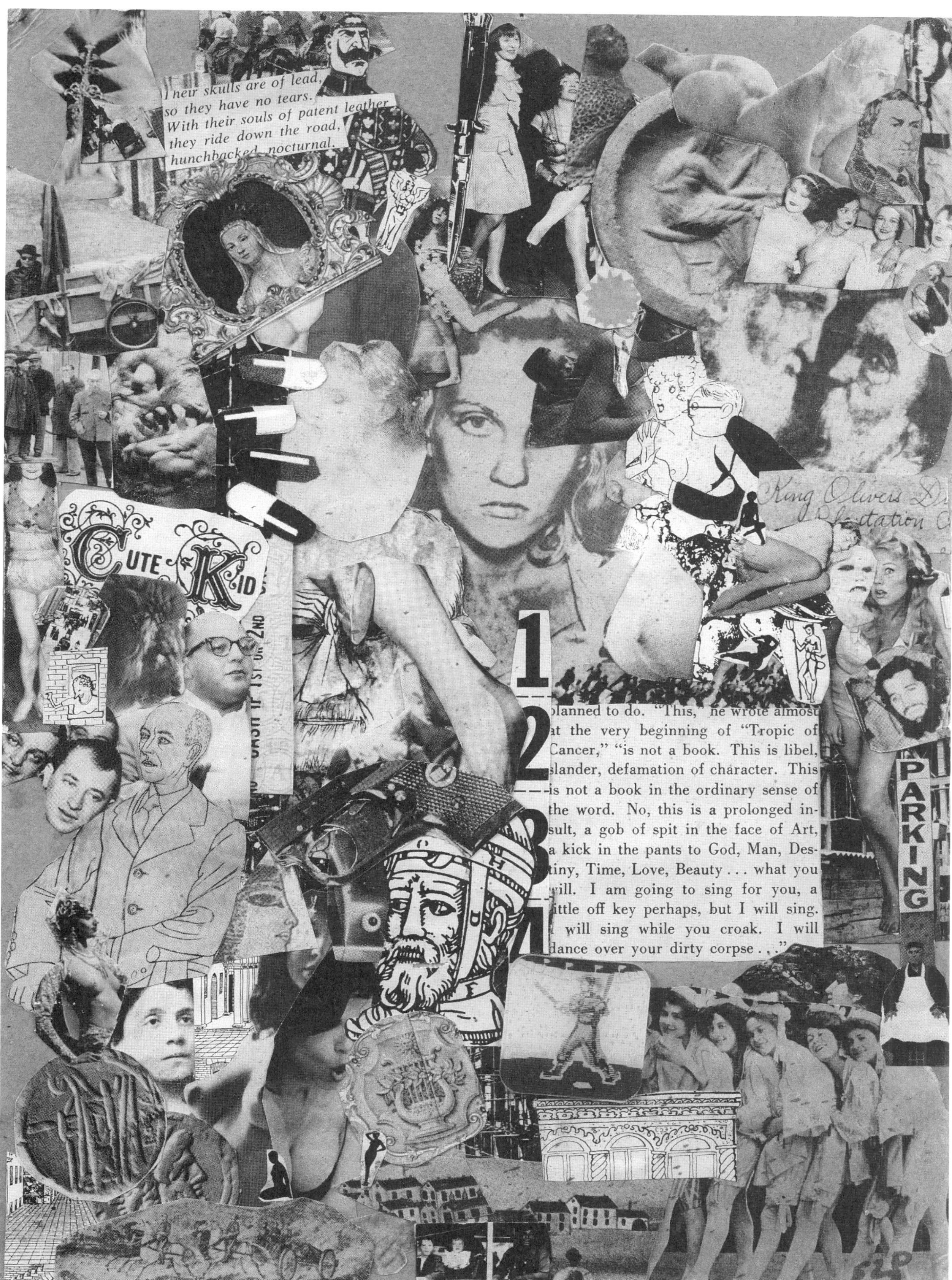

Their skulls are of lead,
so they have no tears.
With their souls of patent leather
they ride down the road,
hunchbacked, nocturnal.
CUTE KID
1
2
3
planned to do. "This," he wrote almost at the very beginning of "Tropic of Cancer," "is not a book. This is libel, slander, defamation of character. This is not a book in the ordinary sense of the word. No, this is a prolonged insult, a gob of spit in the face of Art, a kick in the pants to God, Man, Destiny, Time, Love, Beauty . . . what you will. I am going to sing for you, a little off key perhaps, but I will sing. I will sing while you croak. I will dance over your dirty corpse . . ."
PARKING

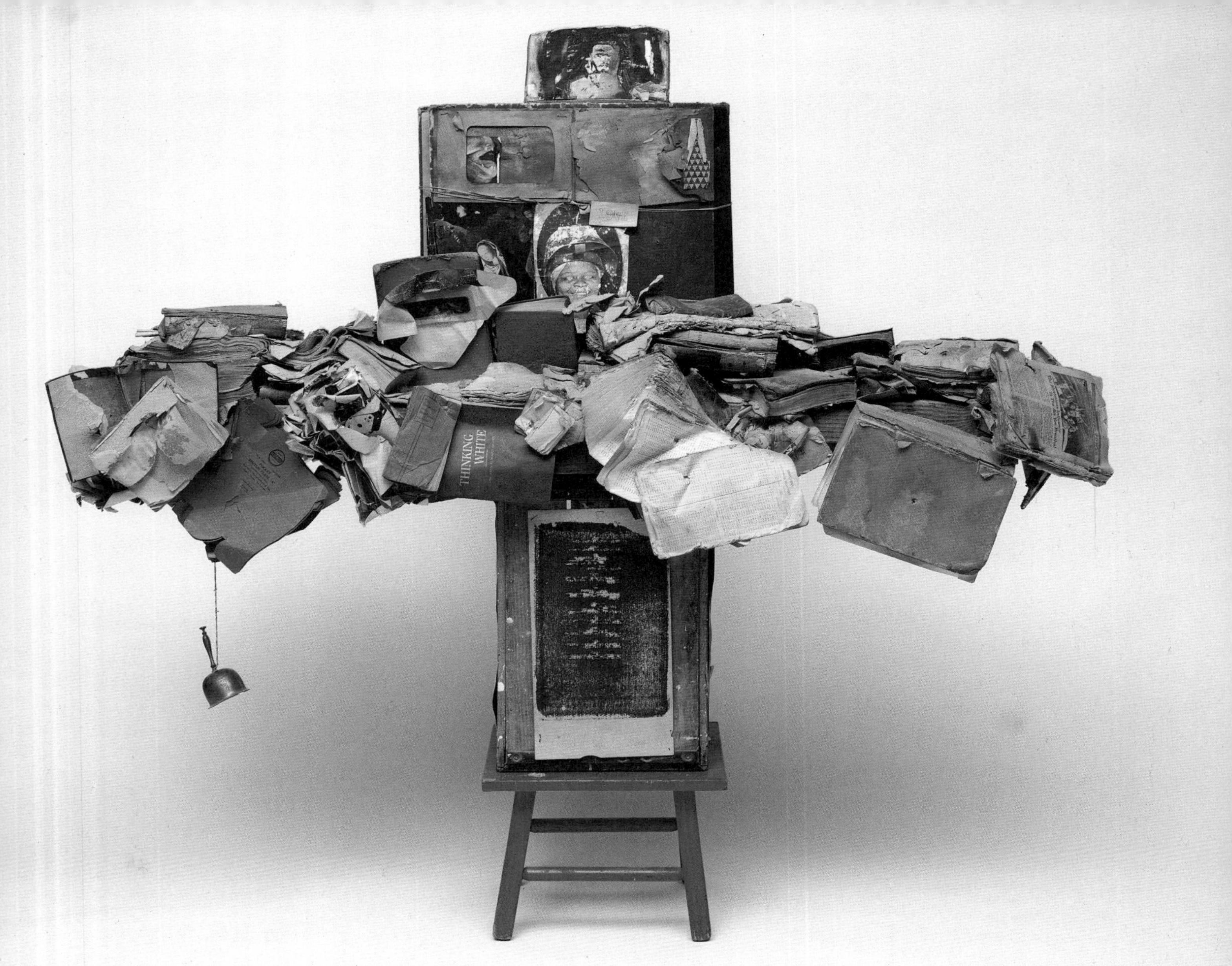

George Herms
The Librarian, 1960
Wood box, paper, brass bell, books, and painted stool, 57 x 63 x 21 (144.8 x 160 x 53.3)
Norton Simon Museum, Pasadena, California; Gift of Molly Barnes, 1969

Edward Kienholz
A Bad Cop (Lt. Carter), 1961
Mixed media, 55 x 16 1/2 x 11 4/5 (140 x 42 x 30)
Collection of Reinhard Onnasch

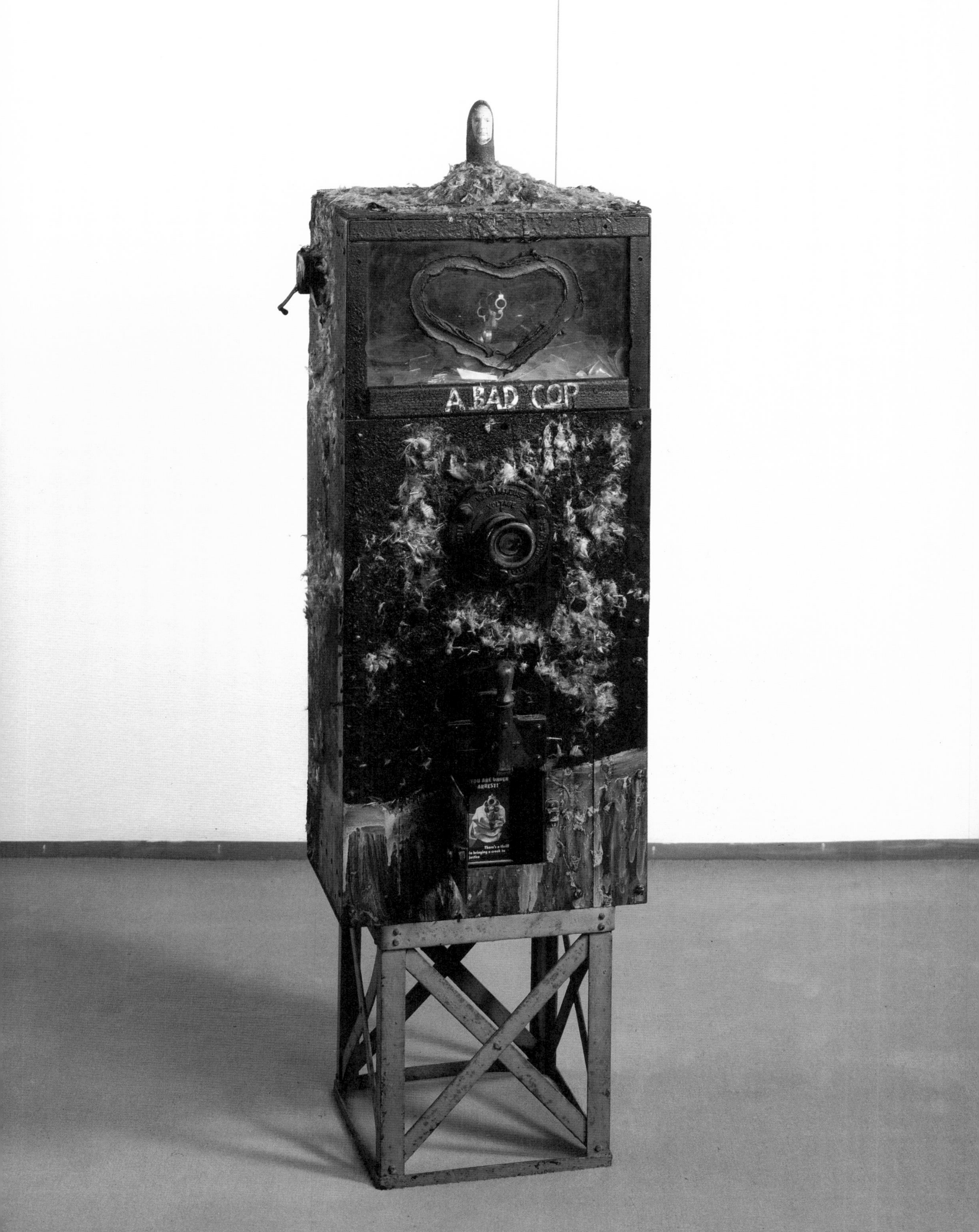
A BAD COP
YOU ARE UNDER ARREST!
There's a thrill in bringing a crook to justice

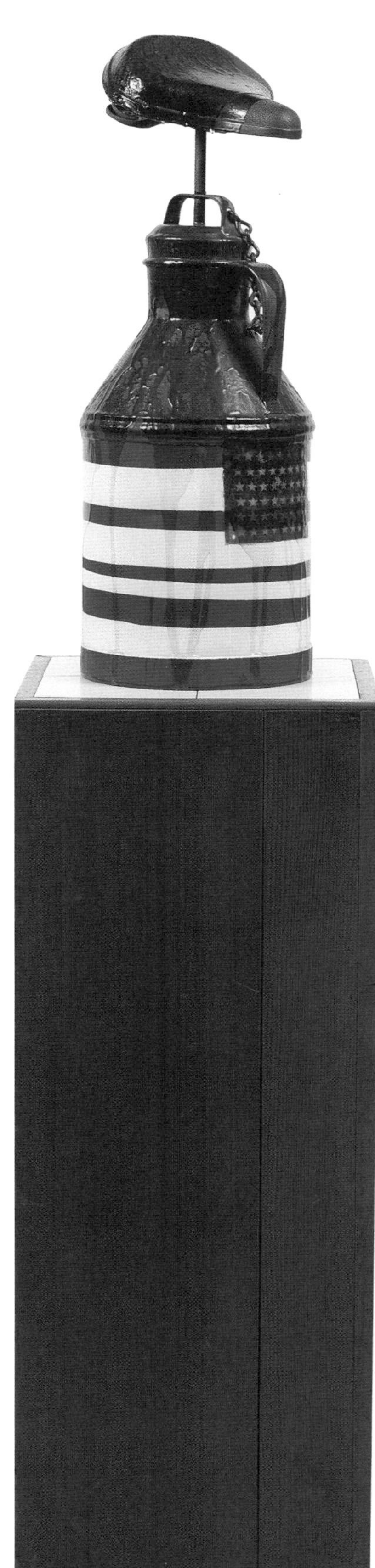

Edward Kienholz
Untitled American President, 1962
Metal, plastic, fabric, paint, and chain on wood with ceramic base,
60 1/4 x 13 1/2 x 13 1/2 (153 x 34.3 x 34.3) overall
Whitney Museum of American Art, New York; Purchase, with
funds from the Painting and Sculpture Committee 93.99a-b

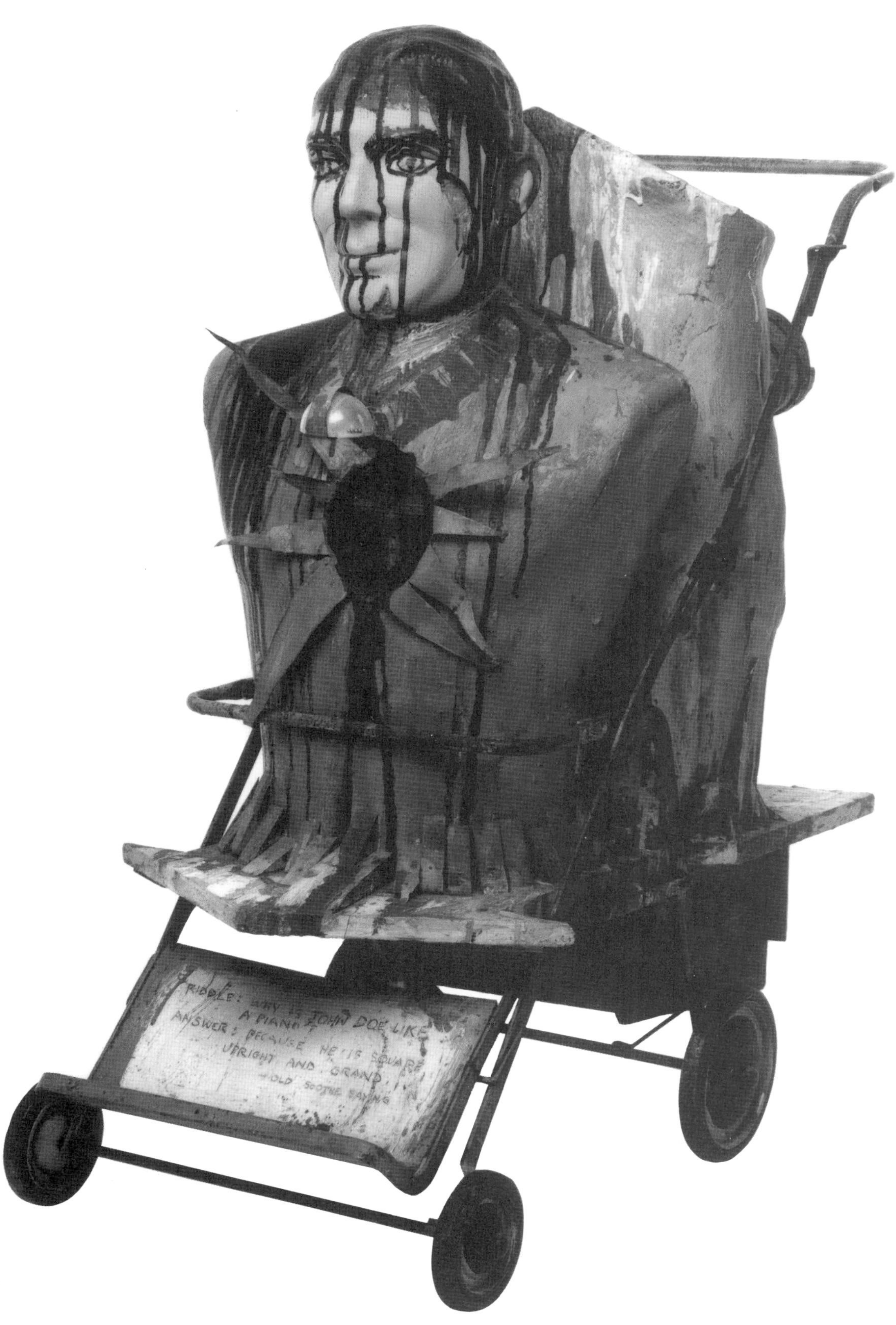

Edward Kienholz
John Doe, 1959
Painted perambulator, toy, and mannequin parts, 41 x 19 x 34 (104.1 x 48.3 x 86.4)
The Menil Collection, Houston

Ben Talbert
The Ace, 1961-62
Artist's easel, bicycle wheel, airplane wings, phonograph, photographs, dolls, collaged papers, oil paint, and crepe paper
96 x 50 x 38 (243.8 x 127 x 96.5)
Collection of Hal Glicksman
(front and back)

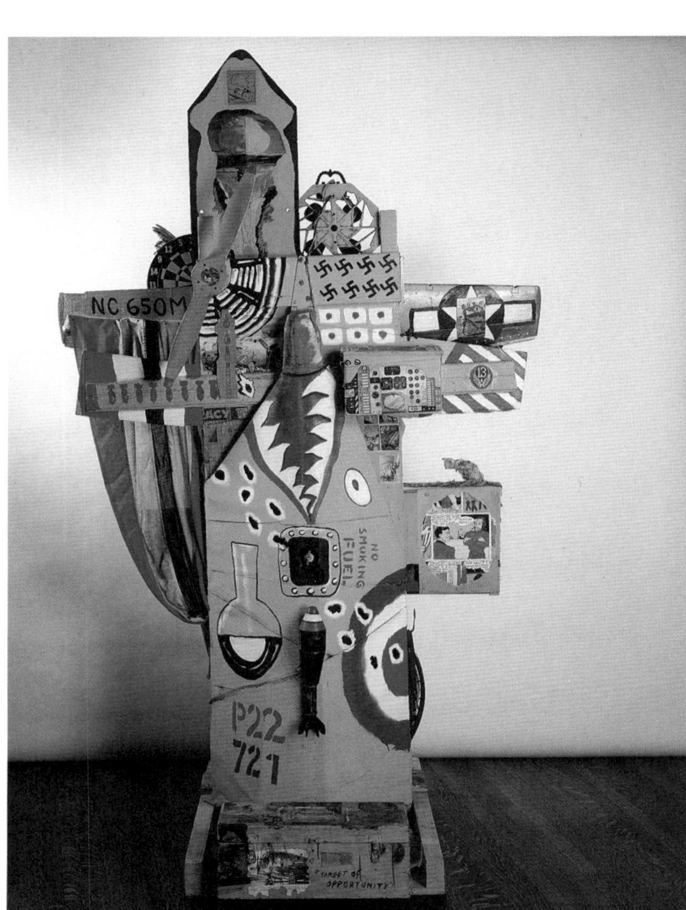

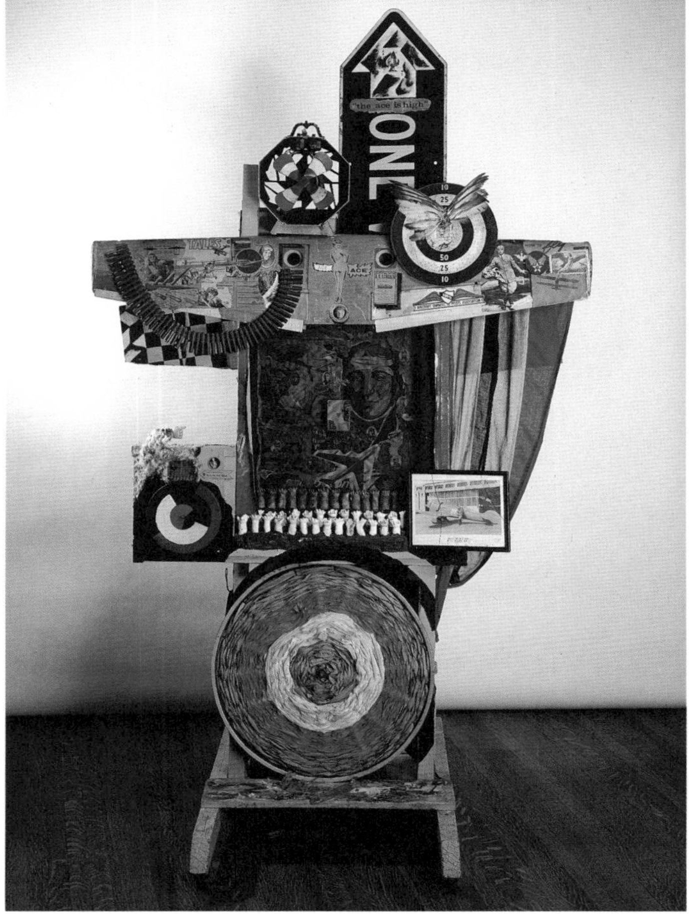

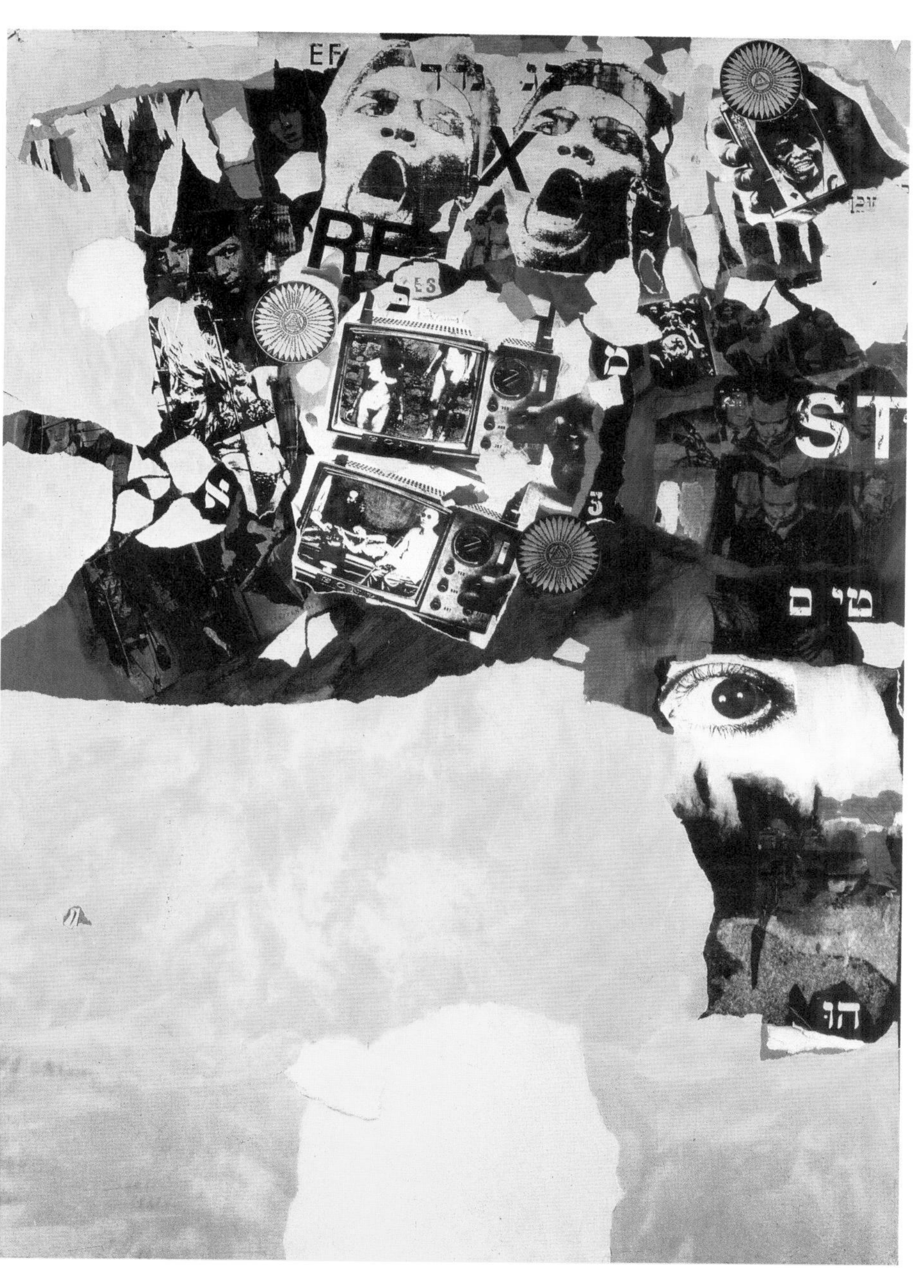

Wallace Berman
Papa's Got A Brand New Bag, 1964
Mixed media collage, 43 x 30 3/4 (109.2 x 78.1)
Collection of Nicole Klagsbrun

Wally Hedrick
Big Dick (Nixon) for President, 1960
Oil on canvas, 110 x 83 (279.4 x 210.8)
Collection of David J. and Jeanne Carlson

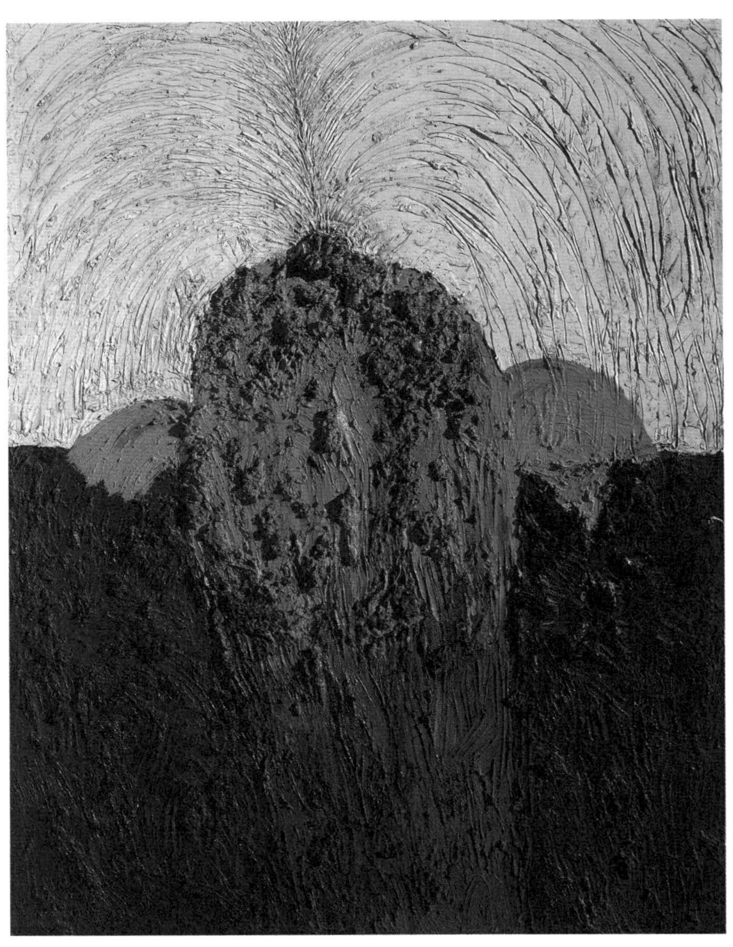

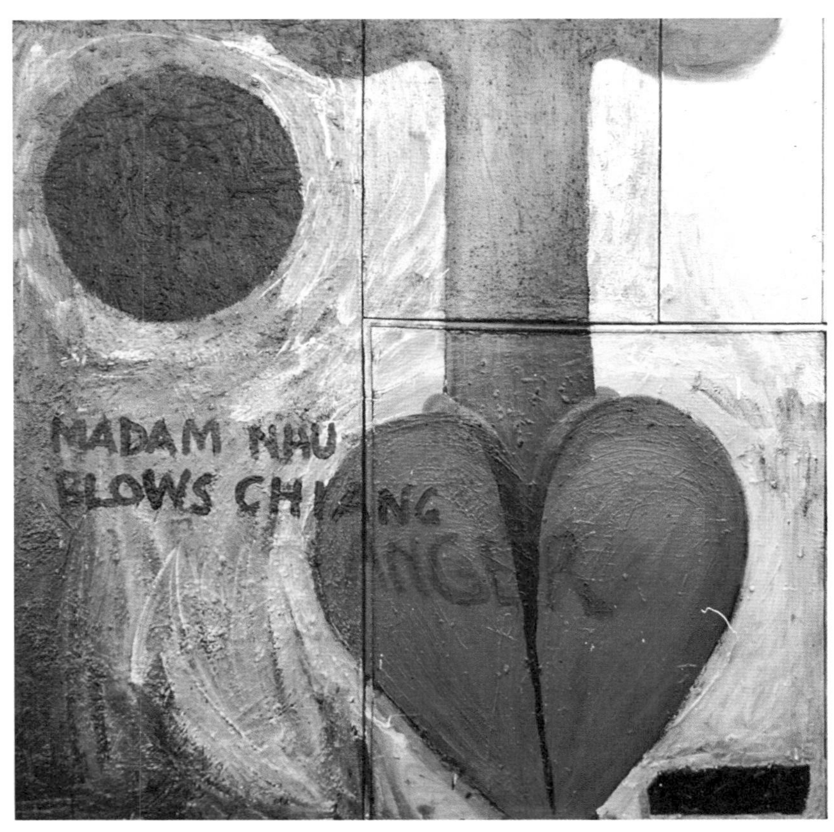

Wally Hedrick
Anger or Madame Nhu's BBQ, 1959
Oil on canvas, 65 3/4 x 65 1/2 (165.1 x 166.4)
Collection of Jay Cooper; courtesy Gallery Paule Anglim, San Francisco

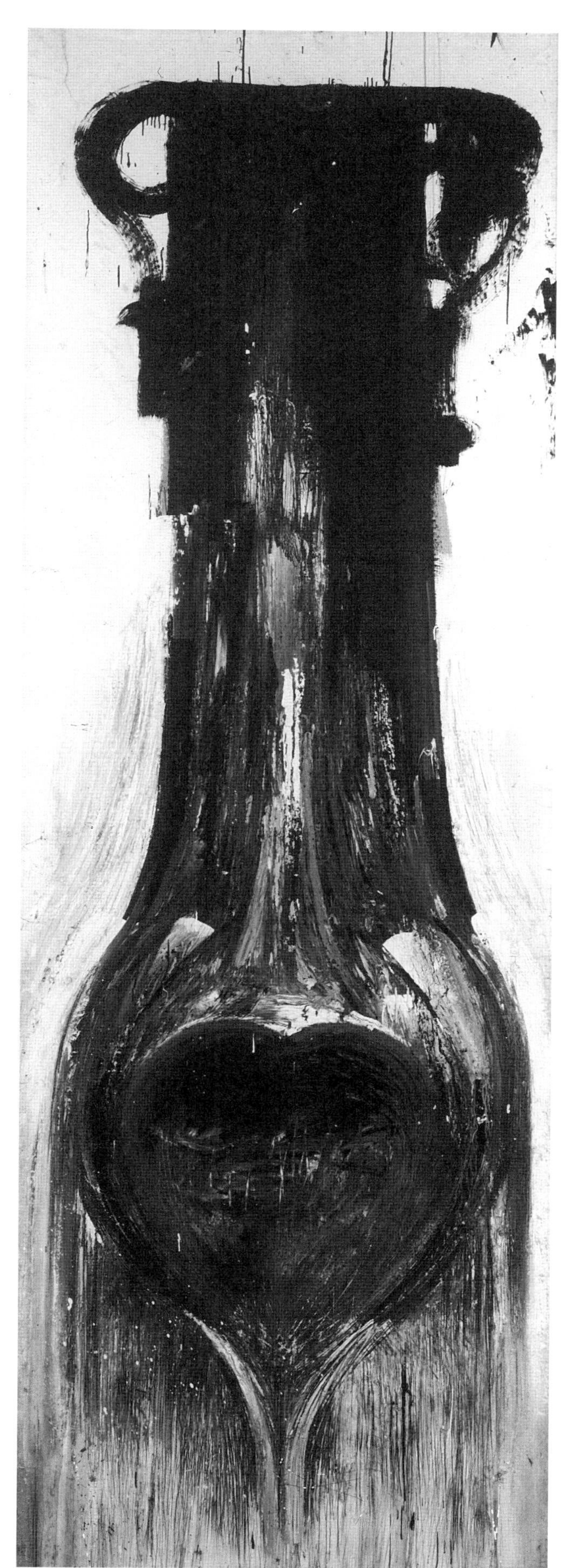

Jay DeFeo
Doctor Jazz, 1958
Oil on paper with tinsel, 125 1/2 x 42 1/2
(318.8 x 108)
Estate of the artist; courtesy Nicole
Klagsbrun Gallery, New York

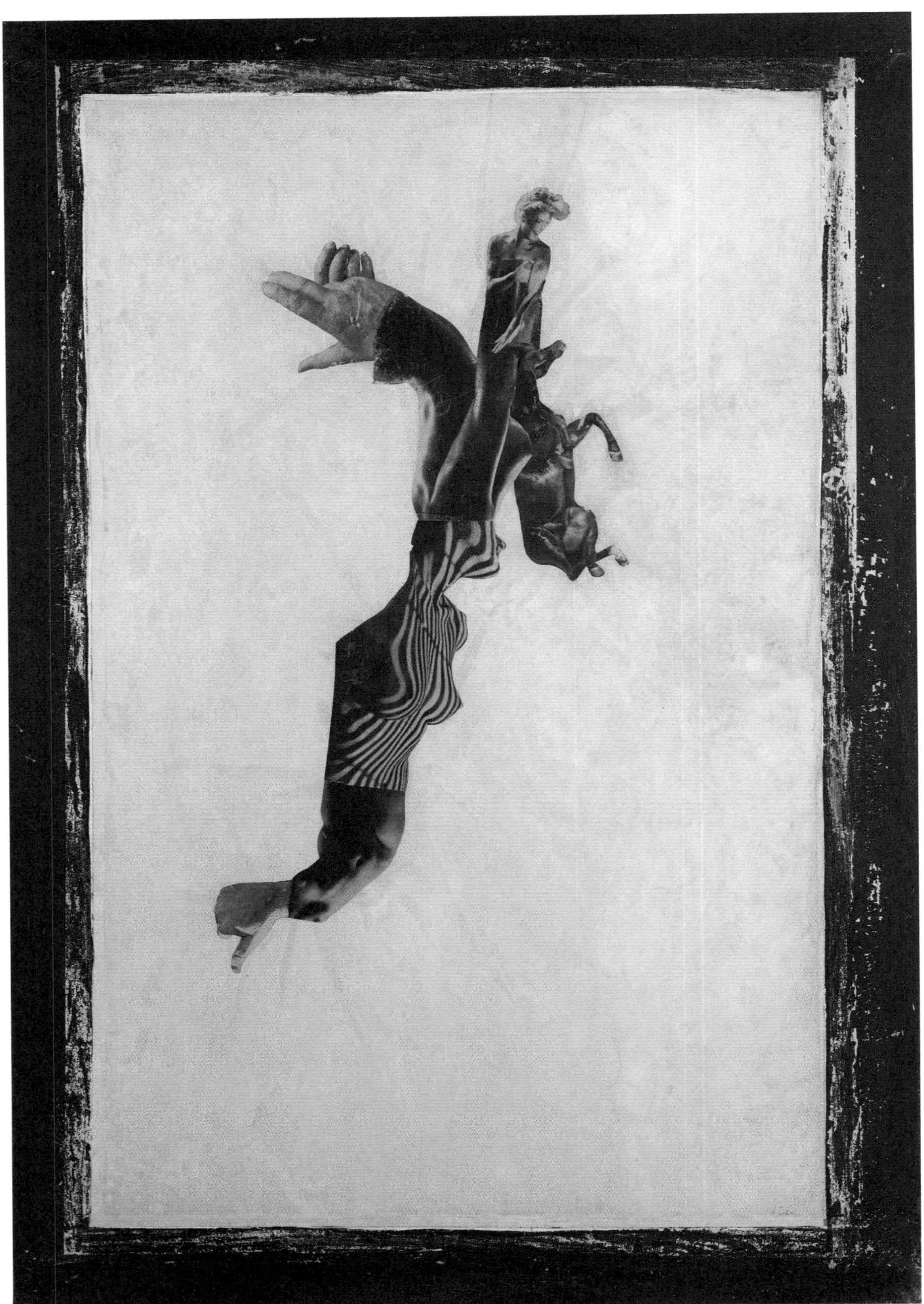

Jay DeFeo
Applaud the Black Fact, 1958
Collage on paper mounted on painted canvas,
50 7/16 x 36 1/8 (128.1 x 91.8)
Whitney Museum of American Art, New York;
Purchase, with funds from the Photography Committee and
the Drawing Committee 93.103

Jay DeFeo
Blossom, 1956
Collage of photomechanical reproductions with mixed media,
43 1/8 x 33 7/8 (109.5 x 86)
The Museum of Modern Art, New York
The Fellows of Photography Fund and The Family of Man Fund

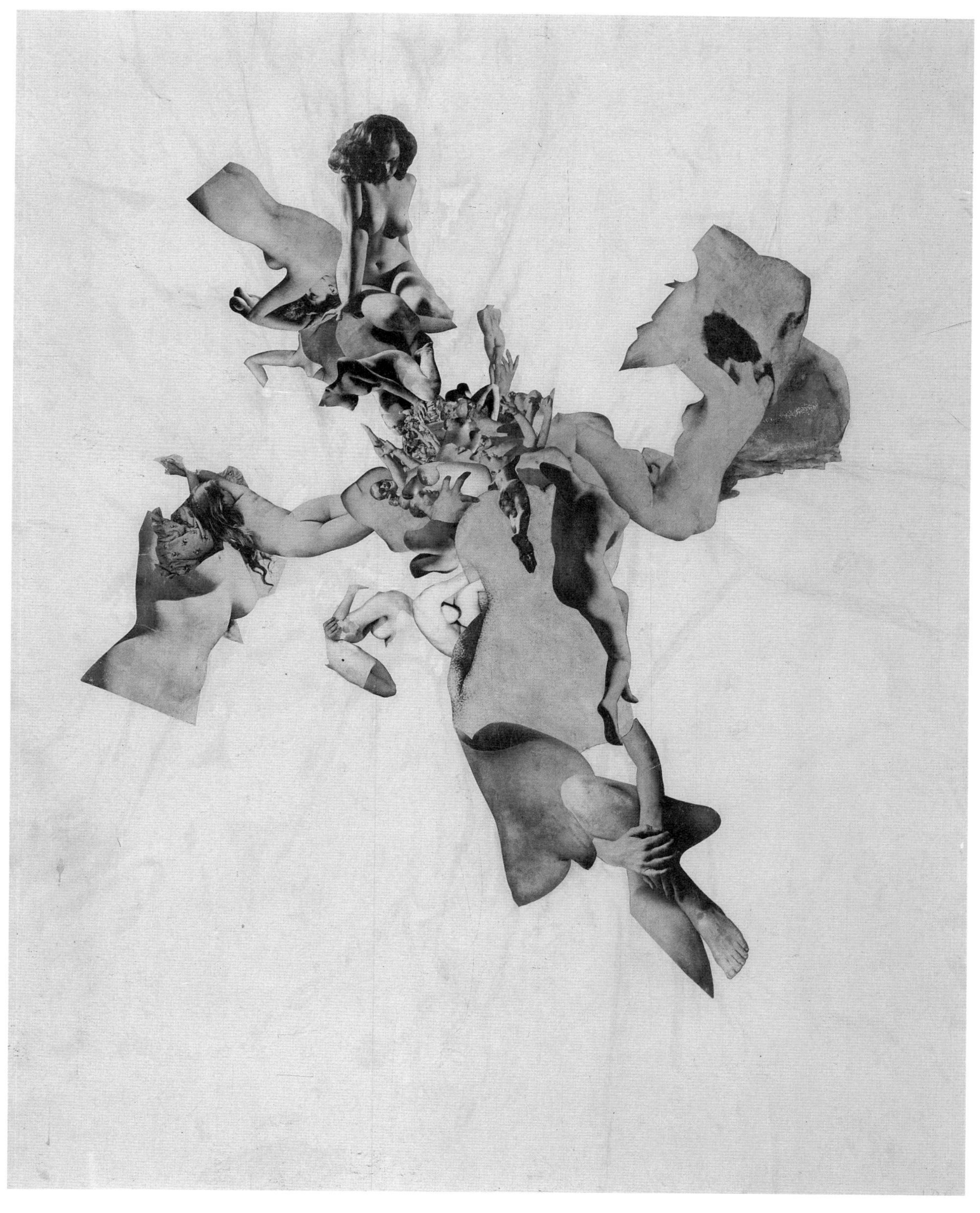

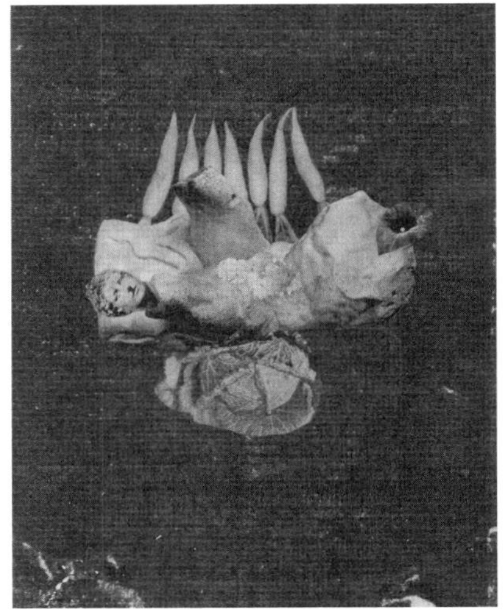

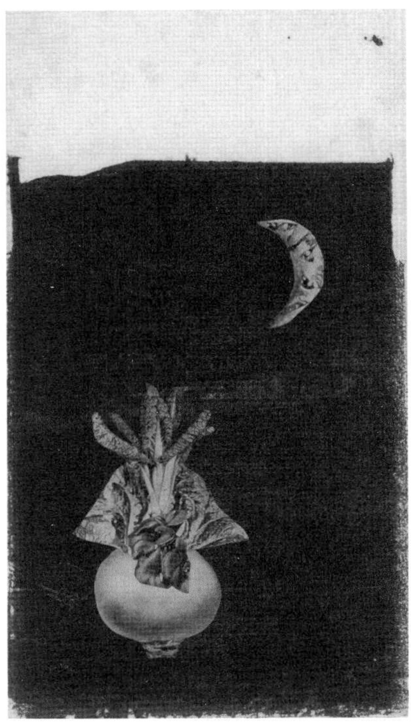

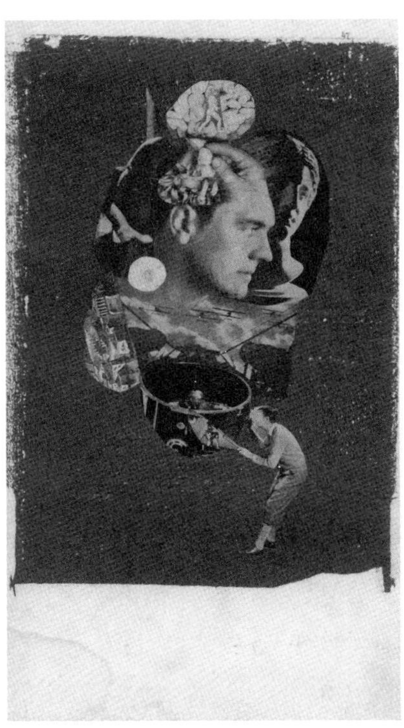

George Herms

Burpee Seed Collages, 1962

Six collages on paper, 10 x 7 1/2 to 16 x 8 1/2 (25.4 x 19.1 to 40.6 x 21.6)

Collection of the artist

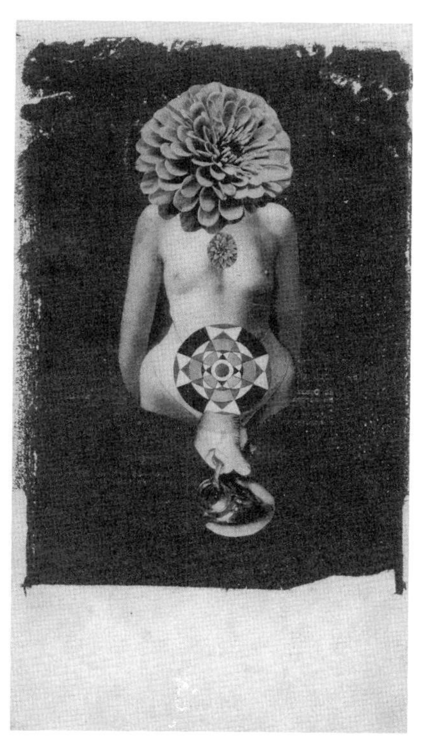

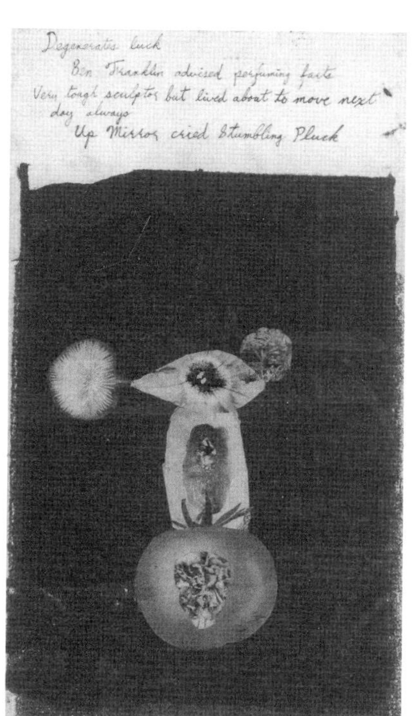
Degenerates luck
Ben Franklin advised perfuming farts
Very tough sculptor but lived about to move next
day always
Up Mirror cried Stumbling Pluck

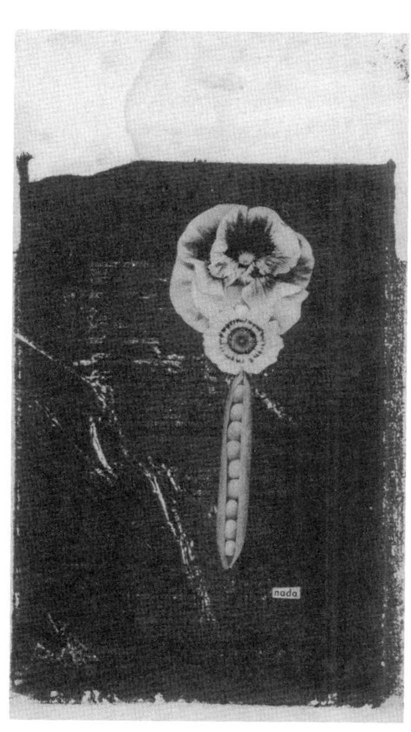
nada

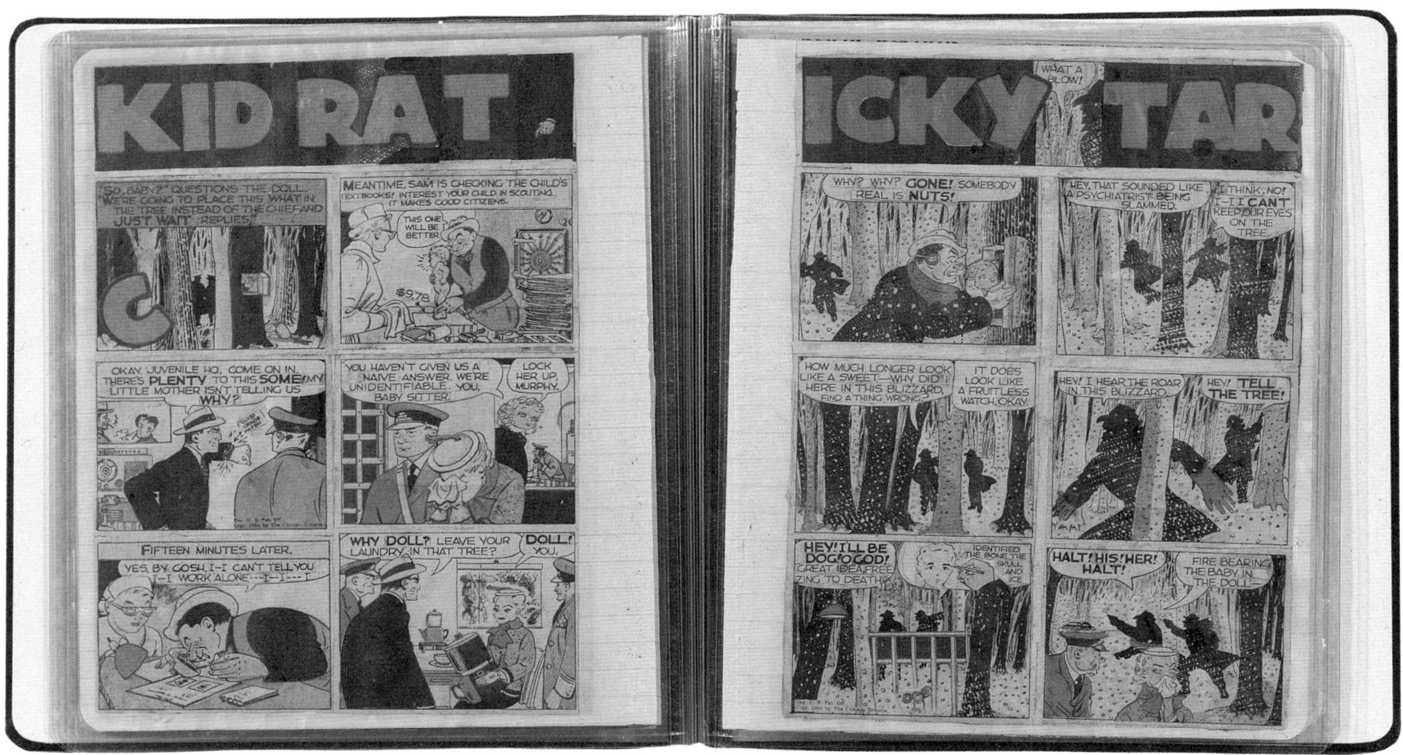

Jess

Tricky Cad, Case I, 1954

Notebook of twelve collages with handwritten title page, 9 7/16 x 7 13/16 (24 x 19.8)

Whitney Museum of American Art, New York; Purchase, with funds from the Contemporary Painting and Sculpture Committee, the Drawing Committee, and the Tom Armstrong Purchase Fund 95.20a-m

Jess

Paranoic Portrait of Robert Creeley, 1955

Paste-up, 26 x 22 (66 x 55.9)

Collection of the artist; courtesy Gallery Paule Anglim, San Francisco

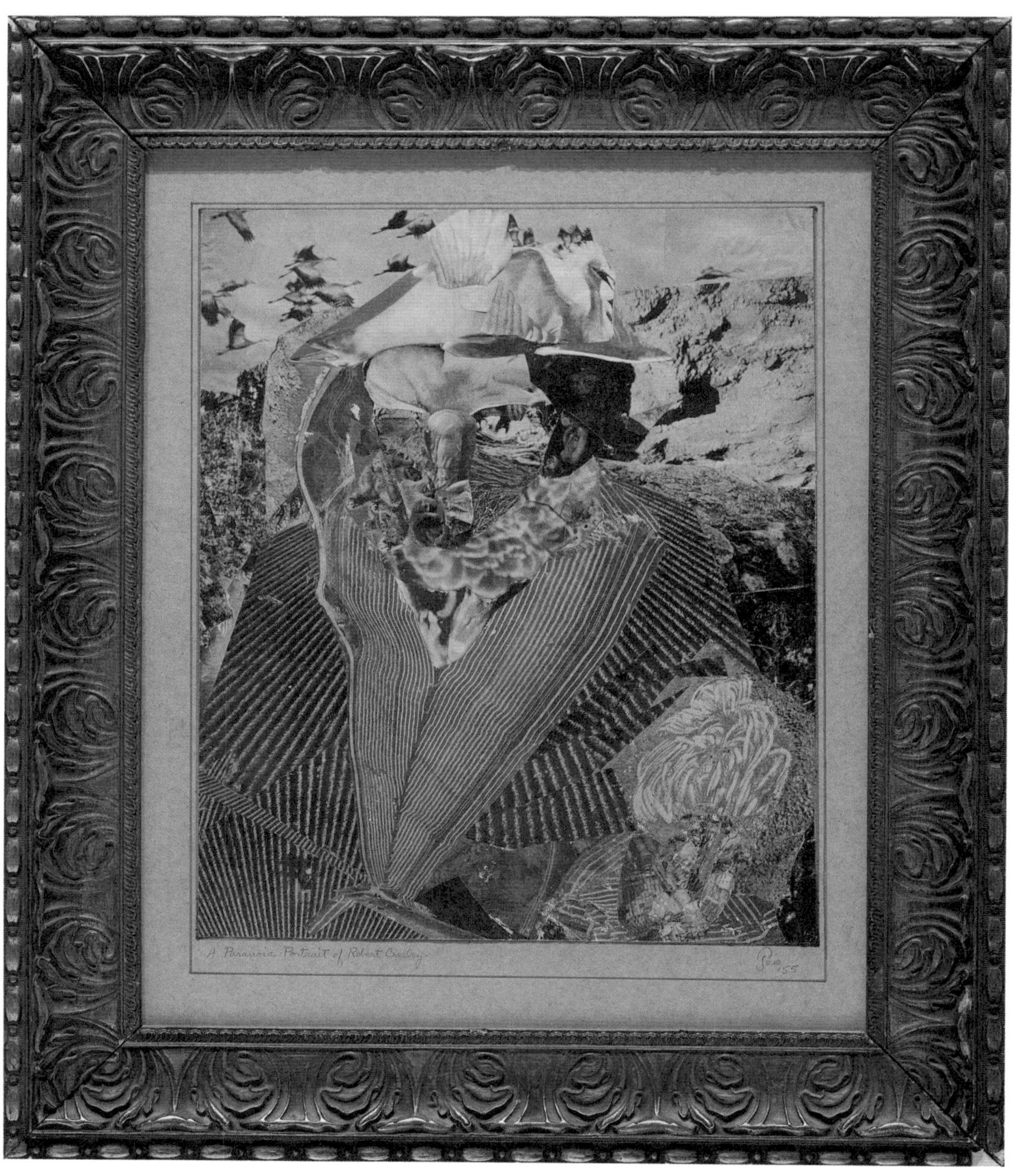
A Paranoic Portrait of Robert Creeley

George Herms
The Meat Market, 1960-61
Table, pickle jar, radio, exposed X-ray plate, doll, butcher's pricing signs, mannequin, picture frame, dress form, cloth, tape, table legs, wood block, wood spool, tin box, sponge, basket, and cow's skull, 58 x 144 x 54 (147.3 x 365.8 x 137.2) overall
Collection of the artist

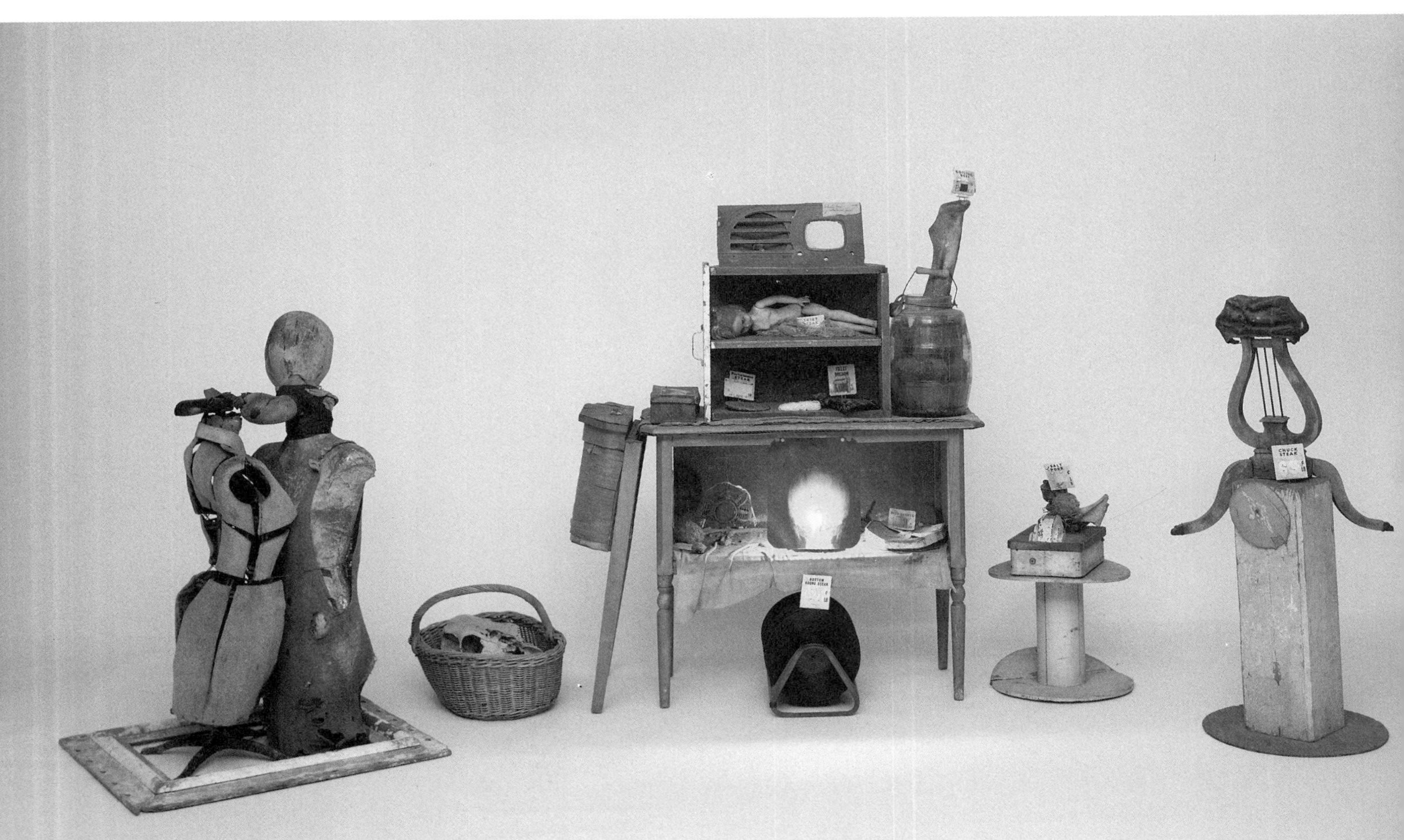

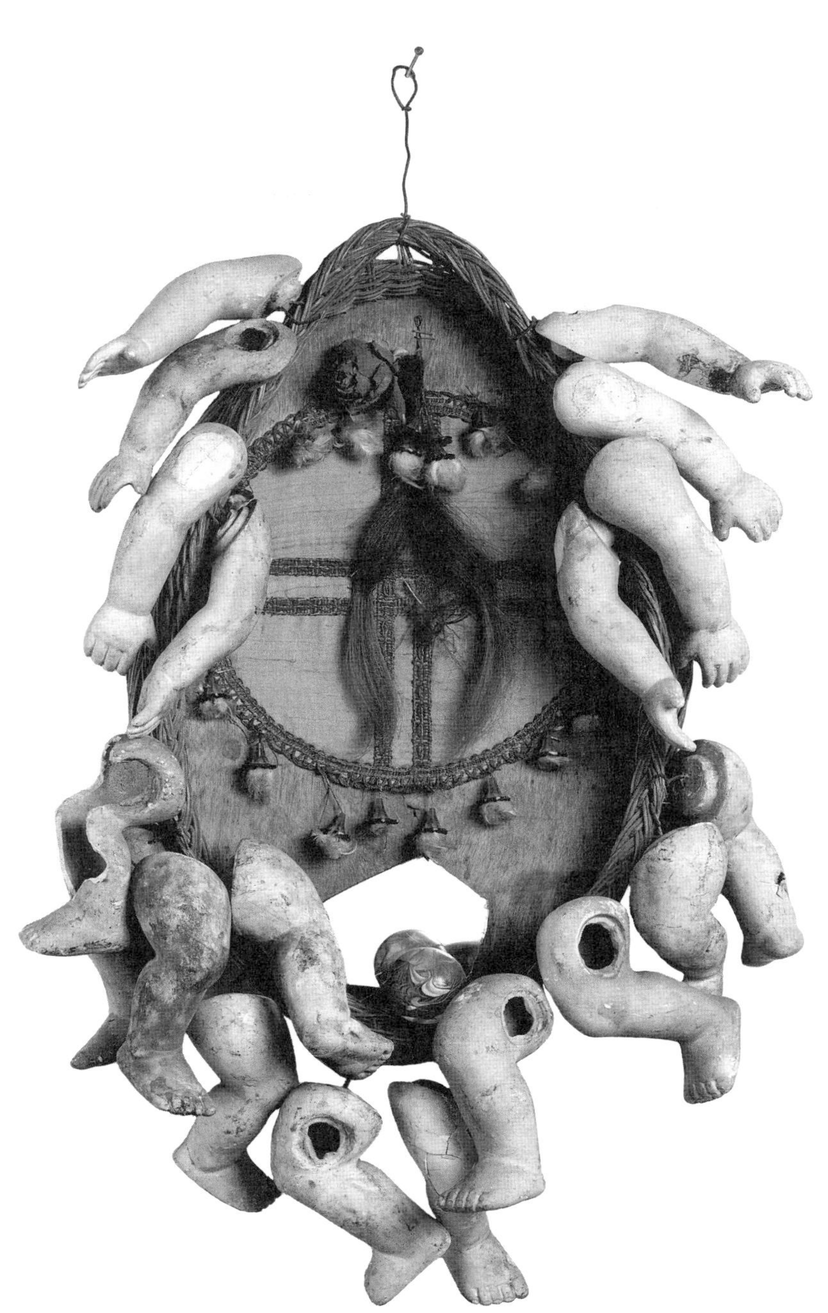

Fred Mason
Superball, 1960
Wood, basket, doll's plaster arms and legs, hair, feathers, mirror, cloth, and dried roses, 26 x 17 (66 x 43.2)
Collection of Hal Glicksman

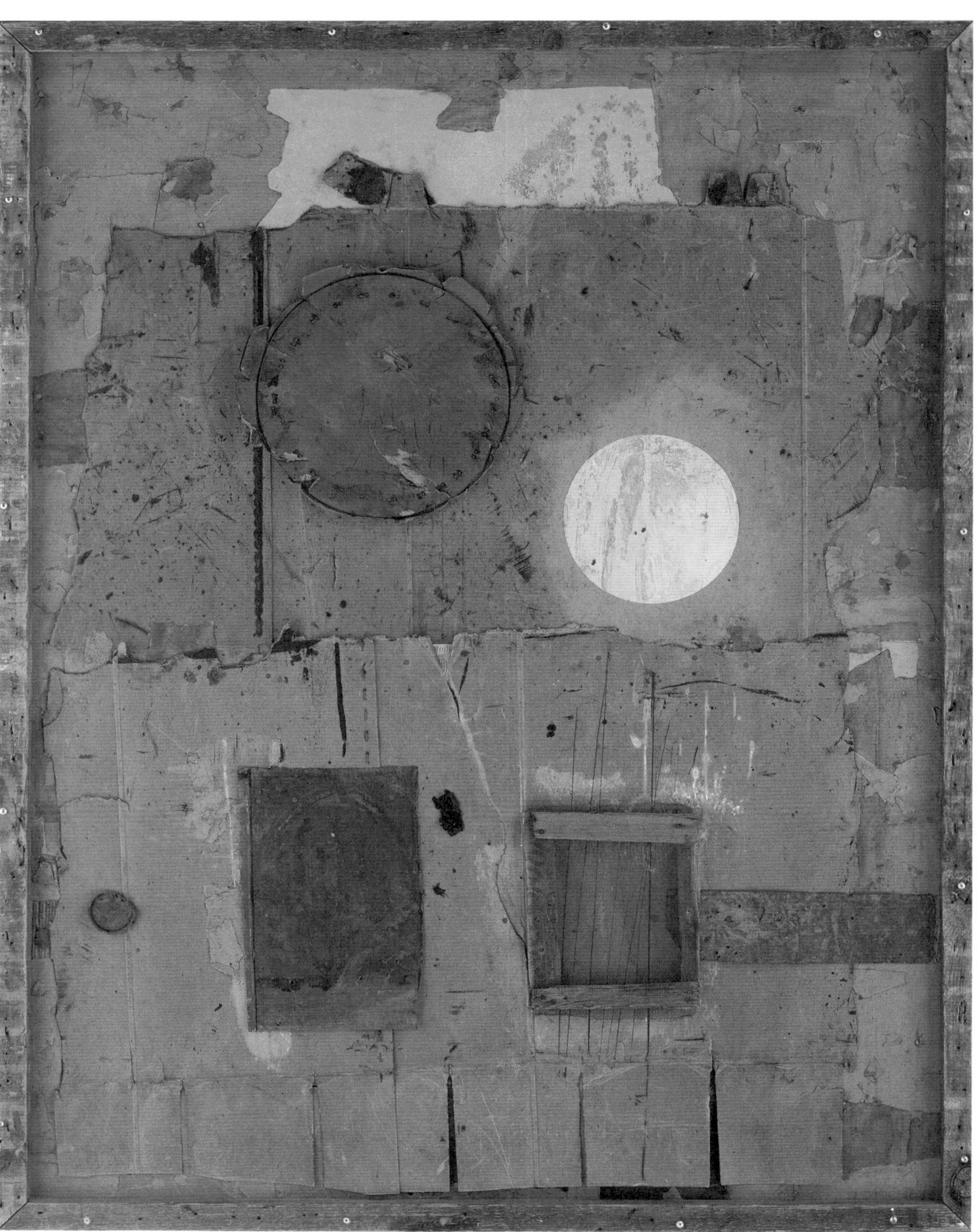

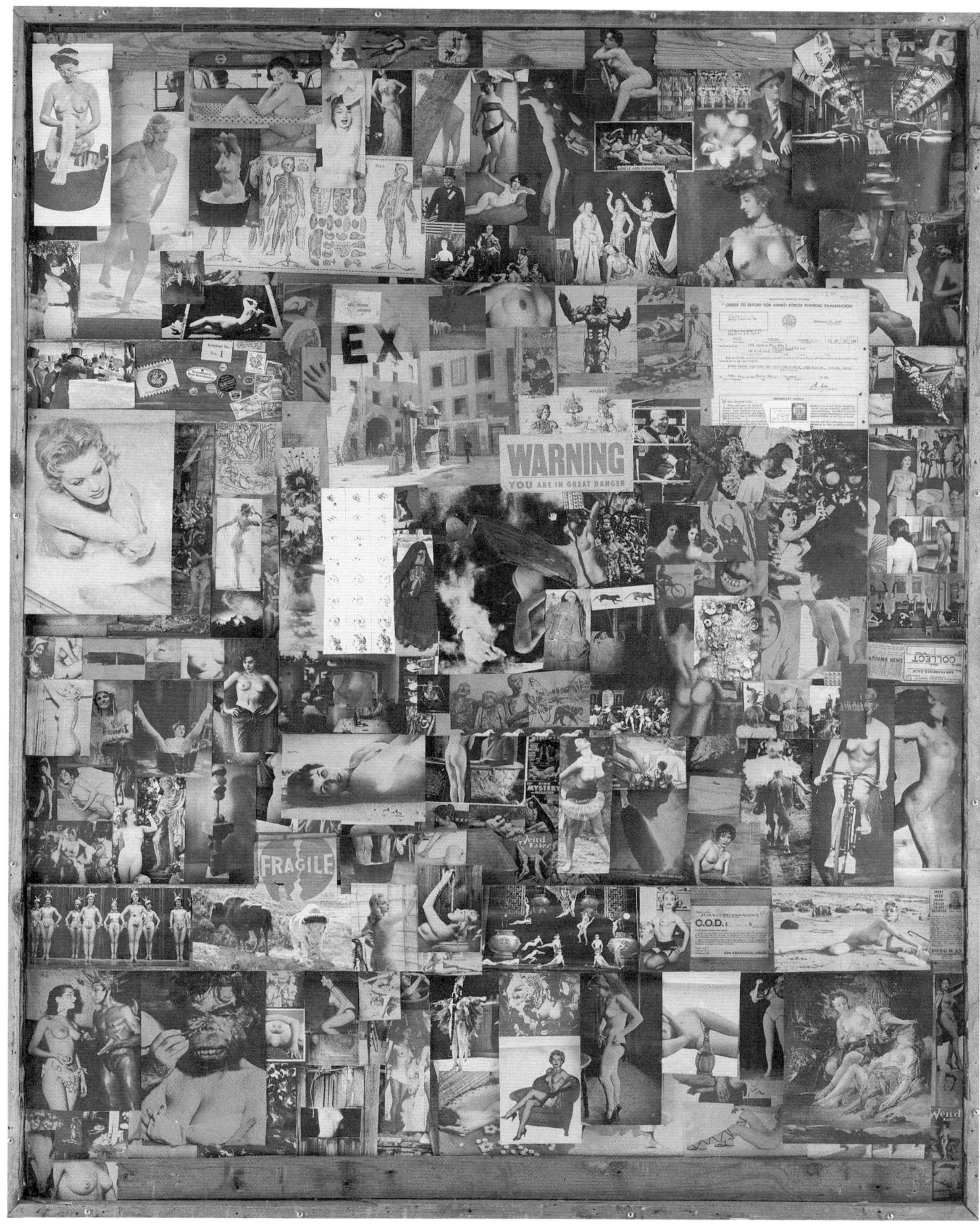

Bruce Conner
UNTITLED, 1954-62
Paper, wood, adhesive, nails, paint, staples, metal, tar,
feathers, and plastic on masonite, 63 7/8 x 49 5/8 x 4 1/8 (162.2 x 126 x 10.5)
Walker Art Center, Minneapolis; T. B. Walker Acquisition Fund, 1992
(front and back)

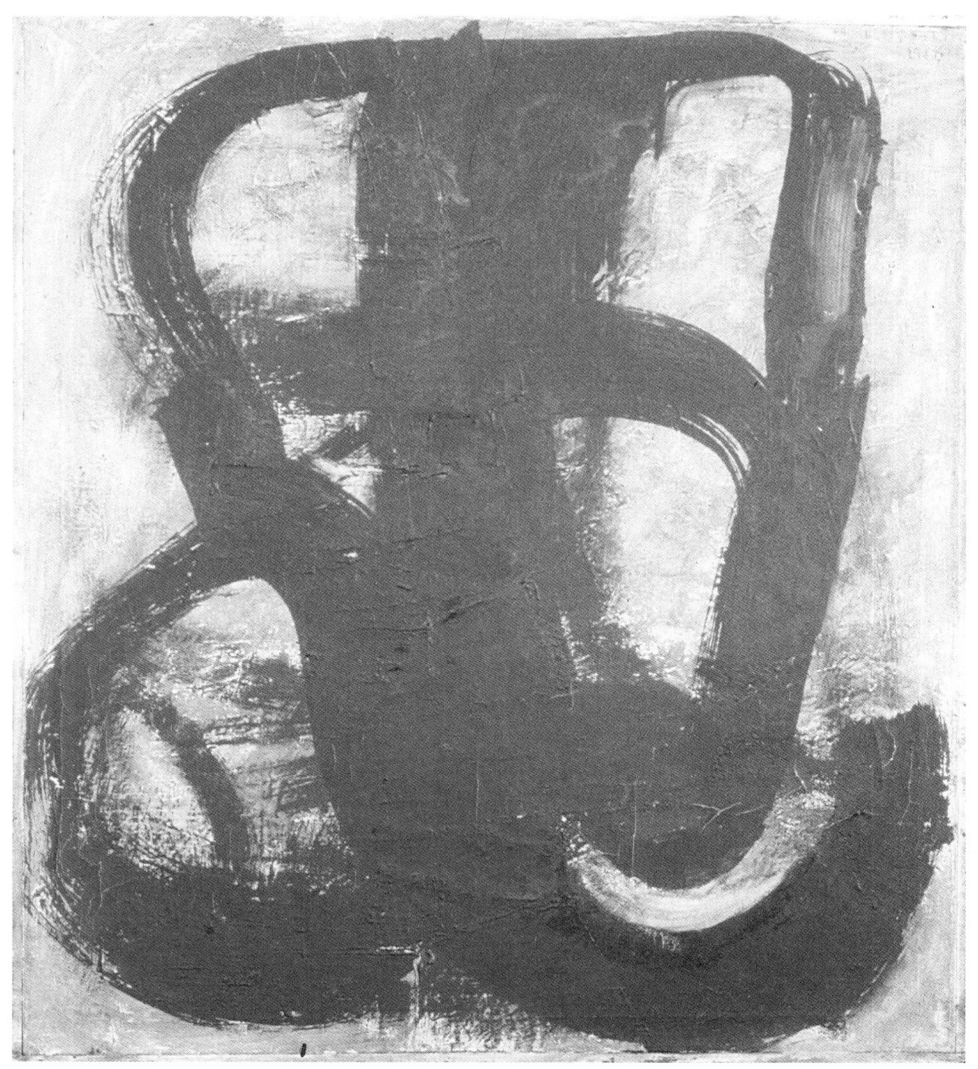

Lawrence Ferlinghetti
Vajra Lotus, 1957-60
Oil on canvas, 48 x 50 (121.9 x 127)
Collection of the artist

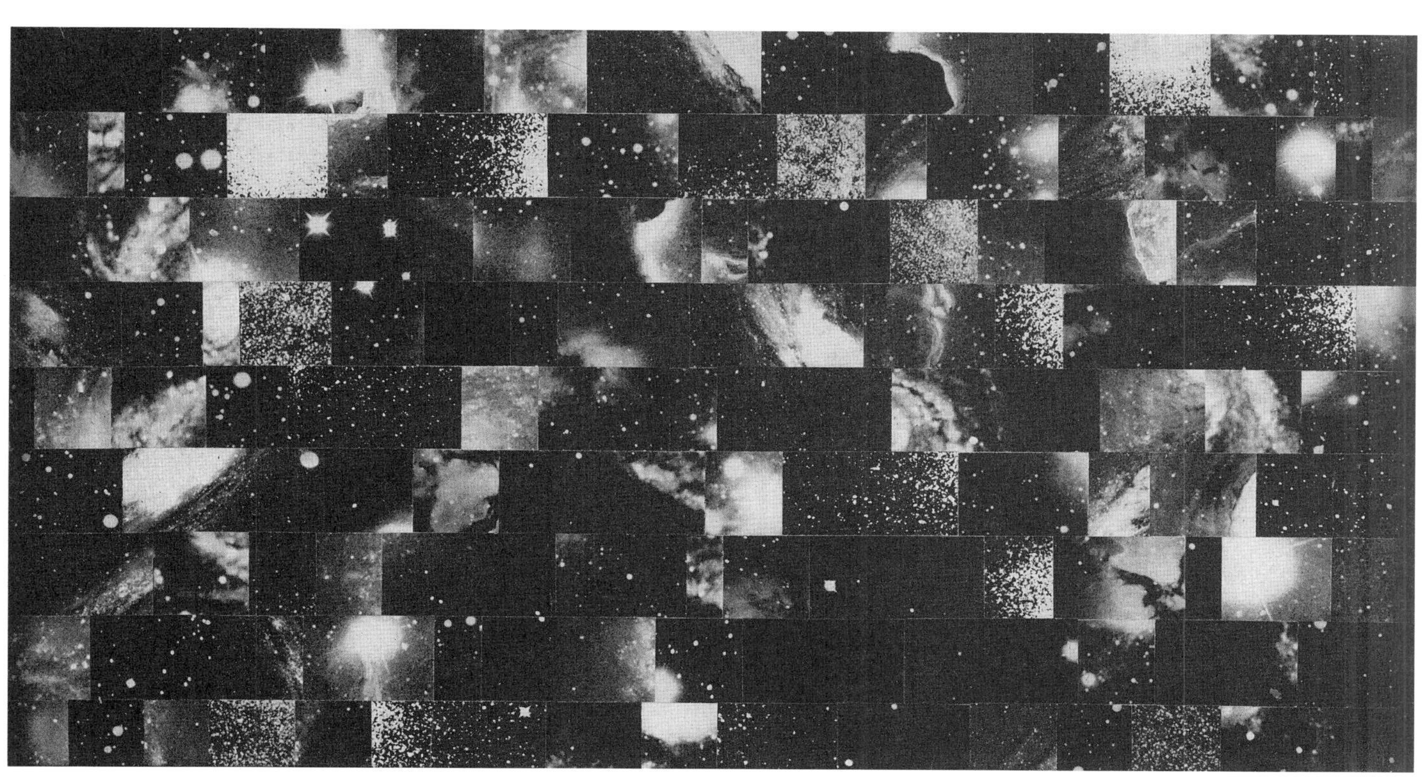

Dean Stockwell
Grid of Galaxies, 1961-63
Photocollage, 9 x 16 (22.9 x 40.6)
Collection of Dennis Hopper

Ray Bremser reading at the Artist's Studio, 1959. Photo © Fred W. McDarrah

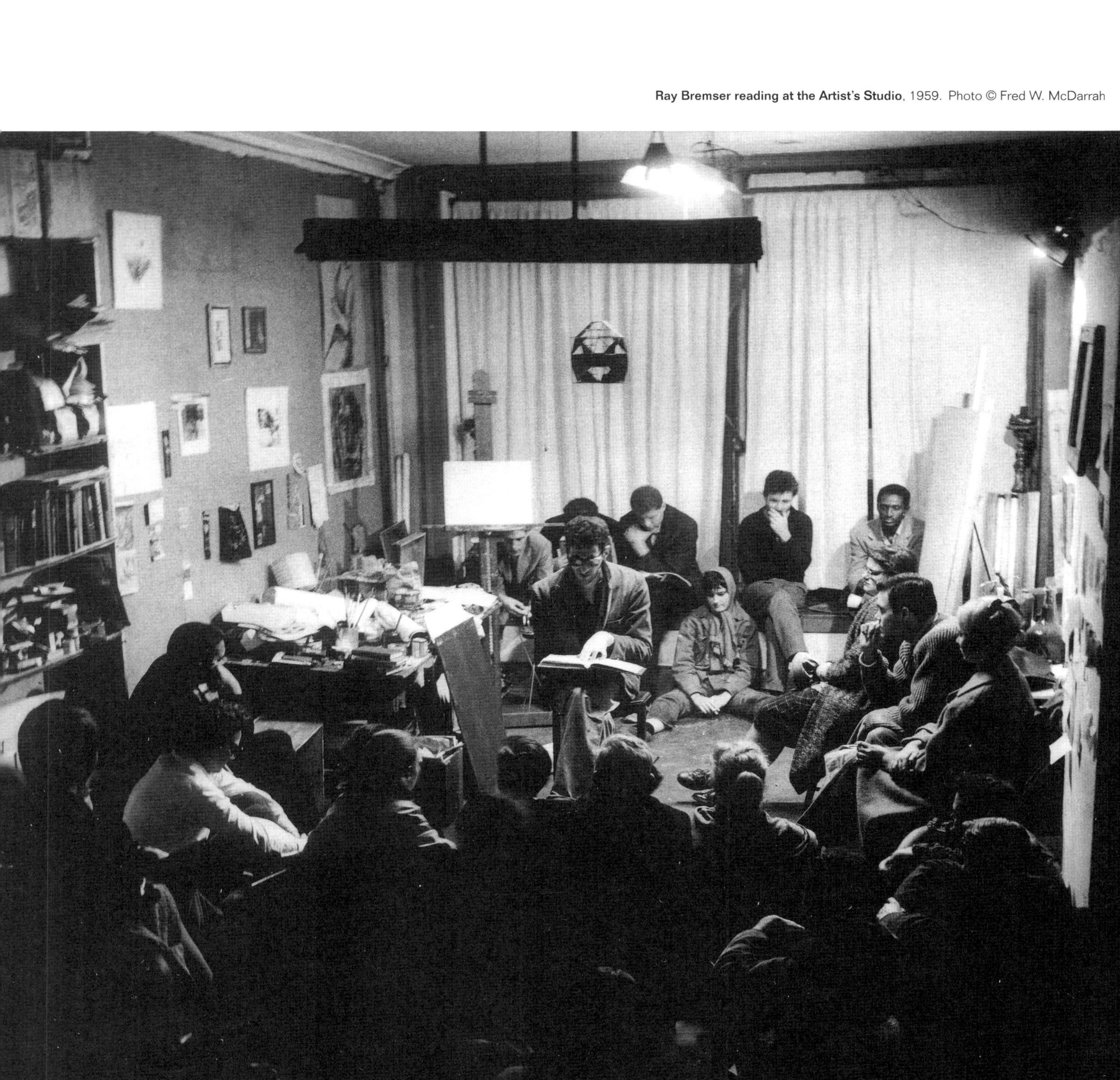

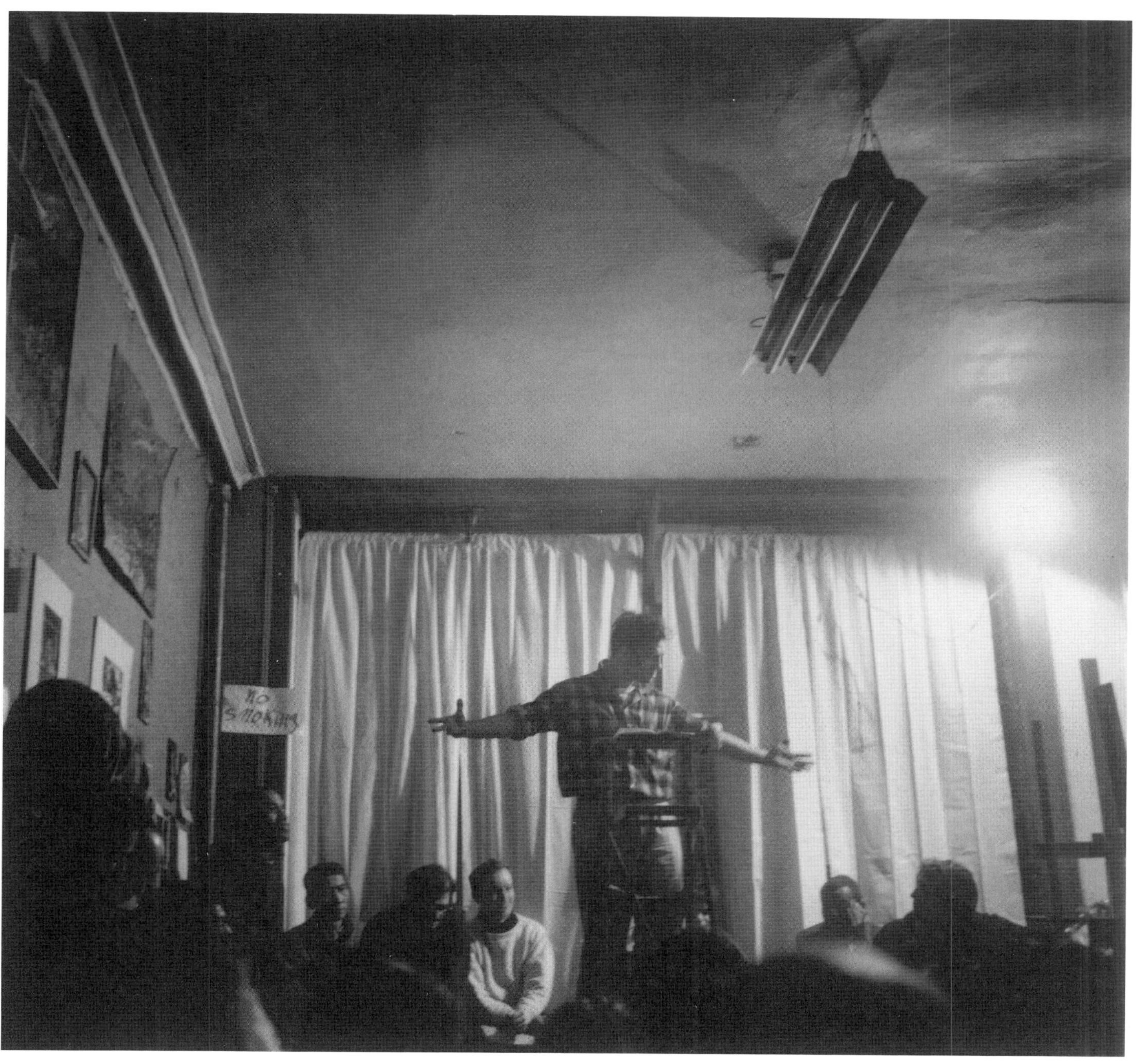

Jack Kerouac at the Artist's Studio, 1959. Photo © Fred W. McDarrah

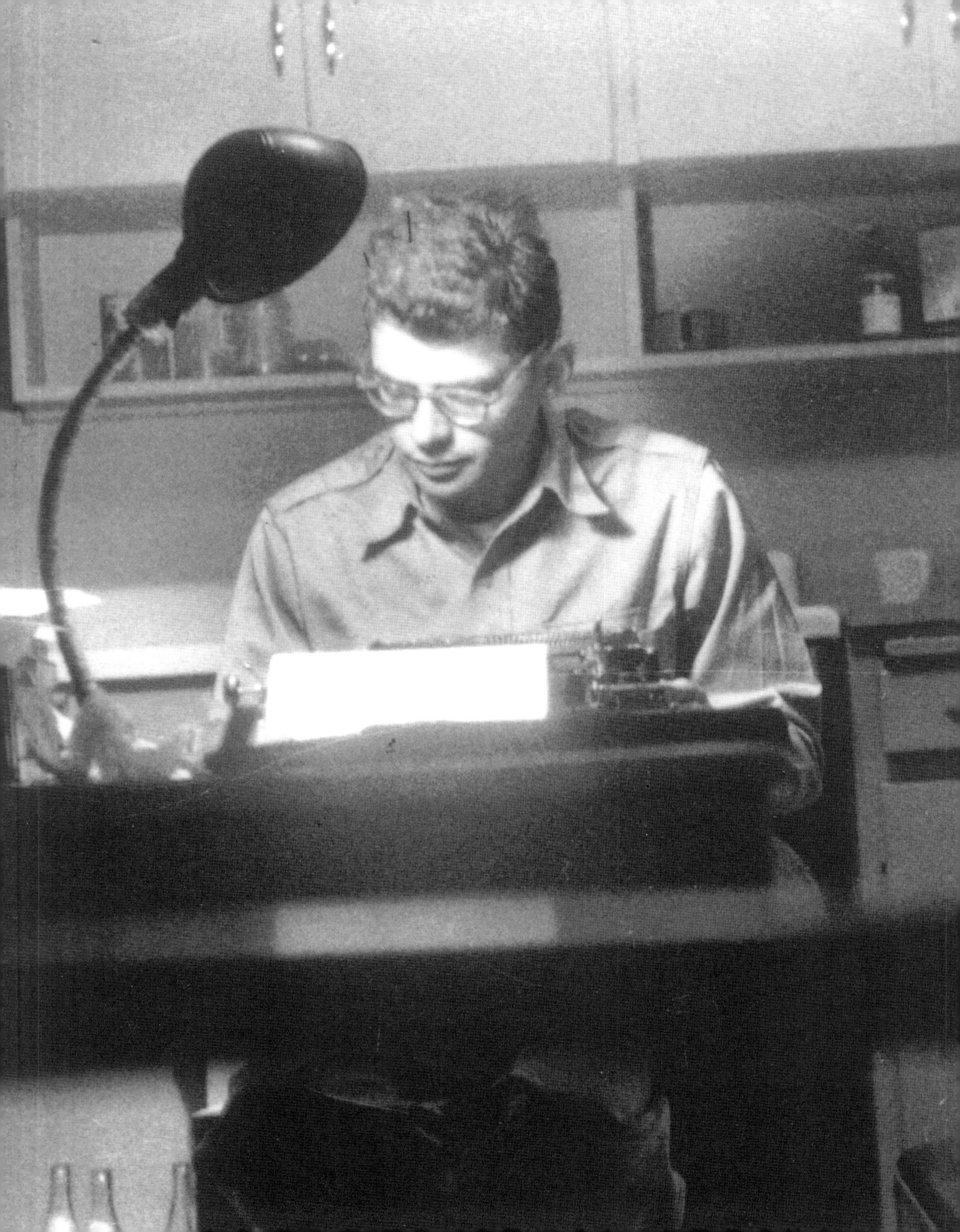

Howl for Carl Solomon

sent by Kerouac to me
Aug. 30, 1955
JCH

I saw the best minds of my generation
generation destroyed by madness
starving, mystical, naked,
who dragged themselves thru the angry streets at
dawn looking for a negro fix
who poverty and tatters and fantastic minds
sat up all night in lofts
contemplating jazz,
who bared their brains to heaven under the El
and saw Mohammedan angels staggering
on tenement roofs illuminated,
who sat in rooms naked and unshaven
listening to the Terror through the wall,
who burned their money in wastebaskets
amid the rubbish of unread Bronx manifestos,
who got busted in their beards returning
through the border with a belt
of marihuana for New York,
who loned it through the streets of Idaho
seeking visionary indian angels
who were visionary indian angels,
who passed through universities
with radiant cool eyes hallucinating
~~anarchy~~ & Blake-light tragedy
among the post-war ~~cynical~~ scholars,
who burned in the hells of ~~poetry~~
whose apartments flared up in the joyous fires
of their heavenly brains,
who purgatoried their bodies night after night
with dreams, with drugs, with waking nightmeares,
alchohol and cock and endless balls,
Peyotl solidities of the halls, backyard cemetary mornings,
wine drunkeness over the rooftops, teahed red light
districts, sun and moon and tree vibrations
in the roaring ~~dusks of winter~~
winter dusks of Brooklyn,
who chained themselves to subways for an endless ride
~~thru~~ from Battery to holy Bronx until the noise
of wheels and children brought them down
~~trembling~~ wide eyed on Benzadrine shuddering
mouth-racked and brilliant brained
in the drear light of Zoo,
who mopped all night in desolate Bickfords
listening to the crack of doom
on the hydrogen jukebox,
who talked continuously seventy hours from park
to pad to bar to Bellevue to museum
to Long Island to
the Brooklyn Bridge, a lost batallion of platonic
conversationalists jumping down the stoops
vomiting out their facts and anecdotes
memories and eyeball kicks and shocks
of hospitals and jails and wars,
who vanished into ~~the Jerseys of~~ the New Jersies of amnesia
posting cryptic picture postcards
of Belmar City Hall and last years sharks,
~~who~~ suffered sweats and bone grindings and migraines
of junk-witdrawel in Newark's bleak frnisjed room,

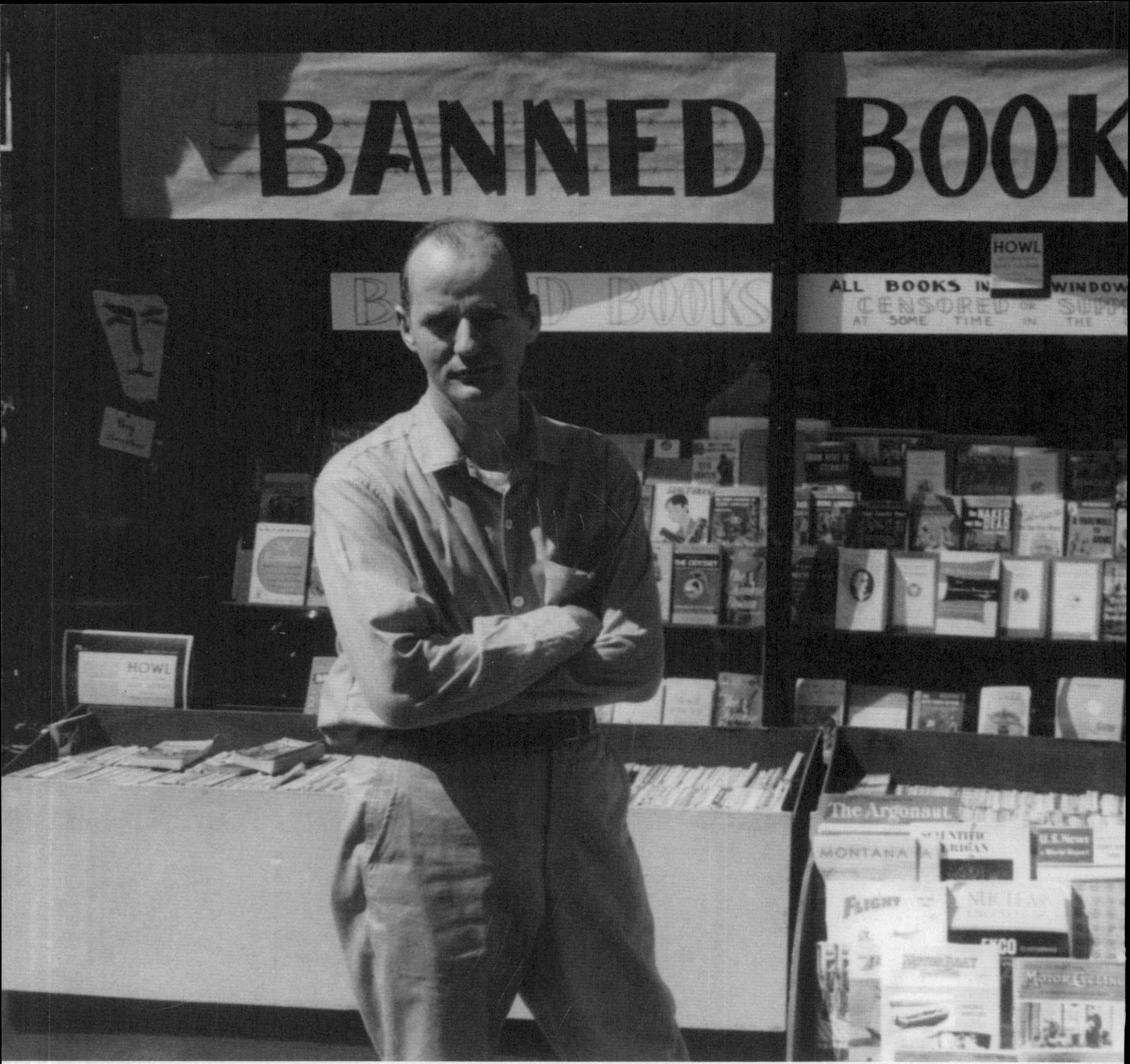

Previous page, left: **Ginsberg typing "Howl," Turner Terrace kitchen table,** 1956 (detail). Photo by Allen Ginsberg;
Right: Allen Ginsberg, **"Howl,"** original manuscript, typescript on paper, 11 x 8 1/2 (27.9 x 21.6). Stanford University Libraries, California

Above: Lawrence Ferlinghetti in front of City Lights Bookstore, San Francisco, 1957. Photo by Harry Redl

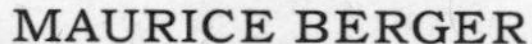

MAURICE BERGER

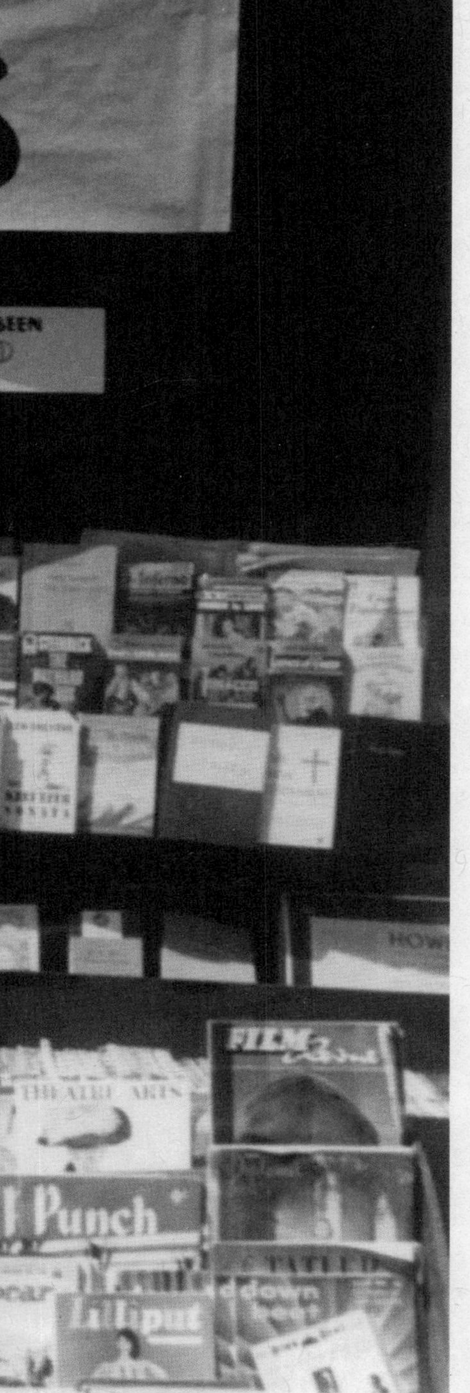

Libraries Full of Tears: The Beats and the Law

America when will you be angelic?
When will you take off your clothes?
When will you look at yourself through the grave?
When will you be worthy of your million Trotskyites?
America why are your libraries full of tears?

Allen Ginsberg, "America," from *Howl and Other Poems* (1956)

At the risk of sounding melodramatic, one could argue that our present-day culture wars actually began on May 21, 1957. For it was on that day that two plainclothes police officers entered the City Lights Bookstore in San Francisco and declared war on a brilliant, albeit marginal, homosexual poet whose only offense was to speak out against what he believed was the repressiveness of American society. The story has been recast many times in recent years: cultural figure creates work that is sexually explicit, homoerotic, and/or outspoken and incurs the wrath of moralizing, right-wing zealots. The central character in this primal scene of cultural repression was Allen Ginsberg; the alleged crime was the publication and sale of his first book, *Howl and Other Poems.*

Lawrence Ferlinghetti, the publisher of *Howl* and owner of City Lights who was arrested along with store clerk Shigeyoshi Murao, had anticipated that the book's four-letter words and references to gay sex and drugs might catch the eye of censors. He submitted the manuscript to the American Civil Liberties Union. He also reluctantly agreed to a demand by his printer that several words in the text be replaced with asterisks. The city's law enforcement community, however, would not be appeased. In March 1957, 520 copies were seized by the San Francisco office of the US Customs, an action that was reversed only after the Washington, DC, office, aware that many intellectuals and artists across the country were outraged, recommended that the case be dropped. Within a few months, perhaps with the intention of compensating for the failure of earlier attempts to suppress the book, the municipal police department moved in on the City Lights Bookstore.[1]

The much-publicized trial of Murao and Ferlinghetti in the summer of 1957 set off a collision of legal and literary forces in a "dreadful mismatch."[2] Assistant district attorney Ralph McIntosh, a hard-line censorship advocate, moralized about Ginsberg's references to homosexuality and the use of such words as "cock," "fuck," and "balls," while the experienced ACLU defense team, headed by noted criminal lawyer Jack Ehrlich, produced an impressive barrage of testimony and letters affirming the social and literary merits of the work. On October 3, 1957, Judge W. J. Clayton Horn, a conservative jurist known for his Sunday school Bible classes, found Ferlinghetti not guilty. (Charges against Murao had earlier been dismissed on the grounds that as an employee he might not have known the actual contents of the book he sold to undercover cops.) Echoing the logic of *Roth* v. *United States*, a landmark obscenity decision handed down four months earlier by the US Supreme Court, Horn concluded that unless "the book [was] entirely lacking 'in social importance' it [could] not be held obscene."[3] In effect, the judge found that while Ginsberg's message was neither entirely convincing nor civil, it was a legitimate expression of social protest that merited constitutional protection.[4]

While Judge Horn's decision underscored the degree to which the legal definition of obscenity was narrowing by the late 1950s, the thorny question of what constituted obscene speech remained unsettled.[5] Within the next decade a number of prominent personalities of the Beat generation found themselves entangled in battles to protect their work from suppression. Despite a series of landmark anti-censorship rulings by the Supreme Court in the mid-1960s, the threat against freedom of cultural expression in the United States exists to this day. Thirty years after the last of these trials, religious fundamentalists and conservative politicians continue to call for the suppression of artists and their supporters. For this reason, there are a number of lessons to be learned from reexamining the persecution of Beat culture—lessons that proffer great insight into the how, and more important, the why of our own present-day reign of repression.

As recent history suggests, the imperative to declare representations obscene and thus illegal inevitably stirs up a torrent of political danger. Well beyond the desire to eliminate offending words and images, these repressive campaigns have easily veered into the realm of ideological manipulation.[6] Ambitious public officials and zealous religious leaders, searching for scapegoats to offer a public angry and frustrated about difficult social and moral problems, have argued that radical or provocative art is "immoral," "obscene," or "blasphemous," that it threatens deeply held political and religious values. This moralistic targeting of words and images can be an effective, even devastating means of social manipulation and control. In selecting particularly provocative depictions that are highly disturbing to conservative elements of the community and whose controversial or elitist nature makes them difficult for their supporters to defend, manipulative politicians and religious leaders have been reasonably successful in gaining public support for repressive actions that might otherwise be seen as questionable or unconstitutional. Even if the First Amendment prevails and efforts at prosecution fail (as is often the case), the resultant chill effect can stifle dissent. In the end, writers, artists, and performers and the institutions that represent them will often turn to self-censorship rather than risk the possibility of public humiliation or bankruptcy.

The Beats' representation of homosexuality, bisexuality, and interracial liaisons, their

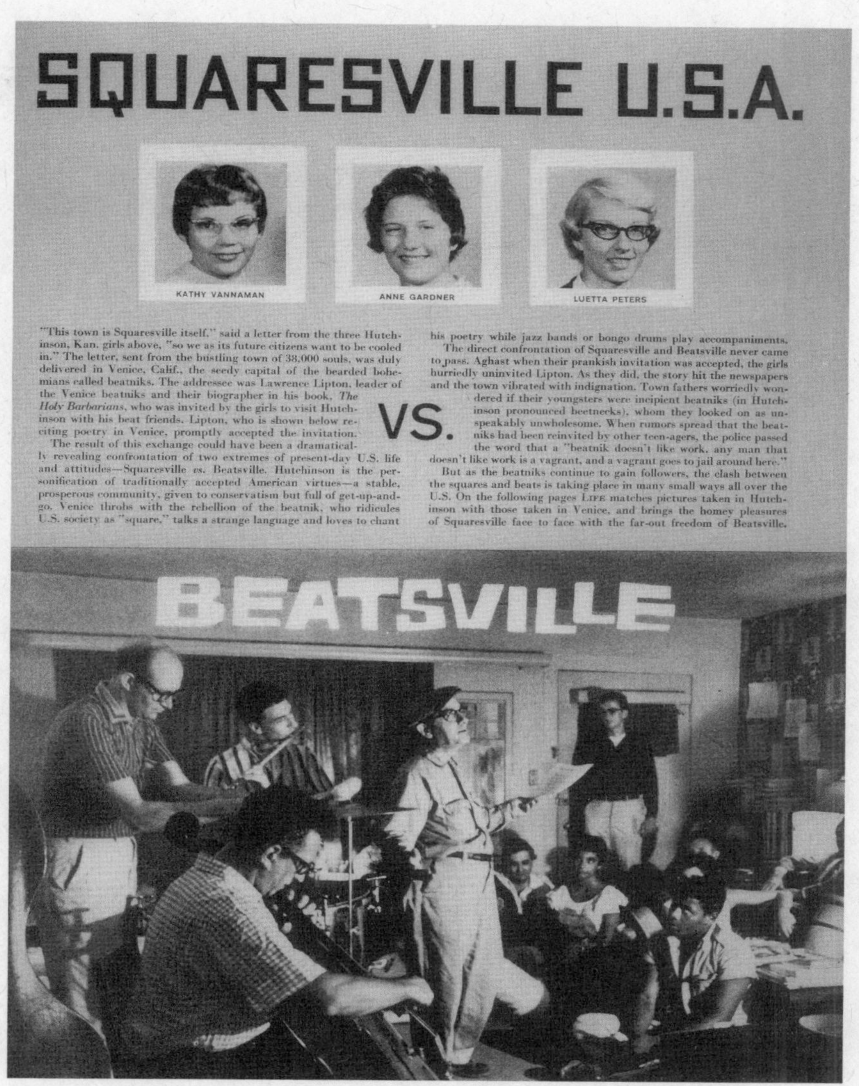

SQUARESVILLE U.S.A.

KATHY VANNAMAN

ANNE GARDNER

LUETTA PETERS

"This town is Squaresville itself," said a letter from the three Hutchinson, Kan. girls above, "so we as its future citizens want to be cooled in." The letter, sent from the bustling town of 38,000 souls, was duly delivered in Venice, Calif., the seedy capital of the bearded bohemians called beatniks. The addressee was Lawrence Lipton, leader of the Venice beatniks and their biographer in his book, *The Holy Barbarians*, who was invited by the girls to visit Hutchinson with his beat friends. Lipton, who is shown below reciting poetry in Venice, promptly accepted the invitation.

The result of this exchange could have been a dramatically revealing confrontation of two extremes of present-day U.S. life and attitudes—Squaresville *vs.* Beatsville. Hutchinson is the personification of traditionally accepted American virtues—a stable, prosperous community, given to conservatism but full of get-up-and-go. Venice throbs with the rebellion of the beatnik, who ridicules U.S. society as "square," talks a strange language and loves to chant his poetry while jazz bands or bongo drums play accompaniments.

VS.

The direct confrontation of Squaresville and Beatsville never came to pass. Aghast when their prankish invitation was accepted, the girls hurriedly uninvited Lipton. As they did, the story hit the newspapers and the town vibrated with indignation. Town fathers worriedly wondered if their youngsters were incipient beatniks (in Hutchinson pronounced beetnecks), whom they looked on as unspeakably unwholesome. When rumors spread that the beatniks had been reinvited by other teen-agers, the police passed the word that a "beatnik doesn't like work, any man that doesn't like work is a vagrant, and a vagrant goes to jail around here."

But as the beatniks continue to gain followers, the clash between the squares and beats is taking place in many small ways all over the U.S. On the following pages LIFE matches pictures taken in Hutchinson with those taken in Venice, and brings the homey pleasures of Squaresville face to face with the far-out freedom of Beatsville.

BEATSVILLE

advocacy of free sex and drugs, and their expressed desire to test the limits of cultural acceptability made them as vulnerable to censorship as any artists of this century. Despite their marginal status, the Beats were constantly the focus of newspaper and magazine articles, radio and television shows, and other mass-media outlets. Their odd manner of dress, stream-of-consciousness rants, and general nonconformity made them fair game for any number of sycophants, satirists, and paranoid cold warriors. The widely reported Beat prosecutions also paralleled and contributed to the gradual liberalization of moral and sexual attitudes then taking place, during a period when district attorneys regularly prosecuted *Playboy* magazine and young innocents could still be scandalized by the sight of Elvis' gyrating hips.[7]

The polarization between the "Beats" and "straights" that occurred in public discussion, as historian Richard Cándida Smith observes, "ritually enacted interior conflicts over the limits of freedom"—an artificial dichotomy between hedonism and chastity promoted by both sides through reductive symbols and stereotypes.[8] In September 1959, for example, *Life* published a photo-essay comparing two "extremes" of American society: the God-fearing citizens of Hutchinson, Kansas, and the "seedy" beatniks of Venice, California.[9] The piece centered around Lawrence Lipton, leader of the Venice Beat community, and the three bored adolescent girls from "squaresville" who invited him and his friends to teach them about the beatnik who

Life, September 21, 1959. Bottom photo by Allan Grant, *Life* ©Time Inc., reprinted with permission.

"throbs with rebellion...ridicules U.S. society...and talks a strange language."[10] The meeting was canceled after the girls were publicly admonished by community leaders for their thoughtless invitation and a police spokesman hinted that the Beats might be arrested for vagrancy if they showed up in Hutchinson. The contrasting shots of clean-as-a-whistle, God-fearing Americans and scruffy, work-fearing beatniks were accompanied by a text that predicted, somewhat ominously, that Beat communities would soon rise across the United States. "We know Beatniks aren't good," teenager Luetta Peters ruefully acknowledged of the lesson she had learned, "but we thought they just dressed sloppy and talked funny. Now we know that they get married without licenses and things like that."[11]

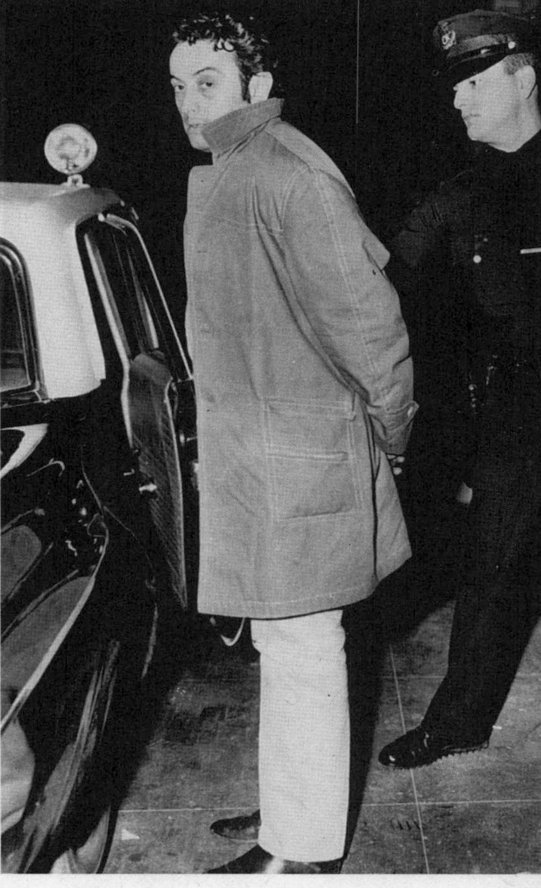

Not surprisingly, the young Miss Peters and her brave protectors pointed to alleged or imagined instances of criminality to justify their disdain for the Beats. Indeed, district attorneys, politicians, clerics, and even prominent intellectuals worked hard to associate Beat culture with criminality. "The spirit of the beat generation," wrote the literary critic Norman Podhoretz, "strikes me as the same spirit which animates the young savages in their leather jackets who have been running amuck in the last few years with switch-blades and zip guns....[I] believe that juvenile crime can be explained partly in terms of the same resentment against normal feeling and the attempt to cope with the world through intelligence that lies behind Kerouac and Ginsberg."[12] When Beat behavior transgressed the threshold of the patently felonious—for example, Lenny Bruce's arrests for narcotics possession in the early 1960s—such associations were even easier to turn into generalizations. Nevertheless, Podhoretz's vague equation between Beat hipsterism and juvenile delinquency became one of the most durable stereotypes of the entire Beat generation.

For the most part, however, law enforcement officials bent on harassing the Beats had little choice but to resort to obscenity charges. Their zeal was often relentless: Barney Rosset, publisher of Grove Press, for example, had to sell off property in order to afford the exorbitant legal fees necessary to defend several of his books in scores of prosecutions, including Henry Miller's *Tropic of Cancer* and *Tropic of Capricorn* and William Burroughs' *Naked Lunch*. In New York City, small Off Broadway theaters, movie houses, and coffeehouses periodically found their licenses revoked or suspended. One institution in particular, the Living Theater, and its directors Julian Beck and Judith Malina, were repeatedly harassed by federal agents. And in San Francisco and Berkeley in the mid-1960s, productions of Michael McClure's play *The Beard*—a lustful and passionate confrontation between two icons of American popular culture, Billy the Kid and Jean Harlow, which culminated in an explicit recreation of heterosexual cunnilingus—were continually hounded by police and prosecutors: over a period of three years, both McClure and the cast were arrested more than twenty times on pornography charges, including arrests on nineteen consecutive nights during the show's Los Angeles run.[13]

The psychological and financial effects of these repeated prosecutions were often devastating. During a twenty-year career in which he challenged what he felt was the hypocrisy of organized religion and other political and social institutions, Lenny Bruce was arrested nearly twenty times on obscenity charges.[14] The rigors of these arrests and prosecutions and the devastating publicity and canceled performances that followed ultimately destroyed Bruce's career. Once able to command more than $3,500 per week, the demoralized comedian was forced to declare bankruptcy in October 1965. Less than a year later, he would die of a morphine overdose at the age of forty.

Lenny Bruce arrested on narcotics charge, 1963

Wallace Berman, too, was shattered after his arrest and conviction in 1957 for exhibiting "pornographic" work at the Ferus Gallery in Los Angeles. After receiving several complaints about Berman's exhibition—a group of three, mixed-media assemblages replete with mystical symbols, Latin and Hebrew inscriptions, and photographs and drawings of genitalia and heterosexual intercourse—the LA vice squad telephoned the gallery and offered the artist the option of removing the offending work. Berman was defiant. So foreign was his art to the arresting officers that they had trouble determining what, in the end, was even obscene. Trial judge Kenneth Halliday, who had earlier found Henry Miller guilty of obscenity, refused a defense motion to present testimony affirming the work's artistic merits, remarking that "we have no need to have an expert tell us what is pornographic."[15] During the trial and its aftermath, Berman received little public support. Judge Halliday's guilty verdict left the artist depressed and unable to leave his studio for weeks. He retreated further into a "highly personal, hermetic language, arcane even to those who knew him"—although the trial itself may not have been the sole cause of this evolution in his sensibility.[16] As critic John Coplans surmised in 1963, Berman had learned a new and complex means of survival: the construction of a vision so internal that it would confuse even the most zealous censor.[17]

These narratives of suppression tell another, more revealing story about the deep and abiding anxieties provoked by radical culture in the fifties and early sixties. American attitudes toward unconventional styles and behavior were, of course, more complex than cold war stereotypes might suggest: a national survey on conformity conducted in 1953, for example, reported that participants ranked academics, writers, and artists higher than business leaders or politicians in social stature because of the "assumed propensity of intellectuals to question things most people took for granted."[18] Even public opinion on obscenity was less than intransigent: in a controversial and much publicized campaign that centered on the issue of obscenity, Justice Horace W. Wilkie of the Wisconsin Supreme Court was reelected in 1964 after his opponent bitterly and continually attacked his earlier, tie-breaking vote to free Henry Miller's *Tropic of Cancer* for sale in the state. In this contest, which became a referendum on conservative Christian values versus the right to free speech, a slim majority of the voting public sided with Wilkie, agreeing with the idea expressed by a number of newspapers across the state that "we do not want right-wingers...setting themselves up as the arbiters of what we and the rest of Wisconsin can read."[19] By this time, the remnants of an entrenched, mostly straight, white, male status quo, people already in command of the legal apparatus necessary to weed

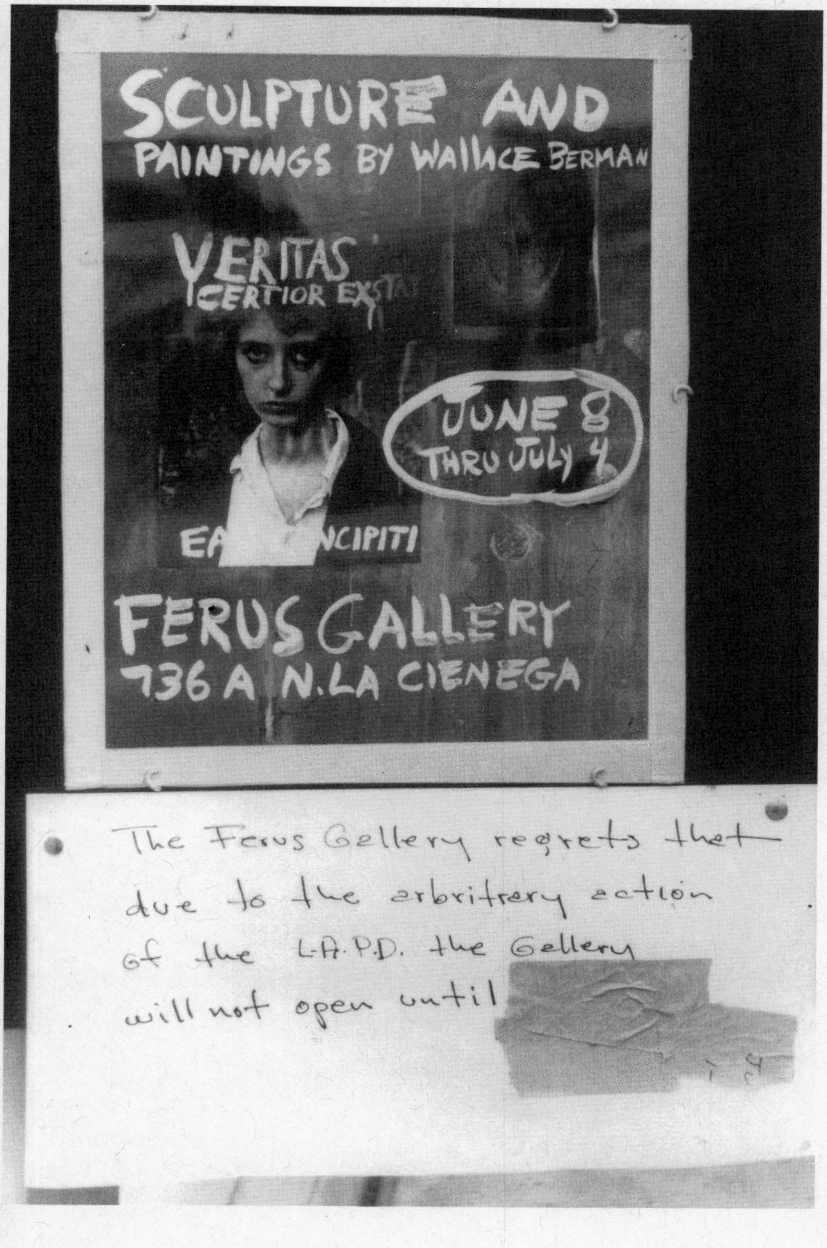

Ferus Gallery notice, 1957. Photo by Charles Brittin

out unwanted words and images, could not shake a deeper, unspoken fear: that the power to control the sensibility and limits of culture was slipping from their grasp.

Cold war America was teaming with cultural watchdogs—members of church committees and parent-teacher associations, Daughters of the American Revolution and American Legionnaires, district attorneys and city councilmen—who prowled the artistic landscape in search of the abnormal, the maladjusted, and the nonconformist. Thus, Congressman George A. Dondero warned of a foreign enemy that wreaked of "all the isms of depravity, decadence and destruction." He continued:

> **Cubism aims to destroy by design disorder. Futurism aims to destroy by a machine myth. Dadaism aims to destroy by ridicule. Expressionism aims to destroy by aping the primitive and insane....Abstractionism aims to destroy by the denial of reason....Abstractionism, or non-objectivity...was spawned as a...Communist product....Who has brought down this curse upon us; who has let into our homeland this horde of germ carrying art vermin?[20]**

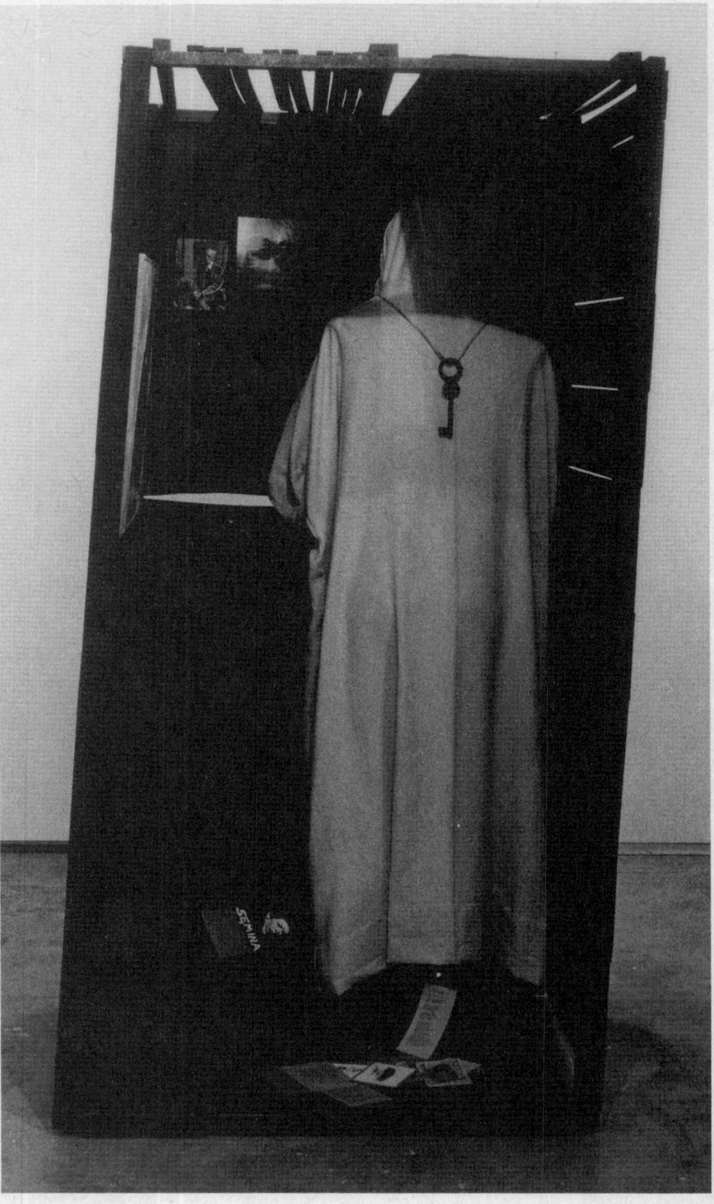

Driven by such paranoid and reactionary logic, rhetoric reminiscent in both tone and content of the Nazi campaigns against "degenerate" art, the legal moralists of the day conscripted the Beats to represent any number of social and cultural ills: to the Massachusetts Supreme Court, they were "brutal, obscene and disgusting."[21] To a judge in Boston, they were fornicators who "portrayed unnatural acts."[22] To the New York Bureau of Narcotics, they were drug pushers.[23] To J. Edgar Hoover, they were violent enemies who had to be reformed, reined in, set straight.[24] Thus it is not surprising that upon Ginsberg's release from Columbia Presbyterian Psychiatric Institute in 1950, where he had been hospitalized for eight months for depression, he was encouraged to "try harder to conform to American norms...[to] go straight, get a job, get married."[25]

Wallace Berman's "Temple" at Ferus Gallery, 1957. Photo by Charles Brittin

Of all the crimes against nature and God, homosexuality was perhaps the most egregious. The homophobia of the 1950s, like the pervasive homophobia of today, often served as a useful tool for discrediting the cultural enemies of the day. Although homosexual sex, through a multitude of local sodomy laws, was (and frequently still is) illegal in many states, obscenity prosecutions against the Beats were not about acts but representations. Yet the innate association between criminality and homosexuality was often used to cast doubt on any words or images that represented gay sexual behavior. It is for this reason that prosecutors in the trials of Burroughs, Bruce, Ginsberg, and others strategically cited passages on gay fellatio and anal sodomy in court in order to prove that the work in question was illegal and dangerous.

Anti-gay hatred was so insidious that even offending artists who weren't homosexual were transformed by censors into handmaidens of the gay conspiracy. When Michael McClure and the cast of *The Beard* were arrested in San Francisco in 1966, for example, the district attorney's office charged them, among other things, with lewd and dissolute conduct in a public place, the

Wallace Berman's "Factum Fidei" at Ferus Gallery, 1957. Photo by Charles Brittin

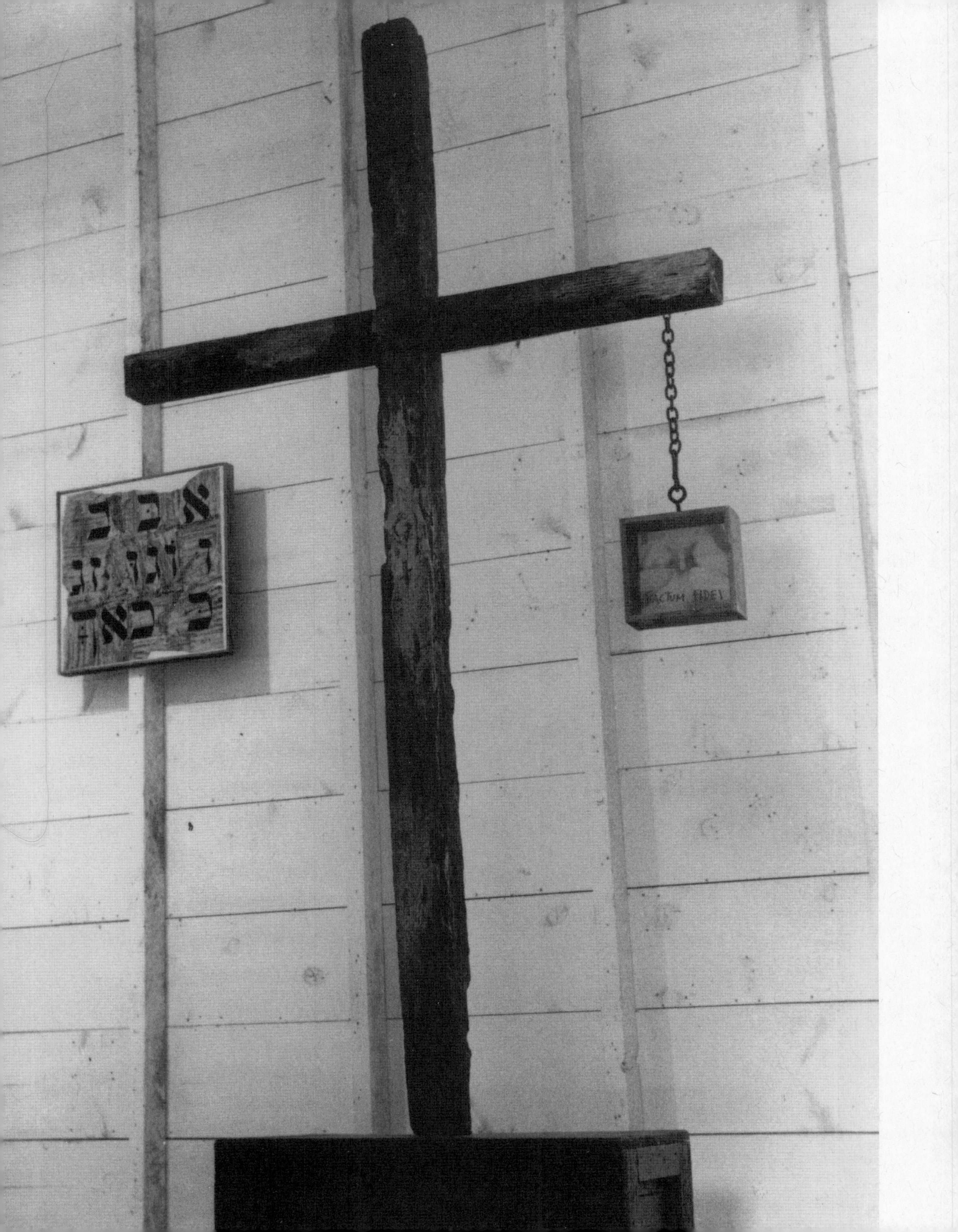
ACTUM FIDEI

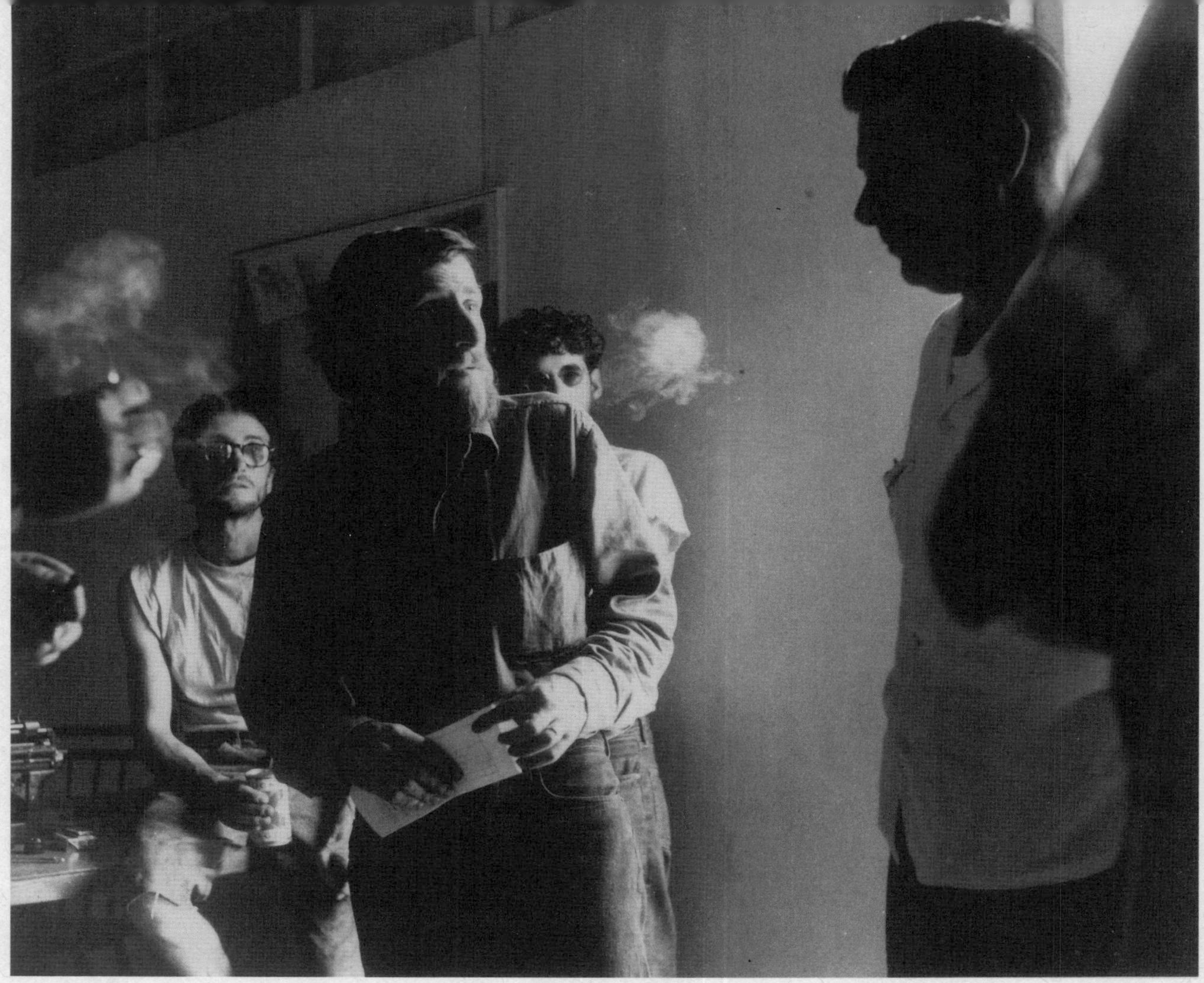

"charge most frequently used against homosexuals arrested in men's rooms."[26] Lenny Bruce recounted that during his first obscenity arrest, over the use of the word "cocksucker," the police officer reminded him that the word signified a "favorite homosexual practice" and was against the law to say in public. During the March 1962 trial in San Francisco, Bruce's attorney, Albert Bendich, attempting to prove that community standards already sanctioned a gay and even homoerotic presence, asked the officer about other clubs he patrolled in the neighborhood. While Bruce had never performed in Finocchio's, a well-known gay hangout, his attorney had the officer describe the club's ever-present coterie of scantily clad transvestites. In effect, Bendich understood the underlying juridical subtext, one that fought hard to equate criminal depravity with homosexuality; he successfully fought back by reminding the court that while some communities would prefer to banish homosexuals, others welcomed them with open arms.[27]

Perhaps the most tragic aspect of the crusade against gays, and the greatest testament to the power of the censor to do considerable political and psychic damage, was the extent to which homophobia was internalized by artists under fire. In a number of instances, prosecutors were able to coax defendants and their witnesses into conceding that homosexuality was in some way immoral or unhealthy. Ginsberg, testifying at the trial of *Naked Lunch* in Boston Superior Court in 1963, for example, attempted to appease prosecutors by citing several examples of how he felt Burroughs exposed the homosexual tendency "to control other people," an impulse he later analogized to Nazism.[28] Similarly, in the *Howl* trial, the chief defense witness observed that

Wallace Berman with Los Angeles sheriff at Ferus Gallery, 1957. Photo by Charles Brittin

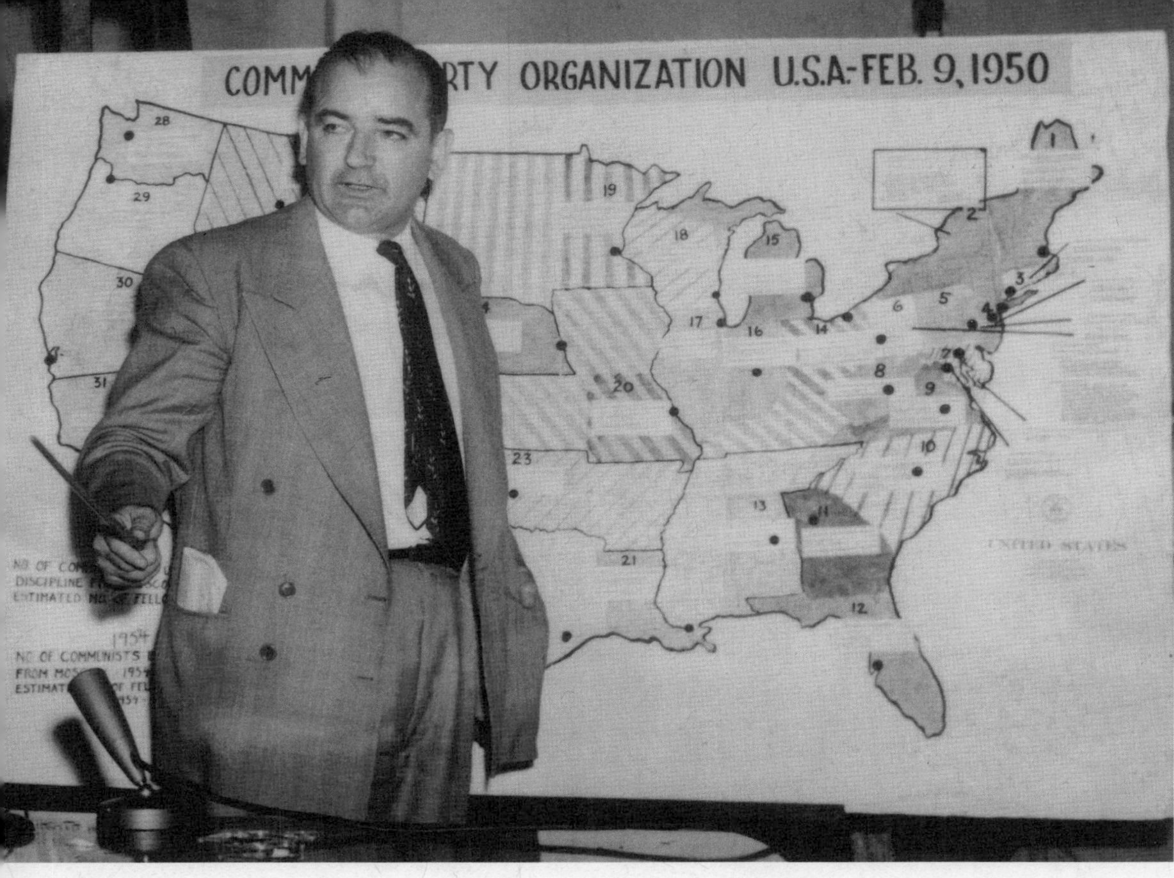

Ginsberg's references to homosexuality indicated a "corrupt sexual act" that contributed to the "picture which the author is trying to give us of modern life as a state of hell."[29]

The ideological need to rid society of gay and lesbian imagery is, in part, motivated by an awareness that these representations, continually announcing, and hence to some extent regularizing, the homosexual presence, are important forces for cultural and political enfranchisement.[30] As anthropologist Carole Vance observes:

> **Diversity in images and expression in the public sector nurtures and sustains diversity in private life. When losses are suffered in public arenas, people for whom controversial or minority images are salient and affirming suffer a real defeat. Defending private rights—to behavior, to images, to information—is difficult without a publicly formed and visible community. People deprived of images become demoralized and isolated, and they become increasingly vulnerable to attacks on their private expression of nonconformity, which are inevitable once sources of public solidarity and resistance have been eliminated.[31]**

That people deprived of this access to self-representation and self-expression become demoralized and isolated, an observation borne out by some of the stories of Beat artists under fire, points to the terroristic power of censorship. The censor, wanting to engender a chilling cultural climate that literally scares artists into submission, exercises immense political power by attempting to forcibly take away the voices of the targets—a reality eloquently challenged by Berman who, after Judge Halliday's guilty verdict was read, mutely walked over to the courtroom blackboard and scrawled the words "There is no justice. There is just revenge."[32]

When it comes to gay men and lesbians and other contested minority groups, it may be muteness (denying the power to represent) rather than physical repression (preventing the act itself) that is the goal of the censor. There is a kind of parallelism between the desire to censor and the need to deny oppressed peoples a voice. The courts have usually interpreted open (i.e.,

Senator Joseph R. McCarthy, 1950

voiced) homosexuality, for example, as dangerous to society's well-being; only when it is closeted (i.e., unspoken) does it have a reasonable chance of falling within the boundaries of legality.[33] The legal permission to proclaim materials "obscene" is also built on the desire to render them speechless, to drive them into a kind of juridical closet. Thus, there is a fine line between the authorized, official power to regulate "obscene" materials and the extralegal power to coerce people into hiding their ideas, their emotions, and even their personal identities.[34]

The idea that censorship often goes hand in hand with an underlying desire to deny minority peoples a voice is underscored by another anxiety about the Beats: their proximity to African-American culture. If the denial of homosexual rights was one of the most overtly stated desires of the Beat censor, the fear of African-American power and of the burgeoning civil rights movement was perhaps the most hidden and unconscious. Unlike homosexuality, drugs, or "obscene" or pornographic representations, being black in the United States in the 1950s was not a crime, despite the vicious realities of segregation and racism. Even miscegenation, an issue strangely central to the Beat ethos, was no longer illegal in most states. Anxieties about race were therefore rarely ever part of obscenity prosecutions; instead, they lay subtly at the margins and below the surface of much hostility toward the Beats.

African-American jazz, styles, and cultural sensibilities were pervasive in the Beat milieu, associations that contributed to numerous critical misreadings. Norman Mailer, in his widely read essay "The White Negro," saw African-Americans as the positive archetypes for Beat bohemianism and juvenile delinquency, an analogy that was both retrograde and racist.[35] "Blacks supplied the argot," writes Richard Pells of Mailer's reasoning, "the worship of 'abstract states of feeling' (nourished by marijuana), and the knowledge of what it meant to live with perpetual danger. Insofar as the hipster had absorbed the 'existentialist synapses' of the blacks, he was in effect a white Negro....his 'intense view of existence' matched the experience of most adolescents, and reinforced their own 'desire to rebel.'"[36]

Mailer's skewed reasoning, deemed "well intentioned but poisonous" by Ginsberg and rejected by most other Beat artists, nevertheless inflected much of the critical thinking about the movement.[37] Podhoretz, dismissing an interracial love affair in Jack Kerouac's *The Subterraneans* as "one long agony of fear and trembling over sex....very primitive, very spontaneous, very elemental, very beat," concluded that it represented one more example of the Beats' romanticized view of interracial love and friendships.[38] To some degree confusing primary texts with Mailer's romanticized interpretation, Podhoretz complained that while blacks and whites "associate freely on a basis of complete equality and without a trace of racial hostility" in the Beat milieu of social defiance, there is in the end only "adulation for the happy, true-hearted, ecstatic Negroes of America."[39] The Beat's love of blacks, he reasoned, was tied to a fetishization of the primitive rather than any real social commitment to civil rights, a sensibility that represented "an inverted form of keeping the nigger in his place."[40]

On one level, Podhoretz's argument is not entirely unfounded. The scarcity of prominent African-Americans in the Beat movement suggests an appropriative, hierarchical, and sometimes disingenuous relationship to black culture. Often, too, the African-American presence in Beat literature and art signified negative or generalized values that rarely considered the complexity of black culture. The association of the "negro streets" as a haven for drug addicts in the opening lines of "Howl" represents a rather typical example of this phenomenon. Yet Podhoretz strategically misses another level of social meaning: in a period galvanized by fears of the mingling of the races (*Brown* v. *Board of Education I* and *II*, the US Supreme Court's landmark and controversial school desegregation rulings, were handed down in 1954 and 1955, respectively), the Beats were advocating an open, interracial culture. Indeed, the Beat milieu was relatively integrated in contrast to virtually all other white-identified avant-gardist movements in the twentieth century.[41] While African-American music, literature, and art did not need validation from whites (except as a means of entering the cultural mainstream), associations with African-

American culture helped spur the Beat's own, sometimes socially astute attitudes toward race and racism. In an analysis of Burrough's *Naked Lunch* at the Boston trial, for example, Ginsberg maintained that a passage singled out by the court as "grossly offensive" (despite its relatively mild language) was, in fact, a "brilliant and funny" satire of the "monstrous speech and thought processes" of the "anti-Negro...anti-Northern, anti-Semitic...Southern, white racist bureaucrat."[42] Such satires and commentaries appeared in the work of a number of other Beat figures, including Ginsberg, Bruce, and LeRoi Jones—writing that often associated racism with the provincialism, philistinism, hypocrisy, and conformity of American life that the Beats so fervently rejected.[43]

Lenny Bruce, for example, often joined Jewish and black idioms in his act as a means of "symbolizing his rejection of a WASP-controlled society that he considered lacking in honesty, decency, mercy, and morality."[44] Incorporating improvisational techniques, slang, and phrases drawn from black jazz culture (as well as attacking anti-black stereotypes in Hollywood, the anti-Communist indifference to the lack of freedom for blacks in the United States, and de facto segregation in liberal communities), Bruce attempted to bring "Jewish ethical and social values to bear on the black movement for civil rights."[45] But the end of Jim Crow segregation was followed by a particularly virulent conservative backlash. That such associations were threatening to reactionary forces in the United States was confirmed by Ginsberg's investigation in the 1970s of extralegal operations of government agencies designed to undermine dissident groups during the cold war period.[46] "In sum," wrote Ginsberg, "there *was* a vast bureaucratic conspiracy to brainwash the public...separate the generations, project obnoxious images of youth, divide black and white citizens, abort and blackmail...[the] social leadership of black citizens, set blacks on each other, provoke whites to murderous confusion, confound honest media, infiltrate, prevaricate and spy on reformist multitudes, becloud understanding and community, and poison public consciousness."[47] There is no doubt that censorship contributed to these repressive goals; reading between the lines of both popular and juridical texts of the day, one intuits the reactive

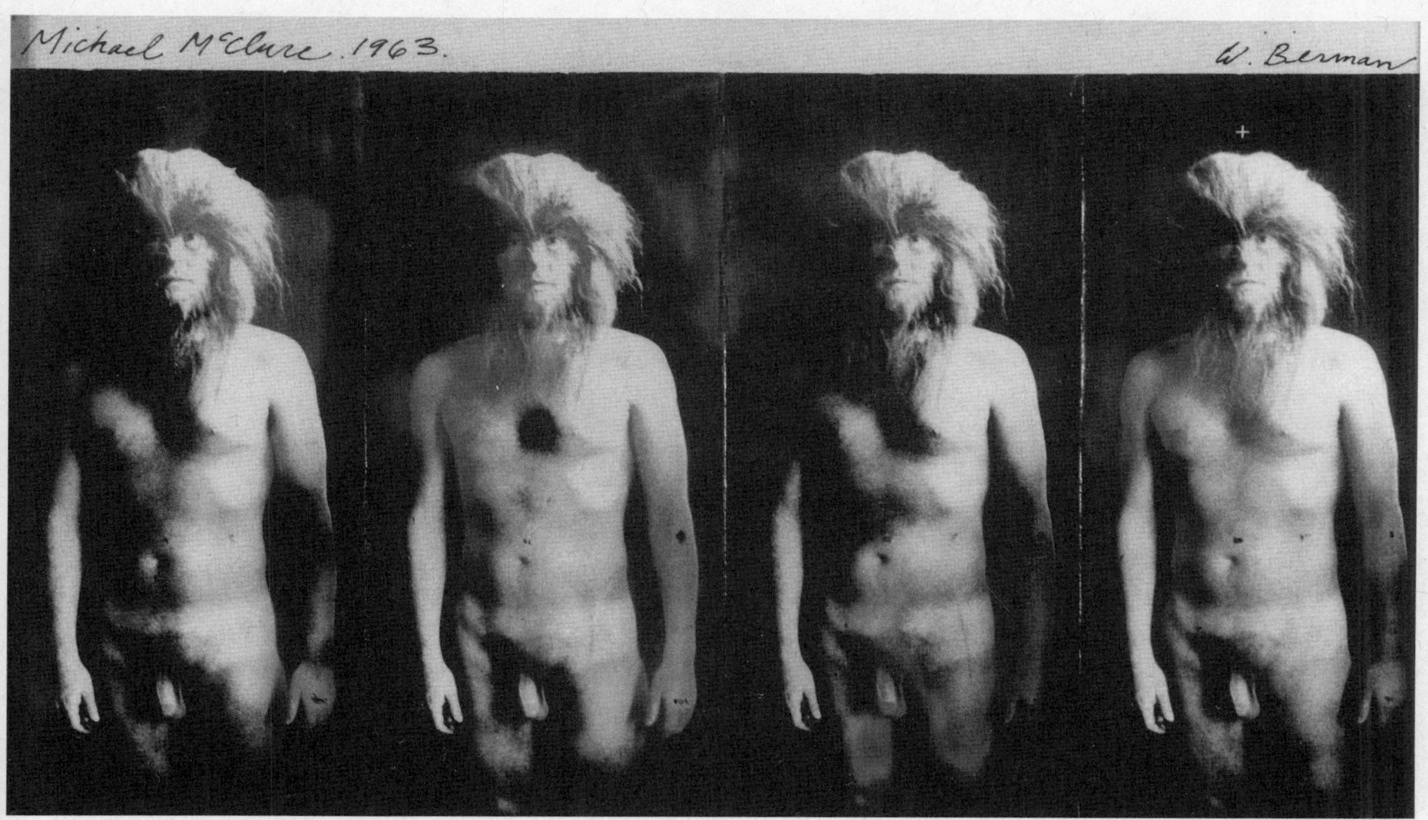

Michael McClure, 1963.
Photo by Wallace Berman

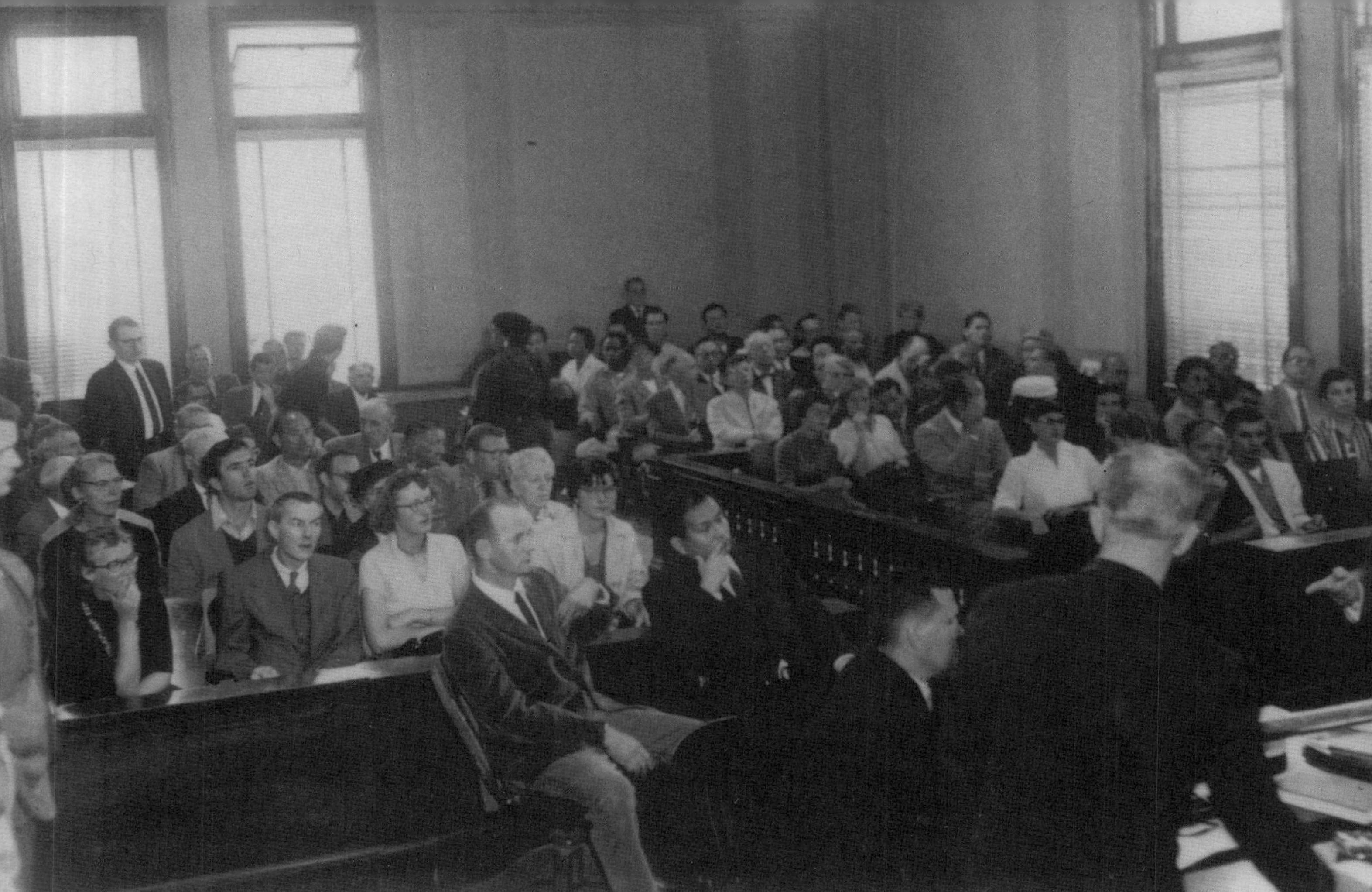

fear of homosexual, black, and erotic bodies then seemingly poised to overtake the power of white, heterosexual, bourgeois men.

Over the past decade, the United States has witnessed a remarkable escalation of censorious actions—aggressive campaigns built on the very apprehensions about homosexuality, race, eroticism, drugs, nonconformity, and the unification of minority voices that fueled the censorship of the Beats forty years ago. Works like filmmaker Marlon Riggs' *Tongues Untied*, a documentary on black, gay men, Andres Serrano's *Piss Christ*, a photograph of a crucifix suspended in urine, performance artist Karen Finley's feminist allegory in which she smeared herself with chocolate, and photographer Robert Mapplethorpe's explicit, homoerotic photographs of African-American men are powerful representations of minority interests expressed through defiant, multiple, and convergent identities. Their direct opposition to the "hegemonic model of straight, white, bourgeois male identity traditionally privileged in Western art history"—has produced a fire storm of vehement, even vitriolic protest.[48]

But as the censorious campaigns of the fifties and early sixties prove, it remains unclear where public opinion actually lies with regard to such issues as "family values," obscenity, or censorship. After Patrick Buchanan proclaimed in a series of articles, speeches, and an address at the 1992 Republican National Convention that America was in the midst of a "cultural war," public opinion polls indicated that he had gone too far in allowing the venomous bigotry of the

Lawrence Ferlinghetti and Shigeyoshi Murao (seated, center) on trial for selling *Howl and Other Poems* at City Lights Bookstore, 1957

far-right to slip out in full view of the nation. Like the crazed Joseph McCarthy at the end of his reign of terror or the hysterical diatribes of Congressman Dondero, one could detect a bit of desperation in Buchanan's sneering screed: "As with our rivers and lakes, we need to clean up our culture: for it is a well from which we all must drink. Just as poisoned land will yield up poison fruits, so a polluted culture, left to fester and stink, can destroy a nation's soul."[49]

If there is one difference between the zealots of the 1950s and contemporary fundamentalists, however, it is that the latter tend to artfully conceal their desire to censor behind an anti-elitist rejection of government funding for the arts. Nevertheless, both hone in on similar issues of sexuality, blasphemy, and obscenity: religious leaders of the Christian right, such as the Rev. Donald Wildmon and his American Family Association, willfully manipulate the public into rechanneling its fears about the Communist menace toward a post-cold war homosexual monster who threatens our children and our moral standing. Hatred for gay men and lesbians consumes conservative social critics—disturbed individuals who, like *Washington Times* writer Richard Grenier, yearn for the moment when they might "set fire to... Mapplethorpe['s body], and not just as a self-expression, but as *performance art*."[50] And others, such as *New Criterion* editor Hilton Kramer, struggle to shore up the cultural status quo against the tide of a presumed multiculturalist erosion of standards and quality.

Within this cultural context, it should not be surprising that more than thirty years after his first confrontation with the law, the radical, outspoken, and openly gay Allen Ginsberg would once again be silenced. In 1988, a reading of "Howl" was bumped off the air, the victim of an Federal Communications Commission regulation intended to ban "indecency" from radio broadcasts. A year later, a still angry Ginsberg wrote to arch-conservative Jesse Helms, protesting the senator's sponsorship of an infamous and draconian "Arts-Control" amendment: "These hypocrite scoundrels have muscled their way into museums already, and plan to extend their own control-addiction to arts councils, humanities programs, universities. How long will Congress, the Public & Arts be held hostage to this cultural Mafia?"[51] If the events of the past forty years are any indication, it may well be that we will always be cultural hostages. For when it comes to the suppression of artistic words and images, there is a tragic propensity for history to repeat itself, the howl of the censor growing louder and more menacing with each assault.

Notes

1 For more on these events, see J.W. Ehrlich, ed., *Howl of the Censor: The Four Letter Word on Trial* (San Carlos, California: Nourse, 1961); Lawrence Ferlinghetti, "Horn on HOWL," *Evergreen Review*, 4 (1957), pp. 145-58; J.G. Fuller, "Trade Winds: Ginsberg Trial," *Saturday Review*, 40 (October 5, 1957), pp. 5-7; and Michael Schumacher, *Dharma Lion: A Critical Biography of Allen Ginsberg* (New York: St. Martin's Press, 1992), pp. 254-55.

2 Schumacher, *Dharma Lion*, p. 260.

3 Horn, as quoted in Edward de Grazia, *Girls Lean Back Everywhere: The Law of Obscenity and the Assault on Genius* (New York: Random House, 1992), p. 337. Associate Justice William Brennan, writing in *Roth*, reasoned that sex, rather than "utterly without redeeming social importance," has "indisputably been a subject of absorbing interest to mankind throughout the ages." Although the Supreme Court ruled that obscenity per se was not protected by the Constitution, it nevertheless attempted to decide what constituted obscenity. As such, it offered a test based on whether the "average person, applying contemporary standards, [would conclude that] the dominant theme of the material taken as a whole appeals to prurient interests." The Court's muddled reasoning—notions of the average person or prurience are always variable and subjective—may have been intentional. By keeping such definitions hazy, the Court left room for juries and judges to protect sexual representations tied to social or cultural content. For more on the case, see Albert B. Gerber, *Sex, Pornography, and Justice* (New York: Lyle Stuart, 1965), pp. 125-33, and Marjorie Heins, *Sex, Sin, and Blasphemy: A Guide to America's Censorship Wars* (New York: The New Press, 1993), pp. 20-21, 30.

4 Horn concluded: "The answer is that life is not encased in one formula whereby everyone acts the same or conforms to a particular pattern....An author should be real in treating his subject and be allowed to express his thoughts and ideas in his own words"; quoted in De Grazia, *Girls Lean Back Everywhere*, p. 338.

5 While the wording of the First Amendment—"Congress shall make no law...abridging the freedom of speech"—would appear to suggest an absolute right to free speech, certain exceptions have always been sanctioned by society and the courts: libel, slander, threats, extortion, perjury, fraud, "fighting words," and, at least since the mid-nineteenth century, "obscenity." For the juridical and societal constructions of obscenity and censorship, see Heins, *Sex, Sin, and Blasphemy*, pp. 1-14.

6 Recently, the concept of what is censorious has grown even more complicated. Advocates of minority groups, for example, arguing that bigoted words and images can wound and endanger already vulnerable minds, have recently called for codes against hate speech. And some feminists, theorizing that degrading images of women can engender misogynist or sexually violent behavior in men, have supported more stringent anti-pornography laws.

7 Through radio and television interviews and trial reports in major newspapers and national magazines—including *Life*, *Saturday Review*, *The Nation*, *New Republic*, and *Newsweek* —the *Howl* prosecution attained national media standing. Ironically, Ferlinghetti's legal problems boosted sales. By the end of the trial, the book was in its fourth printing, and thousands of mimeographed copies were also in circulation.

8 Richard Cándida Smith, *Utopia and Dissent: Art, Poetry, and Politics in California* (Berkeley and Los Angeles: University of California Press, 1995), p. 157.

9 "Squaresville U.S.A. vs. Beatsville," *Life*, September 21, 1959, pp. 31-37.

10 Ibid., p. 31.

11 Ibid., p. 37.

12 Norman Podhoretz, "The Know-Nothing Bohemians," *Partisan Review*, 25 (Spring 1958), p. 318.

13 In another important and harsh application of obscenity laws, Jonas Mekas was prosecuted in 1964 for showing the film *Flaming Creatures* by Jack Smith. For further discussion of this incident, see John Hanhardt's essay, p. 216 below.

14 The judge in the Chicago case, one of several that actually went to trial, imposed such an exorbitant punishment (Bruce was sentenced to a $1,000 fine and a year's imprisonment) that the case was appealed. The Supreme Court of Illinois in 1964 refused to reverse the conviction, basing its decision on a tape recording of Bruce's act in which he joked about Jimmy Hoffa as a Christ figure, the vows of celibacy taken by Catholic priests and nuns, and condoms in toilet vending machines. Less than a week later the US Supreme Court further undercut local obscenity laws with its landmark *Jacobellis* decision. Following the Court's lead, the Illinois judges unilaterally moved to vacate their earlier decision, reasoning that Bruce's "entire performance was [now] immunized" from the possibility of an obscenity conviction because it contained material of "social importance." Another unsuccessful trial in New York became a national media event, with an imposing array of cultural stars testifying for the defense—from newspaper columnist Dorothy Kilgallen (who described Bruce as a brilliant social satirist and "moral man") to Episcopal minister Sidney Lanier (who maintained that Bruce's nightclub act was "in some ways helpful, even healing"). For more on the Bruce prosecutions, see Gerber, *Sex, Pornography, and Justice*, pp. 219-26.

15 For an account of the trial, see Smith, *Utopia and Dissent*, pp. 225-31.

16 Ibid., p. 231.

17 Ibid.

18 Ibid., p. 157.

19 Editorial, *Capital Times*, March 16, 1964; quoted in E.R. Hutchison, *Tropic of Cancer on Trial: A Case History of Censorship* (New York: Grove Press, 1968), p. 229.

20 George A. Dondero, "Modern Art Shackled To Communism," speech given in the US House of Representatives, August 16, 1949, *Congressional Record*, First Session, 81st Congress. I would like to thank Donna De Salvo for directing me to this material.

21 *Attorney General* v. *A Book Named "Naked Lunch,"* Supreme Court of Massachusetts, July 7, 1966; reprinted in Williams S. Burroughs, *Naked Lunch*, Black Cat Edition (New York: Grove Weidenfeld, 1966), p. viii.

22 "Excerpts from the Boston Trial of *Naked Lunch*," in Burroughs, *Naked Lunch*, p. xxiv.

23 In 1965, the Bureau, inspired by Allen Ginsberg's call for the legalization of marijuana and his well-publicized narcotics use, decided that Ginsberg was a drug dealer and launched a harassment campaign; see Schumacher, *Dharma Lion*, p. 449.

24 Ibid., for Hoover's file on Ginsberg.

25 De Grazia, *Girls Lean Back Everywhere*, p. 329.

26 See Smith, *Utopia and Dissent*, pp. 338-39.

27 For the arrest and trial, see Lenny Bruce, *How to Talk Dirty and Influence People: An Autobiography* (New York: Fireside, 1992), pp. 104-28.

28 "Excerpts from the Boston Trial of *Naked Lunch*," in Burroughs, *Naked Lunch*, pp. xxviii-xxix. Burroughs' lurid and graphic novel became embroiled in a number of repressive crusades, including two major obscenity prosecutions, after its US publication in 1962: a 1965 trial in Los Angeles, in which the book was cleared of charges, and a less successful one in Superior Court in Boston in 1963. Despite defense testimony from such expert witnesses as Norman Mailer, Allen Ginsberg, and John Ciardi, the Boston court ruled against Burroughs. On July 7, 1966, the Massachusetts Supreme Court, finding that *Naked Lunch* had not been "commercially exploited for the sake of prurient appeal, to the exclusion of other values," reversed the earlier decision and thus eliminated the threat of a statewide ban; see *Attorney General* v. *A Book Named "Naked Lunch,"* p. ix.

29 Mark Schorer, quoted in Schumacher, *Dharma Lion*, p. 261.

30 There are, of course, a number of other reasons for the imperative to impugn homosexuality. Conservative campaigns to restore traditional social arrangements (or, in present-day parlance, "family values") innately view gay men and lesbians as suspect because they don't reproduce "normal" family life; they are thought to be childless and employed in "frivolous" and economically marginal fields. On these issues, see Allan Sekula, "Gay Bashing as an Art Form" (1989), in Richard Bolton, ed., *Culture Wars: Documents from the Recent Controversies in the Arts* (New York: The New Press, 1992), pp. 118-20.

31 Carole Vance, "The War on Culture" (1989), in Bolton, *Culture Wars*, p. 111.

32 See Smith, *Utopia and Dissent*, p. 227.

33 In *Doe* v. *Casey*, the plaintiff was dismissed from his job as a CIA agent after he voluntarily revealed his homosexuality to a CIA security officer. A federal appeals court, denying that Doe could be stigmatized by his dismissal, reasoned that "the real stigma imposed by [the employer's] action...is the charge of homosexuality." The court, taking a typical "don't ask, don't tell" position, argued that Doe, seeing nothing scandalous in his own homosexuality and thus having no "liberty interest" in evading its consequences, was in some sense to blame for his legal problems. Thus, a self-identified homosexual in government, in order to retain a legally self-protective interest in his or her job, "must (1) subjectively regard his or her homosexuality as degrading and (2) hide it." For more on the case, see Janet E. Halley, "The Politics of the Closet: Legal Articulation of Sexual Orientation Identity," in Dan Danielson and Karen Engles, eds., *After Identity: A Reader in Law and Culture* (New York and London: Routledge, 1995), pp. 33-34.

34 To a great extent, the epistemic violence of censorship can be analogized to the physical violence frequently directed at homosexuals, women, and people of color. If such violence "aims to deform, and often utterly, to destroy, its targets," as Kendall Thomas suggests, censorship results in a kind of representational murder, wherein offending images and words are obliterated. Like the legal structures for outlining and enacting censorious acts, homophobic violence, for example, can also be understood as a kind of coercive "institution," as Thomas has recently argued, a social construction "structured by rules that define roles and positions, powers and opportunities, thereby distributing responsibility for consequences." Thus, the objective and result of violence against lesbians and gays is the "social control of human sexuality through the regulation of the erotic economy of contemporary American society and the enforcement of the institutional and ideological imperatives of what Adrienne Rich has termed 'compulsory heterosexuality.'" Insofar as homophobic assault is motivated by the desire to prevent actual or imagined deviations from heterosexual acts and identities by creating a kind of chill effect, it mimics the imperatives of censorship; both are undeniably powerful tools for undermining homosexual rights by discouraging gay men and lesbians from coming out and reinforcing the negative impression of homosexuality in the public sphere. See Kendall Thomas, "Beyond the Privacy Principal," in Danielson and Engles, *After Identity*, p. 290, and Claudia Card, "Rape as a Terrorist Institution," in R.G. Frey and Christopher W. Morris, eds., *Violence, Terrorism, and Justice* (Cambridge, England: Cambridge University Press, 1991), pp. 297-98.

35 Norman Mailer, "The White Negro: Superficial Reflections on the Hipster," *Dissent*, 4 (Summer 1957), pp. 276-93.

36 Richard Pells, *The Liberal Mind in a Conservative Age: American Intellectuals in the 1940s and 1950s* (New York: Harper & Row, 1985), p. 209.

37 Allen Ginsberg, quoted in Schumacher, *Dharma Lion*, p. 341.

38 Podhoretz, "The Know-Nothing Bohemians," p. 310.

39 Ibid.

40 Ned Polsky, quoted by Podhoretz, ibid., p. 311.

41 I would like to thank Lisa Phillips for pointing out to me this usually misunderstood aspect of the Beat movement.

42 Ginsberg, "Excerpts from the Boston Trial of *Naked Lunch*," in Burroughs, *Naked Lunch*, pp. xxx-xxxi.

43 See, for example, LeRoi Jones, "Correspondence: The Beat Generation," *Partisan Review*, 25 (Summer 1958), p. 473.

44 Frank Kofsky, *Lenny Bruce: The Comedian as Social Critic and Secular Moralist* (New York: Monad Press, 1974), p. 90.

45 Ibid., p. 98.

46 These agencies included the FBI, CIA, Bureau of Narcotics, and the Drug Enforcement Administration; see Schumacher, *Dharma Lion*, pp. 624-25.

47 Ginsberg, quoted in ibid., p. 625.

48 See Kobena Mercer, "Skin Head Sex Thing: Racial Difference and the Homoerotic Imaginary," in *Welcome to the Jungle: New Positions in Black Cultural Studies* (New York and London: Routledge, 1994), p. 191. For the censorship battles of recent years, see Bolton, *Culture Wars*; Maurice Berger, "Too Shocking To Show," *Art in America*, 80 (July 1992), pp. 37-39; and Brian Wallis, "Bush's Compromise: A Newer Form of Censorship?" *Art in America*, 78 (November 1990), pp. 57-63, 210.

49 Patrick Buchanan, "How Can We Clean Up Our Art Act?" *The Washington Post*, June 19, 1989, quoted in Vance, "The War on Culture," p. 109.

50 Richard Grenier, "A Burning Issue Lights Artistic Ire," *Washington Times*, June 28, 1989, reprinted in Bolton, *Culture Wars*, p. 44.

51 Ginsberg, letter to Jesse Helms, August 14, 1989, reprinted in Bolton, *Culture Wars*, p. 92.

Wallace Berman and Jay DeFeo, **Untitled (Jay DeFeo)**, 1958, 5 1/16 x 3 7/8 (12.9 x 9.8), Lannan Foundation, Los Angeles

Hettie Jones and Joyce Glassman at the Artist's Club, 1960. Photo © Fred W. McDarrah

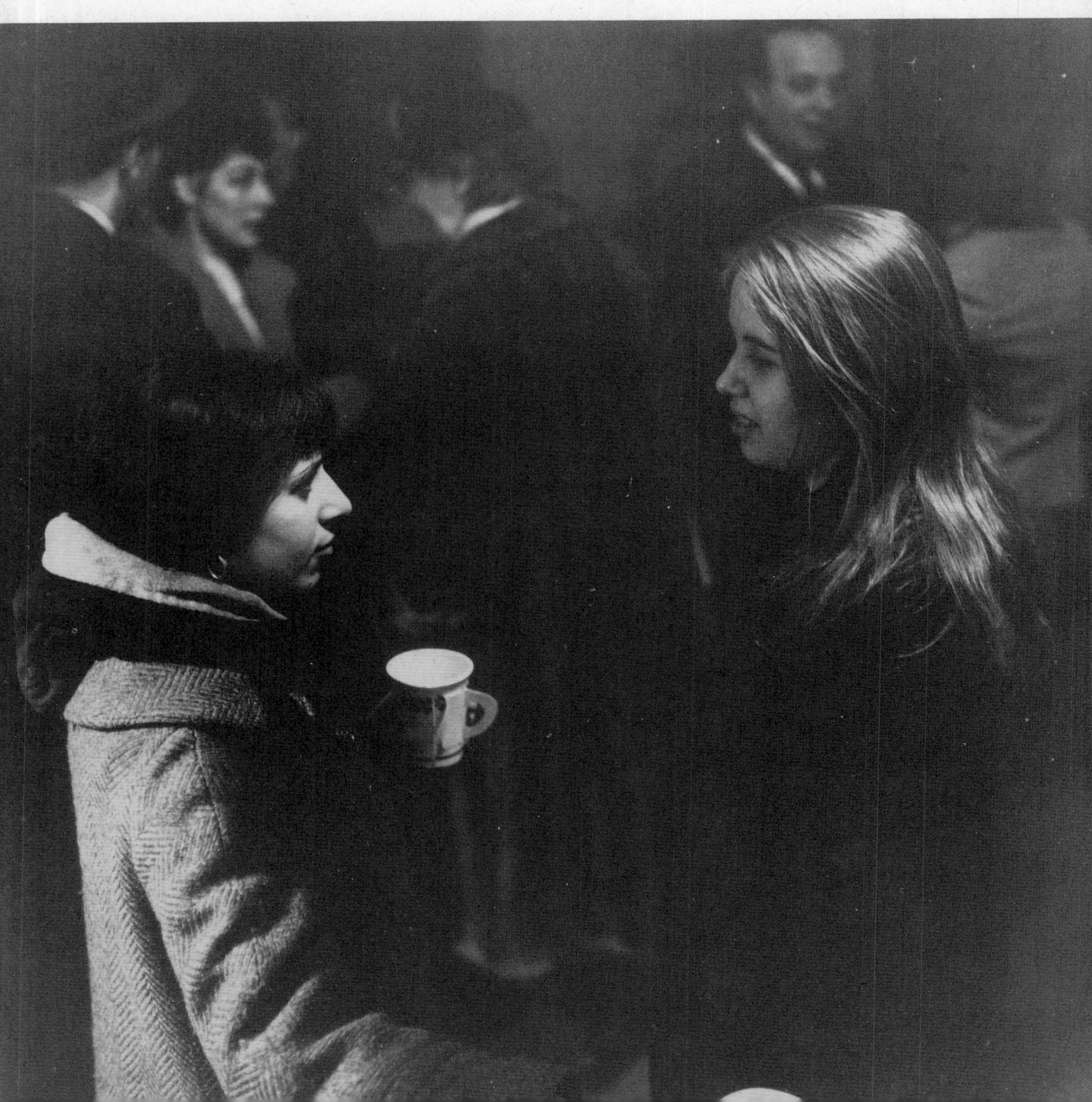

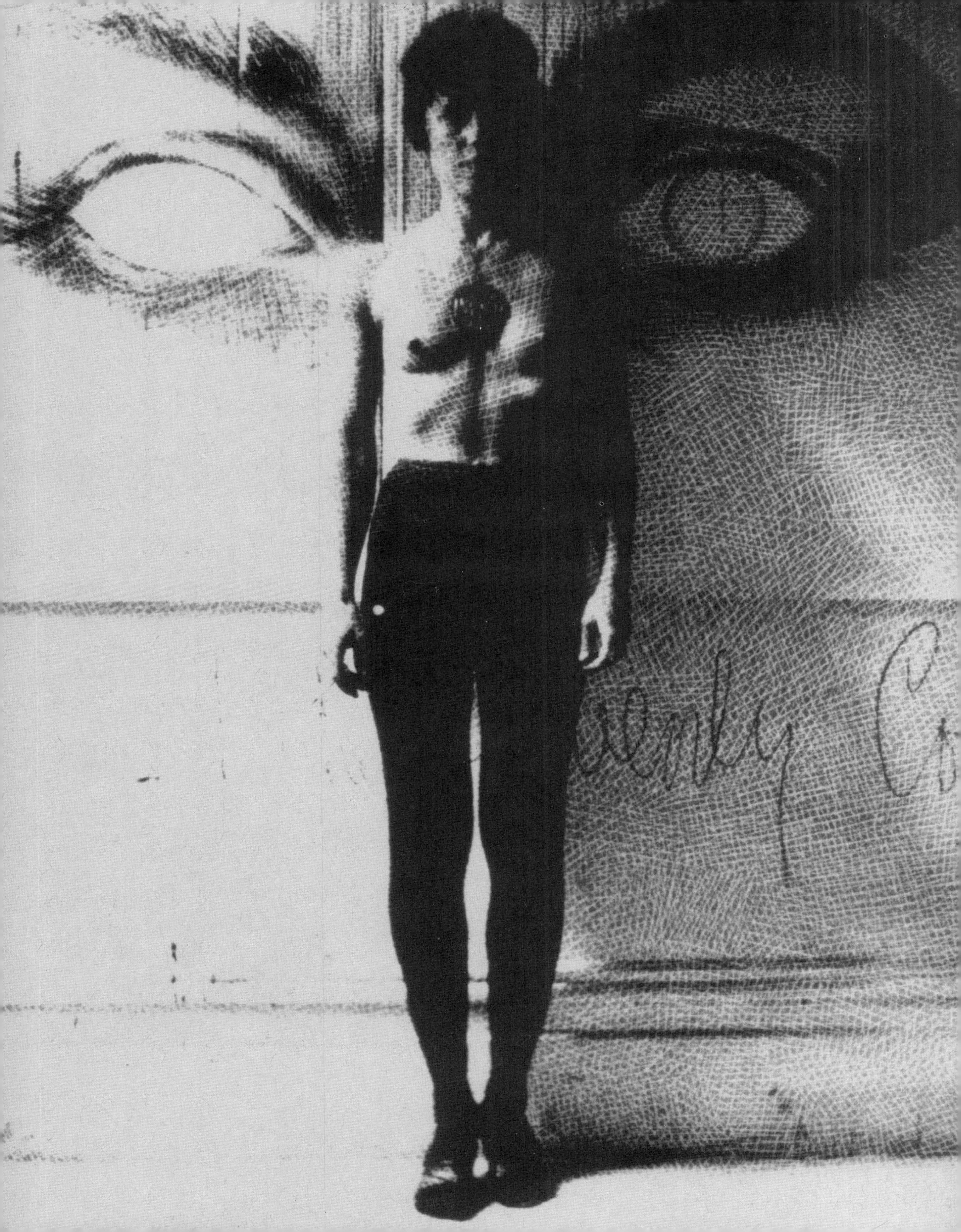

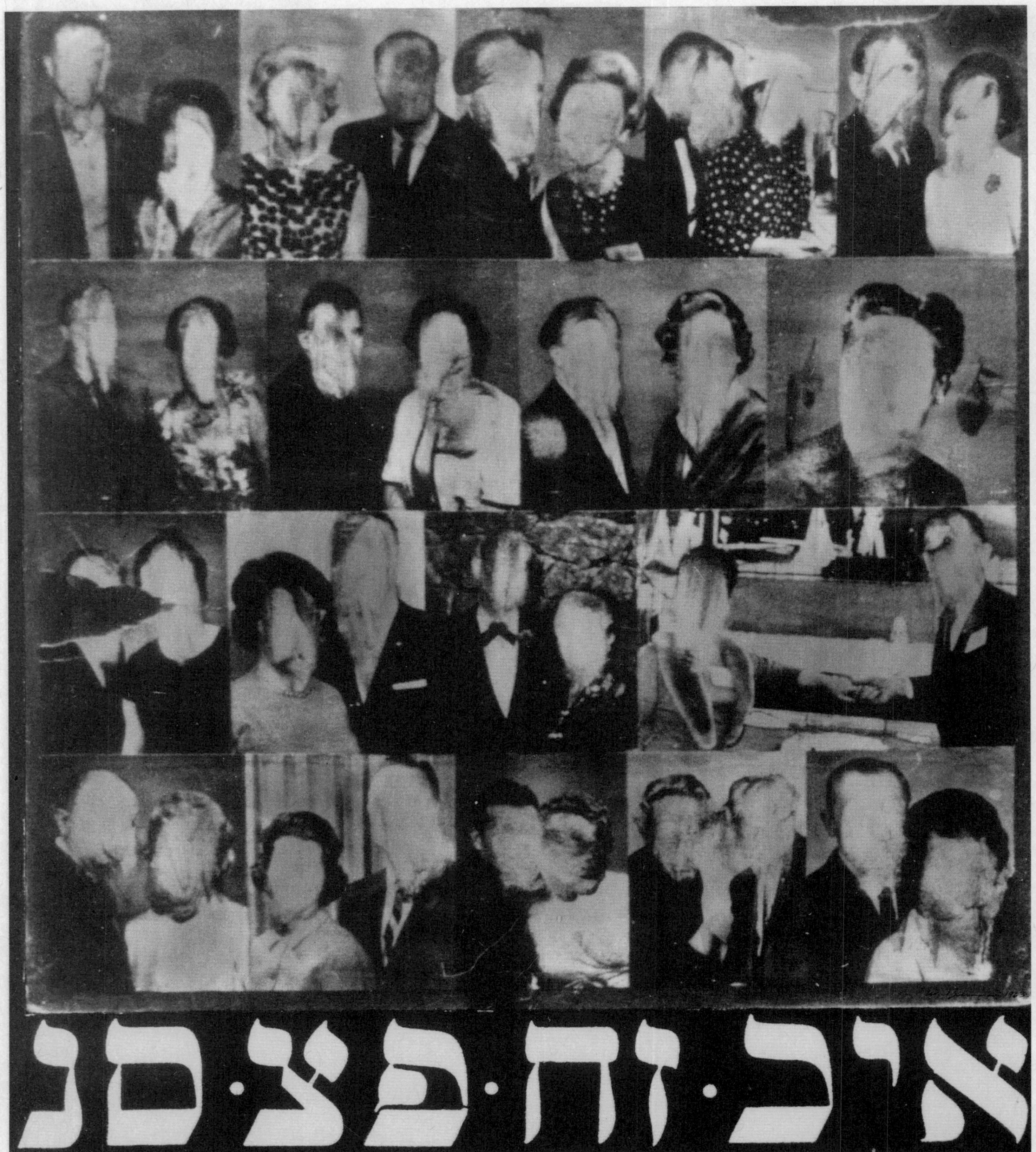

Wallace Berman
Untitled, 1963
Verifax collage, 34 1/2 x 30 1/2 (87.6 x 77.5)
Collection of Nicole Klagsbrun

MARIA DAMON

Victors of Catastrophe: Beat Occlusions

...nothing that has ever happened should be regarded as lost for history....For without exception the cultural treasures [the historian] surveys have an origin which he cannot contemplate without horror. They owe their existence not only to the efforts of the great minds and talents who have created them, but also to the anonymous toil of their contemporaries. There is no document ofcivilization which is not at the same time a document of barbarism.

Walter Benjamin[1]

O mother
what have I left out
O mother
what have I forgotten

Allen Ginsberg[2]

Walter Benjamin's analysis of the task facing those who would reconstruct cultural history from the ground up has become a talisman statement for contemporary students of culture; it lends itself particularly well to an interpretation of Beat culture—its inclusions and exclusions, though cultural studies has come to Beat material relatively late. Most scholars take to heart the distinction between, on the one hand, the "great talents" who produced the "cultural treasures" attributed to the victors of an ongoing historical struggle between the oppressed and the conquering, and, on the other, the "anonymous contemporaries" who toil unlimned. But the Beat aficionado knows that this binary collapses in the countercultural expressions of the Beat era. The great talents are often one and the same as the unsung; and they were unafraid of the abyss. The Beats, known and anonymous, were careful to carve into their documents of civilization—their bodies, their daily comportment, their life stories, as well as their artistic output—the scars of the barbarism of post-atomic, post-Auschwitz American culture. While popular understanding of the Beats comprises primarily the well-known figures of the era—Allen Ginsberg,

William S. Burroughs, Jack Kerouac—the Beats also comprised a tribal ethos of friendship manifested in a widely dispersed network of supporters, fellow travelers, and kindred spirits who, though less famous or entirely unknown, enabled these now prominent men to lead individually creative lives.

Much of the subject matter of acknowledged masterpieces of Beat art and poetry concerns itself with documenting these unknowns. Victors of catastrophe the Beats were; they turned the economy of failure and success upside down. As men who dissented from normative masculinity, they held court in down-and-out milieus and praised the lives of outcasts. Who could contest "Howl's" attempts to capture for literary posterity the lives of junkies and queers of the American underworld?[3] Or "Kaddish's" status as a love letter to an otherwise anonymous Jewish immigrant woman whose traumas of displacement and class mobility American-style finally caught up to her? Or *On the Road*'s mythologizing of innumerable small towns and of a flophouse orphan as Dionysian Adonis?[4] Beat culture, whose jazz-inspired name epitomizes its oxymoronic embrace of sacralized fatigue, rock-bottom soul-poverty and mystic joy (much as the word "shaman" descends from a Sanskrit root, "to exhaust or fatigue"), derived its energy from all explosive marriages of heaven and hell.

Nonetheless, when an African-American Beat poet such as Bob Kaufman stated, in 1981, "I want to be anonymous...my ambition is to be completely forgotten," his words must be read with some sense of double-voiced irony and ambivalence.[5] They do not point only toward an ideal of democratic anonymity and solidarity with the "fellaheen" (a term Kerouac borrowed from Arabic to describe the anonymous working poor he identified with); they are scars that trace the poet's lived experience of poverty and racism. A brilliantly witty poet whose lyricism captured the North Beach scene, Kaufman in fact has been all but forgotten by mainstream literary history, and this critical neglect is due not only to the Beat ideals he embraced or his own disillusionment and disappointment, but also to the fact that he is a person of color. One of his poems, "Bagel Shop Jazz," traces the delicate tensions and alliances among the (nonethnicized) women ("love tinted, Beat angels"), Jewish men ("Caesar-jawed, with synagogue eyes"), and Black men ("the secret terrible hurts, wrapped in cool hipster smiles") who made

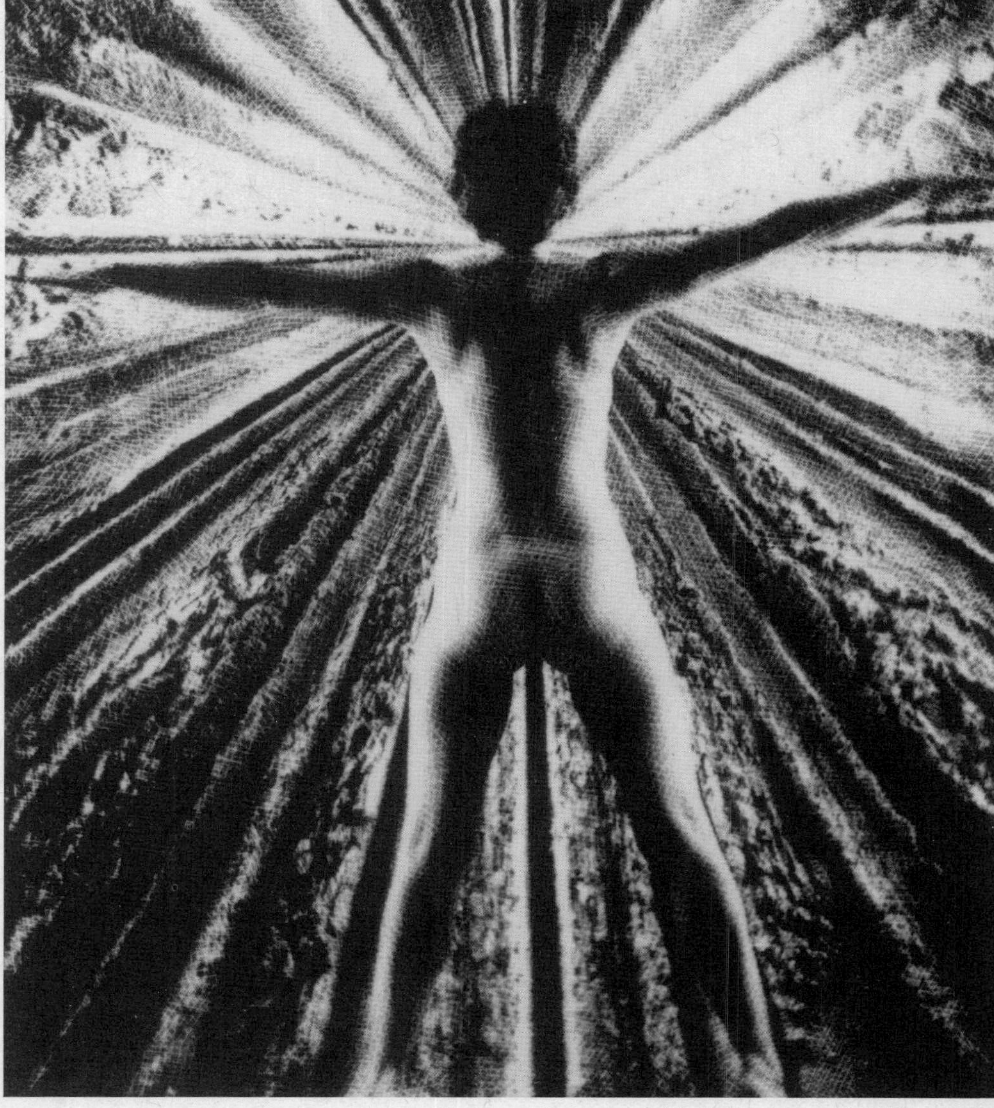

Wallace Berman and Jay DeFeo
Untitled (Jay DeFeo), 1958
Gelatin silver print,
5 1/16 x 3 7/8 (12.9 x 9.8)
Lannan Foundation, Los Angeles

the scene at the Coexistence Bagel Shop, united against the "guilty police" but caught in an uneasy love triangle among themselves.[6] The poem he recited to break ten years of self-imposed silence, "All Those Ships That Never Sailed," traces his attempt to speak through a debilitating experience of physical devastation, the result of street life: "My body once covered with beauty/ Is now a museum of betrayal/...Today I bring it back/ And let you live forever."[7] While Kaufman gains in strength and poetic integrity from his embrace of a fate that may have been thrust upon him willy-nilly, his relative obscurity vis à vis other Beats also represents the de facto situation of racially and economically disenfranchised artists.

This reproduction of larger patterns of exclusionary practices is not, of course, specific to Beat culture, nor can it be attributed to the intentions of the better-known Beats. During the cold war, when the American left had been shattered by the Rosenberg executions, HUAC's anti-Communist excesses, and disillusionment with Stalin's betrayal of socialist ideals, concern with social inequity and with honoring a people's countermemory (the untold story in every historical period) expressed itself culturally and aesthetically rather than in economic or broad sociopolitical analysis. Norman Mailer's notorious "Hipsters," for instance, with its analysis of the white counterculture's debt to "Negro culture," anticipated current scholarship on the "politics of style," arguing for a turn away from classical Marxism's strict, hierarchic separation between economic base and cultural/aesthetic superstructure.[8] Bob Kaufman, who

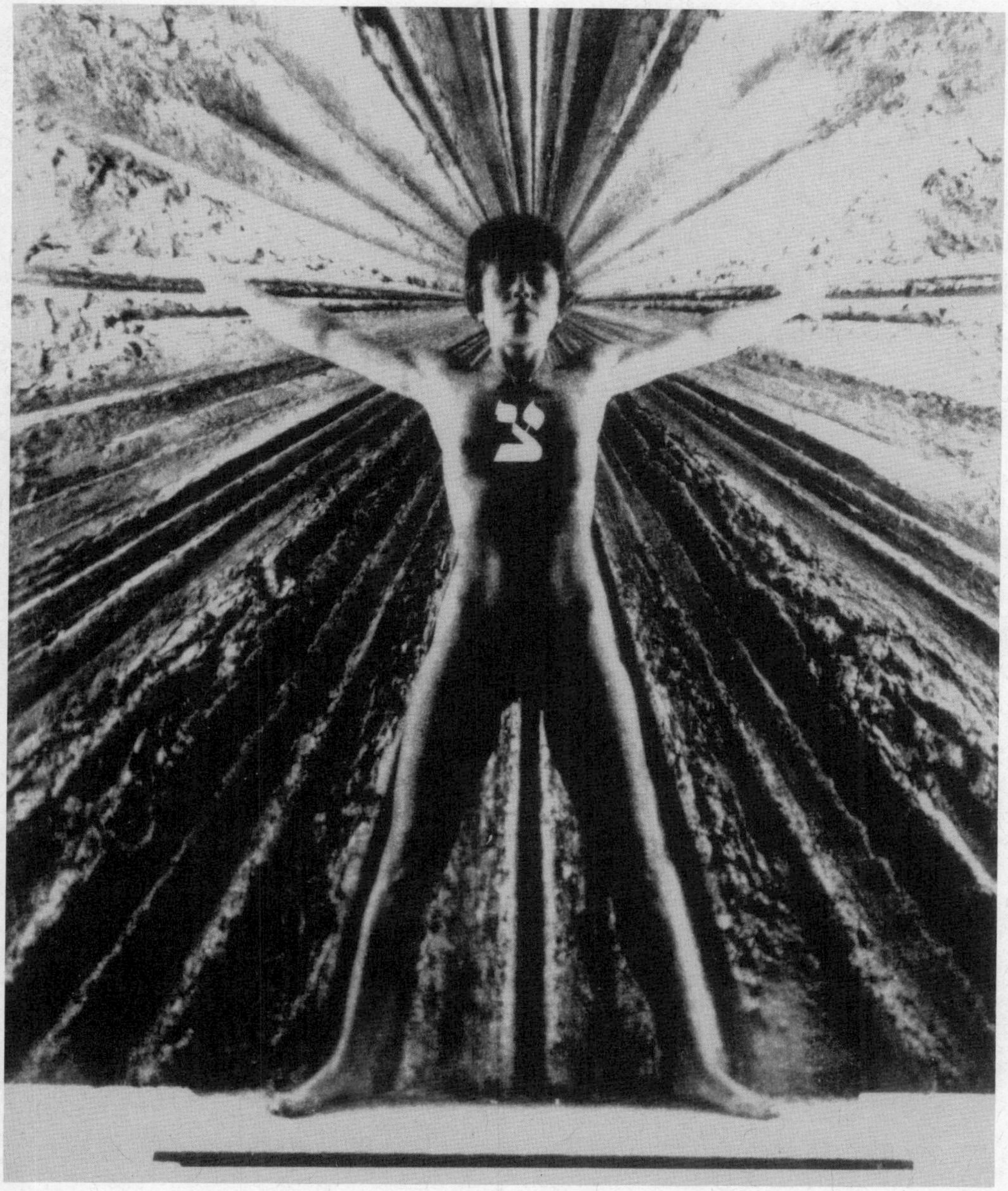

Wallace Berman and Jay DeFeo
Untitled (Jay DeFeo), 1958
Gelatin silver print,
5 1/8 x 4 7/16 (13 x 11.3)
Lannan Foundation, Los Angeles

had been an ardent union organizer for the more left-leaning branch of the International Seamen's Union, quit New York and active politics for San Francisco's poetry scene in the 1950s. Given the era's repression of explicit political challenges to what Eisenhower dubbed the "military-industrial complex," the Beats celebrated the disenfranchised through other strategies. In Benjaminian spirit, for example, Allen Ginsberg has saved every scrap of history and material culture available to him; recently acquired by Stanford University, his collection of tapes, books, manuscripts, photographs, drawings, clothing, and other objects of the period and its denizens provide a rich assemblage-tribute to the friendships and communities that made up the wide Beat network. Kerouac championed and wrote an introduction to Robert Frank's *The Americans*, a collection of photographs capturing the variegated beauties and profundities of anonymous American lives across the continent.[9] However, the subjects of these moving photographs remained anonymous, while Frank and Kerouac did not. Barbara Ehrenreich has described Beat oppositionality as resisting the prescriptive masculinity of the 1950s; mobility, non-monogamy, and voluntary poverty directly challenged the figure of the gray-suited, salaried suburbanite contributing to capital's development in joyless, routinized family life.[10] The Beats were visionary but their visions were, perforce, circumscribed.

When reintroducing Beat material to contemporary study and appreciation, it is thus still necessary to repeatedly and actively go beyond the great-minds-and-talents model that often serves as a primitive but necessary foundation for more textured inquiry (in ethnic and women's studies this is referred to as the "heroes and holidays" approach). From a broader historical perspective, the Beats do not appear as innovative as they once seemed. For example, although they played a role in spreading the influence of Buddhism among white middle-class youth, Gary Snyder, Phil Whalen, Allen Ginsberg, and Jack Kerouac did not introduce Buddhism to the West. A century of importation of Pacific Rim labor—whose construction of the country's railroad system gave the Beats one means of mobility, an important mythic trope, and at times a livelihood—brought these spiritual practices to the West Coast, though they did not spread substantially beyond immigrant use until the convergence of several factors: the return of US servicemen from occupied Japan, often accompanied by Japanese Buddhist wives; the relaxation of immigration laws in 1960, which permitted religious leaders from India, Japan, and the forcibly secularized Tibet to enter the country; the publication and popularity of D.T. Suzuki's books on Zen.

Though Allen Ginsberg's *Howl and Other Poems* and William Burroughs' *Naked Lunch* were both subjects of famous obscenity trials that signaled the end of such forms of literary censorship (both works were acquitted on the grounds of "redeeming social and literary merit"), these authors were not the first writers to bring homoeroticism to the literary and countercultural world (and, interestingly enough, there is still much resistance to acknowledging the homoerotic art and dynamics of Beat life). The Beat and gay subcultures and each one's multiple literary traditions overlapped in sometimes uneasy, sometimes mutually supportive proximity in the bars and cafés of Greenwich Village and North Beach. The large population of discharged World War II veterans in concentrated locations like the Bay Area created a rich milieu of displaced men-in-transition, ripe for a life on the road, in college in unprecedented numbers due to the GI Bill, or in a gay subculture that was beginning to constitute itself as a community that would soon (starting in the late 1960s) achieve political as well as cultural visibility. Some artists, such as poet Harold Norse and painter/diarist Russell FitzGerald, moved comfortably between the two worlds. Although these two worlds were not always in alliance aesthetically (some of the gay "Berkeley Renaissance" poets distanced themselves from what they considered to be the Beats' self-promoting sentimentality, and the straight Beats tolerated rather than actively sought out their gay co-outsiders), the Beat presence created a rebellious atmosphere which, by enabling the gay male community to see itself as actively dissident rather than helplessly deviant, eventually encouraged its politicization.[11]

Joanne Kyger & Gary Snyder Near Japan Sea, 1963. Photo by Allen Ginsberg

What was her name   the goddess I mean
Not that mortal one

Plucking threads
as if they were strings of a harp
Joanne Kyger[12]

And we wear exhaustion like a painted robe
I & my sisters...
Diane DiPrima[13]

Finally, counter to impressions left by uncritical readings of the Beat urtext *On the Road*, women in the Beat movement occupied positions beyond those of, on the one hand, sex objects and, on the other, Momist matriarchal tyrants hellbent on turning apron strings into straitjackets for their male partners and progeny. Beat ideology celebrated the "boy gang" and its freewheeling *communitas*; as Richard Cándida Smith has pointed out, this foregrounding of homosocial and mobile masculinity obscured both the actual domestic arrangements many Beats made and the artistic achievements of their female counterparts and partners. These women raised children, wrote, painted, cooked vast meals for extended families of aesthetic *confrères* and *soeurs*, estab-

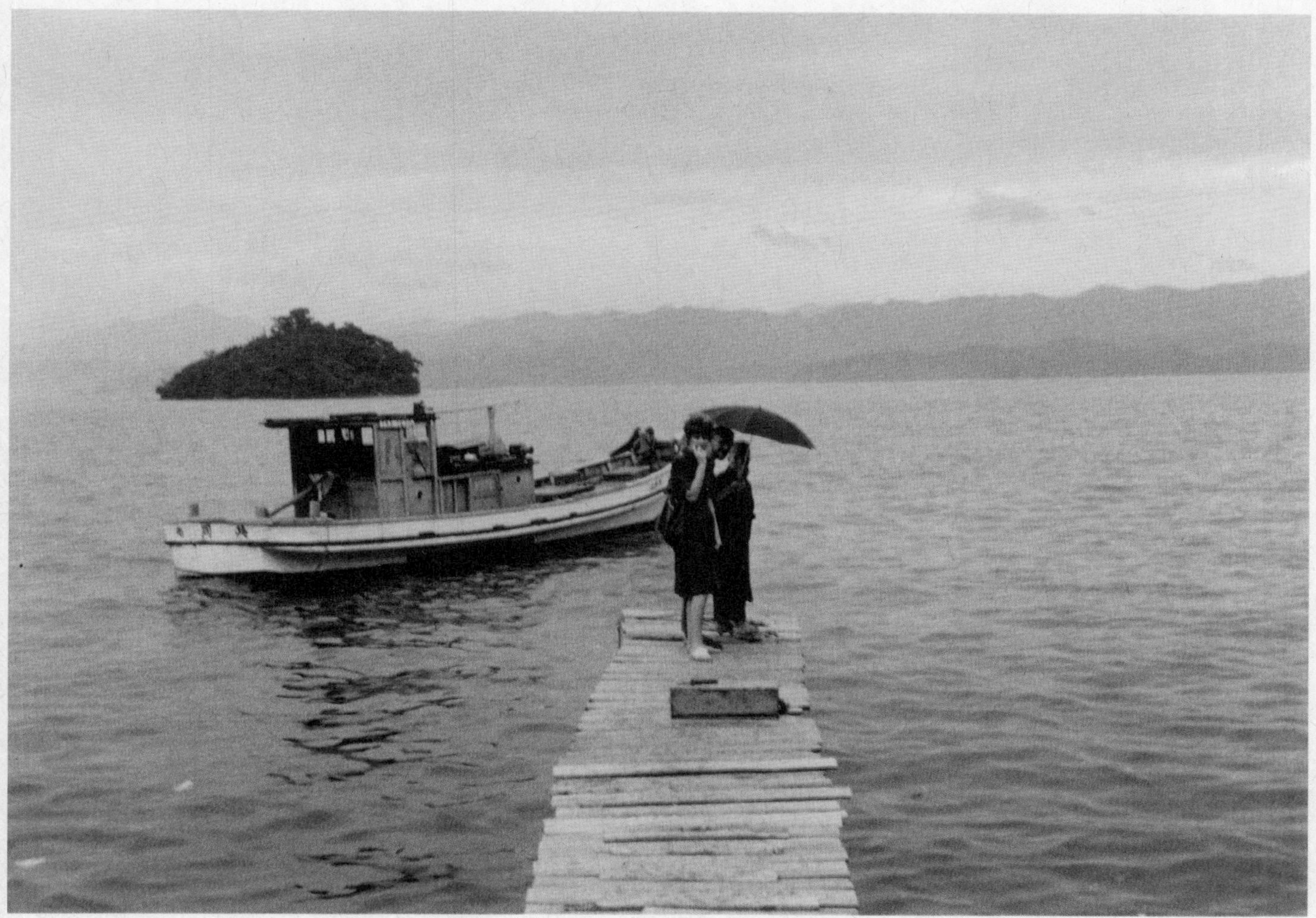

Joanne Kyger, Poet, & her husband Zen student Gary Snyder with local Priest — we visited latter's temple near Sea of Japan, July 1963. Allen Ginsberg lished publishing houses such as Totem Press and The Poets' Press, published or co-published journals and anthologies such as *Yūgen*, *The Floating Bear*, and *Beatitude*. These latter tasks involved incalculable labor hours—anonymous and meticulously skilled toil—of layout, collation, printing, editorial decisions regarding content and format. The women involved had abortions, miscarriages, children, suicides, productive lives; they made clothes, meals, and books, created and managed domestic and performance spaces (sometimes turning the one into the other), and they often worked "straight" jobs in major publishing houses, or turned "tricks" (as did Alexander Trocchi's wife, Lyn, to support his writing and drug habit[15]) to further their partners' creative lives. They hung out, married, cohabited, eloped, drank, drugged, and held it together. In short, they did everything the men did in addition to childbearing and domestic "duties" which, in accord with the tribal ideology of the movement, took on a positive aura.

Joanne Kyger, Diane DiPrima, Janine Pommy Vega, Lenore Kandel, and Anne Waldman (of a slightly younger generation) have considerable poetic oeuvres. Their work, as Kyger's lines suggest, often celebrates traditional women's roles as makers (and the word "poet" derives from the Greek *poiein*, to make) through female deities and mythological characters: Penelope, Athena, Durga, Kali. DiPrima's more recent work has featured the persona of Loba the she-wolf, calling on and being a goddess, wearing the Beat signature—sacred exhaustion—like ceremonial clothing. Just as often, though, the work addresses romantic pain and the centrality of companionate love to modern women's lives: Pommy Vega's delicate lyrics to the Peruvian painter Fernando Vega, written after his death in 1965, trace an ongoing devotion to love that transcends the boundaries of the love object's mortality:

> you have taken him from me & the pain runs
> deep as my life
> & I bless you.[16]

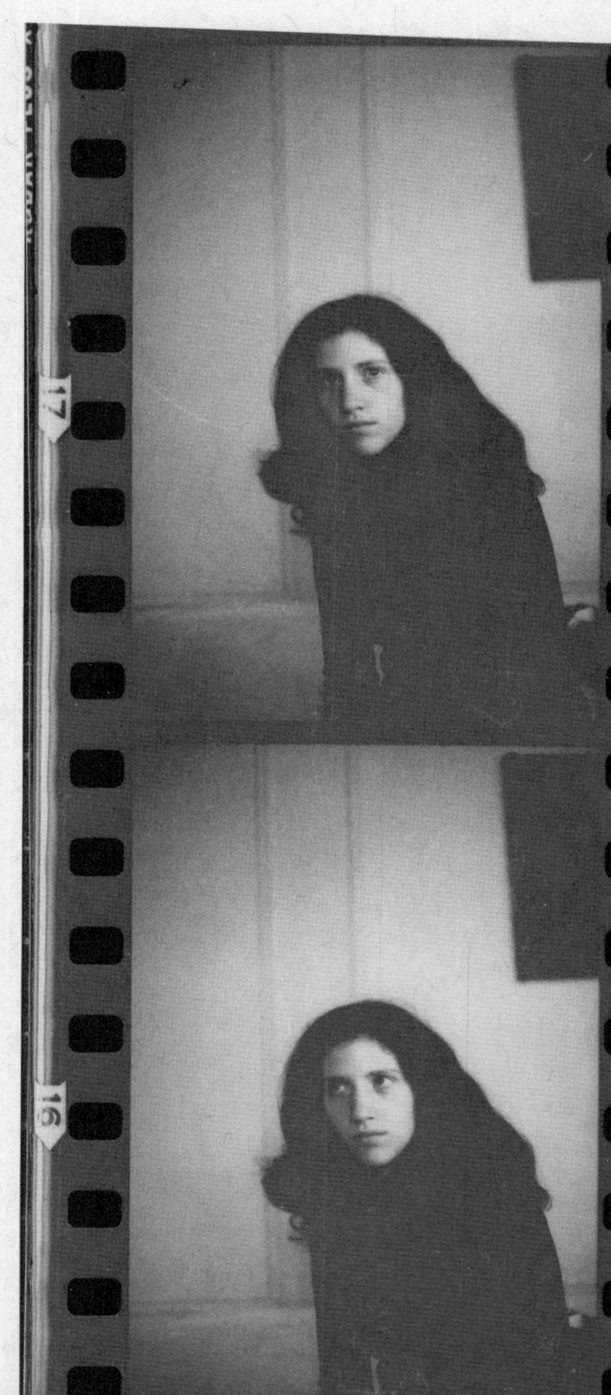

Joyce Johnson, Hettie Jones, Carolyn Cassady, Bonnie Bremser, and Jan Kerouac (again, of a younger generation), the memoirists of the era, demonstrate their then-unacknowledged centrality to the scene in ongoing reinvocations of the period's multivalenced energy. They pull no punches about the difficulty of inhabiting a subculture within a subculture, about creating a covert network invisible even to their larger male-dominated cohort (where, they asked each other sub rosa, can I get an abortion? would *you* look at my poetry? how do *you* find time to write/paint?), about the exhilaration of leaving the certain soul-death of the suburbs in favor of what turned out to be a not entirely free bohemian alternative. Eileen Kaufman transcribed and collected Bob Kaufman's work for publication with New Directions and City Lights, a task he would never have undertaken himself, committed as he was to performing in the absolute present. Alix Geluardi of North Beach and others cared for Beat children when their parents could not do so, and housed, anthologized, and served as companions and comforts to their male counterparts.

Elise Cowen, Natalie Jackson, V.R. ("Bunny") Lang, and Joan Burroughs remain, in portraits by their male and female friends and lovers, significant icons of inspiration, pathos, and creative intelligence for the people in the orbits they inhabited before early deaths

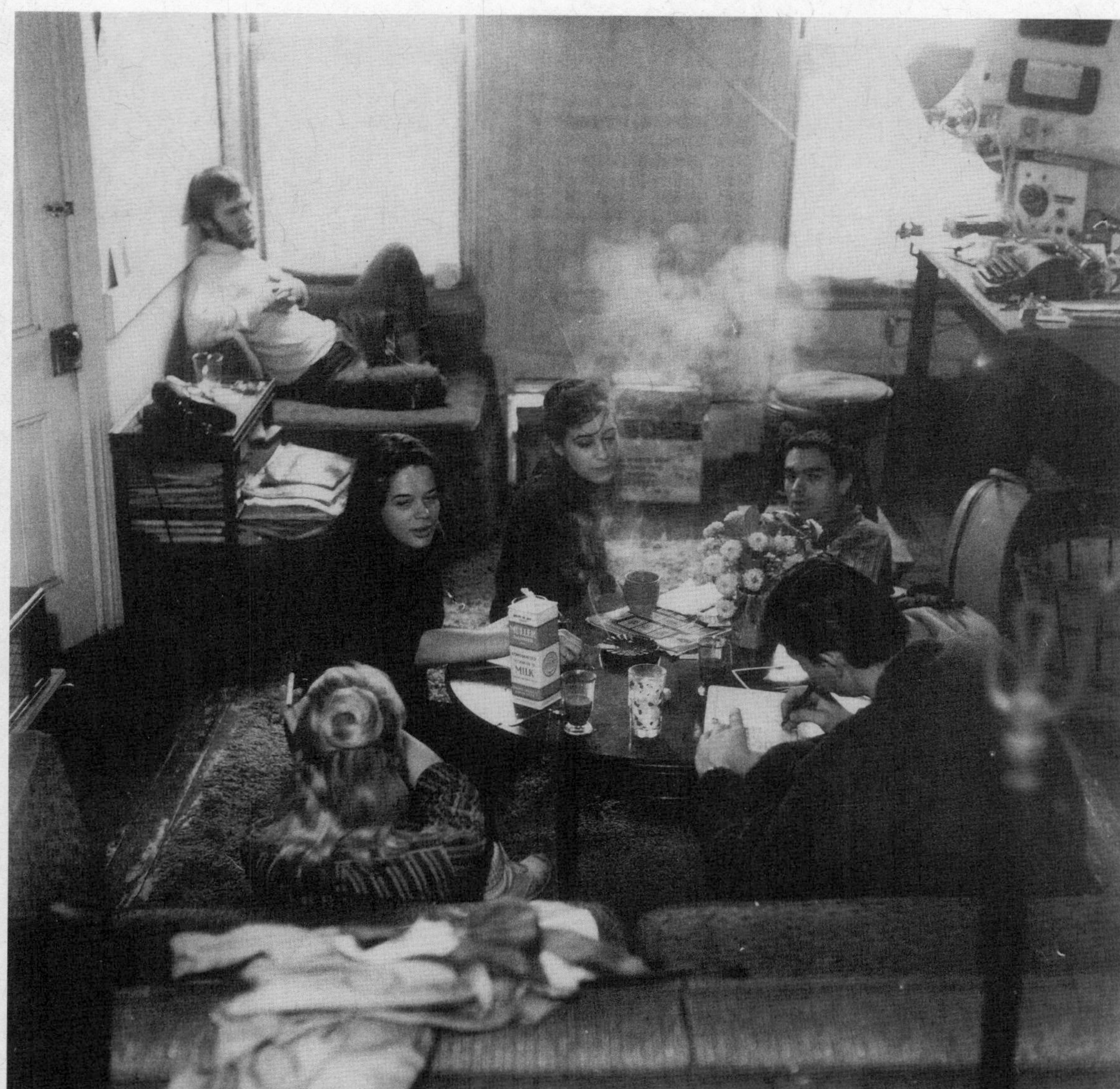

Philip Lamantia and Kirby Doyle visiting from San Francisco, 1959. Photo © Fred W. McDarrah

from illness, suicide, or violence at the hands of loved ones. And while the literary evidence suggests that Beat men may have slighted the creative powers of the women in their immediate circles, Sappho, Emily Dickinson, Gertrude Stein, and Hilda Doolittle ("H.D.") were fully and commonly acknowledged as ma(s)ters of poetic and domestic unorthodoxy; their poetics and their homoerotic lives served as models for experimental writing and transgressive sexual exploration.

Were women, people of color, sexual minorities, and the poor victors or victims, survivors or casualties of that generalized American trauma called "the fifties"? Both, absolutely. A predictably inconclusive answer; the interest lies in the details, the life stories, the art and artifacts, and how these interact with the physical and metaphysical textures of history. I'm concerned that in its current drive for legitimacy Beat culture will lose the beauty of its intrinsic pluralism and debt to the popular—will end up repudiating its rich heritage in its eagerness to align itself with Lionel Trilling, T.S. Eliot, and Ezra Pound (not that these influences weren't there for Ginsberg and Kerouac—but there was much more). I'm concerned that the Beats will miss their own moment, which is now. In the spirit of friendship that Beat culture exemplifies, I want to be mindful of all the life-as-art artists who have enabled Beat "museumification." They're still here, still going on. The angels of history, tatter-winged and resplendently exhausted, are here now.

Diane DiPrima, c. 1953-60. Photo by James O. Mitchell

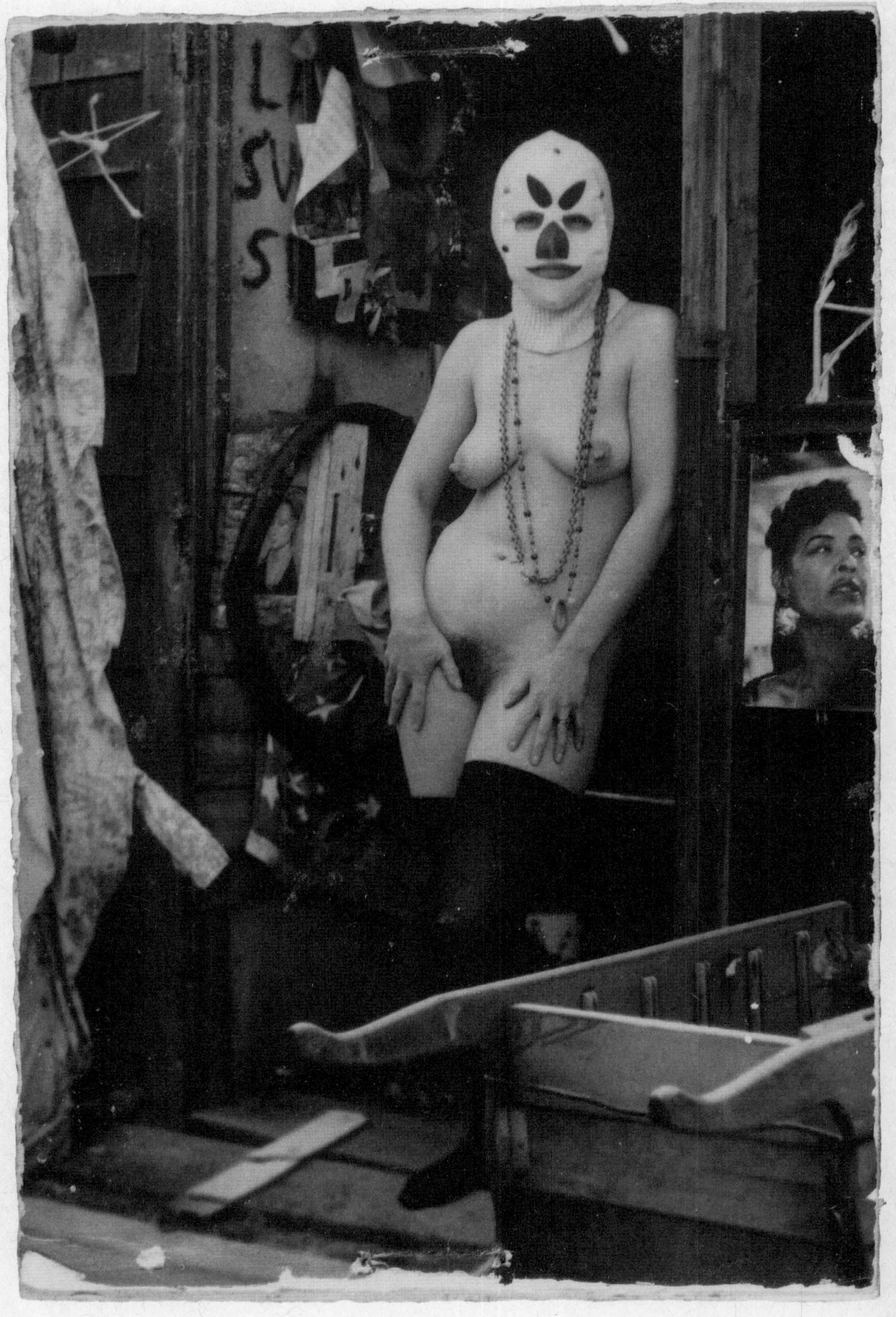

Patricia Jordan, Larkspur, 1960. Photo by Wallace Berman

Notes

1 Walter Benjamin, "Theses on the Philosophy of History," in *Illuminations*, trans. by Harry Zohn (New York: Schocken Books, 1969), pp. 254, 256. Thanks to Ronna Johnson, Ed Cohen, Rob Silberman, and Ann Braude for suggestions and insights.

2 Allen Ginsberg, "Kaddish," in *Kaddish and Other Poems* (San Francisco: City Lights Books, 1961), p. 34.

3 Allen Ginsberg, "Howl," in *Howl and Other Poems* (San Francisco: City Lights Books, 1956), pp. 9-22.

4 Jack Kerouac, *On the Road* (New York: The Viking Press, 1957).

5 Quoted in Raymond Foye's introduction to Bob Kaufman, *The Ancient Rain: Poems 1956-1978* (New York: New Directions Publishing Corporation, 1981), p. ix.

6 Kaufman, "Bagel Shop Jazz," in *Solitudes Crowded with Loneliness* (New York: New Directions Publishing Corporation, 1965), pp. 14-15.

7 Kaufman, "All Those Ships That Never Sailed," in *The Ancient Rain*, p. 55.

8 Norman Mailer, "Hipsters," in *Advertisements for Myself* (London: Panther, 1968), pp. 265-314.

9 Kerouac, "That Crazy Feeling," in Robert Frank, *The Americans* (New York: Grove Press, 1959), pp. 5-9.

10 Barbara Ehrenreich, *The Hearts of Men: American Dreams and the Flight from Commitment* (Garden City, New York: Doubleday and Company, 1983).

11 See John D'Emilio, "The Movement and the Subculture Converge: San Francisco During the Early 1960s," in *Sexual Politics, Sexual Communities: The Making of a Homosexual Minority in the United States, 1940-1970* (Chicago: University of Chicago Press, 1983), pp. 177-95.

12 Joanne Kyger, "Waiting Again," in *Going On: Selected Poems1958-1980* (New York: E.P. Dutton & Co., 1983), p. 4.

13 Diane DiPrima, "The Loba Addresses the Goddess/Or the Loba as Priestess Addresses the Loba-Goddess," in *Pieces of a Song: Selected Poems* (San Francisco: City Lights Books, 1990), p. 186.

14 Richard Cándida Smith, *Utopia and Dissent: Art, Poetry and Politics in California* (Berkeley and Los Angeles: University of California Press, 1995). See especially "The Beat Phenomenon" (pp. 145-71) and "A Woman's Path to Maturation" (pp. 172-211).

15 Greil Marcus,"Foreword," in Alexander Trocchi, *Cain's Book* (New York: Grove Press, 1992), p. viii.

16 Janine Pommy Vega, *Poems to Fernando* (San Francisco: City Lights Books, 1968), p. 16.

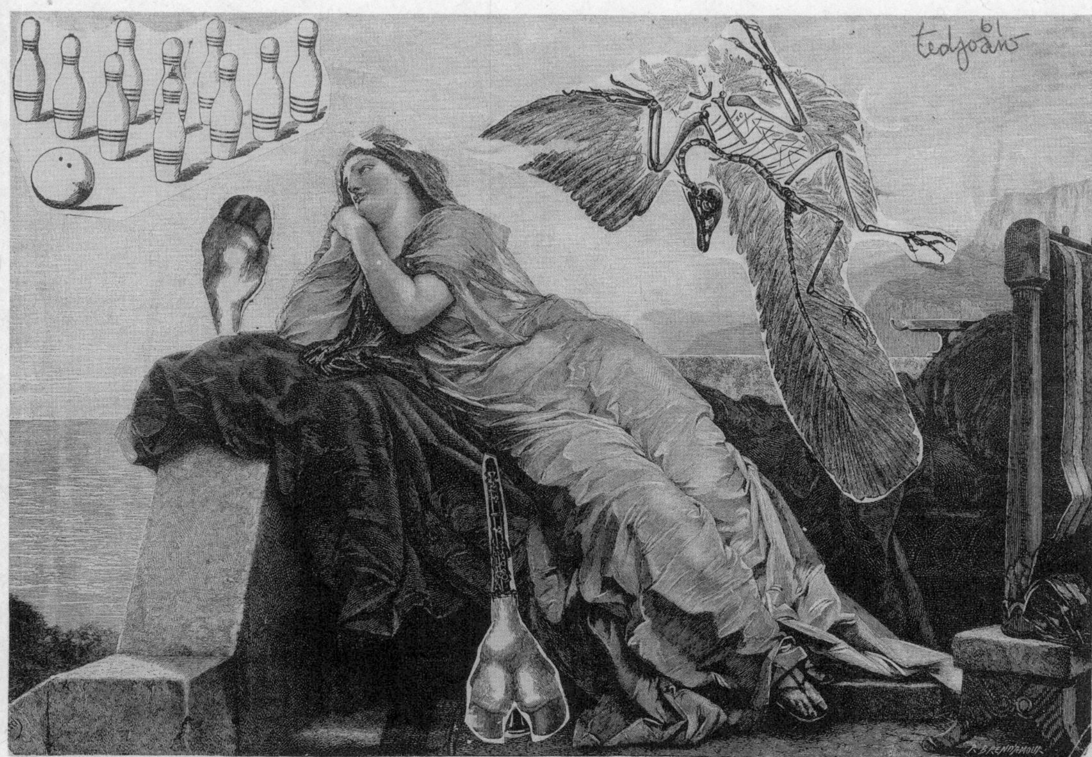

Ted Joans
First Lady Diane DiPrima, 1961
Paper collage,
7 x 9 3/4 (17.8 x 24.8)
Collection of the artist

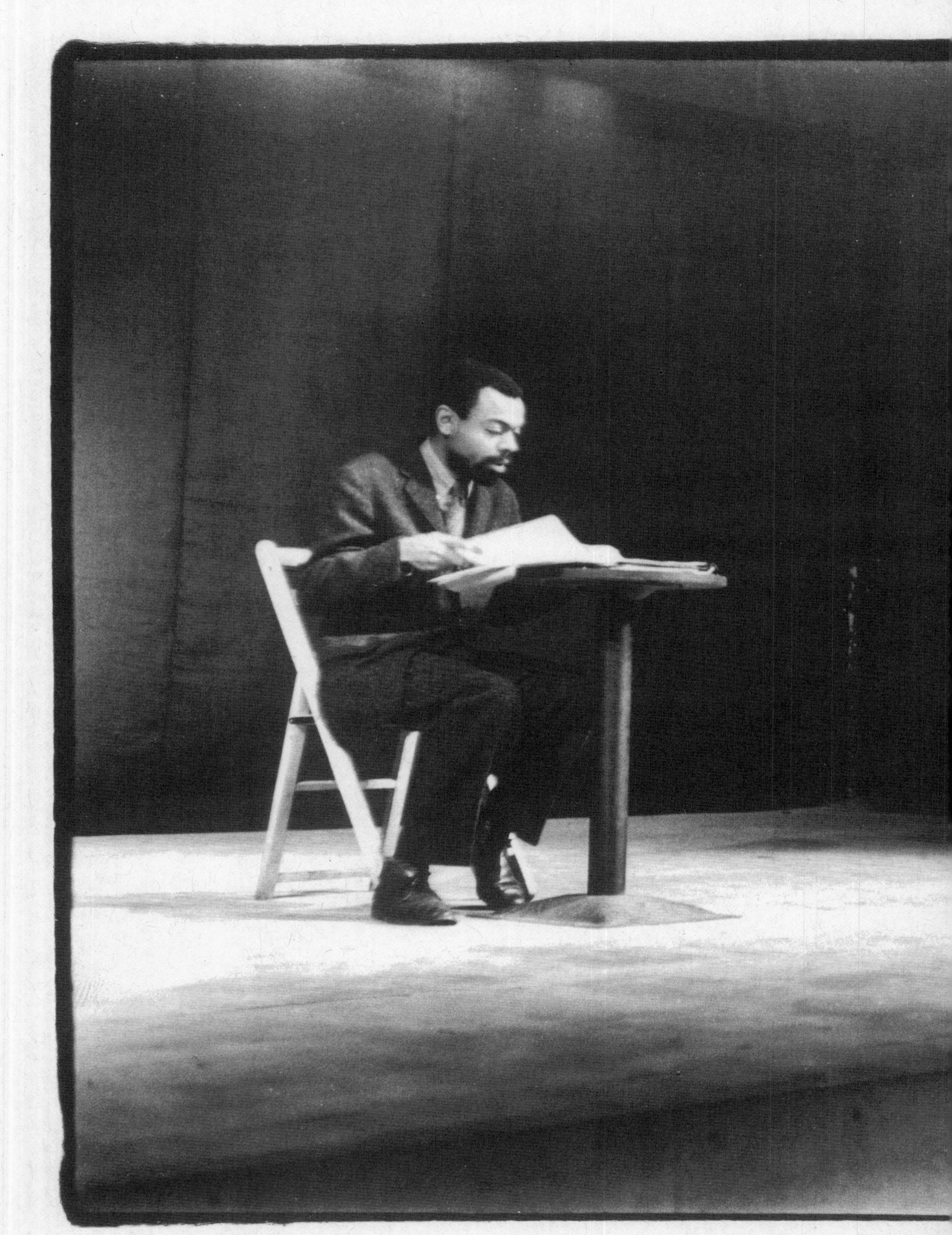

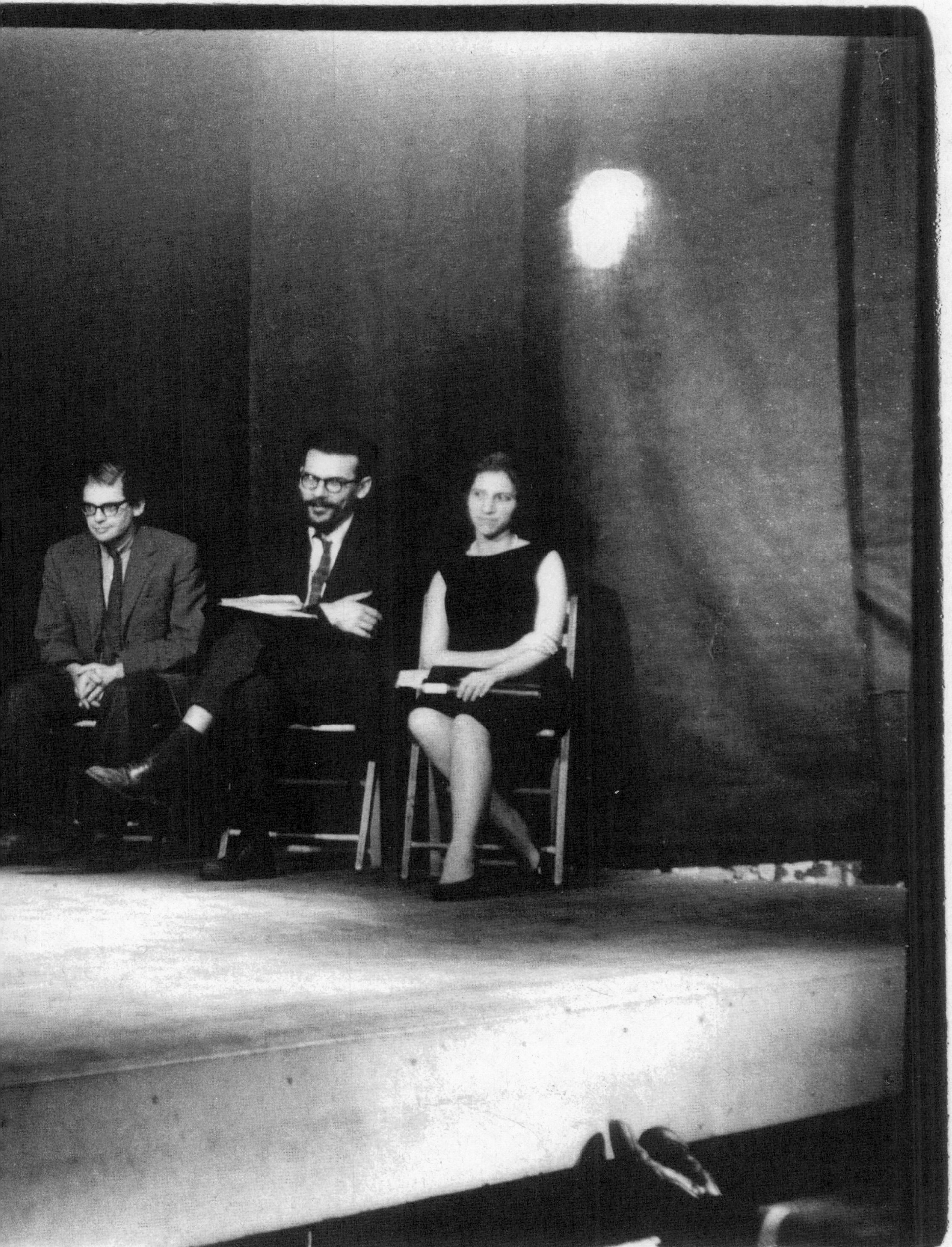

Previous page: **LeRoi Jones reading at the Living Theater**, 1961. Photo © Fred W. McDarrah

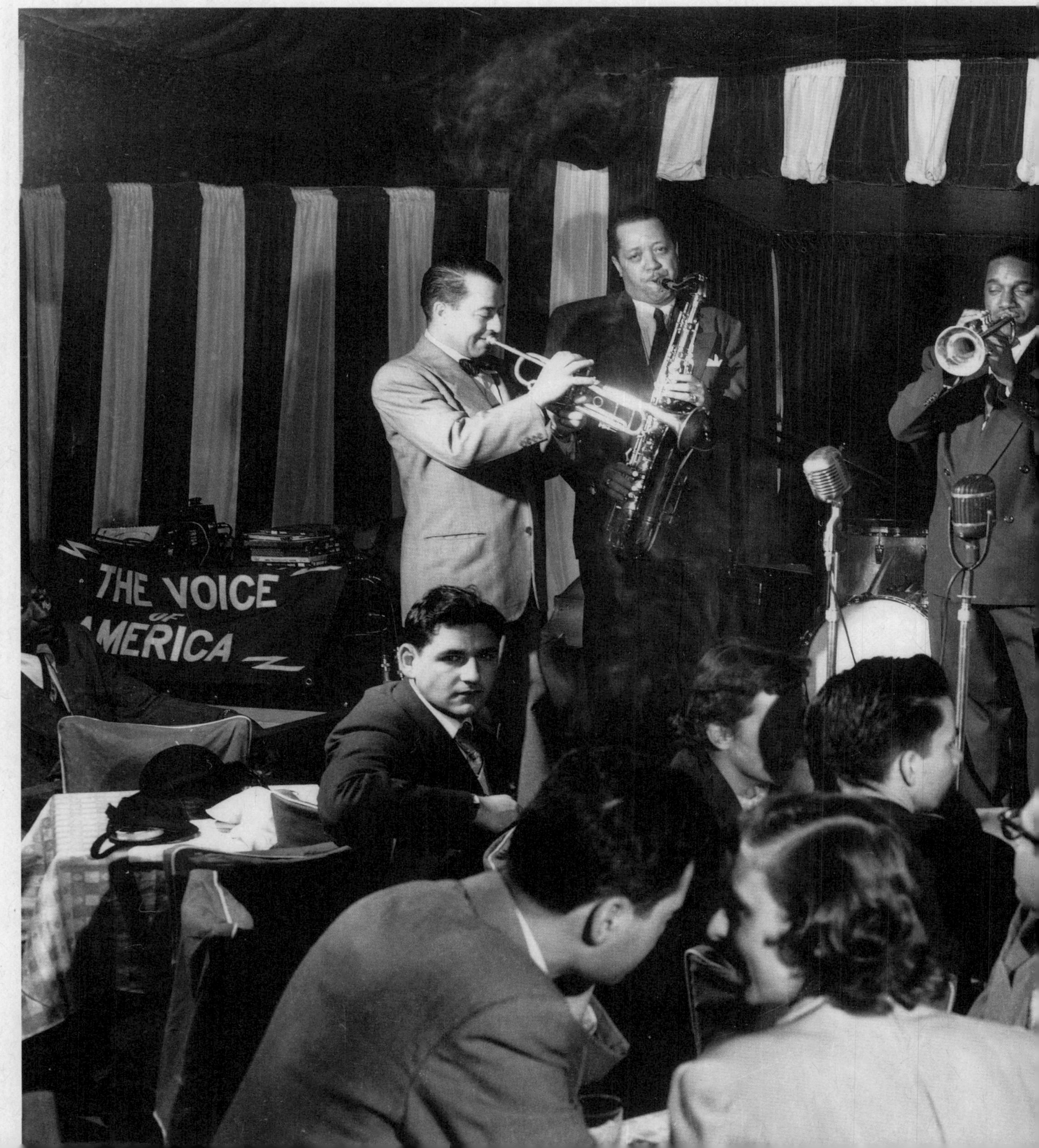

MONA LISA SALOY

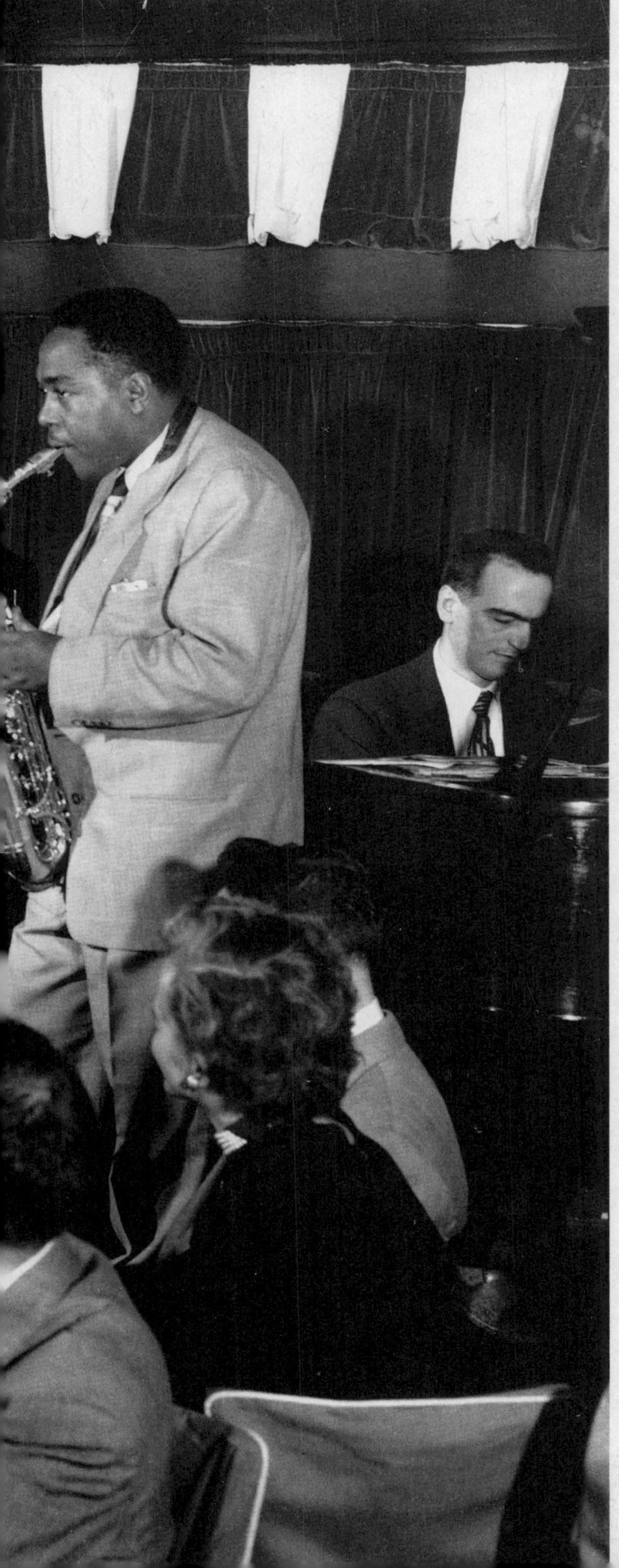

Black Beats and Black Issues

The Black Beats lived through perilous times, feeling much like James Baldwin when he spoke of making a life as an artist: "the world into which he was born is nothing less than a conspiracy against the cultivation of his talent....On the other hand, it is only because the world looks on his talent with such a frightening indifference that the artist is compelled to make his talent important."[1]

And so, the years from 1950 to 1965 are replete at once with Jim Crow rearing its ugly head, in the thick of the deafened ears of democracy. It was a cancerous racial climate that fueled a murderous Mississippi where "14-year-old Emmett Till was abducted, [brutally] beaten, shot in the head and tossed into the Tallahatchie River near Greenwood...for allegedly whistling at a white woman."[2] Yet, the sounds of the new Black music and Black vernacular, a new Black art and literature echoed against the American landscape despite its amnesia.

The Black Beat presence was larger than the preoccupation of "the best minds of" Allen Ginsberg's "generation destroyed by

Charlie Parker at Birdland, 1949

madness/starving, hysterical, naked, dragging themselves through the Negro streets at dawn looking" for a hip fix.[3] For the white Beat intelligentsia, the democratic ideal broke somewhere between concentration camps, Hiroshima and bomb shelters, and Sputnik. The American dream of two-point-one kids, a house in the suburbs with a two-car garage, and a future of empty consumption lacked any meaningful experience. White Beats then turned away from the expected upwardly mobile track, the police state, and took to the road, searching for something better.[4] What they heard was a new Black beat, a new music, and a new language, amounting to a new aesthetic—passionate and humane, expressing new dimensions of feeling, a cultivation of tastes offering an alternative to Standard American English and music, and free from the traditional American ethos. White Beats looked to the East for mystical answers and spiritual truth, to drugs for inner revelation; but within the underside of America, they recognized a black gold, an untapped power that resonated from within the silent invisible depths of Black faces and creativity. The "Negro," as African-Americans were then called, represented a contradictory, double-sided America as yet unveiled, presenting an authenticity as real as American inequality itself.

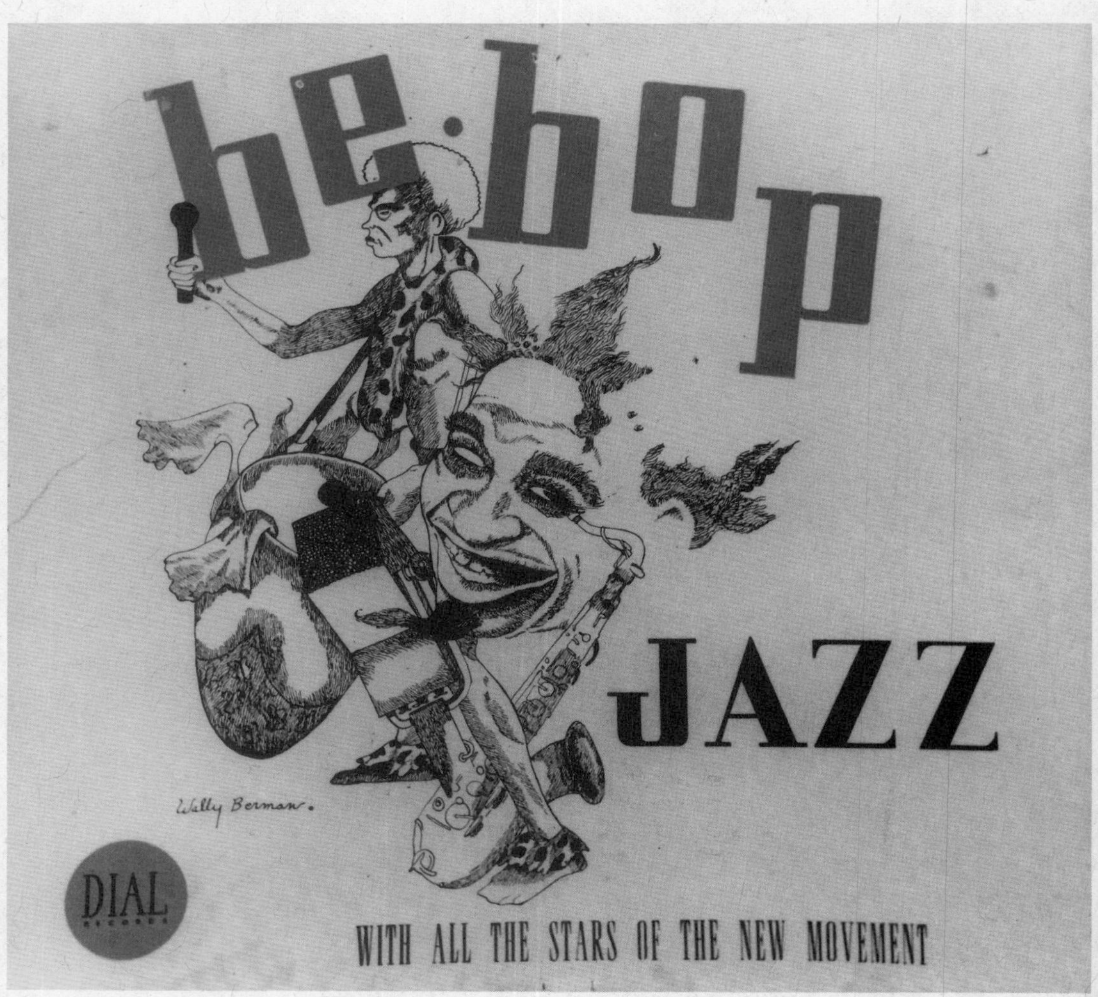

Record jacket by Wallace Berman, c. 1940s. Photo by Charles Brittin

Black Music

The black Beat presence was nowhere more profound than in the new black music, born after swing, in the forties, erupting like a volcano and spilling onto every walk of American life. With bebop, American jazz changed, and it changed all whom it touched. Bebop represented freedom from the traditional jazz of a Louis Armstrong or a Lester Young but evolved from their roots. Bebop was also a great departure from the kind of jazz easily imitated by white musicians. It represented Black bodaciousness in bent notes never played the same way, improvised and original forever. Reed men Charlie "Yardbird" Parker and Dizzy Gillespie embodied bebop along with other pioneers, pianists, Bud Powell, Thelonious Monk, drummers Max Roach and Kenny Clarke, guitarist Charlie Christian, and composer-arranger Tadd Dameron.[5] Charlie Parker was acknowledged by an entire generation. Dizzy Gillespie insists that he "was the architect of the new sound. He knew how to get from one note to another, the style of the thing. Most of what I did was in the area of harmony and rhythm."[6]

Bebop was so innovative that it became what Imamu Amiri Baraka, then a.k.a LeRoi Jones, called the jazz avant-garde, whose "rhythmic diversity and freedom were the really valuable legacies."[7] There are far too many excellent books dedicated to the study of bebop innovations to belabor specifics in this venue. It is important to declare here that, like Armstrong and Young, Parker and Gillespie changed jazz and allowed jazz music to continue a long tradition. According to Martin Williams,

> The music of Charlie Parker and Dizzy Gillespie represented a way for jazz to continue, but that was not just a matter of new devices; it also had to do with a change even in the function of music. Parker's work implied that jazz could no longer be thought of only as an energetic background for the barroom, as a kind of vaudeville, as a vehicle for dancers. From now on it was somehow a music to be listened to....[8]

As a result, the popularity of the music under Parker's innovation spread widely and lastingly.

Bebop gave jazz a new face, and American life a new style, not only of playing but of being. From letter carriers to metal latherers, from hairdressers to coffee drinkers, from teenagers to school teachers, the style of the new jazz and its jazzmen infected American life. For many, like writer Ishmael Reed, "We not only grew up on Be-Bop; Be-Bop raised us. For my generation, Be-bop came on like a light bulb going flash behind the eyes. For us, it was not only an intellectual movement, but a way of life. We walked, dressed, and rapped Be-Bop."[9] It was not uncommon for the Beats, black or white, young or old, to sport black berets, wear dark clothing, and dark sunglasses or shades and walk with the hip air of jazzmen for an obvious surface effect. On a deeper level, this adoption of being "weird" was a "calculated attempt...by Boppers," and "realistic attempts to put distance between themselves and the mindless gibberish of 'square'; i.e., commercial maximum-profit minimum-consciousness values that run the United States."[10] It was, as Baraka calls it, "socio-aesthetic activism." Jazz was no longer simply the black musician's self-expression; instead, jazz as bebop became a motif for expressing man's transcendence of his historical and personal anguish. It is somewhere here, between the imitation of bebop style, that the power of bebop and the black aesthetic give a forceful impact and attraction to black language.

Black Vernacular

The locution of hip had long became the norm for jazzmen and many Black people since the early days of jazz. The strength of hip speech is irrevocably proven in its wide popularity and use today. What is hip? To be hip is to be in the know; or, as Clarence Major puts it, to be hip is to be "sophisticated, independent and wise, in fashion, alert, and courageous."[11] In the jazz lingo, it was not uncommon for someone to yell, "Say man, is this a cool set?" Depending on the circumstance, this translates as: is the situation okay, or is the music good, or can I come inside? Praise for a very fine jazz solo might sound like this: "Man, oh man, can that cat wail!" Of course, the "cat" is a man, the man playing. Wail, to wail, or wailing is another way of expressing the degree of swing, that innate jazz bravado, or the ability to play well. In some cases, swing and wail may be interchanged. Swing, according to Clarence Major, is a "1930s style of white music that developed from hot jazz; also, a type of Black music developed by Duke Ellington; in the 1950s it meant to have fun, to give pleasure."[12] Historically, just as jazz music often runs in direct opposition and rejection to the dominant tradition, black "hep talk" or "hip talk" is filled with reversals to traditional connotations. For an early example, note the following use of "bad": "Oooooooohhhhh, that is a bad brim, Jim."[13] Here, bad is very, very good. Brim is a hat. Jim is a means of addressing a black male.[14] These reversals, oppositions, aesthetics, and values are black values, quite different from the larger society and firmly planted into African-American culture.

Either it was the perversion of the American democratic ideal, the bleak picture of the modern human condition—fated to live with death, losing individuality and personal voice—or the warmth, originality, and cultural force that led a generation to become attracted to the Negro culture and language. Admitting such force in his controversial essay, "The White Negro," Norman Mailer at once admires and insults African-Americans. On the one hand, he concedes to the precarious violence engulfing the life of any Negro, yet reduces the hipster to psychopathic pathology. The lines between the hipster as a Negro and hipster as a "white Negro" are not always clearly drawn. He praises the Negro for his ability to live consciously in the present, hails

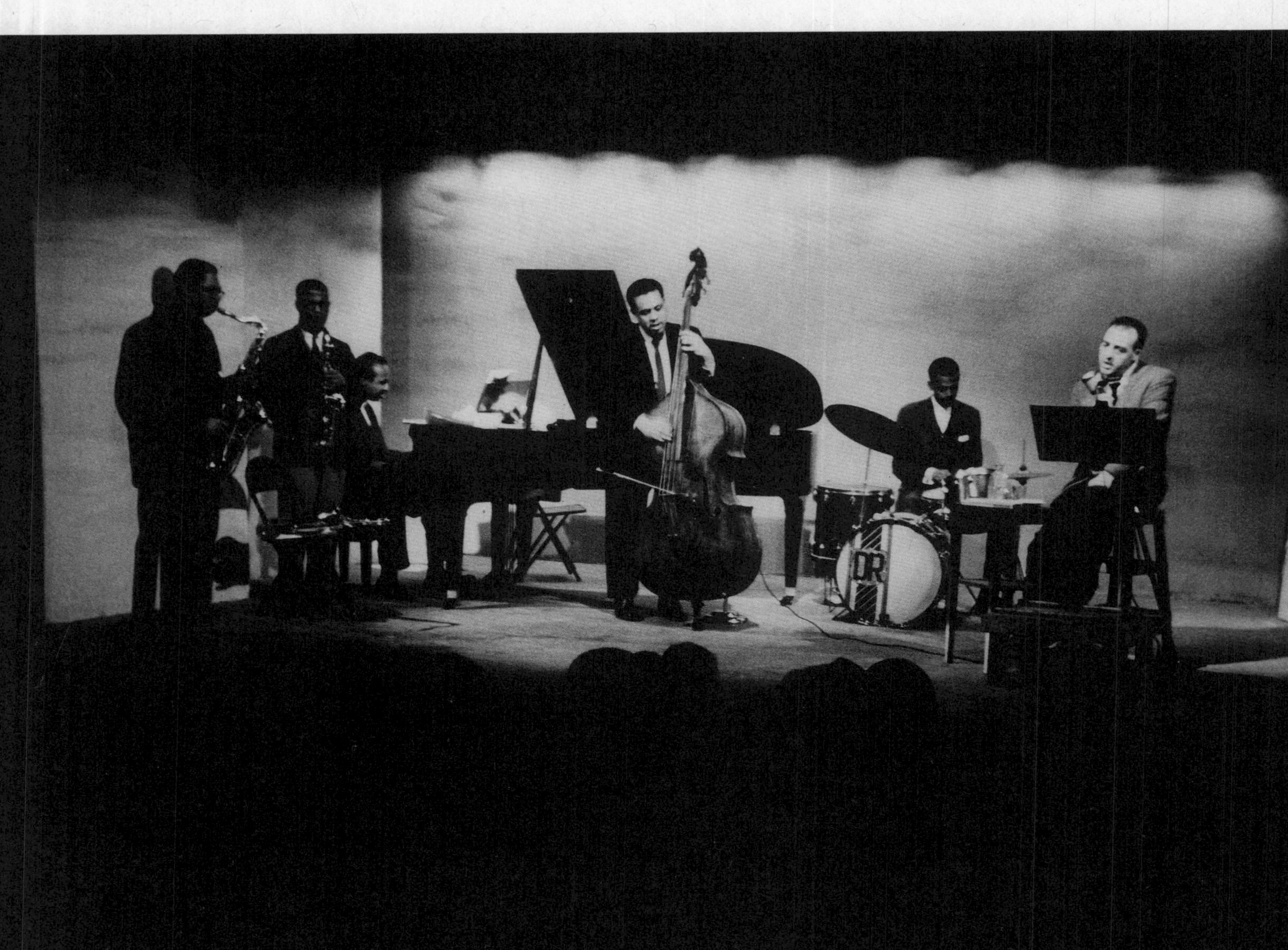

Ted Joans at the Café Bizarre, 1959. Photo © Fred W. McDarrah

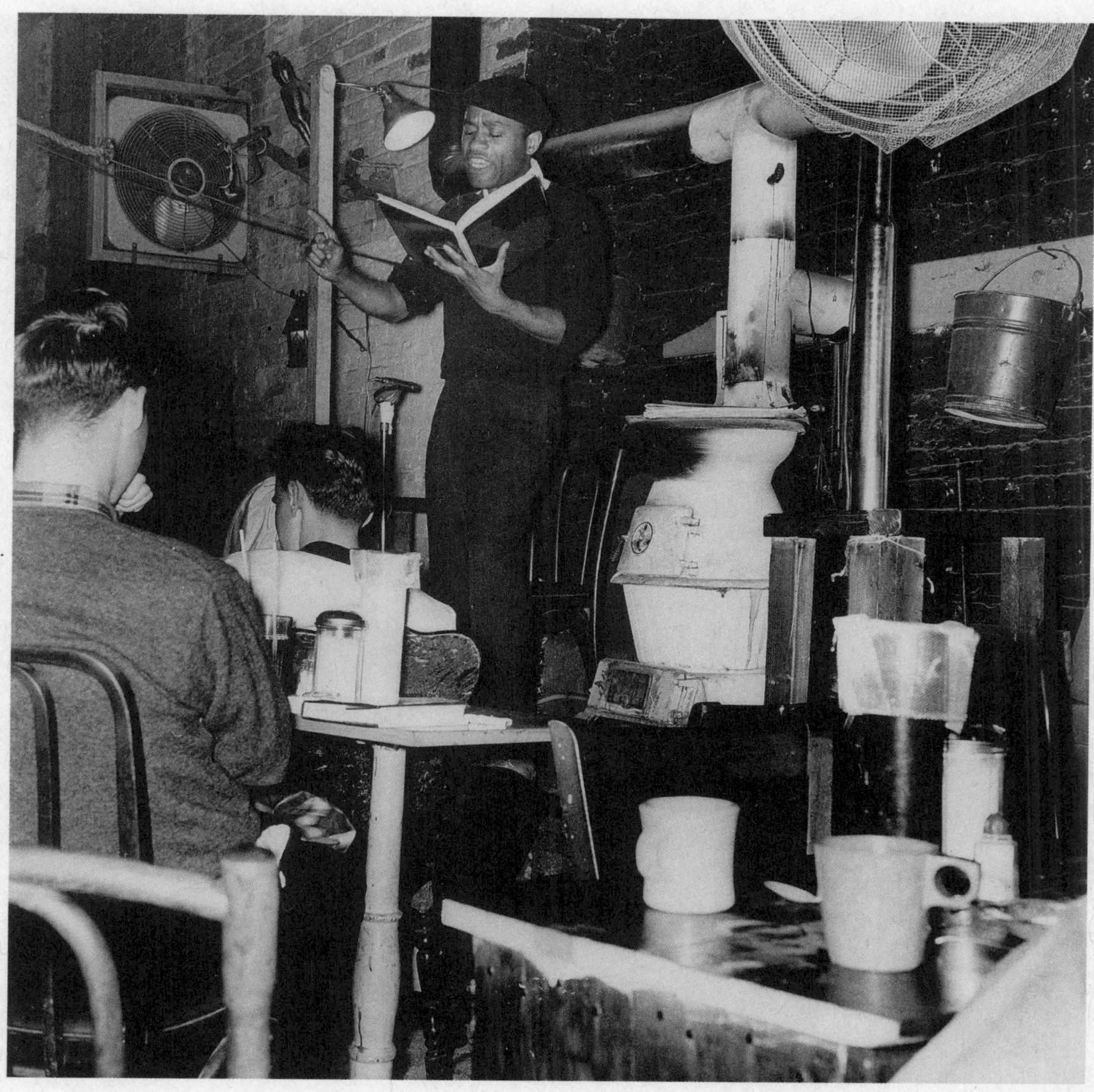

jazz for its ability to express inherent rage, despair, joy, giving voice to "the character and quality of his existence"[15] and declares the hipster an existentialist by the sheer nature of his American dilemma—that the hipster is the only real rebel around. But which hipster is which? The cultural rebels are not all white or black. Though problematic, Mailer rightly credits the Negro:

> the cunning of their language, the abstract ambiguous alternatives in which from the danger of their oppression they learned to speak ("Well, now, man like I'm lookin for a cat to turn me on..."), add even more the profound sensitivity of the Negro jazzman who was the cultural mentor of a people, and it is not too difficult to believe that the language of Hip which evolved was an artful language, tested and shaped by an intense experience and therefore different in kind from white slang....What makes Hip a special language is that it cannot really be taught—if one shares none of the experiences of elation and exhaustion which it is equipped to describe....It is a pictorial language...imbued with the dialectic of small but intense change, a language for the microcosm...man, for it takes the immediate experiences of any passing man and magnifies the dynamic of his movements....[16]

What Mailer hits on the head is the power of black speech and culture.

Charles Mingus and poet Kenneth Patchen at the Living Theater, 1959. Photo © Fred W. McDarrah

Ted Joans
The Ronnie Manhattan Mau Mau Return from Mexico, 1959
Paper collage, 7 x 6 (17.8 x 15.2)
Collection of the artist

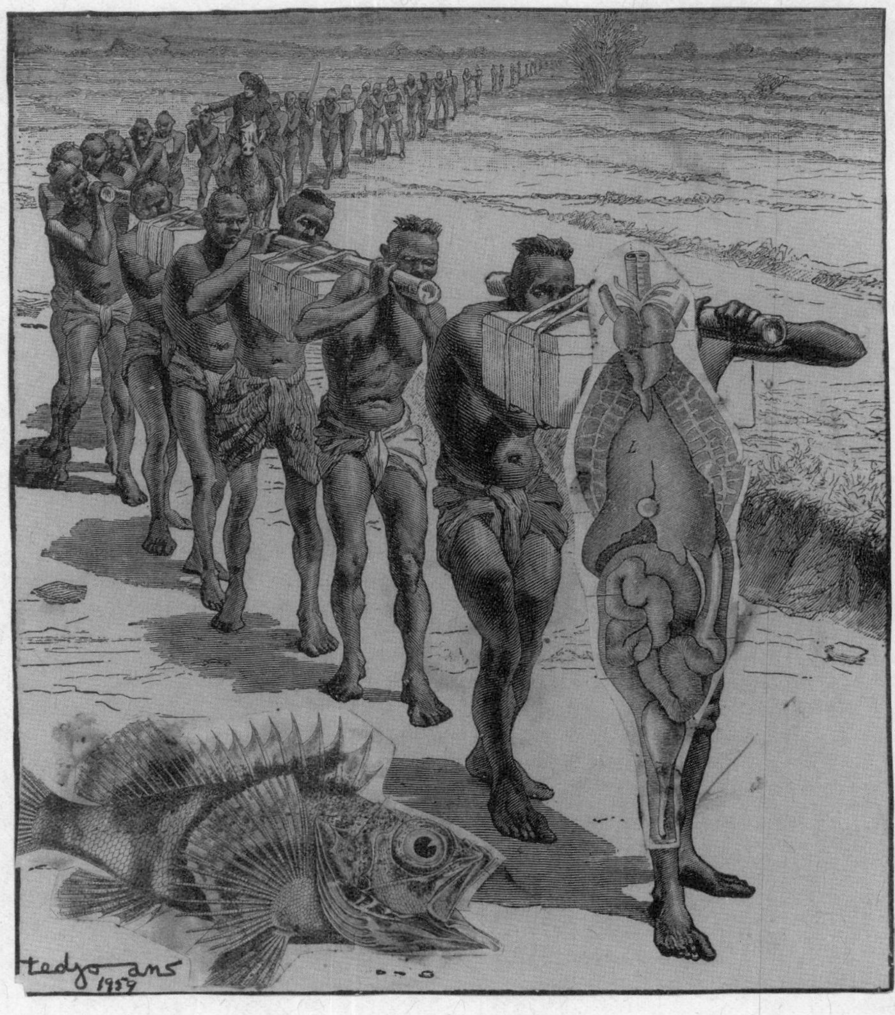

Black vernacular drew the attention of the Beats for many reasons. For the Negro, black talk equaled a personal emancipation of the mind and spirit that enabled a cultural respect and cohesion which spills across classes. Black speech develops a kinship, a creative continuance mechanism that aids cultural growth and cultural self-determination. Vernacular is Black people's signal of subculture, a denouncement of the dominant majority and its values. Though the majority of Negro actions of the 1950s were law abiding, Blacks knew all along that what America said it was and what it actually was to the Negro were very different. Though Black rhetoric gave Negroes no legal power, it built tremendous personal power among many classes: the lower classes, the artistic classes, the intellectual and nationalistic classes. Negroes had no rights but had each other, especially in language. Black English, spoken in barber shops and kitchens, transmitted face-to-face, generation-to-generation, rejects Standard American English. While black vernacular, appropriated by the advertising and communications media, has proven economically viable to all but Blacks, it has elevated African-American culture among Blacks. During the Beat years, it also provided a cultural cohesion within the Beat counterculture and the avant-garde.

Black vernacular is the inner cultural communication vehicle, an instrument of solidarity and political awareness that serves to intensify the obvious or unobvious commitment of a people to their culture; it is an evidence of group consciousness, self-assertion, and group identity. Serving to unite basic values, us versus them, it develops race pride, and provides a direct response to the actual conditions of African-American life. Its social function then is a defensive system of communication, containing beliefs and ideas, supporting and justifying a collective habit. Black talk is a positive gesture that reverses the power of (white American) contempt, giving the language the power to abolish the white world order and release the internal feeling of inferiority and self-contempt. It is a direct reaction against American cultural domination, not subordinate, but an independent expression, a ready springboard to self-congratulation and appreciation, making, as Lerone Bennett suggests, "Blacks become real to themselves and their language an action to make them real to others."[17] Vernacular, then, becomes the honey to the bees for the Beats; it is a language of liberation expressing unique linguistic loyalties. The Beats chose hip language for cultural reasons, "the vernacular as liberation, resistance, and loyalty."[18]

Black Art

The year 1950 brought changes that would provide a keynote for the decade. It kicked off with a Black population that was one-tenth of America's total. Thousands of Blacks attended the National Emergency Civil Rights Conference in Washington. Though two African-American giants, Charles R. Drew and Carter G. Woodson, died, the Supreme Court shook segregation in three landmark cases.[19] Gwendolyn Brooks won the Pulitzer Prize. Charlie Parker was already affectionately known as "Bird." Black artists of the 1950s produced works that hovered between Abstract Expressionism and Social Realism. Just as the fabric of America seemed to break apart with the harrassment of Hollywood filmmakers and stars, the growing lack of freedom in letters, so the visual arts felt the pinch, especially for black artists. Like a large portion of America, they too were influenced tremendously by the new jazz of the day and bent and broke from traditional European molds, searching their innermost recesses for their statements, their authenticity.

It is nearly impossible to generalize fully about black art in the 1950s. As artists living in a separate state of union, cases can be made that their movements ran sometimes parallel yet in contradiction to the movements in literature. Of the leading contributors to African-American art during the decade, Aaron Douglas, Norman Lewis, Archibald Motley, Romare Bearden, Jacob Lawrence, Charles White, Elizabeth Catlett, and Augusta Savage owed much to the support they had received in the forties as Works Progress Administration (WPA) artists.[20] By the fifties, many of them had abandoned the intense historicizing of earlier decades. "Douglas grew into portraiture while building the art department at Fisk, a new romanticism emerged in Norman Lewis and Ellis Wilson, and others began using brilliant colors and stylized semi-abstractions; Charles White expressed 'regenerative forces' that 'symbolized hope and encouragement for the future of his race' in pieces like *The Preacher* and *Mahalia Jackson*."[21]

Many forces during the fifties broadcast the internal racial struggles in the United States and gave international attention to the plight of African-Americans; these same forces also encouraged an increase in black awareness of Africa which, as in literature, affected the works of art. Anti-discrimination laws were passed in New York and Washington, D.C.; bus boycotts occurred in Baton Rouge, Louisiana, and many other southern spots; the US Supreme Court passed the landmark *Brown* v. *Board of Education* decision; Ralph Bunche became Undersecretary of the United Nations; Rosa Parks—a maid who was sick and tired of segregation—became an activist, and her courage generated a momentum toward civil rights that resonates today; Martin Luther King's home was bombed in Montgomery; singer Nat King Cole was attacked by white supremacists on a stage in Birmingham; and the Southern Christian Leadership Conference was born in New Orleans. On the international level, the first conference of black writers and artists met at the Sorbonne in Paris, and Ghana became independent of colonial rule. Boycotts blossomed at home, and the image of Africa was forever changed from the "Tarzan and Jane legend" to a continent of achievement, dignity, and history.

Though bombarded by the racial and social realities of the decade, African-American artists continued to experiment and produce works of art in different directions: some abstract and Beat, some off the picture plane, and some into portraiture. Artists like Norman Lewis, Ed Clark, Arthur Monroe, George Preston, Vincent Smith, and Robert Thompson bridged two worlds. They were at home in their own black communities and branched out into others. Norman Lewis illustrates black artistic growth during the fifties. Like many, he was sensitive to jazz music and incorporated it into his work. He also encompassed everything new with Abstract Expressionism, and was sort of a bridge between the avant-garde and the African-American aesthetic.[22] Art historian Cheryl McKay Dixon calls Norman Lewis "a visionary, of and before the times, right there in Harlem with the musicians and helping at the Harlem Community Art Center"; he was also involved with "white artists like Mark Rothko, Ad Reinhardt, and David Smith—the Abstract Expressionists of the 50s." Ed Clark, from New Orleans, was involved with a co-op gallery called Brata, which meant brother. In 1957, in their first Christmas show, he hung a shaped painting—the painting went outside of the canvas. He is credited as the first to break the picture plane. This cooperative gallery included Japanese artists such as Momiama, and they showed their works in Paris and Tokyo.[23]

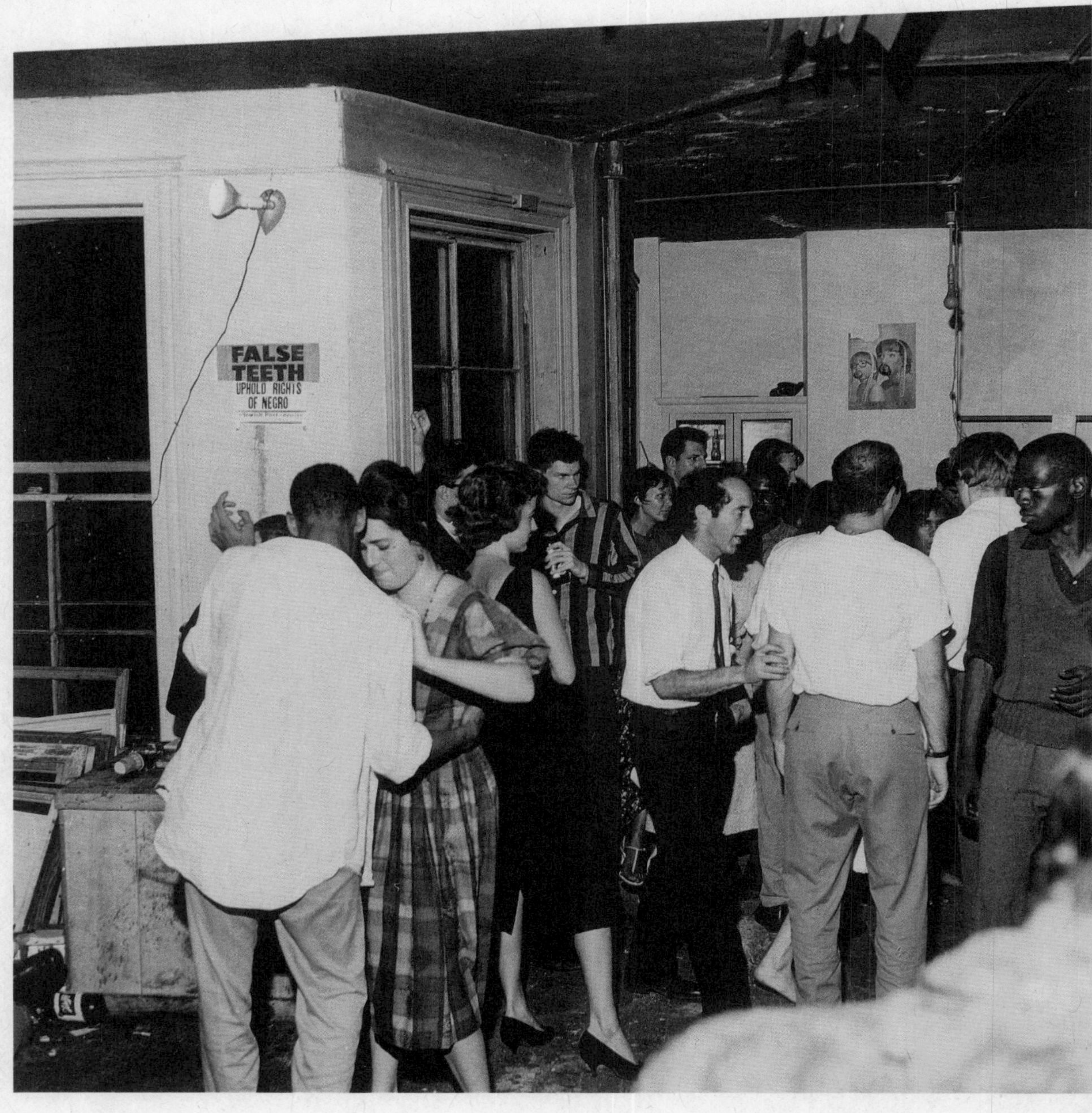

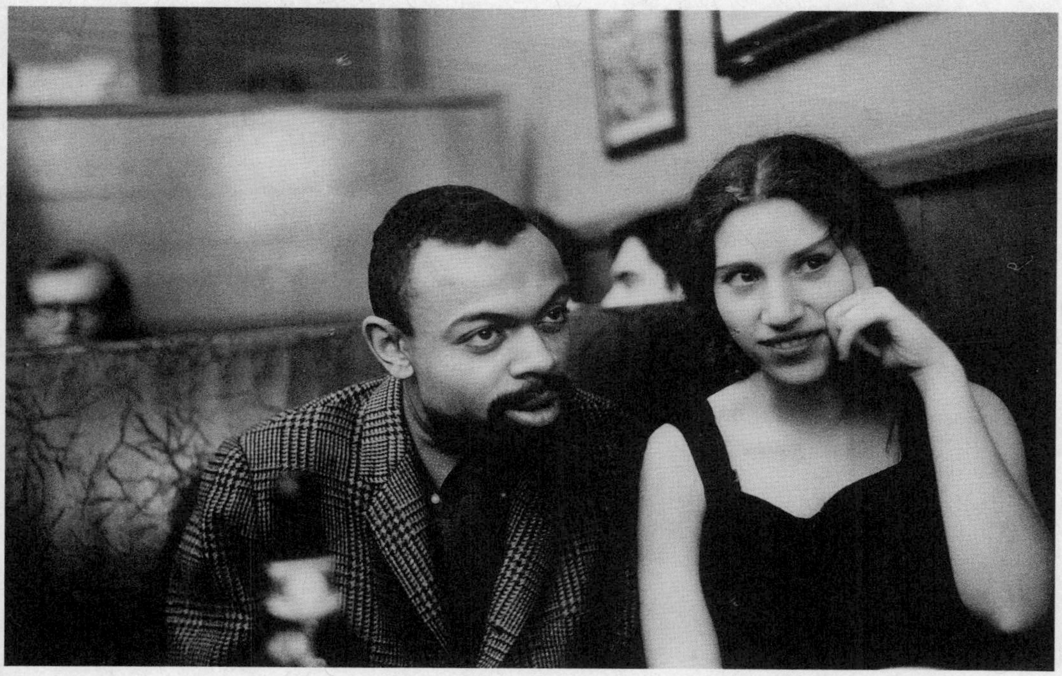

LeRoi Jones and Diane DiPrima in the Cedar Tavern, 1960. Photo © Fred W. McDarrah

Even for the fifties, the arts were not segregated in race or medium. Bicultural friendships and affiliations existed for many during the Beat years. Painter Arthur Monroe, who studied in New York at the time, considered himself an Abstract Expressionist; yet he says the training he received at The Brooklyn Museum School pushed in another direction, and that direction had nothing to do with what or who his personal friends were or what interests he had beyond painting. Of the interrelatedness that occurred between writers and painters and musicians, Arthur Monroe says that "...most people tend to ascribe to the painters things that were happening in the literature. When in fact, they were very separated. What was going on in painting would have happened in painting whether the literature was happening or not. One was not dependent on the other....I hung out with a lot of jazz musicians, probably more jazz musicians than painters, and one of them was Charlie Parker with whom I was very close. In fact, it was Harvey Cropper who introduced me to Charlie Parker, and Harvey Cropper was a [black] painter who taught Charlie Parker how to paint. Bird lived in Harvey's studio for a while...."[24]

Though the fifties was a lean decade, black artists were not deterred. Arthur Monroe insists that their concerns were "how we could enhance and advance the issues in painting. That's all very subjective of course....There never was enough time, and there never was enough money, there never was enough materials. So, a lot of us just scrounged to try to find things."[25] Monroe says there were black artists, tons of them, who identified strongly with Beat and avant-garde ideals: Jimmy DeLoache, Harvey Cropper, Cliff Jackson, Walter Williams, Joseph DuCallier, Vincent Smith, Delaney, Al Hicks, Earl Miller, and others. What pained Monroe about that time? For him, the loss of Charlie Parker and what was happening with America. "One of the things was the rejection...very painful. On several levels, the rejection as an artist, the rejection as a black man...the two of those combined [in a fifties America] was an enormous thing. Remember in the 50s, you still rode in the back of the bus, there were still separate bathrooms and drinking fountains...chain gangs...atomic bombs...the cold war...then when civil rights made its push...the death of John Kennedy...King...Malcolm X...Robert Kennedy....All of those happened at the same time, why? That was something to do with the core of America that was changing, and maybe we (artists, all) put our fingers on that sensitive nerve that was orchestrating the change...."[26]

Ted Joans' birthday party, 1959. Photo © Fred W. McDarrah

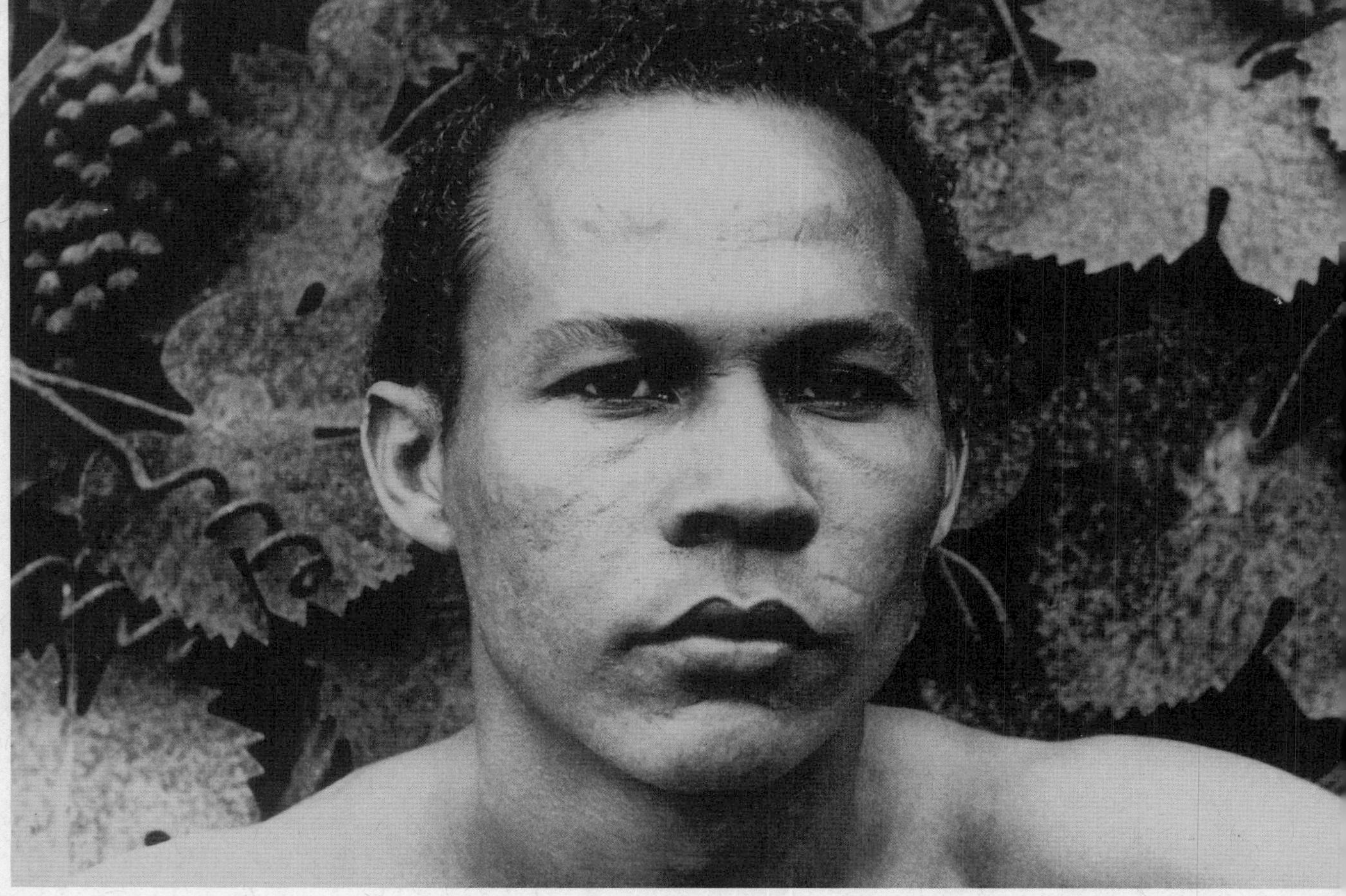

Black Literature

In literature, the 1950s continued the dynamic and penetrating tradition of African-American letters established firmly by Margaret Walker and Richard Wright in the forties. While the literary output was smaller than that of the sixties, the quality far outweighed the meager numbers. It was Ralph Ellison's *Invisible Man* (1952), Gwendolyn Brooks' *Annie Allen* (1950), James Baldwin's *Go Tell It on the Mountain* (1953), *Notes of a Native Son* (1955), and *Nobody Knows My Name* (1961), which jointly pointed out the postwar existential dilemma of the "Negro," and made "the Black man's lack of identity...a *cause célèbre* for Western liberals everywhere."[27] Other notable African-American authors and their works of the day include: (Jay) Saunders Redding's *On Being a Negro in America* (1951) and *Stranger & Alone* (1950); Ann Petry's *The Narrows* (1953); Richard Wright's *The Outsider* (1953), *The Color Curtain* (1956), *Pagan Spain* (1957), *White Man, Listen!* (1957), and *The Long Dream* (1958); Paul Robeson's autobiography, *Here I Stand* (1958); Arna Bontemps and Langston Hughes' *Book of Negro Folklore* (1958).

Because the Negro's plight was coming to light strongly in the fight for civil rights, and Negro fiction and nonfiction prose clearly detailed their dilemma, the world began to recognize the Negro as the essential human, the embodiment of the isolated, invisible modern person, the alienated misfit, aware of the modern fifties situation—the lack of rights, being outside of the mainstream, possessing great discomfort, anxiety, and loneliness—an existential existence. In African-American fiction though, that articulation was not an avowed Beat aesthetic but a human cry of art and angst. It was in the poetry of African-Americans that the Beat notions rang clearest.

Jazz and its language grew as a creative vehicle in poetry far past its initial history during the roaring twenties. Of the pioneers in jazz poetry, Langston Hughes led the pack historically. In his *Montage of a Dream Deferred* (1951), his special *The Sweet Flypaper of Life* (1955) with photographer Roy DeCarava, and *Ask Your Mama: 12 Moods for Jazz* (1961), Hughes pioneered the

Bob Kaufman, 1954 (detail). Photo by Chester Kessler

use of jazz language and Negro colloquial speech, especially in verse, a tradition he had been popularizing since the twenties.

Continuing the jazz poetry tradition, Bob Kaufman used jazz music as a creative vehicle, reading to standing-room-only crowds in San Francisco's North Beach clubs as early as 1953. Called the quintessential jazz poet, Bob Kaufman knew Charlie Parker and Billie Holiday, who often visited his apartment after gigs when he lived in Greenwich Village. In San Francisco, Kaufman was a co-founder of the important Beat literary journal *Beatitude* with Allen Ginsberg, John Kelly, and William Margolis in the spring of 1959. Critic Warren French stresses that *Beatitude* not only documented the Beat writing efforts, but "it was the only cooperative project of prominent Beats."[28] In 1985, the *Silver Anniversary Beatitude* issue was dedicated to Kaufman. In that issue, editor Jeffrey Grossman confirms that Bob Kaufman coined the word "beatnik"—not Herb Caen of the *San Francisco Chronicle*. At the 1994 New York University Beat Conference, Allen Ginsberg, when asked about Bob Kaufman, insisted that it was Kaufman who had been the driving force behind *Beatitude*.

City Lights Books first published Bob Kaufman in a series of three broadsides: *Abomunist Manifesto* (1959), *Second April* (1959), and *Does the Secret Mind Whisper?* (1960). In 1959, the November 30 issue of *Life* magazine, in Paul O'Neil's article "The Only Rebellion Around," a page-and-a-quarter photo defines what is essential for a Beat "pad" or household. Charlie Parker and Miles Davis records are pictured, as is the *Abomunist Manifesto*, unfolded, though Bob Kaufman is not credited. Kaufman's renown nevertheless grew. The French called him "the Black Rimbaud."

In addition to Kaufman, other black poets rallied to the Beat ethic: Ted Joans, who was also a visual artist, wrote *Beat Poems* (1957), *Funky Jazz* (1959), and other books; A.B. Spellman wrote *The Beautiful Days* (1965) and *Four Lives in the Bebop Business* (1966); Calvin Hernton contributed to many journals of the day as well as to *Beyond the Blues: New Poems by American Negroes* (1962) and the seminal anthology *Black Fire: An Anthology of Afro-American Writing* (1969)—edited by Larry Neal and LeRoi Jones. LeRoi Jones describes the newness of the times in his autobiography:

> **I took up with the Beats because that's what I saw taking off and flying and somewhat resembling myself. The open and implied rebellion—of form and content. Aesthetic as well as social and political. But I saw most of it as art, and the social statement as merely our lives as dropouts from the mainstream. I could see the young white boys and girls in their pronouncement of disillusion with and "removal" from society as being related to the black experience. That made us colleagues of the spirit.[29]**

Another black Beat poet, Ray Durem, paints an additional pallet in his poem "Problem in Social Geometry—The Inverted Square!" which is dedicated to Lawrence Ferlinghetti.

> **I have seen the smallest minds of my generation**
> **assume the world ends at Ellis Island,**
> **that its capitol is North Beach,**
> **and Fillmore is a nightown Street**
> **for weary intellectuals.**

Orginally, this poem appeared in *Umbra* in 1967, and again in the 1970 anthology edited by Clarence Major, *The New Black Poetry*. "Problem in Social Geometry" is clearly a Beat portrait dedicated to a Beat publisher.

In 1962, a group of working black writers, Tom Dent with Calvin Hernton and David Henderson, founded the *Umbra* Workshop writers group that edited and produced a fine little magazine of the same name. Participants included other writers, such as Lorenzo Thomas, Brenda Walcott, Askia Mohammad Touré, LeRoi Jones, Ishmael Reed, Jane Poindexter, Joe

Johnson, and the magazine published many writers of color, including Alice Walker, Sonia Sanchez, and Victor Hernandez Cruz. *Umbra* writers gave poetry readings espousing a uniquely black Beat perspective that grew into the Black Arts movement of the sixties.

Black culture has always been noble; it emerged majestic from slave dirges, work songs to blues licks, the integrity of spirituals to the honest praise-singing of gospel, from gutbucket, back-up-in-there blues to rhythm-and-blues popular music, from big band to bebop. American music is black music; black culture is American culture. The market place knows it; the Beats saw, heard, and dug its eloquence and grandeur. With this bodacious music came an integral sacred and special culture of hip, hipness, slick, tipping a dip in their walks, with leaning and rapping diction. Finally, the beat goes on as witnessed in the evolution of jazz, black vernacular in the language of hip, the Beat literature and resultant culture it fostered, and this tribute to the African-American cultural legacy—jazz idiom, music, art, and poetry, as a major and inseparable legacy of Beat culture.

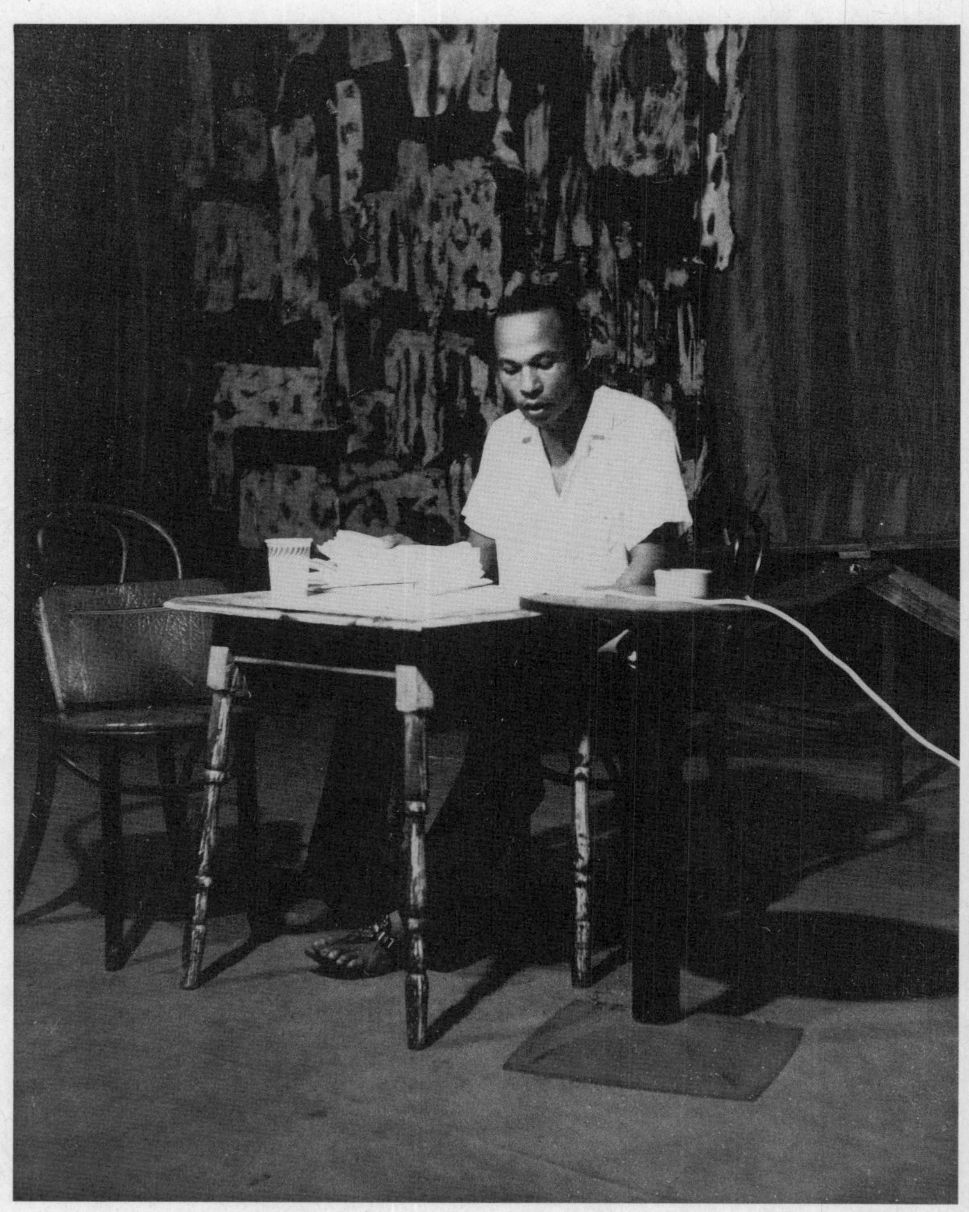

Bob Kaufman reading at the Living Theater, 1960. Photo © Fred W. McDarrah

Notes

1 James Baldwin, *Notes of a Native Son* (Boston: The Beacon Press, 1955), p. 4.

2 George C. Curry, "Killed for Whistling at a White Woman," *Emerge*, 6 (August 1995), p. 24.

3 Allen Ginsberg, *Howl and Other Poems* (San Francisco: City Lights Books, 1956), p. 9.

4 A kind of police force was formed by an uneasy American climate of suspicion on the part of law enforcement, supported by the "red scare," the atmosphere of distrust engendered by Senator McCarthy and the House Un-American Activities Committee trials, and a general attitude of intolerance toward difference.

5 Grover Sales, *Jazz: America's Classical Music* (New York: Da Capo Press, 1992), p. 132.

6 Gary Giddins, *Celebrating Bird: The Triumph of Charlie Parker* (New York: Beech Tree Books, 1987), p. 68.

7 LeRoi Jones, *Black Music* (New York: Quill, 1967), p. 75.

8 Martin Williams, *The Jazz Tradition* (New York: Oxford University Press, 1993), pp. 136-37.

9 Ishmael Reed, *Airing Dirty Laundry* (Reading, Massachusetts: Addison-Wesley Publishing Company, 1993), p. 221.

10 Imamu Amiri Baraka, *The Music, Reflections on Jazz and Blues* (New York: William Morrow and Company, 1987), p. 265.

11 Clarence Major, *Dictionary of Afro-American Slang* (New York: International Publishers Co., 1970), p. 66.

12 Ibid., p. 112.

13 Bad is "a simple reversal of the white standard, the very best"; ibid., p. 22.

14 Ibid., p. 71.

15 Norman Mailer, *The White Negro* (San Francisco: City Lights Books, 1957), p. 4.

16 Ibid., section 3.

17 Lerone Bennett, *Confrontation: Black & White* (Baltimore: Penguin Books, 1965), p. 10.

18 Telephone interview with Dr. Onita Estes Hicks, State University of New York, Old Westbury, March 19, 1994.

19 *Sweatt* v. *Painter*, *McLaurin* v. *Oklahoma State Regents*, and *Henderson* v. *United States*; see Lerone Bennett, *Before the Mayflower: A History of Black America* (New York: Penguin Books, 1988), p. 548.

20 Samella Lewis, *Art: African American* (Los Angeles: Hancraft Studios, 1990), pp. 115-38.

21 Cheryl McKay Dixon, "Afro-American Artists: Themes and Directions Since 1940," MA thesis (Baton Rouge: Louisiana State University, 1973), pp. 27-34.

22 Telephone interview with Cheryl McKay Dixon, June 30, 1995.

23 Ibid.

24 Telephone interview with Arthur Monroe, July 7, 1995.

25 Ibid.

26 Ibid.

27 Richard Barksdale and Keneth Kinnamon, *Black Writers of America* (New York: MacMillan Publishing Company, 1972), pp. 657-58.

28 Warren French, *The San Francisco Poetry Renaissance, 1955-1960* (Boston: Twayne Publishers, 1991), pp. 49-54.

29 LeRoi Jones, *The Autobiography of LeRoi Jones/Amiri Baraka* (New York: Freundlich Books, 1984), p. 156.

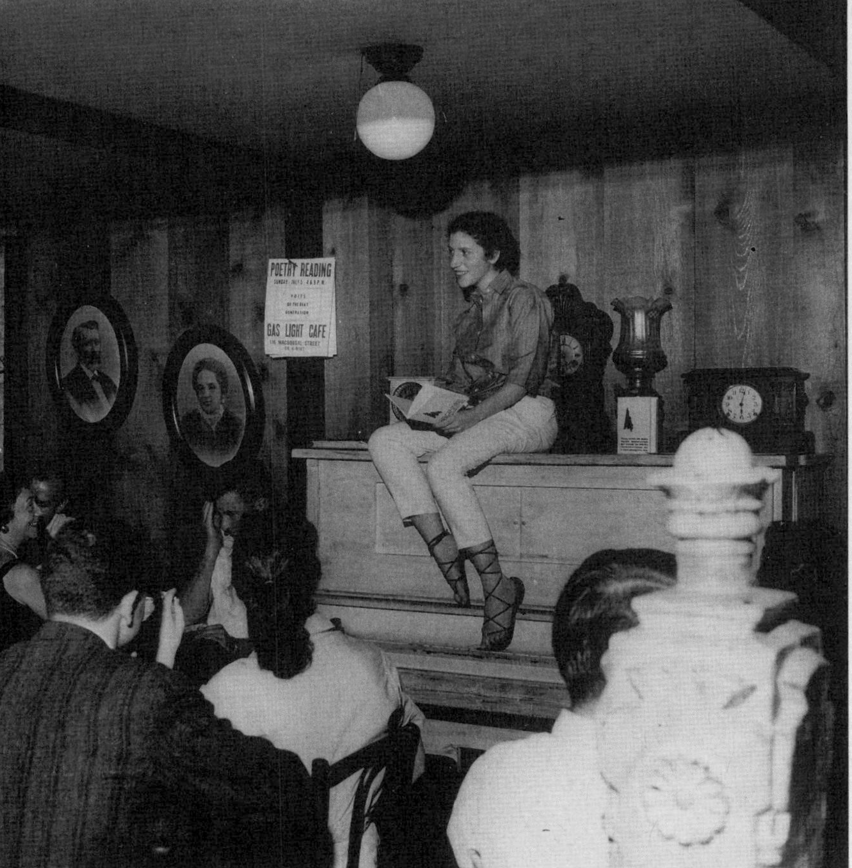

Diane DiPrima reading at the Gaslight Café, 1959. Photo © Fred W. McDarrah

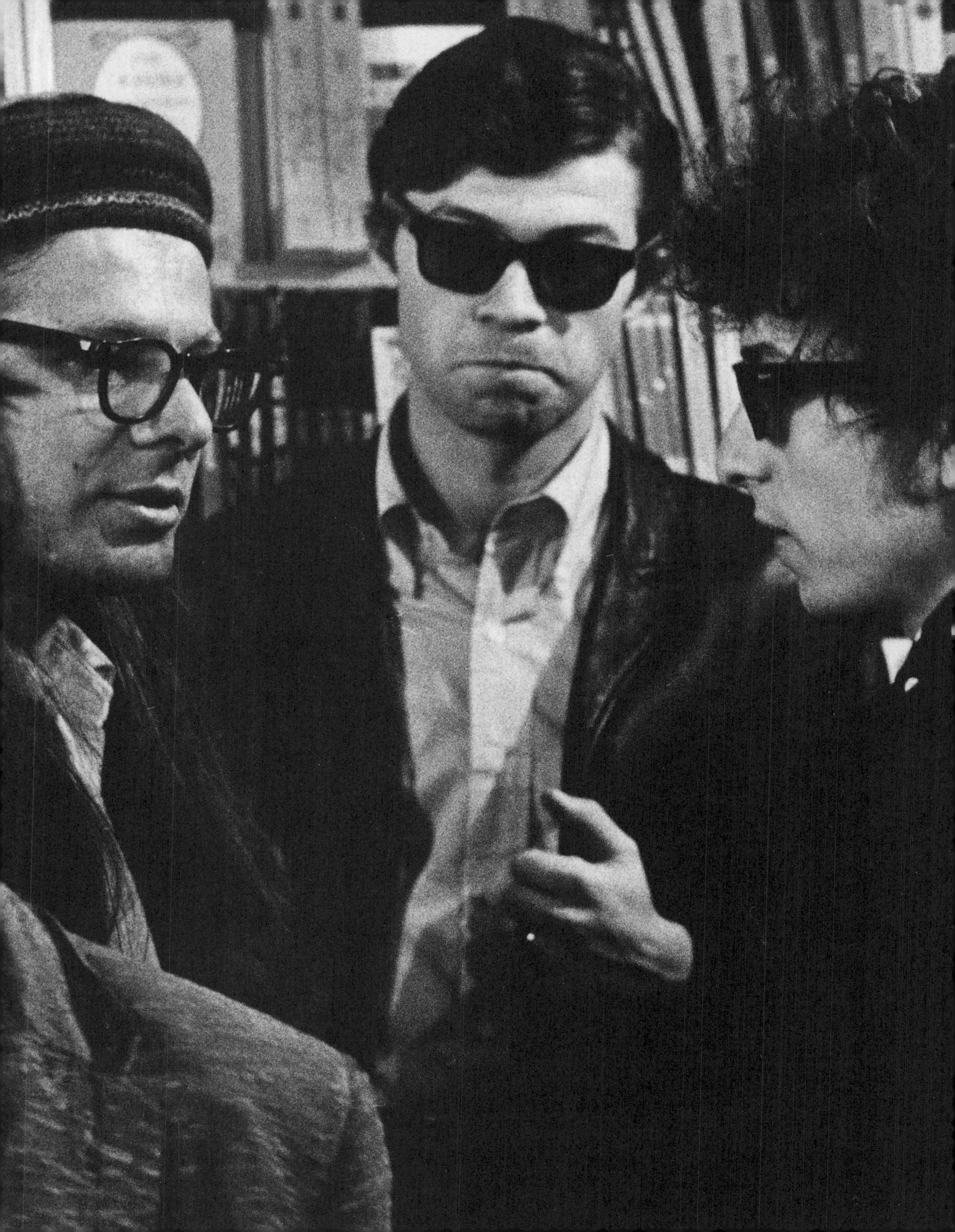

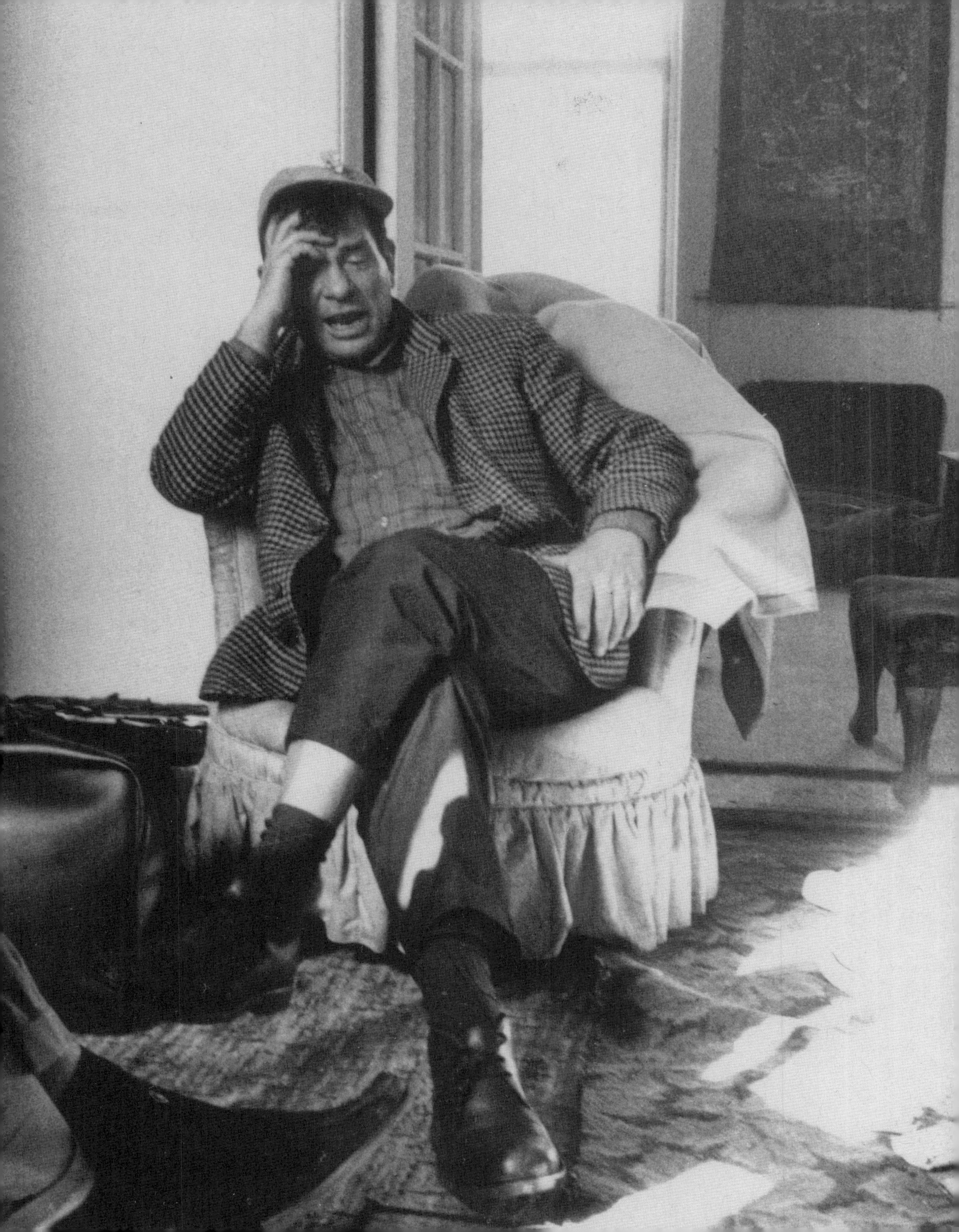

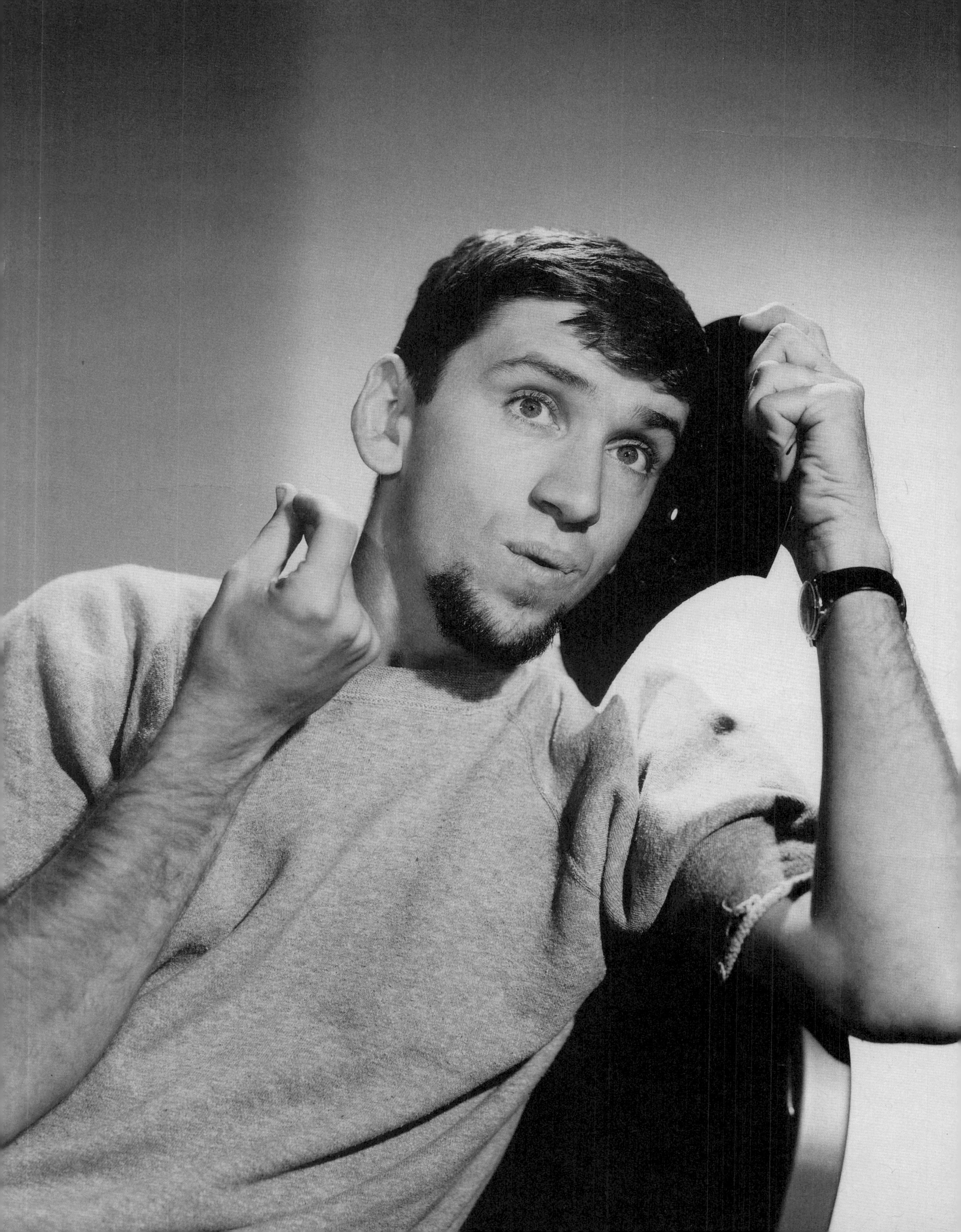

GLENN O'BRIEN

The Beat Goes On

Like Wow

The first beatnik I remember was from the TV series *Dobie Gillis*—Maynard G. Krebs, the cool kooky goateed sidekick of Dobie, the greatest high school romantic in America. Maynard was sloppy, lazy, and did not respond to the mainstream of varsity culture. Maynard was post-romantic, a dreaming realist. I didn't know what a bohemian was, but I knew one when I saw one.

As a preteen, I sensed that a beatnik was what I wanted to be. Maynard G. Krebs was a satire on beatniks, but that didn't matter because beatness shone through. In Krebs I saw the spirit of Dizzy Gillespie. Satori, the essence of Beat, shone through the satire. The Beats were seriously unserious, unseriously serious; there was no way they could be criticized because it did not matter to them. Their detachment was untouchable, legendary. Even in Maynard. Loser Buddha. And somehow I knew that if Dobie Gillis had been capable of learning from Maynard G. Krebs, that is, if he had been hipper and had a more let-it-happen attitude, romance might have happened with Thalia Menninger, the most beautiful high school girl in the world. Because, as cute and charming and cunning as Dobie was, he was the prisoner of his own desires, while Maynard, in his out-of-it irrelevance, was a free man, a king who went on to rule Ginger, Mary Ann, Skipper, the Professor, and the Howells. Maynard preceded everything, in Beat style, with "like." Every utterance being a simile, Maynard spoke always of a Platonic universe—-existential suspension levitating every observation to the metaphysical. Like wow.

It wasn't long after encountering the Maynard way of knowledge that I discovered jazz and genuine Beats. By then I was involved with popular teen forms of rebellion, rock and roll and long hair, and eventual hippiedom. But there was always something about jazz and the Beats that transcended the pop kicks of teenager culture. There was the fine contagion of the twist, the slop, the mashed potatoes, too, and that was rock-and-roll high school at its best. But beyond

Previous page, left: **Peter Orlovsky, Robbie Robertson, and Bob Dylan in City Lights Bookstore**, 1965 (detail). Photo by Larry Keenan; right: **Kerouac's last visit to Ginsberg, yawning**, 1964. Photo by Allen Ginsberg

Bob Denver as Maynard G. Krebs in "The Many Loves of Dobie Gillis"

that was jazz music, which promised graduation into transcendent inspired spontaneity and true cool immunity from a system that was far too neat and orderly.

There were waves of alternative rebel cultures that followed the Beat. Beat begat mod and mod begat hippie and hippie begat punk and punk begat grunge, but that's not really the way it went down; nothing so linear, but there is a conga line of bohemianism stretching down through history and there's always room at the end for one more blip on the scope of grid culture. But in this century it was jazz and the Beats that set the standards by which we shall come to judge the living and the dead. Beat is jazz culture—the literary side of a coin that knows no realm but the kingdom of swing, where art is a living thing. Beat is about the literature of the bop era, where the written word returned from the crypt to the living air of the spoken and heard. Jazz and poetry, though rarely combined with perfection, perfectly coexisted in the same continuum of cool, live spontaneous art forms not made for the can or microwave.

I remember reading Ginsberg and Burroughs in high school and thinking maybe I should be gay for artistic reasons and listening to Miles and Coltrane and thinking about junk. I went to high school in a rough neighborhood and my mother used to tell me not to walk around there because somebody might try to sell me pot and I walked for miles for days and nobody did, but the spirit was willing. I was ready and willing to be a Beat, just born too late and forced to live a

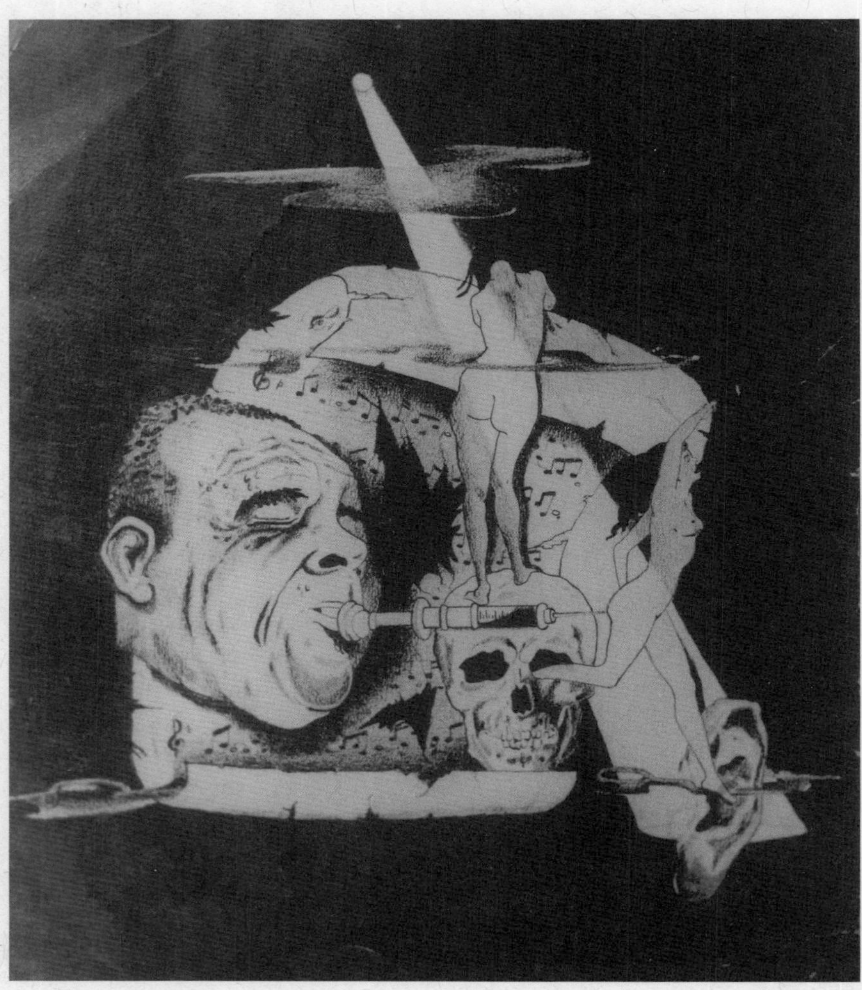

Record jacket by Wallace Berman, c. 1940s. Photo by Charles Brittin

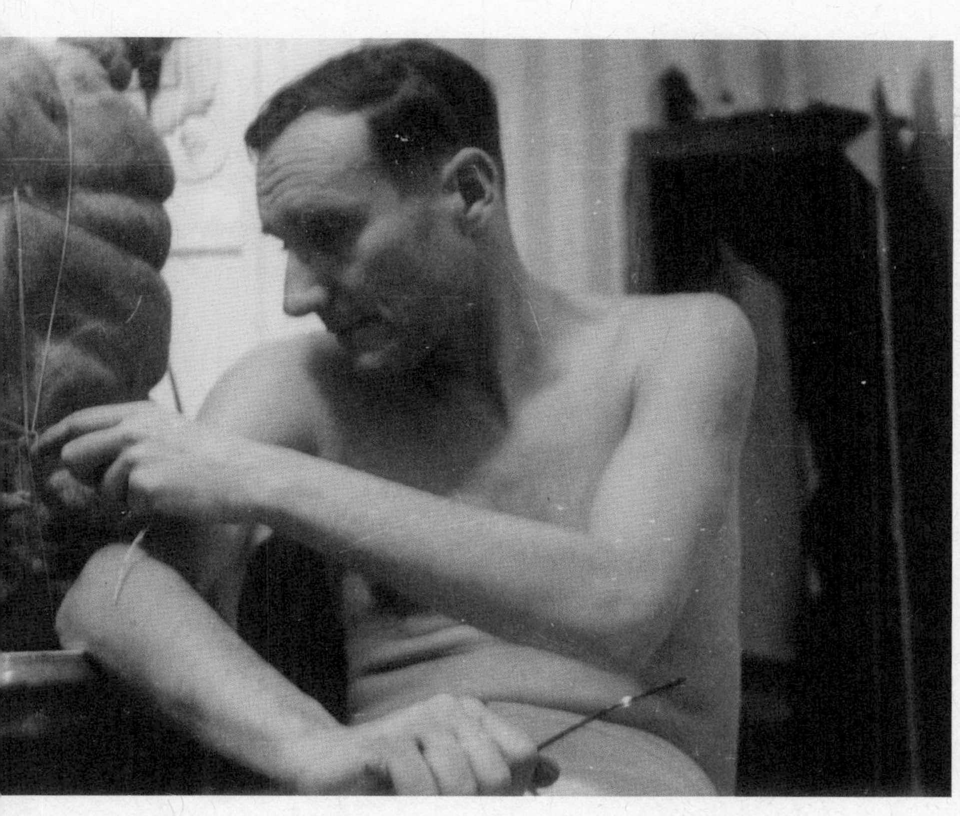

Burroughs with Yage, 1953 (detail).
Photo by Allen Ginsberg

Lafcadio and Peter Orlovsky, San Francisco, 1956.
Photo by Allen Ginsberg

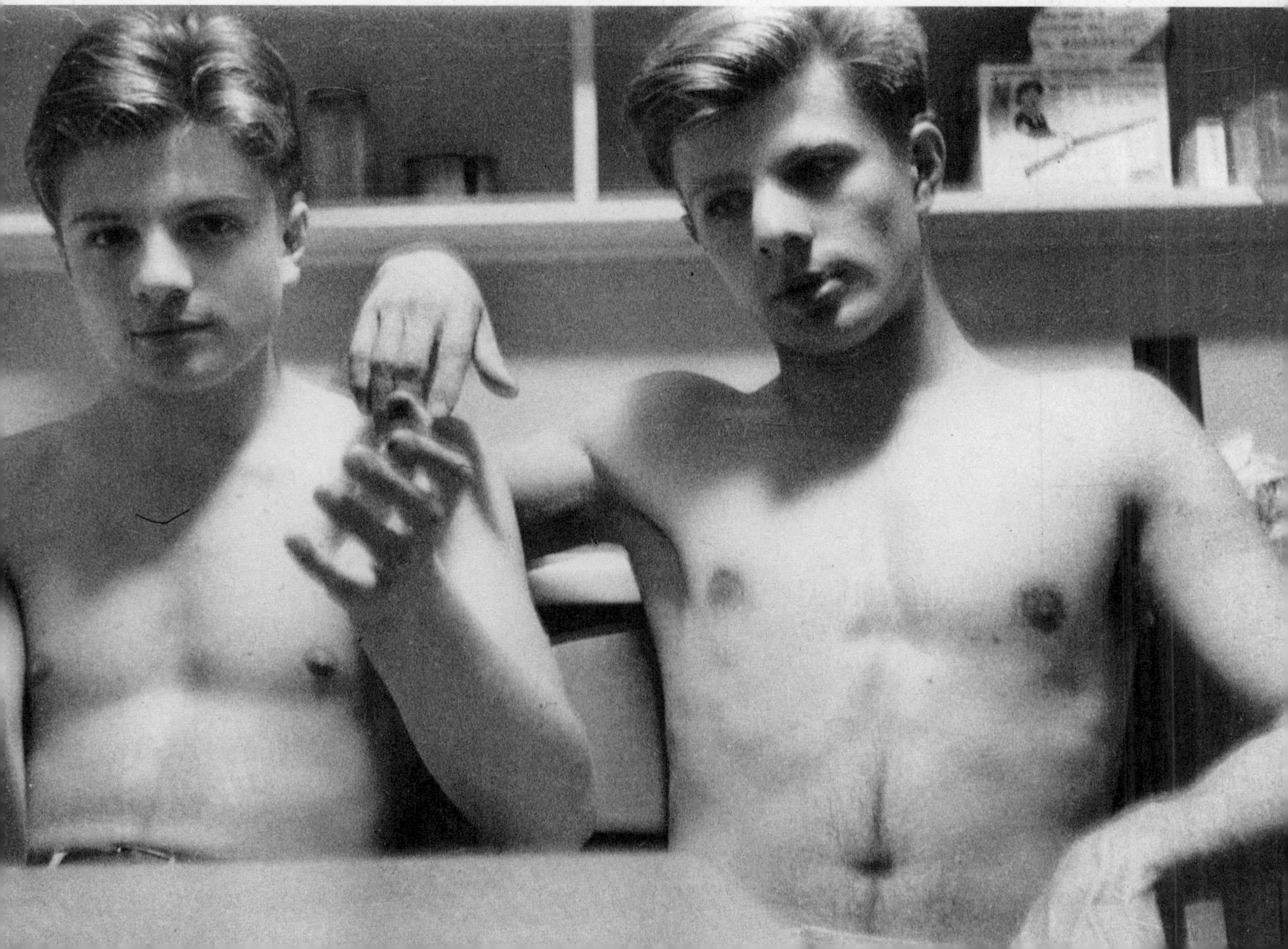

hippie life which was much less to my inclinations.

But in hippie there was Beat. Rhythm and blues and marijuana and all the drugs you could eat. Jimi Hendrix was a Beat. And the Paul Butterfield Blues Band and Canned Heat. And Janis Joplin and Ken Kesey and Merry Pranksters and the tone in Grace Slick's voice and the Fugs and Captain Beefheart. All of that was Beat. Times had changed. Kerouac was a republican in his bottle, but wherever Ginsberg marched or Burroughs discharged a weapon, Beat was there. And it always seemed that the secret heart and mind, the annointed knighthood of hippie was truly Beat.

The Beats were more traditional in their cool state than the excitable armies of faddist atavistic luddite hippies. Hippie, with its extreme and contrary and separatist stance, was a phase. Bill Clinton was probably a hippie for fifteen minutes. Beat was a lifetime of skewed engaged commitment. Bill Clinton is not a beatnik. But, to paraphrase Wyndham Lewis, "A vorticist king? Why not?"

"A Beat president? Dig it."

Look at the Czech Republic.

And listen to Thelonious Monk's "Ugly Beauty."

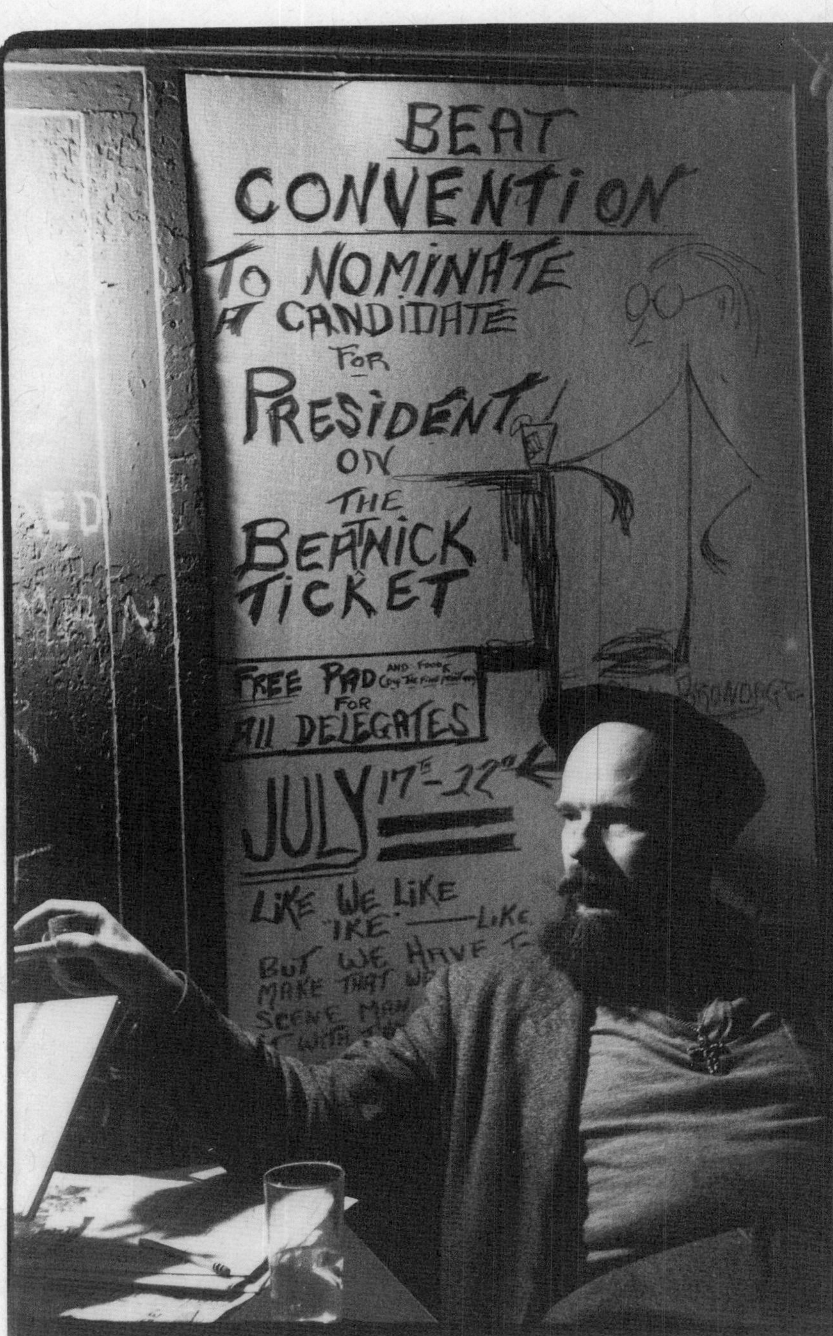

William Smith, a beatnik candidate for president at Ninth Circle Bar, 1960.
Photo © Fred W. McDarrah

James Brown and Oracular Footwork

> **"...they did not understand that the Jes Grew epidemic was unlike physical plagues. Actually Jes Grew was an anti-plague. Some plagues cause the body to waste away; Jes Grew enlivened the host. Other plagues were accompnied by bad air (malaria.) Jes Grew victims said air was as clear as they had ever seen it and that there was the aroma of roses and perfumes which had never before enticed their nostrils. Some plagues arise from decomposing animals, but Jes Grew is electric as life and is characterized by ebullience and ecstasy.Terrible plagues were due to the wrath of God; but Jes Grew is the delight of the gods."**
>
> Ishmael Reed, *Mumbo Jumbo*

A Beat is contagious. Because life is vibration and sometimes you're on the same wavelength and sometimes you tune in a frequency that's a revelation, that lifts you up and you're down with that. Entire cultures transmitted via jungle telegraph, vast libraries transported across seas via drumbeat.

In the 1990s, the Beat doesn't come from a drum, from hand on animal skin on hollow log, from stick on membrane in time in brain. Beat comes from a black box's printed circuits—dial set on BPM. Beats Per Minute. Techno. Rave. House. House. Disco. Old School. New School. Dial it up. Beat comes from a microchip in a box, synthetic, like methadone, or cloned, sampled, appropriated, like ancient waves of Elvin Jones with Coltrane in his head, reduced to a formula, a perfect tone isolated from its creator matrix, perfectly timed at the push of a button, played by a disco technician at a prescribed pace with key words, slogans.

They are isolating the active ingredients from the music and the music is dead. The Beat is a convention, a formula, a pharmaceutic drug over a shaman's dead body, a control panel whose instructions are lost.

The Beat is no longer a syncopation, a subversive way to slip out of step with the arrhythmia of Stars and Stripes forever and into a funky Jes Grew dropstep out of line and into the divine. The Beat is no longer direct connection to the hoodoo godheads. The Beat is no longer time travel machine. The Beat is now disco Sousaphones, sending bio-chem Ecstatics country line dancing into the blast furnaces of planetary clearance sales. They're bargaining that the entertainment will keep you down there.

> **"It's the Beat generation. It's Be-At. It's the Beat to keep. It's the Beat of the heart. It's being Beat and down in the world and like old time lowdown. And like in ancient civilizations the slave boatman rowing galleys to a Beat and servants spinning pottery to a Beat."**
>
> Jack Kerouac

Beat was about the Beat. Reconnection of body and soul with the body and soul of knowledge. A Beat in physics occurs at the intersection of two waves, so maybe we can't expect Beat to be a constant.

Beat occurs in time and has its ups and downs. There is no separating Beat from the Beat. Beat is a religion divined by a rhythm section's sensory perceptions of God and prophesied through the cosmic connections of the soloist.

Beat is always now now, like now. That Beat, that moment of perfect tone and timing. Syncopated, right between when you most and least expect it. Now may be gone, but it will be back.

> **"Bop began with jazz but one afternoon somewhere on the sidewalk maybe 1939, 1940, Dizzy Gillespie or Charlie Parker or Thelonious Monk was walking down past a men's clothing store on 42nd Street or South Main in L.A. and from the loudspeaker they suddenly heard a wild and possible mistake in jazz. That could have only been heard inside their own imaginary head. And that is a new art, Bop. The name derives from an accident."**
>
> Jack Kerouac, *The Early History of Bop*

Allen Ginsberg, Michael McClure, and Bruce Conner chanting in San Francisco at Ginsberg's, 1965.
Photo by Larry Keenan

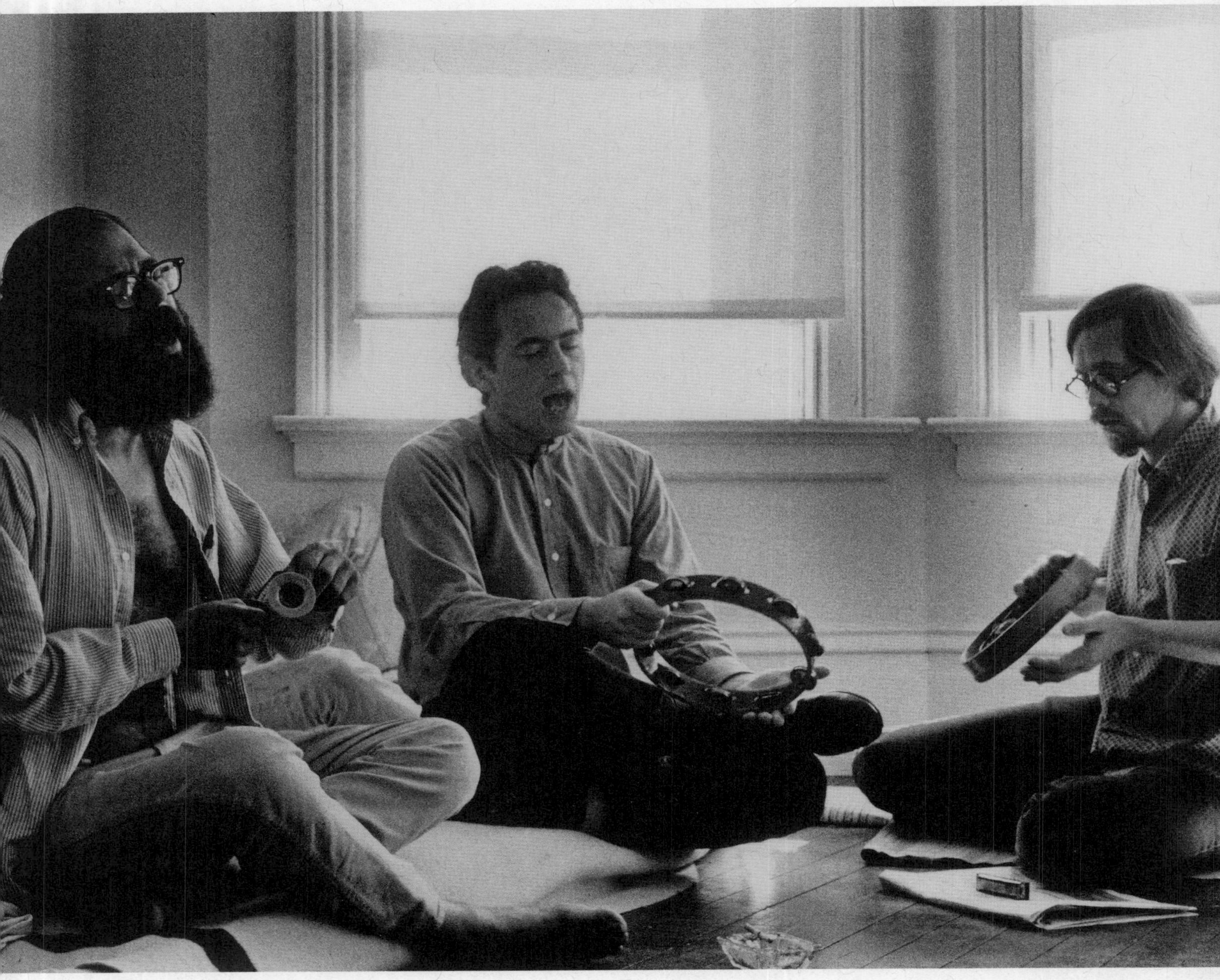

Kerouac, who wrote to a musician's beat, knew that jazz was at the heart of what the writers and artists of his generation were about. It was about the macrowave melting pot, where influences came from Euro-couture/culture and the rhythms brought here in holds of slave ships, from cosmic rays and artificial nuke suns and the glands of gods determined to survive the attempts of mutant humanoids to end all life on the planet. Bebop combined the rhythmic excitement of jazz—the popular dance form—with the most rigorous intellectual invention, becoming, hey boparebop, an irrepressible recombinant life force. Jazz is more powerful than the atomic bomb, more revolutionary than the Afro-derived forms of Cubism; the Cool School is Fro Zen, a still center from which emanates the spontaneous chill of homemade soul food Buddhism.

> "Bop came into being because the girls were leaving the guys and going off to be middle class models or something. And Dizzy or Charlie or Thelonious was walking down the street, heard a noise, a sound, half Lester Young, half rainy fog, that has that chest shivering excitement of shack, or track or empty lot, the sudden vast tiger head on the woodfence rainy no school, saturday morning no school dumpyards. Hey! And rushed off dancing. On the piano that night Thelonious introduced the wooden off key note to everyboy's warm up notes. Minton's Playhouse, evening starts, jam hours later, 10PM, colored bar in hotel next door, one or two white visitors, some from Colombia, some from nowhere, some from ships, some from Army, Navy, Airforce, Marines, some from Europe. The strange note makes the trumpeter of the band lift an eyebrow. Dizzy is surprised for the first time that day. He put the trumpet to lips and blows. "hee, hee, hah" laughs Charlie Parker, bending down to slap his ankle. He puts his alto to his mouth and says "Didn't I tell you?" with jazz of notes. Talking eloquent like great poets of foreign languages, singing in foreign countries with lyres by seas, and nobody understands because the language isn't alive in the land yet. Bop is the language from America's inimitable Africa...."
>
> Jack Kerouac, *The Early History of Bop*

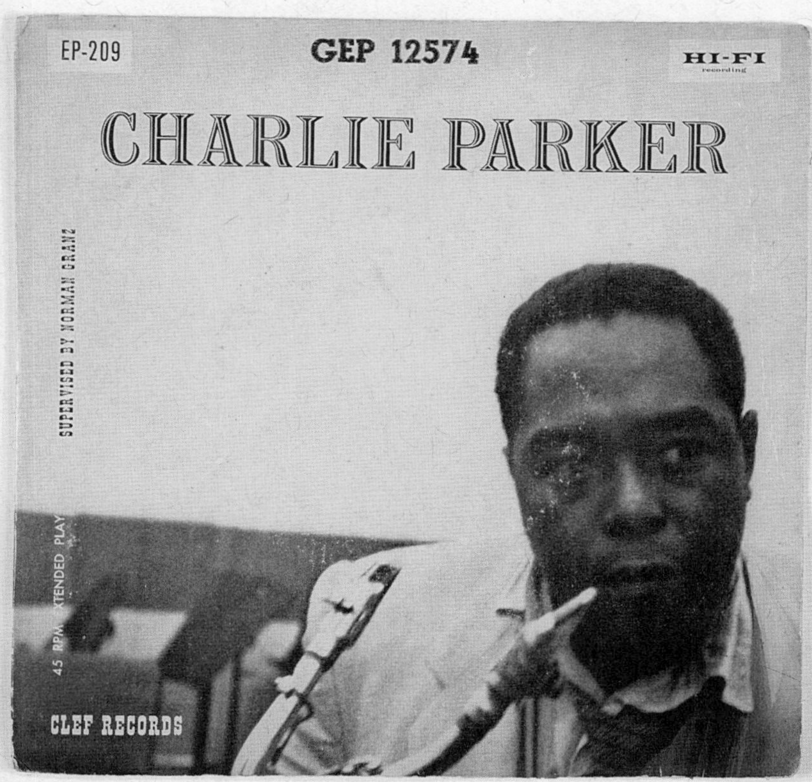

Record jacket for Charlie Parker, Clef Records

Oppenheimer, father of the bomb, sees the atomic light and declares "I am Shiva destroyer of worlds." A real gone daddy-o, he hears the bang where the Beat came from. It's a blast. Can the painful chain of being be halted at last? It's a panic, man. 1957 and Norman Mailer notices that the Beat, the white bohemian is the white negro. Suddenly confronted with the unfamiliar prospect of random and instant annihilation, existential whitey suddenly digs where the brothers are coming from and so with the jazz and the jive talk and the hipster is here. Nonconformism is a necessary adjustment after the unprecedented global mobilization of the Second World War. Like a cramp, a charlie parker horse, a cubist reflex of a hyperextended sensorium.

So here's Red Rodney and Art Pepper and Chet Baker. Devils or angels? Or both. Mailer says the Beat, the white negro, is a psychopath, a cultivated psychopath. Well, maybe not exactly. There goes Gil Evans, jazz arranger to the stars in the skies. Jazz isn't color blind, it's a full spectrum. Black and white are all colors in effect, in abeyance.

Whites turning black without leaving their bodies. Jazz is what Bootsy Collins called the invasion of the bootsynatchers.

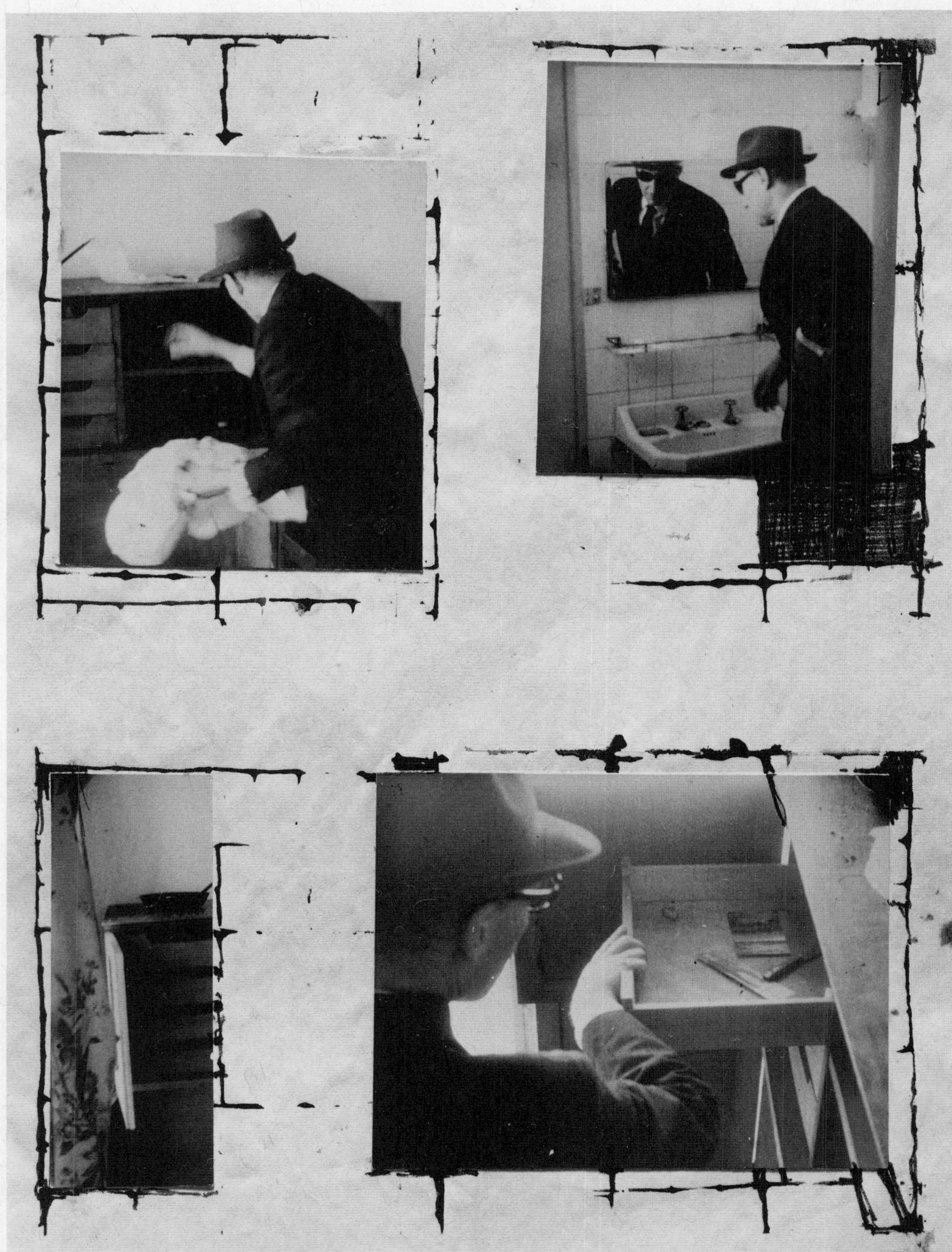

The Cool and the Heat

Like any alternative, the Beat vision got co-opted, got adapted, got made into stage sets, advertising, fashion, and greeting cards, keeping a certain strength in its dilution. Jack Kerouac getting fatter suddenly said there is no Beat generation. But there was Peter Gunn, cool school detective, packing laid-back heat to the jazz sounds of Henry Mancini, wearily ending his makeout sessions with cool blonde Lola Albright to take on another cool case.

And what was it with Jack Webb, Sergeant Friday of the LAPD, the ultimate square, busting homicidal satanic marijuana addicts by day, in another role playing Pete Kelly, hep jazz trumpeter, and in real life being married to sultry Julie London, sex bomb record-cover girl and semi-jazz chanteuse. It's a love-hate thing in Squaresville.

And what is it with Clint Eastwood, the jazz fan superfuzz Dirty Harry, directing the Charlie Parker story, making simple tragedy out of impenetrably divine genius, taking the wit and enormity out of the bottomless soul Charlie Parker. What is it with fuzz and jazz, this love-hate relationship. Is there a Jazz Police?

Jazz more than Beavis and Butthead is here to save us from the music on television, from that really, really big loud music that is about scenic and erotic suffering. Jazz is here to put an end to that and open our ears to the sound of bliss and hanky panky and, when necessary, to start the whole thing over from scratch, from itch.

Want to be a blessed Beat? Put on a beret and wait for inspiration. Hold a pose long enough and it becomes posture, hold that posture long enough and it becomes posterity. Tom Waits started out with a Beat pose (sincere) and grew into its gnarly proportions and today he is one of the few possessors of that methodical madness, one of the few musicians and wordsmithies who starts the itch from scratch and makes original works of art. The Beat is not naive. The Beat is a scholar who, out of desperation, invents what's new.

> **"Charlie Parker pray for me. Pray for me and everybody, in the nirvanas of your brain where you hide, indulgent and huge, no longer Charlie Parker but the secret unsayable name that carries with it merit not to be measured from here to up, down, East or West. Charlie Parker lay the bane off me and everybody."**
>
> Jack Kerouac, *Charlie Parker*

Beatnik Executives

I saw the best minds of *my* generation depressed by lawsuits, dieting, sober, all dressed up, limoing through the negro streets at dawn looking for an angry member of the Screen Actors Guild. We are beatnik executives and we are just doing our job. It's the best job we could find. It's the fucking best we could do. It's the end of the world and we're doing a fucking ad campaign to sell the future only because our pitch is all that's left of it. Maybe if we sell futures in the future we can at least get some arrears in stock.

We are, like it or not, beatnik executives. In the face of certain annihilation we're open for business as usual. According to our medical and artistic training the human body is in the departure lounge. The individual is a lone germ and corporate titans are abroad in the land and somehow we've got to gang up to plague them. No more brush on canvas. Brush on live wires is our painting. We've got to be big and corporate to compete. NovaCorp. Beat Hotels Ltd. Naked Lunch, SA. Howl Inc. Thelonious Power and Light.

Times have changed because the Martian invaders that took over the planet mere decades ago have already changed the presumably immutable nature of time itself. They reset the atomic clock, restructuring our structure. Forget daylight savings time. Our ancestors spent all our savings. They've burned down the future, it just seems that you can't get there from here. "Are we not men?" we quote, handsomely. We have to do something. The Beats are all dead. And

William S. Burroughs and Brion Gysin
Untitled (William Vacates Rooms), from **The Third Mind**, c. 1965-70
Gelatin silver prints and ink on paper, 9 1/2 x 7 1/16 (24.1 x 17.9)
Los Angeles County Museum of Art; Purchased with funds provided by The Hiro Yamagata Foundation

Gregory Corso, Larry Rivers, Jack Kerouac, David Amram, Allen Ginsberg, during filming of "Pull My Daisy," NYC, 1959. Photo © John Cohen

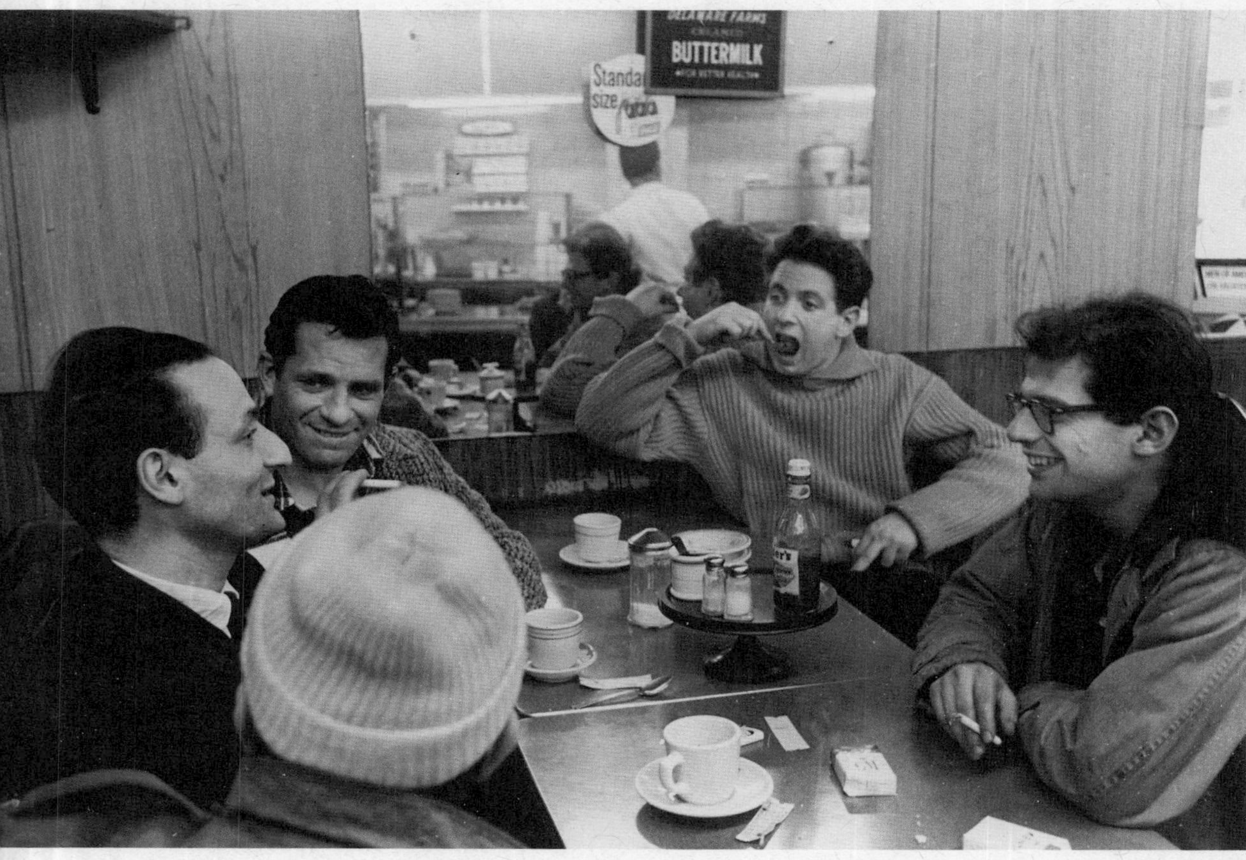

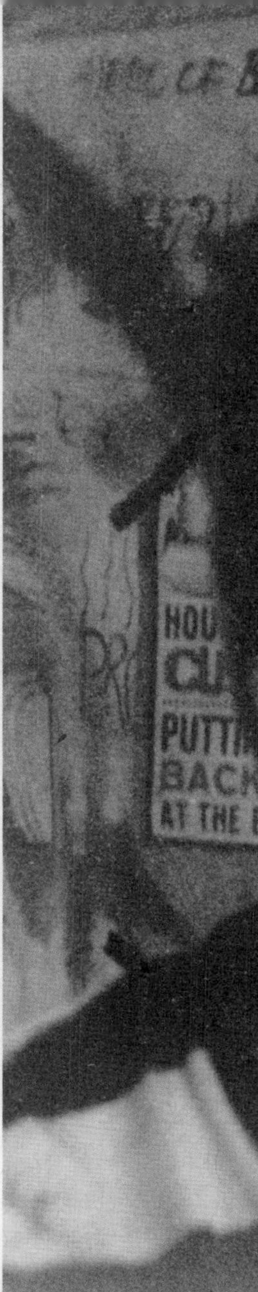

they left us a big job to do and somebody's got to do it if they can find it.

My generation didn't go on the road. There was no road left to go on, only the interstate which seems to describe how we often feel, suspended between modes of being, rebels without a context. The interstate is the road, made all the same. No fifty states of being. Just McDonalds or Burger King. Coke or Pepsi. The cream of the crop got homogenized. Skim milk of human kindness. We're living off the fat free of the land. Born with plastic spoons in our mouth.

The Beats are still our heroes, but we live in a gone world and look back on the adventures of the Beats as a saga, great legendary adventures from a real gone world. Neal Cassady = Gilgamesh. We read their books, of which they are the heroes, and we wonder what's a hero to do and we ask what's new and there's no answer, just a busy signal.

Most of the Beats are gone, real gone. Their work survives them. Their work animates them "safe in heaven dead." But how do you do that kind of work today? What is the essence of Beat? How does Beatness work?

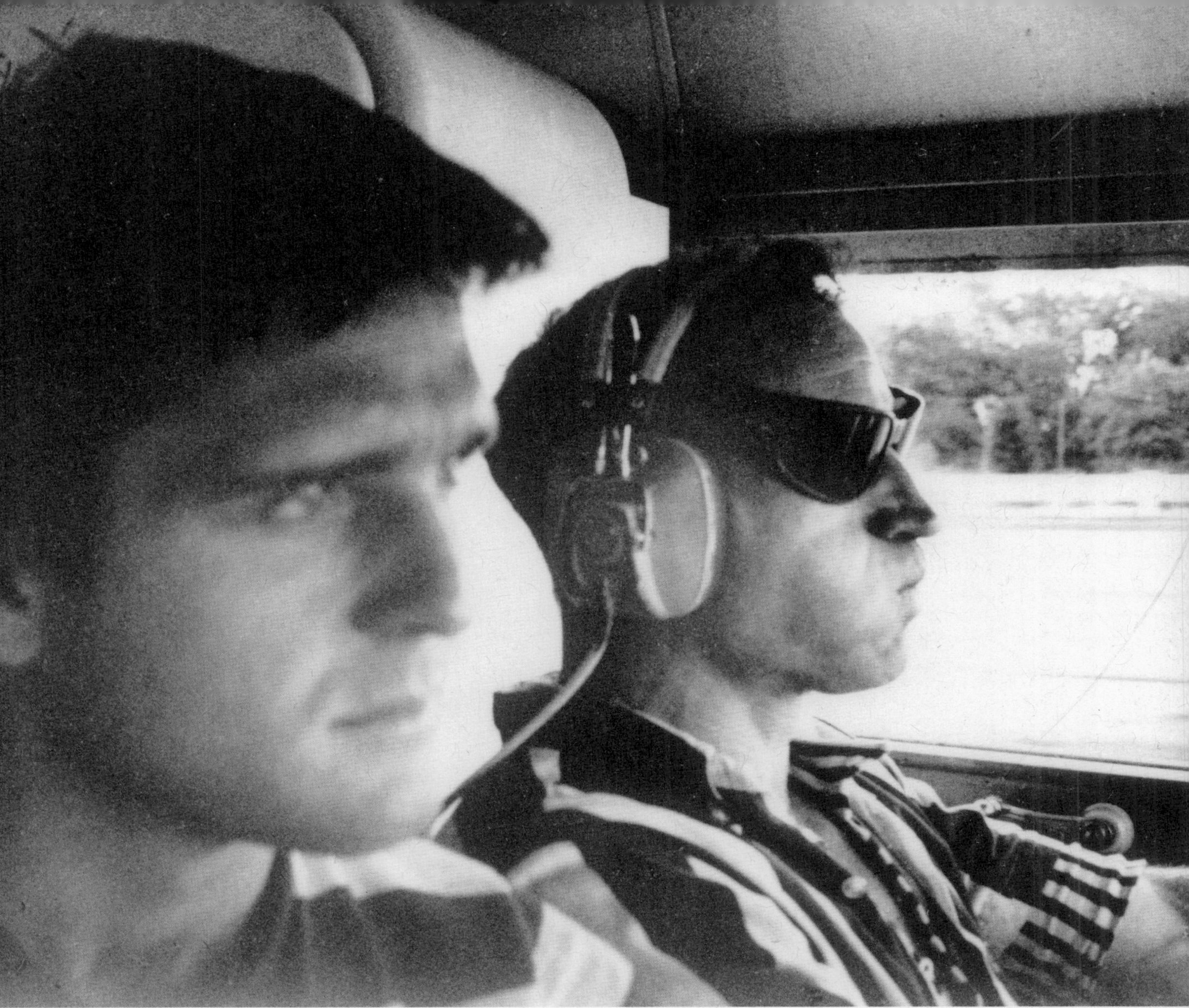

Beatness once worked in opposition to hell-bent consumer culture. Beatness was a holy backwater, an underground of secret society where secrets were sayable but unsalable. But today the underground has been institutionalized and marketed by titanic corporations. There is no underground. There is just the bargain basement bohemia funded by advertising and the Department of Defense.

William Burroughs is in a Nike ad and I'm thinking "Just do what?" There is no road, no antipode rife for revolutionary lounging for us. There is no Paris, no Marrakesh, no Tangier, no Beat Hotel, no Village, no Bowery, no place where tribes can live in mutative cultural symbiotic contemplation. You may be Beat in your heart, but you're white on your face, like egg. They have locked us in the Creative Department and thrown away the PIN number. My friends are signaling me from the beatnik floor at Time Warner. So I'm revolting against revolt. Giving up

Cassady and Babbs, Driver's Seat, Cheeks Blown Out, 1964. Photo by Allen Ginsberg the beatniks that are not beatnik corporations, vertically, i.e., top to bottom.

Having absorbed the old Beat, I want to forget the lives of the saints and just improvise. Forget Kerouac's plaid shirt. Some junkie bought it in a thrift store in Seattle. Forget Paul Bowles and his chic alienated adventures of ugly Americans scouting cheap backroads for future interstates service stations. Paul Bowles, honky academic composer who had the gall to put down Duke Ellington. He deserved to have *The Sheltering Sky* made into that movie.

We have to do better than them anyway. We have to surpass Jack and Neal's quotas. Jack needs to sober up. Neal needs an Infiniti. Corso needs an IRA. Forget the glamour of solo work. Andy Warhol was right. To compete as an artist today you've got to incorporate. Still, as of now there probably are no major beatnik corporations, but it's undoubtedly the future of Beat. Imagine a combination of Microsoft and the Miles Davis Quintet. Imagine a combination of Ben

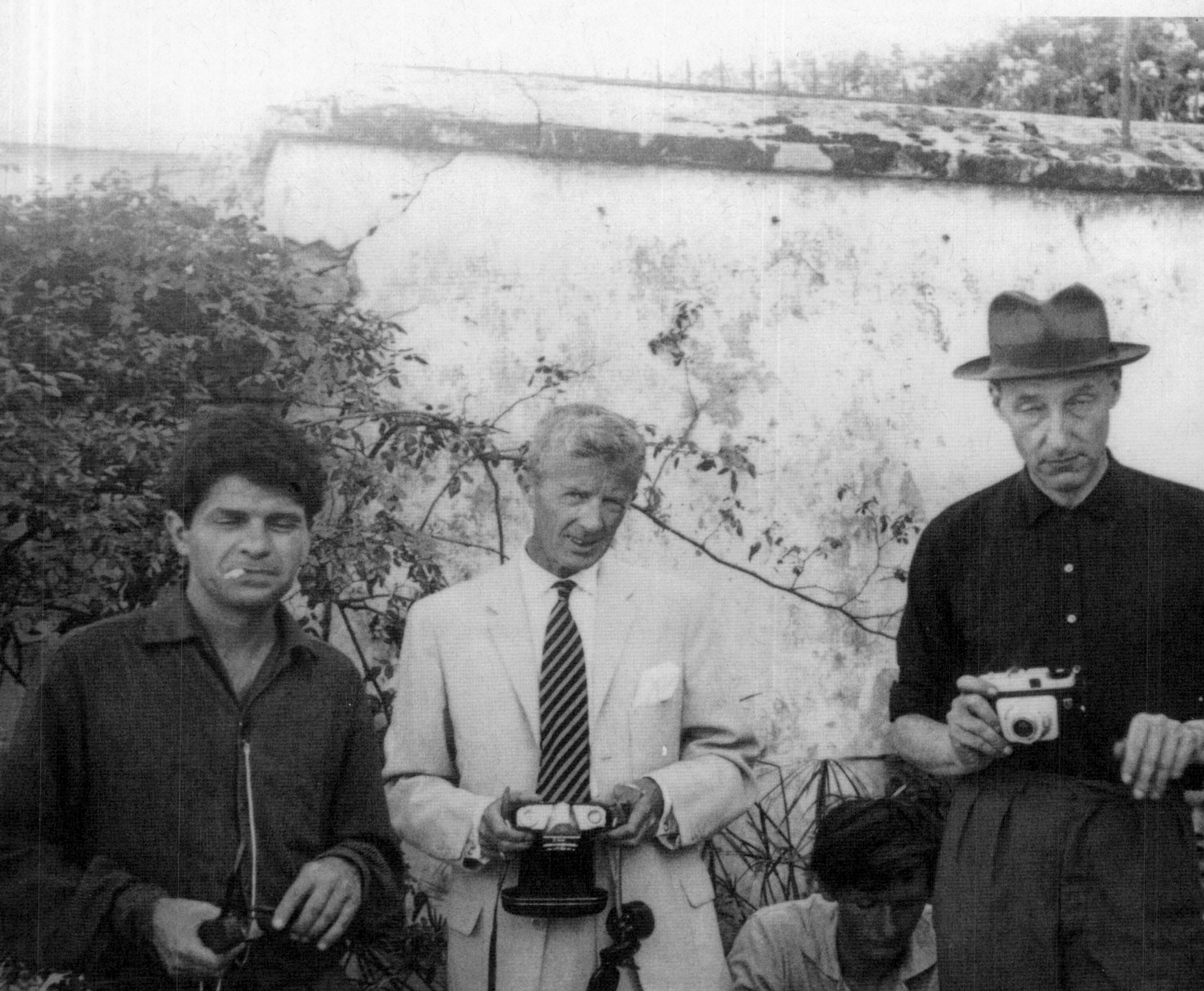

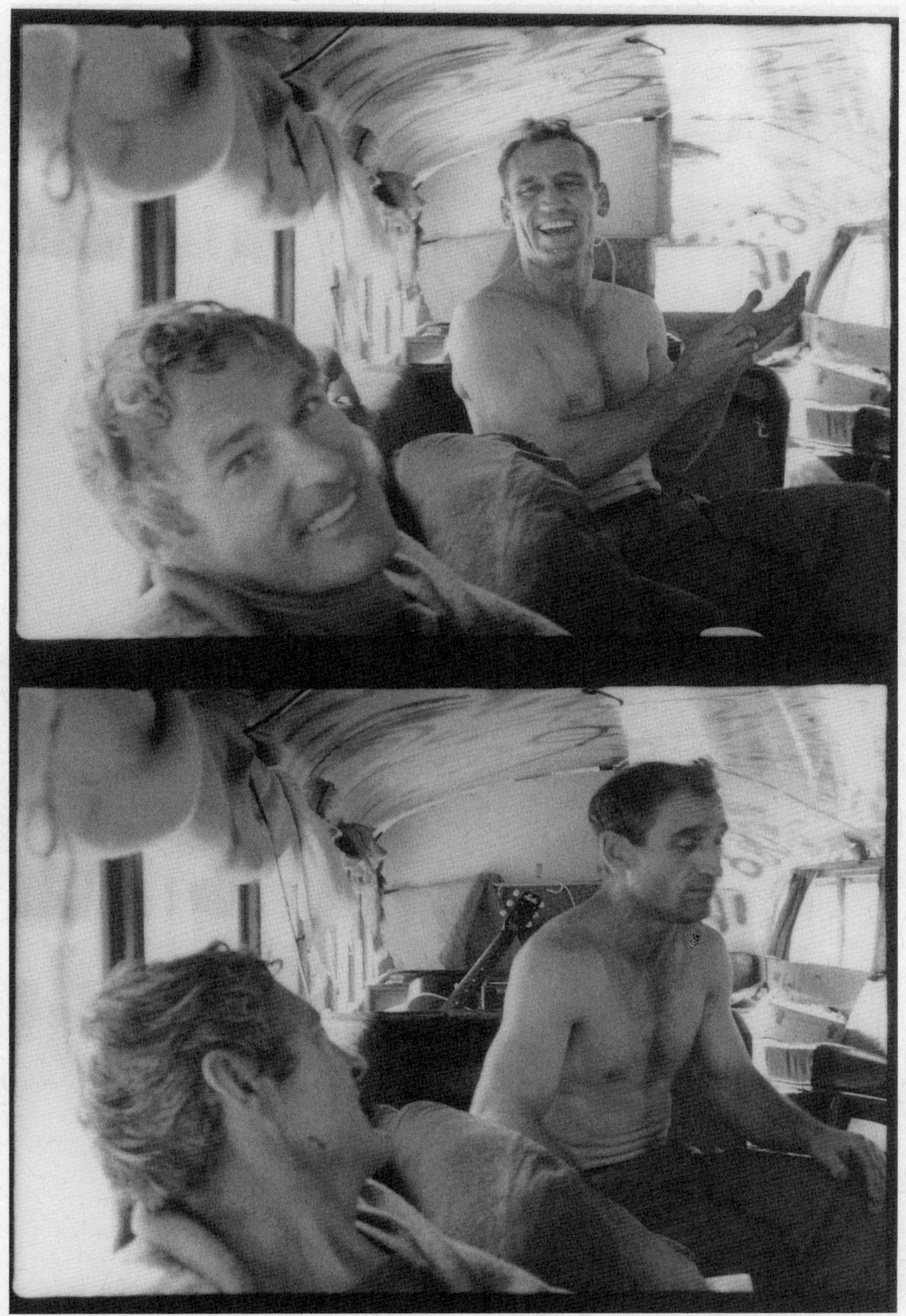

Timothy Leary visiting Neal Cassady on "Further" Bus at Millbrook, 1964. Photo by Allen Ginsberg

Corso, Bowles, and Burroughs with cameras, 1961. Photo by Allen Ginsberg

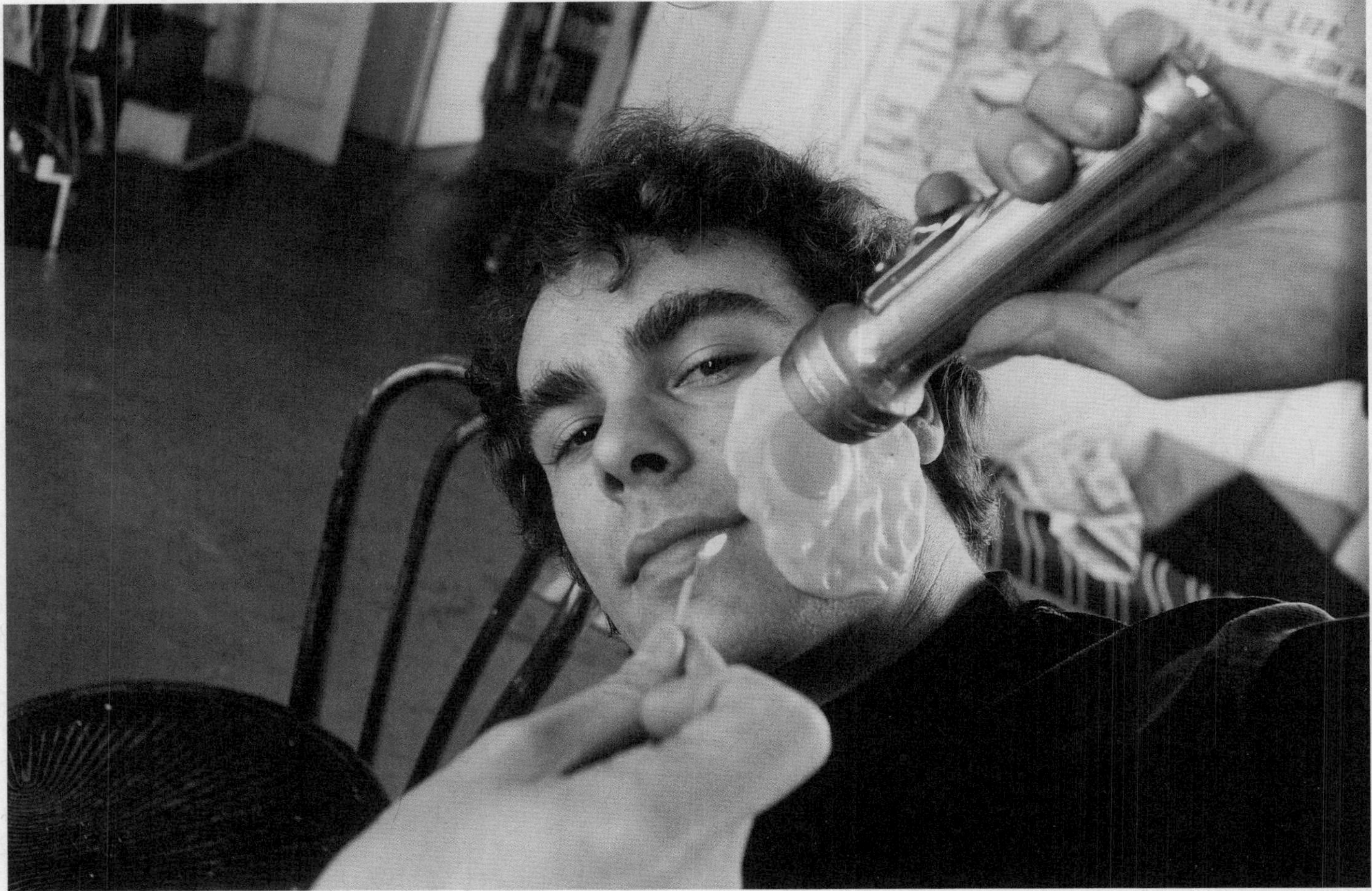

and Jerry and the Chicago Seven.

Whatever is Beat is against the cult of the cute, the naive and the amateur and what's the very latest. The Beat movement is a classical movement, made for the moment to last forever. Its heirs are not interested in rock videos, although occasionally they might appear in one, just as they might appear in the occasional dream or vision.

For Beat to beat the competition we've got to incorporate the incorporeal. Beat corporations will exist to sell art for art's sake. Beat corporations will sell the art of living. Beat corporations will grant new leases on life. Mindblown Industries.

Just remember Charlie Parker had a logo.

Like the Beat Goes on (Before the Name Goes On)

Like the natural law firm of Burroughs, Ginsberg, Corso, Cassady, Kerouac and Orlovsky. And their many associates. Like those pants Eldridge Cleaver designed. Like all true jazz musicians living and dead. Like Ishmael Reed, George Clinton, Bootsy Collins, the Fugs, Sam Shepard, Iggy Pop, Ornette Coleman, Grandmaster Flash, Roy Hargrove, Dennis Hopper, Gena Rowlands, Peter Falk, Q Tip, Dana Bryant, John Lurie, The Lounge Lizards, Neil Young, Sonic Youth, Kiki Smith, Martin Scorsese, Robert De Niro, Willem Dafoe, Lydia Lunch, Quentin Tarantino, Spike Lee, Steven Wright, Lou Reed, John Cale, Diane Arbus, Elliot Erwitt, Peter Hujar, the Estates of Donald Barthelme, John Cassavetes, and Ray Johnson, G. Love and Special Sauce, Booker T and the MGs, Van Morrison, Mac Rebennack, Robert Frank, David Johansen, Kip Hanrahan, Sade, the Digable Planets, Dream Warriors, the Red Hot Chili

Above: **Dean Stockwell**, 1962. Photo by Dennis Hopper

Right: **Robert Alexander**, c. 1961-67 (detail). Photo by Dennis Hopper

Peppers, Marisol, Larry Rivers, Nan Goldin, Jim Jarmusch, KRS One, John McLaughlin, Phoebe Legere, Emily XYZ and Myres Bartlett, the Jazz Passengers, the Redmans, Victor Bockris, the Marsalises, Jeffrey Mermelstein, Lester Bowie, Tuesday Weld, their corporations and staffs, and hundreds of others for whom art is life, including those outside what is usually recognized as the arts, many of whom I know personally.

Beatitudes

Nirvana is a Beat name for a band. And Kurt might have been Beat, if he had lived. Beats die by accident or by-product. Junkies don't fall down or commit suicide. Patti Smith is Beat. Keith Richards is Beat by virtue of still being alive. The Beat is by definition an endangered species, screened for the psychopathic genes that will ensure the survival of a species worth surviving.

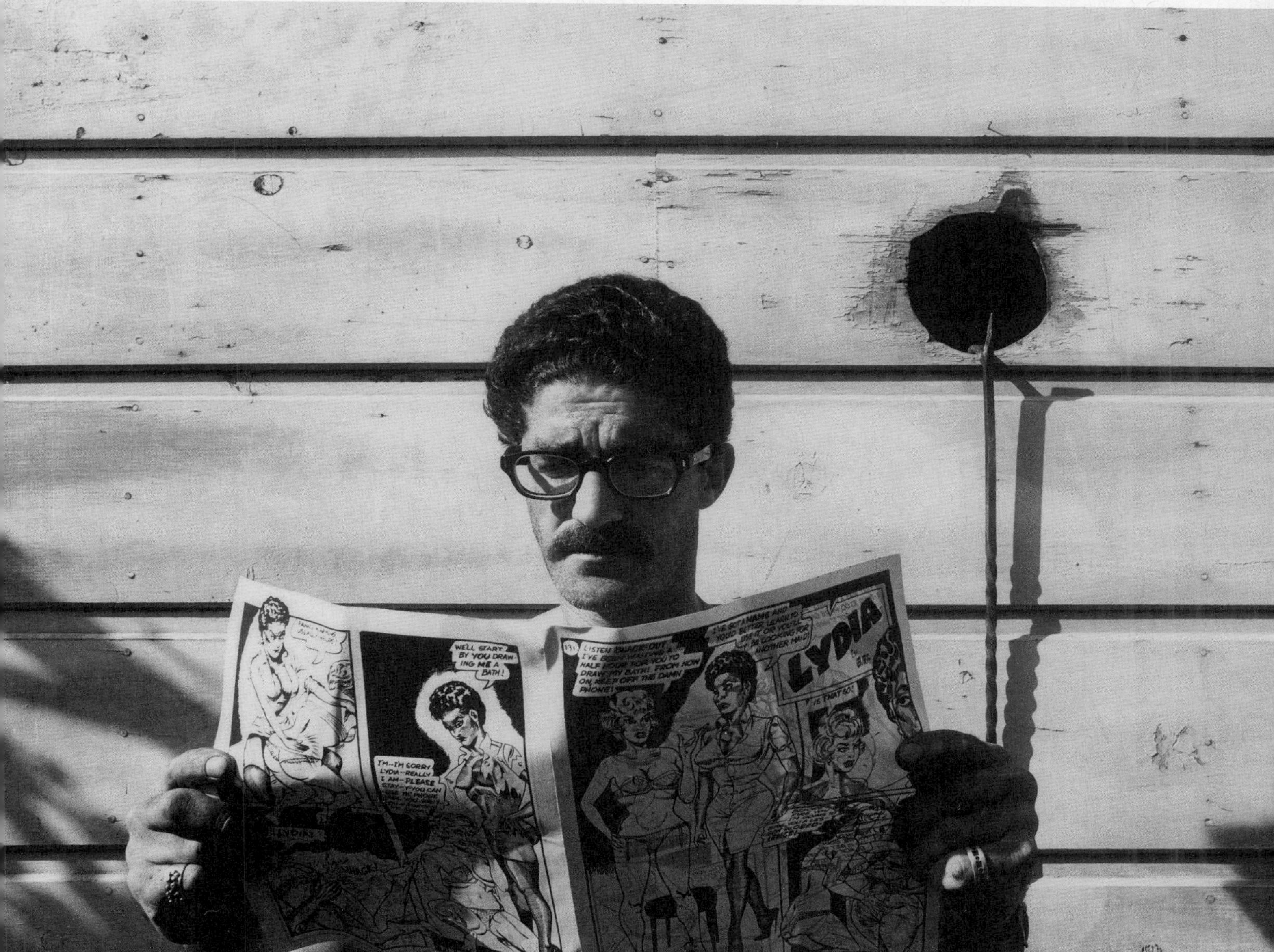

Do You Copy? Dig?

The proof of all of this is Bob Dylan—Beat immaculate and perfectly modest almighty. Bob Dylan is the incarnation of Beatness in our time. Our greatest poet and not a bad guitar player. At every turn, even when it seemed that he had reached the gone locomotive stage talked about by Rimbaud, Dylan made the right moves, guided by spirit and angels scarier than demons. If everybody listened to Bob Dylan, there would be no illiteracy, no hunger, no Tom Petty. No, just kidding Tom. And don't forget to listen to Charles Mingus and Rahsaan Roland Kirk and Sun Ra and to floss daily.

Beat is a joke. The Beat generation is a joke. A sly, infra-dig, sexually satisfied joke. Zen koan, high-heel sneakers, and Afro hairdo melded with Sephardic Schtick in All-American cosmic giggles. Beret, beard, sunglasses and sandals, sipping coffee, grooving high. The great unwashed. Self-satire. Exaggeration of extremities.

Beat is gnosis. In the beginning of Beat is the Word. Accompanied by rhythm section. The Beat movement, wherever it may be working at any time, is about restoring the primacy and validity of the word wherever it is spoken, wherever it is written.

This means poetry, arguments, gossip, jokes, seduction, instructions, suggestions, and copy. Some young whippersnappers don't know and follow living masters Paul Krassner and Ed Sanders and Tuli Kupferberg or past and virtually kicking masters like Lord Buckley or Lenny Bruce. Because young poets hoping to make a CD and poetry video don't know the atomic of Lord Buckley or the divine madness of Lenny Bruce. The brilliance of the Beat word is that it is entertainment, not literature. That it is stand-up. It is more Sam Kinison than T.S. Eliot, and all of those poetry slammers should woodshed with Lord Buckley and Lenny Bruce to raise the level of accuracy in their words and enlightenment in their delivery. Anybody who's really funny, even like Howard Stern and Jerry Seinfeld, is a Beat, like it or not. If you're a Jew you can still be an asshole but you've got Beat genes, like the brothers.

Ralph Rinzler, Bob Dylan, and John Herald at the Gaslight Café, NYC, 1962. Photo © John Cohen

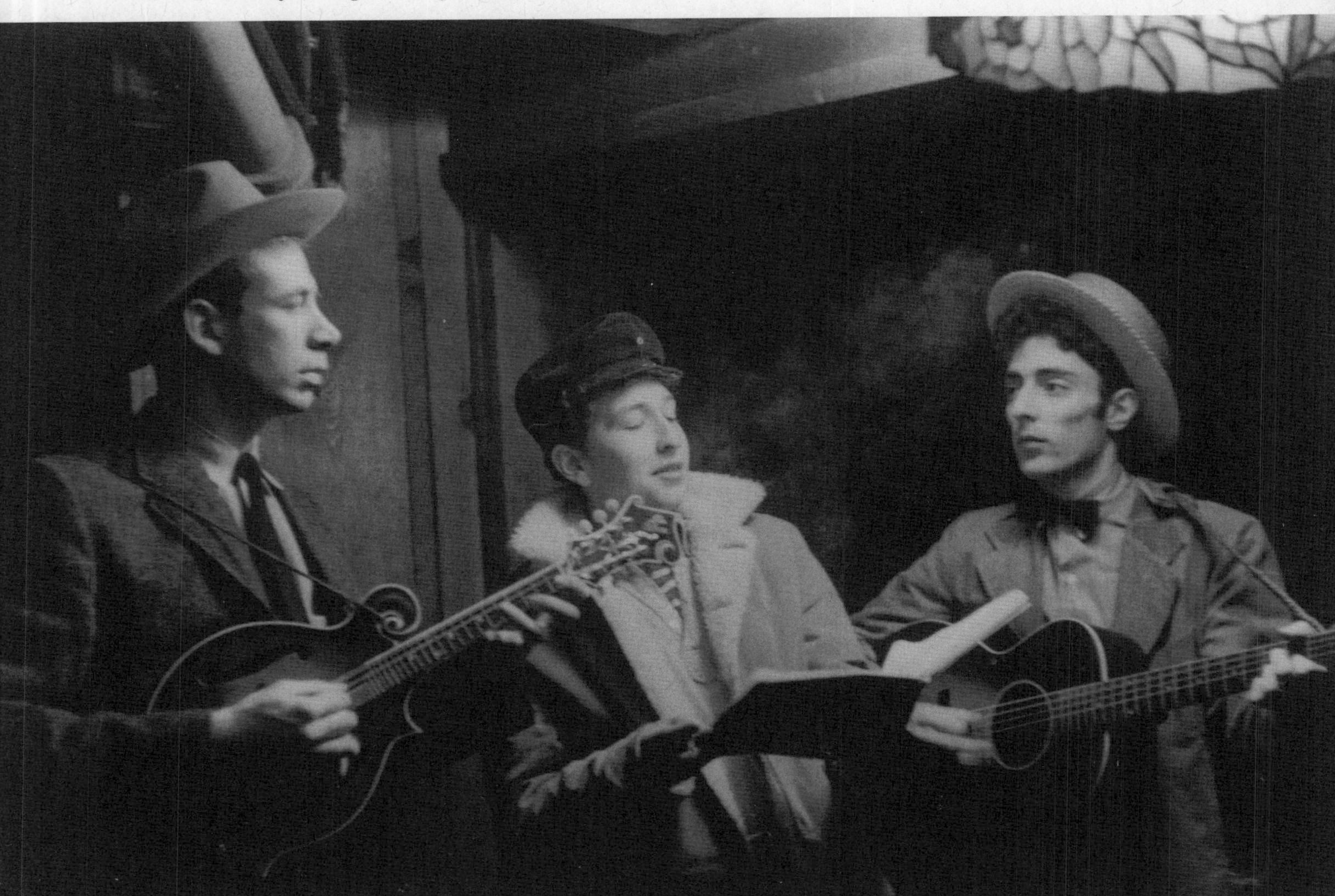

Original

The Beats were about the word. Bringing the written word back into live breath and musical time. Poetry was performed, not filed away. Word was stood by.

And is today, in Black English. Word.

The legacy of the Beats is alive although not yet awesome in today's poetry scene. But maybe it's not there yet because its too reBeat. Don't you think that Beat usage and diction and rhythm grew during the years it spent with Morpheus and Orpheus? Beat work was not inherently uncommercial. It was a commercial. It wasn't made to be sold; it was made to be made on its own terms. It was made to be enjoyed. It would be ridiculous to say that Charlie Parker and Thelonious Monk and Dizzy Gillespie, or Jack Kerouac and William Burroughs revolted against commercial success. Burroughs and Ginsberg have sales figures. They earned it. They did the best they could.

Beat on the poetry scene today is like shipping coal to a nuclear-powered Newcastle. Beat must reform the language of daily life. Beat must inject slang into language to resurrect understanding and truth. Beat words must rewrite the books, the menus, the laws.

Beatniks must conduct Nuremburg trials of advertising. Then the architects will be next!

The Fine Arts

In "The White Negro," 1957, Mailer pointed out that hipsters are rarely visual artists. Of course, Mailer probably never met Brion Gysin, who made up for the lack of numbers. But why does that judgment still ring true today? Is it because psychopaths are no longer able to penetrate the formal parameters of the defined art world? Is it because it's harder to tell if you can dance to paintings? No wait, actually there's Mike Kelley, Richard Prince, John Chamberlain, Nan Goldin, Basquiat in absentia and dozens more who qualify as happening hipster artists, a truly elite status.

And there is still hope for countless others. Just the other day I saw Julian Schnabel in a beret and sandals, starting a goatee.

Compton's Pharmaceutical Encyclopedia of Slang

Ishmael Reed says that the Jes Grew virus returns, seeking its text, from which it was separated. The hip-hop movement, although very unBeatlike in many ways, is a profound reunification of rhythm and blues and text, the rhythmically spoken word. Certainly hip-hop culture is less Zen than Beat culture, but evolution is about adapting to current conditions (or community standards). The fact that "gansta rap" is now under political attack should lead us to at least consider that as alien as it might appear to some, it may have something important in common with

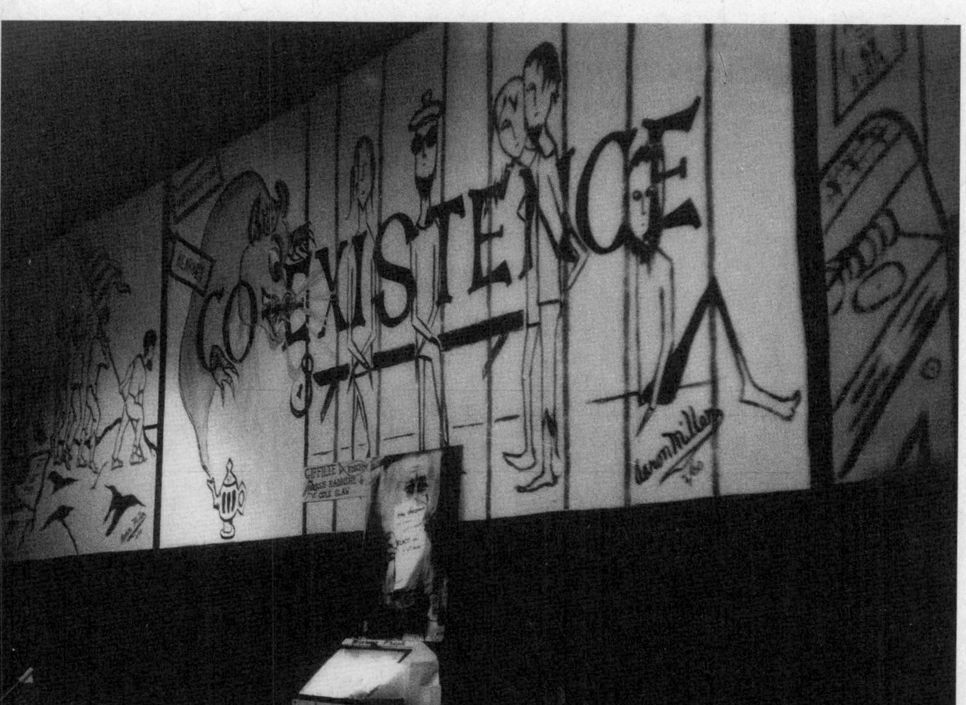

Mural by Aaron Miller in Coexistence Bagel Shop, North Beach, San Francisco, 1960.
Photo © Fred W. McDarrah

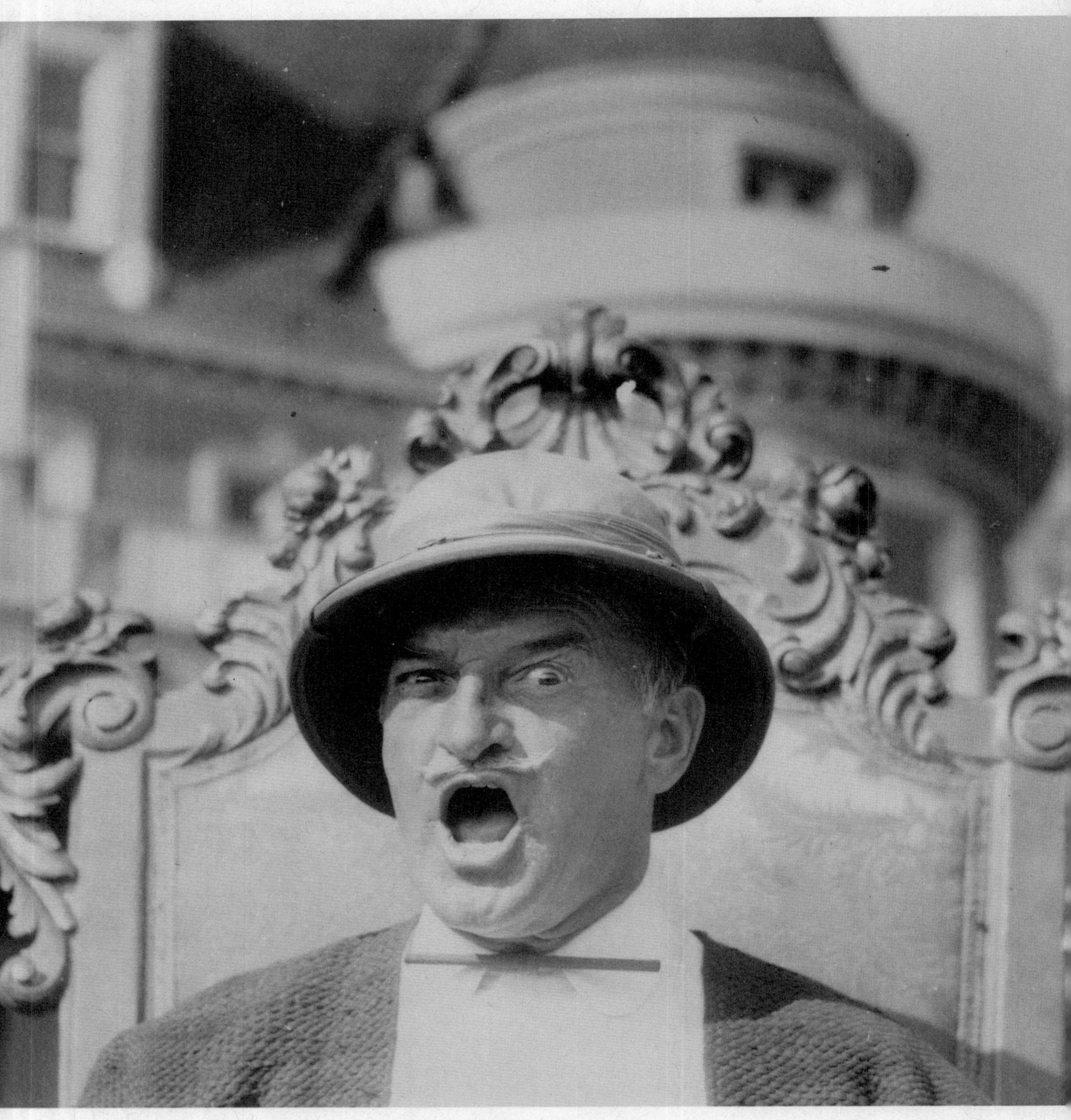

Lord Buckley, comedian/performer, 1950s

Naked Lunch or *Howl* or *Ulysses* and other works that have been subject to censorship.

> **"They are murdering all the young men.**
> **For half a century now, every day,**
> **They have hunted them down and killed them.**
> **They are killing them now.**
> **At this minute, all over the world,**
> **They are killing the young men."**
>
> Kenneth Rexroth, "Thou Shalt Not Kill"

That was 1953. And the generational genocide has escalated increasingly since then with a marketing push of arms and narcotics to youth and black youth in particular. Although white youth are moved by hip-hop culture, they are free travelers in it, not what NWA might have called "Niggaz 4 Life." So the White Negro '95 is a different breed from the cats of the fifties. There is more cultural segregation among like minds. You've got your Beastie Boys and you've got your House of Pain and they are white and they are not jive, they are practitioners of what they are. But if you are looking for a Miles Davis/Bill Evans relationship, it is not here. Hip-hop is a local mobilization of the life force—a Jes Grew militia. Sometimes people makes mistakes. Eazy E is dead, but Snoop Doggy Dogg is a force for good and the text and the vibration are coming together.

The jazzy hip-hop of De La Soul, the Jungle Brothers, A Tribe Called Quest, Dream Warriors, US 3, etc., which has been called hippieish, is truly Beat in its cool and in its groovy physical literacy and it stands as a model for a survivalist bohemianism for us all.

Beat Theology Is the Theology of the Future

> **"I'm a people worshipper. I think people should worship people. I really do. I went out lookin' for God the other day and I couldn't pin him. So I figured if I couldn't find him, I'd look for his stash. His great lake of love, that holds the whole world in gear. And when I finally found it, I had the great pleasure of finding that people were the guardians of it. Dig that. So with my two times two is four I figured that if people were guarding the stash of love known as God, then when people swing with beauty they become little gods and goddesses. And I know a couple of them personally. And I know that you do too. I think people should worship people. I like to worship something I can see, something I can get my hands on, something I can get my brains on. I don't know about that Jehovah can't. I can't reach him."**
>
> Lord Buckley, *H.Bomb*

God's Headset

God listens to John Coltrane
and Thelonious Monk
every day and Charlie Parker
and Miles Davis every night,
which is why, despite his age,
he remains so cool and
admirably inimitable.

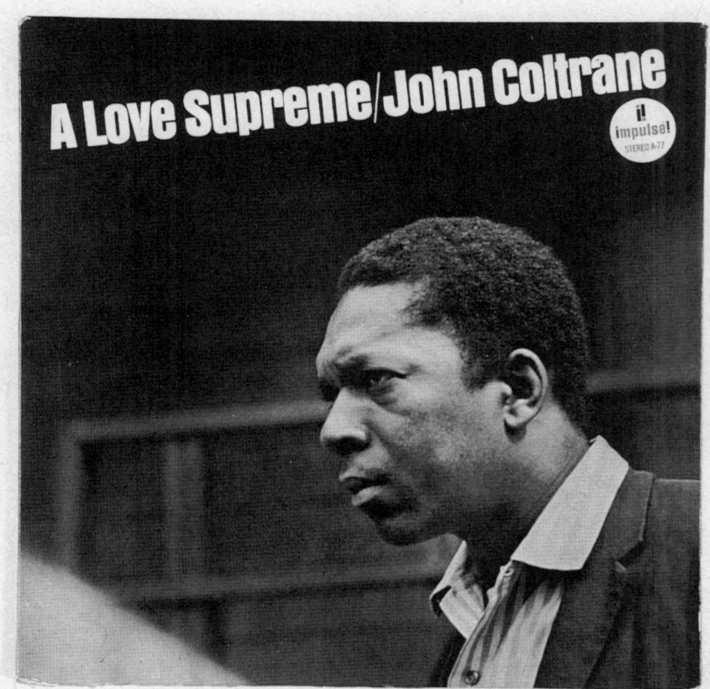

Record jacket for John Coltrane, "A Love Supreme," 1964, Impulse! Records

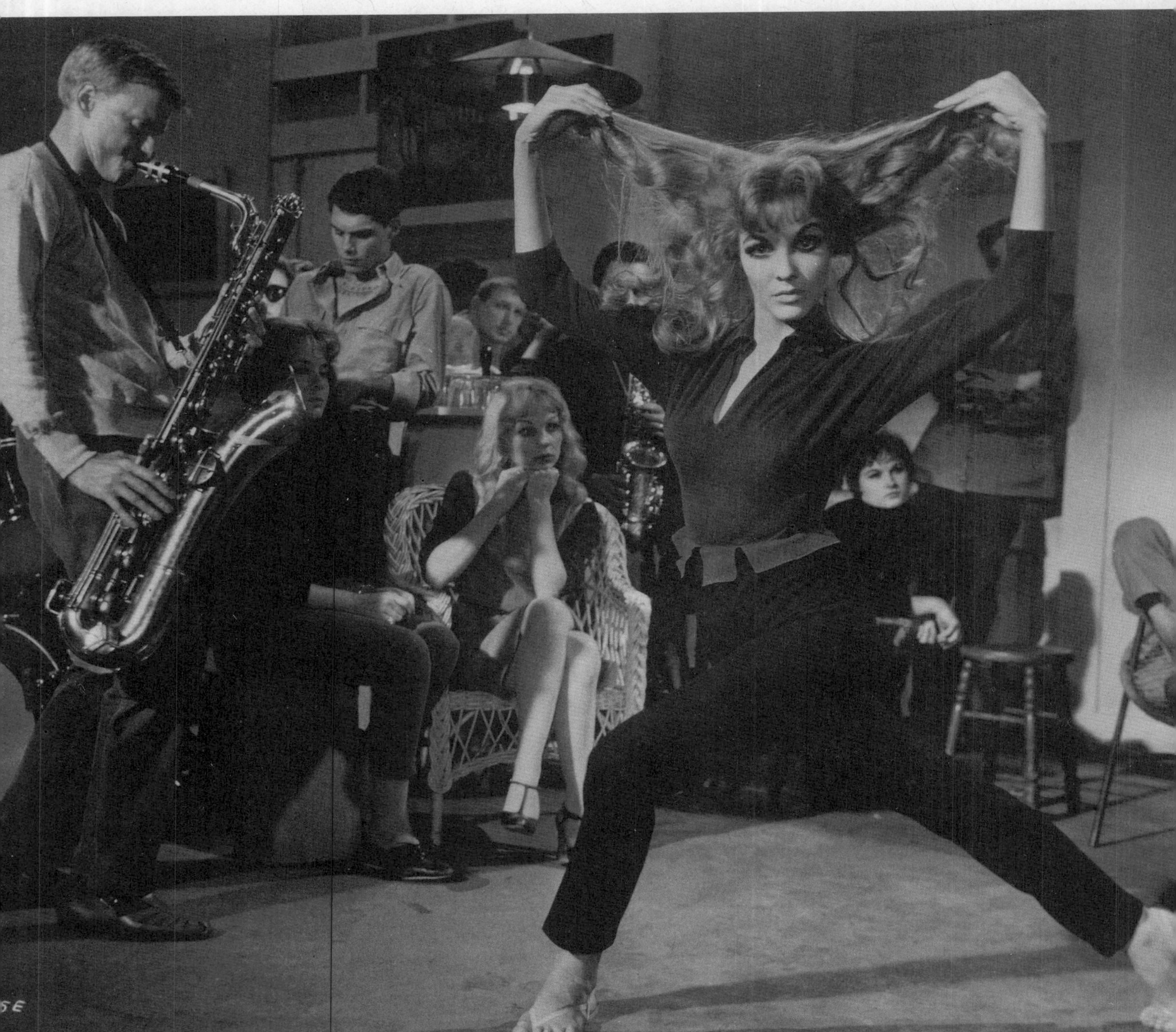

Ranald MacDougall, **The Subterraneans**, 1960

Kenneth Anger, 1954. Photo by Chester Kessler

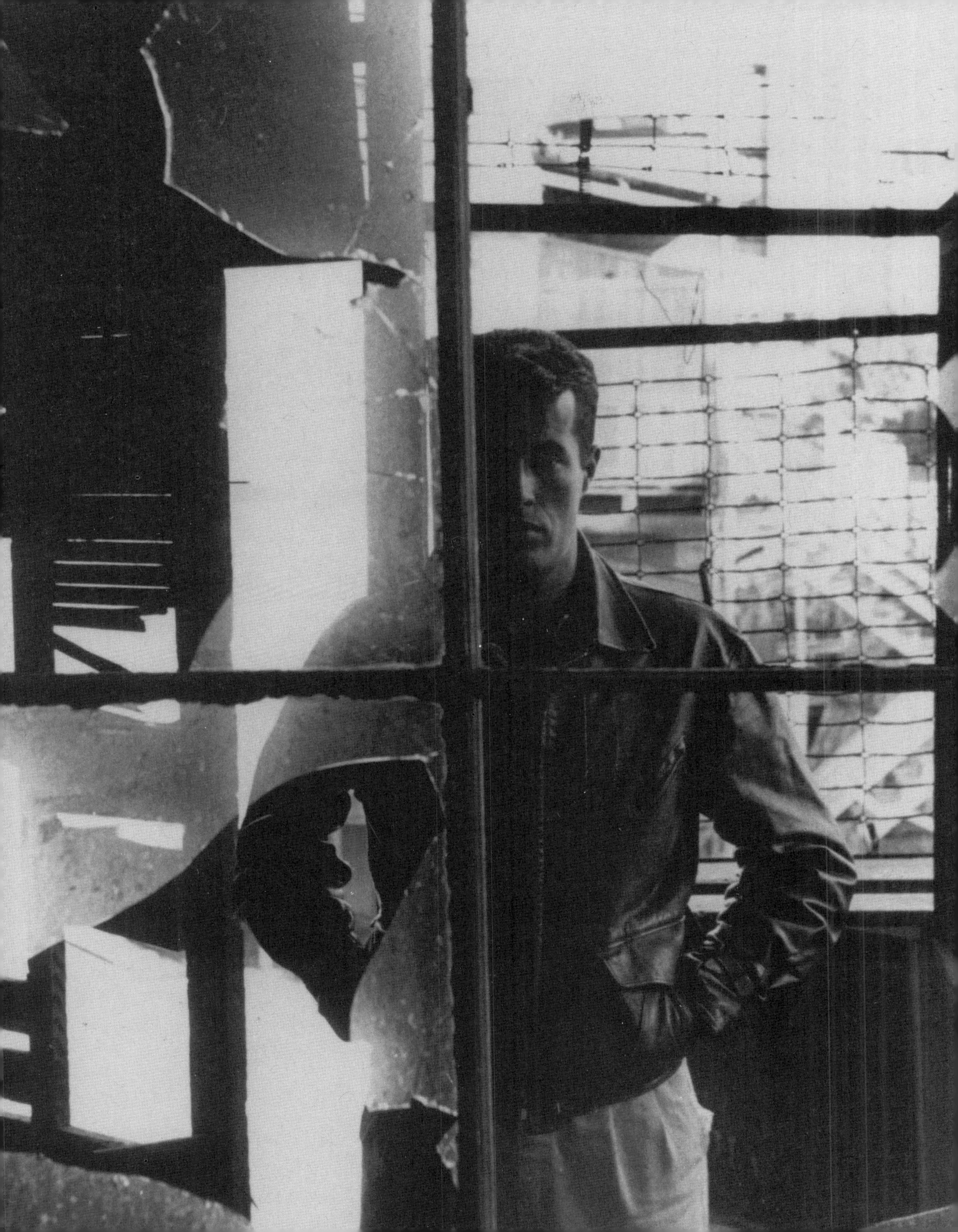

RAY CARNEY

Escape Velocity: Notes on Beat Film

It is a sign of our times, conspicuous to the coarsest observer, that many intelligent and religious persons withdraw themselves from the common labors and competitions of the market and the caucus, and betake themselves to a certain solitary and critical way of living, from which no solid fruit has yet appeared to justify their separation. They hold themselves aloof: they feel the disproportion between their faculties and the work offered them....They are lonely; the spirit of their writing and conversation is lonely; they repel influences; they shun general society....Society to be sure, does not like this very well. It saith: Whoso goes to walk alone, accuses the whole world; he declareth all to be unfit to be his companions; it is very uncivil, nay, insulting. Society will retaliate. Meantime, this retirement does not proceed from any whim on the part of these separators, but if anyone will take pains to talk with them, he will find that this part is chosen both from temperament and from principle; with some unwillingness too, and as a choice of the less of two evils; for these persons are not by nature melancholy, sour, and unsocial...but joyous, susceptible, affectionate. They have even more than others a great wish to be loved. Like the young Mozart, they are ready to cry ten times a day, "But are you sure you love me?"....And yet it seems as if this loneliness and not this love would prevail in their circumstances, because of the extravagant demand they make on human nature....They are the most exacting and extortionate critics. Their quarrel with every man they meet is not with his kind but his degree. There is not enough of him....They prolong their privilege of childhood in this wise: of doing nothing, but making immense demands on all the gladiators in the lists of action and fame. They make us feel the strange disappointment which overcasts every human youth.

Ralph Waldo Emerson, "The Transcendentalist"

What follows is a series of notes intended to be of use to scholars, teachers, and film programmers interested in films connected with the Beat movement and its cultural milieu. The master screening list to which these notes refer (pp. 212-215) is meant to be both comprehensive and selective. On the one hand, the list includes a wide range of films of many different types and genres; on the other hand, a high degree of selectivity has been exercised in compiling it. Works which are clearly second-rate or derivative have not been included. Though a number of Hollywood films are represented, many other depictions of the Beat movement in popular culture, particularly those on television, have been judged not to merit serious attention. It is my belief that each of the works on this list potentially deserves inclusion in a Beat film festival, even as I recognize that probably no single screening series would be able to show all these works.

The first challenge anyone seeking to make such a selection faces is the question of where to draw the boundaries. The definition of what is or is not Beat in film is not at all clear. Compounding the problem is the inherent looseness and vagueness of the Beat movement itself. Much of Beat culture represents a negative rather than a positive stance. It was animated more by a vague feeling of cultural and emotional displacement, dissatisfaction, and yearning than by a specific purpose or program.

It would be a lot easier if we were only looking for movies with "beatniks" in them. San Francisco columnist Herb Caen coined the word (which by sarcastically punning on the recently launched Russian Sputnik was apparently intended to cast doubt on the beatnik's red-white-and-blue-blooded all-Americanness). And the mass media popularized the concept. *Dobie Gillis*, *Life* magazine, and Charles Kuralt and a host of other entertainers and journalists reduced Beatness to a set of superficial, silly externals that have stayed with us ever since: goatees, sunglasses, poetry readings, coffeehouses, slouches, and "cool, man, cool" jargon. The only problem is that there never were any beatniks in this sense (except, perhaps, for the media-influenced imitators who came along late in the history of the movement). Beat culture was a state of mind, not a matter of how you dressed or talked or where you lived. In fact, Beat culture was far from monolithic. It was many different, conflicting, shifting states of mind.

The films and videos that have been selected for the screening list are an attempt to move beyond the cultural clichés and slogans, to look past the Central Casting costumes, props, and jargon that the mass media equated with Beatness, in order to do justice to its spirit. One way to begin defining the Beat spirit is simply to say that it was culturally adversarial. The Beats attempted to stand outside the mainstream culture of the period and to disassociate themselves from most of America's cultural achievements. They were profoundly out of sympathy with most of the values of postwar American society and its institutions, and aspired to position themselves somewhere, anywhere else. (Often it seemed that *where* else hardly mattered.) They aspired to be cultural escape artists.

Since so much of Beat culture was a reaction against mainstream, postwar American society, it seems desirable to begin by setting the stage and providing a cultural background. The first group of films summarizes the feel of the postwar years. Emile de Antonio's *Point of Order!*, made in 1964, looks back at the HUAC hearings of the late forties and early fifties. In a more humorous vein, Kevin Rafferty's *Atomic Cafe* and Obie Benz's *Heavy Petting* capture some of the emotional flavor of the cold war era. On the evidence of these works, American society was united in agreement about two threats to the common welfare: internationally, Soviet Communism and the H-Bomb; domestically, extramarital sex and the alleged decline of morals. It should come as no surprise that when the Beats surfaced in the national consciousness, they were linked with both terrors—suspected, first, of being Communists, and second, of being "perverts" or advocates of "free love" (contemporary code words for homosexuality and extramarital sex, respectively). Although the names of the devils change from year to year, de Antonio, Rafferty, and Benz remind us of one constant: Puritanism perennially rhymes with paranoia.

Greta Schiller, Robert Rosenberg, and John Scagliotti's *Before Stonewall* and Janet Forman's *The Beat Generation: An American Dream* trace responses to this atmosphere of fear and repression. *Before Stonewall* reminds us that the existence of a bohemian cultural underground in America antedates the Beat movement by at least fifty years. In Forman's sociological overview of the Beat response to the Eisenhower era, one of the most interesting points is made by Diane DiPrima, who explains that the notorious "coolness" of the Beats was a symptom not of *not* caring (as depictions of beatniks in the media would have it), but of caring all too intensely. While the middle class used alcohol, sex, and power as narcotics to dull their consciousness of the emotional frustration of their jobs, and accumulated material possessions in an attempt to fill the spiritual void in their lives, the Beats actually faced the truth of their society. Given such an emotionally exposed and vulnerable position, it was necessary to maintain one's "cool" as much as possible.

The next four films in the program illustrate different responses to this malaise from fiction filmmakers contemporaneous with the Beat movement. *The Bachelor Party* (directed by Delbert Mann from a Paddy Chayefsky script) is one of the subtlest presentations of middle-class male anxiety in all of Hollywood film. It is the highest praise to point out that in an era of obligatory "happy endings," the cracks the narrative reveals in mainstream ideals of love and marriage are far from being papered over by the film's sentimental conclusion. Strick, Meyers, and Maddow's *The Savage Eye* is a more tendentious and ultimately less satisfactory work. It is a nightmare depiction of the American dream gone awry—an anti-Hollywood saga of heartlessness and soullessness deliberately set in the camp of the enemy: the streets, shops, and offices of LA.

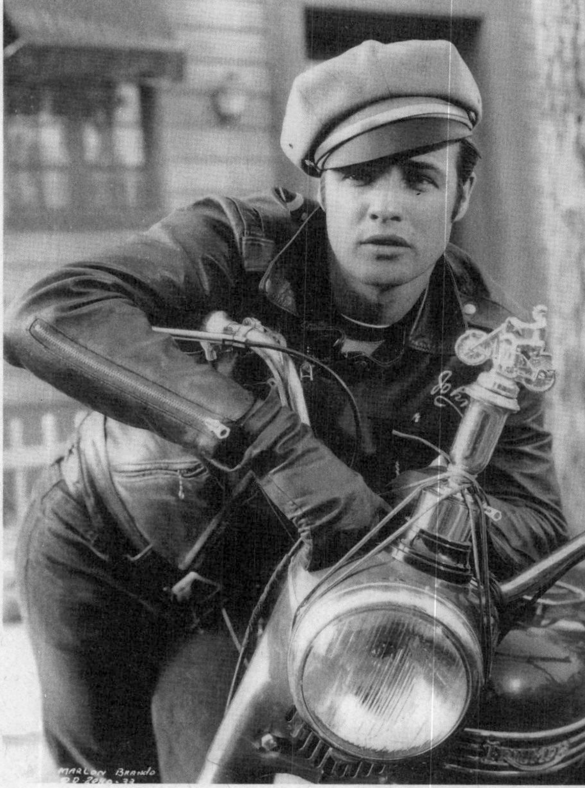

Laslo Benedek
The Wild One, 1954

It is against this background of widespread cultural anxiety and uncertainty that the performances of Marlon Brando in *The Wild One* and James Dean in *Rebel Without a Cause* should be viewed. Brando and Dean were dangerous and exciting actors precisely because they tapped into pervasive undercurrents of dissatisfaction in fifties society. Nicholas Ray's *Rebel Without a Cause* is stunningly in tune with the Beat sensibility. Ray's film demonstrates that if the Beat movement is not confused with its external trappings, its spirit can be captured without even alluding to the Beats. Ray mounts a powerful critique of the social and emotional dysfunctionality of the American family, and, specifically, of the failure of the married-to-his-job father to provide a role model for his son to emulate. (The father as missing person is one of the secret subtexts of many Beat works.) Ray documents the materialism and spiritual aridity of suburban life. In the planetarium scene, he breathtakingly communicates the dread and doom felt by the first generation to grow up in the shadow of the mushroom cloud. And, on the positive side, in the performances of James Dean and Sal Mineo, he captures one of the most important emotional dimensions of Beat culture: its tenderness toward and identification with the weak and disenfranchised members of society.

The scene in *Rebel Without a Cause* that, to my mind, comes closest to summarizing the full complexity of the Beat situation is the extended sequence near the end in which James Dean, Natalie Wood, and Sal Mineo flee to the deserted mansion. Ray suspends his three figures at the same in-between imaginative and tonal place the Beats themselves occupied: between hope and despair, fear and idealism, flight and homecoming, comedy and tragedy, clumsiness and grace. The mansion becomes a special, sanctified playhouse within which Jim, Judy, and Plato live out imaginative possibilities inconceivable within their real families. They play with their old identities, improvise new ones, and try out a shifting series of pretended roles and relationships. (The adolescent awkwardness of their performances only makes them all the more endearing.) They turn life into an ebullient game. As they parody adult tones and voices in a cascade of comic impersonations, they demonstrate that they apparently can be anything—that the notion of a fixed social (or cinematic) identity is an arbitrary limitation on one's true imaginative multiplicity. They show us that personal identity doesn't have to be narrow and formulaic (as it is for the adults in the film), but can be experimental, shifting, open-ended, and playful. They show us that social relations can be stimulating and creative. Their final impersonation is to play at being a family (with Jim and Judy as the parents and Plato as their son)—a family organized along entirely different lines from the families they grew up in: their relationships are not rigid, authoritarian, and hierarchical, but egalitarian, democratic, loving, and sensitively responsive to one another's needs.

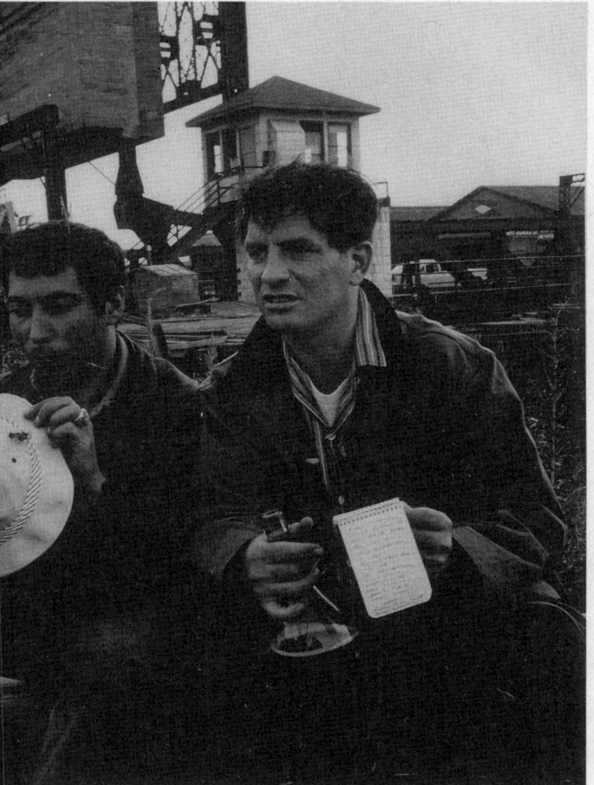

It's a remarkable sequence, deeply revelatory about the essential feel of the Beat situation. The Beats were experimenting with new, flexible forms of selfhood and society in almost exactly the same way as Jim, Judy, and Plato are. (Compare Diane DiPrima's wonderful *Dinners and Nightmares* for a prose analogue to Ray's scene.) What makes the scene so complex and moving is that it captures both the hopefulness and the desperation, both the joy and the sadness of the situation.

Jim, Judy, and Plato are, after all, only playing house. They are only pretending to be a family. They are only experimenting with potentialities of selfhood and social relationship. Their achievement is only imaginative. In the onrush of the plot events, it will last only a few minutes. And yet the scene also convinces us that the possibilities Jim, Judy, and Plato entertain—the new, playful, relaxed forms of personality and relationship they act out—are real. Their identities *are* larger and more fluid, and they *do* display more love than they have been able to express in adult society up to this point in the film. Ray's scene summarizes both the glory and the doom of the Beat dream of creating a society different from that of adult America.

Having written off middle-class culture as emotionally, morally, and socially bankrupt, for their heroes the Beats looked to those whose lives and work fell outside the mainstream. In *On the Road*, Jack Kerouac (thinly concealed behind the persona of Sal Paradise) writes of wishing that he could trade places with Denver ghetto dwellers:

Jack Kerouac, 1963.
Photo by James O. Mitchell

> **At lilac evening I walked with every muscle aching among the lights of 27th and Welton in the Denver colored section, wishing I were a Negro, feeling that the best the white world offered was not enough ecstasy for me, not enough life, joy, kicks, darkness, music, not enough night. I stopped at a little shack where a man sold hot red chili in paper containers; I bought some and ate it, strolling in the dark mysterious streets. I wished I were a Denver Mexican, or even a poor overworked Jap, anything but what I was so drearily, a "white man" disillusioned....I passed the dark porches of Mexican and Negro homes; soft voices were there, occasionally the dusky knee of some mysterious sensual gal; and dark faces of the men behind the rose arbors. Little children sat like sages in little rocking chairs.**

It's an embarrassing, not to say disgraceful, passage—a vision so romanticized that it might be by Disney. Kerouac wishes away every reality of poverty and race in America. The only thing that can be said in his defense is that he and the Beats didn't invent the myth. Similar passages in praise of dusky, mysterious, black sensuousness run throughout American literature, from Harriet Beecher Stowe to William Faulkner to Norman Mailer.

If the black experience was glamorized, the black artist, and in particular the black musician, was idolized by the Beats. As Ed Bland's *The Cry of Jazz* illustrates, the black musician was felt to be in touch with a deeper, more authentic state of being. *Celebrating Bird! The Triumph of Charlie Parker* and *The World According to John Coltrane* make it clear that Bird and 'Trane were appreciated not merely for their technical virtuosity and musicianship, but as kinds of secular saints. They were in touch with spirits (and wrestled with demons) that white society had lost contact with.

Pressed to define Beatness, Kerouac once said that it meant "sensitive." In that sense of the word, the jazz musician was felt by the Beats to be a paragon of almost superhuman sensitivity. He was an antenna that picked up signals no one else could hear, a supremely delicate tuning fork that resonated to invisible cultural and emotional force fields. He heard dog-frequencies and made them audible to the rest of us.

Kerouac's own description of this process in *On the Road* is summarized in his half-comical characterization of George Shearing as being "all ears, opened like the ears of an elephant, listening to the American sounds and mastering them." We will see the cinematic equivalent of this "listening" and "mastering" process in many of the most important avant-garde films of the period. The crucial point with respect to the Beat artist (whether a poet, jazz performer, or filmmaker) is that to make oneself this sensitive—this receptive and alert—one must of necessity put oneself in an extremely exposed and vulnerable position. The artist must let down the walls that normally protect the self, and bravely open up to uncontrollable influences and unpredictable outcomes; must dare to become fluid, transparent, and permeable; and, above all, must give up the comfort of fixed positions and preformulated stances. They would only limit his sensitivity.

The performance of the jazz musician embodied an ideal to which all Beat art (and life) aspired. As a master of second-by-second responsiveness, the jazz performer gave himself over to the flowing energies of the moment. He lived in an eternal now, making himself and his performance up as he went along. Blueprints were out; improvisation was in. Planning and premeditation were the enemies of openness and spontaneity. Art (and life) for the jazz performer became open-ended acts of attention expressed in continuously revised and adjusted acts of mastery.

In this version of American existentialism, Lee Konitz's musical improvisations pointed the way toward Kerouac's verbal ones (typing his "spontaneous bop prosody" at 120 words per minute on an unfurling roll of teletype paper), and both had affiliations with Neal Cassady's lived improvisations (picking up girls on buses, telling stories in bars, or hurtling cars through traffic). The supreme allegiance was to remaining faithful to moment-by-moment movements of feeling and awareness. Organization and structure only got in the way. Since life was only a series of impulses (or so the argument ran), the emphasis was on the truth of impulses over the truth of structures. If the result was, in many cases, appallingly disorganized lives and works, in others (like the finest passages in Ginsberg's, Kerouac's, and DiPrima's writing, Parker's and Coltrane's playing, and Bruce's stand-up routines), the speed and energy of the result were electrifying.

The Beats embraced a variety of Eastern religious practices in an effort to reestablish a relation to the spiritual side of everyday life. Zen Buddhism in particular appealed to them for several reasons: it was not premised on the existence of God to justify its beliefs and practices; and it esteemed nonrational, nonlogical states of mystical awareness (which tied in with the Beat interest in consciousness-altering drugs). At the same time, it was a religion that valued ordinary experience. Zen was not at all a dress-up-and-go-to-church-on-Sunday religion, but had a Whitmanesque love of the prosaic, the mundane, the everyday. Its saints were not otherworldly, but all too worldly—many of them itinerant vagabonds who resembled Beat drifters and rail hoppers. (When it came to dharma bumming, the Beat movement invariably put more emphasis on the bumming than the dharma.) Finally, at least as inflected by its Chinese Sung and T'ang heritage, Zen evinced a great reverence for the natural world. (This proto-ecological aspect was especially appealing to West Coast writers like Gary Snyder and Philip Whalen.)

Three factors were instrumental in raising awareness of Zen in America during the Beat period: the visits of a number of Japanese Zen masters to New York, San Francisco, and Los Angeles in the fifties and early sixties (eventually resulting in the establishment of major Zen centers in all three cities); the popularizations of D.T. Suzuki; and the presentation of a variety of pre-New Age ideas and beliefs by the transplanted British writer Alan Watts, in an influential series of public lectures, radio broadcasts, and books.

None of Watts' talks from the fifties and sixties was preserved on film, but a number of his lectures were filmed in the early 1970s, two of which are included in this series. *Man in Nature* and *Work as Play* give a fair impression of the ideas he presented during the Beat era. The dharma talk by John Daido Loori, Abbott of the Zen Mountain Center in Mount Tremper, New York, is again not contemporaneous with the Beat movement, but can stand as an illustration of many similar talks delivered by Zen monks visiting America during the Beat period.

The various documentaries require less commentary. The first group focuses on four major Beat artists—Jack Kerouac, Allen Ginsberg, William Burroughs, and Lenny Bruce—and each provides a slightly different perspective on the figure at hand. Bruce may seem like the odd man out in this group, but I would argue that his work is in fact deeply in the spirit of the Beat movement. (Indeed, I would argue that he is among the greatest of the Beat artists.) Bruce wages a war against all limiting, rigidifying, life-denying systems of morality and social organization (including but not limited to the system of understandings and relationships called bourgeois values and ideals). It is the same war that the greatest Beat art fights. Like other Beat artists, Bruce calls upon us to recognize vital human qualities that middle-class concepts of virtue and vice only cover up. His work is represented by a film of an on-stage performance and a video of a television appearance. (His records are an even better source of his performance material.) For some reason, no documentary filmmaker has ever chosen to focus on Bruce's life, times, and friendships. (Fred Baker's 1972 *Lenny Bruce Without Tears* is too superficial and sensationalistic to warrant attention.) Another important Beat figure who has been inexplicably overlooked by documentary filmmakers is Lawrence Ferlinghetti (though he hovers in the background of several of the films focusing on other artists).

The next two groups of films are fairly self-explanatory. "Additional Documents from the Period" consists of works that document events contemporaneous with the Beat movement, while the films grouped under the heading "The Beat Goes On" document gatherings of various Beat figures at poetry readings, conferences, and other events in subsequent years, and bring the Beats into the recent past and present. The most poignant of these, to my mind, is *Huncke and Louis*, a work-in-progress by Laki Vazakas. It dives below the inveterate rhetorical posturing and posing of the Beat movement to provide a view of Beatness with the bloom off. Herbert Huncke sadly sums up the death of his youthful Beat dream with his parting words: "I'm not ever going to be positive about anything again." It's a salutary and bracing reality check.

Raymond Saroff's cinematic record of the Happenings staged by Claes Oldenburg, Pat Oldenburg, Lucas Samaras, and others in 1962 is one of the few cinematic documentations of these important artistic events. One of the fundamental goals of Beat art was to break down what were regarded as arbitrary artistic separations—not only between various forms of artistic expression (theater, dance, painting, and sculpture in this case), but between the expressions we call art and those we call life. The point was to take art off the walls of the museums and

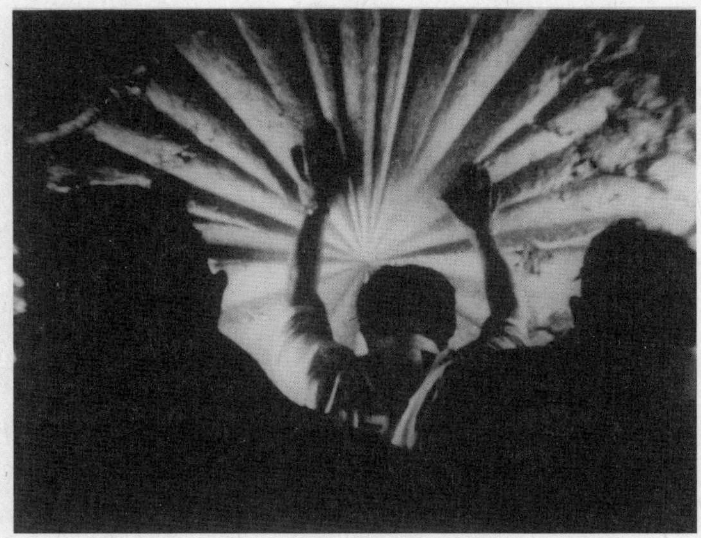

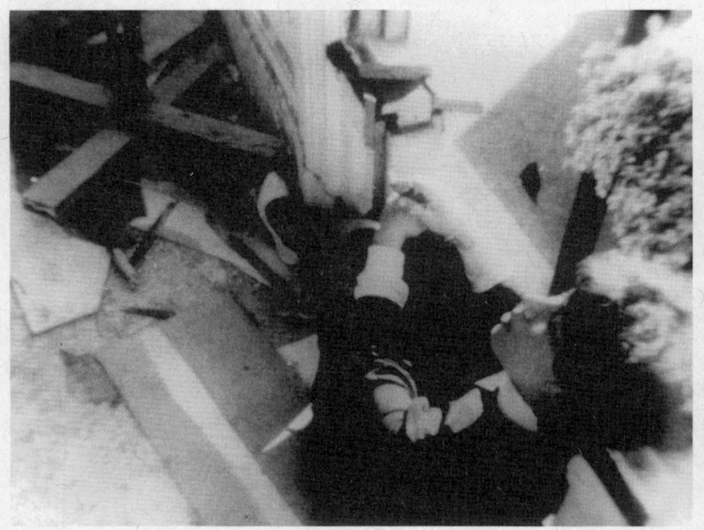

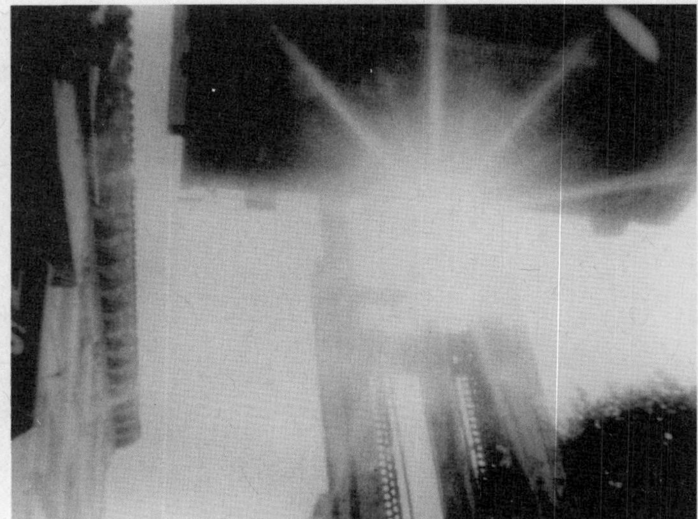

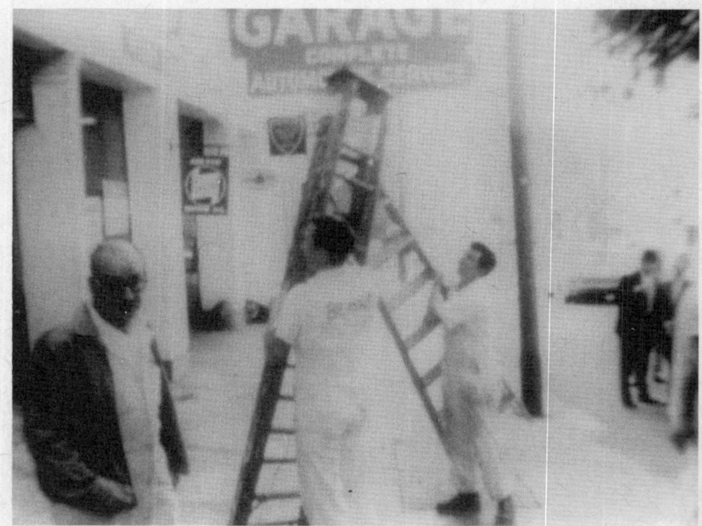

Bruce Conner, **The White Rose**, 1967

galleries and to allow it to reflect and to come into contact with life as it was experienced in the home and on the street. A related goal was to allow the formal roughness, mess, and disjunctions of ordinary life into the work. Rather than emanate from a realm of beauty over and above the clutter and noise of ordinary experience, art was to be lived in real spaces and bodies. It was de-Platonized, taken down off its pedestal of idealism. Oldenburg's Happenings deliberately included events normally excluded from the purview of art: washing your feet, eating supper, changing your clothes, going to bed. The comic tone of the Happenings (though you wouldn't know it from Saroff's film, contemporary audiences were reported to have laughed throughout them) is another way of taking art off its high horse. The Happenings brought art down to earth (like the bodies that keep sliding off the tables in one of the events). They brought it closer to Charlie Chaplin's baggy pants antics. The Happenings did to art what Zen did to religion: they removed its aura of specialness and sacredness. And, as in Zen's blending of the sacred and the profane, the process worked both ways. If art was made ordinary, the ordinary was made artistic. The most mundane events and objects were cherished as being, at least potentially, precious and beautiful. One of the fundamental agendas of the Beat movement was the effort to bring art's powers of renewal and transformation into daily life. (The annual Halloween parade in Greenwich Village is the most obvious manifestation of this attempt to live art, to productively blur its boundaries with life. Jack Smith's *Flaming Creatures* is a cinematic example of an attempt to do the same thing.)

Equally important, the Happening altered the relationship of viewers to the work. Viewers are not allowed to be passive consumers. Not only are they asked to contribute to the event (by bringing a radio and playing music in this instance), but they are forced to engage themselves actively in making sense of it (choosing where to look and what to pay attention to among multiple, simultaneous events). And wherever they do look, the effect is different from traditional museum art. A Happening doesn't lend itself to static analysis. It won't sit still enough to be a still life. It won't stop to be contemplated. Its meanings flow. Its meanings are never completed, never resolved, always in process.

The present-minded, Zen-like fluidity of the experience is one of the most important aspects of much Beat art. Whether one considers Dean Moriarty's driving in *On the Road* (and Kerouac's on-rushing syntactic presentation of it), the metaphoric tumble (to the point of sensory overload) of Stan VanDerBeek's collages, the dramatic mercuriality of the characters Taylor Mead played, the riffs of the jazz virtuosos the Beats admired, or the equally inspired verbal riffs Lenny Bruce improvised on stage—one of the points of the performance is to remain masterfully, meaningfully, and above all, rapidly in motion. There are no rest stops on this journey. There is nothing to hold on to. The artist as the creator of monuments of unaging intellect gives way to the artist as Gingerbread Man. Run, run, as fast as you can, you can't catch him.

Bruce Conner's brilliant and moving *The White Rose* documents another way to take art off the wall. The cinematic Happening he stages has more than superficial similarities with the performed Happenings Oldenburg and his associates stage. As presented by Conner, the work of art overlaps with the work of the world (and also shares the world's sense of "work" as being a verb conflated with art's sense of it as a noun), which establishes a deep connection to Oldenburg. Yet *The White Rose*'s depiction of the relationship of the world and the work, and of the relation of the work of art (noun) and the work of art (verb), is far more complex than Oldenburg's. The physical and spiritual costs exacted by the work of art (noun and verb) have seldom been more succinctly or more movingly expressed than in the juxtaposition of the dark angularity of the moving men's ropes, pulleys, tools, and pallets with the white-on-white curliness of Jay DeFeo's rose.

Conner's film serves as a transition into the next major section of the program: works of film art that are Beat in sensibility. One of the defining differences between mainstream

Hollywood filmmaking and avant-garde works is that Hollywood movies understand experience almost entirely in terms of externalized conflicts and struggles, while in avant-garde films the real drama is almost always inward. In Hollywood movies, characters confront a series of physical obstacles or personal opponents and respond to them with a course of practical actions. Avant-garde films understand that the turning points in life do not usually involve outward actions but inward acts of sensitivity and knowledge, imaginative forms of understanding. The avant-garde filmmaker knows that invisible, intangible, pervasive structures of feeling have much more effect on our destinies than events and objects do. (The mansion sequence in *Rebel Without a Cause* is one of very few scenes in a mainstream movie that presents a deeply inward drama. The house to which Jim, Judy, and Plato flee is haunted by ghosts that are much more insidious, and much harder to exorcise than real ghosts would be: the ghosts of all the "adult" roles, tones, and manners these young adults have internalized.)

Christopher MacLaine's *The End* dramatizes a war between two opposed sets of feelings and tones. One aspect of the film is as dark and apocalyptic as its title. It is a record of obsession, despair, murder, and suicide. Yet the Baudelairian tones, Byronic posturings, and macabre events are so narratively undeveloped and unjustified (who *are* these people? why in the world should we care about them?), and presented in such an overwrought way that the effect is surreal and half-comical. The result of the tonal dissonance is actually more unsettling than if the narrative were presented more normally.

As is also the case in *Beat*, MacLaine's extreme narrative stylizations, eccentric editing, and balletic blocking reveal a witty, graceful, dancelike sensibility. The star of *The End* is none of the self-absorbed young men, but MacLaine himself. The loss we would mourn at the end is not the loss of them, but of him.

It is impossible to do more than hint at the intellectual originality (and emotional challenge) of Stan Brakhage's work in an overview of this sort. Suffice it to say that Brakhage has been selected for inclusion insofar as he attempts to cleanse perception—to escape from the cultural and artistic pollutants that we have breathed into our systems throughout our lives. He represents an artistic strain within the Beat movement that aspires to give us new eyes and ears, to free us from cultural accretions and conventions, even of the most basic sort—like conventions of "realistic" representation and perspective that date back to the Renaissance. The result is a viewing experience like nothing else on film. Brakhage offers an Ur-vision, a vision of experience before it has been cognitively sorted, articulated, and structured into conventional forms of understanding. By the time he made *Anticipation of the Night* in 1958, he was also one of the few Beat artists who had moved completely beyond adolescent concerns, to explore fully adult issues and questions.

Beat art has frequently been diarylike, not only in its content (its intimate autobiographical revelations), but, more important, in its form. Like jazz performance, Beat art is essentially temporal in its understanding of experience and process-oriented in its forms of presentation. The emphasis is on process over destination and performance over product. One result of this process-orientation was the embrace of additive and linear forms of presentation. Beat artists attempted to remain true to the sequential nature of lived experience and the movements of consciousness by deliberately avoiding hierarchical, architectonic, totalizing, or essentializing presentations. Ginsberg's *Kaddish* and Kerouac's *On the Road*, in their different ways, go down the "Open Road" with Whitman in understanding experience as a fundamentally sequential and accumulative process. In this view, life is like a shopping list, a MasterCard statement, a diary, and art must do justice to that aspect of it. In *Lost, Lost, Lost*, Jonas Mekas creates a film that attempts to be true to the time it takes to live a life.

Given the Beats' feelings about American culture, many Beat works communicate a sense of cultural displacement. *Lost, Lost, Lost* and Mekas' *Guns of the Trees* (most of which was filmed after the former but released fourteen years earlier) are deeply affecting portraits of

Jonas Mekas
Lost, Lost, Lost, 1949-63/76

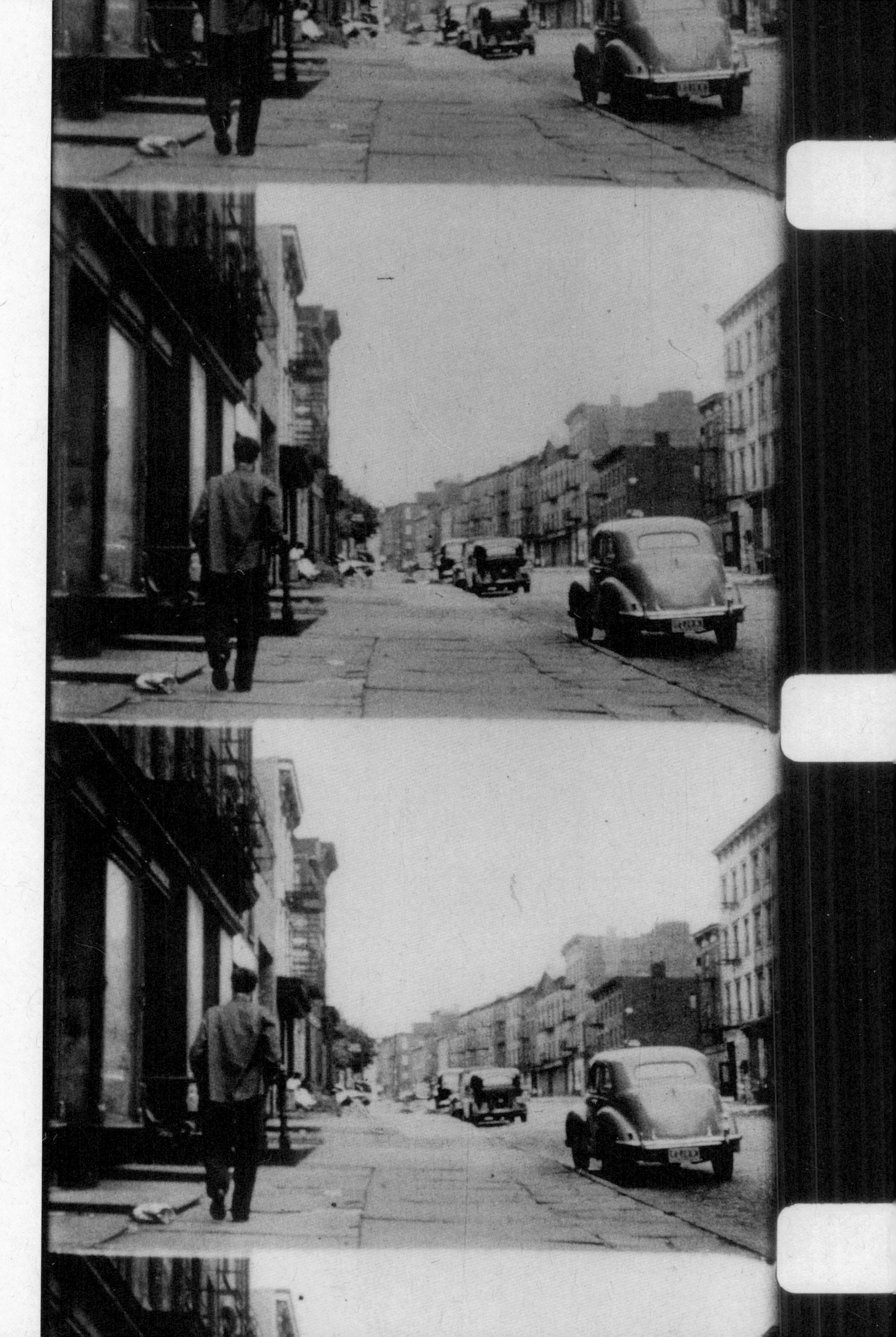

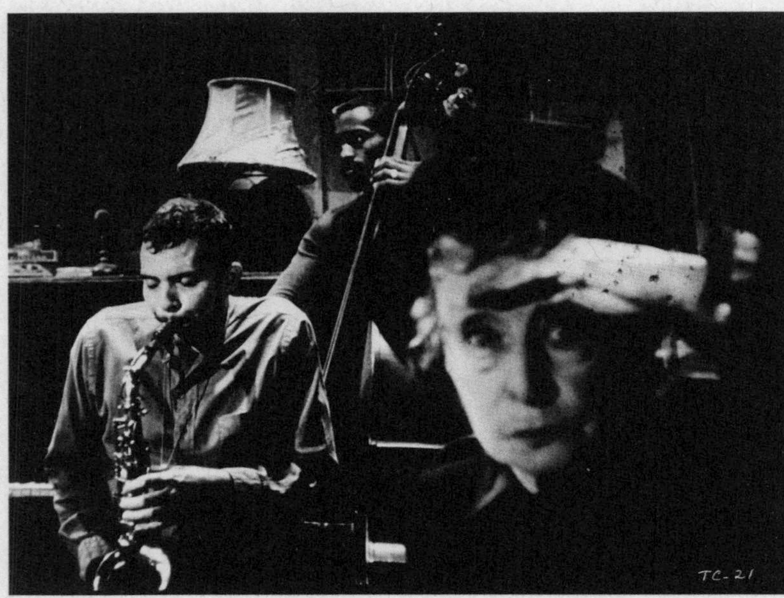

Shirley Clarke
The Connection, 1961

what it felt like in America in the fifties to be a "displaced person"—in all senses: linguistically, culturally, socially, imaginatively, and artistically. For a viewer with the patience to live through the experiences along with Mekas, *Lost, Lost, Lost* is one of the most profoundly sad and moving works of the period. Both *Lost, Lost, Lost* and *Guns of the Trees* also demonstrate how for Mekas and his characters, as in the Beat movement more generally, the state of social marginality and imaginative alienation, however personally painful to experience, conferred some degree of freedom. (With respect to the attitudes toward the black experience already mentioned, one notes that Mekas is as guilty of romanticizing the "other" in *Guns of the Trees* as Kerouac was in *On the Road*.)

Frank Paine's and Shirley Clarke's short pieces capture another mood entirely. They are bebop visions, experiments in visual jazz—attempts to do with film what the jazz performer does with music. Paine's dazzling, propulsive, hilarious *Motion Picture* (which I came across only by accident) puts the viewer on the road and thrillingly on the move with staccato editing to a jazz drum solo. Clarke was trained as a dancer and choreographer and began her filmmaking career by filming dance works. By the time she made *Bridges-Go-Round* and *Skyscraper*, she had discovered the dance of life. She is a choreographer of images, playing visual riffs on the New York skyline, riffs as inventive, ecstatic, and spiritually exultant as those of her personal artistic hero Ornette Coleman (about whom she made a film in 1985).

One of Clarke's strengths as a filmmaker is her tough-mindedness, her refusal to kowtow to the intellectual fad of the week. Her film of Jack Gelber's *The Connection* is remarkable for its utter lack of sentimentality about both the Beats and those who glamorized them on film. In Clarke's vision, the Beat experience is a drug-induced nightmare of frustration and boredom, and even an artistic interest in it is itself potentially an act of voyeurism and exploitation. (Her own film is a clear exception to this generalization.) Nonetheless, I find *The Connection* to be a rather weak work. I suspect that its initial notoriety resulted more from the debates over it in the newspapers than from its accomplishments as a work of art.

Clarke's *The Cool World* (not included on the screening list since it does not reflect a Beat sensibility) is another tough-minded work. Given all the idealizing of the African-American experience by artists during the Beat era, its highly unromanticized view of life in the ghetto is all the more striking. *Portrait of Jason* is another swerve away from cinematic fashion: a reply to the Andy Warhol films in which a character charms the audience with his or her performative panache. Clarke's goal in both works is to let us look deep enough into her characters' eyes to

Shirley Clarke
The Cool World, 1963

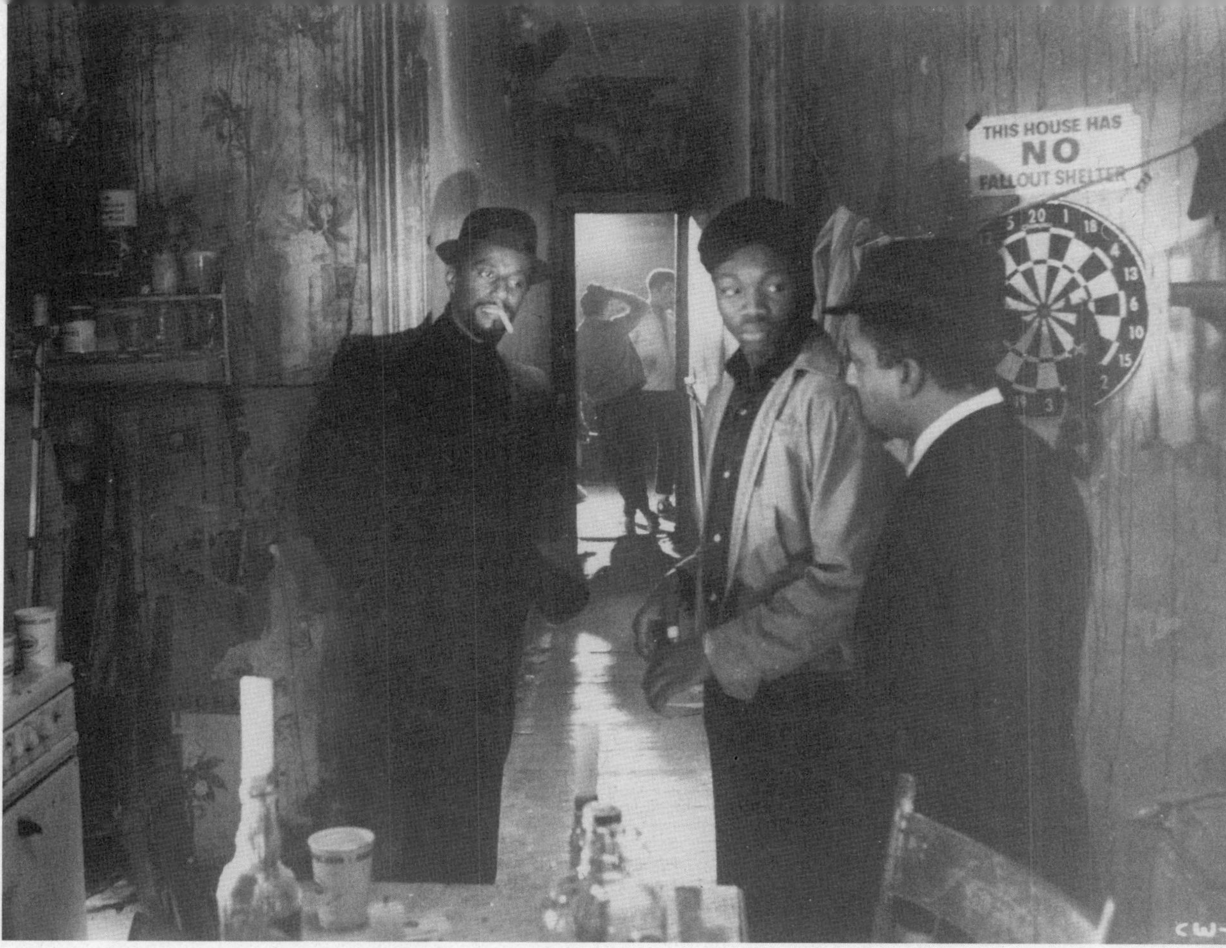

be able to see the skull beneath the skin (to borrow one of her own visual metaphors in *Portrait of Jason*).

Portrait of Jason adds an important additional perspective to an understanding of the Beat movement. As Paul Goodman argued in *Growing Up Absurd* (which is probably the best study of the emotional dynamics of the movement), the visionary and the street hustler, the shaman and the con man, the Beat and the hipster were never very far apart psychologically. To see through bourgeois systems of understanding was to empower oneself to move in either direction, and in fact most Beats included both opposing tendencies within themselves. As evidence of the intimate relationship within the Beat movement of the saint and the scam artist, we not only have the fictional bond between Sal Paradise and Dean Moriarty in *On the Road*, but the real-life symbiosis of Kerouac and Cassady. Like Neal Cassady (as he is devastatingly revealed in his letters to Kerouac or some of Carolyn Cassady's stories), Jason has seen what a game of three-card monte most social interactions are, and he takes that insight as his license for hypocritically manipulating the rules, rigging the game, and ripping off everyone in sight. Jason dazzlingly figure skates the surfaces, after having declared that there are nothing but surfaces. As Goodman points out, the hypocritical role playing of the con man (Neal Cassady/Jason Holiday/Aaron Paine) merges with the sweet quietism of the saint (Kerouac/the gentle young men in Chris MacLaine's work/the Taylor Mead characters in Ron Rice's or Vernon Zimmerman's films) in another way as well: "Role Playing protects a deep conceit of one's abstract powers: one 'could' if one wanted, but in fact is never tested." Like Bennie, the archetypal hipster in John Cassavetes' *Shadows* (whom Jason resembles in other respects as well), Jason *could* do anything—if anything were worth doing. *Jason* explores the limits of hip self-delusion—the scary point where the mask becomes the face. *Jason* is not a time-out from Beatness, but the fulfillment of one of its most lethal and self-destructive imaginative potentialities.

Since they are dealt with at length in separate essays, I will pass over the next two major works on the list, *Shadows* and *Pull My Daisy*, and proceed to the films of Ron Rice and Vernon Zimmerman: *The Flower Thief*, *The Queen of Sheba Meets the Atom Man*, and *Lemon Hearts*. All three feature the best-known Beat actor of the period, Taylor Mead, in the starring role. Though Mead's performances have often been compared with Chaplin's (Rice works in a number of references to *City Lights* and Zimmerman has an extended allusion to *Modern Times*), his true silent film ancestor is not Chaplin but Harry Langdon. The distinction may seem trivial; but it is crucial to understanding the ways in which Mead's work connects with certain imaginative tendencies within the Beat movement. The Chaplin tramp is a comic rendition of mature adulthood; he is sexually, emotionally, and socially mature, and extremely resourceful and knowledgeable about the ways of the world. The characters Mead plays are not adults in any respect. They are eternal children, divine fools, pure-hearted simpletons detached from the world and innocent of its machinations. They illustrate what Kerouac might have had in mind when he defined Beatness as beatitude.

But Mead's characters also illustrate something less flattering about the Beat movement. They summarize a tendency within Beat culture to renounce the social responsibilities and emotional demands of adulthood and become a child again. There are lots of women and a good deal of nudity in Beat film, but representations of mature sexual or social relationships are rare. The characters Mead plays (as well as the male leads in *Adventures of Jimmy*, *Pull My Daisy*, and many other Beat works) display a boyish charm, but to notice that is to suggest why the women in these films all function, more or less, as glorified mommies. They are mainly there to make meals and clean up the messes the little boy or his friends make. (This is essentially the function of women in *On the Road* as well.) It is significant that the closest *The Queen of Sheba* gets to a sex scene is when the Mead character either nurses at Winifred Bryan's breast or physically positions himself as if he were returning to or emerging from the womb. One of Ken Nordine's routines suggests that perhaps it wasn't entirely accidental that the Beats adopted the word "baby" as a slang term of romantic endearment. As Parker Tyler argued, Beat culture was infantile in many respects. In rejecting adult values, many Beats rejected adulthood itself. Like Peter Pan, they never wanted to grow up.

I might note, as a qualification, that *all* Beat culture did not embrace states of terminal arrested development. Clarke's *Portrait of Jason*, as I've already suggested, is quite skeptical about its title character's level of maturity. Cassavetes' *Too Late Blues* takes the choirboy asexuality of its central figure as a dramatic problem to be dealt with. The writing of Diane DiPrima, Herbert Huncke, and John Clellon Holmes also wants us to ask hard questions about the emotional maturity of the figures they present. Furthermore, in the sense in which I have defined the two paradigms, there are Chaplin figures—complex adults—in Beat films as well as Langdon figures. *Lost, Lost, Lost* is an example of a work in which the spirit of Chaplin is alive. But since Chaplin's achievement is itself often misunderstood, I should add that his spirit has nothing to do with pratfalls and comic clowning and everything to do with social displacement, idealistic longing, and romantic vision. If Mead is the Langdon of the Beat movement, its big baby, Mekas is its Chaplin—its great-souled, idealistic adult dreamer (though it may take the work of Chaplin or Mekas to demonstrate that an idealistic dreamer can also be an adult in every respect).

All three of Mead's films can be usefully grouped with the work of Ken Jacobs and Jack Smith (and the Claes Oldenburg Happenings) in terms of their decision to subject the viewer to deliberately "sloppy" artistic experiences. There is a lot of *faux* primitivism on recent radio and television, but the work of Rice, Jacobs, and Smith is clearly different from the calculated awkwardnesses and mannered amateurishness of *The Prairie Home Companion* or *The Late Show with David Letterman*. Real messiness does not look at all like the MTV version.

Needless to say, the goal was not mess as an end in itself. These works wanted to jettison systems of processing and packaging in order to establish contact with states of purity and innocence. But their project raises more than a few questions. Can repressive systems of expression be escaped this way? Can buried impulses be liberated casually and accidentally? Doesn't it take a lot of work and knowledge to do this? The danger, of course, is that a work that rejects basic principles of organization and coherence will simply end up being disorganized and incoherent. In a sermon at the Judson Memorial Church, New York (which I am grateful to David Sterritt, a scholar on the period, for bringing to my attention), the Reverend Al Carmines argued that the Beat movement in general, and Rice's work in particular, was virtually sacramental:

> **[It] is not so much a prophetic thrust into a supersophisticated future as it is a reminder of an elusive [*sic*] and uncompatable [*sic*] past. It finally is conservative in the most natural and ultimate sense. It is a call to remember and to see that the most intimate of daily doings and objects that surround us, and that we use unconsciously are profound and plenteous in meaning, richness, and joy....[The Beats represent] an attempt to strip off the layers of accumulated impersonality—brittle cultivation that winds itself around us as mindlessly and unconsciously as a shell around a snail. Layers that keeps [*sic*] us just right—just proper [*sic*] temperature—for a just proper life."**

Carmines' lapses of diction and loopy syntax might be said to do the same thing he attributes to Rice's sloppy photography: "to strip off the layers of accumulated impersonality." Or they might be said just to make a mess of things.

The argument can be made that Rice, Jacobs, Smith, and Carmines were the victims of an intellectual fallacy. There can be no artistic return to innocence, especially not by the road of casualness or sloppiness. The only way to break free from the accumulations of culture is through a delicate labor of knowledge and awareness. Freedom is attainable only by means of mastery. Anything short of mastery is only a continuation of the misery.

Bruce Conner and Stan VanDerBeek take the road not taken by Rice, Jacobs, and Smith: the path of knowledge, power, mastery. Their work tells us that the way out of limiting forms of experience is not by attempting to leap outside of them and forget them, and not by merely goofing on them (the way Jack Smith fools around with Maria Montez impersonations in *Flaming Creatures*), but by plunging deeply into them, studying them, learning their nuances, learning how to outmaneuver them. The maze of culture must be complexly negotiated if we want to escape it. Conner and VanDerBeek both attempt to employ a kind of jujitsu on inherited experience, by means of which its energy will be turned against itself.

Conner's subject is the consumer packaging of experience. He reveals it everywhere—from the obvious forms that go by the name of advertising, the movies, politics, the newspaper, and the evening news to the somewhat subtler forms that define beauty, artistic value, and sexual attractiveness. He not only shows us how such forms of cultural processing can rob experience of its specialness and mystery, but how a human remnant can miraculously resist absorption. The perceptual retardations and repetitions in works like *Vivian*, *Breakaway*, *Report*, and *Marilyn Times Five* move us into a richly contemplative relation to the sounds and images that encourages us to see beyond the surfaces. In *Marilyn Times Five*, for example, underneath Marilyn's stereotypical cheesecake poses we are able to hear a faint, touching, individual voice that resists being muffled by any amount of packaging. Conner raises Marilyn from her cultural grave. He restores her humanity.

Stan VanDerBeek lives in the same junkyard of images, but displays his mastery of them in a slightly different way. On the one hand, the speed of the experiences he presents borders on being perceptually overwhelming (thus affiliating him more with the Conner of *A Movie* than the Conner of the films that immediately follow); on the other hand, the poise, jauntiness, and wit of VanDerBeek's imagistic redeployments demonstrate how far *he* is from being buried under the cultural trash heap. *Wheels No. 1* emits intermittent nostalgic noises about what may have been lost in the race down the interstate (Greek ideals of beauty, the intricate orderliness of Bach, the balance and harmony of eighteenth-century architecture), but VanDerBeek's overall response is not "woe" or "whoa," but (as his title sequence tells us) "wheeee."

In *Breathdeath*, the metaphoric cascade is almost Shakespearean in its profligacy and suggestiveness. Images of dances/young people/beauty/crowds/Picasso portraits/motion kaleidoscopically transmute into images of skulls/X-rays/war/armies/death/mushroom clouds. However, the exuberance, inventiveness, and agility of VanDerBeek's ability to jump from one realm to the other and back again ultimately communicates not a feeling of doom and destruction, but of power and exhilaration. The strength of this mind is greater and more impressive than the threats it catalogues, no matter how horrible. We are utterly convinced that its nimbleness will always outrun the lead-footed agents of death.

Like the work of Bruce Conner, Marie Menken's *Go Go Go* is an exploration of the ways the mass-produced experiences of contemporary life declare war against the existence of unique personal spaces. Menken's film is deliberately hectic in its pace, external in its view, and dizzying in its scope. Yet it is telling that two fleeting moments of private, personal interiority emerge in the course of it: one when the man at the typewriter touches his brow, and another shortly afterward when two lovers cuddle on the beach. The fugitiveness of the moments makes them seem all the more precious. Menken shows us that personal consciousness withstands the ravages of modern civilization.

Menken's film also reminds us that one of the major artistic developments of the Beat period was the rise of Method acting. The Method represented a decision to turn away from what were felt to be irrelevant or superficial social forms of expression in order to get in touch with almost ineffable private depths of feeling. The Method actor nurtured and drew on feelings that resisted being translated into public forms of expression. Method actors were to established forms of dramatic expression what Charlie Parker or John Coltrane were to received forms of musical expression. Both forms of art turned inward during the Beat period, as if, in a world overrun with standardization and mechanization, the depths of personal consciousness defined one of the last sanctuaries.

The works of Harry Smith and Robert Breer gesture toward other free imaginative spaces. Their hand-painted animations assert the power of personal craftsmanship to stand outside the systems of mass production. Even more important, the puckish wit of Breer's work and the idiosyncrasy of Smith's private iconography remind us that the quirkiness of the individual imagination defies systems of mass production. Watching Smith's animation *No. 10*, for example, is a little like looking into one of those nineteenth-century cabinets of curiosities, or a Joseph Cornell box—which is to say it is like nothing ever produced by a factory. The experience is the opposite of generic.

Both filmmakers create viewing experiences that transport the viewer into a transcendental realm above and beyond daily experience. The title of one of Breer's early works too modestly calls this process of visionary purification "eyewash." It is actually something closer to "mindwash."

Smith and Breer empower viewers, asking them to become highly alert, active, and imaginative participants in the process of meaning-making; Anthony Balch's *Towers Open Fire* series (which includes the titles *Towers Open Fire*, *The Cut-Ups*, *Bill and Tony*, and *William Buys a*

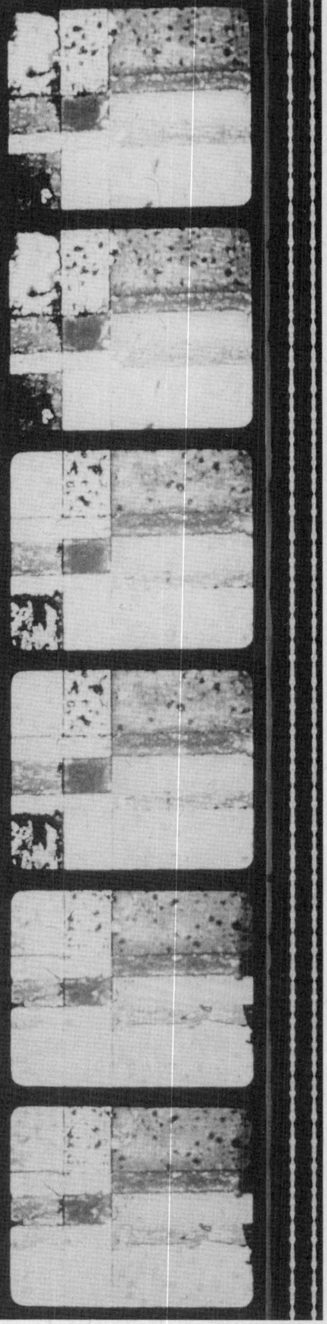

Harry Smith
Early Abstractions No. 3,
excerpt from **Early Abstractions (Nos 1-5, 7 and 10)**, 1939-57

Parrot) moves in the opposite direction. Its strobe editing assaults and batters us into visual and acoustic submission. Its staccato sound and iterative imagery dull our senses into a state of passivity. The rapidity and repetitiveness (and boringness) of Balch's images numb our intellects. (I would note that Bruce Conner's slower repetitions and more imaginative evocations in some of his work have the reverse effect. In *Report* and *Marilyn Times Five*, Conner's loops don't repel, but invite us to move meditatively *into* them, to contemplate their deeper meaning.) Balch's trilogy was created in collaboration with William Burroughs, and was meant to capture the visual effect of Burroughs' writing style on film. Though Balch's visual and acoustic shock tactics are entirely different from Burroughs' narrative shock tactics, the effect of the film and the writing is stunningly similar (in both senses of the adverb). Both artists usher us into a world whirling beyond personal comprehension or control.

The feel of the cinematic art that originated on the West Coast (chiefly from San Francisco) during this period is fundamentally different from that of the East Coast. While New York artists escaped into handcrafted interior spaces (both physical and psychological—the drug experience, the Happening, the pad), West Coast artists moved outside. They could always escape the confinement of alien institutions by going to the ocean, to the desert, to farms and fields, or simply by going—anywhere. While Eastern film is static, Western film tends to be picaresque. It is an art of motion, space, time, and nature. (Winifred Bryan's magical boat ride in *The Queen of Sheba Meets the Atom Man* is the closest New York film of the period gets to this escape into nature, though it is significant that Bryan's immobility during the scene communicates a feeling of entrapment and melancholy that cuts against the visual openness of the sky and the water around her. Even this scene of visual release delivers an East Coast message: you can go out but you can't escape yourself.)

Bruce Baillie's *Mr. Hayashi* might be thought of as a putative East Coast story transformed by a West Coast sensibility. The narrative, slight as it is, mounts a social critique of sorts, involving the difficulty the title character, a Japanese gardener, has finding work that pays adequately. But the beauty of Baillie's black-and-white photography, the misty lusciousness of the landscapes he chooses to photograph, and the powerful silence of Mr. Hayashi's figure within them make the viewer forget all about economics and ethnicity. The shots remind us of Sung scrolls of fields and mountain peaks, where the human figure is dwarfed in

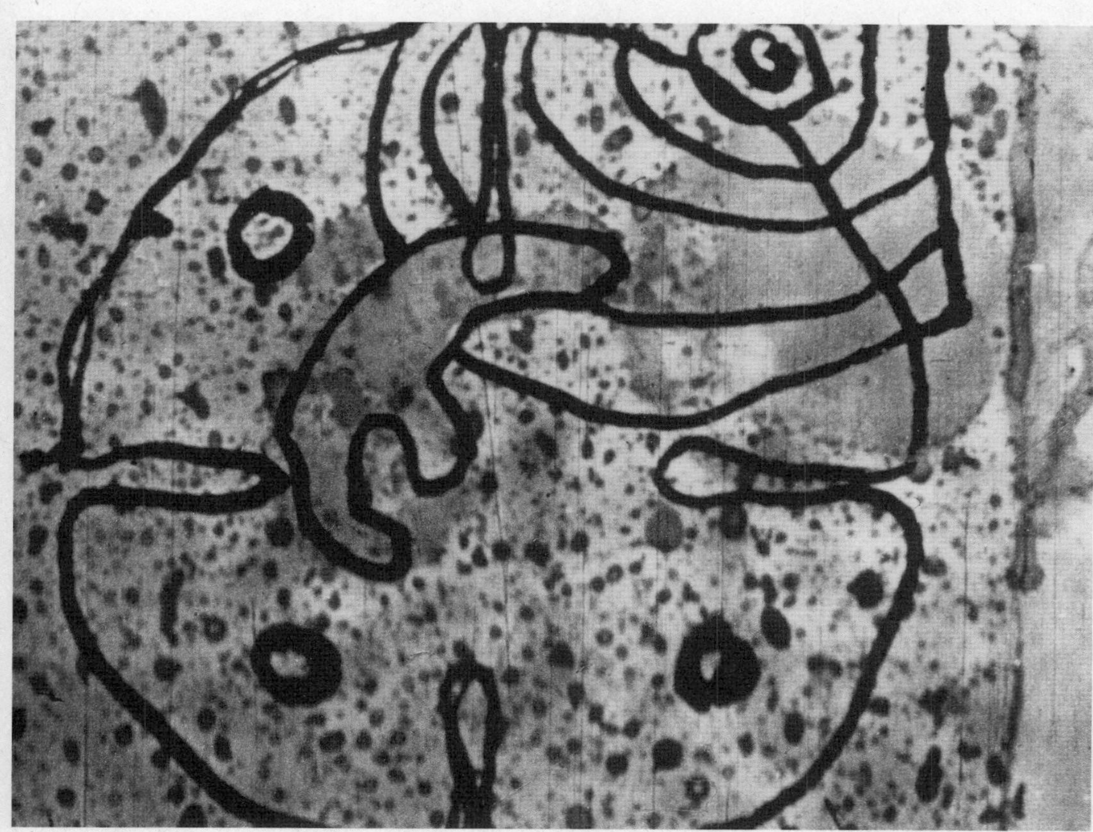

Harry Smith
Early Abstractions No.1,
excerpt from **Early Abstractions (Nos 1-5, 7 and 10)**, 1939-57

Bruce Conner, **Report**, 1963-67

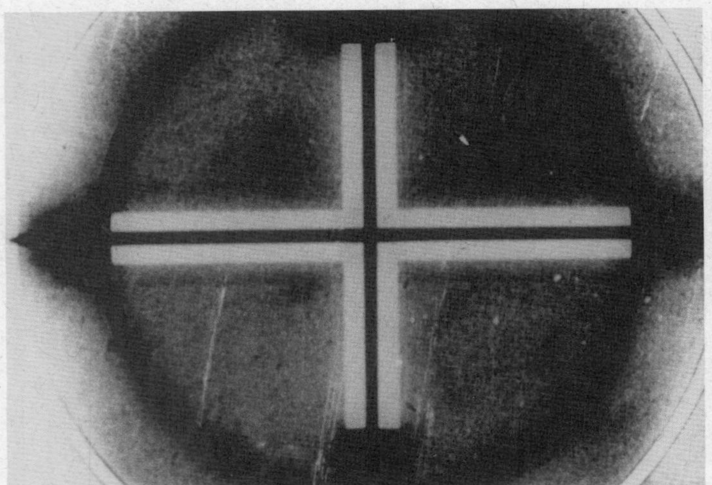

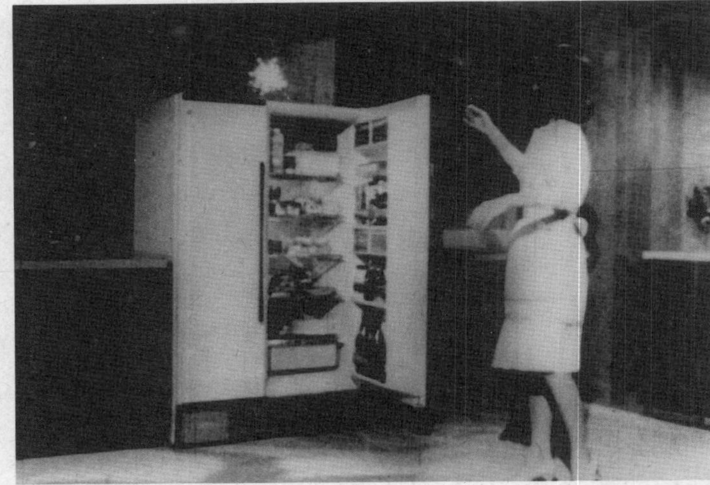

the middle distance. Rather than a study of unemployment, the film becomes a study of nested layers of stillness and serenity (first, the placidity of the photography; second, the brooding calm of the landscape; third, the meditativeness of Mr. Hayashi himself, walking with his head bowed in thought and uttering his thoughtful voice-over narration). The quiet inwardness of it all makes his employment situation seem relatively unimportant by comparison.

Baillie's *To Parsifal*, *Mass for the Dakota Sioux*, and *Quixote* could fittingly be played together as one film. They elaborate on the fundamental dynamic around which *Mr. Hayashi* is organized: the difference between the grandeur, nobility, and serenity of the natural world vs. the shortcomings of artificial social structures and economic arrangements. All three works express a visceral disgust with the so-called achievements of Western culture and a nostalgia for more primitive ways of being. As many other Beat filmmakers did, Baillie identifies with and reserves a special tenderness for the weakest members of society, precisely because they have been largely untouched by these cultural achievements. (Lionel Rogosin's 1956 *On the Bowery*, which is not included on the screening list, displays a similar sympathy toward the socially and institutionally disenfranchised.) The visually cherished figures in *Quixote* are the forgotten and powerless of the earth: an old toothless Native American sitting in a diner; a young woman (whose willowy nakedness is superimposed on an image of a policeman with a billy club); a wrinkled, bleeding, beat-up derelict; nonviolent civil rights protesters marching with locked arms down a city street; a variety of trapped, corralled, or frightened animals being led to the slaughter.

As this list of images suggests, especially the last one, Baillie's work is not known for its emotional subtlety or the absence of clichés. Nonetheless, it is powerful work. Baillie's strength is that he breaks his films free from our culture's pervasive myth of personal agency. The cultural malaise his imagistic superpositions and editorial successions define is beyond any individual's power to create or correct. Baillie imagines a Foucauldian universe that no one is really responsible for creating or capable of opposing. The impersonal systems of technology and history reproduce themselves beyond human desire or control. In this regard, Baillie differs from almost all the other filmmakers on this list. His films deny us the comfort of believing in the power of individual consciousness as an alternative to or an escape from these forces. He imagines a world where not only are there no heroes, but where there *can be* no heroes.

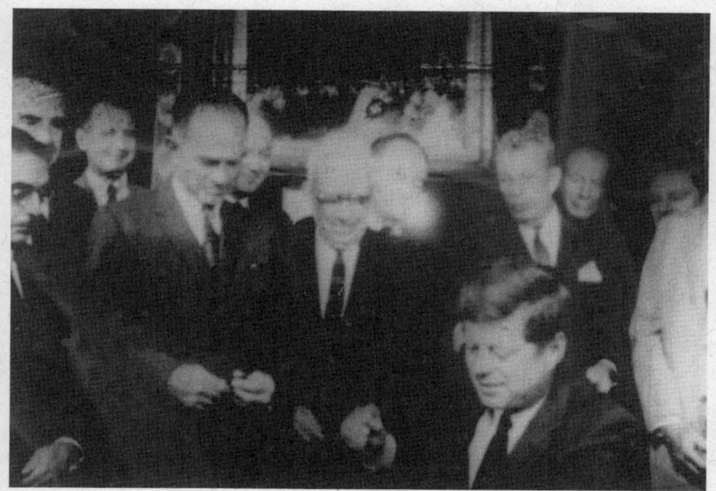

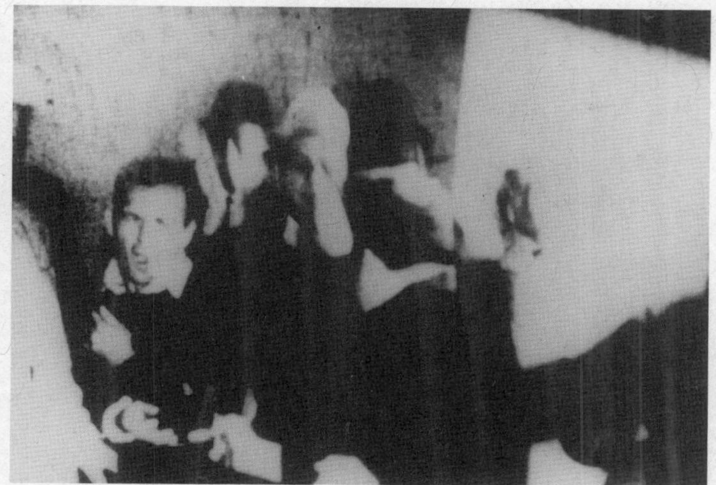

Though it seems weird to group them together because of the difference in their subject matter, the work of Kenneth Anger isn't all that far from Baillie's in its sensibility. Heroism in Anger's work is so thoroughly a cultural artifact (as opposed to being a personal stance) that he might also be said to be a Foucauldian (indeed, he and Baillie are ahead of Foucault, whose major work was later). Anger shows that postmodernism goes further back in American culture (or at least in the culture of Los Angeles) than many of the art history texts acknowledge. For a child of the movies, there is apparently nothing but voguing, role-playing, and style-surfing. Anger's appreciation of the ways life and art interpenetrate has a superficial similarity to Jack Smith's relish of the carnivalesque, but the attitudes of the two filmmakers in this regard couldn't be more opposed. Smith sees costuming, role-playing, and impersonation as ways of expanding our identities and enriching our lives. Anger sees them as limiting us and impoverishing our experiences. For Anger, the movies and other forms of cultural processing represent dead ends for psychological development, emotional traps from which we are unable to escape.

ruth weiss' *The Brink* and John Korty's *The Crazy Quilt*, both Northern California works and therefore not nearly as much under the imaginative sway of the movies, are entirely different. They represent ebullient celebrations of the power of the individual imagination—the imagination of both the characters and their creators—to transform experience idiosyncratically. weiss is a poet and Korty one of the now forgotten pioneers of the American independent film movement. To my mind, these two films actually accomplish what the films Taylor Mead appeared in attempted to do. (Zimmerman's *Lemon Hearts* was made in San Francisco only the year before weiss' *The Brink*.) Like Mead, weiss and Korty use playfulness to enlarge our sense of the possibilities of being. By leaving the straight and narrow of realistic narrative behind, they liberate eccentric, nonstandardized impulses and show us how large and roomy our personalities can be. As was the goal of much Beat art, they free both their characters and their viewers from the repressiveness of overly logical, overly determined, overly causal understandings of experience.

Both weiss and Korty are fundamentally allegorical or symbolic artists. They create fairy tales. The allegory is a way of encouraging the viewer to enter into an especially contemplative or meditative relationship with the story. By encouraging us not to process events realistically, they hope to enhance our ability to understand them imaginatively. Their goal is to stimulate our imaginations to match the level of the characters'.

James Broughton's *Adventures of Jimmy* is another Northern California fairy tale. It is also another addition to the list of "mama's boy" films. Jimmy goes looking for a wife, but comes home with a mother. In fact, with more than one (which only emphasizes the asexuality of his harem).

About the Hollywood movies, the less said the better. It's in the nature of Hollywood filmmaking (along with most radio, television, and print journalism) that it trades in hopelessly reductive clichés and stereotypes. The goal of popular culture is to keep audiences in the clear, and to clear experiences up, even if the experiences must be destroyed in the process. Hollywood translated the inchoate spiritual longings, free-floating anxieties, and vague feelings of alienation that animated the Beat movement into a series of clichéd props, costumes, and Looney Toons cartoon characterizations. The Beats were treated as un-American malcontents, dangerous deviants, comical kooks, or psychopaths—in short, anything but taken seriously. John Byrum's *Heart Beat* (which was based on Carolyn Cassady's memoirs) is sometimes said to be better than this, but that is only because it substitutes a more popular, more recent set of clichés for the somewhat dated Commie/psycho/kook clichés. It turns the Beats into the Young and the Restless. Kerouac, Cassady, and Ginsberg become the stars of a short-running soap opera that never made it to prime time.

The British films dealing with the Beat movement and the "angry young men" (a parallel artistic movement native to the United Kingdom which was linked with the Beat movement during the fifties) treat the subject slightly more seriously and intelligently. These films reflect a fairly different sensibility from American works, but are included to give a sense of how specific cultural and historical conditions affect the development and understanding of an artistic movement. For one thing, British society has always been much more class-conscious than American society, and many of the British films conflate Beat rebellion with working-class discontent. In British film, the Beat stance frequently was linked with practical political issues and sociological realities that Hollywood films to this day studiously avoid (and that the studios were all the more careful to steer clear of during the post-McCarthy, cold war era because of the dangers of being accused of sympathizing with Communism).

The final point to make is that, although every show must of necessity have certain boundary dates set around it, almost any artistic movement worth dealing with has antecedents which anticipate its spirit and successors which carry it into the present. The quote from Emerson's "The Transcendentalist" that heads this essay is meant to suggest that at least as early as 1841 much of the spirit (as well as many of the mannerisms) of the Beat movement could already be detected in American art and life. Thoreau's 1861 "Life Without Principle" is another work that strikingly anticipates Beat feelings and values. (For my money, Thoreau's essay is, in fact, the best summary of the Beat position ever written.) Emerson and Thoreau were Beats before the fact; or to put it the other way around, the Beats were only one of the most recent resurfacings of Emersonian Transcendentalism that have occurred every few decades or so in American culture. It also goes without saying that the Beat spirit lives on in more recent film just as it does in more recent literature and drama. The films of Gus Van Sant, Rick Schmidt, Jon Jost, and Caveh Zahedi come to mind as authentic continuations of the trajectory of the Beat impulse in our own day. Just as Ginsberg himself was following in the footsteps of Whitman, many American filmmakers are even now still on the road with Kerouac. The beat goes on.

I would like to express my appreciation to David Sterritt for his assistance with this essay.

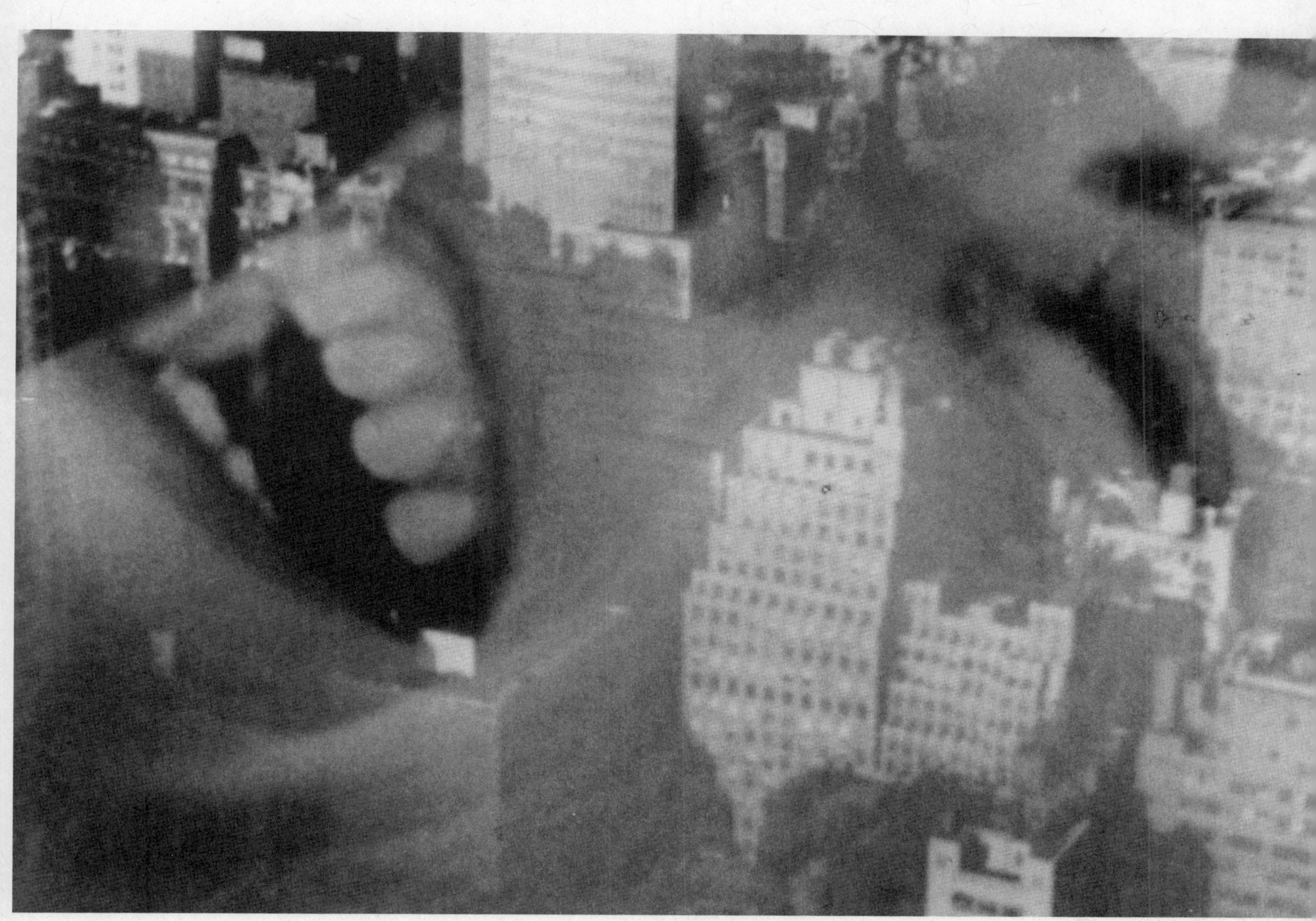

Bruce Baillie, **Quixote**, 1964-65

THE BEAT MOVEMENT IN FILM: A COMPREHENSIVE SCREENING LIST

RAY CARNEY

WORKS INCLUDED IN THE FILM AND VIDEO PROGRAM OF THE "BEATS" EXHIBITION ARE MARKED WITH AN ASTERISK (*).

I. THE BACKBEAT: BEHIND THE BEAT MOVEMENT

THE SOCIAL AND INTELLECTUAL BACKGROUND: THE FEEL OF THE FIFTIES

Point of Order! (1964), Emile de Antonio. Film, black-and-white, sound; 97 minutes. The decade of the fifties begins with the HUAC hearings. Paranoia is rampant.

The Atomic Cafe (1982), Kevin Rafferty, Jayne Loader, and Pierce Rafferty. Film, black-and-white and color, sound; 88 minutes. Comic compilation documentary of various cold war propaganda films. A satire of American optimism and mindless conformism in the face of impending nuclear destruction.

Heavy Petting (1989), Obie Benz. Film, color, sound; 75 minutes. Humorous documentary. Interviews with Allen Ginsberg, William Burroughs, Judith Malina, and others about their loves and lives in the fifties.

Before Stonewall (The Making of a Gay & Lesbian Community) (1984), Greta Schiller, Robert Rosenberg, and John Scagliotti, producers. Film, color, sound; 87 minutes. Sexual repression and the development of a bohemian underground in New York and San Francisco.

**The Beat Generation: An American Dream* (1987), Janet Forman. Film, color, sound; 87 minutes. A sociological overview of the Eisenhower years. Contains archival film footage and more recent interviews with major Beat figures.

AMERICAN CIVILIZATION AND ITS DISCONTENTS: MIDDLE-CLASS ANXIETIES AND FEARS

The Bachelor Party (1957), Delbert Mann. Film, black-and-white, sound; 93 minutes. Hollywood examination of the cracks in the facade of the Organization Man. An important contemporaneous depiction of the self-doubts of the middle-class American male.

The Savage Eye (1959), Joseph Strick, Ben Maddow, and Sidney Meyers. Film, black-and-white, sound; 68 minutes. A relentlessly savage attack on the values of the American middle class: its conspicuous consumption, conformity, and quest for style.

The Wild One (1954), Laslo Benedek. Film, black-and-white, sound; 79 minutes. Starring Marlon Brando, the patron saint of much of the youth movement of the period. His mumbling and brow-furrowing became Beat trademarks.

**Rebel Without a Cause* (1954), Nicholas Ray. Film, color, sound; 111 minutes. The quintessential coming-of-age crisis film. A performance by James Dean that helped to shape Beat manners and mannerisms. (Nicholas Ray's son, Tony Ray, is featured in John Cassavetes' *Shadows*, which appears later on the program.)

CREATIVITY ON THE MARGINS: THE AFRICAN-AMERICAN EXPERIENCE AND THE JAZZ LIFE

**The Cry of Jazz* (1958), Ed Bland. Film, black-and-white, sound; 35 minutes. An early definition of the distinctiveness of the black experience and its link to the aesthetics of jazz. Characteristically Beat in its somewhat romanticized view of the black musician.

Celebrating Bird!: The Triumph of Charlie Parker (1988), Gary Giddins and Kendrick Simmons. Video, black-and-white and color, sound; 59 minutes. Recent interviews and documentary footage of Parker in performance, but more biography than performance.

**The World According to John Coltrane* (1991), Toby Byron and Robert Palmer. Video, black-and-white and color, sound; 59 minutes. Extensive footage of Coltrane in performance on New York television in the fifties. Provides a deep insight into the spirituality of his music.

Jazz on a Summer's Day (1960), Bert Stern. Film, color, sound; 85 minutes. Documentation of the 1959 Newport Jazz Festival. Performers include Anita O'Day, Dinah Washington, Gerry Mulligan, Jack Teagarden, and Louis Armstrong. A major documentary of the period, but slanted toward Dixieland and "hot" jazz and away from the "cooler" or bebop work that was more important to the Beats.

RELIGION WITHOUT GOD—THE QUEST FOR A NEW RELATION TO THE UNIVERSE

Essential Alan Watts: Man in Nature, Work as Play (1973), David Grieve and Henry Jacobs. Video, color, sound; 58 minutes. Visual records of Watts' radio broadcasts and public lectures from the fifties and sixties are not available. This video contains two of a series of filmed talks from the early seventies. Connections with the Beat aesthetic and the work of many West Coast Beat artists in particular are evident.

Zuigan's Permanent Principle (1994), Nita Freidman and Abbott John Daido Loori. Video, color, sound; 54 minutes. A lecture by Abbott John Daido Loori on change, permanence, time, and redeeming the everyday work of life.

II. THE DOCUMENTARY RECORD

PORTRAITS OF THE ARTISTS

Jack Kerouac

Kerouac (1984), John Antonelli. Video, color, sound; 90 minutes. Interviews with Ginsberg, Ferlinghetti, Burroughs, and others; music by Ellington, Mingus, Sims. An upbeat, affirmative depiction of Kerouac's early years, with a salutary emphasis on the young Kerouac.

**What Happened to Kerouac?* (1985), Lewis MacAdams and Richard Lerner. Film, color, sound; 96 minutes. Interviews with Corso, Ginsberg, and others. Focuses on the adult Kerouac. Includes a scene of an older, conservative, alcoholic, beaten Kerouac arguing with Ed Sanders and William Buckley on *Firing Line*. Kerouac's appearance on television on *The Steve Allen Plymouth Show* is also included.

Jack Kerouac's Road—A Franco-American Odyssey (1987), Herménégilde Chiasson. Film, color, sound; 55 minutes. An unusual view of Kerouac entirely from the perspective of his French-Catholic background. An interesting corrective to the view of Kerouac as being rootless and culturally ungrounded. Kerouac speaks French (with English subtitles).

Allen Ginsberg
***A Moveable Feast: Profiles of Contemporary American Authors—Allen Ginsberg** (1991), Bruce Berger. Video, color, sound; 30 minutes. Interviews with and readings by Ginsberg, and an account of his early years in New York and friendship with Kerouac.

***The Life & Times of Allen Ginsberg** (1993), Jerry Aronson. Film, black-and-white and color; 82 minutes. Both a biography of Ginsberg and a comprehensive portrait of the period. A wealth of archival footage and photographs that nicely contextualizes Ginsberg's life and work.

William Burroughs
Burroughs: The Movie** (1983), Howard Brookner. Film, black-and-white and color, sound; 87 minutes, Rare footage of Burroughs' appearance on ***Saturday Night Live, interviews with Burroughs and others who speak about him.

William S. Burroughs: Commissioner of Sewers (1986), Klaus Maeck. Film, black-and-white and color, sound; 60 minutes. Interviews with Burroughs by Jurgen Ploog during Burroughs' 1986 tour of Germany.

Lenny Bruce
"Playboy's" Penthouse (the Beat episode) (1959). Video, black-and-white, sound; 56 minutes. Features Hugh Heffner, Lenny Bruce, Cy Coleman, Charlie Coleman, and others. Bruce conducts an extended (and hilarious) extempore conversation with Heffner.

***Lenny Bruce Performance Film** (1968), John Magnuson, producer. Video, black-and-white, sound; 59 minutes. The only surviving visual record of a Bruce performance on stage. Bruce improvises a jazzlike "riff" based on the transcript of his trial. His intellectual brilliance and agility come through not-withstanding the static camera set-up.

ADDITIONAL DOCUMENTS FROM THE PERIOD

Wholly Communion (1966), Peter Whitehead. Film, black-and-white, sound; 33 minutes. Ginsberg, Corso, Ferlinghetti, and others reading at the Royal Albert Hall in 1965.

The Beats: An Existential Comedy, Philomene Long. Video, sound; 58 minutes. A comic compilation of television and film clips on the Beats, focusing on the West Coast Beats.

The Anatomy of Cindy Fink (1966), Richard Leacock, Patricia Jaffe, and Paul Leaf. Film, color, sound; 12 minutes. Rarely seen documentary about the life of a Greenwich Village dancer.

THE BEAT GOES ON (AFTER-EFFECTS, CONTINUATIONS, REFLECTIONS)

Fried Shoes, Cooked Diamonds: The Beats at Naropa (1978), Costanzo Allione. Video, color, sound; 55 minutes. Burroughs, Ginsberg, Corso, Anne Waldman, Diane DiPrima, and others at Naropa in the early 1970s.

This Song for Jack (1983), Robert Frank. Film, black-and-white, sound; 30 minutes. Documents the 1982 "On the Road, Jack Kerouac Conference" in Boulder, Colorado. Frank creates a deliberate companion piece to his earlier ***Pull My Daisy***. This is, in effect, the same film twenty years later.

West Coast, Beat and Beyond (1984), Chris Felver. Video, color, sound; 59 minutes. Readings by Ginsberg, Kerouac, Ken Kesey, Lawrence Ferlinghetti, and others, on San Francisco's North Beach. Narrated by Gerald Nicosia.

***Gang of Souls** (1989), Maria Beatty. Video, color, sound; 58 minutes. Recent footage of Ginsberg, Burroughs, DiPrima, and others, and tributes to them from a generation of contemporary artists.

Love Lion: Performance with Words and Music by Michael McClure and Ray Manzarek (1991), Sheldon Rochlin and Maxine Harris. Video, color, sound; 70 minutes. On-stage reading that captures the Beat tendency to combine music and poetry in one performance.

***Allan 'n' Allen's Complaint** (1982), Nam June Paik and Shigeko Kubota. Video, color, sound; 30 minutes. Featuring Allen Ginsberg and Allan Kaprow.

***Living with the Living Theater** (1989), Nam June Paik with Betsy Connors and Paul Garrin. Video, color, sound; 28 1/2 minutes. Ginsberg reflecting on the Beat movement.

Gregory Corso Reads from the U.S. Constitution and Bill of Rights (1992), James Rasin and Jerry Poynton. Film, color, sound; 18 minutes. A work in progress. Corso delivers an improvised "riff," somewhat rough and flat in places, on American history.

Huncke and Louis** (1995), Laki Vazakas. Video, color, sound; 10 minutes. A work in progress. A wonderful and disturbing portrait of Herbert Huncke and his companion Louis Cartwright. Cuts beneath the primping and preening of the movement to document the human cost, as Huncke's work also does. Usefully compared with ***The Connection as a study of self-destruction through drugs and life-style.

New Orleans, 1938 (1995), Jerry Poynton. Video, color, sound; 12 minutes. Actor Edgar Oliver reads Herbert Huncke's story, "New Orleans, 1938."

THE HAPPENING: TAKING ART OFF THE WALLS AND BRINGING IT TO LIFE

***Happenings: One** (1962), Raymond Saroff. Film, black-and-white, silent; 21 minutes. Claes Oldenburg, Pat Oldenburg, Lucas Samaras, and others at the Ray Gun Theater.

***Happenings: Two** (1962), Raymond Saroff. Film, black-and-white, silent; 22 1/2 minutes.

***The White Rose** (1967), Bruce Conner. Film, black-and-white, sound; 7 minutes. The removal of Jay DeFeo's massive sculptural piece from her apartment in 1965. A very subtle, deep exploration of art's place in the world.

III. THE BEAT SENSIBILITY IN FILM

Christopher MacLaine
***The End** (1953). Film, color, sound; 35 minutes. Set in San Francisco, a series of surreal episodes deal with suicide and death and the atomic age.

Beat (1958). Film, color, sound; 6 minutes. A boy and girl dance through the streets of a city. Reveals MacLaine's fundamentally choreographic sensibility.

Stan Brakhage
Desistfilm** (1954). Film, black-and-white, sound; 7 minutes. Parker Tyler called it the first authentically Beat film (though the award might actually go to MacLaine's ***The End). Sexual combat and social anxiety among a group of young people.

***Anticipation of the Night** (1958). Film, black-and-white, silent; 40 minutes. The quest for an innocent eye and a form of film that can capture the complexity of lived experience before it has been simplified by the understanding.

Jonas Mekas
***Lost, Lost, Lost** (1949-63/1976). Film, black-and-white and color, sound; 178 minutes. An exploration of terminal marginality, lostness, searching, longing. The first, chronologically, of Mekas' diary films, which capture the movements of time, space, and mind on film.

***Guns of the Trees** (1962). Film, black-and-white, sound; 75 minutes. Two couples—one white, one black—living on the margins. Ties in with Beat anxieties about the A-bomb and the point of work in American society. Narration by Allen Ginsberg. Not nearly as interesting or complex as **Lost, Lost, Lost,** but more obviously Beat. Features Ben Carruthers, who also stars in Cassavetes' **Shadows**.

Frank Paine
***Motion Picture** (1956). Film, color, sound; 4 minutes. The energy and freedom of traveling down the road in an automobile was one of the central Beat metaphors. Paine's mastery of space and time is usefully contrasted with Clarke's in her short films. While Paine lunges through space and eats it up, Clarke balletically dances around in it.

Shirley Clarke
***Bridges-Go-Round** (1958). Film, color, sound; 4 minutes.

***Skyscraper** (1959). Film, black-and-white and color, sound; 20 minutes.

A bebop sensibility. Clarke animates the city and its objects and makes them dance to her tunes.

***The Connection** (1961). Film, black-and-white, sound; 103 minutes. From the Jack Gelber play, acted by The Living Theater. **Waiting for Godot** as a drug-pusher story. Because of some of its language, it was legally ruled obscene and only released after a court battle.

Portrait of Jason (1967). Film, black-and-white, sound; 105 minutes. Jason is the archetypal hipster of the period, the psychopath Norman Mailer's essay "The White Negro" describes, condemned to swing forever.

Andrew Meyer
Shades and Drumbeats (1964). Film, color, silent; 25 minutes. An all-nighter of drugs and sex with a group of young people. Compare with **Shadows** as an evocation of the milieu.

John Cassavetes
***Shadows** (1957-59). Film, black-and-white, sound; 87 minutes. Mixed races, questions of identity. Charlie Mingus and Shafi Hadi (a.k.a. Curtis Porter) perform on the soundtrack.

Too Late Blues (1962). Film, black-and-white, sound; 103 minutes. Jazz milieu. A hero with a Peter Pan complex. Cassavetes tells the story of an artist too idealistic to function in contemporary capitalistic society. Is the problem society or him?

Robert Frank
***Pull My Daisy** (1959), Robert Frank and Alfred Leslie. Film, black-and-white, sound; 28 minutes. One of the best-known Beat films. Although for many years mistakenly believed to be improvised, the film still stands as a paean to spontaneity and freedom.

Me and My Brother (1965-68). Film, black-and-white and color, sound; 91 minutes. Peter and Jules Orlovsky, Christopher Walken, Joe Chaikin, Allen Ginsberg. Raises questions about the boundaries between art and life by forcing the viewer to wonder about what in the film is acted and what is not.

Ron Rice
***The Flower Thief** (1960). Film, black-and-white, sound; 75 minutes. Taylor Mead clowns and improvises his version of Chaplin in **City Lights**.

The Queen of Sheba Meets the Atom Man (1963/1982). Film, black-and-white, sound; 109 minutes. Taylor Mead and Winifred Bryan, who has the most emotionally powerful passage—a ferry ride out into New York harbor.

Vernon Zimmerman
Lemon Hearts (1960). Film, black-and-white, sound; 26 minutes. Taylor Mead house-hunting (and house-haunting) in San Francisco.

Ken Jacobs
***Blonde Cobra** (1959-63). Film, black-and-white and color, sound with live radio; 30 minutes. Jack Smith camping it up in a work that hovers between the comic and the tragic. Where does role-playing end and reality begin?

Little Stabs at Happiness (1959-63). Film, color, sound; 15 minutes. The dark side of the Beat sensibility. Kerouac regarded "goofing"—clowning around—as "holy," but Jacobs wanted to restore its blasphemous potential, and does so in this film.

Jack Smith
***Flaming Creatures** (1963). Film, black-and-white, sound; 45 minutes. A Sternbergian view of life as a form of theater. Relates to the Beat interest in costume and carnival, and the attempt to treat personal identity as a work of art.

COMING TO GRIPS WITH THE TRASH HEAP OF CULTURE: FOUND FOOTAGE AND FOUND-OBJECT FILMS

Bruce Conner
***A Movie** (1958). Film, black-and-white, sound; 12 minutes.

***Cosmic Ray** (1961). Film, black-and-white, sound; 4 minutes.

***Report** (1963-67). Film, black-and-white, sound; 13 minutes.

Marilyn Times Five (1968-73). Film, black-and-white, sound; 13 minutes.

Conner recycles the culture of advertising, Hollywood, and the media to adapt it to his anti-establishment purposes.

Stan VanDerBeek
***Wheels No. 1** (1958). Film, black-and-white, sound; 5 minutes.

***Wheels No. 2** (1959). Film, black-and-white, sound; 4 minutes.

***Science Friction** (1959). Film, color, sound; 9 minutes.

***Breathdeath** (1964). Film, black-and-white, sound; 15 minutes.

Explorations of the American passion for fashion, the lust for motion, and the Faustian push into space—documented and satirized through found footage.

Marie Menken
***Go Go Go** (1962-64). Film, color, silent; 11 1/2 minutes. Making space amid the hecticness and crush for privacy, consciousness, interiority.

WILLIAM BURROUGHS PROGRAM: CAPTURING THE SHOCK SENSIBILITY ON FILM

***Towers Open Fire, The Cut-Ups, Bill and Tony, William Buys a Parrot** (1962-72), Anthony Balch. Film, black-and-white and color; sound; 35 minutes. Written and narrated by William Burroughs. Inspired by Brion Gysin. An attempt to mimic Burroughs' cut-up methods in the medium of film.

Naked Lunch (1991), David Cronenberg. Film, color, sound; 115 minutes. An attempt to do in commercial film what Burroughs does on the page. The film can be compared to Balch's **Towers Open Fire** as evidence of the problems that arise in attempting to translate the Beat sensibility into a mainstream form of expression.

A CLASH OF SENSIBILITIES: BEAT COOL MEETS WARHOL COLD

Andy Warhol
Tarzan and Jane Regained, Sort of... (1963). Film, black-and-white and color, sound; 81 minutes. Wallace Berman and his son appear in the film.

Couch (1964). Film, black-and-white, silent; 54 minutes. Allen Ginsberg, Jack Kerouac, and Gregory Corso appear.

ANIMATION: EAST COAST AND WEST

Harry Smith
**Early Abstractions, Nos. 1-5, 7 and 10* (1939-57). Film, color, sound; 23 minutes. The creation of a transcendental visual style.

Heaven and Earth Magic Feature (1959-66). Film, black-and-white, sound; 66 minutes.

Robert Breer
**Recreation* (1956). Film, color, sound; 1 1/2 minutes.

Eyewash (1959). Film, color, silent; 3 minutes.

Breathing (1963). Film, black-and-white, sound; 5 minutes.

**Fist Fight* (1964). Film, color, sound; 9 minutes.

An attempt to engage the viewer in a playful pursuit of ever-elusive meanings.

IV. VISIONARY PURIFICATIONS AND WEST COAST INFLECTIONS

James Whitney
**Yantra* (1950-55). Film, color, sound; 7 minutes.

**Lapis* (1963-66). Film, color, sound; 10 minutes.

Meditative states translated into the medium of film.

Jordan Belson
**Caravan* (1952). Film, color, sound; 4 minutes.

**Mandala* (1953). Film, color, sound; 3 minutes.

**Séance* (1953). Film, color, sound; 4 minutes.

**Allures* (1961). Film, color, sound; 8 minutes.

Re-Entry (1964). Film, color, sound; 6 minutes.

Larry Jordan
**Triptych in Four Parts* (1958). Film, color, sound; 12 minutes.

**Visions of a City* (1957/1979). Film, black-and-white tinted sepia; 8 minutes.

Bruce Baillie
**Mr. Hayashi* (1961). Film, black-and-white, sound; 3 minutes.

Have You Thought of Talking to the Director? (1962). Film, black-and-white, sound; 15 minutes.

To Parsifal (1963). Film, black-and-white, sound; 16 minutes.

Mass for the Dakota Sioux (1963-64). Film, black-and-white, sound; 20 1/2 minutes.

**Quixote* (1964-65). Film, black-and-white and color, sound; 45 minutes.

A spiritual sensibility, Oriental terseness, love of nature, interest in purity and innocence, and distrust of science, technology, and modern civilization define Baillie's work.

Kenneth Anger
**Scorpio Rising* (1963). Film, color, sound; 29 minutes.

Kustom Kar Kommandos (1965). Film, color, sound; 3 1/2 minutes.

A Los Angeles sensibility: there is no escape from the relentless cultural processing of experience. Culture has become the new nature.

ruth weiss
**The Brink* (1961). Film, black-and-white, sound; 40 minutes. Stan Brakhage called *The Brink* one of the most important San Francisco films of the period. A playful love story about two lonely people. Photographed by Paul Beattie, the painter.

John Korty
**The Crazy Quilt* (1966). Film, black-and-white, sound; 72 minutes.

Funnyman (1967). Film, color, sound; 98 minutes.

Two independent features from the San Francisco North Beach area. A celebration of extravagance, personal eccentricity, and the transforming power of the individual imagination. Beat transmuting into hippie.

James Broughton
**Adventures of Jimmy* (1950). Film, black-and-white, sound; 11 minutes. Mama's boy looks for a match.

V. THE BOUTIQUING OF BEATNESS: HOLLYWOOD GOES BEAT

The Beat Generation (1959), Charles Haas. Film, black-and-white, sound; 95 minutes. Louis Armstrong makes an appearance. A rapist masquerades as a beatnik.

The Subterraneans (1960), Ranald MacDougall. Film, color, sound; 89 minutes. Music by Gerry Mulligan, Carmen McRae, and Shelley Manne. A gentrification of Kerouac's novel of the same title, with a race change (from black to white) of the female lead.

A Bucket of Blood (1959), Roger Corman. Film, black-and-white, sound; 66 minutes. Follows the mass media in treating Beats as deviants, weirdos, psychopaths. A waiter in a coffeehouse murders people and passes himself off as a Beat sculptor.

**Greenwich Village Story* (1961), Jack O'Connell. Film, black-and-white, sound; 95 minutes. The best of the Hollywood adaptations. A love story about a struggling writer and his girlfriend, set in a Beat milieu.

Heart Beat (1980), John Byrum. Film, color, sound; 105 minutes. Hollywood portraits of Cassady, Kerouac, Ginsberg, and others. Adaptation of Carolyn Cassady's memoir of the period. Soap opera on the big screen.

VI. TRANSATLANTIC TRANSFORMATIONS: ANGRY YOUNG MEN (AND WOMEN) IN THE UK

The Rebel Set (a.k.a. Beatsville) (1959), Gene Fowler, Jr. Film, black-and-white, sound; 72 minutes. Rebellious youths get involved in a robbery plot.

Beat Girl (a.k.a. Wild for Kicks) (1962), Edmond T. Greville. Film, black-and-white, sound; 92 minutes. A teenage girl rebels against her father by becoming a beatnik and a criminal.

Saturday Night, Sunday Morning (1960), Karel Reisz. Film, black-and-white, sound; 90 minutes. Starring Albert Finney. One of the best of the "angry young men" films, about a Nottingham factory worker rebelling against his working-class background and surroundings.

Look Back in Anger (1989), David Jones. Video, color, sound; 114 minutes. Starring Kenneth Branagh. The most faithful and dramatically powerful film version of Osborne's play and therefore preferable to the film of the same title made during the period. Arguably the most sympathetic portrait of the British "angry young man" on film.

I would like to express my deep gratitude to Maria Christina Villaseñor for her invaluable help in compiling this filmography.

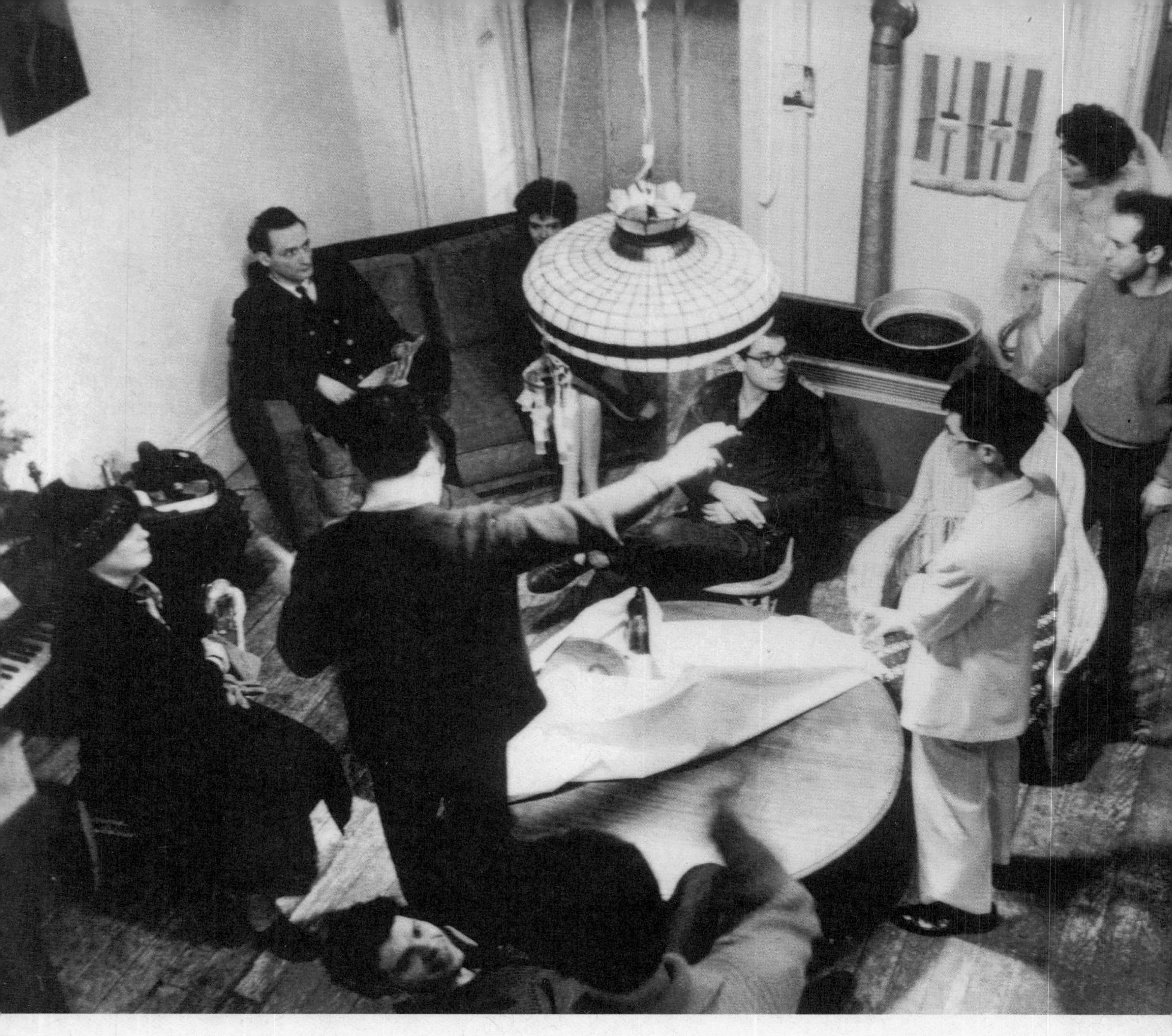

Cast of "Pull My Daisy" in Alfred Leslie's loft, NYC, 1959. Clockwise from lower left: Alice Neel, Larry Rivers, Delphine Seyrig, Allen Ginsberg, Denise Parker, Robert Frank, "Shindey," Sally Gross, Gert Berliner, Richard Bellamy, David Amram, Gregory Corso, Alfred Leslie (back to camera), and Peter Orlovsky (obscured). Photo © John Cohen

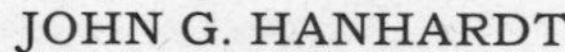

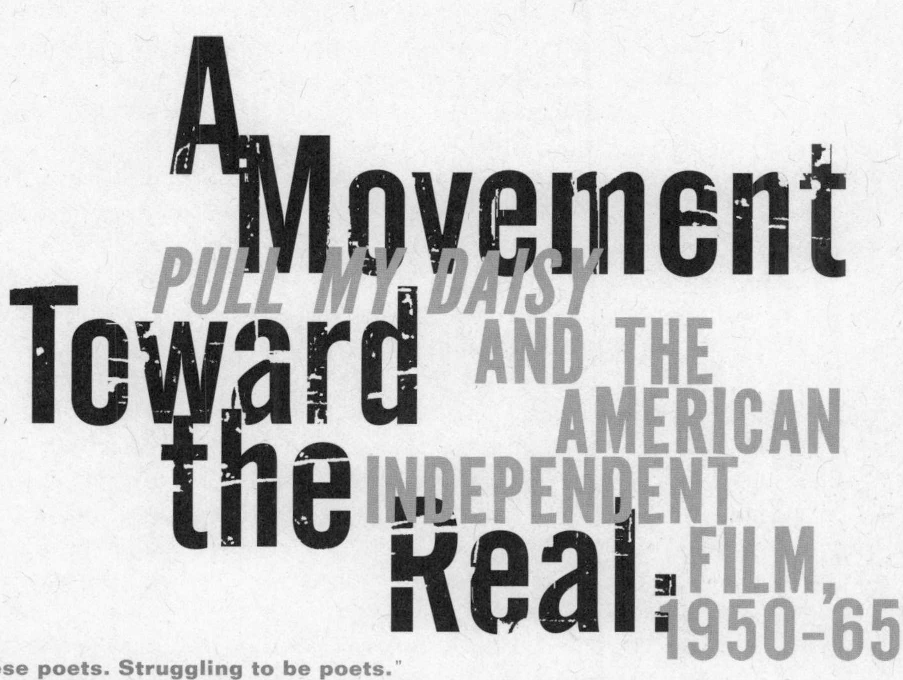

"All these poets. Struggling to be poets."
From Jack Kerouac's script for *Pull My Daisy*[1]

"The picture itself is beatnikness."
Archer Winsten (1960)[2]

"...*Pull My Daisy* clearly point[s]...toward a new thematic, a new sensitivity."
Jonas Mekas (1959)[3]

***Pull My Daisy* holds a special place** in the history of the American cinema. As the above quotes from the time indicate, it is a film that was immediately identified with the Beat movement as perhaps its defining film. Robert Frank's camera and Kerouac's narrative spoke to a new generation of filmmakers. *Pull My Daisy* heralded a new American cinema much as the Beat poets articulated a new American poetics in literature. To better understand Robert Frank and Alfred Leslie's achievement in producing the film, this essay examines the work's historical and critical context, reflecting on filmmakers and their efforts to create an alternative film culture during the late 1950s and early 1960s. It was this dynamic film culture that would shape the world in which the Beats created, freely flowing through their daily life as artists. There was a real sense of change and possibility during this period, which the Beats embodied in their own freely anti-establishment and good-natured rejection of traditional culture and polite society. The changing film community was a key element of the Beat experience—defined as an American phenomenon that set an example for a cultural activism which laid the foundation for the counterculture of the 1960s.[4]

Looking back to 1959, when Robert Frank and Alfred Leslie produced *Pull My Daisy*, is to recall an era in which artists imagined great possibilities for the independent filmmaker. It was a year after Jonas Mekas began writing his regular "Movie Journal" column in *The Village Voice*, which spoke for a new generation of filmmakers working outside the established motion picture industry of Hollywood. The following year saw the establishment of the New American Cinema Group, organized on behalf of filmmakers for whom the cinema was a potentially liberating and poetic, expressive statement. The formation in that same year of Canyon Cinema in San Francisco, an innovative artist-run distribution and support organization for all forms of avant-garde film, demonstrated another initiative by artists, as they created new production and distribution systems for independent filmmakers.

The period of the late 1950s and early 1960s was an active time for artists working in a variety of media, as they turned away from the traditional forms and models of the heroic artist and the romantic abstract text. Instead they directed their creative energies to the everyday world of experience, which became the resource for an emerging set of movements that included Fluxus, Happenings, the avant-garde film, performance, new dance, and music. Within this plethora of vanguard activities, the avant-garde film would create one of the most extraordinary periods in the history of the American cinema, in which a new language of filmmaking flourished and took root in the American film culture.

Filmmakers, seeing themselves as activists, developed new initiatives in creating artist-run organizations through which independent film fashioned a new presence for itself in American culture. As had happened in American jazz and Off Broadway theater, the independent filmmaker established an art practice which reflected the radical changes taking place in American culture. The films produced in the late 1950s did not comprise a single approach to filmmaking. Rather, the communities of filmmakers were contentious, outspoken groups of coalescing and dissolving friendships, relationships, and alliances that met at particular points around shared needs or ideological and aesthetic goals.

During this period certain changes occurred in the filmmakers' relationship to the medium which centered on subject matter, style, and form. This essay seeks to identify certain critical moments that mark an attempt to refashion the cinematic image and reform the cinematic apparatus through the determination of new aesthetic strategies. The relationship of the filmic text to the cinematic apparatus (camera, film, projection system) shifted away from one of support for a symbolic and hallucinatory dream state that represented the unconscious along narrative lines. Instead, filmmakers evoked the abstractions of an unconscious logic, or focused on the material properties of film and the artifice and transparency of the production process. They confronted and dismantled a cinema predicated on European modernist aesthetic models and replaced it with a distinctly American amalgam, in which an activist cinema transformed its sources in order to articulate new models and languages of filmmaking.

The radical developments in independent filmmaking at the end of the 1950s can be introduced through the work of two filmmakers whose individual vision informed, and whose radical differences bracketed the defining ideas of the Beat film. Stan Brakhage evolved a distinctive aesthetic influenced by his interest in the vision of such "authentically" American poets as Charles Olson, Edward Dorn, Robert Creeley, and Robert Duncan. The work of these poets was expressed in an American vernacular evocative of its landscape and culture. The literary critic Sherman Paul, discussing these poets' relationship to American art, characterized their world as being "freer in its attitudes toward the medium, seeing in the random or accidental the beginning of an order."[5] These poets informed and shaped the direct poetics of the Beats, whose voice broke off from the mannered and Europeanized academic poetry of the time, turning instead to the vernacular of American speech and experience. So Brakhage drew from his domestic life, his wife, Jane, and his children, who were the subjects of an evolving abstraction and breakdown of

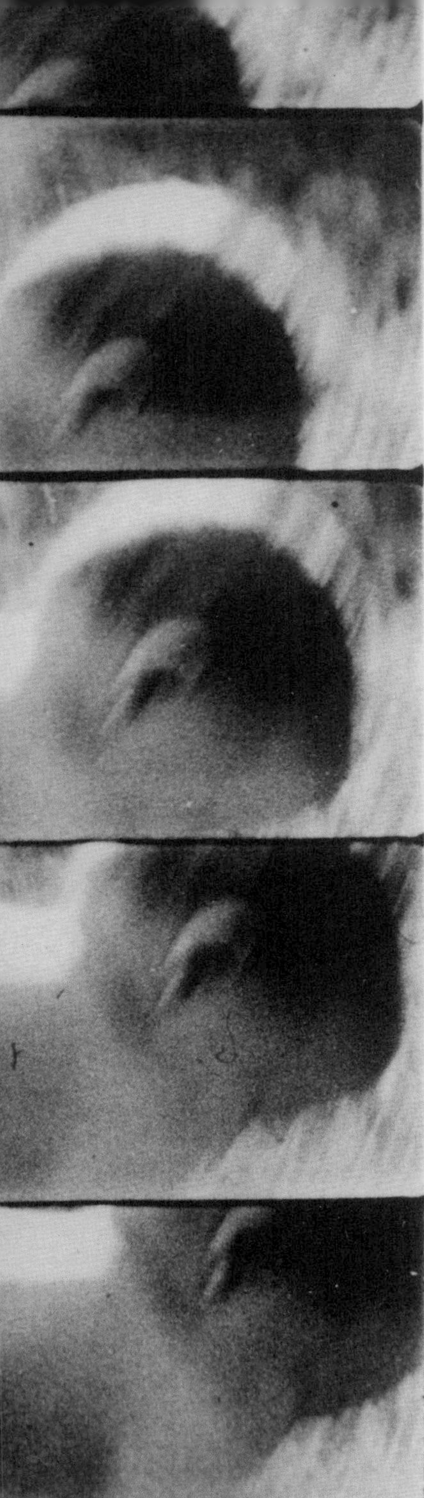

Stan Brakhage
Anticipation of the Night, 1958

the narrative logic of the organization of filmic space and *mise-en-scène*. Brakhage's film *Anticipation of the Night* (1958) is a key work and critical break and change in the perception of filmmaking. This film rejects drama and the notion of narrative, and replaces it with an intuitive and dynamic use of the camera as a means to inject film with a bold, direct acknowledgment of the power of the image, unmediated by the stylistics of outworn formal and modernist strategies.

Brakhage loosens the camera as cascading, fragmentary images of color and light filter throughout the scenes from the artist's life: children, flowers, lawns, home, night and day. The editing movement forms a constant inquiry into images, liberating the film from the narrative constraints of shot-to-shot continuity and point of view.

Brakhage's own words convey the shifting imagery of the film:

> **The daylight shadow of a man in its movement evokes lights in the night. A rose bowl, held in hand, reflects both sun and moon-like illuminations. The opening of a doorway onto trees anticipates the twilight into the night. A child is born on the lawn, born of water, with promissory rainbow, and the wild rose. It becomes the moon and the source of all night light. Lights of the night become young children playing a circular game. The moon moves over a pillared temple to which all lights return. There is seen the sleep of the innocents and their animal dreams, becoming their amusement, their circular game, becoming the morning. The trees change color and lose their leaves for the morn, become the complexity of branches on which the shadow man hangs himself.[6]**

Brakhage places the artist's self within a complex and radical appropriation of the filmic space as he breaks down the perspectival coordinates of the frame. He liberates the camera from the linear language of narrative to an intense, personal space of evolving forms created from light and color and mediated by "metaphors on vision," the title of his manifesto published in 1963 by the journal *Film Culture*. The camera lens refines and distorts reality, collapsing the perspective into an abstract two-dimensional plane and then opening it up into an illusionistic space; the film frame becomes a single space as foreground and background are joined into a continually shifting field of action. Variations in camera speed, from eight, to sixteen, to twenty-four frames per second, and the use of different film stocks create subtle changes and modulations in the image.

The aesthetic stance in *Anticipation of the Night* prefigures many later developments in independent film. In his interplay of camera movement with editing, and with scratching directly on the film surface, Brakhage manipulated the tensions between the recognizable photographic image and the abstraction of light, color, and movement. He thereby freed the image from the parameters of a film frame anchored in the perspectival logic of cinematic narrative space. Brakhage strove to erase the surface and boundaries of illusion and create a new expressive form of filmmaking.

Another film released in 1958 was *A Movie* by Bruce Conner. Conner, a leading figure in the assemblage art movement, lived in San Francisco, which was also one of the centers of the Beat movement. A key element of the Beat movement was the revolution that brought poetry to new audiences outside the academy. The Beats' preoccupation with reinventing language as poetry was achieved by playing with vernacular speech and rejecting European and middle-class mores and notions of poetic decorum. As the poets appropriated words as found objects, Bruce Conner appropriated found footage to articulate a new mode of filmmaking. In *A Movie*, as in his assemblage sculpture, Conner picked up the debris of a consumer society—the detritus of the Hollywood dream factory.

Bruce Conner's films constitute another important and highly distinct development within the independent film movement. His filmmaking was directly influenced by his work as an assemblage artist. The found footage is drawn from entertainment features, television, and educational and scientific films. These sequences are edited together to form a playful new language of visual puns. Conner juxtaposes the actions in unrelated shots in an associative montage which achieves its own narrative continuity with a radically different and ironic meaning: in a shot from a World War II action film, a submarine captain peers through a periscope; this is followed by a shot of Marilyn Monroe in a pornographic short; then a shot of torpedoes being fired from a submarine; the sequence ends with an atomic bomb blast.

A Movie shares the aesthetic strategy of assemblage art—found objects are removed from their everyday contexts and assembled into new sequences to create new constellations of meanings. In Conner's films, each shot differs according to the production qualities of the original film and the kinds of film stocks used. Conner establishes a rhythm as he edits the shots together by adding a contrapuntal soundtrack of pop and classical music that lends further irony to the remade narrative.

Although *Anticipation of the Night* and *A Movie* posit divergent approaches, each constitutes a filmmaking practice liberated from the traditional conventions of the medium. In Brakhage's film, the camera is freed from the constraints of narrative representation. His intensely personal iconography transcends its specificity, rendering the screen as a dynamic illusionistic space reconstructed along the lines of a non-narrative visual logic. Conner acknowledges the pop cultural power of the cinema as he appropriates all its visual idioms and iconographies and transforms them into a vernacular cinematic assemblage tied together through a network of associative references.

Brakhage and Conner represent the two strategic lines along which the independent cinema in 1959 was coalescing, with overlaps occurring through interlocking interests and reference: the personal cinema of short works identified with Brakhage, Bruce Baillie, Ed Emshwiller, Jordan Belson, Carmen D'Avino, Len Lye, and Joseph Cornell; and another cinema, identified with Conner, Robert Breer, Stan VanDerBeek, and Harry Smith, which was appropriating forms from the other arts, popular culture, and quotidian materials to be cinematically reused in innovative ways. The second group of artists sought to transform our perception and understanding of these materials and, in the process, infuse the found object's iconographic powers with new meanings.

Thus this work is particularly relevant to the Beat movement's engagement with language and the power of the spoken word. This cinema included the graphic cutout animation of Harry Smith's hermetic *No. 12*, Stan VanDerBeek's ironic commentary on cold war politics in *Science Friction*, and the free graphic line animation or abstraction and figuration in Robert Breer's films.

Breer was strongly influenced by the currents of modernism in Europe, where he had lived and worked as a painter before returning to New York in the late 1950s, and by his collaborations and friendships with Jean Tinguely and Claes Oldenburg. He created a distinctly American animation which, in its freewheeling line and collage technique, drew from the landscape of daily life and experience. As Breer moved among painting, sculpture, and film, he discovered that "films were very liberating....I wanted to see some things I'd never seen before....For me, film was another medium that permitted mixing of all this extraneous stuff, ideas and words and configurative elements that I couldn't justify putting in paintings anymore."[7]

Independent filmmakers were thus engaged in an aesthetic discourse that emphasized its participation in contemporary art making. Like Breer, many filmmakers crossed over to other art forms to borrow imagery and translate ideas into their own medium, informing the filmic text with a remarkable range of styles, forms, and ideas—just as assemblage, Minimalism, and Pop Art were redefining Off Broadway theater, dance, music, painting, sculpture, and literature, and being redefined in turn. Ed Emshwiller, for example, in *Dance Chromatic* (1959), filmed the movements of a dance and then painted abstractions directly onto the film frames. Here the gestures of dance informed another layer of imagery. Dance was transformed within a cinematic space, and by time, movement and superimposition.

In this rich period of artistic expansion and interdisciplinary movement, new voices arose to champion the American independent cinema. One of the most articulate was that of Jonas Mekas, a Lithuanian immigrant and filmmaker who was to become the leading figure in the American independent cinema during the 1960s and 1970s. Mekas' role as a spokesman for independent film began in 1955 when he founded *Film Culture* magazine. In this journal, one can follow Mekas' shift from a preference for the European art film to a growing appreciation and advocacy of American independent films.

In 1959, Mekas established *Film Culture*'s Independent Film Award "to point out original and unique American contributors to the cinema...."[8] The recipient of the first award was John Cassavetes' *Shadows* (1957–59). The loosely structured narrative follows a group of young people through New York's nightlife and jazz clubs. The freewheeling action moves across the cultural scene of New York City and engages issues of race; with a disarming directness it breaks through the placid politeness and denial of mainstream culture. Mekas presented the award to *Shadows* because in it

Stan VanDerBeek
Science Friction, 1959

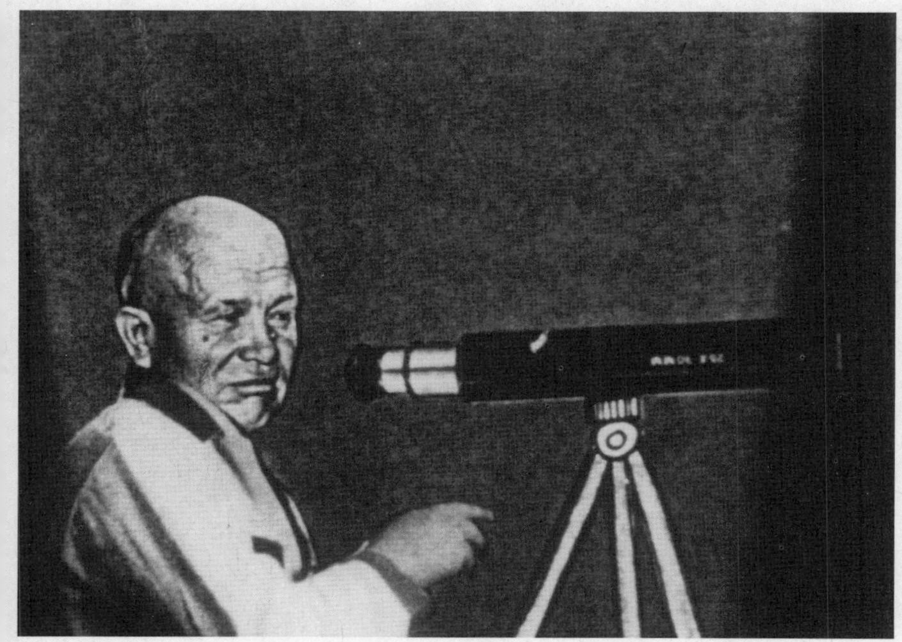

> **Cassavetes...was able to break out of conventional molds and traps and retain original freshness. The improvisation, spontaneity, and free inspiration that are almost entirely lost in most films from an excess of professionalism are fully used in this film. The situations and atmosphere of New York nightlife are vividly, cinematically, and truly caught in *Shadows*. It breathes an immediacy that the cinema of today vitally needs if it is to be a living and contemporary art.**[9]

Shadows marked the emergence of a new narrative cinema, which, although often scripted, conveyed a sense of the real

Jordan Belson, **Allures**, 1961

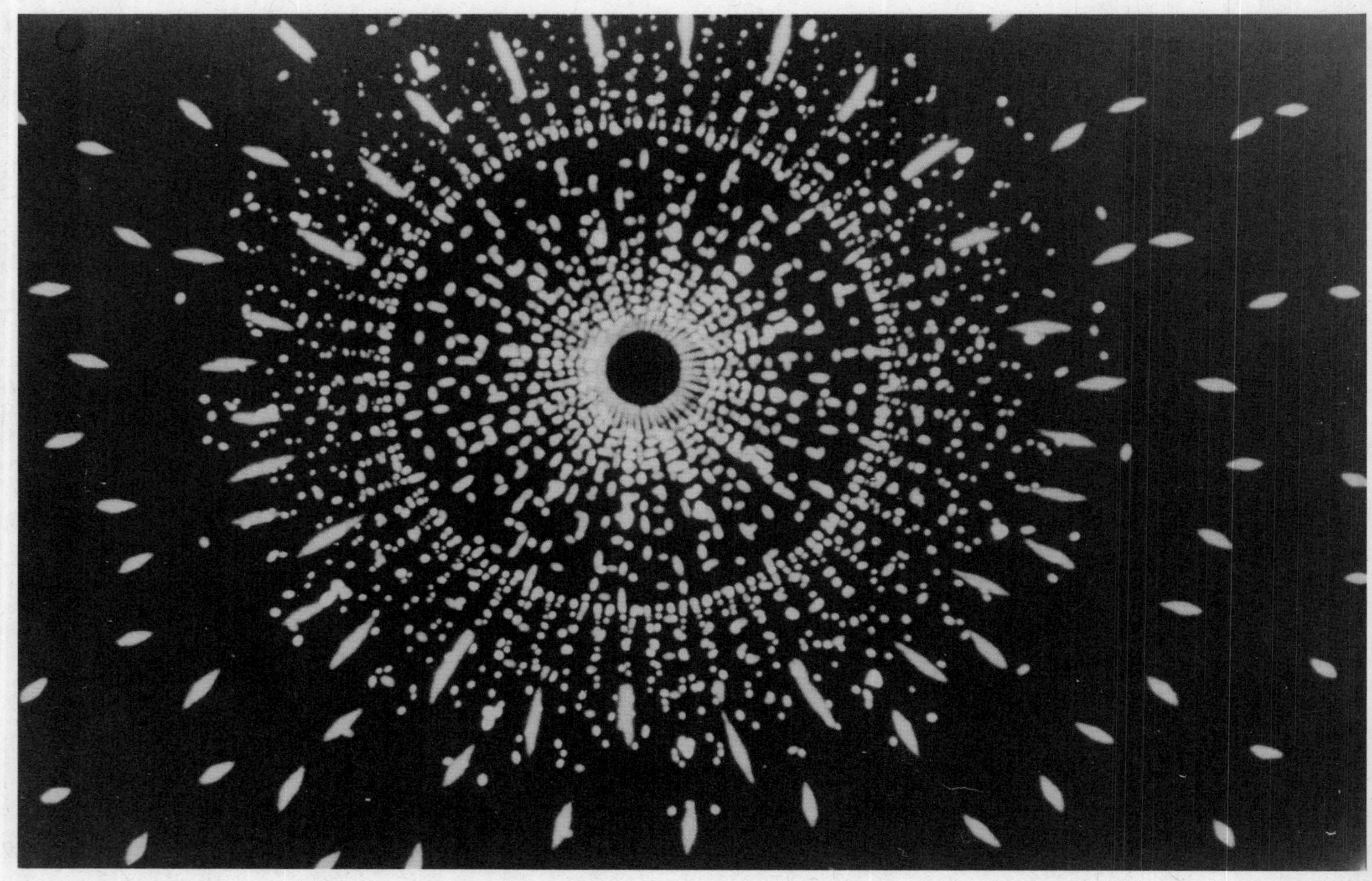

Robert Breer, **Fist Fight**, 1964

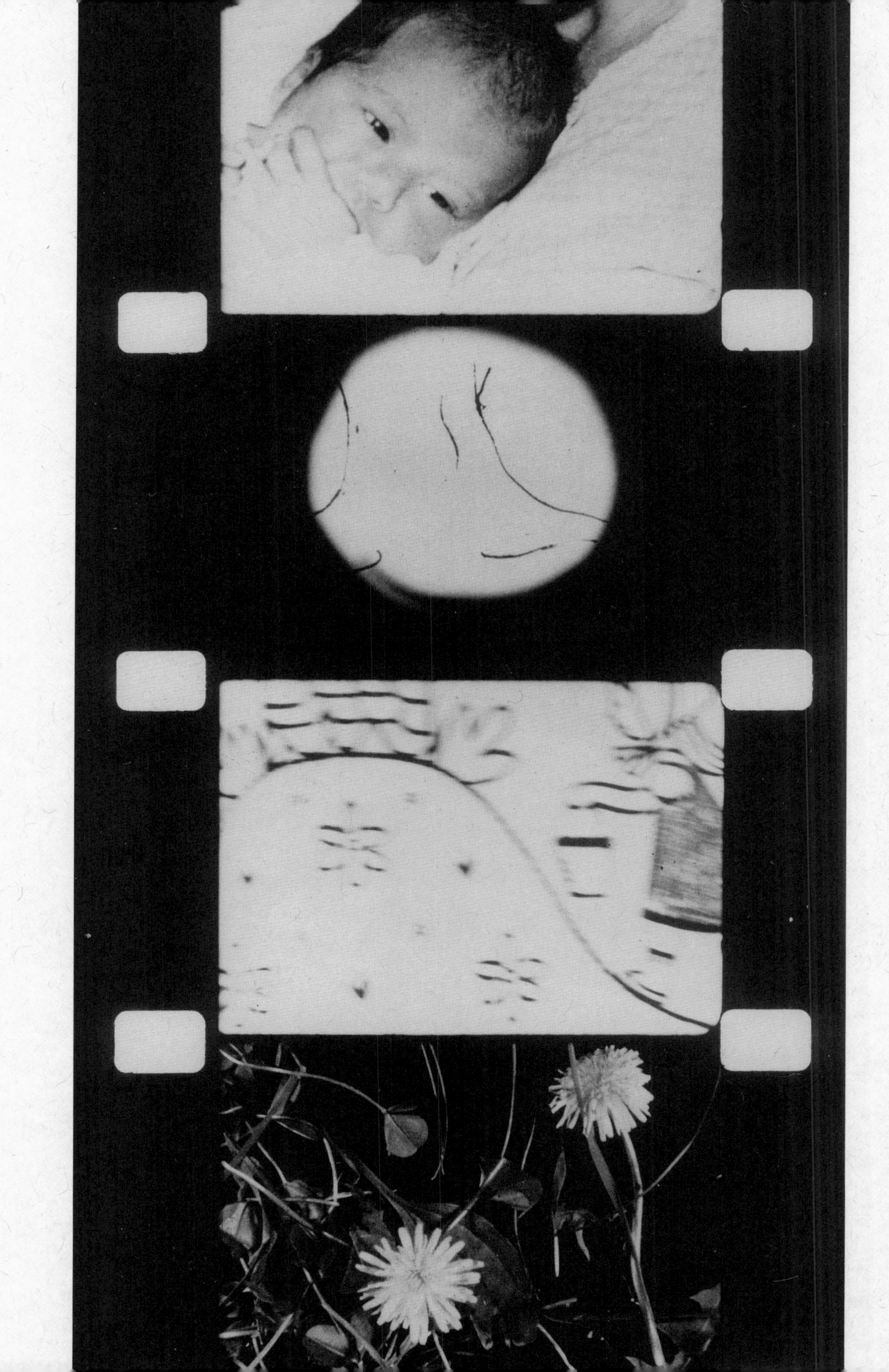

world. The narratives—frequently improvised and recorded on location in apartments, streets, and alleyways with hand-held cameras—achieved a sense of spontaneity, as if the story had been captured on film just as it happened. This semi-documentary fictional style, where actors were filmed on location, outside the studio, reflected stylistic developments taking place in contemporary cinema verité documentary filmmaking. These documentaries employed the technology of the portable camera and the portable sound-recording system to convey immediacy: filmmakers directly responded to the world's events by taking their cameras "on location." In 1961 *Film Culture* gave its third Independent Film Award to *Primary* (1960), a film produced by Ricky Leacock, Don Pennebaker, Robert Drew, and Al Maysles. Mekas cites *Primary*, a documentary film about primary elections that focuses on politicians angling for votes, for its new cinematic techniques of recording life on film.

> **[The filmmakers] have caught scenes of real life with unprecedented authenticity, immediacy, and truth....*Shadows*...indicated new cinematic approaches stylistically and formally. *Primary* goes one step further: By exploring new camera, sound and lighting methods, it enables the film-maker to pierce deeper into the area of new content as well....The techniques of *Primary* indicate that we are entering a long-awaited era, when the budget for a sound film is the same as that of a book of poems, and when a film-maker can shoot his film with sound, alone and by himself and unobtrusively, almost the same way as a poet observing a scene....There is a feeling in the air that cinema is only just beginning.[10]**

The juxtaposition of *Shadows* and *Primary* in a single statement captures something essential about this period. A fictional narrative feature film about an interracial family, two brothers and a sister moving through the worlds of New York jazz clubs, is compared cinematically to a documentary film about the American political system. Mekas' choice of award-winning films

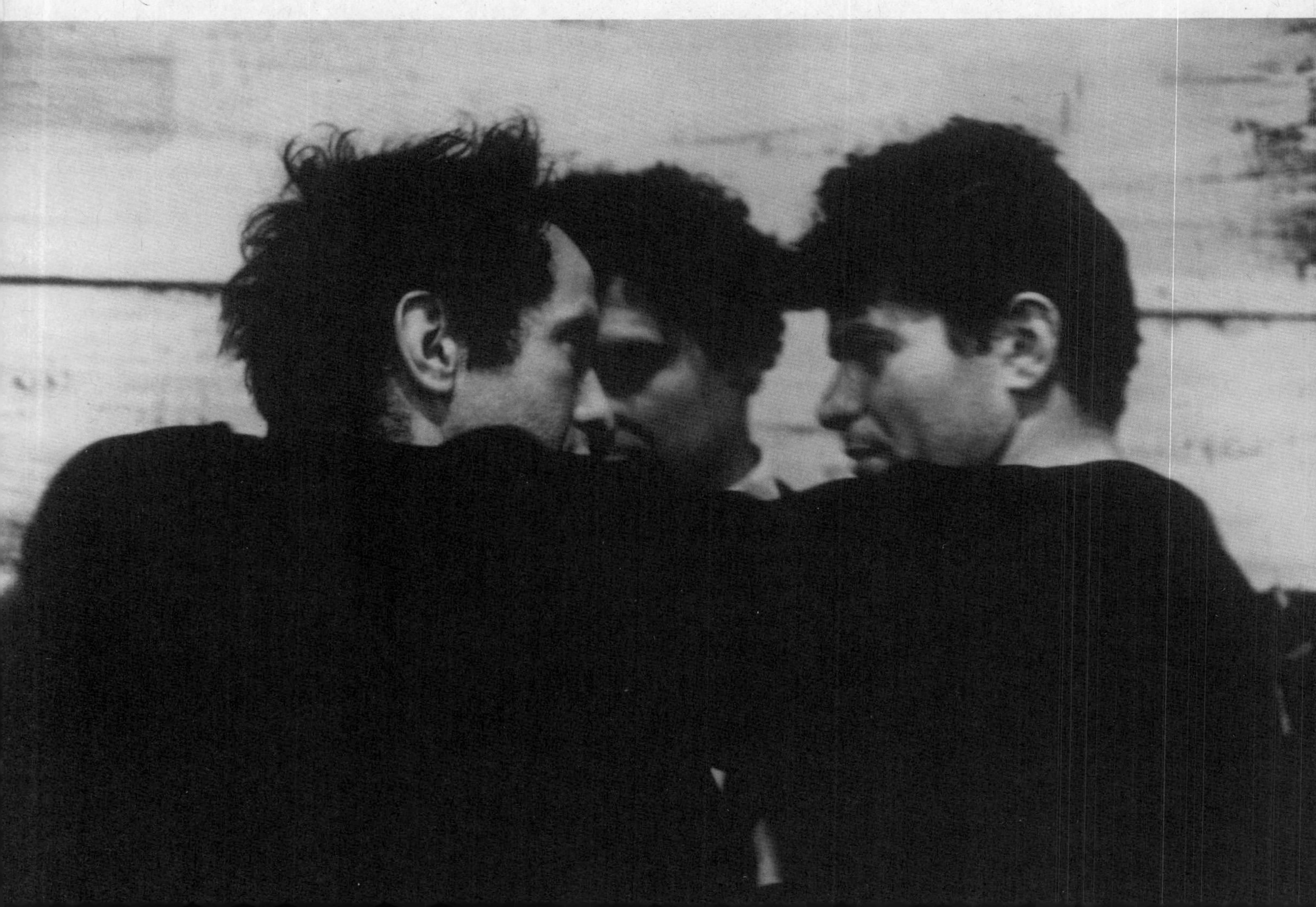

signaled an openness within a redefining film culture that saw genres as fluid and formal innovations which posited a radical new opening onto the world. Like the Beat poets who cleansed American poetry of its bourgeois satisfaction and academic formalism, so these film artists opened up film as an intertextual art practice.

Shadows and such productions as Shirley Clarke's *The Connection* (1961) and *The Cool World* (1963), Lionel Rogosin's *Come Back Africa* (1960), Morris Engel's *Weddings and Babies* (1958), *The Savage Eye* (1959) by Ben Maddow, Joseph Strick, and Sidney Meyers, and *Pull My Daisy* (1959) sparked the formation on September 28, 1960, of the New American Cinema Group. The first meeting included twenty-three independent filmmakers brought together by Lewis Allen (producer of *The Connection*) and Jonas Mekas; a temporary executive board was elected that included Shirley Clarke, Emile De Antonio, Edward Bland, Mekas, and Allen. The New American Cinema Group did not identify itself with any "aesthetic" school and was open to innovation. Its manifesto outlined a number of goals, among them:

1. We believe that cinema is indivisibly a personal expression. We therefore, reject the interference of producers, distributors, and investors until our work is ready to be projected on the screen.

2. We reject censorship....

3. We are seeking new forms of financing, working toward a reorganization of film investing methods, setting up the basis for a free film industry....

4. The New American Cinema is abolishing the Budget Myth....The low budget is not a purely commercial consideration. It goes with our ethical and aesthetic beliefs....

5. We'll take a stand against the present distribution-exhibition policies....

6. We plan to establish our own cooperative distribution center....

7. It's about time the East Coast had its own film festival....

8. We shall meet with the unions to work out more reasonable [requirements for smaller budget films], similar to those existing Off-Broadway—a system based on the size and the nature of the production.

9. We pledge to put aside a certain percentage of our film profits, so as to build up a fund that would be used to help our members finish films or stand as a guarantor for the laboratories.[11]

This manifesto of the New American Cinema Group laid out for the first time a set of goals that would serve as a model for future generations of independent filmmakers. It redefined independent filmmakers—and it redefined independent filmmaking by rethinking all areas of production, distribution, and exhibition. These ambitions were encouraged by viewers, who recognized a freshness and immediacy in these works that had not been seen before in commercial cinema.

There were a number of important interdisciplinary collaborations within this group of filmmakers, including that between the painter Alfred Leslie and the photographer Robert Frank. Frank's collection of photographs, *The Americans*, published in 1959, revolutionized the art of photography as it conveyed a direct and vibrant impression of the edges of daily life. Frank's camera caught from the flow of everyday life an image of great immediacy and intimacy. Like the improvisatory line of jazz, Frank's shooting technique picked out of gesture and incident a powerful visual emblem of American vernacular culture. Frank and Leslie co-directed *Pull My Daisy*, the key Beat film of its generation. This film featured Jack Kerouac, Allen Ginsberg, Gregory Corso, Peter Orlovsky, Alice Neel, and Delphine Seyrig in a story loosely constructed from improvisational antics and spontaneous scenes. It presents a disjointed narrative centered

Robert Frank, Alfred Leslie, and Gregory Corso during production of "Pull My Daisy," NYC, 1959. Photo © John Cohen

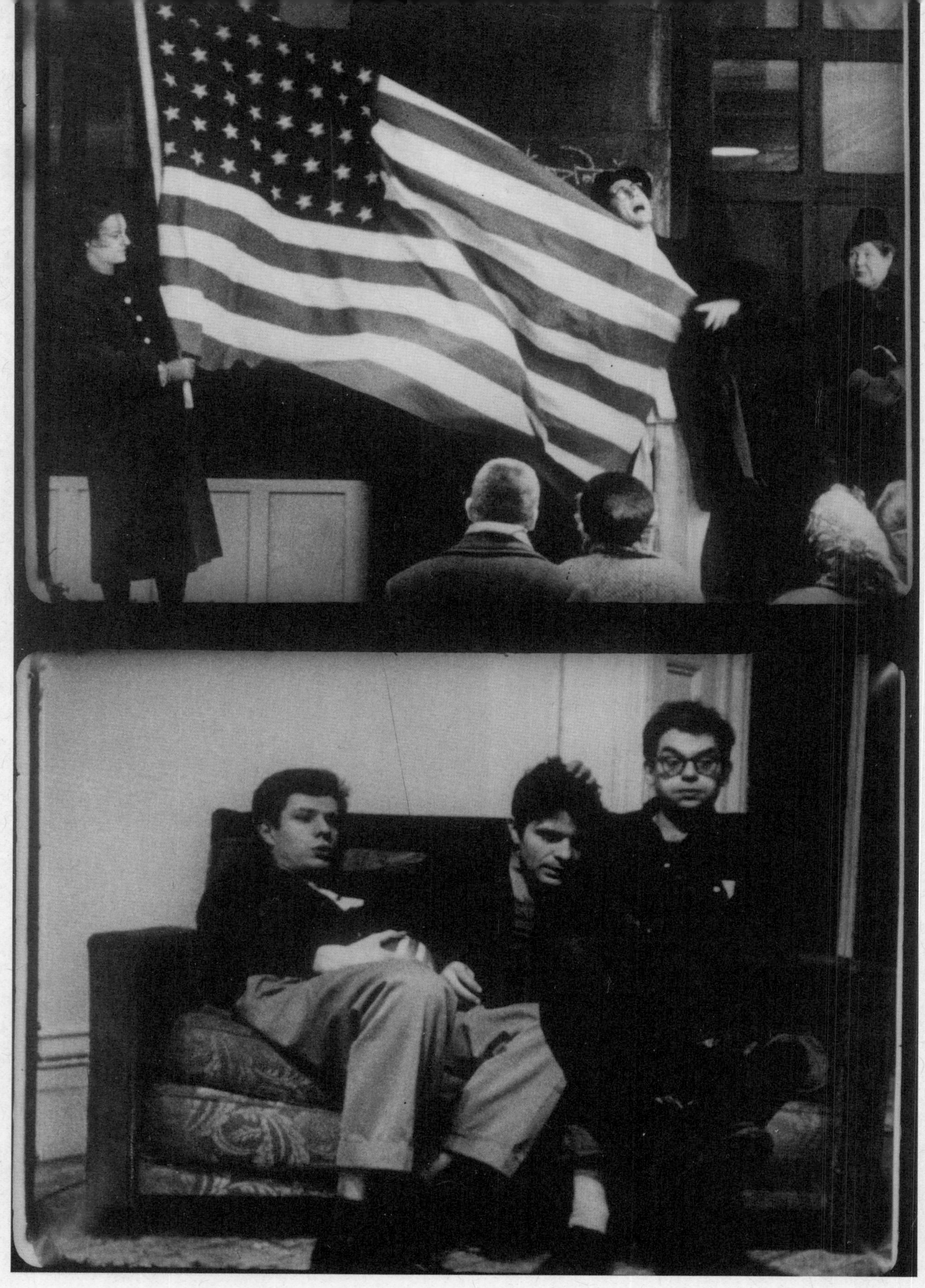

Robert Frank and Alfred Leslie, **Pull My Daisy**, 1959

around a couple and the poets and artists who drift in and out of their loft and lives. The Beat sensibility of anarchic fun and self-parody inspired the lively action of *Pull My Daisy*. In awarding the work *Film Culture*'s second Independent Film Award, Mekas linked the attitude of the film to the look of the film itself, citing its

> ...modernity and its honesty, its sincerity and its humility, its imagination and its humor, its youth, its freshness, and its truth [which are] without comparison in our last year's pompous cinematic production. In its camera work, it effectively breaks with the accepted and 1,000-years-old official rules of slick polished Alton Y Co. cinematographic schmaltz. It breathes an immediacy that the cinema of today vitally needs if it is to be a living and contemporary art.[12]

The distinctive features of *Pull My Daisy* that define its place in avant-garde film history begin with its structure. The film consists simply of action that takes place in a New York Greenwich Village apartment. The black-and-white photography has a grittiness to it that avoids the construction of a "professional" *mise-en-scène* which is characterized by lighting, camera framing of action, and editing that is perfectly mixed to create a seamless narrative whole. Rather, the point of view of the camera—the film is shot from above and assumes a point of view of a visitor to the apartment—perfectly matches the tones of the opening jazz number and Jack Kerouac's narration. The Anita Ellis song sets up a jazz club ambiance—"pull my daisy" refers to the removal of a stripper's G-string; hence also the G-String Production credit line. The lyrics by Kerouac and Ginsberg and the music by David Amram have a playful erotic edge:

> Pull My Daisy
> Tip My Cup
> All My Doors Are Open
> Cut My Thoughts For Coconuts
> All My Eggs Are Broken
>
> Hop My Heart Song
> Harp My Height
> Seraphs Hold Me Steady
> Hip My Angel
> Hype My Light
> Lay It On The Needy[13]

The authors were upset that "Hop My Heart Song" replaced "Hop My Heart On." These lyrics set up a sexual ambivalence within a film that plays itself as narrative constructed around the nuclear family, with the wife preparing meals, the son going to school, and the husband a blue-collar worker. Their movements are the stage for the poets' visit and an emerging social negotiation throughout the domestic space of the apartment.

The action of the film is told through Jack Kerouac's voice-over, which shares the responsibility for determining the shape, feel, and narrative of the action. The discursive strategy of the camera and narration serve to disrupt the master plot of the classical narrative film. The action does not unfold within the space of a traditional narrative, with a story line or psychological underpinning. The space of the apartment becomes a performance space where the tension between Kerouac's language and the action effectively flows from the way the film was made. Kerouac narrated *Pull My Daisy* in its silent film form, providing the improvisatory voice-over to actions which were themselves largely improvised.[14] This resulted in a less-than-perfect fit either in the design of the scenes and dialogue, and in the very fact that two improvisatory levels unfold together. Thus two layers of strategy seen as disrupting the flow of the visuals and soundtrack create an anti-authoritative stance that speaks through a playful, inventive and eclectic use of genres. The story of the family plot is told by Kerouac:

> Early morning in the universe. The wife is getting up, opening up the windows, in this loft that's in the bowery in the lower east side, new york. She's a painter and her husband's a railroad brakeman, and he's coming home in a couple hours, about five hours, from the local. 'Course the room's in a mess. There's her husband's coat on a chair—been there for three days—neckties and his tortured socks.
>
> She has to get the kid up to go to school....[15]

The poets enter the scene:

> Gregory Corso and Allen Ginsberg there, laying their beer cans out on the table, bringing up all the wine, wearing hoods and parkas, falling on the couch, all bursting with poetry while she's saying, Now you get your coat, get your little hat and we're going to go off to school.[16]

The text of the soundtrack/visual then disassembles: the poets speak through Kerouac's voice and Frank's fluid yet punchy cinematography highlights an action, gesture, face, light bulb, tabletop. All the while Kerouac voices a language of jazz-toned improvisations around the circle of his friends in this theatrical-domestic space.

> Meanwhile these guys aren't paying any attention to all that; they're just blowing. But the other cats are over here talking and, you know, being polite. Some of them are saying something and some of them are saying goodbye. Doing something and saying goodbye and doing something are both the same.[17]

The narrative tension between poets and family unravels as guests are treated to the antics of Kerouac's poet buddies.

> She says, All this time we should have fed them some food, we should have done 'em some good, we shoulda—all that time you give 'em wine and beer and give 'em all these beatniks in the house.
>
> He says, Ah, shut up, I didn't do nothing, you know. I didn't do nothing and it's not bad. These are nice fellas. They're just sitting—now they're getting up and they're leaving. I don't blame them for leaving.
>
> You don't understand.[18]

There is a metaleptic disruption of the action where the words stabilize and destabilize the order of actions that explain and do not understand actions. As one critic noted, this is a beatnik version of *Our Town* where Thornton Wilder's omniscient yet friendly neighbor constructs the diachrony and moment of the story of a town.[19] Yet the unacknowledged text within this story is the use of talk, as presented by Kerouac's language and Frank's cinematography, which critique American rationalism through the self-deprecating and not too self-important stance of the artist. While *Pull My Daisy's* informal-seeming structure may belie its organized and carefully planned shooting schedule and editing, the film conveys an anti-establishment boys club atmosphere that shields a homoerotic subtext of relationships and pairing within the Beat movement.

The spirit of anarchy in other films from the period reflects the exploration of technique, acting, and narrative through a radically opened-up production process. Ron Rice's *The Flower Thief* (1960) follows actor Taylor Mead as he moves through assorted landscapes and improvises encounters with a variety of people and objects. Such films were largely derived from the unscripted experience of the production itself—an ongoing dialogue between the filmmaker and actor that was guided only by the framework of a location and the sketchy idea of a gag and story. This same attitude is found in *Hallelujah the Hills* (1963) by Adolfas Mekas, Jonas' brother, in which intrepid New Yorkers cavort through the countryside in an improvised love triangle that parodies the then fashionable high seriousness of European art films.

Ron Rice, **The Flower Thief**, 1960

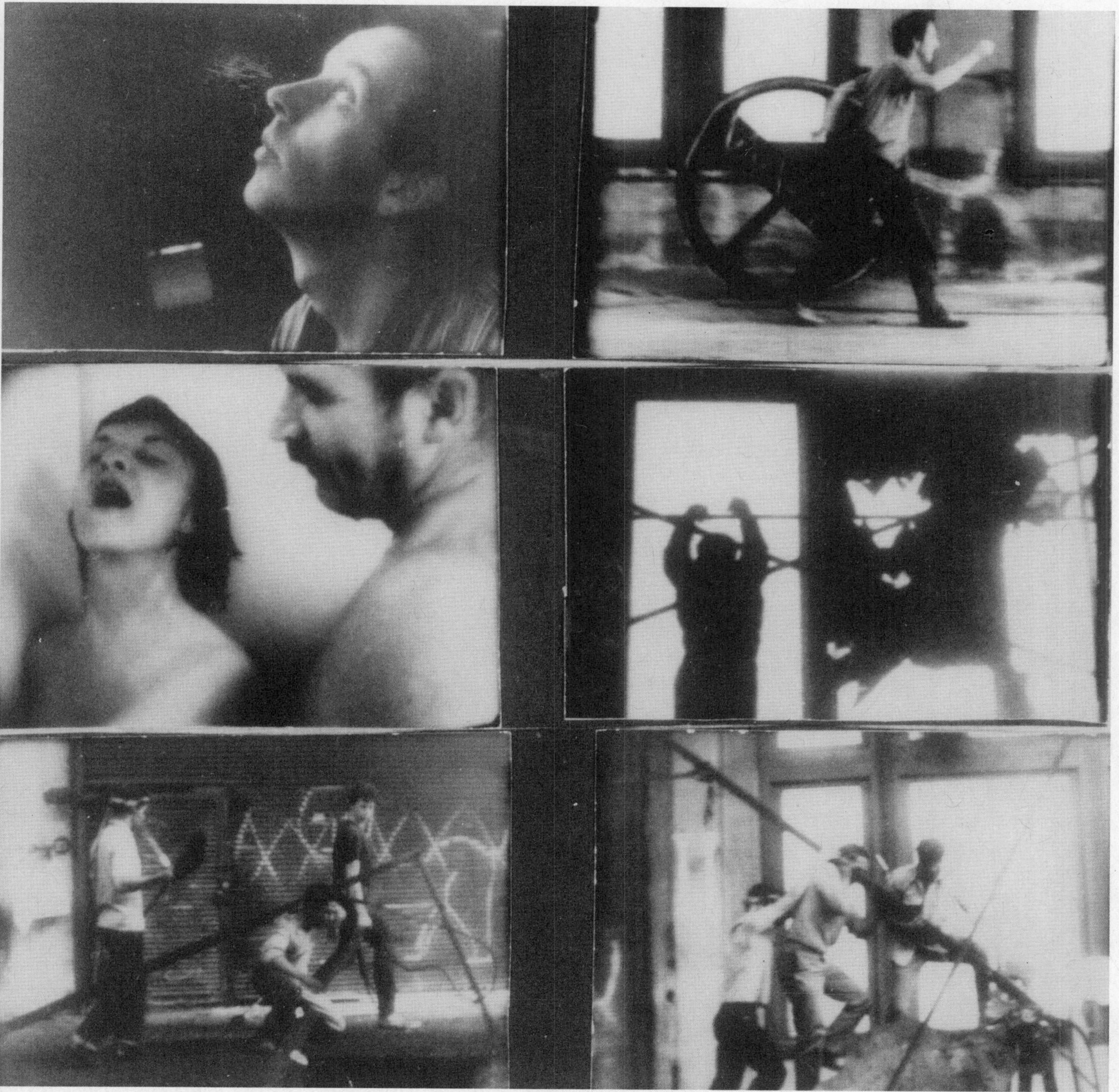

In these independent films actors are not simply directed; rather, they creatively collaborate with the filmmaker. This practice of collaboration extended to other disciplines as well. Shirley Clarke's *The Connection* is based on Jack Gelber's revolutionary Off Broadway play and voiced an underground sensibility of protest against the hypocrisy of the time. Clarke translated Gelber's play into a powerful film about the filming of a documentary. We follow the actions of a group of drug addicts waiting in a room for their fix—as they are being recorded by a documentary film unit which, in order to film them, has given the junkies the money they need for their drugs. The claustrophobic environment and the hostility of the addicts, often directed to the camera, convey the authenticity of documentary, as does the opening up of the film to include the filmmaker. In this compelling exploration of the drug world, the language of the playwright and the vision of the filmmaker merge into a synthesis of language and filmmaking.

The New American Cinema Group eventually dispersed as a movement—by 1962 the filmmakers had gone their separate ways, pursuing individual projects and interests in different parts of the country. In addition to their landmark films, however, the group could claim some success in establishing new outlets for all forms of independent film. As the group's initial manifesto had declared, distribution and exhibition were integrally related to continued efforts to produce new work; since theatrical distribution was dominated by the major commercial conglomerates, the independents were forced to seek other outlets to reach audiences, maintain dialogues with other artists, and remain financially solvent.

During this period, the leading exhibition program in New York City devoted to the independent cinema was Cinema 16. From 1949 to 1963, this independent showcase, under the direction of Amos Vogel, exhibited regularly scheduled film programs every Sunday and Wednesday. Included in its programs were many of the films associated with the New American Cinema Group. The programs were varied and eclectic, often focusing on such topics as censorship and racism. Cinema 16 organized features and short-length films—narrative, avant-garde, scientific, and documentary works—into one-artist, group, and thematic programs. One program on the elevated trains included documentaries as well as Stan Brakhage's *The Wonder Ring* (1955), a lyrical meditation on the light and spaces of the New York els.

Cinema 16 was a nonprofit organization which attracted a large and loyal following that supported the programs and program notes through donations and memberships; Cinema 16 also held symposia, panel discussions, and lectures on independent film. It received considerable press attention and was recognized as the key public outlet for independent and foreign films. But in 1963, unable to maintain its operation and cover increased costs, Cinema 16 was forced to close. There was, moreover, additional competition in New York from television and from the growing number of other showcases for alternative film programming, all of which attracted a new generation of viewers and filmmakers. In 1963 Vogel helped to establish the first "New York Film Festival" at Lincoln Center; he continued to distribute the Cinema 16 film catalogue until he sold it to Grove Press in 1966.

As the New American Cinema Group had stated in its manifesto, there was a great need for alternative systems of distribution and exhibition. In 1960, Bruce Baillie had formed the Canyon Cinema in San Francisco to screen independent films. In New York, Jonas Mekas became involved with the weekend midnight screenings at the Charles Theater, established by Walter Langford and Sol Stein in 1961. These programs featured independent work, including the premiers of films by Ron Rice, Stan VanDerBeek, Robert Breer, Harry Smith, Marie Menken, Brian De Palma, and Ed Emshwiller. Jazz concerts and art exhibitions in the lobby complemented the films and added an air of openness that reflected the interdisciplinary interests of avant-garde artists. Mekas suggested to the theater owners that they hold monthly open screenings to which filmmakers could bring their latest titles. The advocacy of open screenings—the spirit of tolerance for the new—was the major legacy of the Charles Theater, which closed for financial reasons in 1962. The often chaotic reception of these screenings expressed the fluidity

Kenneth Anger
Scorpio Rising, 1963

of this period in film history, when artists, filmmakers, poets, painters, and musicians mingled, argued, and learned from one another's efforts and attitudes.

In 1962, Jonas Mekas played an instrumental role in establishing the Film-Makers' Cooperative in New York, a profit-sharing, non-exclusive national distribution system which accepted all filmmakers who sought an outlet for their films. The Charles Theater experience became a model for the Filmmakers' Cinematheque program, which was also established in 1962 and first showed programs at the Charles Theater before it closed. Every Monday night, "independent, dependent, abstract, neodada, collage, decollage, home, absurd, zen, etc. movies" were shown. The programs included one-artist retrospectives of filmmakers from New York and the West Coast and premieres of Brakhage's *Dog Star Man: Part I* (1962) and *The Sin of Jesus* (1961) by Robert Frank. After the close of the Charles Theater, the Cinematheque organized night exhibitions at the Bleecker Street Theater, from which Cinematheque members were eventually barred in 1963 because the theater owners did not want to be associated with their "controversial" programs.

The major achievement of independent cinema in this period was its realization of new forms, styles, and contents for filmmaking. These independent films are notable for their variety, extending from Brakhage's lyrical cinema to Conner's transformation of found footage to new narrative genres related to avant-garde theater and literature.

During this same period, two filmmakers in particular, Kenneth Anger and Jack Smith, were appropriating the myth of Hollywood into their work, charting somewhat different directions for the art of film in relation to American culture. Kenneth Anger grew up in Hollywood and as a child starred in Max Reinhardt's Hollywood production of *A Midsummer Night's Dream*. In 1960, he published *Hollywood Babylon*, a scandalous history of the underworlds of the "movie

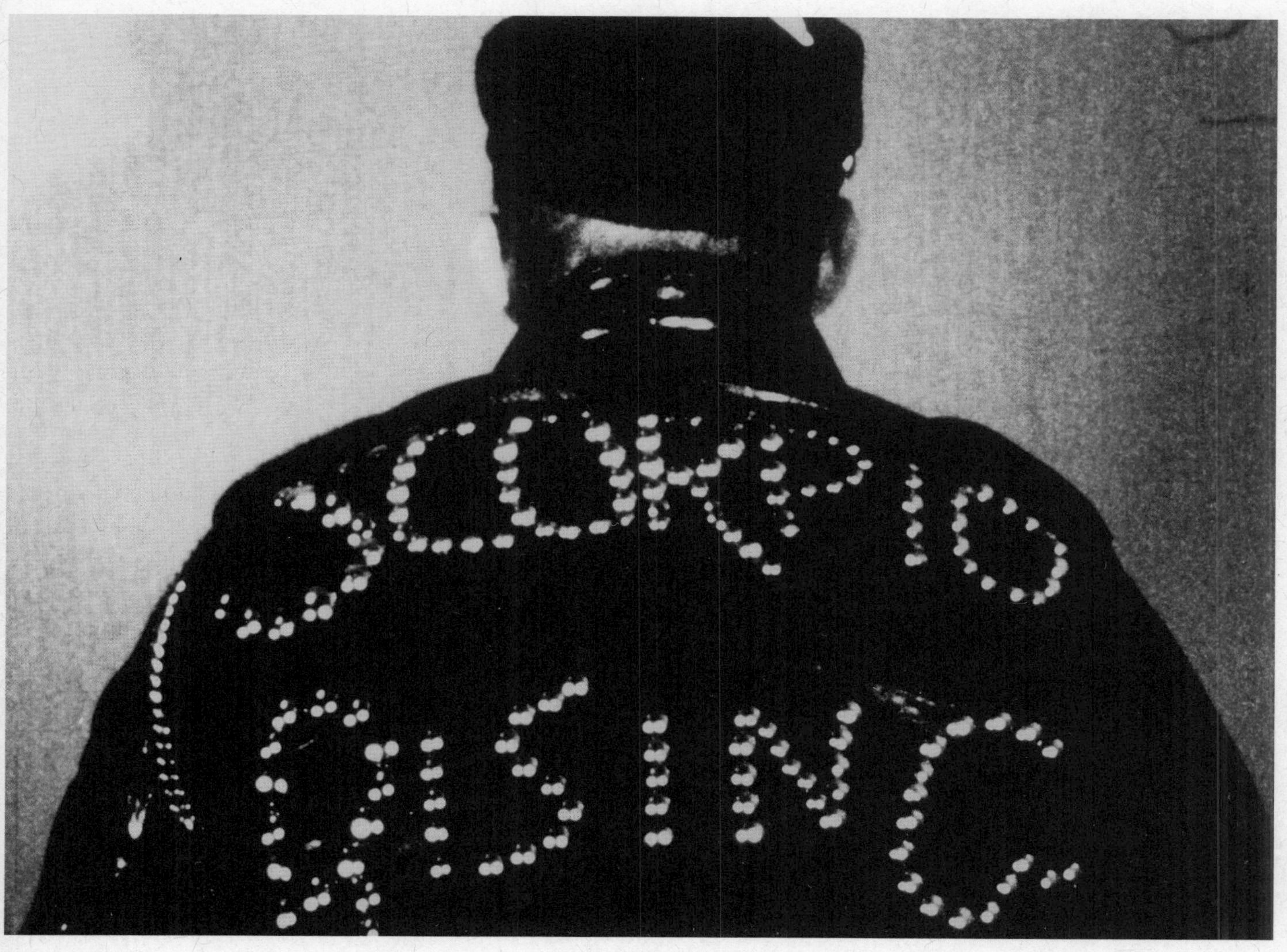

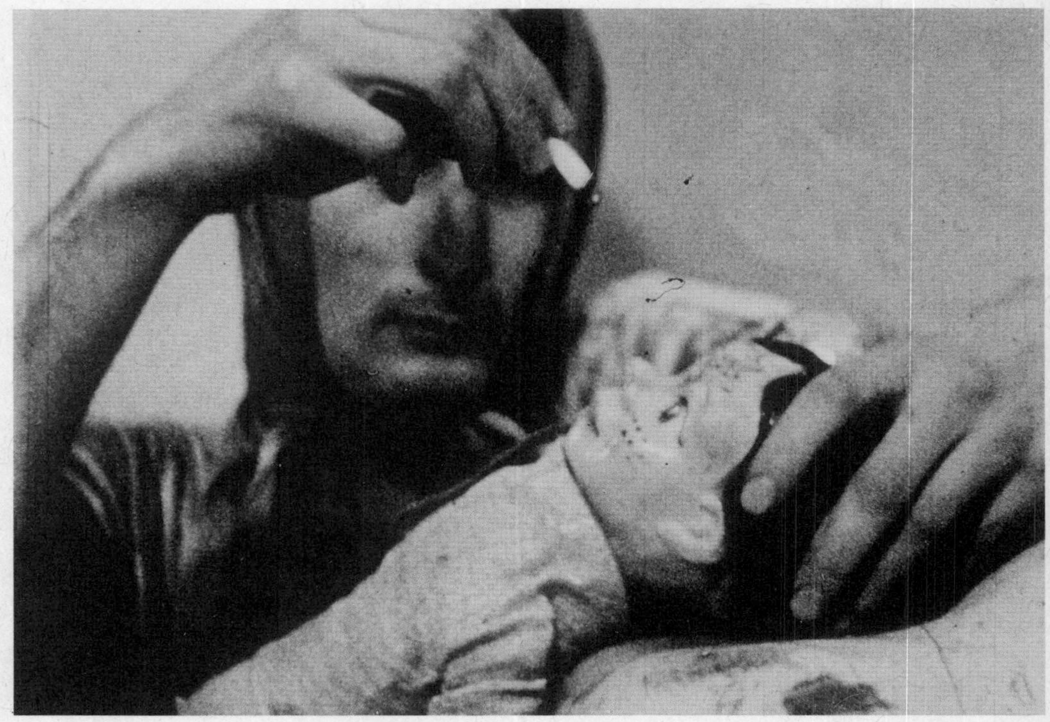

Ken Jacobs
Little Stabs at Happiness, 1959-63

capital." Three years later, Anger produced *Scorpio Rising*, one of the best-known and most influential films of the independent cinema. A soundtrack of thirteen pop songs is heard over a montage of the private and public rituals of a motorcycle gang. Although *Scorpio Rising* was not the first independent film to unite pop hits with visuals, it is a singular work which weaves the private actions and paraphernalia of a leather-jacketed motorcycle gang with images of public mythology such as Western movies, Jesus Christ from a Hollywood epic, and Marlon Brando in *The Wild One.*

Slowly, without hurrying, in poisonously sensuous colors, Anger shows, or more truly lets the subject reveal itself, bit by bit, motion by motion, detail by detail, belts, knobs, chrome, chests, pedals, rings, boots, leather jackets, rituals and mysteries of the motorcycle youth, steel and chrome perversions. The underlying theme is sexual violence. The eroticized appropriation of the icons of popular culture and history—James Dean, Marlon Brando, Hitler, Stalin—is also found in the work of the Beat poets (Ginsberg, Corso), playwrights (Gelber), and visual artists (Oldenburg, Kaprow). It is a strategy designed to eroticize and confront the ideological image of pop culture by destabilizing their meaning within other gendered narratives.

> **A conjuration of the Presiding Princes, Angels, and Spirits of the Sphere of MARS, formed as a "high" view of the Myth of the American Motorcyclist. The Power Machine seen as tribal totem, from toy to terror. Thanatos in chrome and black leather and bursting jeans.[20]**

Controversy surrounded both *Scorpio Rising* and Jack Smith's *Flaming Creatures* (1963). The public viewed them as obscene "underground films." They revealed an outrageous world which, unlike the "movies," did not present the conventional narratives offered in such current films as *Lawrence of Arabia* (1962) or *Cleopatra* (1963). The issue of censorship was topical and highly public in the arts of this time. Jonas Mekas reported on June 18, 1964:

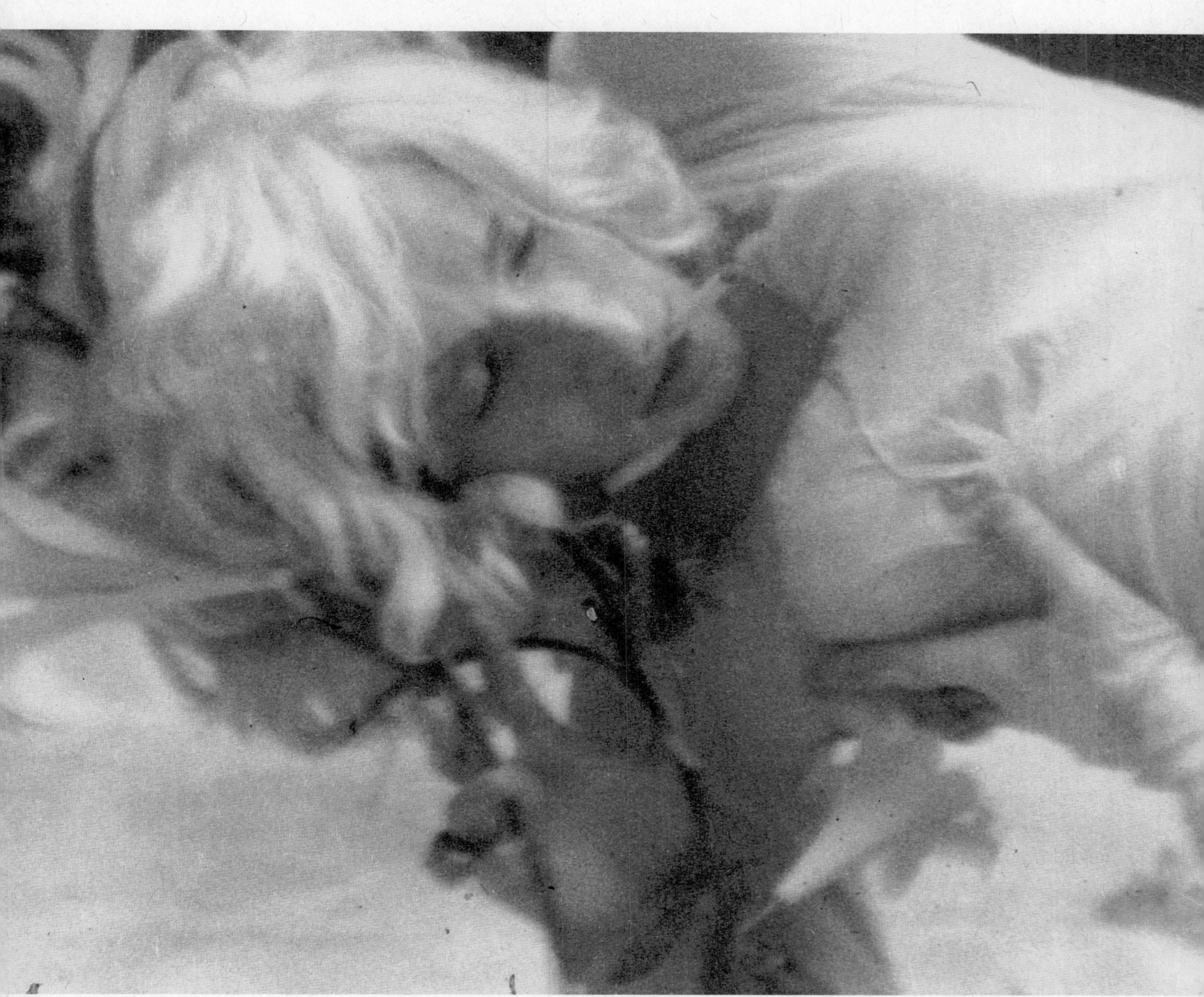

Jack Smith, **Flaming Creatures**, 1963

A verdict was passed in the New York Criminal Court last Friday that Jack Smith's film *Flaming Creatures* is obscene. A similar decision was passed by the Los Angeles court on Kenneth Anger's film *Scorpio Rising*. In practical terms, what this meant is this: From now on, at least in these two cities, it will be a crime to show either *Flaming Creatures* or *Scorpio Rising*, either publicly or privately....During the trial, we had offered—through ourselves and through Lewis Allen, Willard Van Dyke, Herman G. Weinberg, Susan Sontag, Shirley Clarke, Joseph Kaster, Allen Ginsberg, Dr. E. Hornick, and Dr. John Thompson—to explain some of the meanings of *Flaming Creatures* and to give some insight into the meaning of art in general. The court chose to ignore us; it preferred to judge the film by what it called "the community standards."[21]

In its confrontation with the censorship laws and its proclamation of a liberated cinema of images, Jack Smith's *Flaming Creatures* became one of the key works within the American independent cinema. Unlike *Scorpio Rising*, it is not constructed as a complex intellectual montage of symbols and iconography. Susan Sontag described the film:

...in *Flaming Creatures*, a couple of women and a much larger number of men, most of them clad in flamboyant thrift-shop women's clothes, frolic about, pose and posture, dance with one another, enact various scenes of voluptuousness, sexual frenzy, romance, and vampirism...the group rape of a bosomy young woman, rape happily cavorting itself into an orgy. Of course *Flaming Creatures* is outrageous, and intends to be. The very title tells us that.[22]

Jack Smith stands as a major figure who, with his collaborator Ken Jacobs in *Blonde Cobra* (1959-63) and *Little Stabs at Happiness* (1959-63) and his own *Flaming Creatures*, created a cinema that deliberately destroyed conventional narrative plots and structures. Using costumes and imaginary scenes drawn from such cult Hollywood figures as Maria Montez and Marlene Dietrich, Smith and his performers stripped away the narrative of movie myths to reveal the visual texture and erotic subtext of the "dream factory." Smith's *mise-en-scène* was roughened by the use of old (and cheap) film stocks, and faded celluloid that produced ghostlike penumbrae around the images of his imaginary Hollywood.

The fascination that Jack Smith had for Hollywood mythology extended beyond the movies, stories, and plots. These narratives masked the real intrigue on the screen. Smith looked to the sets, lighting, makeup, and costumes as distinctive elements in the vision of the director. The movies and their stars were to Jack Smith a mythopoeic world of desires expressing the extravagant wishes of their directors. Smith's perception of Hollywood films, a view which defines his aesthetic, is perhaps best expressed in his description of Josef von Sternberg directing Marlene Dietrich. It also reveals how Smith viewed himself directing his own films, the world he saw in high imagination and through his camera, a strategy that in its very difference from the Beat sensibility reveals its relationship to a radical reconstruction, and undermining, of the cinematic experience as a mass cultural phenomenon.

[Von Sternberg's] expression was of the erotic realm—the neurotic gothic deviated sex-colored world and it was a turning inside out of himself and magnificent. You had to use your eyes to know this tho because the soundtrack babbled inanities—it alleged Dietrich was an honest jewel thief, noble floosie, fallen woman, etc. to cover up the visuals. In the visuals she was none of those. She was V.S. himself. A flaming neurotic—nothing more or less—no need to know she was rich, poor, innocent, guilty, etc. Your eye if you could use it told you more interesting things (facts?) than those. Dietrich was his visual projection—a brilliant transvestite in a world of delirious unreal adventures. Thrilled by his/her own movement—by superb taste in light, costumery, textures, movement, subject and camera, subject camera/revealing faces—in fact all revelation but *visual* revelation.[23]

Smith's gay epistemology invests gesture and *mise-en-scène* with a meaning that effectively deconstructs the eroticized gaze of the camera lens and *mise-en-scène* of the classic cinematic narrative. The extravagant sensibility of Smith's cinema offers a new vision of American popular myth as reenacted by a troupe of transvestites, male and female personae shuffled and reshuffled within the stage of the screen and the codes of gender identity. Smith's mercurial character and cinema of sexual ambiguities made him a pivotal figure in the independent cinema and an influence on performance and media arts. Andy Warhol and other artists—among them Claes Oldenburg and Ken Jacobs—were attracted to the "on the edge" sensibility, the improvisatory and opened-ended production and creative processes, and the opening up of categories of gender and sexuality. Smith's sets were extravagant versions of Happening environments filled with sexually ambiguous codes.

The variety of influences and contexts that comprise the American independent cinema during the period of the Beats in the 1950s and 1960s offers a rich and provocative history for the Beat sensibility in film. There is no single Beat cinema. Rather, there is a larger Beat culture made possible through a confluence of innovations in performance and language that challenged the visual culture of the cinema. I would offer that *Pull My Daisy* perhaps most clearly embodies the procedures and sensibilities of an authentic Beat cinematic aesthetic. In a sense the American independent film, with its open approach to all film styles and use of collaboration, clearly defines the Beat project. The Beats represented an extraordinary movement that believed in the possibility of an American poetry and art which rejected the closure of cultural pundits or institutions. The Beats believed in the real, the tangible, the double; in the process, they crossed the threshold of the American imagination to be both popular and forbidden, real and illusory—a truly quixotic American dream.

Notes

1 Jack Kerouac, *Pull My Daisy* (New York: Grove Press, 1961), p. 23.

2 Archer Winsten, "Pull My Daisy Bows," *New York Post*, April 10, 1960.

3 Jonas Mekas, "Movie Journal," *The Village Voice*, November 18, 1959.

4 This historical survey of independent film is based in part on my essay "The American Independent Cinema 1958-1964," published in Barbara Haskell, *Blam! The Explosion of Pop, Minimalism, and Performance 1958-1964*, exh. cat. (New York: Whitney Museum of American Art, 1984), pp. 117-36.

5 Sherman Paul, *The Lost America of Love: Rereading Robert Creeley, Edward Dorn, and Robert Duncan* (Baton Rouge: Louisiana State University Press, 1981), p. xiii.

6 Stan Brakhage, quoted in P. Adams Sitney, *Visionary Film: The American Avant-Garde* (New York: Oxford University Press, 1974), p. 181.

7 Robert Breer, quoted in Stuart Liebman, "Program 2," in *A History of the American Avant-Garde Cinema*, exh. cat. (New York: The American Federation of the Arts, 1976), p. 93.

8 "Appendix: The Independent Film Award," in P. Adams Sitney, ed., *Film Culture Reader* (New York: Praeger Publishers, 1970), p. 423.

9 Ibid., pp. 423-24.

10 Ibid., pp. 424-25.

11 "The First Statement of the New American Cinema Group," in Sitney, *Film Culture Reader*, pp. 81-82.

12 Mekas, "Appendix: The Independent Film Award," p. 424.

13 Kerouac, *Pull My Daisy*, n.p.

14 A detailed analysis and description of the production process of *Pull My Daisy* is available in Blaine Allan, "The New American Cinema and the Beat Generation 1956-1960," Ph.D dissertation (Evanston, Illinois: Northwestern University, 1984).

15 Kerouac, *Pull My Daisy*, p. 21.

16 Ibid., p. 22.

17 Ibid., p. 34.

18 Ibid., pp. 36-37.

19 Dwight Macdonald, "Films," *Esquire* (April 1959).

20 Kenneth Anger, quoted in Sitney, *Visionary Film*, p. 116.

21 Jonas Mekas, *Movie Journal: The Rise of the New American Cinema, 1959-1971* (New York: Collier Books, 1972), pp. 141-42.

22 Susan Sontag, quoted in Carel Rowe, *The Baudelairean Cinema: A Trend within the American Avant-Garde* (Ann Arbor, Michigan: UMI Research Press, 1982), p. 127.

23 Jack Smith, quoted in Sitney, *Visionary Film*, p. 391.

Left to right: **Cliff Carnell, Erich Kollmar, and John Cassavetes during the filming of Cassavetes' "Shadows,"** 1957-59

RAY CARNEY

No Exit: John Cassavetes' *Shadows*

[After the initial screenings] I went to Nikos Papadakis who had helped us make the film....I said, "How much money do you have, Niko?" And he said, "I have $2,000. I can get it from friends." And I raised $13,000. [I wrote a script, and] we started shooting again. We shot for ten days and the result...was the final version of *Shadows*.... Now rumor spread that I had made [the second version of] the film for distribution. That we had gone back to make it more commercial. But...the second version was much deeper. I think the greatest things in the film, I mean the best things in the film, were shot in the reshooting, in a ten-day period. Which has to tell you something, because it took us four months to shoot the [improvised] version.

John Cassavetes

Honor the impulse. Trust your instincts. The first draft is the true draft. Never revise, never retract. Blueprints are the death certificates of genius. Just *blow*, man, *blow*....

By now, the litany is familiar. Many of the greatest Beat works were created spontaneously, from the subconscious, without revision or correction. Or were they? About some works, we'll probably never know the truth. When it comes to others, though, the answers are not always the expected ones. It comes as a surprise for many viewers to learn that neither of the two best-known and most celebrated works of cinematic improvisation in the Beat era was actually improvised.

Pull My Daisy was praised for years as a masterwork of free-form "blowing" before Alfred Leslie revealed in a November 28, 1968 *The Village Voice* article that its scenes were as completely scripted, blocked, and rehearsed as those in a Hitchcock movie. The film was shot on a professionally lit and dressed set. The cast worked from a script, and shooting proceeded at the typical studio snail's pace of two minutes of text per day. All camera positions were locked and all movements planned in advance. As many takes and angles were shot, and as much footage exposed in proportion to its final length (3 hours for 28 minutes) as for a Hollywood feature of the period. Probably more. Even Kerouac's wonderfully shaggy-baggy narration was actually written out in advance, performed four times, and mixed from three separate takes. (However, in defense of the man who made "first thought, best thought" a Beat mantra, it must be added that Kerouac is said to have objected when his narration was edited.)

John Cassavetes' *Shadows* comes a little closer to being a true improvisation, but only briefly—in an early, discarded version. The first version of *Shadows* (filmed in 1957) was indeed based on a dramatic improvisation the director and his actors had worked out in an acting class. But Cassavetes was so embarrassed by the filmed result that after screening it just three times late in 1958 he decided the only way to salvage it was to write a series of scenes to cut into it. The revised ninety-minute film retained less than thirty minutes of the original footage. Tipping the balance even further, the little that was retained from the first version was mainly transitional, establishing, or action footage (street and sidewalk shots of characters walking, shots of Central Park and a couple running up a hill, shots of characters racing for trains in Grand Central Station, a fight scene). Most of the important dramatic interactions between the characters were from the new scripted parts.

It should be added that Cassavetes himself was responsible for much of the confusion about whether *Shadows* was or was not improvised, since at the end of the scripted version he retained the same title card that had ended the unscripted version: "The film you have just seen was an improvisation." Although his intention was to express gratitude to his actors for having originated the story, the title card only served to mislead critics and audiences.

Shadows' scenes feel so fresh and spontaneous that viewers can hardly be blamed for the misperception. Consider the following scene. It involves two young people, Lelia and Tony (played by Lelia Goldoni and Tony Ray, son of director Nicholas Ray), who have just met the previous day. They are talking fairly aimlessly as they walk along together. (David is a mutual friend who introduced them.)

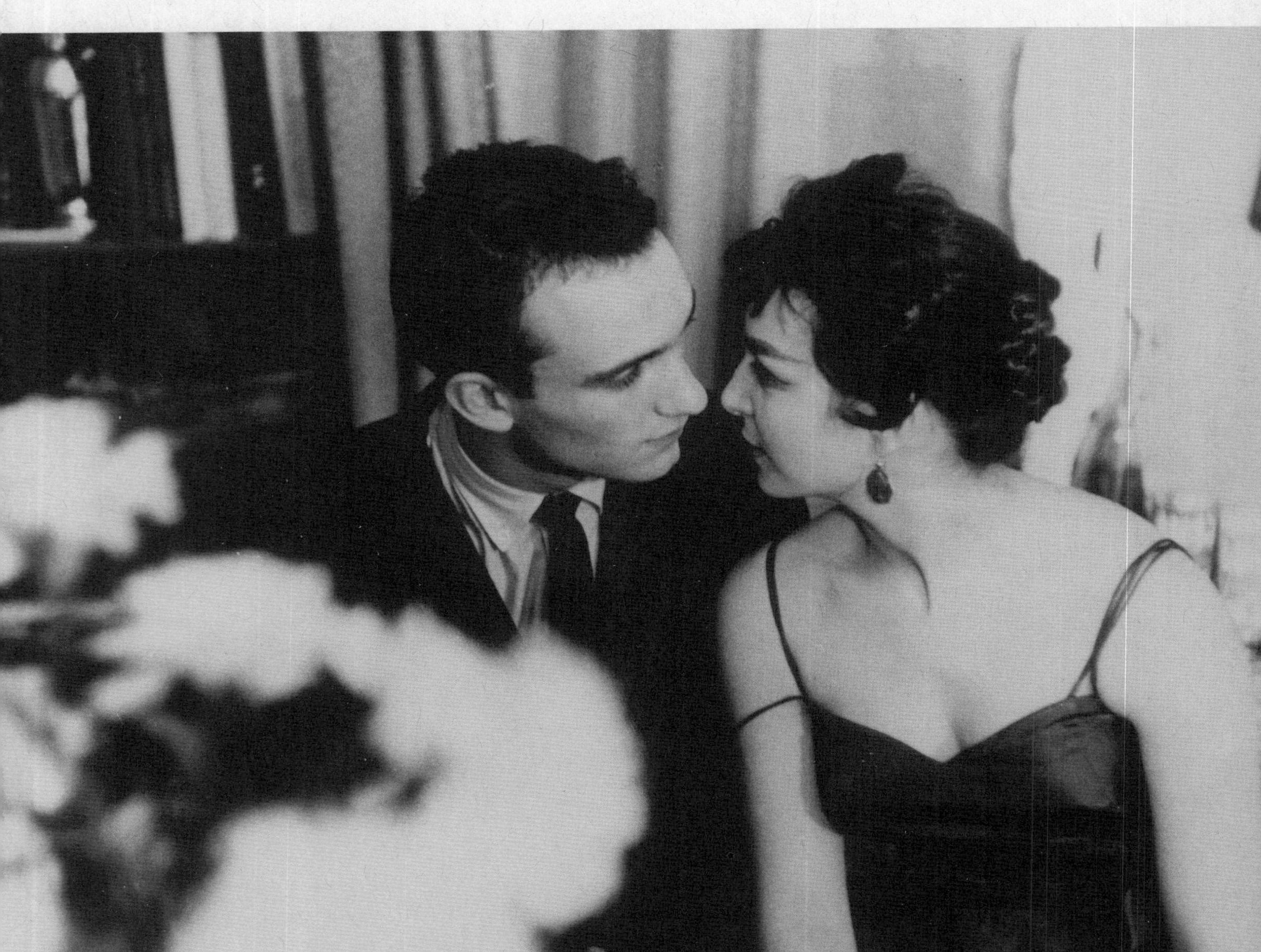

Lelia: I feel I'll never know things. Like...like...

Tony: What do you feel like, tell me what you feel like.

Lelia: I feel like I'm in a...a...

Tony: ...In a cocoon, and you can't get out?

Lelia: That's right....I didn't think boys were supposed to understand things like that....You see I *am* far behind.

Tony: Behind who?

Lelia: Now you sound like David.

Tony: I hope not.

Lelia: Why not? David is one of the most intelligent people I've ever met in my life.

Tony: ...But not very romantic.

Lelia: No, he's not very romantic.

Tony: You know, I'm not a very nice person. I mean I have romantic inclinations. I'm not one of those storybook characters who's supposed to be all noble and righteous. If I see someone I like and she likes me, we accept my romantic inclinations.

It's not hard to see why viewers thought this conversation was being made up by the actors. It has the tentativeness, sprawl, competitiveness, and even occasional flatness of a real conversation between two people who don't know each other very well. We're about as far from Woody Allen or a TV sitcom as we can get. The interaction isn't pointed and witty. It isn't pumped up to make points. It doesn't develop logically or proceed in a straight line. It zigs and zags from one seeming tangent to another. In fact, at least up until Tony's peroration, it doesn't seem to be going anywhere at all. The characters compare opinions, warily jockey for position, make conversational missteps, and even limply repeat each other's phrases ("not very romantic...not very romantic...I have romantic inclinations").

What further adds to the feeling of open-endedness is that, although Tony is consistently smug and cocky in his tones and Lelia is consistently more hesitant and uncertain, their positions keep shifting slightly. While Tony controls the beats in the first four lines, Lelia intermittently seizes control, first with the remark about "boys," then when she chides Tony that he sounds like David, and then again when she defends David's intellect. Tony regains control when he denigrates David as unromantic. Lelia then reestablishes her solidarity with Tony by agreeing with him about David not being romantic. Tony then apparently takes Lelia's concession as an opportunity to up the ante with his final speech.

The reason this scene and so many of the others added to the scripted version of *Shadows* feel improvised (and so different from scenes in most other movies) should be obvious. It is the striking process-orientation of the presentation. While most movie scenes are totalizing and summarizing in their effect, Cassavetes presents an incremental, step-by-step universe of continuous, minute adjustments and discoveries (which are dramatically appropriate insofar as they capture the shifts of position and understanding in an awkward, off-balance, slightly asymmetrical relationship).

I'd note parenthetically that Cassavetes played a kind of trick on his actors to ensure that Lelia's tentativeness and Tony's opportunism would be as convincing as possible. Without telling each actor, he gave Tony his lines well in advance of the scene, while he withheld Lelia's from her until just a few minutes before shooting began. (Cassavetes frequently played similar tricks on his actors when he felt it would contribute to their performances.) The result is that Tony naturally dominates the interaction, takes the lead tonally, and forces Lelia to follow. That is to say, at least a little of the uncertainty in her tone and the slight air of patronization in his were real. As an actor as well as a character, Tony was feeding Lelia some of her lines.

The slippery, accretionary quality of the experience is even more obvious in the scene that follows upstairs in Tony's apartment (which is another of the scripted additions to the film). He

Tony and Lelia (played by Tony Ray and Lelia Goldoni) in John Cassavetes' "Shadows," 1957-59 and Lelia make love, but Cassavetes elides the event itself and dissolves to the postcoital conversation:

Tony: [patronizing, yet concerned] Lelia—really, if I'd known this was the first time for you, I wouldn't have touched you.

Lelia: [wounded] I didn't know it could be so awful.

Tony: [trying to comfort her] Don't be so upset, sweetheart....Baby, it will be much easier next time.

Lelia: [firm] There isn't going to be a next time.

Tony: [saying anything to change the subject and gain control over the beat] Want a cigarette, huh? Come on, have a cigarette.

Lelia: [self-pitying] No.

Tony: [attempting to seize the initiative by playing hurt himself] I'm sorry if I disappointed you. I guess I did.

Lelia: [sympathetic and relenting] I was so frightened. I kept saying to myself you mustn't cry. If you love a man you shouldn't be so frightened.

Tony: [regaining his poise—on familiar ground] It's only natural. [a beat] There isn't a girl in the world that wouldn't feel the same way. She's [a beat, uncertain how to end the sentence]...*got* to.

Lelia: [vulnerable] And what happens now?

Tony: [at sea, taking a beat] What happens? [worried, another beat] Um, well [yet another beat, then blurting out], what do you mean what happens now?

Lelia: [open] I mean do I stay with you?

Tony: [frantic] Lelia, uh. Stay with me? [a worried beat, then suddenly deciding it's flattering] You, you mean *live* with me?

Lelia: Yes.

Tony: [tentative] You...want...to?

Lelia: [weary and hurt] No, I want to go home.

Tony: [vastly relieved, condescending] Okay, baby.

Cassavetes once again drew on his actors' real feelings and personalities to lend authority to their line deliveries: Tony and Lelia had actually had a difficult romantic relationship that had not worked out well. There was still a residue of mixed feelings about their relationship when the scene was shot that undoubtedly added to its authenticity.

The justification for indicating the tones, pauses, and shifts of mood in such detail is that the effect of the scene is attributable at least as much to the continuous permutations of feeling that take place within it as to the mere denotative meaning of the words spoken by the characters. Cassavetes creates the impression that Tony and Lelia truly are making up their lines (and their lives) as they go along. As two virtual strangers who suddenly find themselves in an uncomfortably intimate situation, their interaction is gingerly, awkward, evolutionary, and unpredictable. As in the conversation on the sidewalk, what makes the moment work dramatically is that the fictional characters are in a situation which requires them to function in exactly the same way as actors improvising a scene together.

The scene suggests a deep and intriguing link between the Beat sense of life and the occurrence of continuously shifting dramatic beats in a work of art. To hold oneself as tonally and psychologically open as Tony and Lelia do (both as characters and as actors) is to live the existential ideal of sensory awareness and present-mindedness that so many of the Beats embraced. Tony and Lelia act out an improvisatory vision of experience in which we bravely unmoor our identities from fixed definitions and cut our relationships loose from predictable destinations in order to abandon ourselves to the ever-changing possibilities of the moment. The slipperiness of their relationship, the tonal mercuriality of their interaction, the fugitiveness of each of their momentary emotional rest stops captures a stunningly open-ended vision of experience. Experience will not stand still to have its picture taken. Life will not be turned into a still life. In far more than a

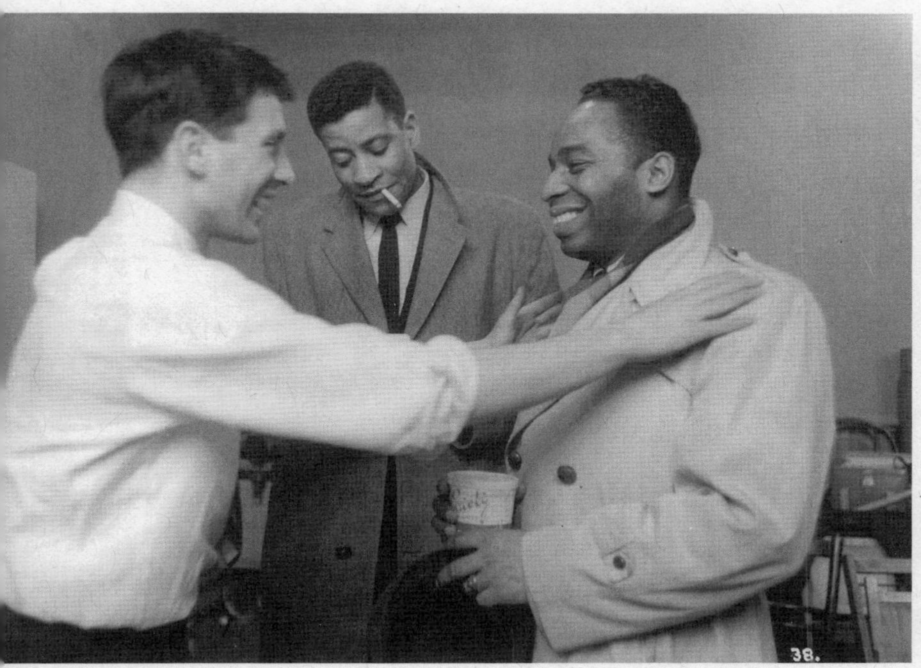

punning sense of the words, the shifts of beats reflect a quintessential Beat appreciation of life in process—of life *as* process. They are the strict equivalent of the jazz performer's incessant, obsessive "changes." Meanings are written in water—continuously recomposed out of ongoing decompositions. The scene communicates the social equivalent of the propulsiveness of some of the driving scenes in Kerouac's *On the Road*: an experiential onwardness that is both exhilarating and more than a little scary to watch. In a sense, Cassavetes outdoes Kerouac. He puts his characters' lives on wheels—without needing to put them in a car.

The further effect of Lelia's and Tony's stammerings and miscues is the more general lesson that great Method acting always communicates: a sense of a fundamental gap between our social and verbal expressions of ourselves and a realm of buried feeling that can only be haltingly and imperfectly expressed by our words and actions. The Method actor sinks a mine shaft into subterranean emotional depths, and goes down to report how much more there is down there than can ever be brought up to the surface. In *On the Waterfront*, when Brando fumbles with Eva Marie Saint's glove in the playground scene or almost starts crying when he talks with Rod Steiger in the cab scene, one of the most important expressive effects of his acting is to convince us that his words and gestures are only the superficial signs of incredibly profound depths of unspoken thought and feeling. In short, Method acting opens a gap between imagination and social forms of expression. It is a form of linguistic skepticism.

This skepticism is another one of the central tenets of Beat art and life. The cultivated inwardness of the hipster and the jazz performer points toward a realm of "pure being" (Kerouac's term) somewhere underneath and beyond verbal and social expression. It is the "beyond" and the "IT" that so many of Kerouac's characters pursue and want to get in touch with. In the Beat aesthetic, this nonverbal, nonsocial interior is a place of purity and spirituality—perhaps the last remaining place exempt from society's predatory systematizations and mechanizations.

Method acting kept the lines of communication open between the interior and exterior realms, so that moving between them, although difficult, was still possible. The unfortunate tendency of much Beat art, however, was to erect a wall between the realms. Many Beat works, especially in film, introduced a reductive schism in which experience was parceled into two mutually exclusive categories: on the one side, private states of imagination and feeling (which were regarded as being pure and valuable); on the other, public forms of social interaction and expression (which were regarded as being flawed and limiting). The private realm was energetic, fluid, playful, and stimulating; the public realm was rigid, mechanical, serious, and frustrating. As different as they are from one another, *On the Road*, *Pull My Daisy*, *The Flower Thief*, and *Howl* consistently dichotomize experience in this way. They imagine the individual either trapped inside established social forms and structures of interaction, or grandly (and nobly) alienated, existing beyond them in some state of pure awareness and being. The Beat vision almost always conceptualizes experience in terms of such dichotomous alternatives—whether the dichotomies are tragic in effect (*Howl*'s angel-headed hipsters versus Moloch) or comic (*Pull My Daisy*'s Peter

Left to right: **John Cassavetes rehearsing Rupert Crosse and Hugh Hurd for a scene in Cassavetes' "Shadows,"** 1957-59 versus the Bishop).

It's a tempting vision. It flatters the individual by making his struggle against society Byronic in its grandeur. But it's just a little too simple. This state of majestic alienation confers easy heroism on everyone. It reminds us that Beat culture was, after all, youth culture, and that it is in the nature of youth to see things in terms of contrasted absolutes, antitheses, and extremes. The either-or opposition of imagination and social expression leaves out the inevitable inbetweenness of adult experience, the middle ground where most of adult life is lived—which is really the most interesting place to be.

The middle ground is the place where the creative individual doesn't repudiate established social and institutional structures of expression, but remains at least partly within them, creatively challenged by and engaged with them, negotiating them. What makes *Shadows* so different from (and its characters' dramatic predicaments so much more complex than) most other Beat works is precisely that Cassavetes rejects the Beat schism. He denies his characters the luxury of a grand alienation from social forms of expression; he forces them to shape their destinies *within* forms of social interaction (however haltingly and imperfectly, as Lelia and Tony demonstrate). Just in case we don't get the point, Cassavetes does include one grandly alienated figure in *Shadows*. Bennie (played by Ben Carruthers) could have stepped right out of the pages of *Howl* or *The Dharma Bums*. Like many another Beatster, he has given up on social interaction and verbal expression in order to tend his private imaginative garden. But rather than want us to admire him, Cassavetes clearly wants us to see how doomed and self-destructive Bennie's obsessively cultivated alienation is.

To put it another way, Cassavetes doesn't allow his characters the comfort of blaming their problems on external relationships and systems of knowledge. The expressive systems that threaten the characters in *Shadows* are within themselves. The danger does not come from external economic, technological, political, or social systems, but from internal systems of understanding and feeling. We do not have the luxury of rebelling against or escaping these systems. In Pogo's words, in a cartoon contemporaneous with the Beat movement, we have met the enemy and it is us.

Bennie illustrates this as well. Throughout *Shadows* he blames his problems on society, while Cassavetes' view is that his real problem is himself. David clearly speaks for the filmmaker when he tells Bennie in the coffee shop scene that he is trapped in an emotional and behavioral "pattern." In Cassavetes' opinion, the real threats to our identities are always within ourselves—especially the tendency of our emotions and intellects to congeal into a static position. We emotionally mechanize and regiment ourselves; it doesn't take capitalism or middle-class values to do it to us. (Tony and Lelia also demonstrate that sort of self-destructive patterning.)

Ironically enough, Bennie's "pattern" is his Beatness—his characteristically Beat attempt to avoid patterns. Cassavetes uses Bennie to demonstrate that strategies of freedom can themselves turn into forms of entrapment. To the extent that Beatness is reduced to a set of prefabricated mannerisms, poses, and styles, Beatness itself becomes only a new form of emotional and psychological imprisonment. That is to say, even our attempts to escape from patterns are themselves continuously congealing into new and confining patterns. In this respect, *Shadows* offers a lesson that many Beat artists and works could have profited from.

For Cassavetes, there is no possibility of breaking free absolutely or permanently. A transcendental stance is simply unavailable. Even at our very best, we walk a perilous razor edge where, on the one hand, we decompose the ever-encroaching patterns that beset us, even as, on the other, our decompositions are continuously recomposing into new patterns. Freedom must constantly be reasserted and reachieved to be maintained.

That is to say, freedom is a complexly achieved state that involves staying *within* the systems that threaten us. Unlike *Howl* or *On the Road*, in *Shadows* there is no outside to society.

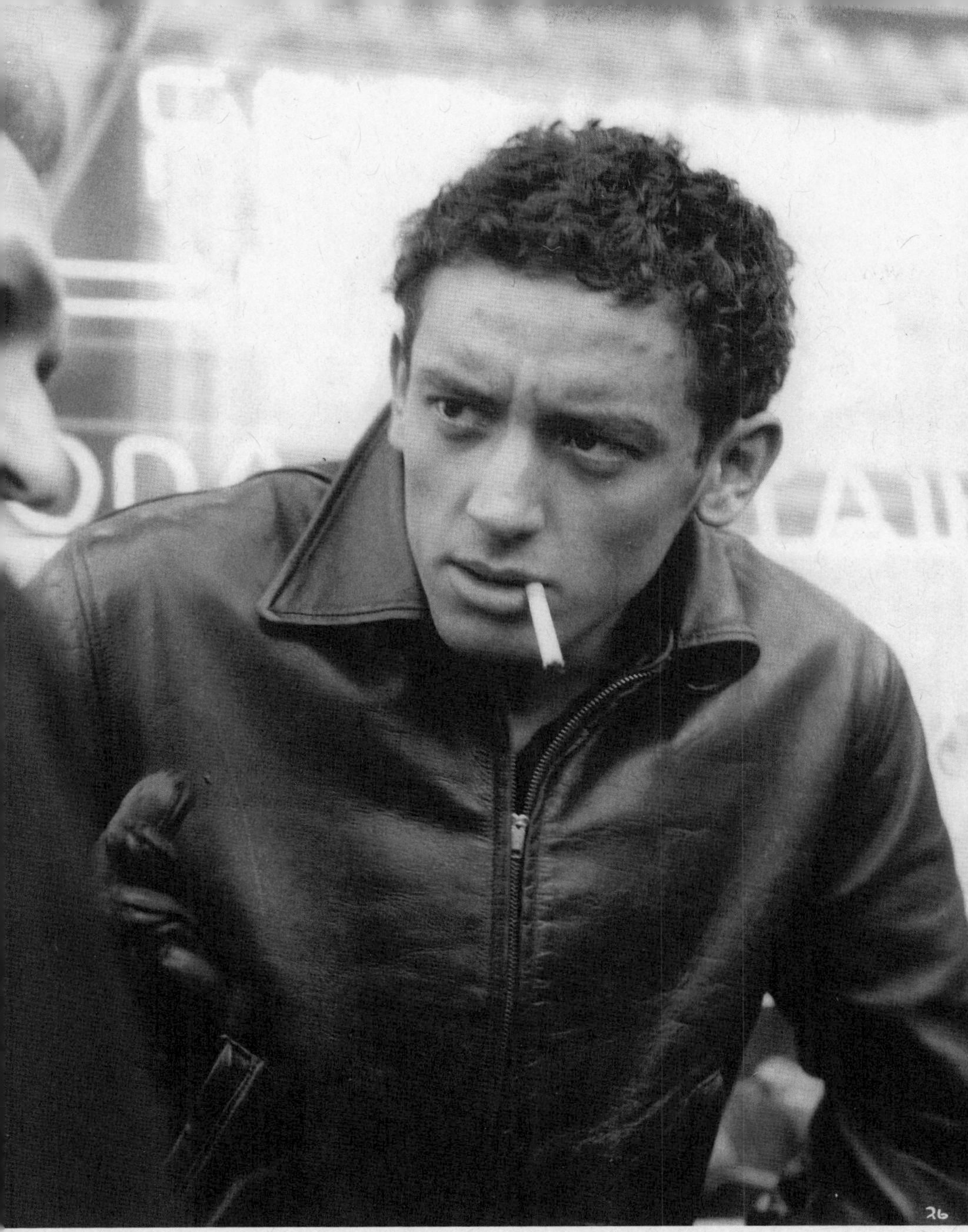

There is no place to escape to, no possibility of withdrawing inward, and no state of "pure being" to liberate. There is no "IT" and no "beyond." That is why all the major scenes in the film involve intricate social interactions between two or more characters. There is no realm outside the social. All of life is mediated and compromised.

I hope it is clear by this point why Cassavetes decided to script, reshoot, and reedit *Shadows*. Because the film takes the expressive middle ground as its territory, it was critical that he be able to delicately modulate his characters' expressions. A genuinely improvised performance could never attain the degree of expressive nuance that this kind of film requires. Subtlety is of the essence for any art that renounces black and white alternatives in order to offer discriminations among grays.

It undoubtedly became obvious to Cassavetes after viewing the improvised version of *Shadows* that he would, paradoxically enough, have to discard most of the scenes of actors improvising their lines in order to be able to suggest the complexity of characters improvising their lives. He would have to use every available device—from subtleties of scripting to playing mind-games with his actors, to drawing on aspects of their personalities that they themselves might not even be aware of—to achieve the subtleties demanded by the characters' states of expressive inbetweenness.

Shadows shows us how much exertion a life of expressive improvisation requires. It demonstrates how hard it is to remain free from ever-encroaching patterns—and that the effort is not something you can wing. It required more work than Cassavetes had ever imagined. *Shadows* proves that the Beat stance was less a way out than a prescription for unending work.

Bennie (played by Ben Carruthers) in John Cassavetes' "Shadows," 1957-59

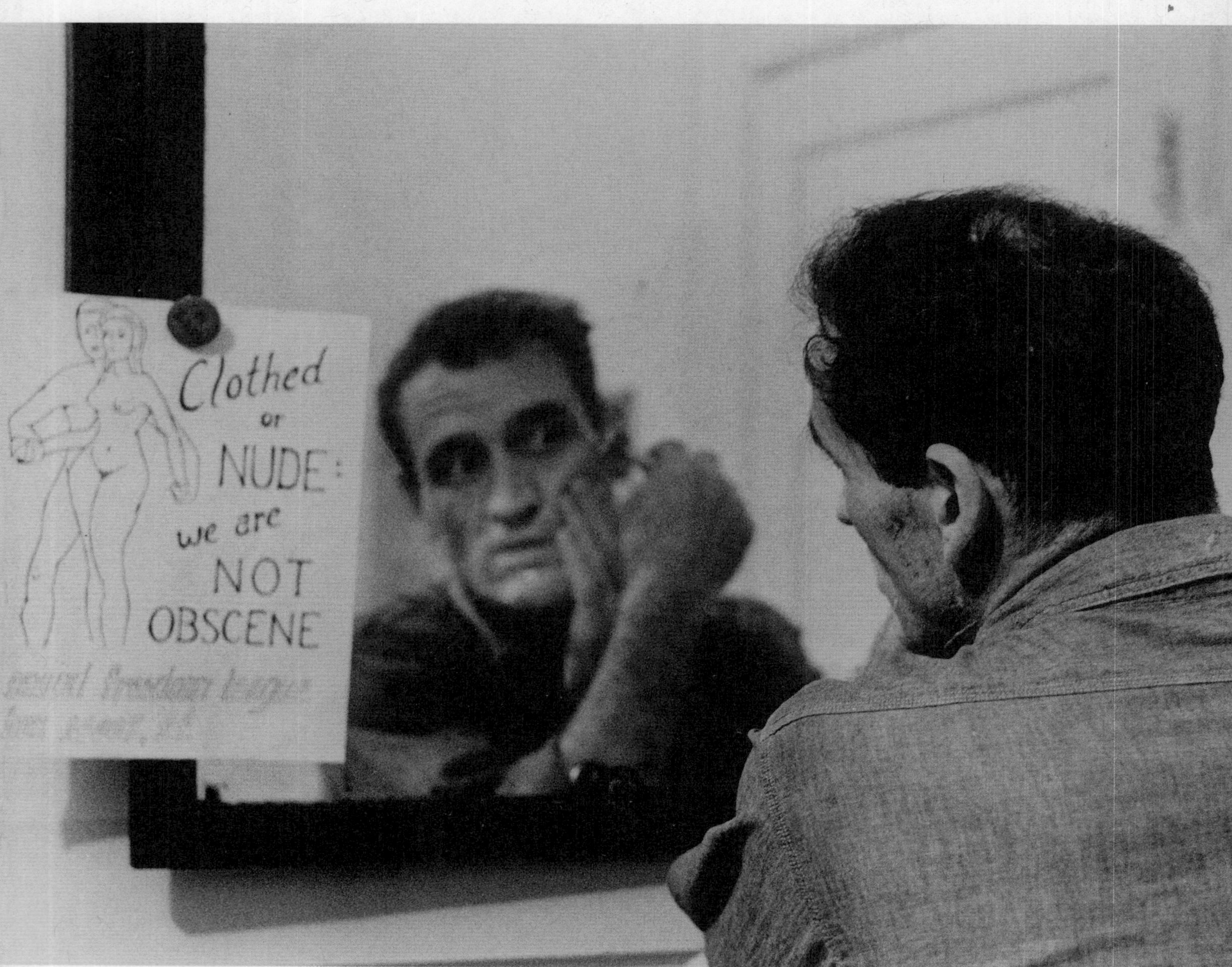

Neal Cassady shaving at Allen Ginsberg's San Francisco apartment, 1965. Photo by Larry Keenan

Robert LaVigne in front of his painting of seventeen-year-old Peter Orlovsky, 1959, at The Hotel Wentley (detail). Photo by Jerry Burchard

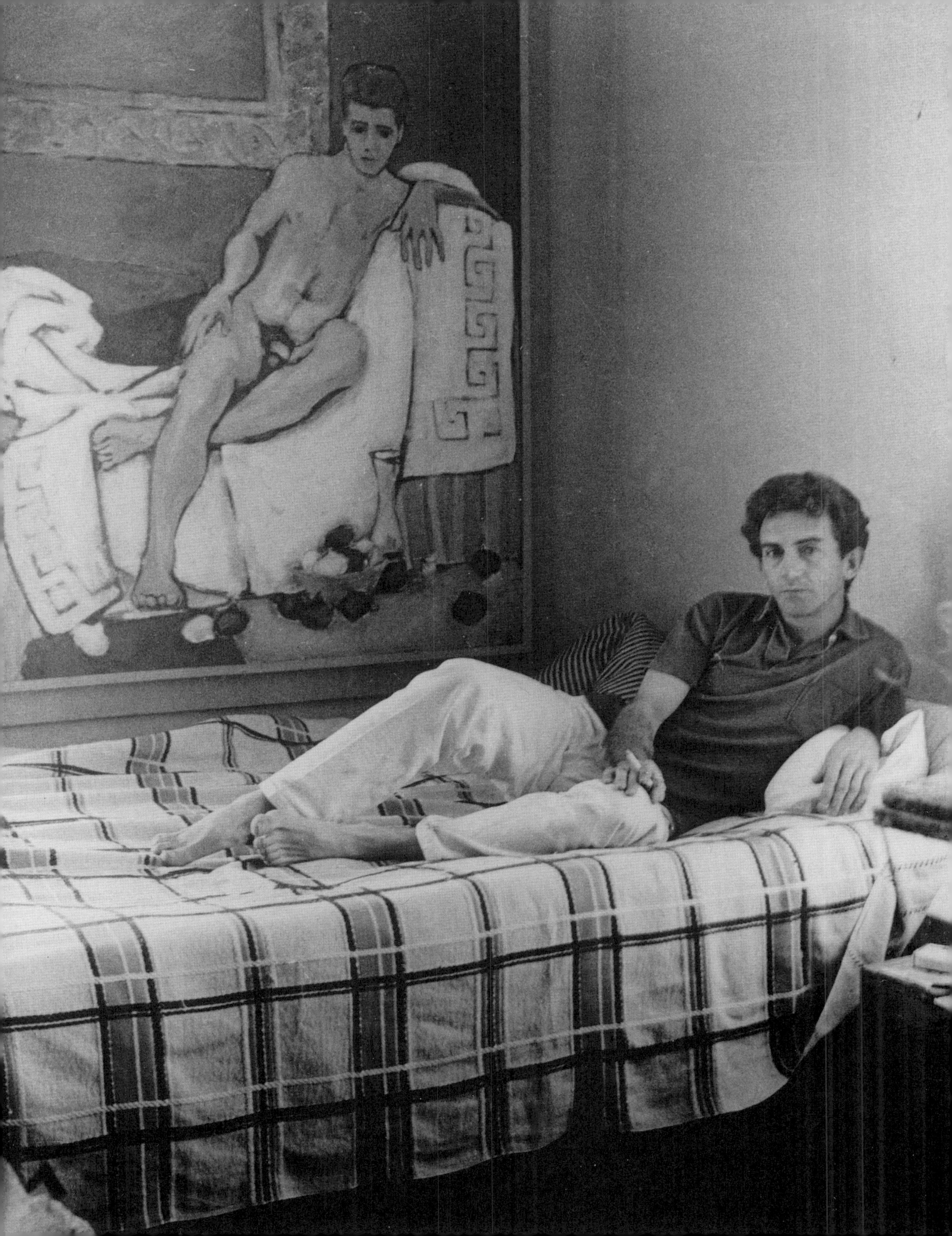

EDWARD SANDERS

THE LEGACY OF THE BEATS

We all filtered
& transformed the impact of the B.G. on our lives
We boosted the volume of some components
lowered the volume of others

We used the Negative Capability
of John Keats
years before
Charles Olson pointed out
that amazing N.C. letter to us
in one of his essays

and we
focused Neg. Cap.
on the thousandfold
aspects of being
a creative rebel

The Beats
brought us
an intoxicating,
lissome & fantastically
appealing *strand*
in the Great Woven Fabric
of the way we lived

We were taught
to escape our shyness
& reticence
& stand up
for better or worse

to the ridicule sometimes bestowed
from an uptight right wing
culture

The Beats in their
sense of public spectacle
drew from a long & complex
tradition
going all the way back
to the public chants
of Archilochus and Sappho
to the prancing dances of
Dionysus
& the Theory of Spectacle
in Aristotle's *Poetics*
to the famous premier performance
of Alfred Jarry's *Ubu Roi* in 1896
to the poèmes simultanes of the
Dadaists in Zurich's Cabaret Voltaire
in 1916—
to Charlie Parker's seething
sax
to the silence of John Cage—
to the calm pushiness of the
Happening Movement
& to the concept that there
was oodles of freedom guaranteed
by the United States Constitution that
was not being used.

That's why I've
written a series of
books called *Tales*
of Beatnik Glory

They were shamelessly
ready to dance
down freedom road

oh glory

Congress
shall make no
law abridging
the freedom of speech,
or of the press
or the right of
the people peaceably to assemble
& to petition the
government
for a redress
of grievances

glory

the right of
the people
to be
secure in their persons,
houses, papers and effects,
against unreasonable
searches & seizures
shall not be violated

GLORY

Nietzsche
pointed out how in

the wild dance
of Bacchus
across the earth
you dissolve
the Capital I
into the
Totality of Gaia.

That was
the message.

The automobile
and the freedom and largesse of America
were
the ballet slippers
of those
testosterone-addled
unselfconfident ego-inflamed
young men

who still lived
haunted by the
near social revolution
of the '30s

& the nightmare
policestate response
to a vastly over-exaggerated domestic
communist threat

We learned from the
Beats how to change
the word No to Go! Go!

We learned
from the Beats
how hard it is
to shade the glare
from what Kenneth Rexroth
called the Light from Plymouth Rock

How hard it is
to overcome
self-revulsion & shame

and that it is the
possibility of
actually finding beauty
experiencing beauty
writing & painting beauty
tasting & hearing beauty
calling forth Beauty

that allows
us to overcome
that harsh
relentless
American glare
of No.

In the
100,000 year
moil of
jealousy, guilt, murder
& abuse
they brought
the word Yes
to sexual history

It's okay to be gay
It's okay publically
to read a poem
about blow jobs or the thrill
of french kissing an elm leaf

It's okay to love
just one mate
in the caverns of galore
It's okay
to explore, to experiment
to laugh at sex
to love love to be ascetic AND erotic
at the same time
It's okay to be sexually confused
to swirl up & down
the yo-yo string of sexual yes-no
like Jack Kerouac

Yes Yes Yes

That spirit of rebellion
helped women to
begin tossing aside
their shackles also

I learned from the Beats
the lesson of the
Rebel Cafe

4 walls of Mystic Fruition

where our words of agitation,
revolution & rebellion
come into the
sharp focus
in an ever-noodling
zone of controlled abandon
Yes!

Everything's excitement
The spine tingles
like thrilling wands
as we come in
through the door
for a night at the
                Rebel Cafe

The Beats taught us
                about the
                        thrill
                            of the
                        Spontaneous Solo

One example
was when
they took fire
from those thrilling
bebop
        lonerhood
        tremble zone
spontaneous
            saxophone solos
on West 52nd

In my own
time it
was having
        Janis Joplin
sing "Amazing Grace"
w/ some bluegrass singers in a bar
holding a bottle of Heineken's

or seeing
Allen Ginsberg
make up a
        25 minute
        spontaneous
        rhymed blues

at midnight
            with the Fugs
    in a recording studio
                on E. 65th
                        in early '66

We learned that
somehow poetry & music
dance & painting
partying & fucking
Bacchus & Barding Around
Traveling in an armchair
& Traveling
            on the lonerhood galores
                of the road

        all were interwoven
        & interconnected

        in a 40, 50, 60, 70 year
        career of art & creativity

They helped teach us about zen
and other forms of
spirituality

We learned about the
Direct Transmission of Mind

and to seek out
            the best minds
            of our own generation

From the Beats we
received a
        new possibility of spirituality
        and visionary experience

I wrote a tune one morning
to "Ah Sunflower, Weary of Time"
when I was
a 20 year
old student at NYU
and walked through
Washington Square
because I knew
that visionary experience
was possible

from A. Ginsberg's
visit from the deep
chanting voice of Blake
in a room in Harlem

The Beats helped
teach us about
the exquisite beauty
of the American countryside

the raw
        thrill
of America
        & its maddened seethe
as a partly poisoned, partly paradisiacal
                raked garden
                between 2 oceans

I learned over the decades

a long and painful lesson
about America
that you can love it and
still be a total rebel

not take its injustices

Kerouac once visited the Merry Pranksters
and saw an American flag
draped casually over
a divan
in the way of the era

and carefully folded it up
in the manner of his era

Although we never used it ourselves, we
loved the word beatnik
We loved it when Civil Rights
marchers in Mississippi were
scorned as "beatnik race-mixers"
There was something especially
taunting & thrilling about its
we-just-might-be-communists
suffix, that wonderful "nik"
that caused police statists
like J. Edgar Hoover to dash
off hot air rigidity memos
on the Beats to the secret
police network.

By 1966 everyone sensed
that in just a few weeks
the reporters in the big
city newsrooms were going
to retire the appellation
w/ which they had gladly rounded
off an entire generation—
Beat**nik** with the "nik"
like a commie serif
on the quadruple meanings
of BEAT
& replace it for
a few years
w/ the word Hippie

Frankly I was
drawn to the Beats
because I wanted
a nonviolent social
revolution

I believed w/ all my
young heart in the
line from A.G.'s *America*
"When can I go into the supermarket
and buy what I need
w/ my good looks?"

A revolution a.s.a.p.
where we wouldn't have to wait
through 10,000 years
of ultra-rightist
micro-improvements

I was hungering for a social democracy
w/ maximum freedom & fun
& the possibility of spirit

in the service of which
I was convinced
the Beats were
part of the
fabric of the vanguard.

****

written
in the morning
in a café
on Union Square East
on May 22, 1994 for
a panel discussion
on the Beats at New
York University's
Eisner & Lubin
Auditorium.

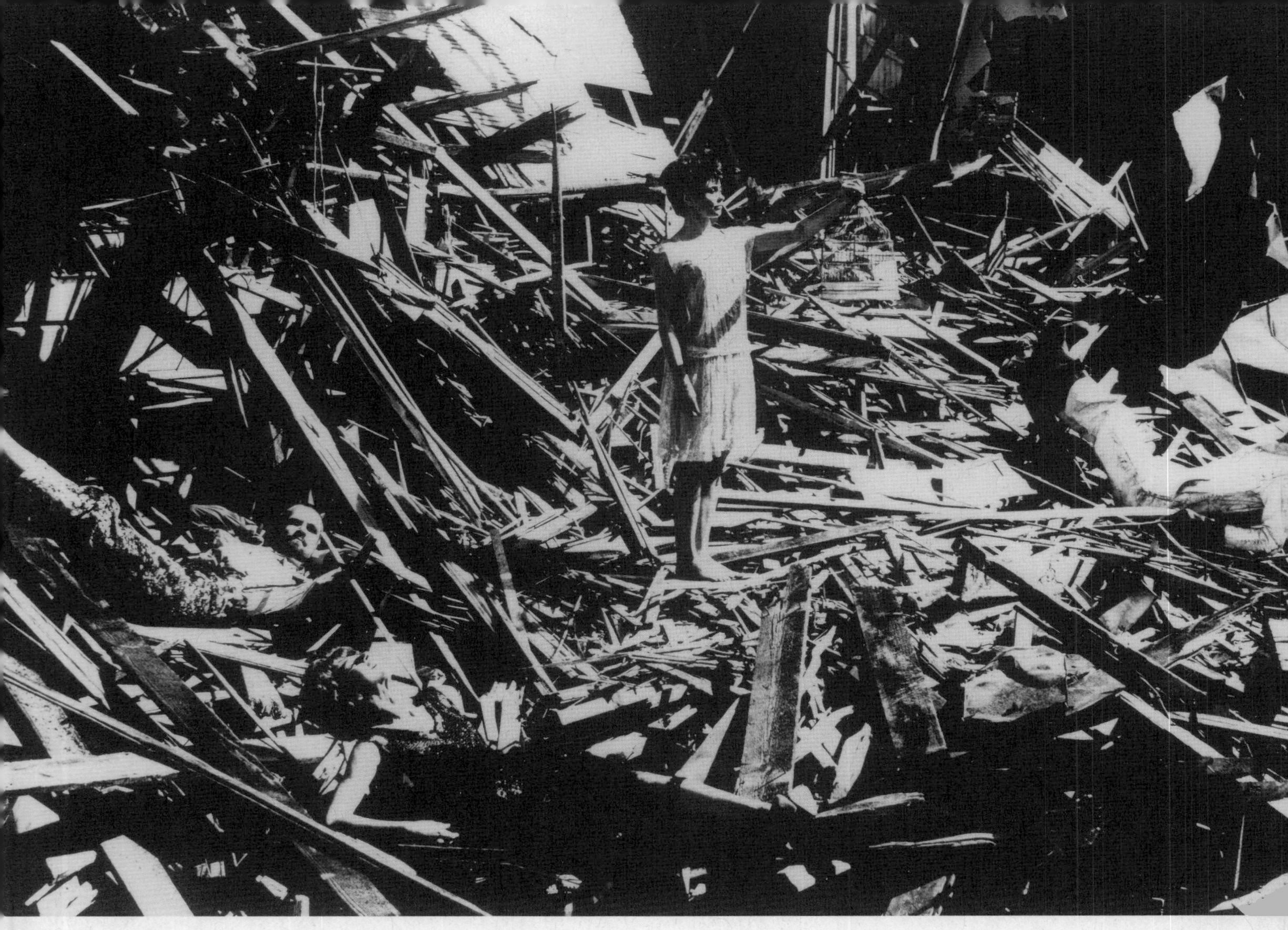

Anna Halprin's Dancers' Workshop, San Francisco, "Improvisations," 1962. Photo by Chester Kessler

STEVEN WATSON

CHRONOLOGY

In compiling this chronology, I have drawn from many sources. For the West Coast artists I am indebted to two pioneering works, Sandra Leonard Starr, *Lost and Found in California: Four Decades of Assemblage Art* (Santa Monica, California: James Corcoran Gallery, 1988), and Rebecca Solnit, *Secret Exhibition: Six California Artists of the Cold War Era* (San Francisco: City Lights Books, 1990). The chronology of the writers drew heavily from Ann Charters' *The Beats: Literary Bohemians in Postwar America (Dictionary of Literary Biography,* 16*)* (Detroit: Gale Research Company, 1983), and from Steven Watson, *The Birth of the Beat Generation: Visionaries, Rebels, and Hipsters* (New York: Pantheon Books, 1995). Other works consulted include: Lois E. Gordon, *American Chronicle: Seven Decades in American Life, 1920-1989* (New York: Crown, 1990); Gorton Carruth, *The Encyclopedia of American Facts and Dates* (New York: Crowell, 1970); John G. Hanhardt's chronology in *A History of the American Avant-Garde Cinema* (New York: The American Federation of Arts, 1976); and Robert Atkins, *ArtSpeak: A Guide to Contemporary Ideas, Movements, and Buzzwords* (New York: Abbeville Press, 1990).

EAST COAST BACKGROUND

The social foundations of the Beat generation were laid in 1944 at Columbia University. The ties formed at this time—among Jack Kerouac, Allen Ginsberg, William S. Burroughs, Neal Cassady, Lucien Carr, Herbert Huncke, Carl Solomon, Joan Vollmer—were literary and romantic, long-lived and seminally important. Lucien Carr introduced Kerouac, Burroughs, and Ginsberg to one another, and the last three lived together in 1946. They spurred one another to write, but only Kerouac completed a major project during this period (*The Town & the City*). In the summer of 1948, Ginsberg had a vision of William Blake speaking to him in a Harlem flat. A year later, after being arrested for possession of stolen goods (which Huncke had left with him), Ginsberg spent eight months in a psychiatric hospital, where he met Carl Solomon, the dedicatee of "Howl." Burroughs began using heroin, and addiction, both metaphorical and literal, became a central theme in his fiction. The word "beat" was introduced by Herbert Huncke in 1946, and the expression "Beat generation" arose out of a conversation between Kerouac and John Clellon Holmes in 1948. This core group became more broadly connected to other writers and artists in the 1950s.

In the visual arts, a new generation emerged, later known as the Abstract Expressionists or the first-generation New York School. They mixed with the wartime expatriates, including many Surrealists, and exhibited at Peggy Guggenheim's Art of This Century and the Egan Gallery. Greenwich Village was the center of the community, especially in such gathering places as the San Remo bar, the Artist's Club, jazz clubs, and the Waldorf Cafeteria. A school in North Carolina, Black Mountain College, provided another focus for the arts community. In its mixture of poetry, art, music, and performance, Black Mountain College became a seedbed for interdisciplinary works.

WEST COAST BACKGROUND

San Francisco had a vital community stretching back to at least the 1930s, in which bohemia, radical politics, literature, and art mixed. By the 1940s, the city contained all the elements of an avant-garde community: hangouts (The Black Cat), modernist academies (the California School of Fine Arts under the leadership of Douglas MacAgy, with staff that included Clyfford Still and Mark Rothko), little magazines (*Circle*, *Ark*), and crossover gatherings of writers, anarchists, and artists (Kenneth Rexroth's social meetings, the Libertarian Circle). The city's geographical distance from New York encouraged aesthetic independence, and its connection to anarchist politics contributed an edge of social engagement.

Los Angeles [hereafter presented in italics] had a less developed art community, but there were direct ties to Surrealism and Dada, thanks to the residence in the city of the artist Man Ray (since 1940) and the collectors Walter and Louise Arensberg (since 1926). The community of artists also connected to popular culture (Wallace Berman, for example, created an album cover for a Charlie Parker recording) and to Hollywood's film industry (Kenneth Anger had been a child movie actor). By the late 1940s the forces of anti-Communism were beginning to be felt in the blacklisting of screenwriters known as the "Hollywood Ten."

GENERAL

WEST COAST

EAST COAST

1950

General

Senator Joseph McCarthy advises President Truman that the State Department is riddled with Communists and Communist sympathizers. Congress passes the McCarran Act, which limits free movement by Communists and their sympathizers.

The illiteracy rate in the United States is at a low of 3.2%.

David Riesman's *The Lonely Crowd* is published, and new terms for social alienation enter the popular vocabulary.

West Coast

***Robert Alexander** opens the Contemporary Bazaar in Sherman Oaks—a shop devoted to dresses, crafts, art objects, poetry readings, and performances.*

Among the faculty in the Bay area are Max Beckmann (Mills College), Clyfford Still, and Ad Reinhardt (California School of Fine Arts).

East Coast

Jack Kerouac's ***The Town & the City*** is published by Harcourt, Brace.

Allen Ginsberg and Gregory Corso meet at the Pony Stable, a Greenwich Village lesbian bar.

Carl Solomon's article, "Report from the Asylum—Further Afterthoughts of a Shock Patient," is published (under the pseudonym Carl Goy) in ***Neurotica.***

Kerouac receives a 23,000-word typewritten letter from Neal Cassady (known as the "Joan Anderson Letter"), and declares it a "novelette" and the "greatest story" he'd ever read by an American writer.

Cinema 16 Film Library is established by Amos Vogel in New York to distribute experimental film.

1951

General

J.D. Salinger's *The Catcher in the Rye* is published.

District Judge Louis Goodman declares obscene two novels by Henry Miller, ***The Tropic of Cancer*** and ***The Tropic of Capricorn***.

Julius and Ethel Rosenberg are found guilty of treason; they are executed in 1953.

The hydrogen bomb is tested in Nevada.

The draft age is lowered to 18.

UNIVAC, the first mass-produced computer, is marketed.

Carl Rogers introduces "client-centered therapy."

West Coast

James Broughton's film *Loony Tom, The Happy Lover.*

The board of trustees of the Los Angeles County Museum of Art demands the removal from exhibition of a Picasso and a Jackson Pollock, due to the works' political and aesthetic unorthodoxy.

Harry Smith, a pioneering director of abstract films, makes a three-dimensional film, ***No. 6.***

Wallace Berman meets his future wife, Shirley Morand, and the poet Cameron; Cameron introduces Berman to the occult.

Jess and Robert Duncan meet and soon become lifelong domestic partners; they collaborate on art and poetry projects.

The first West Coast exhibition of assemblage art, "Common Art Accumulations," is held at The Place, a North Beach bar operated by artists and Black Mountain College graduates Knute Stiles and Leo Krikorian.

East Coast

John Clellon Holmes shows Kerouac his novel *Go*, about members of the Beat generation, with thinly disguised portraits of Ginsberg, Kerouac, Cassady, and Herbert Huncke.

During a three-week writing marathon, Kerouac types on a taped-together roll of teletype paper a second draft of ***On the Road***, which is essentially the version published in 1957.

Robert Rauschenberg holds his first one-artist show (paintings) at Betty Parsons Gallery in New York.

The Frank Perls Gallery mounts the exhibition "The School of New York," for which Robert Motherwell writes the catalogue preface and first coins the term "New York School."

The Living Theater, under the leadership of Julian Beck and Judith Malina, stages its first program of plays (works by Gertrude Stein, Paul Goodman, Federico García Lorca, and Bertolt Brecht).

An exhibition, "Today's Self-Styled School of New York," including many members of the Artist's Club, is organized by Leo Castelli. Held at 60 Ninth Street, it becomes renowned as the Ninth Street Show.

1952

General

Dwight D. Eisenhower elected president.

The Palmer Paint Company in Detroit markets a kit for painting by numbers, and a painting executed in this technique wins third prize in a San Francisco art show.

Color TV sets are marketed.

DNA is discovered to be the basis of genetic material.

The first 3-D movie, ***Bwana Devil***, is released, but the technique quickly loses popularity.

Norman Vincent Peale's ***The Power of Positive Thinking*** is published and becomes a best seller.

The Revised Standard Version of the Bible becomes the biggest-selling nonfiction book in the United States (1952-54).

West Coast

Philip Whalen moves to San Francisco and lives with Gary Snyder on Telegraph Hill.

Wally Hedrick arrives in San Francisco.

King Ubu Gallery, an artists' co-op gallery, is opened by Jess, Robert Duncan, and Harry Jacobus.

Jess begins making collage "paste-ups."

Poet Lawrence Ferlinghetti, under the name Lawrence Ferling, starts a newsletter and writes reviews for ***Art Digest.***

While living with Neal and Carolyn Cassady in San Francisco, Jack Kerouac completes ***Visions of Cody***, his masterpiece of spontaneous prose, and then heads south to visit William Burroughs, who has begun writing ***Queer*** in Mexico City.

East Coast

During the early 1950s, the San Remo bar in Greenwich Village is a main gathering place for writers, artists, and hipsters, including Frank O'Hara, Larry Rivers, Allen Ginsberg, Gregory Corso, Franz Kline, Judith Malina, and Julian Beck.

Among the students and faculty at Black Mountain College are Franz Kline, Robert Rauschenberg, Cy Twombly, and Charles Olson.

Ginsberg sends William Carlos Williams a group of poems he had adapted from journal fragments; Williams is enthusiastic and declares that Ginsberg's poems merit publication.

***Theater Piece No. 1**, subsequently recognized as the first Happening, is performed at Black Mountain College; participants include John Cage, Merce Cunningham, Robert Rauschenberg, Charles Olson, and David Tudor.*

John Clellon Holmes' novel ***Go*** is published. Holmes' "This Is the Beat Generation" appears in ***The New York Times***—the first time the term appears in print.

GENERAL

WEST COAST

EAST COAST

John Cage's *4'33,"* exemplifying the composer's interest in chance, is performed by David Tudor in Woodstock, New York.

The Tanager and the Hansa galleries open; this begins the wave of Tenth Street artist-run cooperatives, including the James Gallery (1954), the Camino Gallery (1956), March Gallery (1957), and the Brata Gallery (1957).

1953

Alfred C. Kinsey publishes ***Sexual Behavior in the Human Female***.

Playboy begins publication.

Jean Dubuffet coins the term "assemblage."

Otto Preminger's film ***The Moon Is Blue*** is denied a seal of approval because it contains the words "virgin" and "seduce."

Earl Warren becomes Chief Justice of the Supreme Court.

Aldous Huxley first experiments with hallucinogenic drugs.

After recovering from a transexual operation in 1952, Christine (formerly George) Jorgensen attracts international attention.

Edmund Hillary and Tenzing Norkay scale Mount Everest.

New vocabulary: girlie magazine, egghead, drag strip, cookout.

After briefly attending *East Washington State and Whitworth College, Edward Kienholz moves to Los Angeles.*

Ruth Witt-Diamant founds the Poetry Center.

Filmmaker Stan Brakhage arrives in San Francisco to study film; moves in with Robert Duncan and Jess. Larry Jordan also begins making films.

Jordan Belson makes the abstract films ***Bop Scotch*** and ***Mandala.***

Lawrence Ferlinghetti and Peter Martin found the City Lights Bookstore, the first American bookshop devoted to paperbacks, at 261 Columbus Avenue.

The Ghost House, the residence of many artists and poets (including Robert Duncan, Jess, Philip Lamantia, and Wally Hedrick) is demolished.

Wally Hedrick marries artist Jay DeFeo and they later move into an apartment at 2322 Fillmore Street, the site of many artists' parties and the home of Michael and Joanna McClure, Joan Brown, Craig Kauffman, James Newman, and Ed Moses.

George Herms visits LA on a break from the University of California, Berkeley and decides to move there.

Walter Hopps transfers from Stanford to UCLA; organizes jazz concerts with Craig Kauffman.

Wallace and Shirley Berman move to a little house at 10426 Crater Lane in Beverly Glen, which becomes a hangout for artists, poets, and musicians.

Burroughs' ***Junkie*****,** begun in 1950 in Mexico, is published in a 35-cent paperback by Ace Books (owned by Carl Solomon's uncle) that also contains ***Narcotics Agent*** by Maurice Helbrant; it receives no reviews but sells well.

After six months spent searching for the hallucinogenic drug yage in South America, Burroughs arrives in New York, intending to stay a month with Ginsberg; they have an intense affair, which Ginsberg ends. Burroughs departs for Tangier in December 1953, where he begins writing ***Naked Lunch.***

Kerouac writes ***Maggie Cassidy*** and ***The Subterraneans*** in New York.

Ginsberg takes up photography seriously, a practice he continues today.

Robert Frank, a native of Switzerland, settles in New York.

At Black Mountain College, Merce Cunningham organizes a permanent troupe of dancers, with John Cage as musical director.

1954

The Supreme Court declares racial segregation unconstitutional in public schools.

New vocabulary: cat music, desegregation, dragster, greaser, togetherness.

Dr. Jonas Salk develops a vaccine to prevent polio.

After a series of widely publicized hearings, the Senate votes to censure Senator Joseph McCarthy.

The Wild One stars Marlon Brando as a juvenile delinquent protagonist.

The first Newport Jazz Festival is held.

Samuel Rodia *(a.k.a. Simon Rodia) stops his thirty-three year-long work on the Watts Towers project.*

Walter Hopps, Ben Bartosh, Betty Bartosh, Michael Scoles, and Craig Kauffman open a storefront gallery in Brentwood, called Syndell Studio.

Edward Kienholz makes wooden relief paintings; meets Robert Alexander.

Lee Mullican and Rachel Rosenthal found a performance-art group called the Instant Theater, based at the Circle Theater in Hollywood, which continues until 1966.

Kenneth Anger makes the film ***Inauguration of the Pleasure Dome****, starring the poet Cameron.*

After the Contemporary Bazaar closes down, Robert Alexander enters a detoxification program for heroin addiction.

Jess and Wally Hedrick have their first one-artist shows at The Place.

The core group of the Beat generation disperses: Ginsberg is in Mexico, Burroughs in Tangier, Kerouac in North Carolina and elsewhere, Neal Cassady in San Jose.

Robert Creeley moves to Black Mountain College to teach and edit ***The Black Mountain Review***.

The first ***The Black Mountain Review*** is published; it is 64 pages long. The journal runs for seven issues, ending in 1957.

Kerouac becomes interested in Buddhism; appoints himself as Ginsberg's guide to Buddhism.

The Cedar Tavern becomes a chief hangout for artists.

The Village Voice *begins publication.*

Robert Rauschenberg begins making combine paintings.

GENERAL

WEST COAST

EAST COAST

West Coast

Wally Hedrick makes a version of his ***Light Machine***, an electronic piano, with lights and speakers that change with pitch, volume, and register.

Wallace and Shirley Berman visit San Francisco, go to the King Ubu Gallery, meet Duncan and Jess.

Berman begins working with photography, learns darkroom technique from photographer Charles Brittin.

*Cameron takes peyote, makes a drawing that is later included in 1957 in Wallace Berman's **Temple**.*

Stan Brakhage makes ***Desistfilm***, described by Parker Tyler as the first authentically Beat film.

*Inspired by Aldous Huxley's **The Doors of Perception**, Robert Alexander uses peyote and mescaline.*

Allen Ginsberg arrives in San Francisco after traveling in Mexico, meets Kenneth Rexroth and Robert Duncan, renews his friendship with Philip Lamantia, and falls in love with the Peter Orlovsky, whom he first sees in a portrait by Robert LaVigne.

Jack Kerouac and Allen Ginsberg separately visit Neal and Carolyn Cassady in San Jose and immerse themselves in Buddhism.

King Ubu Gallery closes and the space is inhabited by the 6 Gallery.

1955

General

African-Americans in Montgomery, Alabama, boycott segregated city bus lines.

Nicholas Ray's ***Rebel Without a Cause*** (1954) is released; its twenty-four-year-old star, James Dean, dies in a car accident.

Disneyland opens in Anaheim, California.

The US Gross National Product reaches a record high.

Bill Haley and the Comets' record, "Rock Around the Clock," introduces rock and roll, and becomes the no. 1 record of the year.

"The Family of Man," organized by Edward Steichen at The Museum of Modern Art, New York, becomes a blockbuster exhibition.

Dr. Martin Luther King, Jr., leads a successful boycott in Montgomery, Alabama, as the civil rights struggle intensifies.

Charlie Parker dies of complications resulting from drug addiction.

On the rise: malls, motels, golf, smog, pizza, suburbs.

West Coast

***Wallace Berman** purchases a 5 x 8-inch Kelly hand press, and, with Robert Alexander's technical assistance, he begins publishing **Semina**, a little magazine featuring poetry, prose, photographs, and drawings.*

Walter Hopps meets Wallace Berman, who in turn sends Hopps to see Robert Alexander in the hope that Hopps might support a vanguard gallery.

At the conclusion of a reading at the 6 Gallery of his play ***Faust Foutu***, Robert Duncan strips.

At seventeen, Joan Brown enters the California School of Fine Arts (BA, 1959; MFA, 1960).

Stan Brakhage lives in the basement of Jess and Robert Duncan's house, where he films ***In Between.***

After detoxing from heroin, Robert Alexander returns to LA, where he lives with Norman Rose and holds midnight light shows and poetry readings.

Edward Kienholz finds Alexander a residence on Santa Monica Boulevard; known as "the Baza shack," it becomes a center for artists, poets, and filmmakers.

Jim Newman, a recent arrival to Los Angeles, helps Walter Hopps operate the Syndell Studio.

George Herms returns from Mexico, lives in Beverly Glen and then Laurel Canyon; meets Wallace Berman and Robert Alexander.

*Excerpts from William Burroughs' **Naked Lunch** are published in **Semina.***

North Beach becomes trendy. Hangouts include the Coexistence Bagel Shop, Gino and Carlos' Bar, The Place, and Vesuvio's. The Cellar and the Coffee Gallery become centers of jazz and poetry performance.

Alan Watts discusses Buddhism on KPFA radio.

East Coast

Stan Brakhage makes two films in New York with Joseph Cornell.

Film Culture magazine, edited by Jonas Mekas, begins publication.

John Wieners enrolls at Black Mountain College.

Robert Duncan teaches at Black Mountain College; leaves and returns in the summer of 1956.

Robert Frank, supported by a Guggenheim award, begins shooting the photographs that will comprise ***The Americans.***

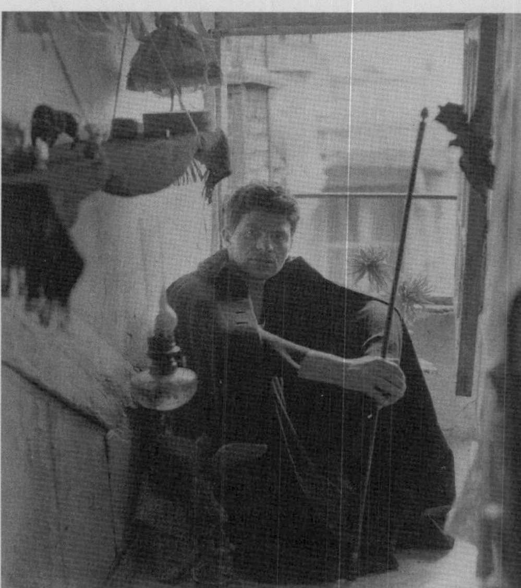

GENERAL

WEST COAST

EAST COAST

Lawrence Ferlinghetti starts City Lights Books; the first publication is his own ***Pictures of the Gone World.***

Epochal poetry reading at the 6 Gallery includes Kenneth Rexroth (emcee), Michael McClure, Gary Snyder, Philip Whalen, Philip Lamantia, and Allen Ginsberg, who read the first section of "Howl." In the audience are Jack Kerouac, Lawrence Ferlinghetti, Neal Cassady, and Peter Orlovsky. This event is usually described as the beginning of the San Francisco Poetry Renaissance.

In Mexico City, Kerouac writes poems, published as ***Mexico City Blues***, and begins his novel ***Tristessa.***

Anna Halprin founds the San Francisco Dancers' Workshop, a pioneer in improvisation and natural movement, and an influence on Trisha Brown, Simone Forti, and Yvonne Rainer.

1956

General

The Methodist Church abolishes racial discrimination.

Harry Belafonte's song "Jamaica Farewell" makes calypso music popular.

New vocabulary: the most, hero sandwich, head-shrinker, lay-off pay.

Elvis Presley debuts on the ***Ed Sullivan Show***, achieves instant stardom, and has a record on the top ten for sixteen consecutive months.

Southdale, the first indoor shopping mall, opens in Bloomington, Minnesota.

William Whyte's ***The Organization Man*** focuses attention on the forces of corporate conformity.

Popular: Dick Clark's ***American Bandstand*** TV show, sack dresses, saddle shoes, bowling, Silly Putty.

Construction begins on Frank Lloyd Wright's Guggenheim Museum.

West Coast

"The New Decade," *an exhibition including Abstract Expressionist painters, opens at the Los Angeles County Museum of Art.*

Allen Ginsberg disrobes at a poetry reading sponsored by Lawrence Lipton.

Stuart Z. Perkoff publishes **Suicide Poems**. *Later founds Venice West, a poetry center (1960).*

Alan Watts and Gerald Heard lecture at the Coronet Theater on Zen Buddhism.

Stone Brothers Printing—founded by Hopps, Alexander, and Berman—becomes a center for artists, poets, and writers. Visitors include Dennis Hopper, James Dean, Harry Dean Stanton, Ed Moses, and Craig Kauffman.

While at the University of California at Berkeley, Herms creates his first freestanding assemblage, a collaged door.

Robert Creeley comes to San Francisco for a few months, stays with Jack Kerouac in Gary Snyder's cabin, and co-edits with Allen Ginsberg the last issue of ***The Black Mountain Review.***

The little magazine ***Ark II-Moby I***, edited by James Harmon and Michael McClure, is published in San Francisco.

Gary Snyder goes to Japan to study Zen and the Japanese language; he remains there for several years.

The first East Coast mainstream recognition of the "Pacific Coast upstarts" appears in Richard Eberhart's article "West Coast Rhythms" in ***The New York Times Book Review.***

East Coast

Black Mountain College is closed down due to lack of funds. The small community there disperses: Duncan and his students go to San Francisco; John Wieners to Boston, where he starts ***Measure***, a poetry magazine the following year.

John Cage begins teaching at The New School for Social Research in New York (continues until 1960), and his class influences future Fluxus artists; students include George Brecht, Dick Higgins, Alison Knowles, Allan Kaprow.

Diane DiPrima and LeRoi Jones, independently, read Ginsberg's ***Howl and Other Poems*** and are inspired by the promise of a new generation of poets.

Jackson Pollock dies in a car crash in East Hampton, New York.

1957

General

Congress approves first civil rights bill for African-Americans since Reconstruction; Federal troops enforce desegregation in Little Rock, Arkansas.

USSR launches Sputnik I and II, first earth satellites. ***Truth or Consequences*** becomes the first nationally televised videotaped production.

The Wolfenden Report on homosexuality and prostitution is published in Britain.

West Coast

Evergreen Review begins publication, *under the leadership of Barney Rosset and Donald Allen, and devotes second issue to the "San Francisco Scene," with contributions by many of the major poets living on the West Coast.*

Bruce Conner, a high school classmate of Michael McClure, moves to San Francisco.

Walter Hopps and Edward Kienholz open the first professional gallery exhibiting the Los Angeles avant-garde at 736A North La Cienega; Robert Alexander names it the Ferus Gallery.

East Coast

September 5, Kerouac's *On the Road* is published by Viking, and ***The New York Times*** gives it a rave review; the book soon rises to no. 7 on the best-seller list.

Norman Mailer's essay "The White Negro" is published in ***Dissent.***

Gregory Corso in his attic room at 9 Rue Git-le-Coeur in Paris, 1957. Photo by Allen Ginsberg

GENERAL

WEST COAST

*Following up on a "citizen's complaint," the Hollywood vice squad visits Wallace Berman's exhibition at the Ferus Gallery. After finding nothing offensive, the police confiscate a reproduction of Cameron's ink drawing from the first issue of **Semina** and arrest Berman for displaying lewd and pornographic material. Alexander, Kienholz, Brittin, Arthur Richer, John Altoon, and David Meltzer are present. Berman is tried and convicted by Judge Kenneth Halliday and Dean Stockwell pays the $150 fine. Refusing to exhibit in censored form, Berman closes the show.*

*Herms installs his assemblage constructions over several square blocks, calls it the **Secret Exhibition** and shows it to only Wallace Berman and John Reed.*

***Collectanea**, a book with poetry by Robert Alexander and a cover illustration by Berman, is published.*

By year's end, most members of the Los Angeles circle around Berman have moved north. New Bay Area residents include the Bermans and George Herms, Bruce Conner, John Reed, Arthur Richer, Robert Alexander.

Joan Brown makes her first assemblage, and has her first one-artist show at the 6 Gallery.

Ginsberg's ***Howl and Other Poems***, published by City Lights in 1956, is seized by US Customs in San Francisco. Publisher Lawrence Ferlinghetti and the manager of City Lights Bookstore, Shigeyoshi Murao, are tried, but not convicted, for obscenity. Judge W.J. Clayton Horn's landmark ruling—that material with "the slightest redeeming social importance" is protected by the first and fourteenth amendments—will allow the publication of D.H. Lawrence's and Henry Miller's works a few years later.

Manuel Neri becomes the informal director of the 6 Gallery and encourages exchange between this gallery and the Ferus Gallery in Los Angeles.

Kenneth Rexroth and Lawrence Ferlinghetti experiment in reciting poetry to jazz music at The Cellar, a subterranean nightclub.

EAST COAST

The final issue of ***The Black Mountain Review*** (no. 7), co-edited by Robert Creeley and Allen Ginsberg, focuses on the San Francisco Renaissance and the Beat generation. Its contributors include Ginsberg, Corso, Burroughs, Kerouac, Gary Snyder, Duncan, Philip Whalen, Philip Lamantia, Louis Zukofsky, and Hubert Selby, Jr.

Kerouac reads at the Village Vanguard in New York, accompanied by Zoot Sims, Al Cohn, and Steve Allen.

Ginsberg, Peter Orlovsky and Corso go to Europe, eventually to Paris, where they live at 9, rue Git-le-Coeur, known as the "Beat Hotel." Together with Kerouac, they visit Burroughs in Tangier and help organize the ***Naked Lunch*** manuscript.

Robert Frank meets Jack Kerouac and asks him to write an introduction to ***The Americans.***

1958

General

The United States launches Explorer I, the USSR Sputnik III; NASA is established.

Brigitte Bardot becomes an international sex symbol.

Elvis Presley is inducted into the army.

The John Birch Society is organized.

The hula-hoop becomes a craze; it is outlawed in Japan.

Xerox markets the first commercial copying machine.

The term "pop art" is first used in print, by Lawrence Alloway.

***The Beat Generation and the Angry Young Men**, edited by Gene Feldman and Max Gartenberg, is the first anthology to link American and English authors.*

Treason charges against Ezra Pound, from 1946, are dropped after he has spent twelve years confined in a mental hospital.

Debuts: bifocal contact lens, Synanon, Grammy awards, Pizza Hut.

West Coast

John Wieners' first book, ***The Hotel Wentley Poems***, is published.

Norman Rose's Paper Editions, a paperback book center, provides employment for many artists and poets, including Robert Alexander, David Meltzer, Arthur Richer, George Herms, and Richard Brautigan.

James Newman starts Dilexi Gallery, named by Robert Alexander, in San Francisco. Berman introduces McClure to peyote, and McClure's poem about the experience fills the next issue of ***Semina.***

Berman photographs Jay DeFeo standing against her painting ***The Eyes***, which was inspired by a poem by Philip Lamantia.

DeFeo begins painting ***The Rose***, her magnum opus, which took seven years to complete.

Berman exhibits at the 6 Gallery, devoting most of his time to postcard art and photography; meets Neal Cassady and Allen Ginsberg.

New Directions publishes Ferlinghetti's ***A Coney Island of the Mind.***

East Coast

Allan Kaprow mounts an environment with sound, light, and odors at the Hansa Gallery, New York. Although not formally called a Happening, it is the first one to be staged in a New York gallery.

Jasper Johns has his first one-artist exhibition, of targets and flags, at the Leo Castelli Gallery, New York.

Robert Rauschenberg designs sets and decor for the Merce Cunningham Dance Company.

Burroughs moves between Paris, London, Tangier (through 1964).

John Cassavetes' film ***Shadows*** wins ***Film Culture***'s first Independent Film Award.

Jonas Mekas begins writing "Movie Journal" column in ***The Village Voice.***

Creative Film Society is founded by Robert Pike in New York to distribute independent film.

Kerouac, Philip Lamantia, Howard Hart, and David Amram do the first "jazz-poetry reading" in New York at the Brata Gallery. City Gallery and Judson Church Gallery open in New York. Allan Kaprow, Claes Oldenburg, and Jim Dine have their first shows at Judson.

GENERAL

WEST COAST

San Francisco Chronicle columnist Herb Caen popularizes the word "beatnik," perhaps originally coined by Sonia Gechtoff's mother.

Bruce Conner's first film, *A Movie*, is created from found footage. He has first one-artist show on the West Coast at the East West Gallery.

Conner and McClure found the Rat Bastard Protective Association; artists Hedrick, DeFeo, Joan Brown, and Manuel Neri are charter members.

Gregory Corso's poem "Bomb" and his book of poems, *Gasoline*, published by City Lights.

EAST COAST

Kerouac's *The Subterraneans* and *The Dharma Bums* are published by Grove and Viking, respectively.

LeRoi Jones and Hettie Cohen start Totem Press and edit the little magazine *Yūgen*.

1959

The national beatnik craze peaks; artifacts include a B-movie called *The Beat Generation*, a beatnik character on a television series (*The Many Loves of Dobie Gillis*), and a spate of articles in such mainstream magazines as *Life*, *Time*, and *Newsweek*.

Motown Records is founded by Berry Gordy.

The first seven US astronauts are selected.

Nikita Khrushchev tours the United States.

Fidel Castro overthrows Fulgencio Batista, to take control of Cuba.

***Kienholz makes his first** important freestanding assemblages.*

Beatitude magazine begins publication under the leadership of Bob Kaufman, Allen Ginsberg, John Kelly, and William Margolis; its end a year later is sometimes used to mark the end of San Francisco's literary renaissance.

The San Francisco Mime Troupe is founded by Ron Davis, beginning with a production of Alfred Jarry's *King Ubu*; the troupe later focuses on radical street theater.

Bruce Conner has a one-artist show at the Spatsa Gallery.

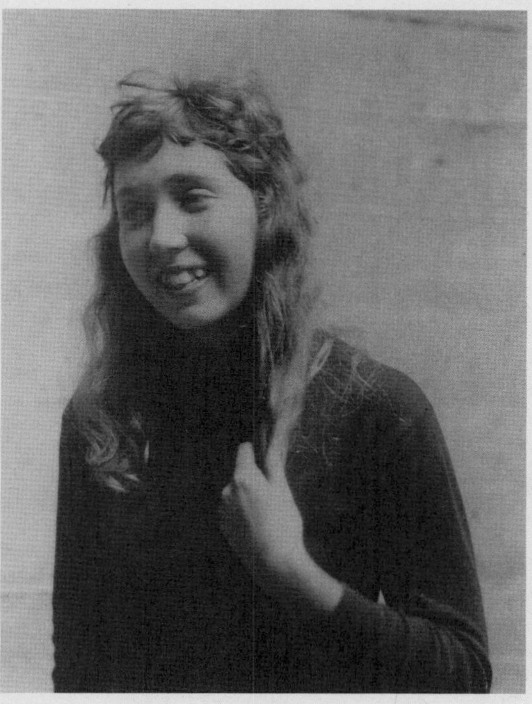

Joan Brown, 1959.
Photo by Jerry Burchard

January 2, the Beat film *Pull My Daisy* begins production (completed six weeks later) in Alfred Leslie's loft; chief participants include cinematographer Robert Frank, musician David Amram, actors Allen Ginsberg, Gregory Corso, Larry Rivers, Peter Orlovsky, Alice Neel, Richard Bellamy, and Delphine Seyrig, and narrator Jack Kerouac. The film is released in June 1959 and becomes a classic of the American independent cinema.

Reuben Gallery opens; before it closes in 1961, it mounts exhibitions by George Brecht, Lucas Samaras, Robert Whitman, and others.

Ginsberg records "Howl" and works on "Kaddish."

Wally Hedrick and Jay DeFeo are included in The Museum of Modern Art's exhibition "Sixteen Americans."

Robert Frank's epochal photo-essay *The Americans*, with an introduction by Jack Kerouac, is published.

Ken Jacobs films Jack Smith camping it up; the material is edited and released in 1963 as *Blonde Cobra*.

In Paris, Olympia Press publishes Burroughs' *Naked Lunch*.

Residing in Paris at the "Beat Hotel," Brion Gysin discovers a means of splicing together lines from previously published works to produce new works; Burroughs explores this method, producing "cut-ups."

The Living Theater produces Jack Gelber's controversial play, *The Connection*.

Frank O'Hara writes an informal poetry manifesto, "Personism."

Allan Kaprow first uses the term Happening in *Something to take place: a happening*, which becomes the script for his participatory environment at the Reuben Gallery. Other artists who create participatory performance works, also called Happenings, include Red Grooms (*The Burning Building*), Robert Whitman (*Small Cannon*), and Al Hansen (*Hi-Ho Bibbe*).

To illustrate Dante's *Inferno*, Robert Rauschenberg begins appropriating images from popular magazines such as *Life* and *Sports Illustrated*.

1960

U-2 spy plane shot down over Russia.

The Nixon-Kennedy presidential debates set viewing audience record and demonstrate television's importance in politics.

***Robert Alexander goes to San Francisco** to help reorganize The Cellar, returns to Venice and lives with Charles Brittin, founds a center for poetry, jazz, and art called the Temple of Man.*

Ginsberg takes LSD with Timothy Leary at Harvard, and the two plan the psychedelic revolution.

Publication of *The New American Poetry*, edited by Donald Allen, introduces to the mainstream canon poets associated with Black Mountain College, San Francisco, and the Beat generation.

	GENERAL	WEST COAST	EAST COAST
	Oral birth control, Enovid, is introduced. On the rise: art galleries, museum construction, bidding levels at art auctions. Nearly 90 percent of American homes have television. The first wave of war babies reaches college, and Pepsi-Cola coins its slogan, "For those who think young." The Student Nonviolent Coordinating Committee (SNCC) and the Students for a Democratic Society (SDS) are founded. C. Wright Mills coins the expression "the New Left." D.H. Lawrence's ***Lady Chatterley's Lover*** is published in the United States following a thirty-year ban.	*Virginia Dwan opens the Dwan Gallery.* *Hopps and Kienholz sell Ferus Gallery to Irving Blum.* William Jahrmarkt founds the Batman Gallery at 2222 Fillmore Street; the first show is devoted to Bruce Conner, followed by a group exhibition, "Gangbang." Although many poets and artists have left San Francisco, tourist fascination with North Beach reaches a new height of popularity. *Berman and Herms move north to Larkspur to join the Jahrmarkts. Berman lives in a houseboat a few doors down from Herms, and sets up an informal, roofless, Semina gallery in a second houseboat.* The Canyon Cinema (experimental film) is organized by Bruce Baillie. Films include Ron Rice's ***The Flower Thief.*** Lenny Bruce is arrested for using obscenities in his nightclub act.	Claes Oldenburg's first one-artist show, "The Street," opens at the Judson Gallery, New York. New American Cinema Group is formed by Jonas Mekas and Lewis Allen as an alternative to the commercial film industry. Jim Dine's ***Car Crash***, a Happening at Judson Gallery. "New Media—New Forms" exhibition at the Martha Jackson Gallery, New York. Claes Oldenburg organizes "Ray Gun Spex," a series of events at the Judson Memorial Church; participants include Jim Dine, Allan Kaprow, Robert Whitman, Al Hansen, and Dick Higgins. Jean Tinguely's ***Hommage à New York*** self-destructs in The Museum of Modern Art garden. Proto-Fluxus events begin to be held in New York; participants include La Monte Young, Jackson Mac Low, Dick Higgins.
1961	**John F. Kennedy inaugurated** as the 35th (and youngest) president of the United States. US breaks off diplomatic relations with Cuba; the Bay of Pigs invasion is a failure. East Germany erects the Berlin Wall. Grove Press publishes Henry Miller's ***Tropic of Cancer*** in the US. A movie version of ***The Subterraneans*** opens, featuring George Peppard as the Jack Kerouac character.	**Caryl Chessman's execution** at San Quentin (in 1960) inspires Berman, Conner, and Kienholz to make works about the event. *Berman returns to Los Angeles.* "Kaddish," Ginsberg's elegy to his mother, is published by City Lights Books (***Kaddish and Other Poems: 1958-1960***). *Herms moves to Topanga Canyon.* *Kienholz has a one-artist show at the Pasadena Art Museum.* Conner makes the film ***Cosmic Ray***, with Ray Charles' music. Conner's ***The Box*** wins first prize in a National Council of Churches competition; images of the assemblage appear in the national media. Jordan Belson films ***Allures.***	**George Maciunas coins the word Fluxus** for a series of interdisciplinary events. Dick Higgins identifies nine criteria for Fluxus works: internationalism, experimentalism, iconoclasm, intermedia, resolution of the art/life dichotomy, play, ephemerality, and specificity. Diane DiPrima and LeRoi Jones publish and edit the monthly poetry newsletter ***The Floating Bear***; with others, found the New York Poets Theater. "The Art of Assemblage" exhibition at The Museum of Modern Art is the first exhibition to recognize assemblage as an art form; John Chamberlain, Bruce Conner, Willem de Kooning, George Herms, Jess, Edward Kienholz, Robert Rauschenberg participate. Shirley Clarke films ***The Connection***; Jonas Mekas films ***Guns of the Trees.***
1962	**Rachel Carson's** ***Silent Spring*** focuses concern on the environment. Closing after 2,717 performances, ***My Fair Lady*** becomes the longest-running musical on Broadway. The Cuban missile crisis. Debuts: Diet Rite, Esalen Institute, Polaroid color film, K Mart. James Meredith is the first African-American student to be admitted to the University of Mississippi. Franz Kline and Marilyn Monroe die. Chubby Checker's song "The Twist" introduces a national dance craze.	***George Herms and Larry Jordan*** *begin working on the film* ***Jewelface*** *(1962-64).* *Jim Newman opens the Los Angeles Dilexi Gallery; gives John Chamberlain his first one-artist show on the West Coast; poor sales force gallery to close before the end of the year.* *The American Legion demands removal of Herms' assemblage,* ***Macks****, from the "California Collage Show" at the Pasadena Art Museum. The museum does not accede and someone breaks into the museum at night and rips the American flag from the work.* *Conner has a one-artist show at the Ferus Gallery.* *Walter Hopps becomes curator, and soon director, of the Pasadena Art Museum; he hires James Demetrion as curator.* *Los Angeles collectors who begin supporting the local avant-garde art include Betty Asher, Mr. and Mrs. Donald Factor, Sidney Felson, Hal Glicksman, Mr. and Mrs. Stanley Grinstein, Dennis Hopper and Brooke Hayward, Edwin Janss, Robert Rowan, Mr. and Mrs. Frederick Weisman, and Diana Zlotnick.* Manuel Neri and Joan Brown marry; remain married until 1966.	**Andy Warhol** begins making silkscreened art works. The Artist's Club closes. Claes Oldenburg exhibits his environmental installation ***The Store*** at the Green Gallery in New York. The Judson Dance Theater is formed, named after the Judson Memorial Church where performances take place. Participants include Trisha Brown, Yvonne Rainer, Steve Paxton, Lucinda Childs, David Gordon, Robert Morris, Carolee Schneemann, Robert Rauschenberg. Three qualities of this wide-ranging work, as described by critic Jill Johnston, are: dancing is physical and bears little relation to the conventional attitudes of dance; the choreography is sometimes created by a non-dancer, giving new emphasis to the event-status of the dance; the whole world of movement can be considered dance. Burroughs' ***Naked Lunch*** published in the US by Grove Press. Ray Johnson initiates a network of mail artists by sending a series of "please respond to" missives; Ed Plunkett names it the New York Correspondence School a few months later, and Johnson creates his variant, the New York Correspondance School.

GENERAL

WEST COAST

EAST COAST

West Coast

John Irwin begins publishing ***Artforum*** in San Francisco. Initially focused on the West Coast, it becomes an important conduit through which California art reaches the East Coast art establishment.

East Coast

A series of three films—***Towers Open Fire, The Cut-Ups, Bill and Tony***—apply the cut-up method to film. The films, inspired by Brion Gysin, are written and narrated by William Burroughs and directed by Anthony Balch in London.

1963

General

The Beatles top the charts with "I Want to Hold Your Hand." Singers Peter, Paul, and Mary are also popular.

Bob Dylan records "The Times They Are A-Changin'."

Timothy Leary and Richard Alpert are dismissed from Harvard University for testing LSD on students.

Martin Luther King, Jr.'s civil rights march takes place in Washington, D.C.; King delivers his "I have a dream" speech.

The University of California Regents abolish compulsory ROTC.

President John F. Kennedy is assassinated in Dallas; Lyndon Johnson becomes president.

The US, USSR, and Great Britain sign a nuclear test ban treaty.

West Coast

Andy Warhol shoots part of his film ***Tarzan and Jane Regained, Sort of...****, featuring Berman and his son, Tosh, at Berman's house on Crater Lane.*

Ed Ruscha publishes his first book, ***Twenty Six Gasoline Stations.***

George Herms films ***Moonstone*** *with Dean Stockwell.*

Bruce Conner begins ***Report***, completed in 1964, a film about the Kennedy assassination.

Kenneth Anger films ***Scorpio Rising***, incorporating pop music into a homoerotic film about bikers.

A nude torso by Kienholz causes scandal during an exhibition at San Fernando Valley State College, Northridge. The exhibition is moved to another site.

Walter Hopps organizes "By or of Marcel Duchamp or Rrose Sélavy," the first major museum Duchamp retrospective, at the Pasadena Art Museum; Duchamp visits Los Angeles for the occasion and meets Ed Ruscha and others.

East Coast

Jack Smith's ***Flaming Creatures*** wins the Independent Film Award and subsequently become a prime case in the censorship wars.

Andy Warhol makes his first films, including ***Haircut*** and ***Kiss.***

Naked Lunch *is banned in Boston, then put on trial for obscenity.*

Charlotte Moorman organizes the first Festival of the Avant-Garde at Carnegie Hall, New York.

The Cedar Tavern closes (it later reopens under different management).

Carolee Schneemann's ***Eye Body*** is her first work to use her body as an extension of painting, anticipating body art, contact improvisation, and feminist performance.

1964

General

Race riots erupt in Harlem.

Stanley Kubrick's film ***Dr. Strangelove*** is released.

Marshall McLuhan writes ***Understanding Media.***

Malcolm X founds the Organization of Afro-American Unity.

The Free Speech Movement is founded at the University of California, Berkeley.

West Coast

Berman experiments with a copy machine *given to him by William Jahrmarkt and makes his first Verifax collages.*

The ***Los Angeles Free Press*** *begins publication.*

East Coast

George Herms comes to New York to work with Diane DiPrima at the American Theater for Poets, designing sets for Michael McClure's play ***Blossom or Billy the Kid.***

Neal Cassady drives Ken Kesey's psychedelic bus "Further"; takes Kerouac from Northport to New York to a party with Kesey and the Merry Pranksters; Cassady and Kerouac never see each other again.

Jonas Mekas is arrested for showing Jack Smith's ***Flaming Creatures*** and Jean Genet's ***Chant d'amour.***

The Film-Makers' Cinematheque is founded. Kerouac moves to Florida and lives with his mother.

1965

General

Malcolm X is assassinated in New York.

Thirty-five people are killed in race riots in the Watts section of Los Angeles.

The United States bombs North Vietnam.

The SDS demonstrates against US business support of apartheid in South Africa and sponsors marches on Washington to protest the war in Vietnam.

"Flower Power" begins in San Francisco, marking the beginning of the hippie movement.

Lenny Bruce delares bankruptcy after being arrested twenty times on obscenity charges; he dies of a drug overdose the next year.

West Coast

Jay DeFeo removes her massive painting, ***The Rose***, from her Fillmore Street apartment; Bruce Conner's film of the event is called ***The White Rose.***

Charles Cowles takes over ***Artforum*** *and runs the magazine from an office over the Ferus Gallery.*

Artist Arthur Richer overdoses in Healdsburg, California.

East Coast

Burroughs lives in New York for the first time in a decade and he is lionized as a literary hero.

Robert Frank begins filming ***Me and My Brother***, about Peter and Julius Orlovsky.

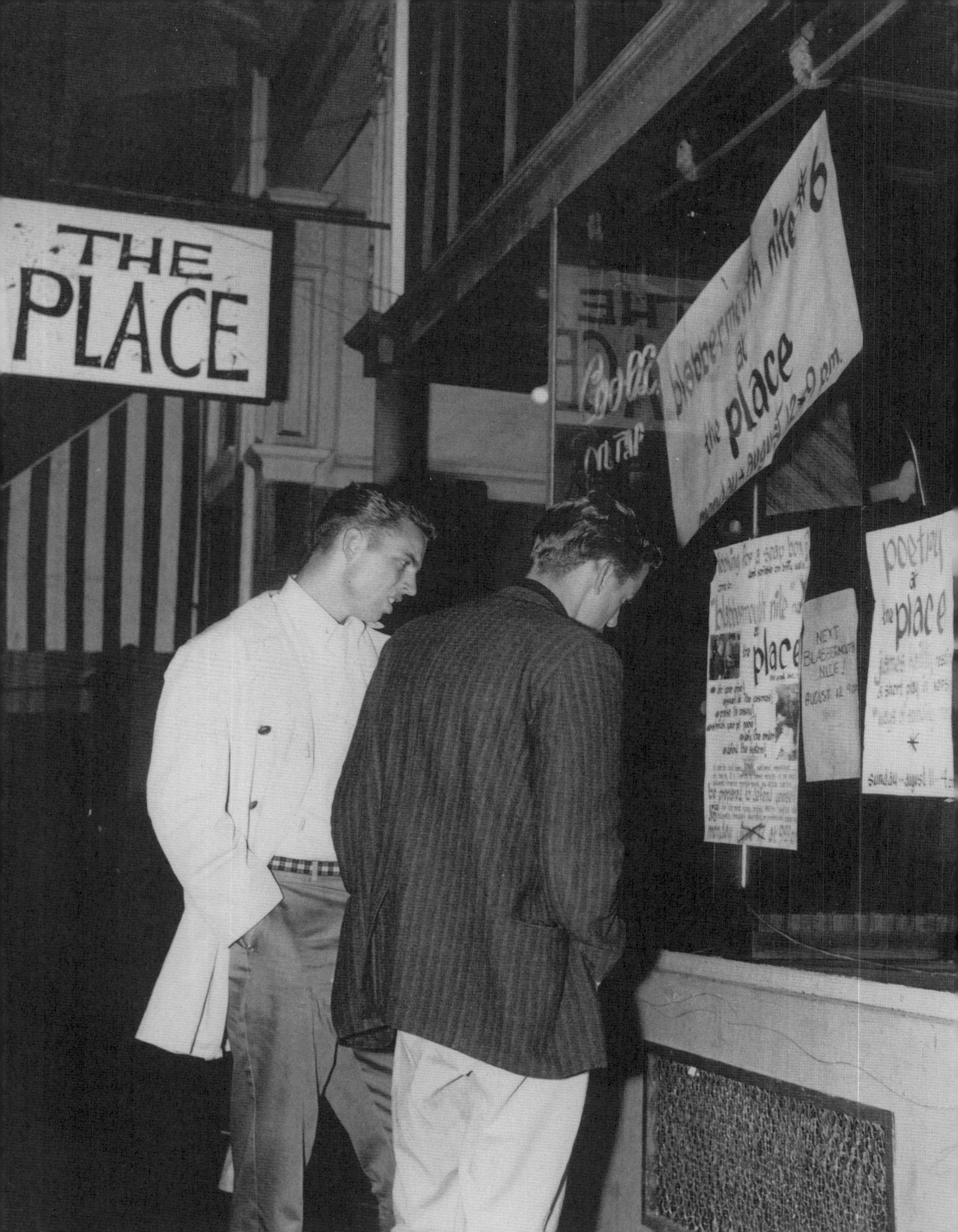
THE PLACE
blabbermouth nite #6
at
the place
August 12
9 p.m.
looking for a soap box?
blabbermouth nite
at
the place
be prepared to defend yourself
NEXT BLABBERMOUTH NITE!
AUGUST 12
poetry
at
the place

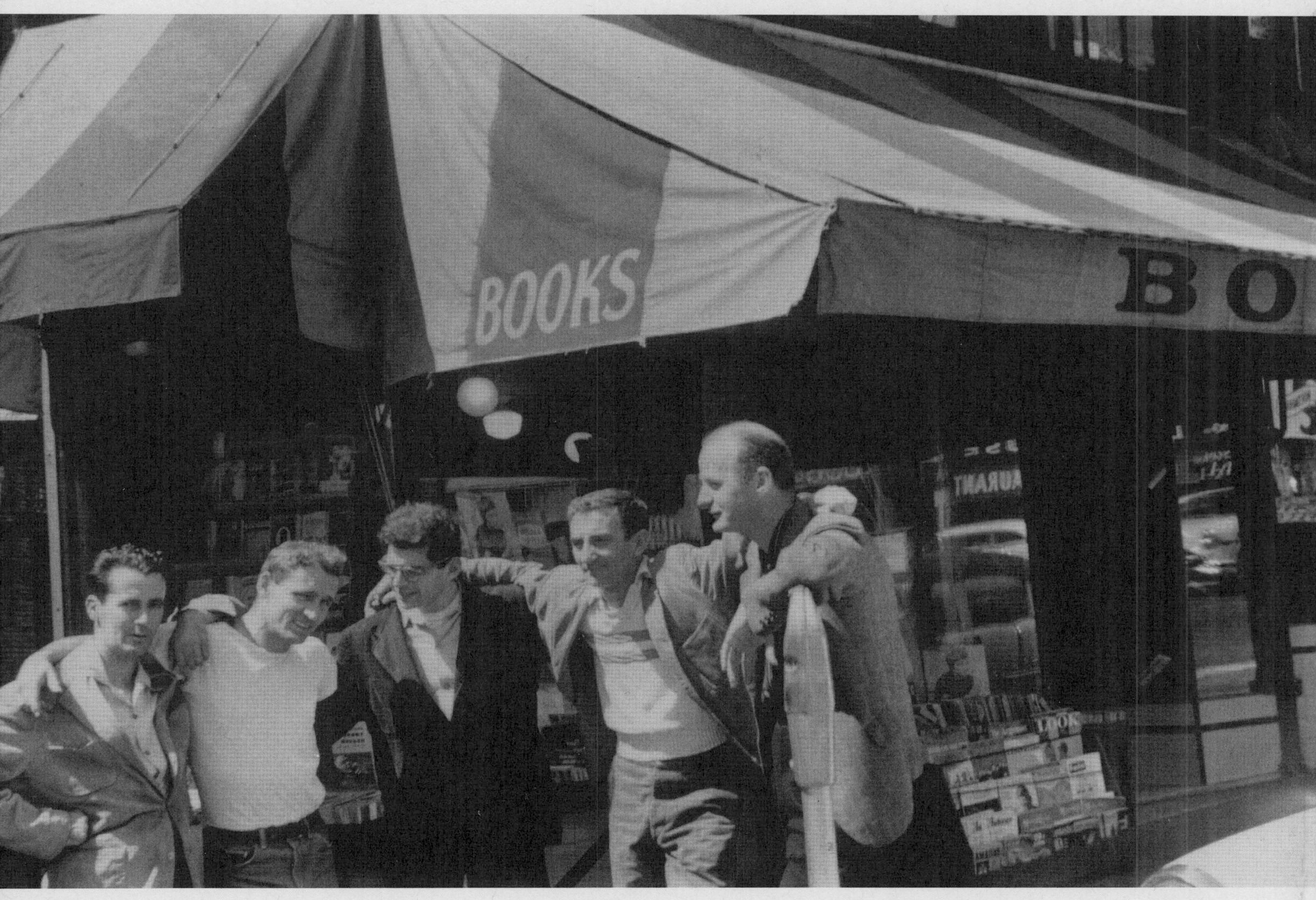

City Lights group portrait, North Beach, San Francisco (Peter Orlovsky held camera), 1955
(Left to right: Bob Donlin, Neal Cassady, Allen Ginsberg, Robert LaVigne, Lawrence Ferlinghetti). Photo by Allen Ginsberg

"Blabbermouth Nite" at The Place, San Francisco, 1957. Photo by Harry Redl

WEST COAST

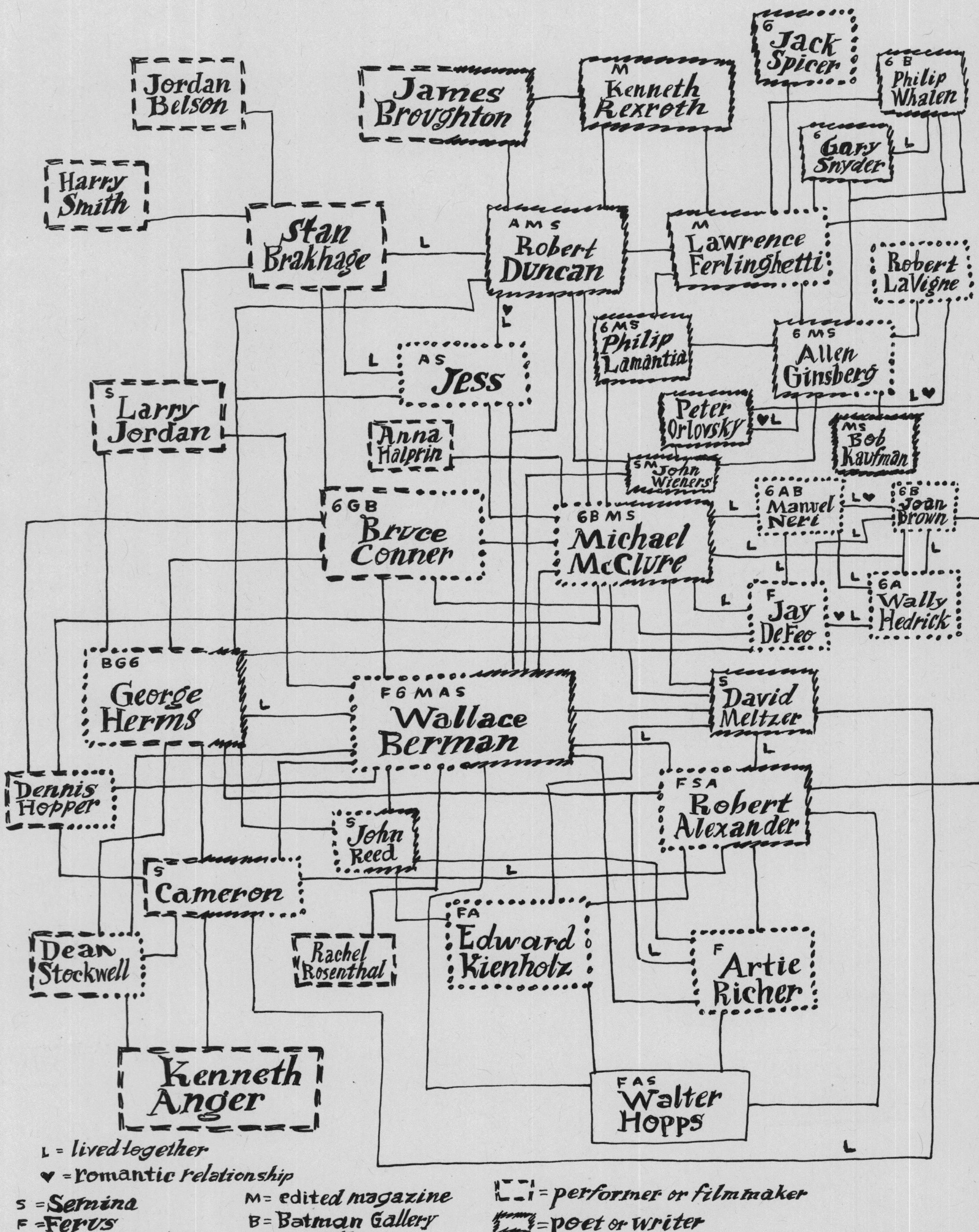

6 Jack Spicer
6 B Philip Whalen
Jordan Belson
James Broughton
M Kenneth Rexroth
6 Gary Snyder
Harry Smith
Stan Brakhage
AMS Robert Duncan
M Lawrence Ferlinghetti
Robert LaVigne
6MS Philip Lamantia
6MS Allen Ginsberg
AS Jess
S Larry Jordan
Peter Orlovsky
MS Bob Kaufman
Anna Halprin
SM John Wieners
6AB Manuel Neri
6B Joan Brown
6GB Bruce Conner
6BMS Michael McClure
F Jay DeFeo
6A Wally Hedrick
BG6 George Herms
F6MAS Wallace Berman
S David Meltzer
Dennis Hopper
FSA Robert Alexander
S John Reed
S Cameron
FA Edward Kienholz
Dean Stockwell
Rachel Rosenthal
F Artie Richer
Kenneth Anger
FAS Walter Hopps
L
♥
L = lived together
♥ = romantic relationship
S = Semina
F = Ferus
A = ran art gallery
M = edited magazine
B = Batman Gallery
6 = 6 Gallery
= performer or filmmaker
= poet or writer
= artist

EAST COAST

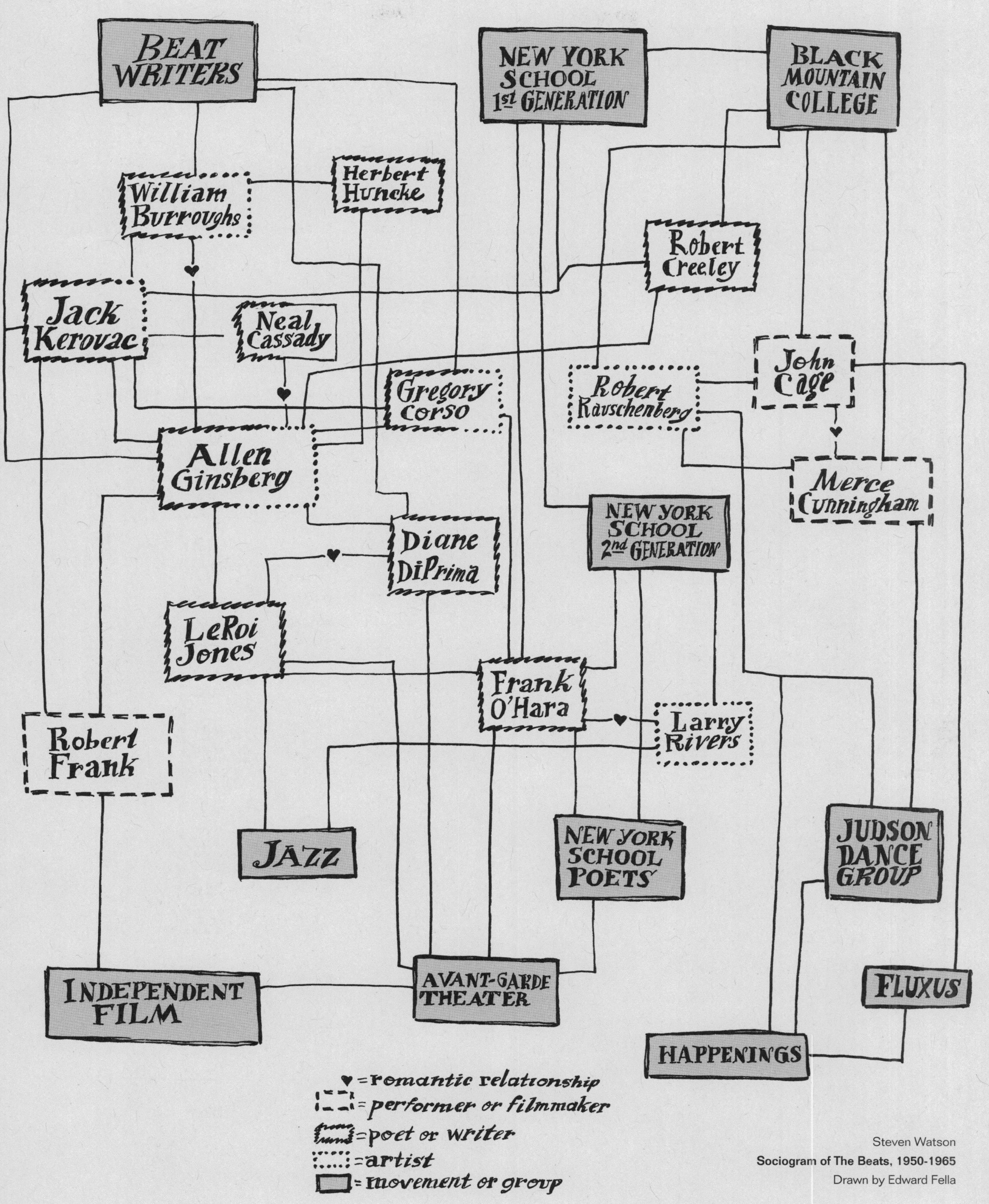

Steven Watson

Sociogram of The Beats, 1950-1965

Drawn by Edward Fella

SELECTED BIBLIOGRAPHY

The Bibliography is divided into eight sections: literary works by Beat writers; articles, anthologies, and cultural studies; literary biographies and autobiographies; visual arts; photographic essays; Beat periodicals; cassettes and compact discs. The items are organized chronologically by year of publication and alphabetically within each year.

SELECTED LITERARY WORKS BY BEAT WRITERS

1950

Kerouac, Jack. ***The Town & the City***. New York: Harcourt, Brace, 1950.

1952

Holmes, John Clellon. ***Go***. New York: Thunder's Mouth Press, 1952.

1953

Burroughs, William S. (as William Lee). ***Junkie***. New York: Ace Books, 1953.

Burroughs, William S. ***Queer*** (first published New York: The Viking Press, 1985).

1955

Ferlinghetti, Lawrence. ***Pictures of the Gone World***. San Francisco: City Lights Books, 1955.

Patchen, Kenneth. ***Poems of Humor & Protest***. San Francisco: City Lights Books, 1955.

1956

Ginsberg, Allen. ***Howl and Other Poems***. San Francisco: City Lights Books, 1956.

1957

Kerouac, Jack. ***On the Road***. New York: The Viking Press, 1957.

Rexroth, Kenneth. "Disengagement: The Art of the Beat Generation." In ***New World Writing***, no. 11. New York: New American Library, 1957, pp. 28-41.

1958

Corso, Gregory. ***Bomb***. San Francisco: City Lights Books, 1958.

_______. ***Gasoline***. San Francisco: City Lights Books, 1958.

DiPrima, Diane. ***This Kind of Bird Flies Backward***. New York: Totem Press, 1958.

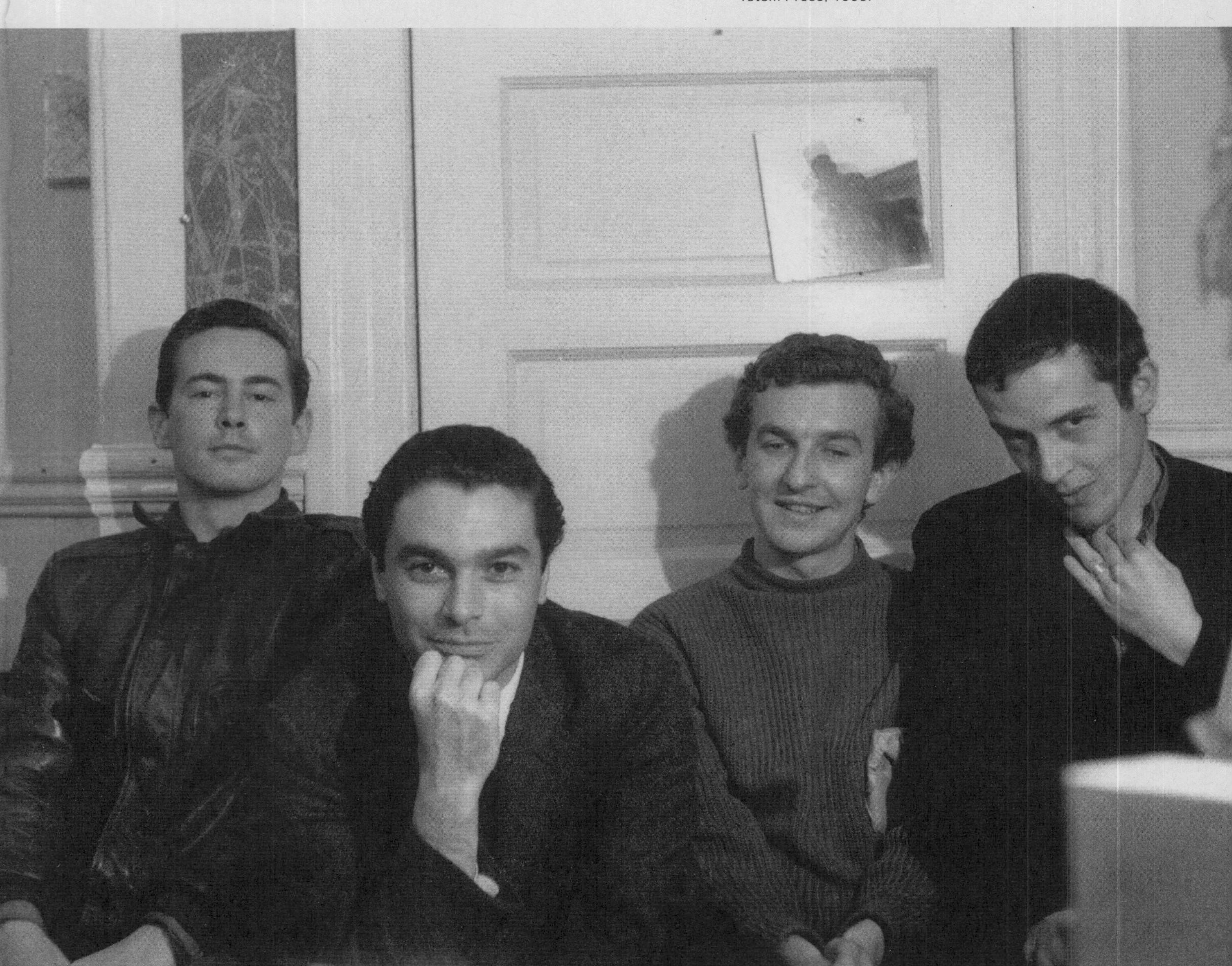

Ferlinghetti, Lawrence. ***A Coney Island of the Mind***. New York: New Directions Publishing Corporation, 1958.

Kerouac, Jack. ***The Dharma Bums***. New York: The Viking Press, 1958.

_______. ***The Subterraneans***. New York: Grove Press, 1958.

Wieners, John. ***The Hotel Wentley Poems.*** San Francisco: Auerhahn Press, 1958.

1959

Burroughs, William S. ***Naked Lunch***. Paris: Olympia Press, 1959 (first American edition, New York: Grove Press, 1962).

Joans, Ted. ***Jazz Poems***. Rhino Review, 1959.

Kaufman, Bob. ***Abomunist Manifesto***. San Francisco: City Lights Books, 1959.

Kerouac, Jack. ***Doctor Sax: Faust Part Three***. New York: Grove Press, 1959.

_______. ***Mexico City Blues***. New York: Grove Weidenfeld, 1959.

Lamantia, Philip. ***Ekstasis***. San Francisco: Auerhahn Press, 1959.

_______. ***Narcotica***. San Francisco: Auerhahn Press, 1959.

1960

Corso, Gregory. ***The Happy Birthday of Death***. New York: New Directions Publishing Corporation, 1960.

Gysin, Brion (with William S. Burroughs, Gregory Corso, and Sinclair Beiles). ***Minutes to Go***. Paris: Two Cities Editions, 1960.

Snyder, Gary. ***Myths & Texts***. New York: Totem Press/Corinth Books, 1960.

1961

Corso, Gregory. ***The American Express***. Paris: Olympia Press, 1961.

DiPrima, Diane. ***Dinners and Nightmares***. New York: Corinth Books, 1961.

Ginsberg, Allen. ***Kaddish and Other Poems: 1958-1960***. San Francisco: City Lights Books, 1961.

Joans, Ted. ***All of Ted Joans and No More: Poems and Collages***. New York: Excelsior-Press Publishers, 1961.

Jones, LeRoi. ***Preface to a Twenty Volume Suicide Note....*** New York: Totem Press/Corinth Books, 1961.

Kerouac, Jack. ***Book of Dreams***. San Francisco: City Lights Books, 1961.

Lamantia, Philip. ***Destroyed Works***. San Francisco: Auerhahn Press, 1962.

McClure, Michael. ***Dark Brown***. London: Auerhahn Press, 1961.

1963

Burroughs, William S., and Allen Ginsberg. ***The Yage Letters***. San Francisco: City Lights Books, 1963.

Ginsberg, Allen. ***Reality Sandwiches: 1953-1960***. San Francisco: City Lights Books, 1963.

1964

McClure, Michael. ***Ghost Tantras***. San Francisco: Privately printed, 1964.

1965

Kaufman, Bob. ***Solitudes Crowded with Loneliness***. New York: New Directions Publishing Corporation, 1965.

1968

Ginsberg, Allen. ***Planet News, 1961-1967***. San Francisco: City Lights Books, 1968.

ARTICLES, ANTHOLOGIES, CULTURAL STUDIES

1952

Holmes, [John] Clellon. "This Is the Beat Generation." ***The New York Times Magazine***, November 16, 1952, pp. 10-22.

1956

Eberhart, Richard. "West Coast Rhythms." ***The New York Times Book Review***, September 2, 1956, p. 7.

1957

"Big Day for Bards at Bay." ***Life***, September 9, 1957, pp. 105-08.

Dempsey, David. "In Pursuit of 'Kicks.'" ***The New York Times Book Review***, September 8, 1957, p. 4.

Ferlinghetti, Lawrence. "Horn on HOWL." ***Evergreen Review***, 1 (1957), pp. 145-58.

Fuller, J.G. "Trade Winds: Ginsberg Trial." ***Saturday Review***, 40 (October 5, 1957), pp. 5-7.

Mailer, Norman. "The White Negro: Superficial Reflections on the Hipster." ***Dissent***, 4 (Summer 1957), pp. 276-93; republished, San Francisco: City Lights Books, 1957.

Podhoretz, Norman. "A Howl of Protest in San Francisco." ***The New Republic***, 137 (September 16, 1957), p. 20.

1958

"Beat Mystics," ***Time***, February 3, 1958, p. 56.

Breslin, James E. "The Beat Generation: A View from the Left." ***The Village Voice***, April 16, 1958, p. 3.

Feldman, Gene, and Max Gartenberg, eds. ***The Beat Generation and the Angry Young Men***. New York: The Citadel Press, 1958.

Gold, Herbert. "The Beat Mystique." ***Playboy***, 5 (February 1958), pp. 20, 84-87.

Holmes, John Clellon. "The Philosophy of the Beat Generation." ***Esquire***, 49 (February 1958), pp. 35-38.

Jones, LeRoi. "Correspondence: The Beat Generation." ***Partisan Review***, 25 (Summer 1958), p. 473.

Kerouac, Jack. "Essentials of Spontaneous Prose." ***Evergreen Review***, 2 (Summer 1958), pp. 72-73.

Leonard, George B., Jr. "The Bored, the Bearded and the Beat." ***Look***, August 19, 1958, pp. 64-68.

Podhoretz, Norman. "The Know-Nothing Bohemians." ***Partisan Review***, 25 (Spring 1958), pp. 305-18.

_______. "Where Is the Beat Generation Going?" ***Esquire***, 50 (December 1958), pp. 147-50.

Rexroth, Kenneth. "Revolt: True and False." ***The Nation***, April 26, 1958, pp. 378-79.

1959

Aronowitz, Alfred G. "The Beat Generation." ***New York Post***, March 9-22, 1959 (12-part series).

"Bam; Roll on with Bam." ***Time***, September 14, 1959, p. 28.

"Bang Bong Bing." ***Time***, September 7, 1959, p. 74.

Baro, Gene. "Beatniks Then and Now." ***The Nation***, September 5, 1959, pp. 115-17.

"California: Heat on the Beatniks." ***Newsweek***, August 17, 1959, p. 36.

"Every Man a Beatnik?" ***Newsweek***, June 29, 1959, p. 83.

Hall, Donald. "It's Not Bohemia or the Beard That Makes the Poem, It's the Poet." ***The New York Times Book Review***, May 3, 1959, p. 4.

Kerouac, Jack. "Beatific: On the Origins of a Generation." ***Encounter***, 13 (August 1959), pp. 57-61.

_______. "Belief and Technique for Modern Prose." ***Evergreen Review***, 2 (Spring 1959), p. 57.

Lipton, Lawrence. ***The Holy Barbarians***. New York: Julian Messner, 1959.

Lyle, David. "Greenwich Village Poets vs. Police." ***New York Herald Tribune***, June 8, 1959, pp. 1-7.

Moody, Howard R. "Reflections on the Beat Generation." ***Religion in Life***, 28 (Summer 1959), pp. 426-32.

O'Neil, Paul. "The Only Rebellion Around." ***Life***, November 30, 1959, pp. 114-30.

Four Beat Poets, (Michael McClure, Philip Lamantia, John Wieners, and David Meltzer), 1957. Photo by Larry Jordan

Roskolenko, Harry. "The Sounds of the Fury." ***Prairie Schooner***, 33 (Summer 1959), pp. 148-53.

Schleifer, Marc D. "Kenneth Patchen on the 'Brat' Generation." ***The Village Voice***, March 18, 1959, pp. 1, 7.

"Squaresville U.S.A. vs. Beatsville." ***Life***, September 21, 1959, pp. 31-37.

1960

Allen, Donald, ed. ***The New American Poetry: 1945-1960***. New York: Grove Press, 1960.

Ciardi, John. "Epitaph for the Dead Beats." ***Saturday Review***, February 6, 1960, pp. 11-13.

Ferlinghetti, Lawrence, ed. ***Beatitude Anthology***. San Francisco: City Lights Books, 1960.

Fisher, Stanley, ed. ***Beat Coast East: An Anthology of Rebellion***. New York: Excelsior Press Publishers, 1960.

Fles, John. "The End of the Affair, or Beyond the Beat Generation." ***The Village Voice***, December 15, 1960, pp. 4, 12.

Krim, Seymour, ed. ***The Beats***. Greenwich, Connecticut: Fawcett Publications, 1960.

Millstein, Gilbert. "Rent a Beatnik and Swing." ***The New York Times Magazine***, April 17, 1960, pp. 26, 28, 30.

"Of Time and the Rebel." ***Time***, December 5, 1960, pp. 16-17.

1961

Baro, Gene, ed. ***"Beat" Poets***. London: Vista Books, 1961.

Ehrlich, J.W., ed. ***Howl of the Censor: The Four Letter Word on Trial***. San Carlos, California: Nourse, 1961.

Parkinson, Thomas, ed. ***A Casebook on the Beat***. New York: Thomas Y. Crowell Company, 1961.

Rexroth, Kenneth. "Bearded Barbarians or Real Bards?" ***The New York Times Book Review***, February 12, 1961, p. 1.

Rigney, Francis J., and L. Douglas Smith. ***The Real Bohemia***. New York: Basic Books, 1961.

1962

Hoffman, Frederick J., ed. ***Marginal Manners: The Variants of Bohemia***. Evanston, Illinois: Row, Peterson and Company, 1962, esp. chap. 4, "The Conventions of Marginality: The 1940's and 1950's."

Scott, James F. "Beat Literature and the American Teen Cult." ***American Quarterly***, 14 (Summer 1962), pp. 150-60.

Wolf, Daniel, and Edwin Fancher, eds. ***The Village Voice Reader***. Garden City, New York: Doubleday and Company, 1962, esp. chaps. 1–3.

1963

Jones, LeRoi, ed. ***The Moderns: An Anthology of New Writing in America***. New York: Corinth Books, 1963.

1965

Howard, Richard. ***Alone with America: Essays on the Art of Poetry in the United States Since 1950***. New York: Atheneum, 1965.

1968

Hale, Dennis, and Jonathan Eisen, eds. ***The California Dream***. New York: The Macmillan Company, 1968, esp. chap. 4, "Life Styles."

1969

Roszak, Theodore. ***The Making of a Counter Culture: Reflections on the Technocratic Society and Its Youthful Opposition***. Garden City, New York: Doubleday and Company, 1969.

1971

Charters, Samuel. ***Some Poems/Poets: Studies in American Underground Poetry Since 1945***. Berkeley: Oyez, 1971.

Cook, Bruce. ***The Beat Generation: The Tumultuous '50s Movement and Its Impact on Today***. New York: Quill/William Morrow, 1971.

Meltzer, David, ed. ***The San Francisco Poets***. New York: Ballantine Books, 1971.

1972

Duberman, Martin. ***Black Mountain: An Exploration in Community***. New York: E.P. Dutton & Co., 1972.

1973

Allen, Donald, and Warren Tallman, eds. ***The Poetics of the New American Poetry***. New York: Grove Press, 1973.

Hassan, Ihab. ***Contemporary American Literature, 1945-1972: An Introduction***. New York: Frederick Ungar Publishing Co., 1973.

1974

Knight, Arthur Winfield, and Glee Knight, eds. ***The Beat Book***. California, Pennsylvania: Unspeakable Visions of the Individual, 1974.

1975

Le Pellec, Yves, ed. ***Beat Generation***. (***Entretiens***, 34.) Paris: Éditions Subervie, 1975.

Sanders, Ed. ***Tales of Beatnik Glory***. New York: Stonehill Publishing Company, 1975.

1976

Tytell, John. ***Naked Angels: The Lives & Literature of the Beat Generation***. New York: McGraw-Hill, 1976.

1977

Knight, Arthur Winfield, and Kit Knight, eds. ***The Beat Diary***. California, Pennsylvania: Unspeakable Visions of the Individual, 1977.

1978

Knight, Arthur Winfield, and Kit Knight, eds. ***The Beat Journey***. California, Pennsylvania: Unspeakable Visions of the Individual, 1978.

1979

McNally, Dennis. ***Desolate Angel: Jack Kerouac, the Beat Generation, and America***. New York: Dell Publishing, 1979.

Saroyan, Aram. ***Genesis Angels: The Saga of Lew Welch and the Beat Generation***. New York: William Morrow and Company, 1979.

1980

Knight, Arthur Winfield, and Kit Knight, eds. ***The Unspeakable Visions of the Individual***. California, Pennsylvania: Unspeakable Visions of the Individual, 1980.

1981

Bartlett, Lee, ed. ***The Beats: Essays in Criticism***. Jefferson, North Carolina: McFarland, 1981.

Nicosia, Gerald. "Focus: The Beats." ***American Book Review***, 3 (May-June 1981), pp. 7-9.

1982

Knight, Arthur Winfield, and Kit Knight, eds. ***Beat Angels***. California, Pennsylvania: Unspeakable Visions of the Individual, 1982.

McClure, Michael. ***Scratching the Beat Surface***. San Francisco: North Point Press, 1982.

Stimpson, Catherine R. "The Beat Generation and the Trials of Homosexual Liberation." ***Salmagundi***, nos. 58–59 (Fall–Winter 1982-83), pp. 373-92.

1983

Charters, Ann, ed. ***The Beats: Literary Bohemians in Postwar America*** (***Dictionary of Literary Biography***,16). Detroit: Gale Research Company, 1983.

1984

Knight, Arthur Winfield, and Kit Knight. ***The Beat Road***. California, Pennsylvania: Unspeakable Visions of the Individual, 1984.

1985

George, Paul S., and Jerold M. Starr "Beat Politics: New Left and Hippie Beginnings in the Postwar Counterculture." In Jerold M. Starr, ed. ***Cultural Politics: Radical Movements in Modern History***. New York: Praeger Publishers, 1985.

Horemans, Rudi, ed. ***Beat Indeed!*** Antwerp: Exa Publishers, 1985.

1986

Weinberg, Jeffrey H., ed. ***Writers Outside the Margin***. Sudbury, Massachusetts: Water Row Press, 1986.

1987

Knight, Arthur Winfield, and Kit Knight, eds. ***The Beat Vision: A Primary Sourcebook***. New York: Paragon House Publishers, 1987.

Weinrich, Regina. ***The Spontaneous Poetics of Jack Kerouac: A Study of the Fiction***. Carbondale, Illinois: Southern Illinois University Press, 1987.

1988

Holmes, John Clellon. ***Passionate Opinions: The Cultural Essays***. Fayetteville: The University of Arkansas Press, 1988.

Knight, Arthur Winfield, and Kit Knight, eds. ***Kerouac and the Beats: A Primary Sourcebook***. New York: Paragon House Publishers, 1988.

1990

Hickey, Morgen. ***The Bohemian Register: An Annotated Bibliography of the Beat Literary Movement***. Metuchen, New Jersey, and London: The Scarecrow Press, 1990.

Lhamon, W.T., Jr. ***Deliberate Speed: The Origins of a Cultural Style in the American 1950s***. Washington, D.C.: Smithsonian Institution Press, 1990.

Stephenson, Gregory. ***The Daybreak Boys: Essays on the Literature of the Beat Generation***. Carbondale, Illinois: Southern Illinois University Press, 1990.

1991

French, Warren. ***The San Francisco Poetry Renaissance, 1955-1960***. Boston: Twayne Publishers, 1991.

Maynard, John Arthur. ***Venice West: The Beat Generation in Southern California***. New Brunswick, New Jersey, and London: Rutgers University Press, 1991.

1992

Charters, Ann, ed. ***The Portable Beat Reader***. New York: Viking Penguin, 1992.

Cook, Ralph T. ***City Lights Books: A Descriptive Bibliography***. Metuchen, New Jersey, and London: The Scarecrow Press, 1992.

Foster, Edward Halsey. ***Understanding the Beats***. Columbia: University of South Carolina Press, 1992.

1993

Halberstam, David. ***The Fifties***. New York: Villard Books, 1993.

Poster for Michael McClure's **"The Beard,"** 1964

McClure, Michael. ***Lighting the Corners: On Art, Nature, and the Visionary: Essays and Interviews***. Albuquerque: University of New Mexico College of Arts and Sciences, 1993.

1995

Tytell, John. ***The Living Theater: Art, Exile, and Outrage***. New York: Grove Press, 1995.

Smith, Richard Cándida. ***Utopia and Dissent: Art, Poetry, and Politics in California***. Berkeley and Los Angeles: University of California Press, 1995.

Watson, Steven. ***The Birth of the Beat Generation: Visionaries, Rebels, and Hipsters***. New York: Pantheon Books, 1995.

LITERARY BIOGRAPHIES & AUTOBIOGRAPHIES

1969

DiPrima, Diane. ***Memoirs of a Beatnik***. New York: Olympia Press, 1969.

1973

Charters, Ann. ***Kerouac: A Biography***. San Francisco: Straight Arrow Books, 1973.

1976

Cassady, Carolyn. ***Heart Beat: My Life with Jack and Neal***. Berkeley: Creative Arts Book Company, 1976.

1977

Ball, Gordon, ed. ***Allen Ginsberg: Journals, Early Fifties, Early Sixties***. New York: Grove Press, 1977.

1979

Cherkovski, Neeli. ***Ferlinghetti: A Biography.*** Garden City, New York: Doubleday and Company, 1979.

1982

Burroughs, William. ***Letters to Allen Ginsberg: 1953-1957***. New York: Full Court Press, 1982.

1983

Johnson, Joyce. ***Minor Characters***. Boston: Houghton Mifflin Company, 1983.

Nicosia, Gerald. ***Memory Babe: A Critical Biography of Jack Kerouac***. New York: Grove Press, 1983.

Smith, Larry. ***Lawrence Ferlinghetti: Poet-at-Large***. Carbondale, Illinois: Southern Illinois University Press, 1983.

1987

Huncke, Herbert. ***Guilty of Everything***. Madras and New York: Hanuman Books, 1987.

1988

Morgan, Ted. ***Literary Outlaw: The Life and Times of William S. Burroughs***. New York: Henry Holt and Company, 1988.

1989

Miles, Barry. ***Ginsberg: A Biography***. New York: Simon and Schuster, 1989.

Stephenson, Gregory. ***Exiled Angel: A Study of the Work of Gregory Corso***. London: Hearing Eye, 1989.

1990

Cassady, Carolyn. ***Off the Road: My Years with Cassady, Kerouac, and Ginsberg***. New York: William Morrow and Company, 1990.

Jones, Hettie. ***How I Became Hettie Jones***. New York: E.P. Dutton & Co., 1990.

Silesky, Barry. ***Ferlinghetti: The Artist in His Time***. New York: Warner Books, 1990.

1992

Bruce, Lenny. ***How to Talk Dirty and Influence People: An Autobiography*** (1963). With introduction by Eric Bogosian. New York: Fireside, 1992.

Schumacher, Michael. ***Dharma Lion: A Critical Biography of Allen Ginsberg***. New York: St. Martin's Press, 1992.

1993

Gooch, Brad. ***City Poet: The Life and Times of Frank O'Hara***. New York: Alfred A. Knopf, 1993.

Miles, Barry. William Burroughs: ***El Hombre Invisible: A Portrait***. New York: Hyperion, 1993.

1994

Weissner, Carl. ***Burroughs: Eine Bild-Biographie***. Berlin: NiSHEN, 1994.

1995

Ginsberg, Allen. ***Journals Mid-Fifties: 1954-1958***. New York: HarperCollins Publishers, 1995.

VISUAL ARTS

1955

Ferlinghetti, Lawrence. "San Francisco." ***Arts Digest***, 29 (August 1, 1955), pp. 26, 30.

1956

Hess, Thomas B. "Great Expectations." ***Art News***, 55 (Summer 1956), pp. 36-38, 62.

1957

Rexroth, Kenneth. "Disengagement: The Art of the Beat Generation." In ***New World Writing***, no. 11. New York: New American Library, 1957, pp. 28-41.

1958

McClure, Michael. "Ode to Jackson Pollock." ***Evergreen Review***, 2 (Autumn 1958), pp. 124-26.

1960

Coates, Robert M. "The Art Galleries: The 'Beat' Beat in Art." ***The New Yorker***, January 2, 1960, pp. 60-61.

1962

3 Beat Poets: Gregory Corso, Allen Ginsberg, Lawrence Ferlinghetti (exhibition catalogue). Providence, Rhode Island: Brown University Library, 1962.

1966

Kaprow, Allan. ***Assemblage, Environments & Happenings***. New York: Harry N. Abrams, 1966.

Kirby, Michael. ***Happenings: An Illustrated Anthology***. New York: E.P. Dutton & Co., 1966.

1967

van der Marck, Jan. ***Pictures to Be Read/Poetry to Be Seen*** (exhibition catalogue). Chicago: Museum of Contemporary Art, 1967.

1968

Finson, Bruce, ed. ***Rolling Renaissance: San Francisco Underground Art in Celebration: 1945-1968***. San Francisco: Intersection, 1968.

Monte, James. ***Late Fifties at the Ferus*** (exhibition catalogue). Los Angeles: Los Angeles County Museum of Art, 1968.

1969

West Coast 1945-1969 (exhibition catalogue). Pasadena: Pasadena Art Museum, 1969.

1973

Ashton, Dore. ***The New York School: A Cultural Reckoning***. New York: The Viking Press, 1973.

1974

Chassman, Neil A. ***Poets of the Cities: New York and San Francisco 1950-1965*** (exhibition catalogue). Dallas: Dallas Museum of Fine Arts, 1974.

Plagens, Peter. ***Sunshine Muse: Contemporary Art on the West Coast***. New York and Washington, D.C.: Praeger Publishers, 1974.

1975

Greene, Merril. ***Art as a Muscular Principle: 10 Artists and San Francisco 1950-1965: Roots and New Directions*** (exhibition catalogue). South Hadley, Massachusetts: Mount Holyoke College, 1975.

1976

The Last Time I Saw Ferus: 1957-1966 (exhibition catalogue). Newport Beach, California: Newport Harbor Art Museum, 1976.

1977

Hopkins, Henry, et al. ***Painting and Sculpture in California: The Modern Era***. San Francisco: San Francisco Museum of Modern Art, 1977, esp. chap. 11, "Expressionism, Bay Area and Los Angeles after 1956"; chap. 12, "Towards the Personal"; chap. 13, "Collage/Assemblage and the Visual Metaphor."

Kuhn, Annette, ed. ***A Voice in the Village: Howard Moody, Twenty Years on Washington Square***. New York: Judson Memorial Church, 1977.

Masheck, Joseph. ***Beat Art: Drawings by Gregory Corso, Jack Kerouac, Peter Orlovsky, Philip Whalen and Others*** (exhibition catalogue). New York: Butler Library, Columbia University, 1977.

_______. "A Note on Surrealism and the Beat Generation." ***Artforum***, 15 (April 1977), pp. 58-59.

Roth, Moira. "The Aesthetic of Indifference." ***Artforum***, 16 (November 1977), pp. 46-53.

1981

Halley, Peter. "Beat, Minimalism, New Wave, and Robert Smithson." ***Arts Magazine***, 55 (May 1981), pp. 120-21.

1982

Lagoria, Georgianna M. ***Northern California Art of the Sixties*** (exhibition catalogue). Santa Clara, California: de Saisset Museum, 1982, esp. "The Beat Era and the California School of Fine Arts."

Pincus, Robert. "The Open Road of Risk: George Herms, Wallace Berman, The Beats and West Coast Visionary Poetics." ***LAICA Journal***, 4 (Fall 1982), pp. 50-55.

1983

Norse, Harold. ***Beat Hotel***. Calexico, California: Atticus Press, 1983.

1984

Allan, Blaine. "The New American Cinema and the Beat Generation 1956-1960." Ph.D. dissertation. Evanston, Illinois: Northwestern University, 1984, esp. chap. 2, "The Beat Generation."

Haskell, Barbara. ***Blam! The Explosion of Pop, Minimalism, and Performance 1958-1964*** (exhibition catalogue). New York: Whitney Museum of American Art, 1984.

1985

Albright, Thomas. ***Art in the San Francisco Bay Area, 1945-1980: An Illustrated History*** (exhibition catalogue). Berkeley and Los Angeles: University of California Press, 1985.

1986

Gallery Paule Anglim. ***Sight, Vision, The Urban Milieu***, no. 3 (exhibition brochure). San Francisco: Gallery Paule Anglim, 1992.

1988

Starr, Sandra Leonard. ***Lost and Found in California: Four Decades of Assemblage Art*** (exhibition catalogue). Santa Monica, California: James Corcoran Gallery, 1988.

1989

Albright, Thomas. ***On Art and Artists: Essays by Thomas Albright***. San Francisco: Chronicle Books, 1989, pp. 40-43.

Kaprow, Allan. ***Assemblage*** (exhibition catalogue). Los Angeles: Wight Art Gallery of the University of California, 1989.

Lyrical Vision: The 6 Gallery 1954-1957 (exhibition catalogue). Davis, California: Natsoulas/Novelozo Gallery, 1989.

1990

Solnit, Rebecca. ***Secret Exhibition: Six California Artists of the Cold War Era***. San Francisco: City Lights Books, 1990.

1992

Berkson, Bill. "Reliquaries Among Friends." ***Artspace***, 16 (September–October 1992), pp. 60-61.

McClure, Michael. "Sixty-six Things About the California Assemblage Movement." ***Artweek***, March 12, 1992, pp. 10-11.

1994

Adler, Edward, and Bernard Mindich. ***Beat Art: Visual Works by and About the Beat Generation*** (exhibition brochure). New York: 80 Washington Square East Galleries, 1994.

Outside the Frame: Performance and the Object: A Survey History of Performance Art in the USA Since 1950. Cleveland: Cleveland Center for Contemporary Art, 1994.

Sterritt, David John. "The Beats, the Fifties, and Film." Ph.D. dissertation. New York: New York University, 1994.

1995

Fineberg, Jonathan. ***Art Since 1940: Strategies of Being***. New York: Harry N. Abrams, 1995, esp. chap. 7, "The Beat Generation: The Fifties in America."

PHOTOGRAPHIC ESSAYS

1959

Frank, Robert. ***The Americans***, introduction by Jack Kerouac. New York: Grove Press, 1959 (originally published without introduction, Paris: Robert Delpire, 1958).

1960

McDarrah, Fred W., photographer, Elias Wilentz, ed. ***The Beat Scene***. New York: Corinth Books, 1960.

1961

McDarrah, Fred W. ***The Artist's World: In Pictures***. New York: E.P. Dutton & Co., 1961.

1966

Gruen, John, and Fred W. McDarrah, photographer. ***The New Bohemia: The Combine Generation***. New York: Shorecrest, 1966.

1970

Charters, Ann. ***Scenes Along the Road: Photographs of the Desolation Angels 1944-1960***. New York: Portents/Gotham Book Mart, 1970.

1975

Green, Mark. ***A Kind of Beatness: Photographs of a North Beach Era: 1950-1965*** (exhibition catalogue). San Francisco: Focus Gallery, 1975.

1978

Nowinski, Ira. ***Café Society: Photographs and Poetry from San Francisco's North Beach***. San Francisco: Seefood Studios, 1978.

1980

Ferlinghetti, Lawrence, and Nancy J. Peters. ***Literary San Francisco: A Pictorial History from Its Beginnings to the Present Day***. San Francisco: City Lights Books and Harper and Row, Publishers, 1980.

1984
Chapman, Harold. ***The Beat Hotel***. Paris: Gris Banal, Éditeur, 1984.

1985
McDarrah, Fred W. ***Kerouac and Friends: A Beat Generation Album***. New York: William Morrow and Company, 1985.

1986
Charters, Ann. ***Beats & Company: A Portrait of a Literary Generation***. Garden City, New York: Doubleday and Company, 1986.
Felver, Christopher. ***The Poet Exposed***. Toronto: St. James Press, 1986.

1990
Ginsberg, Allen. ***Allen Ginsberg: Photographs***. Altadena, California: Twelvetrees Press, 1990.

1993
Ginsberg, Allen. ***Snapshot Poetics: Allen Ginsberg's Photographic Memoir of the Beat Era***. San Francisco: Chronicle Books, 1993.

BEAT PERIODICALS

The following is a selected list of important, small journals that published the works of Beat writers, poets, and artists.

1946
Chicago Review, Chicago, 1946-58. Edited by Irving Rosenthal.

1947
The Ark, San Francisco, 1947-57. Edited by James Harmon.

1948
Neurotica, St. Louis and New York, 1948-52. Edited by Jay Irving Landesman and G. Legman.

1950
Suck-Egg Mule, Taos, New Mexico, 1950-51. Edited by Judson Crews.

1952
City Lights, San Francisco, 1952-55. Edited by Peter Martin and others.
Merlin, Paris, 1952-55. Edited by Alexander Trocchi.

1954
The Black Mountain Review, Black Mountain, North Carolina, 1954-57. Edited by Robert Creeley.
The Miscellaneous Man, Berkeley and Los Angeles, 1954-59, 1968. Edited by William J. Margolis.

1956
Ark II / Moby I (issue no. 2 of ***The Ark***), San Francisco, 1956-57. Edited by Michael McClure and James Harmon.
Neon, New York, 1956-60. Edited by Gilbert Sorrentino.

1957
Evergreen Review, New York, 1957-73. Published by Grove Press; edited by Barney Rosset and Donald Allen.
Hearse, Eureka, California, 1957-72. Edited by E.V. Griffith.
Measure, Boston, 1957-62. Edited by John Wieners.

1958
Yūgen, New York, 1958-62. Edited by LeRoi Jones and Hettie Cohen.

1959
Big Table, Chicago, 1959-60. Edited by Irving Rosenthal and Paul Carroll.
Exodus, New York, 1959-60. Edited by Bernard Scott and Daniel Wolf.
Nomad, Culver City, California, 1959-62. Edited by Donald Factor, Anthony Linick, and John Daly.

1960
The Hasty Papers, New York, 1960. Edited by Alfred Leslie.
Kulchur, New York, 1960-65, 1966. Edited by Marc D. Schleifer and Lita Hornick.

1961
The Floating Bear, New York, 1961-71. Edited by Diane DiPrima and LeRoi Jones.
Journal for the Protection of All Beings, San Francisco, 1961-78. Published by City Lights Books; edited by Michael McClure, Lawrence Ferlinghetti, David Meltzer, and Gary Snyder.
The Outsider, New Orleans and Tucson, Arizona, 1961-68, 1969. Edited by Jon Edgar Webb.
Set, Gloucester, Massachusetts, 1961, 1962-63, 1964. Edited by Gerrit Lansing.

1962
Blue Grass, Dobbs Ferry, New York, and Georgetown, Kentucky, 1962-64. Edited by Hank Chapin.

1963
City Lights Journal, San Francisco, 1963-66. Published by City Lights Books; edited by Lawrence Ferlinghetti.
Stolen Paper Review, San Francisco, 1963-65. Edited by Jeff Berner.
Wild Dog, Pocatello, Idaho, 1963-66. Edited by Geoffrey Dunbar, John Hoopes, and others.

1964
Gnaoua, Tangier, Morocco, 1964. Edited by Ira Cohen.
Grist, Lawrence, Kansas, 1964-67. Edited by John Fowler.
Notes from Underground, San Francisco, 1964-66. Edited by John Bryan.

1965
The Marijuana Newsletter, New York, 1965. Edited by Randolfe Wicker, Ed Sanders, Peter Orlovsky, and C.T. Smith.

CASSETTES AND COMPACT DISKS

1990
The Jack Kerouac Collection (cassette). Produced by James Austin. Santa Monica, California: Rhino Records, 1990.

1992
The Beat Generation (cassette). Produced by James Austin. Santa Monica, California: Rhino Records, 1992.

1993
Howls, Raps & Roars: Recordings from the San Francisco Poetry Renaissance (CD). Produced by Bill Belmont. Berkeley, California: Fantasy Records, 1993.

1994
Allen Ginsberg: Holy Soul Jelly Roll: Poems and Songs 1949-1993 (CD). Produced by Hal Willner. Santa Monica, California: Rhino Records, 1994.

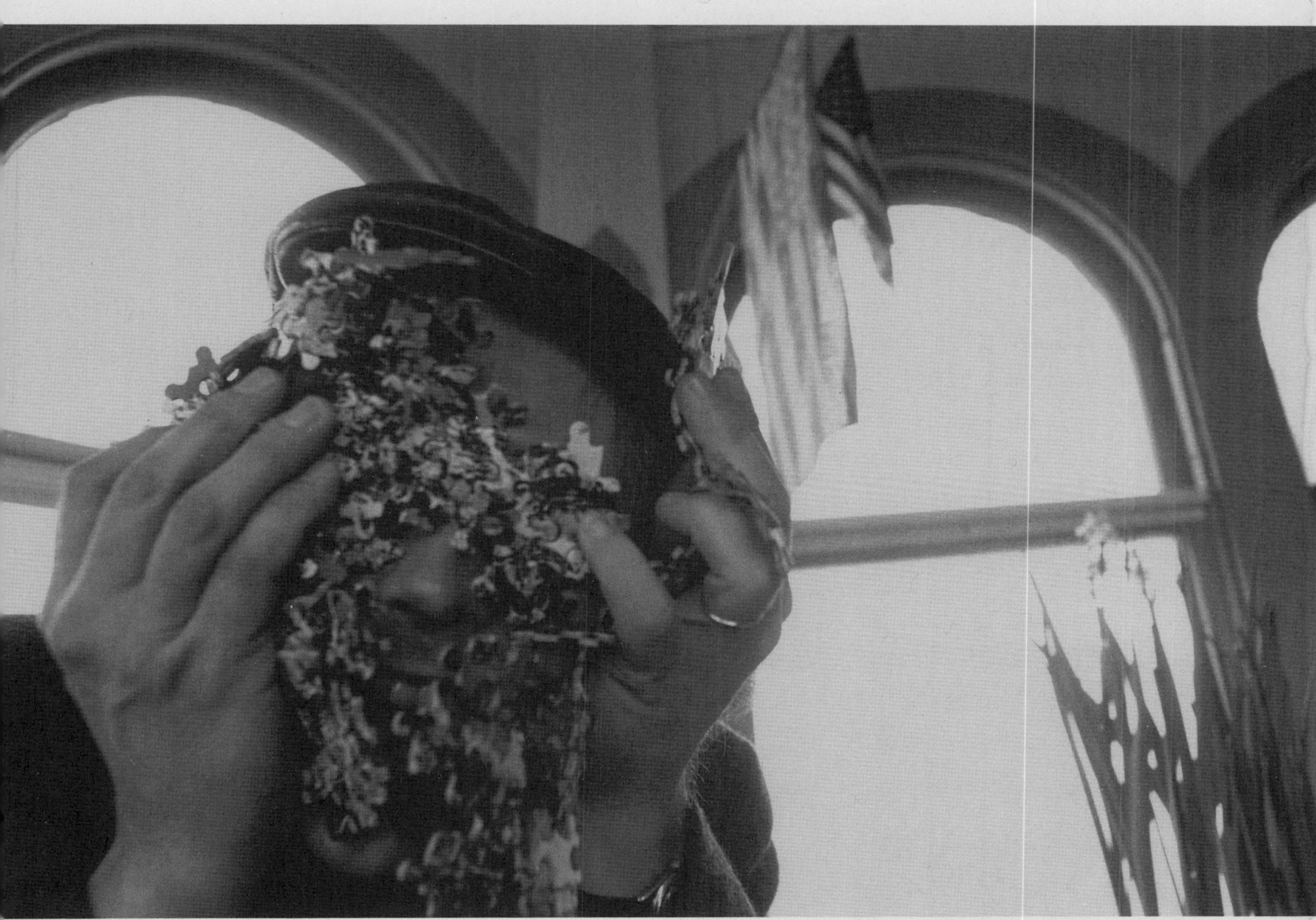

Bruce Conner, 1964. Photo by Dennis Hopper

WORKS IN THE EXHIBITION*

DIMENSIONS ARE IN INCHES, FOLLOWED BY CENTIMETERS; HEIGHT PRECEDES WIDTH PRECEDES DEPTH.

LOS ANGELES

PAINTING, SCULPTURE, AND WORKS ON PAPER

Robert Alexander (1922-1987)
Untitled, c. 1959
Three solarized photograms,
7 x 5 (17.8 x 12.7) each
The Oakland Museum, California

Wallace Berman (1926-1976)
Semina, 1955-64
Printed papers, nine issues total,
5 1/2 x 3 1/8 to 11 x 9 (14 x 7.9 to 27.9 x 22.9)
Collection of Hal Glicksman

"Darkroom Drawings," 1957
Six light-exposed and chemically processed drawings on gelatin photographic paper, dimensions vary
Collection of Walter Hopps

Untitled, 1957
Collage of rubber stamps, letters, and gelatin silver prints, 27 x 24 (68.6 x 61)
Collection of Shirley and Tosh Berman

Collage from the film entitled "Semina" addressed to Larry and Patricia Jordan, 1960
Cardboard and gelatin silver prints,
9 1/2 x 8 1/2 (24 x 21.6)
Archives of American Art, Smithsonian Institution, Washington, D.C.; Patricia Jordan Papers

Semina Suitcase, c. 1960
Metal suitcase with collaged gelatin silver prints, 8 x 10 x 4
(20.3 x 25.4 x 10.2)
Collection of Shirley Berman

Untitled, 1963
Verifax collage, 34 1/2 x 30 1/2
(87.6 x 77.5)
Collection of Nicole Klagsbrun

Untitled, 1963
Verifax collage, 12 x 9 (30.5 x 22.9)
Collection of Dennis Hopper

Untitled, 1963
Collage, 5 1/2 x 5 (14 x 12.7)
Collection of Dennis Hopper

Papa's Got a Brand New Bag, 1964
Mixed-media collage, 43 x 30 3/4
(109.2 x 78.1)
Collection of Nicole Klagsbrun

Untitled, 1964
Verifax collage, 5 1/2 x 7 (14 x 17.8)
Collection of Dennis Hopper

Untitled, c. 1964
Mixed media and verifax,
5 1/2 x 7 (14 x 17.8)
Collection of Dennis Hopper

Scope, 1965
Verifax collage on canvas,
38 x 32 (96.5 x 81.3)
Collection of Dennis Hopper

Postcard to Ray Johnson from Wallace Berman announcing studio exhibition, n.d.
Printed cardboard, gelatin silver print, ink, and stamp, 4 1/2 x 6 (11.4 x 15.2)
Archives of American Art, Smithsonian Institution, Washington, D.C.; Wallace Berman Papers

Wallace Berman (1926-1976) and Michael McClure (b. 1932)
Untitled, 1964-65
Two verifax collages with gelatin silver prints and poems,
12 x 9 (30.5 x 22.9) each
Lannan Foundation, Los Angeles

Cameron (1922-1995)
Untitled, c.1957
Ink on paper, 18 1/2 x 24 (47 x 61)
Estate of the artist

James Eller (b. 1943)
Miss April 1962, 1962
Mixed media, 20 x 24 1/8 (50.8 x 61.3)
Collection of Hal Glicksman

George Herms (b. 1935)
The Librarian, 1960
Wood box, papers, brass bell, books, and painted stool,
57 x 63 x 21 (144.8 x 160 x 53.3)
Norton Simon Museum, Pasadena, California; Gift of Molly Barnes, 1969

Poet, 1960
Wood, stack of papers tied with string, rusted klaxon and wire, 27 x 27 x 27
(68.6 x 68.6 x 68.6)
Collection of Arthur J. Neumann

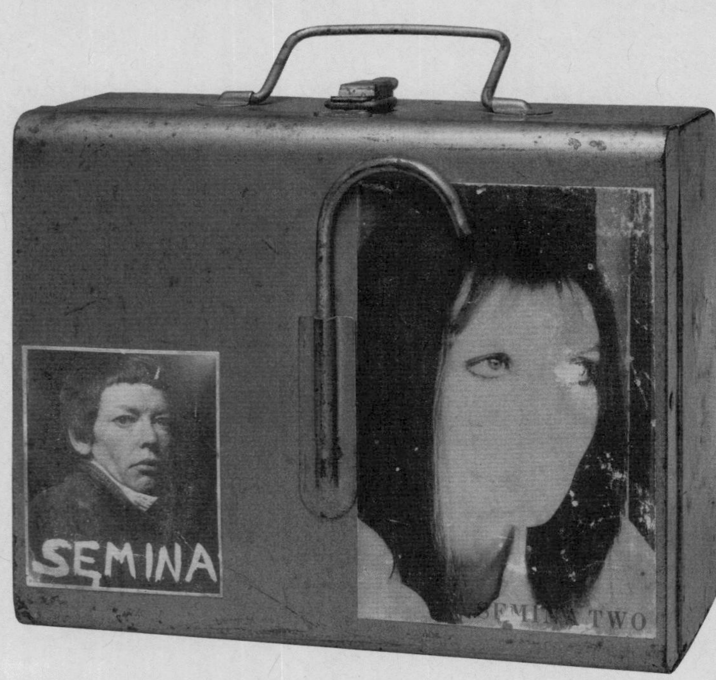

Wallace Berman
Semina Suitcase, c. 1960
Metal suitcase with collaged gelatin silver prints, 8 x 10 x 4 (20.3 x 25.4 x 10.2)
Collection of Shirley Berman

*as of September 20, 1995

The Meat Market, 1960-61
Table, pickle jar, radio, exposed X-ray plate, doll, butcher's pricing signs, mannequin, picture frame, dress form, cloth, tape, table legs, wood block, wood spool, tin box, sponge, basket, and cow's skull, 58 x 144 x 54 (147.3 x 365.8 x 137.2)
Collection of the artist

Burpee Seed Collages, 1962
Six collages on paper, 10 x 7 1/2 to 16 x 8 1/2 (25.4 x 19.1 to 40.6 x 21.6)
Collection of the artist

Edward Kienholz (1927-1994)
The Mort Soul Searcher, 1960
Mixed media, 26 x 55 7/8 x 22 (66 x 141.9 x 55.9)
Collection of Reinhard Onnasch

The Psycho-Vendetta Case, 1960
Painted wood, canvas, tin cans, and handcuffs, 23 x 22 x 16 (58.4 x 55.9 x 40.6)
Museum Moderner Kunst Stiftung Ludwig, Vienna

A Bad Cop (Lt. Carter), 1961
Mixed media, 55 x 16 1/2 x 11 4/5 (140 x 42 x 30)
Collection of Reinhard Onnasch

Untitled American President, 1962
Metal, plastic, fabric, paint, and chain on wood with ceramic base, 60 1/4 x 13 1/2 x 13 1/2 (153 x 34.3 x 34.3) overall
Whitney Museum of American Art, New York; Purchase, with funds from the Painting and Sculpture Committee 93.99a-b

Fred Mason (b. 1938)
Superball, 1960
Wood, basket, doll's plaster arms and legs, hair, feathers, mirror, cloth, and dried roses, 26 x 17 (66 x 43.2)
Collection of Hal Glicksman

Stuart Perkoff (1930-1974)
Untitled, 1959
Collage, 11 x 7 7/8 (27.9 x 20)
Collection of Hal Glicksman

Dean Stockwell (b. 1935)
Grid of Galaxies, 1961-63
Photocollage, 9 x 16 (22.9 x 40.6)
Collection of Dennis Hopper

Ben Talbert (1935-1974)
The Ace, 1961-62
Artist's easel, bicycle wheel, airplane wings, phonograph, photographs, dolls, collaged papers, oil paint, and crepe paper, 96 x 50 x 38 (243.8 x 127 x 96.5)
Collection of Hal Glicksman

PHOTOGRAPHS

All photographs are gelatin silver prints, unless otherwise noted; dimensions vary.

Wallace Berman (1926-1976)
John Reed, San Francisco, 1958,
Archives of American Art, Smithsonian Institution, Washington, D.C.; Wallace Berman Papers

John Wieners, Beverly Glen, 1959
Archives of American Art, Smithsonian Institution, Washington, D.C.; Wallace Berman Papers

Patricia Jordan, Larkspur, 1960,
Archives of American Art, Smithsonian Institution, Washington, D.C.; Wallace Berman Papers

Michael McClure, 1963
Collection of Michael McClure

Wallace Berman and Jay DeFeo
Untitled (Jay DeFeo), 1958
Nine gelatin silver prints, dimensions vary
Lannan Foundation, Los Angeles

Charles Brittin (b. 1928)
Record jacket by Wallace Berman, c. 1940s
Collection of the artist

Wallace Berman's living room, c. 1954
Collection of the artist

Berman house at Crater Lane, 1956
Collection of the artist

Robert Alexander and Wallace Berman writing on the walls in Venice, California, 1956
Collection of the artist

Wallace Berman in front of a poem in Venice, California, 1956
Collection of the artist

Ferus Gallery notice, 1957
Collection of the artist

Robert Alexander, Arthur Richer, Walter Hopps, and Wallace Berman with tire in alley behind Ferus Gallery, 1957
Collection of the artist

Stone Brothers Printing with Wallace Berman in window, 1957
Collection of the artist

Veritas Crown of Flames, 1957
Collection of the artist

Wallace Berman's "Factum Fidei" at Ferus Gallery, 1957
Collection of the artist

Wallace Berman's "Temple" at Ferus Gallery, 1957
Collection of the artist

Wallace Berman with Los Angeles sheriff at Ferus Gallery, 1957
Collection of the artist

Wallace Berman with Los Angeles sheriff outside of Ferus Gallery, 1957
Collection of the artist

Wallace Berman's Larkspur Gallery, Larkspur, California, 1960
Collection of the artist

Dennis Hopper (b. 1936)
Biker, 1961
Collection of the artist

Biker Couple, 1961
Collection of the artist

Double Standard, 1961
Collection of the artist

Shattered Glass, 1961-67
Collection of the artist

Newspapers and Streamers, c. 1961-67
Collection of the artist

Shop Interior, c. 1961-67
Collection of the artist

Wallace Berman, 1964
Collection of the artist

SAN FRANCISCO

PAINTING, SCULPTURE, AND WORKS ON PAPER

Ronald Bladen (1918-1988)
Two *Earth Drawings*, c. 1950
Earth on paper, 17 15/16 x 14 15/16 (45.6 x 37.9) each
Collection of Barbara Bladen Porter

Untitled, c. 1955
Oil on board, 47 1/2 x 35 3/4 (120.7 x 90.8)
Collection of Connie Reyes

Untitled #50C, c. 1955
Oil on canvas, 35 1/2 x 38 (90.2 x 96.5)
Collection of Connie Reyes

Joan Brown (1938-1990)
Untitled (Bird), 1957-60
Cardboard, twine, gauze, wood, and wire, 12 x 6 x 8 (30.5 x 15.2 x 20.3)
Collection of Noel Neri; courtesy George Adams Gallery, New York

Bruce Conner (b. 1933)
UNTITLED, 1954-62
Paper, wood, adhesive, nails, paint, staples, metal, tar, feathers, and plastic on masonite, 63 7/8 x 49 5/8 x 4 1/8 (162.2 x 126 x 10.5)
Walker Art Center, Minneapolis; T.B. Walker Acquisition Fund, 1992

RATBASTARD, 1958
Nylon, wood, coat hanger, cloth, nails, canvas, newspapers, and photocopy, 9 5/8 x 8 x 2 (24.4 x 20.3 x 5.1)
Lannan Foundation, Los Angeles

BLACK DAHLIA, 1959
Mixed media, 26 3/4 x 10 3/4 x 2 3/4 (67.9 x 27.3 x 7)
Collection of Walter Hopps

CHILD, 1959
Wax, nylon, cloth, metal, twine, and a highchair, 34 5/8 x 17 x 16 1/2 (88 x 43.2 x 41.9)
The Museum of Modern Art, New York; Gift of Philip Johnson, 1970

NARCOTICA, 1959
Wood, wax, feathers, rubber tubing, silk, and glass, 34 1/2 x 15 3/8 x 3 1/2 (87.6 x 39.1 x 8.9)
Indiana University Art Museum, Bloomington; Gift of Mr. and Mrs. G. David Thompson

PORTRAIT OF ALLEN GINSBERG, c. 1960-61
Wood, nylon, tin can, candle, wax, spray paint, and assorted detritus, 20 x 19 x 11 1/2 (50.8 x 48.3 x 29.2)
Collection of Robert Shapazian

FROM THE DENNIS HOPPER ONE MAN SHOW, c. 1961
Seven collages from wood engravings, dimensions vary
Collection of Dennis Hopper

DRUM, 1962
Mixed media, 9 5/8 x 8 x 2 (24.4 x 20.3 x 5.1)
Courtesy Curt Marcus Gallery, New York, and Smith Andersen Gallery, Palo Alto, California

COUCH, 1963
Cloth-covered couch with wood frame, figure, cloth, and paint, 32 x 70 3/4 x 27 (81.3 x 179.7 x 68.6)
Norton Simon Museum, Pasadena, California; Museum Purchase with funds donated by Mr. David H. Steinmetz, III and an Anonymous Foundation, 1969

Jay DeFeo (1929-1989)
Applaud the Black Fact, 1958
Collage on paper mounted on painted canvas, 50 7/16 x 36 1/8 (128.1 x 91.8)
Whitney Museum of American Art, New York; Purchase with funds from the Photography Committee and the Drawing Committee 93.103

Blossom, 1958
Collage of photomechanical reproductions with mixed media, 43 1/8 x 33 7/8 (109.5 x 86)
The Museum of Modern Art, New York; The Fellows of Photography Fund and The Family of Man Fund

Deathwish, 1958
Oil, graphite, and charcoal on paper mounted on canvas, 88 x 42 3/8 (223.5 x 107.6)
Lannan Foundation, Los Angeles

Doctor Jazz, 1958
Oil on paper with tinsel, 125 1/2 x 42 1/2 (318.8 x 108)
Estate of the artist; courtesy Nicole Klagsbrun Gallery, New York

The Rose, 1958-65
Oil and mixed media on canvas, 129 x 92 x 8 (327.7 x 233.7 x 20.3)
Estate of the artist

Lawrence Ferlinghetti (b. 1919)
Deux, 1950
Oil on canvas, 10 1/2 x 13 3/4 (26.7 x 34.9)
Collection of the artist

Vajra Lotus, 1957-60
Oil on canvas, 48 x 50 (121.9 x 127)
Collection of the artist

Wally Hedrick (b. 1928)
Around Painting, 1957
Oil on canvas, approximately 69 3/4 (177.2) diameter
The Museum of Modern Art, New York; Larry Aldrich Foundation Fund, 1959

Anger or Madame Nhu's Bar-B-Q, 1959
Oil on canvas, 65 3/4 x 65 1/2 (165.1 x 166.4)
Collection of Jay Cooper; courtesy Gallery Paule Anglim, San Francisco

Big Dick (Nixon) for President, 1960
Oil on canvas, 110 x 83 (279.4 x 210.8)
Collection of David J. and Jeanne Carlson

Madame Nhu's BBQ, 1962
Oil on canvas, 66 x 48 (167.6 x 121.9)
Gallery Paule Anglim, San Francisco

Jess (Collins) (b. 1923)
Tricky Cad, Case I, 1954
Notebook of twelve collages with handwritten title page, 9 7/16 x 7 13/16 (24 x 19.8)
Whitney Museum of American Art, New York; Purchase, with funds from the Contemporary Painting and Sculpture Committee, the Drawing Committee, and the Tom Armstrong Purchase Fund 95.20a-m

Civilization of Insects, 1955
Paste-up, 26 x 22 (66 x 55.9)
Collection of the artist; courtesy Gallery Paule Anglim, San Francisco

Paranoic Portrait of Robert Creeley, 1955
Paste-up, 26 x 22 (66 x 55.9)
Collection of the artist; courtesy Gallery Paule Anglim, San Francisco

St. Nick, 1962
Mixed media, 18 x 6 x 6 (45.7 x 15.2 x 15.2)
Collection of the artist; courtesy Gallery Paule Anglim, San Francisco

The Dios Kuroi, 1963
Paste-up book, 9 3/8 x 6 1/2 (23.8 x 16.5)
Odyssia Gallery, New York

Robert LaVigne (b. 1928)
Peter Orlovsky: Six Sketches, 1954
Graphite on paper, 8 x 5 (20.3 x 12.7) each
Rare Book and Manuscript Library, Columbia University, New York; Robert LaVigne Collection

Nude with Onions (Peter Orlovsky), 1954
Oil on canvas mounted on wood, 59 x 47 1/8 (149.9 x 119.7)
Collection of the artist

Portrait of Allen Ginsberg, 1956
Ink on paper, 13 x 12 1/2 (33 x 31.8)
Rare Book and Manuscript Library, Columbia University, New York; Robert LaVigne Collection

Portrait of Gregory Corso, 1956
Ink on paper, 10 1/2 x 8 (26.7 x 20.3)
Rare Book and Manuscript Library; Columbia University, New York; Robert LaVigne Collection

Portrait of Jack Kerouac, 1956
Ink on paper, 8 x 10 1/2 (20.3 x 26.7)
Rare Book and Manuscript Library, Columbia University, New York; Robert LaVigne Collection

Cover design for John Wieners' "The Hotel Wentley Poems," 1957
Ink, wash, and halftone on paper, 8 x 12 1/2 (20.3 x 31.8)
Rare Book and Manuscript Library, Columbia University, New York; Robert LaVigne Collection

Michael McClure (b. 1932)
Self-Portrait with Ghost, 1956
Ripolin enamel on paper, 30 x 20
(76.2 x 50.8)
Collection of the artist

Red Visionary Profile, 1957
Ripolin enamel on paper, 122 1/2 x 116
(311.2 x 294.6)
Collection of the artist

A New Book/A Book of Torture, 1961
Ripolin enamel on paper, 42 x 27 1/2
(106.7 x 69.9)
Collection of the artist

Black Quick Silver Diptych, 1964
Ink on paper, 11 1/4 x 11 1/4
(28.6 x 28.6)
Collection of the artist

Arthur Monroe (b. 1935)
Untitled, 1959
Oil on canvas, 54 x 70 (137.2 x 177.8)
The Oakland Museum, California

Harold Norse (b. 1916)
Cosmograph VII "Burroughs," Paris, 1960
Ink on paper, 12 3/4 x 9 3/4
(32.4 x 24.8)
Collection of the artist

Karma Force, 1960
Ink on paper, 13 x 7 (33 x 17.8)
Collection of the artist

Kenneth Patchen (1911-1972)
Now when I get back here..., c. 1960
Mixed media, 24 x 21 (61 x 53.3)
University Library, University of California, Santa Cruz;
Special Collections, The Kenneth Patchen Archive

Keith Sanzenbach (1930-1964)
Mandala, 1960
Oil and lacquer on burlap, 46 x 52
(116.8 x 132.1)
The Oakland Museum, California;
Gift of Reidar Wennesland

PHOTOGRAPHS

All photographs are gelatin silver prints, unless otherwise noted; dimensions vary.

Jerry Burchard (b. 1931)
Bruce Conner in his studio, 1959
Collection of the artist

Jay DeFeo in her studio in front of "The Rose," 1959
Collection of the artist

Jay DeFeo with shattered glass filled with rose petals, 1959
Collection of the artist

Robert LaVigne in front of his painting of seventeen-year-old Peter Orlovsky, 1959, at the Hotel Wentley, 1959
Collection of the artist

Larry Jordan (b. 1934)
Four Beat Poets (Michael McClure, Philip Lamantia, John Wieners, and David Meltzer), 1957
Collection of the artist

Poetry is Jazz (Michael McClure, Philip Lamantia, and Larry Jordan), 1957
Collection of the artist

Patricia Jordan (d. 1988)
George Herms, Larkspur Mud, 1960
Archives of American Art, Smithsonian Institution, Washington, D.C.; Patricia Jordan Papers

Wallace Berman, 1960
Collection of Jess

Larry Keenan (b. 1943)
Allen Ginsberg, Michael McClure, and Bruce Conner chanting in San Francisco at Ginsberg's, 1965
Collection of the artist

City Lights Bookstore, last gathering of poets and artists, North Beach, San Francisco, 1965
Collection of the artist

Lawrence Ferlinghetti, City Lights Bookstore basement, North Beach (I Am the Door), 1965
Collection of the artist

Michael McClure, Bob Dylan, and Allen Ginsberg in North Beach, San Francisco, 1965
Collection of the artist

Neal Cassady shaving at Allen Ginsberg's San Francisco apartment, 1965
Collection of the artist

Chester Kessler (1919-1979)
Bob Kaufman, 1954
Collection of Robert E. Johnson

Kenneth Anger, 1954
Collection of Robert E. Johnson

Anna Halprin's Dancers' Workshop, San Francisco, "Improvisations," 1962
Collection of Robert E. Johnson

James O. Mitchell (b. 1933)
Diane DiPrima, c. 1953-60
Collection of the artist

Jack Kerouac, 1963
Collection of the artist

Harry Redl (b. 1926)
Michael McClure, 1956
Collection of Michael McClure

Allen Ginsberg and "Moloch," 1957
Collection of the artist

"Blabbermouth Nite" at The Place, San Francisco, 1957
Collection of the artist

David Meltzer and family, San Francisco, 1957
Collection of the artist

Gary Snyder, San Francisco, 1957
Collection of the artist

Lawrence Ferlinghetti with Bruce Lippincott and band at "Jazz-Poetry" at The Cellar, 1957
Collection of the artist

Michael McClure and Gary Snyder at a reading, Berkeley, California, 1958
Collection of the artist

NEW YORK

PAINTING, SCULPTURE, AND WORKS ON PAPER

Julian Beck (1925-1985)
History, 1957
Collage on canvas, 40 x 58
(101.6 x 147.3)
Janos Gat Gallery, New York

Romeo and Juliet, 1957
Collage on canvas, 40 x 22
(101.6 x 55.9)
Collection of Sietske and Herman Turndorf; courtesy Janos Gat Gallery, New York

William S. Burroughs (b. 1914)
Rub Out the Word, c. 1958-59
Color marker on paper, 10 x 8
(25.4 x 20.3)
Private Collection

Self-Portrait, c. 1959
Ink on paper, 11 x 8 1/2 (27.9 x 21.6)
Rare Book and Manuscript Library, Columbia University,New York;
Allen Ginsberg Collection

Untitled, c.1960s
Photomontage
Collection of Robert Jackson

William S. Burroughs (b. 1914) and Brion Gysin (1916-1986)
Untitled (In America), from *The Third Mind*, c. 1965-70
Gelatin silver print and ink on paper, 9 1/8 x 7 (23.2 x17.8)
Los Angeles County Museum of Art;
Purchased with funds provided by The Hiro Yamagata Foundation

Untitled (Plan Drug Addiction), from *The Third Mind*, c.1965-70
Gelatin silver print, typescript, offset lithography, newsprint, letterpress, crayon, and ink on paper, 12 5/16 x 9 3/8 (31.3 x 23.8)
Los Angeles County Museum of Art; Purchased with funds provided by The Hiro Yamagata Foundation

Untitled ("Primrose Path?"), from *The Third Mind*, c.1965-70
Gelatin silver prints, typescript, newsprint, and ink on paper, 9 7/16 x 6 11/16 (24 x 17)
Los Angeles County Museum of Art; Purchased with funds provided by The Hiro Yamagata Foundation

Untitled ("Recommend a Restaurant?"), from *The Third Mind*, c. 1965-70
Negative photostatic print, 9 3/8 x 7 3/16 (23.8 x 18.3)
Los Angeles County Museum of Art; Purchased with funds provided by The Hiro Yamagata Foundation

Untitled ("Rub Out the Word"), from *The Third Mind*, c. 1965-70
Typescript and ink on paper, 10 1/16 x 6 13/16 (25.6 x 17.3)
Los Angeles County Museum of Art; Purchased with funds provided by The Hiro Yamagata Foundation

Untitled (The Energy of a Hurricane), from *The Third Mind*, c. 1965-70
Offset lithography, newsprint, ink, letterpress, and graphite on paper, 9 1/8 x 7 3/8 (23.2 x 18.7)
Los Angeles County Museum of Art; Purchased with funds provided by The Hiro Yamagata Foundation

Untitled (Tornado Dead: 223), from *The Third Mind*, c. 1965-70
Offset lithography, newsprint, ink, letterpress, and graphite on paper, 8 3/4 x 6 3/4 (22.2 x 17.1)
Los Angeles County Museum of Art; Purchased with funds provided by The Hiro Yamagata Foundation

Untitled (William Vacates Rooms), from *The Third Mind*, c. 1965-70
Gelatin silver prints and ink on paper, 9 1/2 x 7 1/16 (24.1 x 17.9)
Los Angeles County Museum of Art; Purchased with funds provided by The Hiro Yamagata Foundation

Untitled (W.R. Hearst, Jr.), from *The Third Mind*, c. 1965-70
Gelatin silver print, typescript, offset lithography, letterpress, crayon, and graphite on paper, 12 1/4 x 9 1/2 (31.1 x 24.1)
Los Angeles County Museum of Art; Purchased with funds provided by The Hiro Yamagata Foundation

John Chamberlain (b. 1927)
Manitou, 1959
Painted steel, 13 x 13 x 3 (33 x 33 x 7.6)
Dia Center for the Arts, New York

Swannanoa/Swannanoa II, 1959
Painted and chromium-plated steel, 45 1/2 x 66 x 25 1/2 (115.6 x 167.6 x 64.8)
Dia Center for the Arts, New York

Ed Clark (b. 1926)
Untitled, 1957
Oil on canvas, 48 x 66 (121.9 x 167.6)
Collection of the artist; courtesy G.R. N'Namadi Gallery, Birmingham, Michigan

Gregory Corso (b. 1930)
Portrait of Robert LaVigne, 1956
Ink on paper, 10 1/2 x 8 (26.7 x 20.3)
Rare Book and Manuscript Library, Columbia University, New York; Robert LaVigne Collection

Untitled, c. 1962
Collage, 29 x 41 (73.7 x 104.1)
Collection of Abby and B.H. Friedman

Self-Portrait, n.d.
Ink on paper, 11 x 8 1/2 (27.9 x 21.6)
Rare Book and Manuscript Library, Columbia University, New York; Gregory Corso Collection

Willem de Kooning (b. 1904) and Dody Müller (b. 1927)
Untitled, 1960
Torn bank check, metallic paper, and ink, 17 3/4 x 12 (45.1 x 30.5)
Collection of Dody Müller

Jim Dine (b. 1935)
Bedspring, 1960
Mixed media on wire bedspring, 52 1/4 x 72 x 11 (132.7 x 183 x 28)
Solomon R. Guggenheim Museum, New York; Purchased with funds contributed by the Louis and Bessie Adler Foundation, Inc., Seymour M. Klein, President

Ted Joans (b. 1928)
Bird Lives!, 1958
Oil on canvas board, 24 x 19 7/8 (61 x 50.5)
Collection of the artist

Leroi Jersey Jones, 1959
The Ronnie Manhattan Mau Mau Return from Mexico, 1959
Afraid of Fred McDarrah, 1960
The Treble Clef Cat (David Amram), 1960
First Lady Diane DiPrima, 1961
Perfidious Portrait of Allen, 1961
Six paper collage portraits, dimensions vary
Collection of the artist

Ray Johnson (1927-1995)
Elvis Presley #2, c. 1956-57
Tempera and ink wash on magazine page, 11 x 8 1/2 (27.9 x 21.6)
Collection of William S. Wilson

James Dean, 1957
Paper collage, 14 7/8 x 11 7/16 (37.8 x 29)
Estate of the artist; courtesy Richard Feigen Gallery, New York

Letter from Diane DiPrima to her landlord with lease, c. 1961-62
Ink on paper and envelope, 11 x 8 1/2 (27.9 x 21.6)
Collection of William S. Wilson

Mouse on the Wall, 1963
Dead mouse in frame, 15 5/8 x 9 5/8 (39.7 x 24.4)
Collection of William S. Wilson

Jack Kerouac (1922-1969)
Buddha, 1956-60
Oil on canvas, 17 x 13 1/2 (43.2 x 34.3)
Collection of The Sampas Family; John Sampas, legal representative

Untitled, c. 1950s
Oil on board, 16 x 12 (40.6 x 30.5)
Collection of The Sampas Family; John Sampas, legal representative

Untitled, late 1950s
Crayon on paper, 11 x 8 1/2 (27.9 x 21.6)
Rare Book and Manuscript Library, Columbia University, New York; Allen Ginsberg Papers

Untitled, c. 1958-62
Oil on board, 15 3/4 x 13 (40 x 33)
Collection of The Sampas Family; John Sampas, legal representative

Untitled, c. 1959
Watercolor and oil on paper, 12 x 9 (30.5 x 22.9)
Collection of The Sampas Family; John Sampas, legal representative

Untitled, c. 1959
Watercolor on paper, 12 x 9 (30.5 x 22.9)
Collection of The Sampas Family; John Sampas, legal representative

Untitled, c. 1960
Graphite on paper, 12 x 9 (30.5 x 22.9)
Collection of The Sampas Family; John Sampas, legal representative

Larry Rivers and Frank O'Hara
Us, from **Stones**, 1957
Lithograph
Sheet, irregular: 18 7/8 x 23 3/4 (47.9 x 60.3);
Image, irregular: 13 7/8 x 18 (35.2 x 45.7)
Whitney Museum of American Art, New York; Gift of Mr. and Mrs. Joseph L. Braun 77.123.1-77.123.13

Untitled, c. 1961
Graphite and oil on paper,
8 1/2 x 11 (21.6 x 27.9)
Collection of The Sampas Family;
John Sampas, legal representative

Franz Kline (1910-1962)
Mahoning, 1956
Oil and paper collage on canvas, 80 x 100 (203.2 x 254)
Whitney Museum of American Art, New York; Purchase, with funds from the Friends of the Whitney Museum of American Art 57.10

Dahlia, 1959
Oil on canvas, 82 x 67 (208.3 x 170.2)
Whitney Museum of American Art, New York; Purchase, with funds from an anonymous group of friends of the Whitney Museum of American Art 66.90

Alfred Leslie (b. 1927)
Dr. Orta, 1960
Oil on canvas, 36 x 60 (91.4 x 152.4)
Whitney Museum of American Art, New York; Gift of Sylvia Winifred Staub in commemoration of the post-World War II Abstract Expressionists 93.129

Jackson Pollock (1912-1956)
Number 27, 1950
Oil on canvas, 49 x 106 (124.5 x 269.2)
Whitney Museum of American Art, New York; Purchase 53.12

Robert Rauschenberg (b. 1925)
Mother of God, c. 1950
Oil, enamel, printed paper, newspaper, and metallic paints on masonite,
48 x 32 1/8 (121.9 x 81.6)
Collection of the artist

Yoicks, 1953
Oil, fabric, and paper on canvas,
96 x 72 (243.8 x 182.9)
Whitney Museum of American Art, New York; Gift of the artist 71.210

Satellite, 1955
Oil, fabric, paper, and wood on canvas with stuffed pheasant, 79 3/8 x 43 1/4 x 5 5/8 (201.6 x 109.9 x 14.29)
Whitney Museum of American Art, New York; Gift of Claire B. Zeisler and purchase with funds from the Mrs. Percy Uris Purchase Fund 91.85

Robert Rauschenberg (b. 1925) and Susan Weil (b. 1930)
Untitled (Feet and Foliage), c. 1950
Cyanotype, 58 1/4 x 41 (148 x 104.1)
The Museum of Modern Art, New York; Gift of Carolyn Brown and Earle Brown

Larry Rivers
O'Hara Nude with Boots, 1954
Oil on canvas, 97 x 53 (246.4 x 134.6)
Collection of the artist

Cedar Bar Menu I, 1960
Oil on canvas, 47 1/2 x 35
(120.7 x 88.9)
Collection of the artist

Larry Rivers (b. 1923) and Kenneth Koch (b. 1925)
New York 1950-1960, 1961
Oil and charcoal on canvas, 69 x 84
(175.3 x 213.4)
Private collection

Larry Rivers (b. 1923) and Frank O'Hara (1926-1966)
Stones, 1957-59
Portfolio of 12 lithographs plus title page, with text by Frank O'Hara, dimensions vary
Whitney Museum of American Art, New York; Gift of Mr. and Mrs. Joseph L. Braun 77.123.1-13

Carolee Schneemann (b. 1939)
Quarry Transposed—Portrait of N., 1960
Fabric, glass, photos, and paint on canvas, 57 x 34 3/4 x 5
(144.8 x 88.3 x 12.7)
Collection of the artist

Harry Smith (1923-1991)
Untitled, c. 1956
Watercolor on paper, 11 x 14
(27.9 x 35.6)
Collection of Raymond Foye

Untitled, c. 1956
Watercolor on paper, 11 x 14
(27.9 x 35.6)
Collection of Raymond Foye

Untitled, c. 1960
Watercolor on paper
Courtesy of Jonas Mekas and Anthology Film Archives

Tree of Life, c. early 1960s
Watercolor on paper, 18 1/2 x 3 3/4
(47 x 9.5)
Collection of Allen Ginsberg

Vincent Smith (b. 1929)
The Jazz Café, 1954
Oil on canvas, 30 x 36 (76.2 x 91.4)
Collection of the artist; G.W. Einstein Company, New York

Robert Smithson (1938-1973)
Algae, c. 1960
Paint and photocollage on masonite,
27 x 23 (68.6 x 58.4)
Estate of the artist; courtesy John Weber Gallery, New York

Spaceman, Laser, Moonscape, 1961-63
Gouache and collage on paper,
23 x 29 (58.4 x 73.7)
Estate of the artist; courtesy John Weber Gallery, New York

Bob Thompson (1937-1965)
Portrait of Allen, 1965
Oil on canvas, 20 x 16 (50.8 x 40.6)
Collection of George Nelson Preston

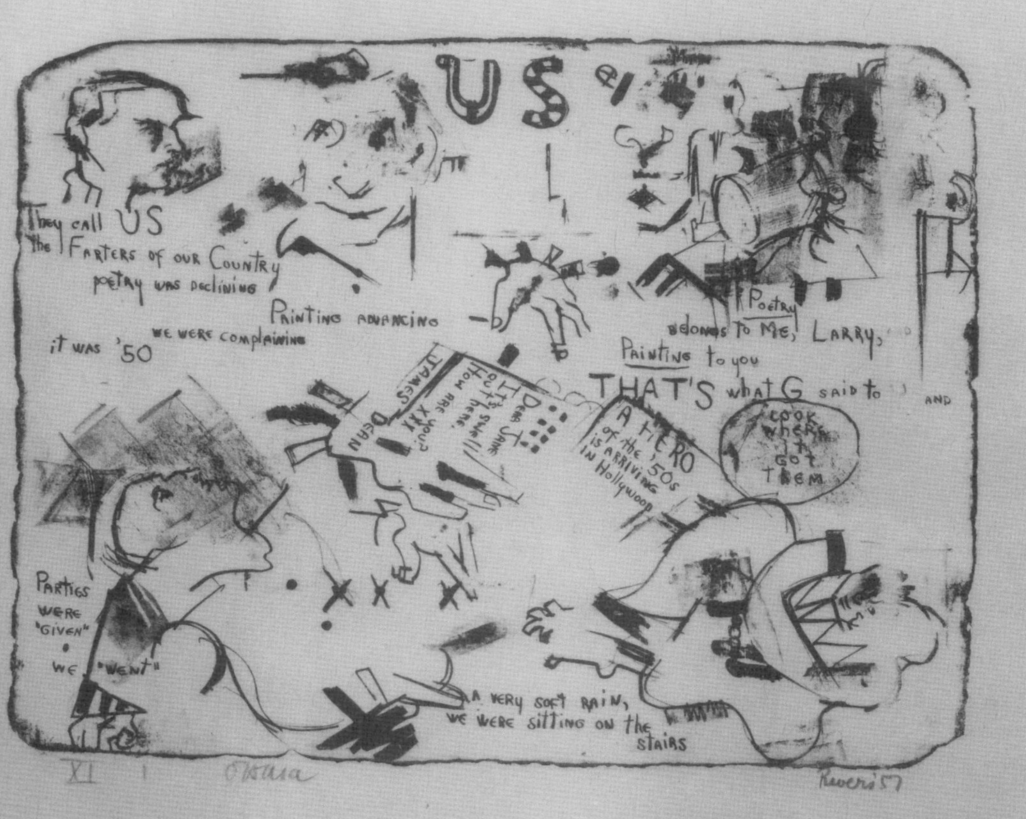

PHOTOGRAPHS

All photographs are gelatin silver prints, unless otherwise noted; dimensions vary.

John Cohen (b. 1932)
*Cast of "Pull My Daisy" in Alfred Leslie's loft, NYC,*1959. Clockwise from lower left: Alice Neel, Larry Rivers, Delphine Seyrig, Allen Ginsberg, Denise Parker, Robert Frank, "Shindey," Sally Gross, Gert Berliner, Richard Bellamy, David Amram, Gregory Corso, Alfred Leslie (back to camera), and Peter Orlovsky (obscured)
© John Cohen/Courtesy Deborah Bell Photographs, New York

Gregory Corso, Larry Rivers, Jack Kerouac, David Amram, Allen Ginsberg during filming of "Pull My Daisy," NYC, 1959
© John Cohen/Courtesy Deborah Bell Photographs, New York

Jack Kerouac, Dody Müller, and Cessa Carr at cast party in Alfred Leslie's loft for "Pull My Daisy," NYC, 1959. Painting in background by Alfred Leslie.
© John Cohen/Courtesy Deborah Bell Photographs, New York

Robert Frank, Alfred Leslie, and Gregory Corso during production of "Pull My Daisy," NYC, 1959
© John Cohen/Courtesy Deborah Bell Photographs, New York

Robert Frank and Larry Rivers, NYC, 1959, during production of "Pull My Daisy"
© John Cohen/Courtesy Deborah Bell Photographs, New York

Claes Oldenburg and Jim Dine in a Happening, NYC, 1960
© John Cohen/Courtesy Deborah Bell Photographs, New York

Red Grooms in his Happening, "The Magic Train Ride," at the Reuben Gallery, NYC, 1960
© John Cohen/Courtesy Deborah Bell Photographs, New York

Ralph Rinzler, Bob Dylan, and John Herald at the Gaslight Café, NYC, 1962
© John Cohen/Courtesy Deborah Bell Photographs, New York

Robert Frank (b. 1924)
Long Island (Walter Gutman, Jack Kerouac, and friends), 1959
© Robert Frank; courtesy Pace/MacGill Gallery, New York

Kerouac with Flamingos, Florida, 1963
© Robert Frank; courtesy Pace/MacGill Gallery, New York

Allen Ginsberg (b. 1926)
Hal Chase, Jack Kerouac, Allen Ginsberg, and William S. Burroughs, Morningside Heights, Budapest Degenerates, 1945
Collection of the artist; courtesy Fahey/Klein Gallery

Bill and Jack in Mortal Combat, 1953
Collection of the artist; courtesy Fahey/Klein Gallery

Burroughs Lying Down in Bedroom, 1953
Collection of the artist; courtesy Fahey/Klein Gallery

Burroughs with Yage, 1953
Collection of the artist; courtesy Fahey/Klein Gallery

Jack Kerouac, Heroic Portrait, 1953
Collection of the artist; courtesy Fahey/Klein Gallery

Rare Glimpse of Storyteller Herbert Huncke, 1953
Collection of the artist; courtesy Fahey/Klein Gallery

Sad in Love, 1953
Collection of the artist; courtesy Fahey/Klein Gallery

City Lights group portrait, North Beach, San Francisco (Peter Orlovsky held camera), 1955
(Left to right: Bob Donlin, Neal Cassady, Allen Ginsberg, Robert LaVigne, Lawrence Ferlinghetti)
Collection of the artist; courtesy Fahey/Klein Gallery

Neal Cassady and Natalie Jackson under cinema marquee, San Francisco, 1955
Collection of the artist; courtesy Fahey/Klein Gallery

Ginsberg typing "Howl," Turner Terrace kitchen table, 1956
Collection of the artist; courtesy Fahey/Klein Gallery

Lafcadio and Peter Orlovsky, San Francisco, 1956
Collection of the artist; courtesy Fahey/Klein Gallery

Gregory Corso in his attic room at 9 Rue Git-le-Coeur in Paris, 1957
Collection of the artist; courtesy Fahey/Klein Gallery

Burroughs in Tangiers Under Hot Shadow, 1961
Collection of the artist; courtesy Fahey/Klein Gallery

Corso and Ginsberg, Shy 1961
Collection of the artist; courtesy Fahey/Klein Gallery

Corso, Bowles, and Burroughs with cameras, 1961
Collection of the artist; courtesy Fahey/Klein Gallery

Peter Orlovsky, William Burroughs, Allen Ginsberg, Alan Anson, Gregory Corso, and Paul Bowles (seated), 1961
Collection of the artist; courtesy Fahey/Klein Gallery

Joanne Kyger & Gary Snyder Near Japan Sea, 1963
Collection of the artist; courtesy Fahey/Klein Gallery

Cassady and Babbs, Driver's Seat, Cheeks Blown Out, 1964
Collection of the artist; courtesy Fahey/Klein Gallery

Kerouac's last visit to Ginsberg, yawning, 1964
Collection of the artist; courtesy Fahey/Klein Gallery

Timothy Leary visiting Neal Cassady on "Further" Bus at Millbrook, 1964
Collection of the artist; courtesy Fahey/Klein Gallery

Fred W. McDarrah (b. 1926)
Jack Kerouac leaving the Artist's Club after New Year's Eve party, 1958
© Fred W. McDarrah

Café Bizarre, 1959
© Fred W. McDarrah

Cedar Tavern, 1959
© Fred W. McDarrah

Charles Mingus and poet Kenneth Patchen at the Living Theater, 1959
© Fred W. McDarrah

Diane DiPrima reading at the Gaslight Café, 1959
© Fred W. McDarrah

Jack Kerouac at the Artist's Studio, 1959
© Fred W. McDarrah

Jack Kerouac typing, 1959
© Fred W. McDarrah

Philip Lamantia and Kirby Doyle visiting from San Francisco, 1959
© Fred W. McDarrah

Ray Bremser reading at the Artist's Studio, 1959
© Fred W. McDarrah

Ted Joans at the Café Bizarre, 1959
© Fred W. McDarrah

Ted Joans' birthday party, 1959
© Fred W. McDarrah

Beat & Hipster Fortune Cookies for sale at the Living Theater, c. 1959
© Fred W. McDarrah

Bob Kaufman reading at the Living Theater, 1960
© Fred W. McDarrah

Hettie Jones and Joyce Glassman at the Artist's Club, 1960
© Fred W. McDarrah

LeRoi Jones and Diane DiPrima in the Cedar Tavern, 1960
© Fred W. McDarrah

Mural by Aaron Miller in Coexistence Bagel Shop, North Beach, San Francisco, 1960
© Fred W. McDarrah

William Smith, a beatnik candidate for president at Ninth Circle Bar, 1960
© Fred W. McDarrah

LeRoi Jones reading at the Living Theater, 1961
© Fred W. McDarrah

Robert R. McElroy
Allan Kaprow's "An Apple Shrine," at the Judson Gallery, 1960

MANUSCRIPTS AND NOTEBOOKS

William S. Burroughs (b. 1914)
Naked Lunch, 1958
Original manuscript, 11 x 8 1/2 (27.9 x 21.6) each
Collection of Robert H. Jackson

Pages from "Grids and Experiments," 1959-61
Paper, 12 1/2 x 9 1/2 (31.8 x 24.1)
Collection of Robert H. Jackson

Envelope of cut-ups of his own manuscripts sent to Barry Miles, c. 1960s
Paper
Collection of Robert H. Jackson

Scrapbook #84, c. 1960s
Paper, 12 1/2 x 7 3/4 (31.8 x 19.7)
Collection of Robert H. Jackson

Gregory Corso (b. 1930)
Notebook
Leather cover, 6 leaves, 4 1/2 x 7 (11.4 x 17.8)
Rare Book and Manuscript Library, Columbia University, New York; Gregory Corso Collection

Notebook, 1956
12 3/16 x 7 11/16 (31 x 19.5)
Private Collection

Allen Ginsberg (b. 1926)
Howl, 1956
Original manuscript, 11 x 8 1/2 (27.9 x 21.6), 11 pages
Stanford University Libraries, California

Jack Kerouac (1922-1969)
Book of Dreams, c. 1952-54
Bound typescript with crayon on paper, 11 x 8 1/2 (27.9 x 21.6)
The New York Public Library; Astor, Lenox and Tilden Foundations, Henry W. and Albert A. Berg Collection of English and American Literature

Book of Sketches, c. 1952
Holograph pocket notebook, 6 x 3 3/4 (15.2 x 9.5)
The New York Public Library; Astor, Lenox and Tilden Foundations, Henry W. and Albert A. Berg Collection of English and American Literature

On the Road, 1951
Original manuscript, teletype paper scroll
Collection of The Sampas Family; John Sampas, legal representative

Dharma Bums, 1958
Original manuscript, teletype paper scroll
Collection of Anthony G. Sampas

Mexico City Blues, c. 1955
Typing paper, 11 x 8 1/2 (27.9 x 21.6) each
The New York Public Library; Astor, Lenox and Tilden Foundations, Henry W. and Albert A. Berg Collection of English and American Literature

Some of the Dharma, n.d.
Bound typescript, 11 x 8 1/2 (27.9 x 21.6); six spiral notebooks, 5 x 3 (12.7 x 7.6) each
The New York Public Library; Astor, Lenox and Tilden Foundations, Henry W. and Albert A. Berg Collection of English and American Literature

NOTES ON THE CONTRIBUTORS

Maurice Berger is a senior fellow at the Vera List Center for Art and Politics of the New School for Social Research in New York. He is the author of *Labyrinths: Robert Morris, Minimalism, and the 1960s* and *How Art Becomes History*.

Ray Carney is a professor of film and American studies at Boston University. His most recent book is *The Films of John Cassavetes: Pragmatism, Modernism, and the Movies*.

Maria Damon is associate professor of English at the University of Minnesota. Her recent book is *The Dark End of the Street: Margins in American Vanguard Poetry*.

Allen Ginsberg is Distinguished Professor at Brooklyn College, City University of New York. He is the author of numerous books of poetry, beginning with the landmark *Howl and Other Poems* in 1956. He is currently preparing an edition of selected poems.

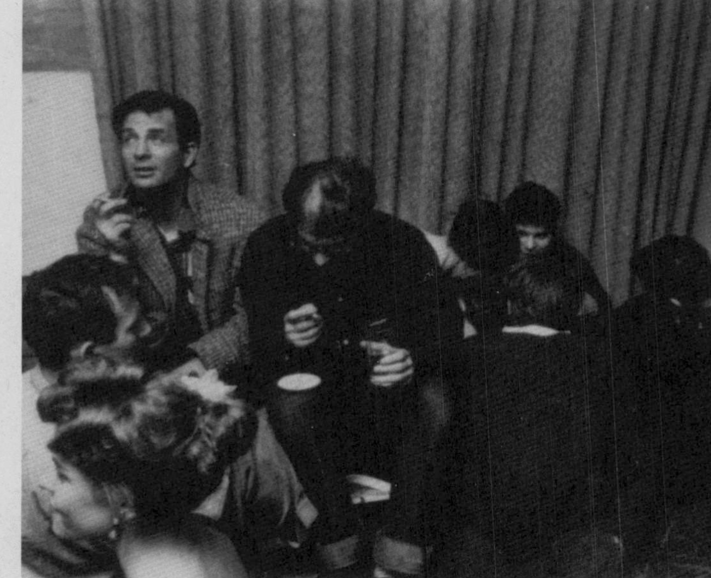

John G. Hanhardt is curator, film and video, Whitney Museum of American Art, where he has curated numerous exhibitions, including the Nam June Paik retrospective and *The Films of Andy Warhol*.

Glenn O'Brien is a beatnik executive. He is a former editor of *Interview* and *Rolling Stone*, a contributor to *Details* and *Harper's Bazaar*. He has written catalogue essays on Jean-Michel Basquiat, Keith Sonnier, and Christopher Wool, among others.

Lisa Phillips is a curator at the Whitney Museum of American Art. Her previous exhibitions and exhibition catalogues include *Richard Prince*, *Terry Winters*, and *Image World: Art and Media Culture*.

Mona Lisa Saloy is assistant professor of English at Dillard University. Her poetry has been published in *The Southern Review*, *African American Review*, *Word Up*, and *The Black Scholar*, among other publications.

Edward Sanders is an American bard. His most recent books of poetry are *Hymn to the Rebel Cafe* and *Chekhov*, both published by Black Sparrow Press.

Rebecca Solnit is a critic and historian who has published extensively on contemporary art. Her recent books include *Savage Dreams: A Journey into the Hidden Wars of the American West* and *Secret Exhibition: Six California Artists of the Cold War Era*.

Steven Watson has written widely on modern art and literature. He is the author of *Strange Bedfellows: The First American Avant-Garde* and *The Birth of the Beat Generation: Visionaries, Rebels, and Hipsters*.

WHITNEY MUSEUM OF AMERICAN ART

OFFICERS AND TRUSTEES

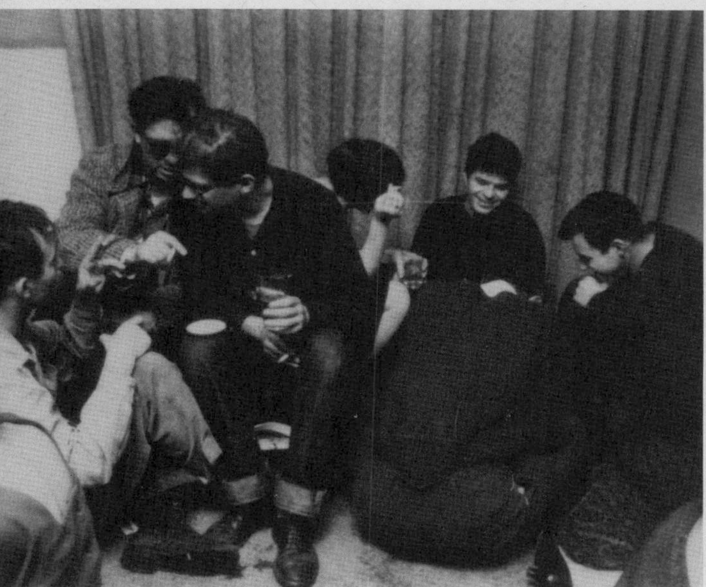

Left and right: **Kerouac, Ginsberg, Corso at Julian Beck's apartment**. Photo by Don Loomis

This publication was organized at the Whitney Museum by Mary E. DelMonico, Head, Publications; Sheila Schwartz, Editor; Heidi Jacobs, Copy Editor; Nerissa Dominguez, Production Coordinator; José Fernandez, Assistant/Design; and Melinda Barlow, Assistant.

Design: ReVerb/Los Angeles
Printing: Herlin Press
Binding: Mueller Trade Bindery (softcover) Acme Bookbinding (hardcover)
Paper: French Dur-o-tone, Monadnock Dulcet, and French Construction
Printed in the USA

PHOTOGRAPH CREDITS

Anthology Film Archives: 201, 206-7, 217, 220, 227, 230, 231, 234, 236, 239, 241; Archive Photos/APA: 126, 131; Archive Photos: 21, 188, 192; Benjamin Blackwell: 93 (bottom); Erni Burden, courtesy of Bruce Conner: 92; City Lights Books: 134; Geoffrey Clements: 3, 12, 22-23, 24, 39 (right), 42, 44, 50, 72, 77, 79, 82, 100, 106, 110, 127, 128, 129, 130, 149, 154, 158, 162, 170, 189, 248, 258, 265, 275; © John Cohen/Courtesy Deborah Bell Photographs: 1, 39 (left), 178, 184, 214-15, 222, 224; Grey Crawford: 108-9, 112; D. James Dee: 52, 63; Susan Einstein: 32, 93 (top), 139, 142, 143; Everett Collection: 168; Todd France: 175, 187, "A Love Supreme" album cover courtesy of Impulse! Records; © Allen Ginsberg: 2, 4, 8, 25, 26, 27, 31 (top), 30-31 (bottom), 120, 145, 167, 171, 178-79, 180-81, 252; Paula Goldman: 84, 85, 91, 97, 102, 113, 117, 269; Allan Grant, *Life* Magazine © Time Inc., Reprinted with permission: 125; H. Armstrong Roberts: 22; Sung-Pyo Han: 62; David Heald © The Solomon R. Guggenheim Foundation, New York: 54; George Hixson: 55, 101; © Larry Keenan, Jr.: 6, 7, 87, 166, 174, 242; *MAD MAGAZINE* and all related elements are the property of E.C. Publications, Inc. copyrighted © 1960. All rights reserved: 24; © Elliott Erwitt/Magnum Photos: 29; Photographs © Fred W. McDarrah from *The Beat Generation: Glory Days in Greenwich Village* published by Schirmer Books, 1996: 12, 15, 33, 34, 35, 118, 119, 138, 147, 150-51, 156, 157, 160, 161, 164, 165, 172, 185; Robert R. McElroy: 41, 64, 65; © James O. Mitchell: 5, 146, 193; © 1995 The Museum of Modern Art, New York: 96, 107; Michael Ochs Archives: 186; Claes Oldenburg: 41 (top); © Nata Piaskowski: 78, 80; Eric Pollitzer: 56; © 1995 Robert Rauschenberg/Licensed by VAGA, New York, NY: 42, 43, 51; © Harry Redl: 16, 22-23, 38, 72, 122; © 1995 Larry Rivers/Licensed by VAGA, New York, NY: 46, 47; L. Schopplein: 111; Steven Sloman: 37; Frank J. Thomas: 83; Michael Tropea: 43; UPI/Bettmann: 20, 152-53; Thomas P. Vinetz: 133; Dorothy Zeidman: 51

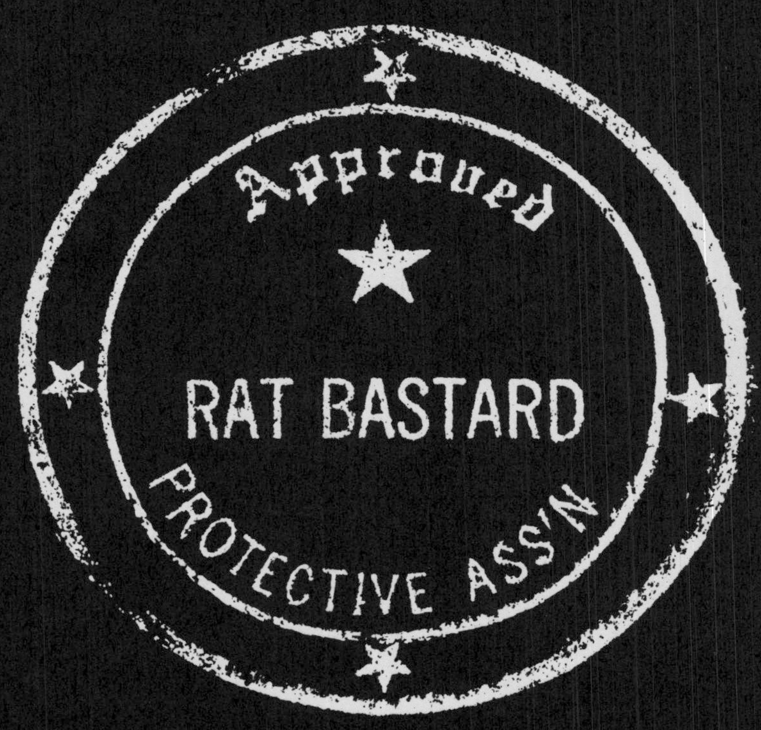

recycled paper

Bruce Conner "**Rat Bastard Protective Association**" stamp, c. 1958